BALKAN WORLDS

Sources and Studies in World History

Kevin Reilly, Series Editor

THE ALCHEMY OF HAPPINESS
Abu Hamid Muhammad al-Ghazzali
translated by Claud Field
Revised and annotated by Elton L. Daniel

LIFELINES FROM OUR PAST
A New World History
L. S. Stavrianos

NATIVE AMERICANS BEFORE 1492
The Moundbuilding Centers of the Eastern Woodlands
Lynda Norene Shaffer

GERMS, SEEDS, AND ANIMALS
Studies in Ecological History
Alfred W. Crosby

BALKAN WORLDS
The First and Last Europe
Traian Stoianovich

AN ATLAS AND SURVEY OF SOUTH ASIAN HISTORY
Karl J. Schmidt

TRAIAN STOIANOVICH

BALKAN WORLDS

THE FIRST AND LAST EUROPE

M.E. Sharpe
Armonk, New York
London, England

Library of Congress Cataloging-in-Publication Data

Stoianovich, Traian.
Balkan worlds: the first and last Europe / Traian Stoianovich.
p.   cm. — (Sources and studies in world history)
Includes bibliographical references and index.
ISBN 1-56324-032-7.—ISBN 1-56324-033-5 (pbk)
1. Balkan Peninsula—Civilization.
I. Title. II. Series.
DR23.S758   1994
949.6—dc20
94-16917
CIP

Printed in the United States of America

The paper used in this publication meets the minimum requirements of
American National Standard for Information Sciences—
Permanence of Paper for Printed Library Materials,
ANSI Z 39.48-1984.

BM (c)   10   9   8   7   6   5   4   3   2   1
BM (p)   10   9   8   7   6   5   4   3   2   1

TO

MARCELLE

CONTENTS

LIST OF TABLES

LIST OF MAPS AND DIAGRAMS

FOREWORD

It is a great personal as well as professional pleasure for me to introduce Traian Stoianovich to readers of world history. It is a special honor for me to introduce this book. I was one of Traian Stoianovich's graduate students in 1967 when he published *A Study in Balkan Civilization*, a short precursor of the present work, and along with his teaching, it changed the way I thought about history forever.

Like its model, *The Mediterranean and the Mediterranean World in the Age of Philip II,* by his teacher and mentor, Fernand Braudel, Traian Stoianovich's interpretation of Balkan history is not intended as a history of the world. But, like Braudel, Stoianovich chose a region of enormously varied nations and cultures and, by inventing new categories of historical meaning, treated it as a single unit. The freshness of those categories and the brilliant way in which they integrated and gave meaning to diverse histories, which are typically treated separately, was what appealed to this graduate student. It was, of course, a route to world history.

Greek and Balkan history have long offered routes to world history, if not since Herodotus, certainly in the twentieth century. One thinks of Arnold Toynbee, William H. McNeill, and L.S. Stavrianos. The Balkans are a microcosm of the world. The region cries out for analysis that transcends the boundaries of nation states, language, and confessions of faith. To understand the Balkans is to understand a world.

Balkan Worlds is, however, much more than a *route* to world history or a history of a world in miniature. It is, in and of itself, a world history in significant and striking ways. It is a world history, for example, in its chronological scope; it surveys the Balkans over a period of ten thousand years. To make sense of so many millennia, Stoianovich does not narrow his focus, however; he widens it. He chooses to discover every possible route to historical knowledge, to devise a "total history" that excludes nothing on principle. But total history is not a prescription for the gathering of ever more trivial data; in Stoianovich's hands it is the reverse. It allows him to decipher the most important changes, those that a concentration on the usual array of "historical events" belies. Stoianovich asks about such things as climate, the balance between seeing and hearing, and the use of gas lighting in cities—to cite just a few topics—in order to understand the most profound changes in the Balkans over these millennia. This is an approach that depends on a prodigious knowledge of historical sources and processes both inside and outside the region, and it is one which cannot fail to suggest broader processes that may be at work throughout larger realms, certainly throughout much of Eurasia.

World history or Balkan history, this work is a joy to read. On almost every page one is dazzled by Stoianovich's topics, examples, connections—by the range of his questions as well as the richness of his evidence. It is the kind of book that fires the mind while it engages the heart.

Kevin Reilly

PREFACE

The present study is not a conventional history. It aspires to be a "total history" even though it surely will fall short of exploring all possible avenues and categories of Balkan experience.

The book makes use of anthropological and sociological theory and grapples with the problem of economic change. The subjects range from folklore and climate to birth techniques, pedagogy, and demography; from the role of salt in Neolithic cultures to the role of silver in the medieval world and of price and wage movements in the premodern era; from status groups to kinship, clanship, and men's and women's societies; from millenarian movements to revolution; from archaic to modern notions of work, time, and space; from the Balkans as the primary area of European economic achievement during the Neolithic era to the area's industrial devolution.

The Balkan societies possess overly rich histories. Provincial, religious, ethnic, national, and ideological discords abound. Such discords at present divert attention from the more important question of how to make the leap from an outmoded industrialization to cybernetic technology. They frustrate the need to relate that leap to ecological demands and also maintain an equilibrium between the good of freedom and the good of social justice. A lesson to be learned from the partial failures of the past is that outside models are unlikely to work unless they take cognizance of local peculiarities.

The book is divided into two parts. Part One is a substantially revised and enlarged version of *A Study in Balkan Civilization* (New York: Alfred A. Knopf, 1967), with numerous additional notes wherever the lapse of a quarter-century has not impeded their recovery. Part Two is wholly new.

Part Two includes two chapters, one on the liberties and constraints of culture and a second on the interaction of human, plant, animal, and man- and woman-made "populations." The chapter on liberties and constraints shows how the reinvented goal of a "higher man and woman" has been both realized and obstructed. The chapter on interacting populations shows how changes in the spatial distribution and quantity of human populations alter the distribution, quantity, and function of other populations, and vice versa. One of its main concerns is ecology.

Part Two presents in a new light some of the problems raised in Part One. Both parts show how the problems of the past impinge upon those of the present. Part Two in particular examines the possible consequences for the Balkans, Europe, and the world of the dissolution of the Soviet Union and old federal Yugoslavia.

Anthropological interests pervade both parts of the book. The work differs from most anthropological studies, however, in its focus on large regional sub-cultures despite its pervasive concern for "little communities." A work of history and a study of space-time relationships, it differs from historical studies of the traditional type by its embrace of eight to ten millennia instead of the customary short periods delineated by historians. It recognizes the importance of war and states. In the final analysis, however, it is a history of peoples, of local little cultures, and of the meeting of competing civilizations or great cultures. If not a world history, it may be a means toward its achievement.

I hope this book can be a guide but not a mold. It is daring. I dare hope it is sound, a challenging synthesis of working hypotheses.

ACKNOWLEDGMENTS

Without the work of fellow historians, anthropologists, sociologists, psychologists, archaeologists, economists, political scientists, and geographers, this study would have been impossible. For providing a stimulating intellectual environment during the research phase of the first version of my work, I thank in particular a former colleague and departed friend, Warren I. Susman. Both for his personal interest in my work and for his inspired teaching and inspiring scholarship, I remain indebted to my distinguished mentor, Fernand Braudel. I thank Michael Weber and Kevin Reilly for their enthusiastic reception of my manuscript, Ann Grogg for her scrupulous copyediting, Cameron Paquette for his skillful execution of my maps and diagrams, Nancy Connick for her meticulous typesetting, and Ana Erlić for the care with which she proceeded to turn a manuscript into a book. For their ungrudging patience while I have been writing this book, and for the inspiration of their presence even when we have been physically distant from each other, I shall be ever grateful to Marcelle, Diana, Tripp, and Alexander.

INTRODUCTION

The subjects of our study are the Balkans and civilization. Both require definition.

The term "Balkans" lacks precision. Derived through Turkish from two Persian words meaning "high house" or "mountain," it applies to an area of four or five different mountain systems: the Pindus and Dinaric Alps in the west, the Rhodope Mountains in the center and southeast, and the Carpatho-Transylvanian and Balkan Alps in the northeast. Four seas also bound the Balkans: the Adriatic and Ionian to the west, the Aegean to the south, and the Black to the east. As one approaches the sea, one leaves the Balkans. At the same time, Balkan aspects linger on in the Aegean and Adriatic islands. Similarly, upon confronting the steppe to the northeast, one bids the Balkans adieu. But a few typically Balkan cultural traits extend into the steppe, and steppic geographic and cultural traits are manifest in eastern Thrace and even south of the Danube and Sava rivers. Some scholars exclude Greece, Dalmatia, Transylvania, or Moldavia and Wallachia (Romania) from the Balkans, often with considerable justification. Even fewer will admit to the inclusion of Hungary. Our own approach is more flexible. There is a core area that no one may exclude: whatever is not sea or steppe between the four seas and the Sava and Danube. However, we shall often traverse these limits.

The term "Balkans" gained currency only after the middle of the nineteenth century following the use, in 1808, by the German geographer Johann August Zeune, of the word *Balkanhalbinsel* (Balkan peninsula), and the publication, in 1831, by Major George Thomas Keppel, earl of Albemarle, of a book entitled *Narrative of a Journey across the Balcan*.[1] The area to which the name "Balkans" alludes previously lacked a general name. In classical antiquity, the western portion was called Illyricum. The eastern portion was called Thrace. Medieval European travelers knew several Balkan regions as Romanie, while the Ottoman Turks called the eastern and central portions Rumelia. Both names derive from the history of the Balkans as part of the Roman Empire. In the eighteenth century, European travelers called most of the area Turkey-in-Europe, in obvious reference to its inclusion within the Ottoman Empire since the fourteenth, mid-fifteenth, or early sixteenth century. A narrow region along the Adriatic coast remained Venetian from the Middle Ages to the time of Napoleon, and during the sixteenth, seventeenth, and eighteenth centuries a northwestern area was joined to the Habsburg dominions.

Of many possible definitions of "civilization," two are especially relevant. First is the identification of culture by an anthropologist as "an open system in a state of stable but moving equilibrium." The system maintains a boundary and accepts inputs or innovations and discharges older traits at approximately equal rates. It changes continuously but gradually in content but remains stable in structure or complexity of total arrangement.[2] A historian adds that "civilization" (his term for "culture") is "first of all a space, a 'cultural area,' a dwelling," filled with "a mass of very diverse 'goods' or cultural traits": the form and substance of a house and roof, tools and weapons, a dialect or group of dialects, culinary tastes, manners of belief, ways of love. "The regular arrangement, the frequency of certain traits, their ubiquity in a precise area are the first signs of cultural cohesion. If to the spatial coherence there is added a temporal permanence, the total repertory, the set, is a civilization or culture."[3]

Geologists, archaeologists, and psychoanalysts are concerned with rock strata, cultural objects, or thoughts and feelings. They reject the view that what is most exposed is what is most important, contending that what is buried deep is often more significant. Historians usually stress surface phenomena. Unlike Gestalt psychologists, who study human behavior in terms of total configurations, they emphasize unique individual occurrences.

Geological, archaeological, and psychological principles enter into the organization of the book. The chapters should therefore be read consecutively, for each is a view into a particular system of coherences that must exist before the next system can arise. The deepest structure relates to the earth and cosmos. Above it is a biological layer, above the biological a technological, above the technological a social, above the social an economic stratum. The geographical and biological structures change most slowly, and only after the rise of an economic structure can there be a personality culture, the most fragile of all systems of coherence.

To understand the Balkans, one must also know what Europe is. One may regard Europe, wrote Sir Ernest Barker, from at least "two points of view: the southern, which was that of the Greeks and their successors the Romans, and the northern, which has established itself since the end of ancient history, and more particularly since the beginning of what we call modern history some 500 years ago." The term "Europe" means "wide prospect" or "broad field of vision." At first, however, "the wide prospect" was "a narrow field," being applied "only to central Greece." The Greeks later extended it to the entire northern land mass of which Greece was a part. But because "the dark northern area beyond the Balkans was unsurveyed and uncircumscribed," to be a European meant for the Greeks "to be an inhabitant of the sunnier countries which bordered the northern shores of the Mediterranean Sea."[4]

Two thousand years later, many Greeks embraced the northern view of Europe, confining it to the group of cultures lying north of the Balkans. From that perspective, however, Greece was part of Europe because it was part of what I call the "first" Europe. Its classical tradition also legitimized its inclusion in the new Europe. It may be excluded from Europe, however, because of its Byzantine and Orthodox heritage. The Balkan cultures lying north of Greece customarily have been excluded both from the old Europe and from the new (western, Roman Catholic, Protestant, and Germanic) Europe. This book depicts the Balkans as an integral part of the first Europe. Their exclusion from the new Europe and the organization of the new Europe on the basis of money and power rather than culture may result, in fact, in the suicide of Europe itself.

Notes

1. Zeune, *Gea: Versuch einer wissenschaftlichen Erdbeschreibung*, pp. 32, 53; Foucher, "Changements et continuité dans la géopolitique du Sud-Est de l'Europe"; Keppel, *Narrative of a Journey across the Balcan*.
2. Wallace, *Culture and Personality*, p. 142.
3. Braudel, "L'Apport de l'histoire des civilisations," p. 20.12–7, my translation.
4. Barker, "Space," pp. 295–307.

PART ONE

Let us proceed from the deepest to the less deep and finally to the recent layers of history. Let us embrace the premise that the past is "reversible," that it can be known and understood in new ways not only by the discovery of new data but also by asking new questions, identifying and analyzing new sets of relationships, employing methods new and old appropriate to questions new and old.

1 EARTH CULTURE

In the lore of the Pelasgian pre-Greeks, black earth was the most fertile of soils. By way of homeopathic logic, the opaque or black acquired among them a wondrous quality. Among the Slavs, the words for "magic" and "black" exhibit an identical root, *čar(n)* or variations thereof,[1] and possess a cognate in Latin *carmen* or English "charm." Associated with the Crnojević (*crn* = black, magical) lords, the territory (Zeta) inland from the Bocche di Cattaro (Boka Kotorska) and from what was known as Venetian Albania came to be called Crna Gora (Black [or Enchanted] Wooded Mountain), translated into the western European languages as Montenegro. In Anglo-America, one refers to the black art and to black magic. Wicked from the viewpoint of the Christian churches, the black art is awesome and uncanny in the world vision of pagans.

Earth Mother

To the ancient Arcadians of the Peloponnesus, the Earth Mother was Melaina, the Black Divinity, a fitting title for the deity of fruitfulness and "mistress of the earth and sea"—black like the black-earth ritualistic pottery of Lesbos.[2] Wearing black robes and a horse's head in order to achieve communion with the ocean of ancestors, the legendary Melaina—or Demeter—retires to a cave (Paleolithic temple) to mourn the disappearance of her daughter Persephone. The fruits of the earth perish. Famine threatens. But a miracle occurs. The god of the underworld restores Persephone to her earthly abode. In exchange, she promises to rejoin him annually. Upon her return the earth dons a garment of green. Fruits grow again.

Under Roman rule, the peoples of Pannonia and Dalmatia honored three goddesses: the "mothers of the Pannonians and Dalmatians" of Roman inscriptions, replicas of the Greek Moirai (the trinity of spinners, or dividers,[3] of time, space, and fate) or of the Celtic *Matres Deae*.[4] A veiled memory of this tradition persists in Serbian riddles in which the secret names for earth are mother *(mama)*, earth *(zemlja)*, *dodola* (discussed below), friend *(druga)*, mistress *(gospa)*, bride *(neva)*, or parent's sister *(tetka)*.[5]

7

The clay, bone, stone, and ivory female figurines of the Aurignacians suggest that the Earth Mother cult goes back to the prenomadic Aurignacian mammoth hunters of Eurasia. Aurignacian figurines honor two dissimilar but complementary aesthetic principles, the round and the cylindrical. Of the two goddess types, one is short legged, obese or pregnant, and broad hipped; the other is tall, long legged, and slender.[6] Both figurines draw attention to the areas of fertility. One is the Mother. The other is Kore, daughter ready for initiation to womanhood. In the Balkan Neolithic cultures, the female figurines with egg-shaped buttocks represent a fusion of the human form and the form of a bird goddess, with buttocks resembling an egg (the cosmic egg) to symbolize fertility.[7]

The role of the Aurignacian cult of the Great Mother may have been designed to obtain, by mimetic ritual, an abundance of wild herds, thereby ensuring the biological continuity of the band. In the postglacial period, with the rise of nomadism and downgrading of women, the cult declined. When it was revitalized after the introduction of hoe farming by women, it gained added significance as a mimetic ritual designed to secure an abundance of crops.

Little is known of Balkan Paleolithic art. Balkan Neolithic art shifted from naturalism to symbolism, even in representations of the Great Mother or of the "supreme god," often portrayed as a stylized tree or cross.[8] Participants acting ritually divested themselves of their individuality by putting on a mask, a device for achieving communion with the collective totem.[9] Tattoos—the sculpture of the body—and painted designs on Neolithic figurines discovered at Gradac in Serbia, Cucuteni in Moldavia, and Sesklo in Thessaly proclaim their sacral character. Extant Neolithic clay stamps suggest that magical designs likewise were applied to the human body. In any event, Thracians, Dacians, Agathyrsi, Sarmatians, Illyrians, and Celto-Illyrian Japodes practiced the art of puncturing or tattooing the body in the time of Cicero, Virgil, Pliny, and Strabo. In Bosnia, home of the ancient Illyrians, the custom of tattooing persisted among Roman Catholics of the Vrbas valley to the twentieth century. It was also common among Catholic and Muslim Albanian tribesmen. Tattoo patterns were known in Bosnia as the cross, ear of corn, twig, fir tree, circle, and ring fence. Symbols of regeneration and procreation, with an overlay of a later sun cult,[10] they are the archetypal mandala symbols of Jungian psychology.

Kouros

Under complex circumstances, including the appearance of bronze and iron technologies and horse-breeding nomads, emphasis shifted between 2500 and 1500 B.C. from an Earth Mother to a Sky Father. Never complete, the shift was aided by the subsequent development of cities, the growth of enlightenment, the displacement of totemism by anthropomorphic religion, and the spread of Christianity and Islam.

The transformation came through the evolution of the totemic cults (tree, ivy, serpent, wolf, dog, deer, goat, bull, boar, bear, horse, etc.) into a cult of the reborn male youth or Kouros[11]—Dionysos of the tree, Dionysos Zagreus,[12] the Thracian Sabazios, and Attis, Adonis, Osiris, and Hermes, or the rider of the "green horse" *(hippos chloros)*, the three-headed Thracian cavalier, the three-headed Slavic god Triglav (a taboo name), the three-headed "tsar" Trojan (or Trajan), and their Christian successors: St. George, St. Theodore, St. Martin, St. Michael, St. Nicholas, and St. Sava. The latter are all horsemen. St. Sava was reputed in Serbian legend to have as companions a horse and hound. St. George was known as the rider of the green horse Zelenko.[13]

The Illyrians, on the other hand, may have maintained an identity with their old totem, the serpent, and hence with the cult of the bird and snake goddess.[14] They derived their very name from their word for serpent, *ilur,* for which a similar term exists in Basque *(luur)* and in Hittite *(ilu* or *illu)*. As Ilion, it was also the local name for Troy.[15]

The Kouroi were underworld demons who were resettled in the skies. All were messengers of death and resurrection—culture heroes, inventors, teachers, saviors, prometheans. First to domesticate animals, they were the first to teach man to yoke oxen to the plow and practice the art of metallurgy. First of the millers and weavers, they were the first to cultivate the vine and olive. Inventions earlier credited to the Earth Mother were reassigned to these males or, as among the Serbs, after their conversion to Christianity, to such successors of the "supreme god" as St. Sava or the "devil."[16] They were venerated for the invention of such fetishes (material manifestations of the supernatural) as the hammer, ax, scythe, millstone, mill wheel, anvil, trammels *(verige)*, and implements of war such as the shield, which aided the transition from an Earth Mother to a Sky Father cult.[17] The function of the Minoan double ax thus changed from a rain charm to an instrument of battle and sacrifice of the sacred bull.[18]

The enactment of the mimetic death and resurrection of Dionysos and Osiris lived on in the Christian story of the resurrection of Christ. The Christ in effigy of the Easter holy days is one of the few sculptured (hence, three-dimensional) figures retained in the Orthodox church after the partial victory over iconoclasm, in the ninth century, by the partisans of the cult of icons.

Wooden and other three-dimensional idols or images disappeared from the social and religious practices of Byzantium after the compromise between the image breakers and the advocates of the cult of icons and just before the conversion to Orthodox Christianity of the greater part of the South Slavs.[19] In Athens, however, where paganism lingered longer than in almost any other part of the empire, wooden idols known as *xoana* were borne in processions conducted to ensure communal health and wealth even as late as the Greek revolution of 1821. This practice was a carryover from the procession of the twelve *xoana* of the east Parthenon frieze. Such processions were accompanied in Greek antiquity by a sacrifice and communal meal designed to ensure the health and prosperity of the city.[20]

Rites of the death and resurrection of the male youth were enacted in Greek girls' spring initiation ceremonies until a half-century ago. In the Zagori district of Epirus, the Kouros was known as Zaphiris. A girl normally played his part. Sometimes, however, he was a wooden doll (idol) or a bundle of leaves in the form of a cross. The ritual suggests an older rite of the death and resurrection of Kore, the Earth Daughter. Covering Zaphiris (girl, boy, idol, or cross) with leaves and flowers in a ceremony purporting to portray his (her, its) death, a band of local adolescent "May girls" would burst into a threnody bewailing his legacy: a house in ruins and a grieving bride *(kouremadia)* "with a belly [stretching] to the mouth." Of a sudden, Zaphiris miraculously would come to life.[21]

Green George

The Balkan Slavs link growth and fertility rites with St. George's Day (April 23). In Macedonia and Bulgaria, young people celebrate the day by swaying on swings. Like dancing and jumping over fire, swaying symbolizes growth, vitality, virility, fertility. In Balkan mountainous areas, young men and maidens set up swings from tree branches and sing songs.[22] In one such Bulgarian song, the Sun's Mother instructs him how to win a maiden "more radiant" than he—presumably with the generative qualities of a daughter of the Earth Mother, Baba or Kubaba of the Sumerians, Baba the Radiant:[23]

> Coming are the sacred days,
> Will come also holy George's day.
> Lower then the hammocks from the sky,
> On that wondrous day, St. George's Day.
> To swing and sway for their health,
> All the girls will come to play.
> Maid Dobrinka will also come!
> Lift then the hammock up, up, up,
> And raise the maiden to the skies![24]

In Croatia, a "Green George" leads a company of "Georges" in a *kolo* or round dance from one village house to the next. The dancers sing songs welcoming nature's rebirth. In Slovenia, a "Green George" and a company of goatskin-clad youths, or *koranti*, enact the struggle between winter and spring.[25] In parts of Carinthia, a "Green George" covered from head to foot with leafage was symbolically drowned in punishment for the infertility of the cattle or for not having brought enough rain.[26]

The "Green George" of the Balkans corresponds to the "Green One" (al-Khudr) of Muslim Arabs, the spring deity whom Syrian Christians associate with St. George. There also may be a connection between the Croatian Georges or Slovenian *koranti* and the Phrygian *korybantes* (medicine men who cured madness by orgiastic dancing and the music of the flute and kettle drums and were associated with the cult of Cybele), Cretan *kouretes* (orgiastic dancers), and Roman *salii* (leapers)—magical fraternities or cult societies of male seers or medicine men or youthful members of a men's society who play the role of fertility demons, driving out the old year and bringing in the new, possessing gear simultaneously musical and military: a stretched skin to serve both as shield and timbrel, and a cudgel, sword, or spear that was also a drumstick.[27]

St. George's Day was a day of fun and frolic. The spring festival also required precautionary measures to assure the fertility of cattle and crops. In parts of Serbia, even until the mid-twentieth century, it was the solemn duty of the master and mistress of each household to perform certain rites, either on the eve or morning of St. George's Day. They would place a small stone on each fruit tree to make it taboo to caterpillars, pass some milk through a hole in an oak bark to assure the family of cream *(kajmak)* thick as the bark for the rest of the year, make crosses of hazelnut branches and stick them in the fields in order to obtain a plentiful harvest, place a bucket of water in the cattle enclosure to entice each cow to yield an equivalent quantity of milk, and rub the udders of milch cows and sheep with nettle.

Serbs and Croats thus designated St. George's Day as the "herdsman's holiday" or "feast of the herds." On this day they observed the traditions of baking a ritual cake for the health of their cattle, ceremonially milked their sheep and made their first cheese of the year, weaned the lambs born during the previous winter, and drove their herds and flocks from the lowlands to verdant mountain pastures. St. George was known to them as the shepherd, as lord of the forest, and, like St. Sava of popular belief, as the protector of wolves.[28]

Rain and Fire Rites

St. George's Day was an occasion for the lighting of bonfires, as were St. John's or Midsummer's Eve (June 23/24, the summer solstice of the old Roman calendar), the feast of St. Vitus (June 28), the three days preceding and following the feast of St. Peter (July 12), the Bulgarian fire feasts or *goreshtnitsi* (July 15, 16, and 17), and the three days before and after the feast of the prophet Elijah (July 20), known in Ireland as the feast of Baaltin and in Scotland as the feast of Beltin in honor of the Syro-Phoenician god Baal.[29] The lighting of the fires was designed to purify, exalt, and kindle anew the forces of life.[30] It was a general practice of the peoples of the preindustrial Old World.

Almost everywhere in the Balkans, the participants in fire rites shouted, sang, and leaped over the fire. Sometimes they danced or raced wildly through the woods and over the hills. Erotic in appearance, their behavior was ritualistic. The singing, dancing, hopping, turning, and shouting were intended to demonstrate the health, vigor, and virility or femininity of the actors and magically procure for them future health and vigor, a bride or husband, a long life, and even

THE LAST FIRE I SAW — WAS IN LATE
1944 — CELEBRATING THE RED ARMY
ENTERING CROATIA (VIROVITICA). BY
1945 CUSTOM DISAPPEARED

12 BALKAN WORLDS

immortality. In Athens and in the vicinity of Florina, purifying fires were lit in village and town streets and in private yards as late as the 1950s.[31] The chief participants were then small boys. The practice had become a children's game or a spectator's delight.

The traditional ritual fire was a special fire variously known as the living, sacred, or divine fire. It was produced in several ways—basically, however, by the Paleolithic method of rubbing two pieces of wood. In the Balkans, the common wood was hazel, willow, oak, linden, or dogberry.

Of an apotropaic nature, the fire rites assumed different forms. In some places, the fire was made on a special day of each year. In others, the building of a new house was the occasion for a fire to symbolize the passage from one residence to another. An epidemic also required a rite of passage to enable the survivors to leave behind a world of calamity for a world of well-being.[32] Fire rites for cattle such as the so-called shrine of the ox *(volovska bogomolja)* were also common. In the event of an epizootic—and in some places at a fixed time of the year—Slavic villagers passed their cattle, sheep, goats, pigs, and horses through a tunnel covered by a fire or led them between two trees whose branches had been set ablaze.[33]

The making of a living fire, or needfire, was generally preceded by the quenching of the old fires and followed by the lighting of the hearths with the new fire. The practice prevailed in the nineteenth century among both the Balkan Slavs and the Albanians, but it was very old, having been known to all the ancient Mediterranean and Indo-European cultures.

The classical Greeks kept an ever-burning sacred fire in their Prytaneion or civic hearth building, the ancestor of our town hall.[34] Among the Romans, Hebrews, and Greeks of antiquity, the living fire was normally created by rubbing two pyrites. The Romans generally made the fire at the feast of the Paliliae (or Pariliae) on April 21, an occasion for confession, purification, and renewal, resembling in many ways the later pagan-like pastoral and agricultural festival of St. George.[35]

Both water and fire purify. Water, however, is needed for life. The practice of a "procession round" a community or holy place with the aim of achieving a desired goal, known to the ancient Greeks as *perperia*, was associated later with the specific end of obtaining rain. Following the Slavic invasions, the rain procession was linked to the rain god Perun, giving rise to the use among the Greeks of the terms *perperouna* and *papparouna* for such processions. In Epirus, Thessaly, and Macedonia, a boy or girl stripped naked and dressed in wreaths and festoons of leafage was escorted from house to house by a group of children who danced and sang an invocation:

> Perperia all fresh bedewed,
> Freshen all the neighbourhood;
> By the woods, on the highway,

> As thou goest, to God now pray:
> O my God, upon the plain,
> Send thou us a still, small rain;
> That the fields may fruitful be,
> And vines in blossom we may see;
> That the grain be full and sound,
> And wealthy grow the folks around.

A member of the visited household poured water over the rain child, rewarding it with some sweetmeats or a few coppers. The procession then continued to the next dwelling to repeat the performance.[36]

In Bulgaria, eastern Serbia, and parts of Macedonia, the rain maiden was called Peperuda, Peperudja, or Peperuga, literally "butterfly."[37] As the procession of singing and dancing girls moved from house to house, the residents similarly poured water over the "butterfly," threw flour over her head, and gave flour, butter, and cheese to her companions.

A Briton, Andrew Archibald Paton, commented on the custom of the rain maiden in Serbia of the 1840s, where the maiden was known as Dodola. "When a long drought has taken place," he wrote,

> a handsome young woman is stripped, and so dressed up with grass, flowers, cabbage and other leaves, that her face is scarcely visible; she then, in company with several girls of twelve to fifteen years of age, goes from house to house singing a song, the burden of which is a wish for rain. It is then the custom of the mistress of the house at which the Dodola is stopped to throw a little water on her. This custom used also to be kept up in the Servian districts of Hungary, but has been forbidden by the priests.[38]

Regarded by the higher clergy as a pagan rite and attacked by the secularized "intelligentsia" as a superstition, the custom of the rain maiden in towns was passed on to the Gipsies.[39] Until the second half of the nineteenth century, children were mainly responsible for the performance of rain and other fertility rites. As the Balkan societies were more fully commercialized, however, age, gender, and ethnic roles were revised or the rite was desacralized. The rite became a children's game or children progressively were excluded from the "real" world as that world itself was fragmented.[40]

Neolithic Culture

The culture of the Earth Mother, Kouroi, Green Georges, and the rekindling of fires was a culture of Paleolithic origin but so thoroughly remodeled that we may call it Neolithic. Until the mid-nineteenth century, the folk culture of the Balkans was fundamentally an earth culture of this kind, a culture of survivals and anachronisms. Neolithic culture embodied a gradual but basic shift from food gathering as a primary way of life to the cultivation of plants and domestication of animals, which in turn led to the formation of settled farming communities—the constitution of what Ernest Gellner has called *agraria*.[41]

Until the mid-twentieth century, archaeologists placed the beginning of the Balkan Neolithic during the first half of the third or in the fourth millennium. Since then, on the basis of the radiocarbon dating technique devised by Willard F. Libby in 1952 and the corrections provided by dendrochronology or the annual growth in tree rings, they have updated the period.

The radiocarbon method is based on the hypothesis that radioactive carbon-14 atoms present in living matter are lost at a fixed rate when a plant or animal dies. By measuring the residual radioactivity in organic matter, scientists determine the approximate date at which the matter was part of a living plant or animal. What reduces the method's reliability without the aid of dendrochronology is the fact that the radioactivity level has not always been constant.[42] By and large, however, scientists consider radiocarbon dates for the Neolithic period more trustworthy than dates for the Paleolithic period and the period of the last two millennia.

Table 1.1 presents a chronological ordering of the earliest Balkan and western Asiatic Neolithic based on current data.

Many eminent scholars reject the notion that a Neolithic farming culture developed independently in Europe. Vladimir J. Fewkes, for example, concluded that a Neolithic culture arose in the central Balkan and middle Danubian areas only after the advent of farmer immigrants from the south. The probable route of migration between the Near East and the Danube, he believed, was by way of the valley of the Meander (Menderes) in Anatolia to Milet and the Cyclades, thence to Thessaly and Macedonia and by way of the Vardar and Morava valleys to the middle Danube.[43] Accepting this hypothesis in part, V. Gordon Childe stressed the likelihood of "several streams" of migration from "different starting-points." He also contended that the Neolithic culture of the middle Danube contained not only cultural traits introduced from the south—cereals (one-corn wheat and millet), farming methods, clay seals, vase-painting techniques, and a preference for Spondylus shells—but a number of indigenous traits. The very possibility of the self-sufficiency of a community promoted the formation of distinctive culture areas,[44] each serving the wants of its inhabitants.

More extreme than Childe, Richard Pittioni rejected the view that the Neolithic culture was transplanted to the Danube by immigrants from other regions. He also refused to accept the view that it arose through the spread of ideas from abroad (stimulus diffusion). Convinced that the transmission of ideas presumes prior relationships between peoples, Pittioni advanced instead a theory of "historical convergences." He thus maintained that Danubian dwellers developed a Neolithic culture when local conditions, including ecological and climatic factors, prompted them to want to borrow elements from other cultures. A stimulus from abroad occurred only after the affirmation of a demand for stimulation by

Table 1.1

Chronology of Balkan and Western Asiatic Neolithic Cultures

Place	Location	Complex	Date B.C.
Jarmo	Iraq		6750 ± 200
Nea Nikomedeia	Greek Macedonia near Verroia		between 6220 ± 150, or 6475 ± 150 and 7200
Jericho	Dead Sea valley		6480 ± 160
Achilleion	Thessaly, near Pharsala	Proto-Sesklo	ca. 6500
		Early Sesklo	ca. 6300
Anza	Yugoslavian Macedonia between Veles and Štip	Proto-Sesklo and Early Vinča (Starčevo)	between 6000 and 6400
Belt Cave	Northern Iran		5840 ± 330
Lepenski Vir	Serbian Danube at Iron Gate	Starčevo with Danubian Mesolithic elements	between 5600 and 6050
Vršnik III	Yugoslovian Macedonia north of Štip	Starčevo	ca. 5900
Karanovo	Central Bulgaria near Nova Zagora	Karanovo II (Starčevo)	between 5550 and 5850
Khirokitia	Cyprus		5685 ± 100
Hacilar IX, (deepest level)	Central Anatolia		5600
Gyálarét	Hungary	Körös	5332 ± 100
Obre	Bosnia	Obre II (Butmir)	between 4850 and 5100
Gornja Tuzla	Bosnia	Starčevo	4889 ± 75
Vinča	Serbian Danube	Early and Mid-Vinča: Starčevo	between 4800 and 5100
Cernavodă	Romanian Danube northwest of Constanţa	Pontic-Anatolian Cycladic: Hamangia III	ca. 4800
Hăbăşeşti	Moldavia	Cucuteni A	ca. 4360
Csöszhalom	Hungary	Tisza	3647 ± 60

Sources: For most of the Balkan Neolithic dates, see Gimbutas, *The Goddesses and Gods of Old Europe*, pp. 241–55; for Nikomedeia, Rodden, "An Early Neolithic Village in Greece"; Weinberg, "The Relative Chronology of the Aegean and Early Bronze Ages," p. 310. For the Neolithic in Macedonia, see Hammond, *A History of Macedonia*, I, 215–33. For Yugoslav scholars on the Balkan Neolithic cultures, see Narodni Muzej, *Neolit Centralnog Balkana*.

some members of the borrowing culture.[45] Pittioni's views have found support among such prehistorians and archaeologists as Robin Dennell, Jean Guilaine, and Marija Gimbutas.[46]

Salt of the Earth

Crucially pertinent to the theory of historical convergences is the fact that a Neolithic culture could not arise in Europe until after the transformation of a cold climate into a moist temperate one and of tundra vegetation into deciduous forest unsuitable for hunting in large bands. People thus were impelled to settle along river and lake banks and near marshes, where shells, fish, and aquatic plants like the water chestnut and yellow nenuphar were available as food.

The earliest Balkan Neolithic communities huddled close to rivers and lakes (see Figure 1.1). Nea Nikomedeia emerged near the mouth of the Haliakmon and Axios (Vardar), at the edge of the former Yiannitsa Lake. Otzaki, Tsani, and Magoulitza arose in the valleys of several small Thessalian streams to the south, and Sesklo appeared to the southeast, near a lake and close to the sea. Vršnik sprang up near the Bregalnica; Vinča, Starčevo, Kličevac, and Žuto Brdo, near the confluence of the Danube and the Sava or the Danube and the Morava; Gornja Tuzla, near the two Tuzla rivers. Archaeologists have appropriately named several networks of cultures—Körös (Criş), Tisza, and Maros (Mureş)—after rivers.

After an initial existence as food gatherers around lakes, marshes, and rivers, the people of Nea Nikomedeia, Sesklo, Vršnik, Starčevo, and Tuzla learned to domesticate both plants and animals. According to Robert J. Rodden, the Nea Nikomedeia dwellers domesticated sheep, goats, pigs, and kine some nine thousand years ago. They grew wheat, barley, lentils, and peas, and they fished and gathered pistachio nuts and acorns in the surrounding forests. They spun and wove and made pottery and statuettes of fertility goddesses.[47] The earliest Starčevo levels show similar evidence of fishing, domestication of plants and animals, pottery making, and spinning and weaving.

Following the innovation of hoe farming and the taming of animals, men altered their food habits. Hunters had roasted their meat—for man had known the use of fire in the Paleolithic era—or had eaten it raw. In either case, they had obtained the salts needed by their bodies without adding sodium chloride. Neolithic men, on the other hand, were obliged to add salt to their foods after their adoption of the practice of boiling their vegetables, cereals, and meats.[48] They likewise required salt for their animals and for the preservation of meats, fish, and vegetables from season to season. Because it was not available everywhere, salt may have been the most important article of human commerce for thousands of years.[49]

A vegetable that mankind preserved quite early was the cabbage, from which people may have made a kind of sauerkraut similar to the *kiselo zele* of the later

Figure 1.1. Rock Structures and Mountain Systems and the Balkan Neolithic and Medieval Cultures

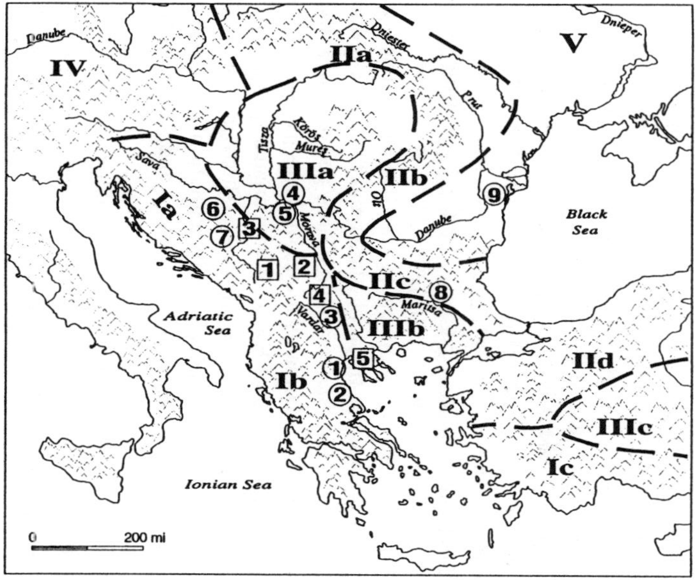

KEY

I Dinaric-Pindus-Taurus rock structures and mountain system (folded mountains):

Ia Dinaric Alps. Mountains follow a northwest-southeast direction.

Ib Pindus. Mountains follow a north-south direction.

Ic Taurus. Mountains follow a west-east direction.

II Carpathian-Transylvanian-Balkan-Pontic system (folded mountains):

IIa Carpathians.

IIb Transylvanian Alps.

IIc Balkan mountain system. Mountains follow a west-east direction.

IId Pontic mountain system. Mountains follow a west-east direction.

III Uplifted or downthrust median blocks lying between two or more folded mountain systems:

IIIa Pannonian Plain, an ancient sea basin.

IIIb Rhodope Mountains.

IIIc Anatolian Plateau.

IV Central European Alps.
V East European Platform.

NEOLITHIC SITES

① Nea Nikomedeia
② Sesklo
③ Vršnik
④ Starčevo
⑤ Vinča
⑥ Tuzla
⑦ Butmir
⑧ Karanovo
⑨ Hamangia

MEDIEVAL MINE SITES

[1] Brskovo
[2] Novo Brdo
[3] Srebrenica
[4] Kratovo
[5] Siderocapsa

☐ Mountains

⌐ Rock structure and mountain systems

Bulgarians, the preparation of which may require as much as six kilograms of salt to a hundred head of cabbage.[50] As late as 1900, when the annual per capita consumption of potatoes in Bulgaria was 2.3 kilograms, the consumption of cabbage stood at 11.2 kilograms, constituting one-third of the per capita vegetable consumption in the country. In the centuries before 1800, when the Bulgarians had no potatoes, cabbage may have represented two-fifths of the Bulgarian vegetable diet.[51]

The storage and boiling of cultivated foods created a need for containers and may have been a significant stimulus to the making of pottery—pots for Neolithic man's soups, cereals, and other food that had to be cooked or stored.

A few human societies started to add salt to their foods about ten thousand years ago. The cultural traits suggesting a need for sodium chloride—farming, domesticated animals, and pottery—became manifest in the Balkans between nine thousand and five thousand years ago. The fact that so many of the words for salt in the Indo-European languages are cognates lends support to the view that the Indo-Europeans were familiar with salt before their migrations from a possible common hearth.

Requiring salt in their daily diet, the earliest farmers either had to settle in an area where they could easily procure it or they had to produce, or otherwise obtain, a surplus of goods that they could give in exchange for gifts of salt. One may infer from the current place names of Balkan and central European Neolithic sites that the earliest Neolithic communities were located close to salt supplies. Haliakmon, the river site of Nea Nikomedeia, thus contains the Greek word for salt (hals). The river presumably was so named in recognition of the presence of salt at its mouth. Similarly, the first syllable of Tuzla (Gornja and Donja), a center of salt wells (in the valleys of the Great and Little Tuzla rivers) on territory of the Butmir Neolithic culture, is the Turkish name for salt. The Illyrian bos, from which is derived the name of the province of Bosnia, in like manner may have signified salt. Bosnia (the former Butmir culture) thus literally would be "the salt country." The dwellers of the areas of the onetime Starčevo and Körös cultures, on the other hand, may have fulfilled part of their salt needs during the last two millennia from the mines of neighboring Wallachia —from saltworks such as those of Slanic and Doftana in Muntenia or Ocnele Mari in Oltenia.[52] The Starčevo and Körös peoples may also have obtained salt supplies from the Marmaros mines of Transylvania, which in the fifteenth century provided the king of Hungary with annual revenues of a hundred thousand florins.[53] The salt mines of Moldavia, Bukovina, and Galicia fulfilled the needs of the Cucuteni and later Tripolye culture of the steppic region between the Siret River and Danube delta in the west and south and the Dnieper in the east.

In historical times, marine salt was gathered at the mouth of the Hebrus (Maritsa) in the northern Aegean, along the eastern Adriatic coast and its Mediterranean continuation—at Trieste; at Piran, Koper, and Milje in maritime

Slovenia; at Pag and Šibenik; at the mouth of the Neretva (ancient Narenta); at
Ston (Stagno), to be shipped out from Ragusan Gruž (Gravosa); at Novi (Castel-
nuovo) and Kotor (Cattaro); at Durrës (Dyrrachium) and Avlona (Vlorë); at
Corfu, Santa Maura, and Zante; in the Gulf of Arta and at Clarenza and Patras; in
the Gulf of Smyrna; at Naxos, Phocaea, and Mitylene (Lesbos); at Enos in
maritime Thrace; at Burgas (ancient Anchialos); and in Cyprus.[54]

An English traveler, John Locke, relates his impressions of the Cypriot salt
lagoons in the year 1553:

> . . . we hired horses to ride from Arnacho to Salina, which is a good mile. The
> salt pit is very neere two miles in compasse, very plaine and levell, into the which
> they let runne at the time of raine a quantitie of water comming from the
> mountaines, which water is let in until the pit be full to a certaine marke,
> which when it is full, the rest is conveyed by a trench into the sea. This water
> is let runne in about October, or sooner or later, as the time of the yeere doth
> afforde. There they let it remaine until the ende of July or the middest of
> August, out of which pits at that time, in stead of water that they let in they
> gather very faire white salt, without any further art or labour, for it is only done
> by the great heate of the sunne. . . . The most part of all the salt they have in
> Venice commeth from these Salines, and they have it so plentifull, that they
> are not able, never a yeere to gather the one halfe, for they onely gather in July,
> August, and September, and not fully these three monethes. Yet notwithstand-
> ing the abundance that the shippes carie away yeerely, there remaine heapes
> like hilles, some heapes able to lade nine or tenne shippes, and there are heapes
> of two yeeres gathering, some of three and some of nine or tenne yeeres
> making, to the value of a great summe of golde. . . . This salt as it lyeth in the
> pit is like so much ice, and it is sixe inches thicke: they digge it with axes, and
> cause their slaves to cary it to the heapes.[55]

Locke was describing the salt lagoons of the plain of Larnaca. A similar lake,
with a poorer grade of salt, was situated to the west of Limassol.

For the Romans of the first century A.D., the salt of Cyprus was the best of all
marine salts. From the location of Neolithic Khirokitia, halfway between the
lagoons of Limassol and Larnaca, one may infer that salt also was known to the
Neolithic folk of the area.

Like the western Asiatic sites of Jericho and Jarmo, the Balkan and Aegean
Neolithic sites were situated close to salt marshes or mines or in places to which
salt could be brought by boat, cart, or horse. One may infer, on the other hand,
that communities near but not actually at a salt site were prodded into producing
surpluses in order to exchange them for salt. Later, the salt gatherers may have
been inspired to produce goods resembling those they had acquired at first by
exchange. Gift exchange presumably evolved into economic exchange. Neolithic culture spread in these ways from one community to another. The process
of cultural diffusion was inextricably entangled with the process of historical
convergences.[56]

Permanence of Culture Areas

To the concept of historical convergences, let us add the concept of the spatial continuity of cultures or "permanence" of culture areas. Despite ethnic migrations, the modification of techniques, the appearance of new elite cultures, the creation of empires, and the disappearance of old and appearance of new tongues, the total number of basic world culture areas probably remained approximately the same from the latter part of the Neolithic era to the close of the eighteenth century. Culture areas have tended to remain as distinct entities, with only slightly shifting frontiers, even when the total culture of an area has been altered by the influx of new ethnic groups or the intrusion of other cultures.

Culture is an organized and partly integrated way of life, a system of learned or conditioned human behavior and the processes and patterns of communicating basic system values to succeeding age cohorts. All persons sharing a common system of behavior and a common language or other forms of communication (religious beliefs and practices) are thus members of a separate and unique culture. Accepting innovations and giving up older traits, changing continuously in terms of content or detail but remaining relatively constant in terms of structure,[57] a culture has both territorial and temporal dimensions. As "a space, a 'cultural area,' a dwelling, filled with a mass of very diverse 'goods' or cultural traits," it is able to retain its identity or coherence for a long time despite changes in detail.[58]

Culture is also bipolar, at once catholic and parochial. Its catholicity finds expression in an ecumenical world vision, in knowledge, things, and symbols that can be transmitted easily from one society to another through the medium of culture bearers in both. Its parochial configuration derives from its ethnocentric vision of the world. On the one hand, it is for export. On the other, it can belong to no other people.

What is exported is never an entire culture, only individual culture traits. When a people moves from one area to another, it has to divest itself of many traits. In the new area, it acquires many new traits. Each culture area thus tends to persist as an entity even though the culture it lodges may change.

Culture areas also tend to preserve their distinctiveness through the constant need of the societies they lodge to make crucial decisions. A society may have a choice of several courses of development. Once a decision is made, however, and the society starts off on a particular course, it is difficult to switch to a different course. The choices objectively open to a society are theoretically large. In practice, however, they are limited by the experiences it has already had, and especially by those decisions that constitute a "psychohistorical focus"—the choices that foster a distinctive emotional pattern, a specific complex of cultural values, a precise way of organizing a particular environment; in short, the choices that allow the society to assert its basic identity even as it changes in detail.[59]

Examples of a psychohistorical focus are the "Greek Miracle," the Renaissance, Calvinism, the French Revolution, the Russian Revolution (despite the momentary demise of the Soviet Union), and the Relativity Revolution and age of data-gathering and processing devices, probing into the subconscious and manipulating the mind and mobilizing alternately promising and frightening nuclear sources of power. Of all the foregoing, the last is probably the most crucial. Only one psychohistorical focus approaches it in importance: the Neolithic view of the world.

A psychohistorical focus is a special vision of the world, a way of occupying and manipulating space, a complex of attitudes toward the earth and cosmos. Among elite groups, it changes more frequently than at the folk level. In either case, we confront what Fernand Braudel aptly called *la longue durée*, for a psychohistorical focus can last hundreds and thousands of years and "exceed in longevity all other collective realities."[60]

A folk psychohistorical focus that has lasted until our own time came into being in the central Balkans between the end of the Upper Paleolithic era and the Neolithic of the sixth, fifth, and fourth millennia. Until the Upper Paleolithic era, or until the development of articulate language, cultural change "had been so immensely slow," according to the British archaeologist Jacquetta Hawkes, "that traditions could spread over half the globe, providing a universal culture to which we are only beginning to return today." Though a considerable number of cultures—each with its own set of tools and weapons, art styles, burial rites, and symbolisms—came into being in the Upper Paleolithic, it was not until the growth in Europe of dense forests, the diffusion of pottery making, the introduction of farming, and the development of territorial communities in the Neolithic era that there arose between one forest barrier and another a veritable "patchwork of small cultures, each with its distinctive products."[61]

Distinctive cultural areas were constituted long before the initial development of cities, and they generally have had a longer continuity of cultural experience than city cultures or makers of what are sometimes called the "great traditions." [62] Culture areas were ultimately identified in terms of one or more model cities. They had existed as autonomous culture areas, however, before the rise of these cities, and they often would continue to exist after the political demise of the same cities. Culture areas are thus units of long duration.

The Neolithic folk culture was everywhere much alike, a culture of fisherfolk and farmers, long free of the culture of cities. After the rise of cities that were more than ceremonial centers or fortified places during the second and first millennium B.C., the folk cultures became peasant cultures. Peasant cultures differed from the folk cultures by being dominated from without. They retained, however, the basic psychohistorical focus of the older folk cultures.

The Neolithic folk cultures of the Balkans constituted in some respects a single civilization or system of cultures. It was also in the Neolithic period, however, that the Balkans split into several culture areas. One may identify five of these areas with a fair degree of assurance: a central folk culture—Starčevo— in what today are Serbia, Macedonia, and a portion of Bulgaria; a northern complex of Danubian cultures—Körös, Maros, and Tisza—in Hungary and Transylvania; an eastern culture of the steppes—Cucuteni in Moldavia, Hamangia and Boian along the lower Danube, and Tripolye in the western Ukraine; a southern Aegean culture; and a northwestern culture—Butmir—in Bosnia. The steppic culture extended southward from the Danube across eastern Bulgaria and Thrace into Thessaly. The central or Morava-Vardar culture (in its Vinča forms) ran from northeastern Bosnia or from the Serbian Drina in the west to Troy and western Anatolia in the east and Macedonia and Thessaly in the south. Eastern Bulgaria thus was a zone of encounter between the central Balkan and the Moldavian or steppic culture. Thessaly was a zone of encounter of three culture areas: central Balkan, Moldavian, and Aegean.

The steppic complex of cultures showed a preference for obese female figurines, painted pottery, and spiral design; later it embraced a zoomorphic art. In the Danubian cultures, painted pottery was rarer; incised or banded ware (with textile and basketry motifs) was more frequent; and spirals occurred in repetition patterns. The central Balkan cultures favored incised pottery, finger-impressed designs in white paint, spirals, and slender female figurines; there were few repetition patterns. The Butmir culture was like the Danubian and central Balkan in its appreciation of incised spiral designs, like the Danubian in its choice of repetition patterns, and like the Anatolian in its predilection for black-earth statuettes of Hittite-like physical type. The justly renowned Aegean Neolithic culture had its own set of distinctive characteristics.

For the English social anthropologist J. A. Pitt-Rivers, however, the problem of the proper unit of area analysis "is one of the hoariest problems of social anthropology and like most of its kind it turns out on closer examination to be a pseudo-problem. One delimits the area of one's data according to the techniques which one intends to use." [63] Pitt-Rivers's pragmatism, however, and his focus on social relations stood in the way of an appreciation of culture.

More interesting for an appreciation of culture areas is the mind of Leo Frobenius. According to Frobenius, culture areas maintain their distinctiveness through their geographical separateness, retaining their own particular style even when they give up one style for another. [64] Despite changes in techniques and traditions or even an influx of new populations, adds Robert W. Ehrich, culture areas tend to preserve their separateness through the fact that the old "geographical forces of isolation, internal contact systems and environmental possibilities which make for regional cultural differentiation . . . soon reassert themselves." [65]

Culture areas also conserve their distinctiveness as havens for societies that have made different kinds of crucial decisions, or even similar decisions but at different times. One might also say that culture areas obtained a general size, shape, and identity as whole cultures only after they made the most crucial decision they would ever make until their choice of an industrial society. What will happen to culture areas once the twentieth-century communications revolution has exerted its full impact remains to be seen. However, the separation of the world, including the Balkans, into distinctive culture areas is one of the indisputable facts of history. An internal reason for the breakup of Yugoslavia and for the civil wars in that country during 1941–46 (until the capture of the anticommunist guerrilla leader Draža Mihailović) and 1991–94 (and beyond?) may be the persistence in its territories of such archaic cultural-geographic divisions.

Anthropologist Conrad M. Arensberg defines a culture area as an area in which many of the inhabitants possess "common forms of subsistence and technology, common forms of social organization and of institutional specialization, common religious practices, concepts, and symbolisms."[66] A culture area thus is one whose inhabitants possess a common set of social and cultural structures—a common self-regulating "system of transformations." The latter is Jean Piaget's term for such sets of social and cultural relationships as are governed by laws applicable to the whole rather than the parts and are conserved and revitalized by the very interplay of self-regulating transformations.[67] Examples of systems of cultural and social transformation would include modes of production, common articles and ways of consumption, common beliefs and ritual practices, common ways of exchanging women (or men), values, information, and goods. The actual "system of transformations" is what some anthropologists, among them Margaret Mead and Dorothy Demetracopoulou Lee, call a "whole culture."[68]

Writing about two thousand years ago, the Greco-Roman geographer-historian Strabo perceived the larger European system of systems of transformation as the product not only of conquest by the Romans but of cultural and ecological diversity, which itself was the source of cultural and economic intercommunication and enrichment:

> Now the whole of Europe is habitable with the exception of a small part, which cannot be dwelt in, on account of the severity of the cold, and which borders on the Hamaxoeci [dwellers in waggons, or huts fixed on wheels for the purpose of transportation from one pasturage to another, as necessity might require], who dwell by the Don, Maeotis, and Dnieper. The wintry and mountainous parts of the habitable earth would seem to afford by nature but a miserable means of existence; nevertheless by good management, places scarcely inhabited by any but robbers, may be got into condition. Thus the Greeks though dwelling amidst rocks and mountains, live in comfort, owing to their economy in government and the arts, and all the other appliances of life. Thus too the Romans, after subduing numerous nations who were leading a savage life, either induced by the rockiness of their countries, or want of ports, or severity of the cold, or for other reasons scarcely habitable, have taught the arts of commerce to many who were formerly in total ignorance, and spread civilization amongst the most savage. Where the climate is equable and mild, nature herself does much towards the production of these advantages. As in such favoured regions everything inclines to peace, so those which are sterile generate bravery and a disposition to war. These two races receive mutual

advantage from each other, the one aiding by their arms, the other by their husbandry, arts, and institutions. Harm must result to both when failing to act in concert, but the advantage will lie on the side of those accustomed to arms, except in instances where they are overpowered by multitudes. This continent is very much favoured in this respect, being interspersed with plains and mountains, so that everywhere the foundations of husbandry, civilization, and hardihood lie side by side. The number of those who cultivate the arts of peace, is, however, the most numerous, which preponderance over the whole is mainly due to the influence of the government, first of the Greeks, and afterwards of the Macedonians and Romans.[69]

Soil, Forest, and Climate

More important in the shaping of cultures, therefore, than cultural anthropologists normally admit is geography. But once a psychohistorical focus has been chosen and the culture of an area is established, minor changes in fauna, flora, and works of man and nature will not significantly alter the culture unless other factors—technology, sociology, and economics—also intervene.

In the Cambrian period of the Paleozoic era, several hundred million years ago, the Balkans were an uninterrupted continental land mass with Asia Minor. During the Silurian period, a vast inland ocean extending from Sumatra to the Atlantic usurped most of the land. Geological folding in the Carboniferous period produced the Carpatho-Balkan mountain system and a partial recession of the sea. Subsequently, during the Tertiary period, the Carpatho-Balkan system and the Slovenian, Dinaric, and Pindus Alps were uplifted, and the Cambrian core, or Rhodope Massif, was altered. These upheavals culminated during the Tertiary and Pleistocene in the formation of the Adriatic and Aegean seas and in the submersion of Pannonia and adjacent areas in a revived but shallow inland sea. As the continental glaciers withdrew, the sea was slowly drained off by the Danube, which cut a gorge (Iron Gate) through the Carpatho-Balkan system, thus dividing it into two parts, a Carpatho-Transylvanian system to the north and a Balkan system to the south (see Figure 1.1, p. 17.)

The Balkans began to acquire their present physical appearance only in Pleistocene times and just prior to the Neolithic. Residues of the former inland sea remained, however, as lakes or lake basins, such as the now-drained and tilled Lake Copais of Boeotia (first drained in Minoan times and then again, at the close of the nineteenth century, by the English Lake Copais Company, Ltd., in order to promote cotton cultivation); the Vardar-Morava and Maritsa depressions, which once were lake basins (the drainage and irrigation of the Salonika plain was begun in 1925 by the American Vardar Concession); and many Macedonian lakes.[70] Until a hundred years ago, remnants of the old sea were evident also in the Hungarian Plain, a portion of which, including stretches of the Danube and a zone east of the Tisza, from the Bega to the Njírség, lay under water for more than eight months of the year.[71]

Also formed in interglacial times and after the final withdrawal of the continental glaciers (8000 B.C.), just before the Neolithic, were the loess soils of
Pannonia and the northeastern Balkans and Ukraine. Either because the area was
widely forested during the Pleistocene and loess was never deposited there or
because the loess has since been carried away by erosion, it is now rare in the
western and southern Balkans.[72]

Loess comprises fine, porous particles of mud that were dried up after the
glacial retreat and blown by winds to various foothills or dropped in relatively
treeless steppe areas. Generally rich in humus, loess soils are very fertile. But
several conditions must be met before they support a long-lasting forest cover.
They must occur at a fairly great depth (more than the usual ten feet common in
Pannonia), the water table in the area should not be too low, and rainfall should
be fairly abundant. Aware of many of these needs, an astute British observer of a
century ago noted an important distinction between the forest-bearing and alluvial soils of north-central Serbia and the loess of the Banat:

> The soil at Požarevac is remarkably rich, the greasy humus being from twenty
> to twenty-five feet thick, and consequently able to nourish the noblest forest
> trees. In the Banat, which is the granary of the Austrian empire, trees grow
> well for fifteen, twenty, or twenty-five years, and then die away. The cause of
> this is that the earth, although rich, is only from three to six feet thick, with
> sand or clay below; thus as soon as the roots descend to the substrata, in which
> they find no nourishment, rottenness appears on the top branches, and gener-
> ally descends.[73]

During the eighteenth and part of the nineteenth century, sand and clay soils
gained ground in Hungary to the detriment of loess as trees were felled and
marshes drained to further the growth of a cereal economy and fulfill the requirements of new colonists and of a generally expanding population. For a fine study
of Mediterranean forests between the seventh and eleventh centuries, one may
turn to Maurice Lombard.[74] Lombard errs, however, in regard to the central
Balkans and western Greece, where forests were far more widespread than
shown on his map. For example, during the First Crusade (1096), the troops of
Walter Sans-Avoir and his uncle Walter of Poissy took eight days to traverse the
densely wooded Silvae Bulgarorum—so named for their location in an area once
forming part of the Bulgarian Empire—between Belgrade and Niš.[75] These forests are missing from Lombard's map.

In 1433, another traveler from western Europe, Bertrandon de la Broquière,
counselor to Philippe le Bon of Burgundy, was impressed less by the magnitude
of Serbia's forests—the Silvae Bulgarorum—than by Serbia's allure as "a very
pretty and well inhabited country," with a "great profusion of villages and good
foods and especially good wines."[76] Colonization had transformed the Mačva
plain, Morava valley, and right bank of the middle Danube into one of the most
densely settled Balkan regions.

Three centuries later, the same territory was perhaps more sparsely settled than any other Balkan land. Where there once had been people, there were again forests. The wife of the English ambassador to the Porte, Lady Mary Wortley Montagu, accordingly spent seven days in 1717 passing through the thick woods between Belgrade and Niš.[77]

In 1830, Serbian forests were thinner in consequence of the recolonization undertaken after 1750. But an English major, George Keppel, received a letter from a friend describing the area between Niš and Belgrade in terms similar to Lady Montagu's. Trees became more frequent as one moved northward from Niš. Low oak brushwood lay on each side of the road for many miles, and "immense oak forests" covered "the face of the whole country" between Jagodina (Svetozarevo) and Belgrade. "The vast quantity of timber which lay felled on the side of this road to rot" grieved him: "If we had but all these useless trees in England!" But signs of the imminent decline of Serbian forests were already at hand: "We repeatedly saw the finest oak trees in blaze: a hole is cut near the bottom, and a fire lighted in it. This is the easiest way of clearing the ground."[78]

More lyrical in his enthusiasm for the Serbian woods after his trip of 1833 from Niš to Belgrade was the French poet politician, Alphonse-Marie-Louis de Lamartine. Traversing an "ocean" of "virgin forests," Lamartine traveled for six days through "magnificent and perpetual umbrages with no other spectacle than the endless colonnades of enormous and lofty trunks of beech, the waves of foliage swayed by the winds, [and] the avenues of hills and mountains in the uniform garb of their secular oaks." Upon orders of the government of the new principality, however, the people were cutting roads, a sight that made him feel as if "in the midst of the forests of North America, at the moment of the birth of a people or the founding of a new colony."[79]

The proud woods of the Silvae Bulgarorum, of the Morava basin and of Šumadija, or Serbian Sylvania, are no more. In place of forests of oak and beech now stand patches of šibljak, deciduous brushwood. Southward, šibljak yields to pseudomacchie or evergreen brushwoods, then to hard-leaved evergreen shrubs, or macchie, and low, shrubby phrygana.

We do not know how much deforestation occurred before 1830. Even for the period since then, information is scarce. For some regions, there is no information on the deforestation that took place before the end of the nineteenth century. We therefore present with some reservation the data in Table 1.2 showing the decline of Balkan forests between 1830 and 1950 and the partly successful effort in Serbia and Bulgaria during the twentieth century to revive them. Moreover, on the basis of two sets of figures, we may conclude either that deforestation continued in Bulgaria until the mid-1920s or that it was halted between 1910 and 1920. The forest coverage of Greece seems twice as extensive in 1920 as in 1910, but the increase is illusory, being solely a reflection of the annexation to Greece in 1912 of the more widely forested areas of southern Macedonia and Epirus. In the

Table 1.2

Territorial Extent of Forests in Various Balkan Areas, 1830–1950 (percentage of total area)

Area	Year									
	1830	1850	1870	1890	1900	1910	1920	1930	1940	1950
Bosnia-Hercegovina	—	—	—	—	—	50.0	48.0	45.5	43.5	41–45.9
Bulgaria	—	—	—	—	31.0	29.0	23.5	—	—	—
(alternate data)	—	—	—	—	32.0	28.0	27.0	28.0	32.0	—
Croatia-Slavonia	60.0	—	—	—	—	—	34.0	33.5	33.0	32.4
Greece										
Pre-1912	—	—	—	12.0	11.0	9.5	—	—	—	—
Post-1912	—	—	—	—	—	—	19.0	18.0	17.0	14.5–16.5
Montenegro	—	—	—	—	—	—	52.5	—	—	28.9
Moldo-Wallachia	—	—	—	—	—	15.0	19.0	—	18.0	—
Serbia	65.0	50.0	35.0	22.5	19.0	—	18.0	20.5	23.0	25.8
Vojvodina	—	—	—	—	—	—	5.1	—	5.0	5.0

Sources: For some of the sources on which the table is based and for an overall view of the problem of forests and deforestation in the Balkans, see Borchgrave, *La Serbie administrative, économique et commerciale*, pp. 126–31; George, *L'Europe Centrale*, II, map on p. 724; Jardé, *The Formation of the Greek People*, pp. 25–29; Branislav Jovanović, "O šumama Srbije početkom XIX veka"; pp. 17–35; Logio, *Bulgaria Past and Present*, pp. 169–77; Markert, ed., *Osteurope-Handbuch: Jugoslawien*, p. 246; Martonne, *La Valachie*, pp. 295–98; Philippson, *Das Mittelmeergebiet*, pp. 147–55; Stead, ed., *Servia by the Servians*, pp. 255–59; Sugar, *Industrialization of Bosnia-Hercegovina*, pp. 129–38, 160–61, 211–12; Sweet-Escott, *Greece*, pp. 94, 124, 178; Turrill, *The Plant Life of the Balkan Peninsula*, pp. 135–216; Zagoroff, Végh, and Billimovich, *The Agricultural Economy of the Danubian Countries*, p. 239.

Serbian case, several estimates depict a less sharp decline of forests during the nineteenth century than shown in the table and therefore a less notable recovery in the twentieth. Part of the problem stems from the insuperable difficulty of arriving at a precise and universally satisfactory definition of a forest.

A human problem since the taming of the sheep, goat, and pig, and since man's use of slash-and-burn methods to clear the ground of trees, deforestation has sometimes also been an opportunity, as in the case of Attica, where, according to Arnold J. Toynbee, it was the challenge that inspired Athens to become the mentor of Hellas:

> When the pastures of Attica dried up and her ploughlands wasted away, her people turned from the common pursuits of stock-breeding and grain-growing to devices that were all their own: olive-cultivation [actually learned from the inhabitants of southwestern Asia] and the exploitation of the subsoil. The gracious tree of Athena not only keeps alive but flourishes on the bare rock. Yet Man cannot live by olive-oil alone. To make a living from the olive-groves, the Athenian must exchange Attic oil for Scythian grain. To place his oil on the Scythian market, he must pack it in jars and ship it overseas— necessities which called into existence the Attic potteries, and the Attic merchant marine, and also the Attic silver-mines, since international trade demands a money economy and thus stimulates an exploration of the subsoil for precious metals as well as for potter's earth. Finally, all these things together— exports, industries, merchant ships, and money—required the protection and defrayed the upkeep of a navy. Thus the denudation of their soil in Attica stimulated the Athenians to acquire the command of the sea from one end of the Aegean to the other, and beyond; and therewith the riches which they had lost were recovered a hundredfold. [Furthermore], the extinction of the Attic forests compelled Athenian architects to translate their work from the medium of timber into the medium of stone and so led them on to create the Parthenon instead of resting content with the commonplace log-house which Man has always built in every place where tall trees grow.[80]

Numerous factors have made for deforestation: accidental and naturally provoked fires; the building of houses and navies; the burning of limestone and charcoal; the smelting of gold, silver, lead, and iron; the collection of resin to make pitch; the building of roads; the drainage of marshes and consequent lowering of the water table; the kindling of forest fires to catch brigands or enemy troops; the exportation of timber—from Prevesa, for example, to the navy yard at Toulon between 1788 and 1795 [81]—and fuel wood; the ravages of sheep, pigs, and goats; and slash-and-burn farming and forestry, including the use of the ashes of trees as fertilizer for two or three harvests before moving elsewhere to repeat the process. Behind some of these factors loom economic development and population growth, requiring the replacement of forests by crops of hemp, maize, and tobacco.[82]

For some seven or eight thousand years before 1850, however, the forest was a dominant aspect of much of the Balkans. "Both in South Slavonic and Alban-ian lands," wrote anthropologist Mary Edith Durham,

> many places take their names from trees and plants. It is hard for us, now that Europe is disforested and the woods which exist are tamed and trained, to realize that in ancient days the forest was an almighty power. It blocked routes; it forced vast torrents of shifting peoples to swerve aside and skirt it; it almost completely separated one group of tribes from another, and is often responsible for the many dialects and race differences which torment us to-day.
>
> It was terrible. It harboured wild beast, wolf, bear, wild-cat, lynx, which harried the flocks and the herdsmen; it sheltered even wilder men who preyed on their fellows; and it spread and spread relentlessly, devouring grass land, damming streams with fallen trunks, and making mud-swamps. The little army of men struggled with flint and bronze and fire continually to keep it at bay. They fought the forest—but they could not do without it. Fuel they must have. The Arab in the south may manage with dried dung. In the hard frosts of the north man must have a real fire and plenty of it. From the forest, too, man got his building material, the means of making his rude implements: ploughs, carts, sleds, his tool-handles. An Albanian proverb says: "The forest gave a handle to the axe and the axe felled the forest." The tree-trunk hollowed by fire and axe still forms [in 1928], in some places, the ferry-boat in the Balkans. All food was cooked, all pottery baked, all metal smelted with a wood-fire. Man's life was bound up with the forest; it meant more to him than do the oil-wells and coal-fields of to-day. You cannot make a boat, nor a sled, of coal and oil; nor hunt game in its depths. No wonder that in early days man looked on trees as things to be propitiated and imagined spirits in sacred groves. Those of us who have ridden for hours through what is left of the Balkan primeval forests —even now almost pathless—know the awe inspired by the silence, the gold green light, and the endless army of mighty grey trunks towering erect from the soil that is muffled and bedded with the dead leafage of a thousand years and echoes no tread. The horse sinks knee-deep. You dismount and plunge through it with difficulty. Only the tapping woodpecker breaks the silence. Gladly you strike a marked trail tramped by countless generations, and reach a huddled group of charcoal-burners, who squat in huts of bark and branch at the forest edge, and—save that they have fire-arms and tobacco—live much as their forbears a thousand years ago.[83]

A question that comes to mind is, Were deforestation and afforestation mani-festations of climatic change? And, did deforestation and afforestation in turn produce climatic change?

Balkanologists have given less attention to climate as a factor of historical change than scholars of Scandinavian, North American, and alpine studies. In his monumental *Méditerranée*, however, Fernand Braudel pointed to several facts that may have signified a deterioration of the Mediterranean or European climate during the latter part of the sixteenth century.[84] More unreservedly, Scandinavian scholars hold that there was a climatic deterioration in Scandinavia, and one of them—Gustaf Utterström—supposes a simultaneous improvement of climate in an intermediate zone extending from England to the southern Baltic. Utterström thus links the need for grain in the Mediterranean toward the close of the century to climatic impairment, and the ability of the Baltic countries to place grains in Mediterranean markets after 1580 to climatic improvement in the Anglo-Baltic zone.[85] Data on Balkan climate are meager, as shown in Table 1.3.

Inconclusive though they are, the available facts tend to support the view of a more humid and cooler climate in the more northerly Balkan regions from the close of the sixteenth to the end of the eighteenth century, indeed, almost to the mid-nineteenth century in Hungary and Serbia. Until about 1840, observers continued to describe Serbia as a land of bogs and swamps, some of which never dried, notably in the Sava, Drina, Kolubara, and Morava lowlands. Its later transformation was achieved in part by private and public reclamation projects. In a more profound sense, it may have been the result of the contraction of the alpine glaciers, which began in earnest around 1840.

The fluctuations in the level of the Caspian Sea call for an explanation that may also clarify the general problem of climatic fluctuations in the northern hemisphere. Some of these fluctuations may have been the result of changes in the intensity of solar activity, with consequent shifts in the location of the cyclonic depression corridor. When solar activity is strong, the cyclonic depression takes a subpolar route, passing over Scotland, Scandinavia, and the White and Kara seas, depriving the Volga of precipitation in favor of the northern Eurasian steppe. Under conditions of moderate solar activity, the corridor traverses France, Germany, and central Russia, causing a wetter and colder climate in these regions, especially during the growing season, but bringing on drought in the southern Asian steppes. Under conditions of weak solar activity, the cyclonic depression runs across the Mediterranean, the Black Sea, the Caucasus, and Kazakhstan, causing aridification in the more northerly areas and a decline in the level of the Caspian Sea.[86]

Cyclical climatic fluctuations are of many types. The most well known are those of long duration associated with the glacial epochs. Among the less well known except in the nineteenth and twentieth centuries are the thirty-five- or thirty-six-year (actually, between seventeen and fifty years) Brückner cycles, so named after Eduard Brückner, who identified three short-term cycles of drought in western and central Asia in the nineteenth century: 1830–40, 1865–75, and 1887–97.[87]

The fluctuations in the water level of Lake Ostrovo in western Greek Macedonia since the mid-nineteenth century suggest that a modified Brückner cycle may have a wider territorial application. In any case, Lake Ostrovo lay at 538–539 meters above sea level in 1848, at 545.5–547.5 meters between 1858 and 1862, 534 meters in 1875, 534.26 in 1887, 525.67 in 1893, 526.02 in 1899, 525.67 in December 1903, and 540.88 meters in June 1923. Drought cycles of short-term duration thus may have occurred there between 1840 (in 1839, the lake is said to have stood at a high level) and 1847, perhaps for several years before and after 1875, and between 1887 (or earlier) and 1903.[88]

Table 1.3

Climatic Variations, 1558–1830

Date	Area	Data
1558–87	Caspian Sea	Caspian Sea rose by 1 meter; indicative of moister climate to north, the process was still going on in the 1620s. Lying at 32 meters below sea level in A.D 600, the sea lay at –29 meters in 1000, at –19 meters in 1300, at –23 meters in 1500, at –29 meters in 1558, at –28 meters in 1587, and was still rising in 1623. From a level of 23 meters below sea level in the eighteenth century, it sank to –25.9 meters in 1890.
1564–68	Ottoman Empire	Famine years.
August–November 1572	Greece and Black Sea region	Continual rains impeded the sowing of cereals.
1580, 1589, 1594–1604, 1608–10, 1640–44, 1664, 1676–79, 1700–3	Alps	Alpine glaciers expanded until 1720, presumably producing cooler and wetter springs and summers in Balkans, as in France and central Europe.
1593, 1596, 1597, 1598, 1601, and 1605	Balkans	Famine years. In 1605, family members sold each other into slavery to obtain food.
June 1601	Balkans	Torrential rains ruined crops, making people fear "a corruption of the air."
Fall 1605–harvest 1609	Persia	Famine, especially between the summer of 1606 and fall of 1608, preceded by a locust invasion and accompanied by drought. Modifications in intensity of solar activity may have caused changes in the latitudinal position of the Atlantic corridor of low cyclonic atmospheric pressure, causing the climate to become drier in some latitudes of northern hemisphere and wetter in others. The effects included a "little ice age" in most of Europe beginning about 1550 or earlier and perhaps a "drought age" in areas farther south and east, such as Persia.

Date	Area	Data
December 10, 1631	Salonika	Twenty-four-hour rain of ashes fell on Salonika, probably the consequence of the eruption of Mount Vesuvius on same day. In same month, a similar rain fell on Istanbul. (Violent explosions of volcanic dust reflect away much of the sun's energy, causing the climate to cool for a time.)
Winter 1678	Cyprus	Dearth in Cyprus. Famine in Syria, Palestine, and Judea.
July 1686	Istanbul	Dearth; by July 1686, grain prices were three times as high as in 1683 (Turkey was at war).
1690	Bosnia	Famine forced people to eat dog meat, horse meat, and even human flesh.
Summer 1694	Northern Balkans	Notation in a prayer book found in Valjevo district (Serbia) in 1820s: "So the Turk came to Varadin but ran away again because of the heavy rain; rain fell for forty days in the summer of 1694."
Fall 1695 and winter 1696	Levant, Egypt, Istanbul, Aegean, and Asia Minor	Drought prevented germination of wheat in the Levant and Aegean. In Asia Minor, rats ate wheat reserves, threatening Anatolia with famine. In Cairo, eight hundred people died daily of starvation. Dearth in Istanbul. (In England, Scotland, France, and Scandinavia, the growing seasons were much abbreviated and unusually humid in the 1690s, with dearth or famine as a consequence and the loss of one-fourth of Finland's population.)
1707	Island of Santorini (Thera)	Emergence from sea of the islet of Nea-Kaimeni (other recorded irruptions in 197 B.C. and A.D. 19, 46, 726, 1570–73, 1650, 1707, 1866–70, and 1925–28; earthquake in 1956).
Autumn 1713 and winter 1714	Salonika	Dry, cold winter without rain or snow. Drought continuing until June 1714 caused wheat prices to soar.
February 1714	Athens and island of Milos	No rain for last ten months.
Spring and summer 1714	Arta, Lepanto, Negrepont, Volo(s), and Salonika	Abundant harvest in Arta district, but a long drought in the other areas forced the peasants to feed their animals with prematurely harvested grains.

Date	Area	Data
July 27, 1714	Patras	Earthquake ruined 280 houses and church belfries and porticoes.
August 1714	Istanbul	Food riot.
Winter 1725	Istanbul	Wet, cold, stormy winter, worst in years, possibly worse than in Baltic.
March 1729	Istanbul	Grains were scarce; food riots at bakeries, several persons were killed.
September–October 1729	Banat	Continual rains and storms. In late September, "terrible" hail storm caused damage to public buildings in Timişoara (Temesvár) valued at several million florins.
Winter 1730	Istanbul and Thrace	Rude, snowy winter transformed Bosporus into "glacial sea."
July 1732	Tripolitsa and Modon	Poor grain harvest in the plain of Tripolitsa (Peloponnesus), dearth in Modon.
Spring 1733	Salonika	Famine caused Jews of Salonika to riot.
April 21–August 1735	Famagusta (Cyprus)	Violent earthquake on April 21 with repeated shocks until August. On July 5 there were several shocks at intervals of two to three minutes, each lasting four to five seconds. The earthquake of April 21 caused earth to rise and fall like the waves of the sea, water wells to boil over, and mulberry and other trees to dash against each other. Mosques, churches, and three-quarters of the freestone houses were damaged or destroyed, but houses of sun-baked mud remained intact.
April 11, 1739	Aegean and Macedonia	Snow fell. Frost destroyed fruit and vegetable crops but spared cereal crops. The snowfall was preceded and followed by dry weather.
April 22, 1739	Salonika	Turks began public prayers for rain.
May 17, 1739	Salonika	Still no rain.
May 21–28, 1739	Salonika	Rained the entire week.
June 15, 1739	Bucharest	Violent whirlwinds, lightning and thunder between 5:00 and 5:30 A.M., causing roofs of some houses and churches to collapse and uprooting many trees. No one remembered the like of this brief storm.

Date	Area	Data
February–December 1740	Peloponnesus	As of February, the grain harvest of the previous year was exhausted and grain prices were much higher than at Marseille. By December, the Peloponnesus was again threatened by famine.
August 1740	Istanbul and "most of the Turkish provinces"	Dearth.
Summer 1743	Aegean and Macedonia	Rain interrupted the drought on an unspecified day before August 17. (Precipitation in northwestern Europe was above normal from 1735 to 1739 and below normal from 1740 to 1744).
1752	Istanbul and Adrianople	Earthquake caused heavy destruction, especially in Adrianople (Edirne).
Summer 1753	Adrianople and Istanbul	Water damage ruined grainaries in Adrianople, caused grains in Istanbul to rot.
December 24–25, 1754	Alexandria coast	Eighteen French and more than twenty other boats wrecked in a storm.
Winter 1755	Istanbul	Hard winter.
Spring 1755	Balkans and Anatolia	Drought; public prayers for rain.
July–September 1772	Istanbul	North wind continued to blow without interruption.
Winter 1781	Morea, especially southern coast	Strong SSW and southerly winds combined with "continual rains" dangerous for navigation. No one remembered a more humid winter.
Fall 1782–winter 1783	Southern Mediterranean	For last three months (prior to January 11, 1783), frightful winds forced numerous ships headed westward to turn back to Zante, Corfu, or Izmir; numerous shipwrecks.
1782, 1784, 1803, 1822, 1823, 1828, 1829	Lika province	Famine.

Date	Area	Data
1788–94	Rhodope Mountains, Macedonia	Drought and war provoked famine and attacks upon grain depots of landlords.
Spring 1789– spring 1790	Levant and Dardanelles	Storms destroyed a "prodigious quantity" of merchant ships.
August 1790	Istanbul	Dearth.
August 1813	Epirus	Earthquake, followed by early rainy fall, a common occurrence in this region.
1813	Serbia	People reduced to eating the crushed bark of oak.
1813–18	South Slav provinces	Six consecutive famine years in one or more provinces. John D. Post explains the occurrence as part of a worldwide phenomenon, marked by "abnormally high volcanic activity of almost epochal proportions" between 1812 and 1815. It induced "the first modern pandemic cholera" in Bengal in 1816–17; the "most extensive typhus epidemic in European history," striking in two waves (1813–15 and 1816–19); a summerless 1816 in north Atlantic on heels of violent eruption in 1815 of Tomboro, in Indonesia; and plague epidemic in Balkans, along Adriatic, and in southern Mediterranean lands. (In world perspective, the *partial* effect of this meteorological catastrophe was "three decades of economic pause punctuated by recurring crises, distress, social upheaval, international migration, political rebellion, and pandemic disease.")
End January 1816	Hungary	Two-day blizzard of brownish snow (colored by volcanic dust), causing hundreds of thousands of sheep, kine, and horses to perish; followed by cold, moist growing season and reduced harvests in Hungary, Croatia, Slavonia, and Transylvania.
Latter half of 1816	Tripopotamos region of Greece, near Erymanthe glaciers	Famine preceded by savage attack of extraordinarily large band of rats upon provisions of Pouqueville's company.
October 1829– April 1830	Moldavia	Winter of "unheard-of rigor," temperature falling at one place below –30°R (–35.5°F, –37.5°C) on December 12, 1829.

Sources: For 1558–87 and 1605–9, see Gumilev, "Les Fluctuations du niveau de la mer Caspienne"; Brooks, *Climate throught the Ages, pp. 321–23; Stoianovich, Between East and West,* IV, Final chapter. For the Alps and western Europe in general in the sixteenth, seventeenth and eighteenth centuries, in addition to Braudel, *La Méditerranée* I, 225–30, and Utterström, "Climatic Fluctuations and Population Problems," see Le Roy Ladurie, "Histoire et climat," pp. 3–34; Le Roy Ladurie, "Pour l'histoire de l'environnement," pp. 1459–70; Le Roy Ladurie, *Histoire du climat depuis l'an mil;* and an updated translation entitled *Times of Feast, Times of Famine;* and John D. Post "MeteoorologicalHistoriography," pp. 721–32. For the sixteenth century in general and for 1564 to the 1580s see Stojanović, *Stare srpske povelje i pisma,* Vol. I, pt. 2, p. 354; Tradić, *Španija i Dubrovnik u XVI v,* pp. 19, 35–36, 65, 71–72, 87; Radonić, *Fontes rerum Slavorum meridionalium,* II, 459, 471; Emmanuel, *Histoire des Israélites de Salonique,* I, 221–22; Aymard, *Venise,* pp. 47, 133–39, 143–46. For 1593, 1596, 1597, 1598, 1601, and 1605, see Stojanović, *Stari srpski zapisi i natpisi,* I, 248–67. For June 1601, see Braudel, *La Méditerranée,* I, 249. For December 1631, see Emmanuel, *Histoire des Israélites de Salonique,* I, 266. For 1678, see AN, AÉ, B¹ 377, February 12 and March 17, 1678. For 1686, see AN, AÉ, B¹ 379, Girardin, July 17, 1686. For 1690 in Bosnia, see Filipović, "Odlaženje na prehranu," p. 80. For the summer of 1694, see Vujić, *Putešestvije po Serbiji,* II, 37. For 1695 and 1696 in the eastern Mediterranean, see AN, AÉ, B¹ 382, Castagnères, December 26, 1695, and other consular documents. For the 1690s in northern and western Europe, see Parry, *Climatic Change, Agriculture, and Settlement,* pp. 162–68; Jutikkala, "The Great Finnish Famine in 1696–97," pp. 48–63. For 1707, see Wegner, *Land der Griechen,* p. 116; Schmieder, *Die alte Welt,* pp. 182–83. For the autumn of 1713 and winter and spring of 1714 in Salonika, see AN, AÉ, B¹ 990, Boismont, February 28, 1714, and June 2, 1714. For February 1714, see AN, AÉ, B¹ 904, Goujon, February 2, 1714. For the spring and summer of 1714, see AN, AÉ, B¹ 170, Du Broca, July 1, 1714. For July 27, 1714, see Pouqueville, *Voyage dans la Grèce,* V, 295–96. For August 1714, see AN, AÉ, B¹ 388, Desalleurs, August 4, 1714. For 1725, for October 1729, for the winter of 1730, and for 1754, 1755, 1772, and 1789–90, see Stoianovich, *A Study in Balkan Civilization,* pp. 35–36. For March 1729, July 1732, and the spring of 1733, see respectively AN, AÉ, B¹ 399, Villeneuve, March 14, 1729; AN, AÉ, B¹ 864, Clairambault, July 9, 1732; and AN, AÉ, B¹ 994, Bayle, June 4, 1733. For 1735, see AN, MAR, B⁷ 322 (Levant et Barbarie: Journaux et mémoires du sieur Granger 1733 à 1737), Granger memoir on the "état présent de l'île de Chypre," September 1, 1735. For April and May 1739, see AN, AÉ, B¹ 995, Thomas, April 22, May 17, and May 28, 1739. For June 15, 1739, see DaPontès, *Éphémérides daces,* II, 219. For 1735–44 in northwestern Europe, see Post, *Food Shortage, Climatic Variability, and Epidemic Disease in Preindustrial Europe;* pp. 55–57. For February to December 1740, see AN, AÉ, B¹ 865, Clairambault, February 10, 1740, and December 17, 1740. For August 1740, see AN, AÉ, B¹ 417, Villeneuve, August 23, 1740. For 1752, see Flachat, *Observations sur le commerce et sur les arts,* I, 596–97. For the summer of 1753, see AN, AÉ B¹ 432, Desalleurs, August 1, 1753. For the winter of 1781, see AN, AÉ B¹ 906, Chateauneuf, March 17, 1781. For the fall of 1782 and winter of 1783, see ibid., Chateauneuf, January 11, 1783. For 1782, 1784, 1803, 1822, 1823, 1828, and 1829 in Lika province, see Filipović "Odlaženje na prehranu," p. 82. For 1788–94 see Ferrières-Sauveboeuf, *Mémoires historiques, politiques et géographiques,* I, 128–30; Atanasov, *Selskite vŭstaniia v Bŭlgariia,* pp. 26–29; Mutafchieva, "Feodalnite razmiritsi v severna Trakiia," pp. 204–5. For August 1790, see AN, AÉ, B¹ 448, Choiseul-Gouffier, August 4, 1790. For August 1813, see Pouqueville, *Voyage dans la Grèce,* II, 255–58. For 1813 in Serbia, see Jovanović, "O šumama Srbije početkom XIX veka," p. 21. For 1813–18, see Jeremić, *Zdravstvene prilike u jugoslovenskim zemljamado kraja devetnaestog veka,* p. 13. For the great Hungarian blizzard, see Post, *The Last Great Subsistence Crisis,* p. 22. For the latter half of 1816, see Pouqueville, *Voyage dans la Grèce,* IV, 328–29. For October 1829 to April 1830, see Soutsos, *Mémoires du Prince Nicolas Soutzo,* p. 66. See also Post, "A Study in Meteorolgoical and Trade Cycle History," pp. 315–49. For the effect of volcanic eruptions on climate, see Bryson and Murray, *Climates of Hunger,* pp. 144–45.

Table 1.4

Average Temperatures, 1851–1950

Town	Base Years	Average Temperature*	Base Years	Average Temperature*	Increase or Decrease*
Ljubljana	1851–1900	9.06°	1901–1950	9.5°	+0.44°
Zagreb	1872–1908	10.9°	1909–1945	11.5°	+0.6°
Belgrade	1888–1916	11.1°	1917–1950	11.8°	+0.7°
Athens	1858–1903	17.6°	1894–1929	17.4°	−0.2°

* Temperatures in degrees centigrade.

From a longer-term perspective, the cold humid phase came to an end in Europe by 1850, yielding to a warm dry phase of secular duration. Since that time, the average yearly temperature has increased everywhere in the Balkans except in peninsular Greece by half a degree centigrade every fifty years. In Attica and peninsular Greece, a slight cooling of the climate may have occurred (see Table 1.4). If typical, the changes in the average yearly temperatures of the Balkan and fringe-Balkan towns listed above would imply a trend toward a warmer climate in the northern bulk of the peninsula and an unaltered or slightly cooler climate in the extreme south.

Temperatures in Sofia have followed the pattern set at Belgrade, Zagreb, and Ljubljana, and at distant Kazan in the former Soviet Union where the average yearly temperature rose between 1828 and 1934 by 1.5 degrees. In fact, the Balkan climatic trend reflects a worldwide tendency toward a warmer climate.[89]

Many scholars ascribe the warmer and drier Balkan climate since 1850 to deforestation and urbanization. But in Attica and peninsular Greece, where urbanization was speedier and more intense than in the rest of the Balkans and where deforestation has continued despite the government's efforts to infuse in people a rational "love and respect" for trees (differing from old tree worship), the already warm climate has not become warmer. Deforestation and reforestation may provoke local alterations of climate, but the "causes" of general climatic change are more complex.

Space: Mana and Taboo

Man's vision and organization of space change in accordance with fluctuations in his notions of the cosmos. But since Neolithic times, man's conception of the cosmos has been almost everywhere basically identical, steeped in the principle of the sacred or mythical space, the system of symbolically if not always geometrically concentric zones, Mircea Eliade's "architectonic symbolism of the Center."[90]

In the Neolithic period the house arose around or beside a symbolic familiar center such as the hearth. Around each house was maintained a space needed to ensure the psychological tranquillity and biological survival of household members. Apart from the temple cave of Paleolithic times, temples may not have appeared in the Balkans until the second millennium B.C., assuming at first the form of a sacred place with the sky as a roof, as on the island of Crete or at the hill settlement of Sultan in Bulgaria and at Paraćin and Rudnik in Serbia.[91] Whether with a natural sky roof or with the man-made sky of the later buildings, the new temple was both a special place of congregation and a special time of communion. It was in fact a spatial expression of the temporal and cosmic outlook of a group that was so large (relatively) that it could not be brought together in an ordinary house and so separated physically that it could be easily assembled only at special (normally seasonal or vegetative life-cycle) intervals.

Perhaps a survival of the prehistoric temple is the South Slavic institution of the *zapis*. A sign of the cross carved in a holy communal or ancestral tree, usually a linden, the *zapis* existed in almost every Serbian rural community, among many Bulgarians, and among some Romanians. In Serbian villages where settlers originated from widely different areas, a *zapis* existed for each group with a sense of its own specific traditions.[92]

The fruit of a *zapis* tree was normally sacred or taboo, and climbing the holy tree was forbidden. As the residence of an underworld demon (daemon or mythical ancestor), it was a place of resort for the satisfaction of collective or communal needs, the holy place at which members of a community gathered especially at harvest time. Joining a procession led by an Orthodox priest, the community circled the tree three times, performed a sacrifice, and ate a common meal. In the Slavonian county of Požega, according to a Roman Catholic priest who visited the district in 1629 or 1630, Christians and Muslims alike assembled at a secluded linden *zapis* on a Sunday of the ninth month of each year to hear an Orthodox priest say mass and collectively honor the sacred tree, kissing it like a relic and sometimes making sacrifices to it. The yearly procession around the communal *zapis* tree has persisted into the twentieth century.[93]

Rarely a geographical center, the *zapis* was always a symbolic center. The sacral center of the community, its only rivals were the graveyard and the church.

In early historical and probably in prehistoric times, a community was defined essentially in two ways: in terms of its inner hallowed space, and in terms of its outer boundaries. From the latter notion grew the Greek, Latin, Celtic, Germanic, and Slavic terms for community: the Greek *polis;* the Common Germanic *tun* (English "town," German *Zaun*, and Dutch *tuin*); the Celtic *dunum, dun,* or *dum;* and the Germanic *gard* and Slavic *grad* and *ograda.* All these terms originally referred to a physically or symbolically fortified ring fence or hedge.

Denoting a commune, the word *verv'* may have alluded in Kievan Rus to the ritual wreaths or strings attached to trees or posts defining the outer limits of a community. The expression lives on in the South Slavic *vrvca*, which ordinarily designates a string but also signifies a wreath or marker. The Polish word for commune—*opole*—may be a cognate of the Greek *polis*, while the South Slavic *okolina*, like the Latin *orbis* and *urbs*, denotes a circle, the outer ring of a community. *Okolina*, however, may contain not only the sense of wheel or circle—from Slavic *kolo*, cognate of Anglo-Saxon *hweol* and English "wheel"— but also an earlier sense of stake. From this point of view, an *okolina* was the network of posts (or trees), the outposts identifying the outer limits of an organized human collectivity.[94] If not accompanied by special propitiatory rites, penetration by outsiders from the *strana* (a word related to Latin *stratum*), or polluted outside world, into the zone protected by the *okolina* was tantamount to an invasion of the outermost ring of the sacred space.

The hearth, the *zapis*, the *prytaneion*, the cemetery, and the temple, church, mosque, or *tekke* were the sacral centers. Around one or more of the sacral centers later grew civic and commercial centers. Beyond the religious, civic, and commercial nuclei arose the residential quarters, and beyond these quarters extended the limits of the city. But these limits were a succession of boundaries, ending only when the outermost boundary, the *okolina*, was reached.

A similar focus of sacral and social attention was the delimitation of properties. To mark the boundary between the fields of two or more farmers, the ancient Greeks made use of diverse objects and natural phenomena—statues, wayside altars, sanctuaries, watersheds, watercourses, and confluences of rivers. But the customary markers of places sacred and taboo were posts erected at regular intervals. Known to the Greeks as an *omphalos* and to the Romans as a *mundus*, the post, pillar, column, or obelisk was usually set above or beside the grave mound of an underworld demon or ancestor. It was often ringed at the top with a wreath (resembling the Serbian *vrvca*). It was in fact a symbolic tree, characteristically a fruit tree. Believed to be the possessor of mana, or generalized supernatural power, it was always a focus of collective emotion and sacral fervor.[95]

In Albania, at least until World War II, the designation of clan, family, and village boundaries required the participation of village or tribal elders and the performance of a precise ritual in which the persons charged with the erection of limits had to lay a curse upon themselves as assurance that their acts would conform to local precepts of justice. Albanian markers consisted of small stones, rocks, and boulders, small "witness" stones buried beside a larger stone, big stones with charcoal buried beneath them, deep holes, old trees, trees with notches, roads, and irrigation canals. In some districts, the younger members of a family were ceremonially shown the traditional markers at the spring festival of Summer's Day. Boundary disputes were frequent and sometimes settled by the shedding of blood, for no group honorably could permit the loss of land consecrated by an ancestor.[96]

Among Albanians, wrote Margaret Hasluck,

> Every tribe, village, house, field, meadow, pasturage, vegetable garden, vineyard, forest and spinney required a fixed boundary. Some boundaries were centuries old, but ancient or modern, they could in no circumstances be moved. The stones that most often indicated their line were, in the absence or rarity of title-deeds written on paper or engraved on copper, the chief tokens of ownership of property. Consequently they were . . . as sacred and immovable in the eyes of the law. . . . Brothers, cousins or villages might quarrel over a boundary and keep up the shooting until it had cost a hundred lives—nevertheless, the boundary remained where it had been when the first shot was fired.[97]

North of the Danube, boundary markers no less sacred than those dividing families, villages, and clans separated territorial states. The Imperial (Austrian) consul to Bucharest describes the frontiers of Transylvania, Wallachia, and Moldavia in the 1780s as follows: "The sources that spring from the summits of the Carpathians form the natural limits of Transylvania. Those to the south belong to the two principalities [Wallachia and Moldavia] while the transmontane sources belong to Transylvania. The latter plants an [image of its] eagle and the former plant a large wooden cross to mark their boundaries."[98]

The wooden boundary cross of the Romanians probably was a symbol of an underworld spirit like the *omphalos* of the ancient Greeks. It was indeed a special form of the *omphalos* and of the memorial marker known to the South Slavs as *potka*, a term related etymologically perhaps to Latin *postus* or *positus* (from *ponere*) and English "post."

Embracing three distinct meanings—post marker, taboo, and penalty for the breaking of a taboo—the *potka* spells out (in my own hypothetical text): "I am the ancestral demon of this community or family. If you are not of my community or family, do not go and do not allow your animals to go beyond the point where I stand because I have the magical power of law to inflict evil and harm upon those who do not heed the sacred taboo. The community in turn will impose a penalty or fine upon anyone who offends me or disregards my inviolate instructions."

Performing for a preliterate folk what the term "posted" did for a literate population in New England, the *potka* presumably is an old South Slavic institution. An explicit reference to it occurs in the mid-fourteenth-century code of Emperor Stephen Dušan with the sense of fine or penalty.

The material from which a *potka* was made and the form it assumed varied. A tree, branches (especially of the hazelnut) stuck in a heap of earth, a post, or a mere heap of earth were the most common materials in the zone of central Balkan culture—Serbia, western Bulgaria, Macedonia, and adjacent territories in Albania, Montenegro, and Vojvodina. This was also the zone where the most common term for boundary marker was *potka*, whereas in some parts of Bulgaria it is *počka (pochka)*, *bočka (bochka)*, and *botka*. In Dalmatia, the term was *cilj*.

In most areas the *potka* assumed several forms, but one form generally prevailed in each region. The dominant form in the Morava area of southern Serbia was a post or pillar with a cross carved on it. In the Timok district of eastern Serbia near the Romanian frontier, it was a post with a wreath of grass tied near the top. In Srem (Syrmium), it was a post, stake, or pillar, and attached to it was a wreath (as in many other parts of Europe), a sheaf of straw, or a board with a cross carved on it. In Kosovo and in the Skopje (Skoplje) district of Macedonia, the *potka* assumed the form of a mound of earth. In Dalmatia and Montenegro, it was a mound of stones with a cross erected over it or carved on one of the stones.

Geographic and topographic variations account for the different forms. Trees and posts thus prevail in the middle forest zone, imported boards in denuded eastern Vojvodina, mounds of earth in deforested plains areas, and mounds of stones or individual stones in the Dinaric-Mediterranean karst region.

Since the nineteenth century the *potka* has been modified in two ways. First, the cross has tended to vanish from the markers of Dalmatia, Montenegro, and Vojvodina, and perhaps of Macedonia (where the disappearance may have begun earlier, perhaps under the impact of Islam). In Vojvodina, the board on which a cross was formerly carved started to bear the inscription—and several decades before the advent of communism—*zabranjeno* (forbidden).[99]

The primitive purpose of the *omphalos* or *potka* was magical: to procure abundance and fertility and ward off alien and evil spirits. Already in the Neolithic period, however, the institution may have acquired a proto-economic significance—to keep strangers and their herds off the meadows and fields of a given human group. But the magico-religious and economic functions were so intricately intertwined that the purely economic role of the *potka* failed to be appreciated until the nineteenth century, when it started to lose its magical role by being desacralized, secularized, rationalized.

The *potka* reflected the premodern world view of the Balkan peoples. That view also embraced the notion of a holy or cosmic mountain (or mountains) as a link between heaven and earth. Vestigial beliefs current among Serbs until a half-century ago suggest that their ancestors once (but not in "earliest" times) may have imagined the earth and sky as being joined by hooks reaching out from four cosmic mountains lying at the four corners of the earth. Montenegrins believed that Mount Durmitor was one of the mountains holding up the sky. Dalmatians ascribed a similar function to Mount Otres. Serbian poetry suggests a liaison between earth and sky by way of a mythical "iron mountain" *(gvozdena planina),* while Serbian mythology creates a vision of a "wooded mountain of naiads" *(vilina gora),* protector of a primeval cosmic order, presumably reaching up from the earth to the moon.[100]

In their notion of a cosmic mountain, the premodern Serbs participated in a common premodern Mediterranean, Asiatic, and European, perhaps even all-human, view of the universe. Their Durmitor and Otres, their iron mountain and mountain of nymphs have parallels if not equivalents in the Mount Sumeru of Uralo-Altaics, in the pyramids of the pharaohs, in the ziggurat and holy mount of Sumerian history and mythology, in mounts Olympus and Parnassus and Delphi of the Greeks, in mounts Sinai and Zion of the Jews, and Rila and Pirin (from Perun) of the Bulgarians and eastern Macedonian Slavs, and in the sacred Christian mounts of Tabor, Athos, and Golgotha.

Although the conception of a sacred space is common to all peoples, the fourfold view of the world—four holy mountains, four heavenly rivers, four seas (northern, southern, eastern, and western), four suns, four points of the compass, four seasons of the year, four city quarters, four factions (Blues, Greens, Reds, and Whites in Byzantium), and four tribes—was predominantly an oriental notion. In Europe, Africa, and parts of America, the prevalent world view was in terms of three. Like Indo-Europeans in general, the Slavs and Serbs counted the passage of time in terms of nights and of the three crowings of the cock *(prvi, drugi, i treći petli)* and divided the day (daylight) into morning, noon, and evening.[101]

The Indo-European numerical notion probably also pervaded the thought of the ancient Hellenes until they came into intimate contact with the culturally Asian world of the Aegean, whereupon the European and Asian notions were drawn into a synthesis, allowed to exist symbiotically, or one prevailed over the other. The Achaeans thus came to regard themselves as divided into four tribes and grouped their ships in multiples of four. Less influenced by Aegean culture, the Dorian communities of later Hellenic invaders regarded themselves as members of one of three tribes and grouped their ships in multiples of three. In classical Greece, tragedy as a literary discourse at first also took the form of a trilogy, as in the *Prometheus Bound, Prometheus Unbound,* and *Prometheus the Torchbearer* of Aeschylus.[102] The Balkan Slavs ultimately incorporated into their culture—the date of occurrence remains unknown—the presumably Asian image of four cosmic mountains.

A product of the Neolithic cultures, the Balkan rural world remained a system of earth cultures until the end of the nineteenth century, bound religiously, psychologically, and economically to the soil and surrounding space. The intruding elite cultures of the early metallurgical ages, of classical Antiquity, of Roman, Byzantine, and Ottoman rule, and of Mithraic, Judaic, Christian, and Muslim teachings and institutions, transformed many rural folk into a peasantry. Not until after 1850, however, did groups of new elites succeed in institutionalizing a succession of rival productivist ideologies—capitalist (1840–1940), war economic and socialist (1940–90), and (from a short-term perspective) capitalist again (since 1990)—that would cause a radical transformation of the old Neolithic cultures. Submerged as they now are, however, the old folk cultures may still condition the deepest thoughts and feelings of peasants, workers, writers, and thinkers, and of men of action and politics—in short, of Balkan men and women in general—in regard to the definition of space.

Notes

1. Čajkanović, *O srpskom vrhovnom bogu*, pp. 50–51, 55, 71, 119, 197.
2. Vasić, "Htonski kult, Vinča i naš folklor," pp. 267–69.
3. Thomson, *Studies in Ancient Greek Society*, I, 334–39; Cornford, *From Religion to Philosophy*, pp. 15–17. On the Moirai and other spinners of time and fate, see Onians, *The Origins of European Thought*, pp. 303–415.
4. Oliva, *Pannonia and the Onset of Crisis in the Roman Empire*, p. 145; Blum and Blum, *Health and Healing in Rural Greece*, pp. 130–31.
5. Janković, *Astronomija u predanjima*, p. 15.
6. Maringer, *The Gods of Prehistoric Man*, pp. 153–56, 203–10.
7. Gimbutas, *The Goddesses and Gods of Old Europe*, pp. 106–7.
8. Čajkanović, *O srpskom vrhovnom bogu*, p. 136.
9. Romaios, *Cultes populaires de la Thrace*, pp. 174–79; Cornford, *From Religion to Philosophy*, pp. 47–48, 56–59, 75–77, 80.
10. Durham, *Some Tribal Origins, Laws, and Customs*, pp. 101–31.
11. Maringer, *The Gods of Prehistoric Man*, pp. 153–60, 203–16.
12. Harrison, *Themis*, pp. 14–18; Frazer, *The Golden Bough*, p. 449.
13. Čajkanović, *O srpskom vrhovnom bogu*, pp. 17–33, 61, 81, 119, 124, 147–48, 158, 165–66; Janković, *Astronomija u predanjima*, pp. 74–75.
14. Durham, *Some Tribal Origins, Laws and Customs*, pp. 131ff.; Gimbutas, *The Goddesses and Gods of Old Europe*, pp. 113–37. For a concise view of the Neolithic era, see Gimbutas, "The Neolithic Cultures of the Balkan Peninsula," pp. 9–49.
15. Rafo, "Prilog poznavanju ilirske mitologije," pp. 419–29.
16. Djordjević, *Priroda u verovanju i predanju našega naroda*, II, 210.
17. Čajkanović, *O srpskom vrhovnom bogu*, pp. 70–77, 108–13, 144; Harrison, *Themis*, p. 27; Stoianovich, *Between East and West*, III, chapter entitled "Material Foundations of Preindustrial Civilization in the Balkans"; Mijatović, *Zanati i esnafi u Rasini*, p. 211.
18. Thomson, *Studies in Ancient Greek Society*, I, 251, 290; Čajkanovič, *O srpskom vrhovnom bogu*, pp. 75–77, 180 n. 5.
19. Čajkanović, *Studije iz religije i folklora*, pp. 99–108.
20. Harrison, *Themis*, p. 138.
21. Romaios, *Cultes populaires de la Thrace*, p. 163.
22. Kemp, *Healing Ritual*, pp. 155–56.
23. Matossian, "In the Beginning God Was a Woman," pp. 332, 341 n. 36.
24. Kremenliev, *Bulgarian-Macedonian Folk Music*, p. 131. Differing somewhat from Kremenliev's, the translation is my own. Both translations convey the same essential meaning.
25. Kurath, "Dance Relatives of Mid-Europe and Middle America," pp. 88–100; Schneeweis, *Serbokroatische Volkskunde*, I, 137.
26. Dumézil, *Le Crime des Lemniennes*, pp. 45, 57; Frazer, *The Golden Bough*, pp. 145–47.
27. Cornford, *From Religion to Philosophy*, p. 94; Harrison, *Themis*, pp. 13–29, 54, 193–204; Dodds, *The Greeks and the Irrational*, pp. 77–79; Romaios, *Cultes populaires de la Thrace*, p. 73.
28. Čajkanović, *Studije iz religije i folklora*, pp. 157–65; Schneeweis, *Serbokroatische Volkskunde*, I, 136–37.
29. Romaios, *Cultes populaires de la Thrace*, p. 96n.
30. On fire rites and the geographic distribution of terms for fire—*oganj* or a variant thereof among the Serbs of eastern Serbia and among the Croats and the South Slavs of

Montenegro and Macedonia, and *vatra* among Albanians and most of the western Serbs—
see Trojanović, *Vatra.*
31. Sanders, *Rainbow in the Rock*, p. 181.
32. Kemp, *Healing Ritual*, pp. 145–55.
33. Schneeweis, *Serbokroatische Volkskunde*, I, 170.
34. Thomson, *Studies in Ancient Greek Society*, I, 363.
35. Trojanović, *Vatra*, pp. 120, 190–91; Kemp, *Healing Ritual*, p. 154.
36. Frazer, *The Golden Bough*, p. 80.
37. Djordjević, *Priroda u verovanju i predanju našega naroda*, I, 79–80; Schneeweis, *Serbokroatische Volkskunde*, I, 161–63.
38. Paton, *Servia*, pp. 270–71.
39. Schneeweis, *Serbokroatische Volkskunde*, I, 161–63.
40. Stahl, ed., *Nerej*, I, 387.
41. Gellner, *Plough, Sword and Book*, p. 17.
42. Gimbutas, *The Goddesses and Gods of Old Europe*, pp. 13–15; Dolukhanov, *Ecology and Economy in Neolithic Eastern Europe*, pp. 28–30.
43. Fewkes, "Neolithic Sites in the Moravo-Danubian Area," pp. 5–81; for similar views, see Popovitch (Popović), "Sur la chronologie de la civilisation proto-historique," XLIX, 129–46, L, 1–24.
44. Childe, *The Dawn of European Civilization*, pp. 61–66, 88, 342–44; Childe, "Archaeological Documents for the Prehistory of Science," p. 755. On the origins of weaving, see Wilford, "Site in Turkey Yields Oldest Cloth Ever Found."
45. Pittioni, "Southern Middle Europe and Southeastern Europe," pp. 220–23. See Braidwood and Willey, "Conclusions and Afterthoughts," pp. 346–48, for a critique.
46. Dennell, *European Economic Prehistory*; Guilaine, *Premiers bergers et paysans de l'Occident méditerranéen*, pp. 22–26; Gimbutas, *The Goddesses and Gods of Old Europe*, passim.
47. Rodden, "An Early Neolithic Village in Greece," pp. 83–92.
48. Anati, *Palestine before the Hebrews*, p. 38.
49. Waterbolk, "The Lower Rhine Basin," p. 244.
50. Maurizio, *Die Geschichte unserer Pflanzennahrung*, pp. 151–53; Maurizio, *Histoire de l'alimentation végétale*, pp. 220–22.
51. Danaïlow, *Les Effets de la guerre en Bulgarie*, p. 92.
52. Martonne, *La Valachie*, pp. 308–10.
53. Selection from the 1432 travel account of Bertrandon de la Broquière, in *Monumenta Hungariae Historica*, Diplomataria, IV, 312 (301–23).
54. Stojanović, *Stare srpske povelje i pisma*, Vol. I., pt. 2, pp. 314–15, 317–18, 327–28; Šamić, *Les Voyageurs français en Bosnie*, p. 216; Tadić, *Dubrovački portreti*, pp. 20–21, 66, 185–87; Kostić, "Domaće životinje kao transportna sredstva u srpskim zemljama za turskog vremena," pp. 58–59; Chaumette des Fossés, *Voyage en Bosnie*, pp. 4–5; Kritovoulos, *History of Mehmed the Conqueror*, pp. 108–9; Marciana (Venezia), MSS Ital., Cl. 6, No. 176, "Relatione e descrittione del Sangiacato di Scutari," account by the Venetian noble of Cattaro, Mariano Bolizza, 1604–1612 (microfilm copy belonging to Fernand Braudel); Academia Scientiarum et Artium Slavorum Meridionalium, *Monumenta Spectantia Historiam Slavorum Meridionalium*, Vol. VIII, Ljubić, ed., *Commissiones et Relationes Venetae*, II, 205 ("Itinerario di Giovanni Battista Giustiniano," 1553), on purchase of salt from the salt pans of Šibenik by the Morlaks of the interior; Geštrin, "Économie et société en Slovénie au XVIe siècle," p. 676.
55. Hakluyt, ed., *Principal Navigations*, Vol. II, pt. 2 (1599), p. 108, or III (1927), 26–27.
56. Leroi-Gourhan, *Milieu et techniques*, p. 465.

57. Wallace, *Culture and Personality*, p. 142.

58. Braudel, "L'Apport de l'histoire des civilisations," p. 20.12–7, my translation.

59. Barbu, *Problems of Historical Psychology*, pp. 9–10, 102, 200.

60. Braudel, "L'Apport de l'histoire des civilisations," pp. 20.12–10 to 11, my translation. See also Braudel, "Histoire et sciences sociales: La Longue durée," pp. 725–53; Stoianovich, "Longue durée."

61. Hawkes, *Prehistory*, pp. 50–52. For similar view, see Sapir, "Culture, Genuine and Spurious," pp. 113–14.

62. Redfield, "Little Community," pp. 1–182.

63. Pitt-Rivers, *The People of the Sierra*, p. 208.

64. Frobenius, *Le Destin des civilisations*, pp. 90–91.

65. Ehrich, "Culture Areas and Culture History," p. 4.

66. Arensberg, "The Old World Peoples," pp. 75–99.

67. Piaget, *Le Structuralisme*, pp. 6–14.

68. Lee, "Studies of Whole Cultures," pp. 77–114.

69. Strabo, *The Geography of Strabo*, I, 191–92 (chap. 5, section 26).

70. Turrill, *The Plant Life of the Balkan Peninsula*, pp. 218–19.

71. For an overview of the geography and culture of the Hungarian Plain, see Den Hollander, "The Great European Plain."

72. Houston, *A Social Geography of Europe*, p. 88.

73. Paton, *Servia*, pp. 255–56.

74. Lombard, "Un Problème cartographié," pp. 234–54 and end map.

75. Turrill, *The Plant Life of the Balkan Peninsula*, p. 193.

76. Bertrandon de la Broquière, *Le Voyage de Bertrandon de la Broquière*, ed. Charles Schefer, pp. 203–11, my translation.

77. Lady Mary (Pierrepont) Wortley Montagu to Princess Caroline of Wales, Adrianople, April 1 [O.S.], 1717, in Montagu, *Complete Letters*, ed. Robert Halsband, I, 310.

78. Keppel, *Narrative of a Journey across the Balcan*, I, 456–58.

79. Lamartine, *Voyage en Orient*, II, 257, 264, my translation.

80. Toynbee, *A Study of History*, II, 39–41.

81. Semple, *The Geography of the Mediterranean Region*, p. 281.

82. Haumant, *La Formation de la Yougoslavie*, pp. 286–87.

83. Durham, *Some Tribal Origins, Laws and Customs*, pp. 231–32.

84. Braudel, *La Méditerranée*, I, 245–52.

85. Utterström, "Climatic Fluctuations and Population Problems," pp. 3–47. On a short-term Mediterranean climatic change during thirteenth and twelfth centuries B.C. as the basic factor in the decline of Minoan culture, taking the form of drought in most of mainland Greece and enticing Mycenaeans to migrate, see Carpenter, *Discontinuity in Greek Civilization*, esp. pp. 61–67.

86. Gumilev, "Les Fluctuations du niveau de la mer Caspienne," pp. 331–66; Gumilev, "Heterochronism in the Moisture Supply of Eurasia in the Middle Ages," pp. 81–90. For a brilliant argument on the extent and level of the Black Sea that may nonetheless have to be discarded, see Huntington, *The Pulse of Asia*, pp. 329–58.

87. Huntington, *The Pulse of Asia*, pp. 366–67, 373.

88. Hasluck, "Historical Sketch of the Fluctuations of Lake Ostrovo in West Macedonia." pp. 338–47.

89. Stoianovich, *A Study in Balkan Civilization*, p. 37. On temperature variations in the Aegean and Adriatic areas and in the Mediterranean in general, see Philippson, *Das Mittelmeergebiet*, pp. 104–23. On mean monthly temperatures in several dozen Balkan, Aegean, and eastern Mediterranean cities, see Turrill, *The Plant Life of the Balkan Peninsula*, pp. 57–60.

90. Eliade, *Cosmos and History*, pp. 12–17.

91. Garašanin and Garašanin, *Arheološka nalazišta u Srbiji,* p. 116; Coulborn, *The Origin of Civilized Societies,* p. 154.

92. Kemp, *Healing Ritual*, pp. 111–12; Schneeweis, *Serbokroatische Volkskunde,* I, 15, 153.

93. Lettenbauer, "Bemerkungen in Volksglauben und Brauchtum der Südslawen," pp. 68–82.

94. Niederle, *Manuel de l'Antiquité slave*, II, 174, 178; Hencken, "Indo-European Languages and Archeology," p. 44.

95. Harrison, *Themis*, pp. 165–69, 396–424; Jardé, *The Formation of the Greek People*, pp. 15–16.

96. Margaret Hasluck, *The Unwritten Law in Albania*, pp. 95–109.

97. Ibid., p. 95.

98. Raicevich, *Osservazioni storiche naturali, e politiche intorno*, pp. 33–34, my translation.

99. Trojanović, *Psihofizičko izražavanje srpskog naroda poglavito bez reči*, pp. 118–22; Barjaktarović, " 'Potka' Dušanova Zakonika," pp. 232–33, with résumé in English.

100. Janković, *Astronomija u predanjima*, pp. 35–38.

101. Ibid., pp. 153–54; Niederle, *Manuel de l'antiquité slave*, II, 332; Djordjević, *Priroda u verovanju i predanju našega naroda*, II, 66.

102. Jaeger, *Paideia*, I, 254, 280.

2 BIOTECHNICS AND SOCIAL BIOLOGY

Balkan views of space may provide an insight into Balkan world views in general. One may sharpen this insight by ascertaining the relative importance for Balkan men and women of the various senses, and the significance of different parts of the body and different bodily techniques and gestures.

Marcel Mauss defined techniques as "*traditional efficacious*" acts.[1] The appropriate technique varies with gender and age. It also varies, according to André Leroi-Gourhan, with "the ideal mechanical function" that it is expected to achieve. The latter expectation depends in turn on the ethnic or individual style or aesthetic of the performers and on their conception of the relationship between the materials used in the performance of the technique and the expected result. It similarly depends on the performance itself or ways of making contact between the body or bodily parts and the materials used for the purpose of obtaining the intended result.[2] A group's perceptions and conceptions of the body and individual bodily parts thus reflect its own image of the group and proper role in it of the individual.[3]

Man (in the generic sense) relates his environment to his own biological need for comparatively unbroken activity or mobility and for group life. Except theoretically, therefore, one may hardly discuss biotechnics—the manner of mobilizing various parts of the body—without some reference to sociology and technology. Group life requires the formalization of techniques, while the need for mobility, given the character of man's brain and hand, results in technical activity. Even when highly formalized, however, biotechnical acts retain their biological foundations.

For the foregoing reasons, and because gestures sometimes are a more important mode of psychophysical communication than verbalization, we turn to biotechnics. We shall probe into some aspects of the ill-defined discipline lying at the frontiers of biology and sociology, closely related alike to social psychology and dynamic sociology.

Illustrious or Tarnished Face

Three dominant personality value orientations have characterized Balkan society for several thousand years: shame, guilt, and courage, or views hieropolitical, sacral, and heroic. As Table 2.1 demonstrates, each of these value orientations is bipolar. The negative pole sometimes is the feminine pole. Some of the negative qualities thus may have been thought to be becoming in, or "natural" to, a woman. By and large, however, males were expected to behave—although they often failed to do so—in terms of the positive pole. Each value is identified by an abstraction in current use, of which we cite only the Greek and Serbian forms.

The customary expression in Serbo-Croatian and Bulgarian for the honor-shame or hieropolitical value orientation, the most widely prevalent of the three value systems, is *obraz*. This term is closely related to Latin *imago* or Greek *eidolon* or εἰκών,[4] and to Latin *persona* and Greek πρόσωπον. The *imago* was the mask of wax molded on the face of a deceased ancestor and deferentially treasured in the family home. The *persona*, deriving perhaps from Etruscan *farsu* and less immediately from Greek *prosopon*, similarly defined a ritual or ancestral mask.[5] As inferred from medieval Slavic documents, the various meanings of *obraz*—form, image, character, person, symbol, face, figure, statue, idol, guise, and mask—suggest a history not unlike that of *imago* and *persona*.[6] The etymology of *obraz*—"cut-about" or "carving-around"—suggests on the one hand an image or idol, perhaps of an ancestral deity. It points on the other to χἄρακτήρ, the Greek term for a carving tool that was later applied to the image shaped by the tool and ultimately given the meaning of "character."[7]

Two expressions—*svetao obraz* and *crn obraz*—recur in Serbian heroic poetry, the chief vehicle of the courage culture. They denote, respectively, a face of illustrious reputation or a tarnished face.[8] For the Balkan populations, Slavic and non-Slavic alike, the face was "the focus of honor." Until the opening of the twentieth century, Serbian male peasants customarily raised their right hand or middle and index fingers to their face to seal a pledge.[9] The focus of a man's honor if he and his family were honorable, the "face" became the focus of his shame if he or his family betrayed a trust or violated the folk culture.

The precedence of the honor-shame over the philanthropy-guilt orientation is demonstrated by an enumeration of sins in the peasant's system of values: disrespect for one's elders or older brothers; beating or striking one's parents; incest; desecration of the prescribed forms of behavior toward one's godparent, godchild, and foster brother or sister; neglecting to make a ritual visit to the home of a newly married daughter or sister; the commission of almost any act injurious to the existing family system; a transgression against any firmly rooted family, village, or clan way of life; niggardliness in the exchange of gifts; and killing the lead ram of a flock. The last was sinful because it frequently led to the dispersion of an entire flock and to economic loss for one or more families.[10]

Even the sinful was what was shameful, while the shameful included all human thought and action that was a threat to the existing social values and forms of social integration. One may note in this connection that the South Slavic term for "shame"—*sram* or *sramota*—is a cognate of the Old Icelandic

Table 2.1

Positive and Negative Poles of Balkan Value Orientations

Pole	Positive		Pole	Negative	
	Greek	Serbian		Greek	Serbian
Honor and glory, honor and esteem	kleos and time (privileged office, reward, esteem); philotimia, philotimo	čast i slava or čast i poštenje	Shame, modesty, humility	entrope	sramota
Philanthropy, pious donation, good deeds, benevolence	philanthropia and eusebia	dobro delo or sevap (derived from eusebia and Arabic 'asabiyya)	Ritual inadequacy, pollution, sin, guilt	hamartia or miasma	grehota
Virility, nobility, manliness, courage in terms of the needs of patriarchal society and "humanity"	arete or andreia	čojstvo or vala i junaštvo (renown and heroism), more inclusive than either heroism (junaštvo) or chivalry (viteštvo)	Wanton violence, excessive pride, use of power without moderation, "inhumanity," self-assertion, violence of temper	hybris	ljutina or nečoveštvo and inat (anger without remorse)

Sources: For the value orientations of the Greeks, see Comford, *From Religion to Philosophy,* p. 118; Jaeger, *Paideia* 1, 3–14, 22, 41, 44, 47, 92–94, 120, 201, 286–93, 308–9; Wheelwright, *Heraclitus,* p. 5; Moore, *Sophocles and Areté,* pp. 14, 27–28, 52–55; Dodds, *The Greeks and the Irrational,* pp. 17–18, 35; Wassermann, "Thucydides and the Disintegration of the Polis"; Blum and Blum, *Health and Healing,* pp. 46–47. For the value orientations of the Serbs and other South Slavs, see Gesemann, *Heroische Lebensform,* pp. 116, 163. On this subject, see also Brkić, *Moral Concepts in Traditional Serbian Epic Poetry,* pp. 34–137, 154–65; Jugoslavenska Akademija znanosti i umjetnosti (JAZU), *Rječnik hrvatskoga ili srpskoga jezika,* 1, 904–7 (čast); Djordjević, *Beleške o našoj poeziji,* p. 189; Mićić, "Zlatibor: Antropogeografska ispitivanja," p. 426; Desitej Obradović, in a letter dated Vienna, October 30, 1799, in Skerlić, Dragutinović, and Ivković, eds, *Dela Dositeja Obradovića,* p. 541; Novaković, *Istorija srpske književnosti,* p. 182; Morison, *The Revolt of the Serbs against the Turks,* pp. 133, 135; Guzina, *Knežina i postanak buržoaske države,* p. 76 n. 4; Čubrilović, *Istorija političke misli u Srbiji XIX veka,* pp. 41–44. On philanthropy, *eusebia,* and *'asabiyya,* see Constantelos, "Philanthropia as an Imperial Virtue in the Byzantine Empire," pp. 1–15; Bell "Philanthropia in the Papyri of the Roman Period," pp. 31–37; Frye, "Introduction," in Frye, ed., *Islam and the West,* p. 3.

harmr and German and English "harm."[11] The infrastructural or old meaning of *sram* and *sramota* is "harm," while the superstructural meaning is "shame," a sense acquired by the word through the influence of the Christian sacral culture.

The two poles of the the honor-shame culture thus originally were the management of one's household in a way that either did honor to the community of householders or conversely hurt them. In the first case, one became a *kućić* or *odžaković*, a man of a distinguished family. In the second, one became a *nečovek* or "nonman," a man "without a face"—*bezobrazan*.[12]

A value developed especially in Montenegro, *čojstvo* was little evident before the seventeenth century. It did not imply valuation of "the 'free,' unbound personality," a nineteenth-century western European value, but rather embraced "the cult of the great, strong personality," the man who personified his family or clan by sharply carving out a more highly renowned image of it.[13]

Throughout the Balkans, individualism defined as the conception of the individual as the elementary unit of social organization was almost totally absent until the second half of the eighteenth century. Even among the Greeks, who in classical Antiquity had come close to a conception of individuality, the notion of an autonomous self was still in a reemergent form as late as the mid-twentieth century. The so-called *egoismos* of the Sarakatsani (Saracatsan) males of Zagori is little other than an extreme sensitivity to public mockery,[14] that is, to loss of face.

Dorothy Demetracopoulou Lee defines twentieth-century *philotimo* as a tridimensional "self-esteem" that embraces self, family, and nation. Out of fear of *entrope* (disorder), "a Greek avoids saying things and doing things which would reflect on the philotimo of himself, his family, his country. For example, the self-made man in Greece does not boast of his rags-to-riches progress. This would expose the poverty of his village, the inability of his family to help him, the fact that his uncle or his godfather could not or did not do his duty by him; it would expose much that should remain decently covered, and would further prove him to be lacking in *philotimo*."[15]

The ordinary speech of the South Slavs lacked a word for person or individual until the latter part of the eighteenth century. The Bulgarian monk Paisii borrowed Latin *persona* but gave it the sense of a person of good stature or other distinctive physical features.[16] Apart from the similarly recent borrowing of the learned term *persona*, the Serbs and Croats also lacked an expression for the individual person. In the nineteenth century, they borrowed for that purpose from Russian and Czech literature the word *osoba*.[17] In a play written in 1883, the Serbian writer Branislav Nušić introduced the word *individua* in a play.[18] It never became popular and was not included in the dictionary of the Zagreb Academy of Sciences and Arts.

Earlier in the century, the term *obrazovanost* was introduced into Serbo-Croatian from Russian with the meaning of German *Bildung*.[19] The relationship between *obrazovanost* and *obraz*, however, was only etymological. *Obrazovanost* referred to high culture, whereas *obraznost* continued to identify the paideia of good householding, as understood in a pastoral-agricultural society. As against the local, familial, and clan focus of *obraznost*, the spatial focus of *obrazovanost* was at least superficially the nation. Inferentially, it contained a sharp critique of the old *ponos* (not to be confused with Greek πόνος, meaning "hard work") or traditional mind set, favoring instead a new national and work-oriented outlook *(nacionalni ponos)*.[20]

Reasonable Ear, Willful Eye, and Righteous Hand

One of the ways by which the old Balkan cultures were revised during the nineteenth century was through a skillful reformulation by the literary culture of the proverbs of the oral culture. For example, one Serbian proverb held that "Fear has big eyes" *(u straha su velike oči)*. By changing the case of one noun, the literary culture gave a new meaning to the proverb: "When one is afraid, one has big eyes" *(u strahu su velike oči)*.[21] By this change, Fear was depersonalized, demoted from its status as a deity.

The distinctive attitudes of elite cultures and popular cultures toward the face, and primarily toward the ear and eye, may enhance our understanding of the Balkan cultures. In *La Jeunesse de la science grecque*, Abel Rey describes the Greek imagination as "remarkably visual."[22] This visualism is a structural characteristic of the maritime and insular peoples of Aegean culture. We thus may distinguish between the cultures of the maritime fringes, where visualism goes back to the seventh and sixth centuries B.C., and the cultures of the Balkan interior (often close to the sea), where visualism is of recent origin.

The emergence in ancient Greece of individuals who consciously or unconsciously set a higher value upon the visual function than upon the other senses, a partial consequence of the quality of the Aegean light, led a portion of Greek society to perceive each object as an independent or clearly differentiated plastic unit. It allowed the Greeks to create a discipline of philosophy and develop the sciences of mathematics, physics, biology, history, politics, and a rudimentary form of anthropology.

The affirmation of a visual or optical stress, however, did not result in a much-diminished stress of the acoustical. Moreover, the mass of Greeks retained their beliefs in the gruesome sisterhood of Cholera, Plague (Panoukla), and Smallpox (Vlogia), in the ubiquity of capricious and sometimes cruel nymphs and nereids, in dryads or maiden inhabitants of fruit-bearing trees, in Sir Boreas (the North Wind), in the "Bad Hour"—noontime, but also night, a whirlwind, a shadow, a woman, a baby, a dog, a donkey, a black cat, or a bear, that is, something capable of assuming many different forms[23]—in half-human and half-animal centaurs *(kallikantzaroi)*, who, like Chiron of old, effected cures with potions and incantations.

The Greek centaur occasionally assumed the guise of a wolf or *lykokantzaros* (and *vrykolakas*, revenant),[24] a creature like the werewolf or wolf-haired man *(vukodlak, vlăkodlak, vrkolak)* of the South Slavs.[25] The latter was reputed in some districts to thirst for the blood of young maidens and was said to be the mate of a fire-winged gnome called *v(j)eštica* (literally, "the wise one," related to the ancient British *wica*). Outbreaks of lycanthropy, a form of madness in which the sufferer imagined himself to be a wolf or some other beast, were in fact frequent in western and eastern Europe alike during the Middle Ages. It was commonly held among the South Slavs that a werewolf in life became a vampire at death.

Still widely current among the Slavic, Greek, and other peasantries of the Balkans at the beginning of the twentieth century, these beliefs were the product of long tradition. More fundamentally, they derived from a specific kind of mental structure: from the dominance in their societies of the nonvisual senses— hearing, smell, taste, and touch, which normally give rise to a diffuse, fluid, indeterminate, intuitive conception of subjects—and of an oral tradition, exemplified by Homeric and post-Homeric oral poetry (800–500 B.C.), by the Akritan epic cycle of ninth- and tenth-century Byzantium (known to us only through later written versions), and by the ballads and epic cycles of Serbian poetry (1400– 1850).

Without necessarily lacking good vision, Balkan peasants were "visually backward." Like pre-Enlightenment Europeans in general, they perceived "visually" not only the objects that were there but the zoomorphized and personified things that supposedly lay behind the "objective" things: pure and impure spirits, fortune and misfortune, nymphs and werewolves, the echo and the nightmare, the guardians of marshes, caverns, and cemeteries (that is, the vivid images evoked by phosphorescent sparks), and a host of other subjective phenomena.

Distinctions are sometimes made between the visual Greeks and the auditory-minded Hebrews, who were made aware of God's presence by the clap of thunder and the blast of trumpets. Among the Greeks too, however, visual-mindedness remained a minority phenomenon. Particularly in the village, the sense of vision, as a cultural device, failed to achieve an appreciable superiority over the other senses. An anthropologist thus aptly identifies the basic mental structure of a Boeotian village in the mid-twentieth century by reference not to its visualism but to its sense of smell:

A sprig of basil is a common offering to a guest, with the admonition, necessary only for non-Greeks, to rub a bit of it between the fingers to release its aroma. Indeed, the sense of smell is a far more frequently functioning mode of perception in [the Boeotian village of] Vasilika than in America. The villagers investigate unrecognized substances by smelling them, the quality and freshness of food is tested partly by smell, the decision as to when food is properly seasoned or as to when it is cooked sufficiently is partially determined in the same way.[26]

But of all the nonvisual senses, the most significant in the previsual era and in societies with a previsual orientation is the sense of hearing. The members of such societies frequently believe that "reason" or even the source of life itself is localized in the ear. Hesiod, for example, relates that the medicine man Melampous gained his prophetic knowledge by allowing snakes to lick his ears. The Albanian Ghegs (Gegs) of a later era reduce the snake to the size of a worm and contend that this vital worm, lodged in the ear, is the agent of life and that the individual dies when the worm dies. In the Middle Ages, a Latin hymn to the Virgin promulgated the idea of the immaculate conception in the ear. Almost universally people have worn earrings to protect the ear against the Evil Eye.

In Serbian society, the practice prevailed in schools—until the early decades of the twentieth century—of "pulling children by the ear." In the nineteenth century, teachers customarily ordered a pupil correctly answering a question to pull the ear of schoolmates who had previously given a wrong answer. As this custom was sometimes practiced, it mirrored the personal inadequacies of teachers, who were largely divorced from the ancient folk and peasant culture but insufficiently immersed in the ways of modernity. The original intent of the pulling of the ear, however, was not to exhibit sheer cruelty or to demonstrate where power and authority lay, or even to be harsh toward mental indolence. It was rather to fortify the power of memory and reasoning of pupils who displayed a deficiency in that respect by extending the hand of the more industrious, more gifted, or craftier student to the ear of the less industrious, less gifted, less crafty, or otherwise less fortunate one. When the future Serbian grammarian and folklorist Vuk Karadžić attended primary school in Loznica in 1796, it was common practice for teachers to impose on pupils a ritual beating every Saturday— *subota: djačka bubota.* This beating, from which no pupil escaped, was administered with a hazelwood rod, for Serbs regarded the hazelnut as the "tree for knowing good and evil." The function of the hazelwood rod was to transfer to pupils a feeling of the importance of knowing in the formation of a strong and healthy community.[27]

Two words served to designate a witness in medieval Serbia: *svedok* and *posluh.* The first was an individual who knew something about a given event or person (like the English term itself). The second was a person who provided hearsay evidence or simply was heard. Neither term clearly designated an observer,[28] for the best evidence was long believed to be hearsay evidence and the reputation of a person or his family. On the other hand, an early nineteenth-century Serbian proverb—perhaps an invention of the incipient literary culture—contended that it was "better to believe the eyes than the ears." Other proverbs seemingly of older origin held that the eyes are "deceivers," that they "see everything but themselves," or that they are "[deceptive as] water." Contrarily, a good reputation was "better than a golden belt," and the word went out to the young: "Marry with your ears, not with your eyes."[29]

In the 1840s, when Serbian art was beginning to develop along western European lines, an English observer visited a house in Šabac containing paintings of contemporary Serbian political figures. He was much amused by an oil painting of Prince Miloš:

> It was altogether without *chiaro scuro;* but his decorations, button holes, and even a large mole on his cheek, were done with the most painful minuteness. In his left hand he held a scroll, on which was inscribed *Ustav,* or Constitution, his right hand was partly doubled *à la* finger post; it pointed significantly to the said scroll, the fore-finger being adorned with a large diamond ring.[30]

From the point of view of Renaissance canons of art founded on the principle of a single source of light illuminating a scene and one immobile eye looking at that light and so giving an apparent depth to the scene, the picture was "primitive." More exactly, it was based not on visual perception but on the reputation and status of the person portrayed. "Byzantine" and "Slavo-Byzantine" ecclesiastical art of the eighteenth and early nineteenth century differed from Balkan secular art in medium and subject matter, but the two converged in their baroque or rural-seigniorial style and symbolic conceptions of nature.

It is wrong to suppose, however, that the Balkan peoples minimized the importance of the eye. Indeed, they may have agreed with conclusions of modern research that the dilation of the pupil of the eye not only reflects changes in light intensity but measures the emotional involvement of the viewer. Like many other peoples, they have been intuitively aware for thousands of years of the power of the Fascinating Eye—the βασκανία or ὀφθαλμός βάσκανος of the ancient Greeks, the *fascinatio* of the Romans, the κακὸ μάτι of Greek peasants of a later time, or the *urokljivi oči* (fascinating eyes) of the Serbs.

In classical Antiquity, the Fascinating Eye was attributed to entire communities and ethnic groups, notably to Cretans, Thebans, Cypriots, Illyrians, and Triballi.[31] Archaeological evidence suggests that Evil Eye beliefs were current in Anatolia at least as early as 6000 B.C. They were still a widespread Greek and Mediterranean phenomenon in the closing decades of the twentieth century.[32]

Localizing human reason in the ear, South Slavic peasants associated will and pathos with the eye, the principal nonoral agent for the expression of anger, surprise, interest, contentment, indolence, mockery, disdain, deceit, humility, coquetry, or desire. The eye was a mirror of the human emotions and passions. It was commonly believed that a *zloočnik* or possessor of the Evil Eye (animal or human being) could inflict distress upon domestic animals, especially horses, or upon a pretty maid or strong or handsome youth.[33] It could provoke an epizootic or cause a small child to fall ill or die. In rural areas, when a person admired a child, he or she was expected to spit in the direction of its face or make a pretense of doing so. The mother or other protector of the child would retort with the formula: "The fascination back to your eyes!" Until 1900, many South Slavic peasant girls were in the habit of wearing a pendant or necklace of phallic, fertility, and power symbols, including images of such objects as cowrie shells, crosses, trees, hands, steps, cocks, tools, and weapons, as a means of warding off the Evil Eye.

One of the most effective symbols against the Evil Eye, according to popular tradition, was the right hand, with the palm facing outward toward the foreign eye and fingers and thumb retained in their natural position (thus differing from the procreative Sabazios hand in which the little finger and its neighbor bend slightly toward the palm).[34] This gesture is found on some of the tombstones or funereal monuments (stećaks) of the western Balkans—22,000 such massive hewn stones have been found in Hercegovina and 38,000 in Bosnia—which are sometimes represented as expressions of the religion and art of the Bogomil heresy of medieval Bosnia. They may well be of earlier origin, however, for the outspread hand they portray is a common Mediterranean and Near Eastern apotropaic symbol.[35]

As a symbol of protection and vitality,[36] the hand—especially the right hand —is sacred. Pious Muslims rarely use a knife or fork for eating. When they do, they invariably employ the right hand, for Muslim tradition forbids the taking of food with the left hand, just as Muslims may not touch certain portions of their body with the right.

The right hand was similarly a symbol of justice and contract. A sale or purchase was often sealed in rural Serbian areas, even at the beginning of the twentieth century, with a ritual handshake or clasping or striking of right hands. Slavic nuptial rites also required a handshake between the contracting parties (the families concerned). Moreover, the South Slavic terms for betrothal (poroka, zaruke, etc.) and for an order of goods (poruka) both contain the root "hand."

The hand protects and binds. It also counts and measures. In the Homeric era, the Greeks made use of their fingers in varying positions to express numbers mounting to the thousands. The Romans likewise employed the complex art of manual enumeration.[37] In Serbian, there is a special word for the weight that a person can carry on his back (zametica), for the quantity of wood he can transport in the same manner (breme), or for the quantity of wood he can bear on his shoulder (naramak). But measures of length or quantity easily translatable into units of the body are expressed primarily in terms of the hand (ruka), arm (rame), or foot (noga), or portions or aspects thereof. For example, dlan or dlaka represents a palm's length; nokat, the length of a fingernail; prst, a finger's length; palac, a thumb's length; rasteg or rastegljaj, an elbow's length; stopa, a foot or step; korak, a pace; pedalj, the distance from the end of the thumb to the end of the middle finger when extended; čeperak, the distance from the end of the thumb to the end of the index finger when extended; šaka, a fistful; and pregršt, a quantity that can be held in both arms.[38] Similar words exist in Bulgarian, but such expressions are not confined to any specific ethnic group. They rather reflect a general pattern in archaic cultures (of which vestiges remain in modern ones): a tendency to relate units of measure to the body and, above all, to the just or righteous hand.

Narcotics and Stimulants

The intrusion under Ottoman rule of the pleasures and pressures of an urban culture produced a need for stimulation and forgetfulness alike. Until the mid-sixteenth century the Turks were noted for their sobriety.[39] Between 1550 and 1650, however, they became consumers of wine, coffee, tobacco, and opium. By the second half of the seventeenth century, observed Sir Paul Rycaut, the English consul to Smyrna (Izmir), "the vice of drunkenness" had become "more common amongst the Turks than amongst the Germans or our selves"—namely, among the Turks of the cities, especially the soldiery and young males. In town and country alike, however, males were expected to turn from wine to opium at the age of thirty or soon thereafter. Taken in the morning "in a small quantity, about the bigness of a tare," the opium "superinduces at first a strange cheerfulness about the heart." But as the opium

> begins to digest, the vapour becomes more gross, and consequently a kind of stupefaction is induced over the brain and nerves, which with drowsiness and sleep passes away like a drunken fit. The youth amongst them which drink wine abhor opium, until growing into years, and to the care of a family (as a sign of which they suffer their beards to increase) they are taught by their imaum *[imam]*, and more by example of others, that wine being against their [Muslim] law, is only dispensable in wild and unbridled youth, but in those of riper age is a vice to be reproached by all sober and well-governed men. In the place of which they take up the lawful and innocent pill of opium, which makes men serious and settled (as they say) because that it operates not like wine, which makes men mad, and rash, and violent, but disposes them to be sots, and to sit grave and quiet without doing hurt to any man, which is a qualification accounted very laudable amongst them, and is one of the greatest virtues which they endeavour to acquire in their tekkés *[tekkes]* or monasteries. This being the reason for which it is taken and allowed, it is grown a common custom almost amongst all the country-people, who in the morning before they go to work take first their opium, and upon it three or four dishes of cofee *[sic]*; for it is observable, that none eats opium but who accompanies it with great quantities of coffee, which is doubtless a kind of opiate in it self, and partakes very much of a narcotick quality; by this means and constant use some arrive to take strange quantities; the most that ever I knew any man take was three drams in twenty-four hours, viz. a dram and a half or thereabouts in the morning, and as much an hour afternoon: the which for more exactness I had the curiosity to see weighed.[40]

The consumption of wine, coffee, and tobacco became a threat to the agents of political order—not, however, to the political system—because it usually was done in such places of congregation as the coffeehouse and tavern—coffee, tobacco, and opium in the coffeehouse and wine in the tavern—where loose talk might provide the occasion for insurrection against one or more political authorities. Himself an inveterate drinker of wine, Murad IV (r.1623–40) repeatedly issued injunctions proscribing the drinking of wine, coffee, and tobacco (the last by means of the narghile). The prohibitive or restrictive measures were directed, wrote Rycaut, against taverns, coffeehouses, tobacco shops, and "other idle places of concourse," to wit, barber shops, where no more than one person "was suffered to enter at a time; for these being places of resort, treason was frequently vented there, men of that profession being notorious through the world for their talk and intemperance of language." To inhibit fires, often the occasion of disorders in the capital, orders were issued that all fires and candles should be extinguished within two hours after nightfall.[41]

These measures of high police, wrote Joseph von Hammer-Purgstall, were "designed to prevent gatherings of the unemployed and suppress all places of reunion where the state of public affairs might be a subject of discussion. Not without reason, the despot [Murad] feared that, in the midst of cups and pipes, there might develop a spirit of turbulence and resistance difficult to arrest."[42]

Such earlier orders were repeated between 1622 and 1670, applicable sometimes not only to the capital but also to other large cities. Despite the death penalty and other cruel punishments, opposition to the injunctions continued. Epigrams abounded in the capital, calling in particular for the restoration of the free status of "the Negro" (the unhindered consumption of coffee). Only toward the end of the 1660s did the coffeehouse finally prevail as an Ottoman institution against which actions by the government were bound to fail.[43]

In 1670, elaborated Rycaut, a government order to the *kadi* of Izmir prohibiting the consumption of wine in places with Muslim inhabitants further castigated the practice, affirming:

> that wine and games at dice and figured cards, and of arrows without feathers, which are lotteries, are the filthiness of diabolical work . . . , are fomenters of malice and wickedness, and are the ferment of that faction & sedition which corrupt and seduce the servants of God, which being prohibited by authority, and yet used, provokes the anger and disdain of Almighty God against us . . . .
>
> [Therefore] . . . , when this royal command comes to your hands, wheresoever there are taverns of wine, let them be raised [that is, razed] and thrown down in all cities and towns ennobled with Musulmin [Muslim] Moschs, let the buying and selling thereof be prohibited, with all drinking and use of wine; and likewise I command, that in Constantinople [Istanbul], Brusa [Bursa], and Adrianople [Edirne] the imposition thereupon be wholly taken off. And that in all other cities and towns adorned with Musulmin Moschs, there be not a drop of wine suffered or admitted in; and that Musulmins neither privately nor secretly drink wine.

A year later, Christian priests and all Franks (Frenks, Europeans) were allowed to make wine in their own homes. In 1672, taverns were allowed to reopen.[44]

The campaign against wine, coffee, and tobacco—this last item introduced perhaps to the Ottoman Turks by the Dutch—could not succeed for two important reasons. First, too large a public and too strong powerful interests—the Christian church, the soldiery, and the *ulema* or Muslim religious leaders—had a stake in their consumption. Second, the government itself levied sales taxes on one or more of these items. It also licensed the right to vend or distribute them, presumably in order to limit their sale but, from a practical point of view, in order to augment the state's revenues. As its share in the taxes collected declined, the government became less eager to deprive itself of the revenues brought in by licensed coffeehouses and taverns, by grants of monopolies, and by sales taxes and taxes on the raising of tobacco.[45]

The government's position toward opium is less clear. It may not to have been averse to its consumption except to the extent that much of it occurred in coffeehouses. Moreover, its consumption disinclined consumers to rebel, an achievement not disadvantageous to the government. Many consumers of opium ultimately may have been incapacitated. But since unemployment was a perennial problem, the withdrawal of consumers of opium from the labor market may not have seemed a great evil.

Gestures, Technics, and Civilization

Peoples with similar languages sometimes misunderstand and distrust each other. A different alphabet may be one source of misunderstanding, as in the case of the Serbs, Bosnians, and Croats, the first with a tradition of Cyrillic characters; the second with a mixed tradition of "Bosnian," Latin, Cyrillic, and Arabic scripts; and the third with a tradition of Glagolitic (a script slightly older than the Cyrillic, now largely restricted to the liturgical books of a few Dalmatian communities) and Latin. Another source of discord is a different set of gestures.

An early nineteenth-century chaplain to the British embassy in Istanbul, Reverend Robert Walsh, perceived the importance of gestures in distinguishing Ottoman from European civilization: "The Turkish barber pushed the razor from him—ours draws it to him; the carpenter, on the contrary, drew the saw to him, for all the teeth are set in—ours pushes it from him, for all the teeth are set out; the mason sat while he laid the stones—ours always stands; the scribe wrote on his hand, and from right to left—ours always writes on a desk or table, and from left to right."[46] The source of such differences may be technological. But once tools adapted in a certain way to the hand or other parts of the body are diffused within a society, a predisposition is created in their favor which makes it difficult for members of the society to accept tools requiring a different form of manipulation.

Some gestures have no direct relationship to technology but are such an essential part of intracultural communication that they will be altered with the greatest reluctance and only in periods of tremendous cultural stress. Such gestures include the manner of saying yes and no. The classical Greeks, who possessed a highly developed art of gesture, brought the head down to indicate acknowledgment and turned it sideways to show disapproval. Under oriental influences, they later modified their gestures.

By the latter part of the sixteenth century, the Balkans were divided into three broad cultural areas: (1) a northwestern zone, where the old gestures were preserved, as in most of the rest of Europe; (2) a southern and southeastern zone, in which Greeks and Orthodox Albanians brought their head down to say yes and threw it back to indicate no; and (3) a central and eastern zone, in which Serbs, Bulgarians, and some of their immediate neighbors shook their head in affirmation and nodded to demonstrate negation.

Since the Enlightenment, and especially since the Serbian and Greek revolutions (wars of independence), the eastern and southern modes of expression have receded before the northwestern, particularly in the cities. Around 1900, the zone of eastern gesture was limited to the area north of Greece, as that country was then constituted, and south of a line running from Bar (Antivari) on the Adriatic to the Morava at Ćuprija and then continuing eastward. To the north and west of this line was an expanding area in which the gestures of the urban male youth were "western" and those of the old folk and women were "eastern." Since 1900, the "eastern" gestures have continued to disappear. The southern or southeastern gestures of the Greeks (and of many Turks) have been more tenacious.[47]

Emotional States

Like the peoples of other European premodern societies, Balkan man was impulsive and inclined to violence. A nineteenth-century Serbian statesman, Ilija Garašanin, thus called upon God to "slay" his enemies. The Orthodox church of Greece invoked against Eleutherios Venizelos, for his espousal of the Allied cause during the First World War, "the ulcers of Job, the whale of Jonah, the leprosy of Naaman, the bite of death, the shuddering of the dying, the thunderbolt of Hell, and the malediction of God and man."[48] Montenegrins, who—like the Turks, Albanians, and inhabitants of the Bay of Kotor—engaged in headhunting when at war, until their government took steps to put a stop to the custom in 1862, are known to have torn Muslims to shreds with their teeth in hand-to-hand combat in boat battles on the waters of Lake Scutari (Shkodër, Skadar).[49]

Even more than violence, what characterizes the Balkan peoples is their impulsiveness, especially the ease with which they can pass from one emotion to its opposite. Joy gives way to tears and lamentations, the tearing of hair, and the beating of breasts. Tears and lamentations yield to rejoicing, as at the wake (*strava*, both an expression and a shaking off of the dread of death) of Attila the Hun in A.D. 453: "After having grievously mourned him, they [his subjects] proceeded to regale in banquetry, performing over his tomb the ritual that they call *strava*. Freely coupling opposite extremes of feeling, they passed from moments of funereal sorrow to moments of gaudy joy."[50]

Culturally, such joy is religious-magical, intended to reanimate the dead. The cultural response, however, may be an expression of a psychological need. Grief must yield to joy, even hysterical joy, or else there is no more life. To paraphrase the French historian Lucien Febvre, every human feeling is at once itself and its contrary,[51] while the character of a given culture and the play of personal attitudes determine whether, at a specific moment, hate prevails over love or pity over cruelty. These contrasting states, however, are unified. One of them cannot manifest itself without engendering its opposite, at least at a latent level.

Certain cultures discourage the expression of the opposite poles of man's emotional states. The Puritan tradition provides one example of such a culture. Other traditions have likewise attempted to unify opposites in a middle way or to free man from opposites: the Chinese *tao (dao)*, the Hindu *nirvana*, the Greek *sophrosyne*, the European Enlightenment. We shall deal with the attempts to create a middle way in the Balkans in a later chapter. Suffice it to say here that the dominant way of the Balkans was not the middle but the polar way: the way of honor and shame, ritual inadequacy and philanthropy, humanity and inhumanity.

A French doctor, Gabriel Frilley, who served at the court of Prince Nikola of Montenegro from 1870 to 1880, has left a medical portrait of the mental state of Montenegrins, which, in modified form, may also have held true of the other Balkan peoples: "Neuroses appear to dominate the pathology of Montenegrins: neuroses of the understanding [the French term is "intelligence"] in considerable proportions for such a small population; neuroses of the sensibilities, and especially of the head, [such as] migraine [and] the most varied kinds of neuralgia; add to this infantile paralysis, hysteria among at least a third of the womenfolk, troubles of the nervous system among many men, [and] nervous beatings of the aorta, almost universal in both sexes."[52]

So prevalent among women in ancient Hellas that the Greeks associated it with the stoppage of the womb, hysteria often took the form of a mass phenomenon. George Thomson relates that "Cases of mass hysteria are recorded from Sparta and Lokroi Epizephyrioi, and in both the victims were women. At Sparta they were cured by the medicine-man Bakis under instructions from the Delphic Oracle. At Lokroi they would be sitting quietly at their meal, when suddenly, as though in answer to a supernatural voice, they would leap in a frenzy and run out of the town. They were cured by singing paeans to Apollo."[53] Cases of neurasthenia and hysteria might have been more numerous had it not been for the Dionysiac ritual of "mountain dancing" at regular times of the year, which provided a ritual outlet for irrational impulses.

Evidence of such "mountain dancing," particularly in regions that did not come under the influence of the "middle way" of Greek antiquity—notably, in Thrace, where the cult of Sabazios and Semele was transformed into the cult of St. Constantine and St. Helen, and in the Scythian steppe—persisted until the mid-twentieth century. In several Thracian villages, for example, between the night of May 2 and the week of May 21 (the feast of St. Constantine and St. Helen), the inhabitants, especially the women and girls, engaged in public singing and dancing. On the nights of May 20–21, barefoot medicine men and women *(nestenaria)* entered into an orgiastic dance over hot embers. Reminiscent of the Gaelic May Day festival of Beltane (Baaltin, Beltin), the Thracian fire dance was followed by a cathartic week of fun, frolic, festivity, and frenzy, the chief aim of which was ritual purification or renewal.[54]

As the ritual outlets for the expression of irrational impulses were slowly removed during the nineteenth century through the spread of rationalism and what is sometimes called "westernization," there may have been an increase in manifestations of hysteria. In any event, anthropologist Mary Edith Durham has described a curious form of neurasthenia among the women of Macedonia and Montenegro, often psychologically exhausted by their unenviable lot of childbearing, lactation, and toil:

> It begins as a hiccough, and becomes more and more intense until it is a violent and fast-recurring spasm of the diaphragm. The hiccoughs become louder and louder till they are an uninterrupted crowing like that of a hoarse rooster. So quick are they that the patient cannot breathe. Just as she appears to be in danger of choking, she suddenly pulls herself together, draws a long breath, gives a gasp or two, and recovers in a few minutes. At intervals the attacks may go on all day; nor, when the habit is acquired, is it easy to cure. To a certain extent it is under the patient's control; but, not entirely.[55]

This neurasthenia was a form of protest, culturally permissible because the patriarchal society, then under attack from abroad and from the youth and "intelligentsia" in its midst, failed to realize how much the emotional behavior of its women similarly could constitute a threat to its continued existence.

Childbirth and Pedagogy

Childbearing and lactation constituted an important part of the functions of the Balkan woman. The basic birth technique in many ancient cultures is exemplified by the birth of Buddha to Maya while she stood upright holding on to a tree branch.[56] With certain modifications, this technique of childbirth persisted in many rural areas of the Balkans until the latter part of the nineteenth century and sporadically for a half-century longer. Especially in Montenegro and some rural districts of Macedonia, women often gave birth while working in the fields. During the 1860s, the usual technique in Montenegro, when the woman was at home, was to give birth while standing up, her legs spread apart and her arm resting on some piece of furniture, the domestic "tree branch." Another practice, reported a half-century later, similar to the American birthing-chair technique of the 1980s and 1990s, was childbirth with the assistance of old women who served as midwives. The old women would walk the mother endlessly up and down the hut, supporting her under the armpits if she was too weak to go on but refusing to let her sit or lie down lest the child fail to drop out. If the floor of the hut was of stone, they spread straw over it to prevent the cracking of the child's head. The day after giving birth, or on the second day, Montenegrin women resumed their customary occupations. In other regions, they returned to their tasks a day or two later.[57]

In southern Macedonia, along the present-day frontier between Greece and what until 1991 was Yugoslavia, the pregnant woman enjoyed a relatively privileged position if data for the past half-century also apply to earlier periods. She owed this status to the desire of her family and community to improve her chances of bearing a healthy child. Efforts thus were made to exempt her from hard work, spare her unpleasant sights, and gratify her sense of taste. The most careful attention was given to this last point. It was believed that a pregnant woman's culinary cravings were, in reality, expressions of the needs of the fetus or unborn child.

Almost everywhere in the Balkans the infant was swaddled, lightly in Albania, round and round in Macedonia. After forty days or after its first smile, it was allowed to have one hand free. In some districts of Albania infants were strapped to a board until their baptism or, in Muslim families, for the first forty days after birth.[58]

The naturalist Pierre Belon du Mans offers an invaluable short description of the child-rearing practices of the Turks, presumably in the towns, in the early part of the sixteenth century. After comparing Turkish and "Latin" (western European) methods of pedagogy, Belon concluded that Turkish children were "never so stinky" nor so difficult to raise as the children of the "Latins." Turkish mothers breast-fed their children until the infants were at least ten months old, refraining from giving them cereals or milk from a nonhuman source until that time, whereas in western Europe cereals and the milk of domestic animals were given to infants much earlier. Instead of featherbeds, Turkish infants had cradles of taut leather with a round opening over which were placed their nude bottoms. Below the opening was set a large pot, and a hollow pipelike tube of boxwood less than an inch thick and almost six inches long, with a round or elongated hook at one end depending on the sex of the infant, was joined to the urinary member of the child, with the straight end of the pipe being passed between its legs into the opening of the cradle. Keeping them cradled until their infants were able to control their physiological needs, the Turks avoided the soiling of their carpets, so essential a part of the Turkish home. They also diminished their need for linens and were able to keep their infants relatively clean, comfortable, and contented.[59]

In Montenegro and southern Macedonia, children were not weaned until they began to teethe and very often not until their third or fourth year.[60] During the first two or three years, the upbringing was basically the task of the mother. The earliest experiences of children born in southern Macedonia appear to have been happy, for their mothers normally changed them as soon as they wet themselves, fondled or tapped them playfully, tickled them around the lips to give them oral pleasure, and told them stories. A happy early childhood may account for the esteem in which Balkan men held mothers and sisters, even when their attitude toward women in general was ambivalent or negative.

As the child grew older, and especially after the weaning, other authorities prevailed, and this shift may account for the reluctance of some Balkan women to wean their children. Normally, however, the mother herself began the process of accustoming the child to the acceptance of other authorities and the learning of principles essential to the preservation of the community, namely: (1) to be economical and, in particular, "not to drop crumbs when it eats"; (2) to honor its elders and cultivate a consciousness of age categories, give priority to the advice of elders, sit down at table in accordance with age and sex, and express conventional wishes of good luck to everyone (especially members of its own family and community) it met or found at work; (3) to be diligent in terms of the needs of the family and larger community.[61] This last requirement took the form in certain other Balkan societies, especially in Albania and Montenegro, of being provident in warfare or thievery.

Mobility

Hunger was an ever-present problem. To cope with this bane, the Slavic and Albanian peasantry of the western provinces developed the custom of sending younger family members to spend the winter in a more fertile region or with a more prosperous branch of the family; in spring these migrants would return to their primary homes.[62] Migratory peasant workers *(argati*, from Greek ἐργάτης) from many different regions left their homes in the spring to work on farms or estates in the more fertile central and eastern areas, rejoining their families in late autumn. Indeed, Belon du Mans relates that while traveling between the Maritsa (Hebrus, Evros) River and Istanbul in the mid-sixteenth century, he ran into many "large bands" of poor Albanian harvesters, locally known as *Ergates*, who were on their way home with their sickles from the wheat plains of Rumelia and Anatolia.[63]

Such population movements were more or less regularized, occurring at stipulated times of the year. In his epochal study of the Mediterranean, Fernand Braudel sketches a remarkable portrait of the role of St. George's Day (April 23, Old Style) and St. Demetrius's Day (October 26, O.S.) as the terminal dates of the winter and summer seasons throughout the eastern Mediterranean and the zone of Byzantine and Ottoman civilization. As St. Demetrius' Day drew near, the Turks brought their campaigns to a close. From then until St. George's Day, navigation diminished, epidemics were sometimes appeased, war yielded to diplomatic negotiations and correspondence, and rumors abounded. Between St. George's Day and St. Demetrius's Day, commerce and agriculture were reactivated, war was resumed, and epidemics threatened again.[64] Rents and debts became payable on one or both of the two holidays. Apprentices quit their homes on one of the two occasions to enter the service of a master craftsman. Village craftsmen departed from their homes at the time of the spring festival to offer their services in distant towns and provinces, generally returning for the autumn festival. Farmhands hired out their labor on St. George's Day, returning home for St. Demetrius's Day. Depending upon climatic differences, shepherds and shepherd folk abandoned their summer pastures on the occasion of one of the two festivals and their winter pastures on the occasion of the other festival. The two feasts, along with the feast of the Assumption (August 15), were also occasions for group marriages. A Serbian proverb attests, moreover, to their importance in the life of the outlaw (commonly called *hajduk*), so characteristic a feature in Balkan society between the mid-sixteenth and the mid-nineteenth centuries:

> MITROV DANAK-HAJDUČKI RASTANAK
> On St. Demetrius's *hajduks* disband,
> On St. George's *hajduks* together band.[65]
> ĐURĐEV DANAK-HAJDUČKI SAJTANAK

War, shepherds' migrations, agriculture, commerce, and marriage were thus endowed with a regular rhythm. Bandits, marriageable girls, farmhands, craftsmen, apprentices, shepherds, mariners, and warriors moved from one home, from one community, from one kind of activity to another on the occasion of the two feasts. The Balkan peoples of the premodern era, notably, during the resurgence of pastoralism between 1400 and 1800 or 1830, were extraordinarily mobile.

In addition to the seasonally regulated mobility of the pre-1830 era (and yet later), there was the mobility provoked by fiscal and seigniorial pressures, by the looting and personal affronts of armies, by famine, and by plagues and other epidemics. But even mobility in response to epidemics was characterized by regularity, for the crisis recurred after a few years, often continuing for two or three years in succession. In the mountainous areas, hunger was a graver threat than plague. In the lowlands and maritime regions, plague, often preceded and accompanied by hunger, was a constant menace. Provinces along the routes of war, such as Thrace, Macedonia, and Serbia, were areas where plague spread quickly from one region to another. In some places, however, rural and urban alike, plague was endemic.

The prevalence of plague in most of the Balkans until the mid-nineteenth century had a detrimental effect on the rural and urban economy. In the cities, the plague was generally severe, resulting in the replacement of many older urban residents by peasants without urban traditions and skills.[66] In plague-stricken lowland villages, shepherd peoples from the highlands, without a farming tradition, replaced the agriculturists—or the villages were abandoned.

There were also other categories of wanderers: migrant teachers and monks, moving periodically from one community to another, and migrant beggars, prophets, and healers. In years of economic and political crisis, tens of thousands of peasants and unemployed artisans from smaller towns flocked to the capital and larger cities. The Ottoman government reacted to this concentration of "useless and unemployed people" in Istanbul, the former Constantinople or Byzantium, by summarily executing several thousands of persons and deporting tens of thousands to the Asian shores of the Bosporus or to the European provinces.

The periodic exportation of trouble from the capital created trouble for the provincial towns, which reacted in like manner. Often in the service of local commanders *(ağas)* or great landlords *(beys)*, adventurers, brigands, homeless vagabonds, unemployed or impoverished artisans and farmhands then took to roaming the countryside, seizing land and other properties, offering "protection" to frightened peasants in return for a portion of their crop.[67] Wanderers who succeeded in the latter form of enterprise, generally with the complaisance of a provincial governor or of local authorities or notables, were primarily of the Muslim faith, but a few were Christians.

In 1788, while the Ottoman Empire was at war with Russia and Austria, the Turkish soldiery so thoroughly terrified the inhabitants of Bulgaria that many of them took flight to the mountains of Macedonia.[68] Similarly, many thousands of Orthodox Serbs and Macedonians and Roman Catholic Bulgarians and Albanians sought refuge north of the Sava and Danube during the Austro-Turkish war of the closing decades of the seventeenth century. In the Morea, Muslim landowners dispatched much grain to Istanbul, Trieste, and western Mediterranean ports following the abundant harvest of 1788, causing a local scarcity of cereals in 1789. The recurrence of such exports by provincial authorities and the "*capitalistes du païs*" provoked a famine during 1790, causing some poor Greek peasants to sell their meager belongings to obtain bread and inciting others to desert their old villages for new lands of promise.[69]

Such desertions often were followed by a return to the old community, although rural settlements were sometimes totally abandoned. But more significant than the actual fact of abandonment was the act of moving to and fro—from country to town or to other countrysides, from low country to mountain, from mountain to low country, from forest and cave to the plain and then back to forest or cave.

To this history of flights (and sometimes returns) characteristic of the premodern era, one might add the Serbian emigrations of World War I, so poignantly described by Dragoljub Jovanović:

> The most vivid picture left by the War in the memory of the Serbs is not of a cemetery or a blood-stained battlefield, although Serbia had given a formidable number of victims and had been the scene of the fiercest fighting. The most clear-cut impression of the Serbian campaign is the motley, pitiful spectacle of the *bežanija*, that endless, disorderly flight of fugitives muffled to the eyes, old women, children, on foot or in wooden carts patiently drawn by emaciated and exhausted oxen, driving in front of them some cattle and carrying on their backs or under their arms some chattels, the number and importance of which grew less with every stage of this removal which was always beginning again

and never coming to an end. In short, the outstanding event of the Serbian war is not a great battle, such as Verdun, but the Great Retreat, that retreat which led the Serbs into exile through Albania—the last after so many others following on each advance of the enemy.[70]

Freed of the political picture, Yugoslavia's participation in World War II was similarly an account of retreats, of operations shifting from one part of the country to another, of expulsion and repeated migration of peoples, of starvation and disease, compounded by acts of genocide. In the Greek civil war of 1946–48, poor villagers from the plains defected to the guerrillas in the hills. Prosperous and conservative villagers from the hills fled to the towns and villages of the plains in search of the protection of the army and gendarmerie.[71] The Yugoslav civil war of the early 1990s in the territories of the former Military Frontier (Slavonian as well as Croatian) and in Bosnia and Hercegovina produced similar dislocations of hundreds of thousands of people.

The focus of this chapter has been psychological polarity and physical mobility. The face, ear, eye, and hand, and certain bodily techniques, have received special consideration because they provide an insight into the emotional states, as well as the cultural values, of the Balkan peoples. We have further probed into the traditional, seasonal, and critical situations that give rise to, or encourage, the physical mobility of the Balkan peoples, for they duplicate and reinforce their psychological mobility and polarity.

Balkan men and women may not be more mobile either physically or psychologically than their neighbors. Studies of deserted villages, migrations, urbanization, colonization, decolonization, and historical psychology show that man in general is mobile. Even though, as we shall see, the Balkan peoples were not well equipped with vehicles, they continued to be highly mobile *as members of collectivities* as late as 1830 even in times of peace. In western Europe, on the other hand, mobility under peacetime conditions has been largely on an individual or small-group basis for hundreds of years.

Notes

1. Mauss, "Les Techniques du corps," p. 371, Mauss's italics.
2. Leroi-Gourhan, *Le Geste et la parole*, II, 104–6, 128, 133.
3. Douglas, *Natural Symbols,* pp. 93–112.
4. Cornford, *From Religion to Philosophy*, pp. 109–10, 115.
5. Mauss, "Une Catégorie de l'esprit humain," pp. 348–54.
6. Miklosich, *Lexicon Palaeoslovenico-graeco-latinum*, p. 473 *(obraz)*. For the use of the word in the sense of mask, guise, or disguise, as in the phrase, "he put on the monastic guise," see Jagić, *Entstehungsgeschichte der kirchenslavischen Sprache*, p. 29.
7. Gesemann, *Heroische Lebensform*, pp. 26–27; Milićević, *Život Srba seljaka*, p. 14; Dvorniković, *Karakterologija Jugoslovena*, p. 40; Liddell and Scott, comps., *A Greek-English Lexicon*, II, 1977.
8. Brkić, *Moral Concepts in Traditional Serbian Epic Poetry*, pp. 36, 84–85, 96 n. 72, 99 n. 2, 127.

9. Trojanović, *Psihofizičko izražavanje srpskog naroda poglavito bez reči*, p. 19.

10. Brkić, *Moral Concepts in Traditional Serbian Epic Poetry*, pp. 34–60, 73–74, 81–82.

11. Sadnik and Aitzenmüller, *Handwörterbuch zu den altkirchenslavischen Texten*, p. 307 *(besrama)*.

12. Gesemann, *Heroische Lebensform*, pp. 116, 163.

13. Ibid., pp. 26–27, 35–40, 116, 163–64, 208–26.

14. Campbell, *Honour, Family, and Patronage*, p. 281; Herzfelfd, "Honour and Shame," pp. 339–51.

15. Lee, "View of the Self in Greek Culture," in *Freedom and Culture*, pp. 141–42.

16. Milev, "Grŭtskite i latinskite dumi v Istoriiata na Paisii Khilendarski," pp. 406, 408.

17. JAZU, *Rječnik*, IX 237 *(osoba)* and 796 *(persona)*.

18. Nušić, "Narodni Poslanik", p. 44.

19. Gesemann, *Heroische Lebensform*, p. 163; JAZU, *Rječnik*, VIII, 454 *(obrazovanost)*.

20. Domanović, "Razmišljanje jednog običnog srpskog vola," pp. 110–14.

21. Stevović, "U straha su velike oči," pp. 50–52.

22. Rey, *La Jeunesse de la science grecque*, pp. 27–28.

23. Hartog, *The Mirror of Herodotus*, pp. 273–80; Blum and Blum, *The Dangerous Hour*, pp. 54, 101–4, 116–17.

24. Blum and Blum, *The Dangerous Hour*, pp. 70–76.

25. Djordjević, *Priroda u verovanju i predanju našega naroda*, I, 41; Janković, *Astronomija u predanjima*, pp. 62, 110.

26. Friedl, *Vasilika*, p. 41.

27. Čajkanovič, *Studije iz religije i folklora*, pp. 43–55; Kemp, *Healing Ritual*, p. 156. For the ritual box on the ear or "switching" or slapping of children by adults, of husbands by wives, and of wives by husbands, at Easter among Czechs in the fourteenth and fifteenth centuries—variously known as *mrskačka, šlehačka*, or *pomlázka*—see Jakobson, "Medieval Mock Mystery," p. 254.

28. Novaković, ed., *Zakonik Stefana Dušana cara srpskog 1349 i 1354*, pp. 64 (art. 80), 167, 196, 251. The classicist-folklorist Margaret Hasluck relates that among early twentieth-century Albanians, criminal questions were resolved either by oath or by a witness and that the informant (*këpucar*, "man who gets shoe-money" for the traveling he had to do to serve as a witness while remaining virtually unknown to all but the accuser) had to be an observer. Whether, in fact, he had been in the past—or was even at the time of her observations—primarily an observer, remains a question. Cf. Hasluck, *The Unwritten Law in Albania*, pp. 196–201.

29. Karadžić, ed., *Srpske narodne poslovice i druge različne kao one y običaj uzete riječi i zagonetke*, pp. 29, 273–74, 380.

30. Paton, *Servia*, pp. 114–15.

31. Trojanović, *Psihofizičko izražavanje srpskog naroda poglavito bez reči*, p. 25.

32. Hasluck, "The Evil Eye in Some Greek Villages," pp. 160–72; Blum and Blum, *The Dangerous Hour*, pp. 145–49, 309, 360—63, 366; Blum and Blum, *Health and Healing*, pp. 131–32.

33. Djordjević, *Priroda u verovanju i predanju našega naroda*, I, 138–41, 165, 175–76, 265, 279–80; Kemp, *Healing Ritual*, pp. 132–41; Hasluck, "The Evil Eye in Some Greek Villages," pp. 160–72.

34. Onians, *The Origins of European Thought*, pp. 496–98.

35. Soloviev "Bogomilentum und Bogomilengräber in den südslawischen Ländern," pp. 173–98. Raditsa, review of Mandić, *Bogomilska crkva;* Thomson, *Studies in Ancient Greek Society*, I, 56.

36. Onians, *The Origins of European Thought*, pp. 97 n. 10, 494–98.

37. Elworthy, *The Evil Eye*, pp. 236–40.

38. Vlajinac, *Rečnik naših starih mera*, II, 168–71 *(breme)*, 240–41 *(grs, grst)*, 265 *(dlaka, dlan)*, 302 *(zametak, zametica)*, III, 465–69 *(korak)*, 645–46 *(naramak)*, 646–49 *(noga)*, 649 *(nokat)*, IV, 704–7 *(ped, peda, pedalj)*, 763–67 *(prst)*, 787–88 *(rasteg, rastegljaj)*, 802 *(ruka)*.

39. Busbecq, *The Life and Letters*, I, 221.

40. Rycaut, *The History of the Turkish Empire*, pp. 223–24.

41. Ibid., pp. 22, 32, 38.

42. Hammer-Purgstall, *Histoire de l'empire ottoman*, IX, 208–10.

43. Ibid., VIII, 287; Kreševljaković, "Gradska privreda i esnafi u Bosni i Hercegovini," pp. 194–95.

44. Rycaut, *The History of the Turkish Empire*, pp. 224–26.

45. Young, *Corps de droit ottoman*, V, 188.

46. Walsh, *Narrative of a Journey from Constantinople to England*, p. 95.

47. If my memory does not fail me, one of the sources for the gestures of negation and affirmation is Trojanović, *Psihofizičko izražavanje srpskog naroda poglavito bez reči*.

48. Durham, *Some Tribal Origins, Laws, and Customs*, p. 281.

49. Trojanović, *Psihofizičko izražavanje srpskog naroda poglavito bez reči*, p. 40.

50. Iordanis, "De Origine Actibusque Getarum," p. 124; Iordanis, *De Origine Actibusque Getarum*, pp. 58–59, my translation.

51. Febvre, "La Sensibilité et l'histoire," pp. 221–38.

52. Frilley and Wlahovitj, *Le Monténégro contemporain*, p. 417, my translation.

53. Thomson, *Studies in Ancient Greek Society*, I, 227.

54. Romaios, *Cultes populaires de la Thrace*, pp. 11–118.

55. Durham, *Some Tribal Origins, Laws, and Customs*, p. 273.

56. Mauss, "Les Techniques du corps," p. 376.

57. Durham, *Some Tribal Origins, Laws, and Customs*, p. 187.

58. Schneeweis, *Serbokroatische Volkskunde*, I, 52–53; Biometric Laboratory Staff, "Discussion of Miss M. L. Tildsley's Measurements on the Northern and Southern Albanians," pp. 32–33.

59. Belon du Mans, *Les Observations de plvsievrs singularritez et choses memorables*, pp. 179–80 (1554 ed.).

60. Schneeweis, *Serbokroatische Volkskunde*, I, 53; Frilley and Wlahovitj, *Le Monténégro contemporain*, p. 156.

61. Tanović, "Domaće vaspitanje u Južnoj Makedoniji," pp. 348–51.

62. Filipović, "Odlaženje na prehranu," pp. 76–93.

63. Belon du Mans, *Les Observations de plvsievrs singularritez et choses memorables*, p. 65 (1553 ed.).

64. Braudel, *La Méditerranée*, I, 225–38.

65. Milićević, *Život Srba seljaka*, p. 144; Schneeweis, *Serbokroatische Volkskunde*, I, 137, my translation.

66. Stoianovich, *Between East and West*, II, 106–8.

67. On "protection production," see ibid., II, 17–20; Lane, "Economic Consequences of Organized Violence," pp. 401–10.

68. Ferrières-Sauveboeuf, *Mémoires historiques*, I, 128–30.

69. AN, AÉ, B¹ 473 (Coron), Taitbout, July 9, 1790.

70. Jovanović, *Les Effets économiques et sociaux de la Guerre en Serbie*, p. 28; trans. Mitrany, *The Effect of the War in Southeastern Europe*, p. 243.

71. Laiou, "Population Movements in the Greek Countryside," pp. 55–103.

3 TECHNOLOGY

Techniques are designed to achieve some specific mechanical, chemical, or physical effects. They thus must be regularly efficacious and regularly transmissible. They may be further divided into two broad categories: (1) techniques in conformity with the body and instrumental techniques, or techniques in conformity with nature and (2) techniques designed to give nature a different form.[1] To move from the first type of technique to the second requires a new time orientation, notably a sacrifice of current advantage to the goal of some future advantage. A further obstacle to the acceptance of the second type of technique was the prevalence among the Greeks of classical Antiquity—despite their propensity for innovation—of the view that a human work or τέχνη *(techne)* acquires a useful and intelligible form only to the extent that its maker aspires to conform to nature even though, as Plato contended, the work itself can be only an imperfect translation of nature.[2] In this chapter, I shall deal mainly with the second type of technique.

Much is known about ancient Greek, Roman, and even Byzantine technology, but comparatively little about the technology of the Balkan peoples of the areas lying beyond the maritime urban centers. We shall therefore give due attention to the rural sector. At the same time, we shall try to determine how and why the Balkans, once one of the technologically most advanced regions of the world, became a technologically backward area. Finally, we shall describe the efforts made by the Balkan states since the nineteenth century to reduce or eliminate their technological backwardness.

Hoe, Ard, and Plow

From the perspective of agricultural implements, the history of Balkan agriculture between 7000 B.C. and A.D. 1900 is to a large extent a history of the hoe, spade, ard, and plow. In the course of thousands of years, however, the hoe and spade were modified and other tools were invented. By the classical era, Greek peasants employed at least six different implements for penetrating the soil and turning it over, breaking up soils of different types, and removing weeds: the *skapane* or pickax; the *dikella*, a two-pronged hoe, which the South Slavs later adopted along with the name *(dikelj)*; the *miskhos*, a heavier hoe for use in the deeper soils of Thessaly; the *skalis*, a weeding hoe; the *thrinax*, a three-pronged pitchfork for turning over the soil; and the *sphyra*, a sledge for breaking up clods of earth.[3]

The ard and the plow are both plowing implements but differ from each other in several notable respects. An ard possesses a long beam, a plow a short beam. An ard plows symmetrically, pushing the earth aside in both directions. A plow functions unsymmetrically, turning the earth over to one side. An ard is a light instrument, normally not requiring more than a pair of oxen for traction. A plow is a heavier instrument, requiring two or more pairs of oxen and often using the power of horses rather than of oxen or asses. An ard scratches the surface of the earth, a plow penetrates more deeply. The ard is a more suitable instrument for contour plowing, for in hilly regions and in areas where the soil is not deep, the momentum of the plow brings into cultivation both fertile and infertile soils. Generally situated in hill country, fields under ard cultivation tend to be irregular, rounded, or rectangular. More common in the plains, those under plow cultivation generally assume the form of long strips.

It is not clear whether the earliest ard invented by man or woman was an altogether new tool or whether it evolved directly from the spade in some regions and from the hoe in others. The early history of Balkan ards is similarly obscure. However, ards were in use in the Balkans at the time of Hesiod (ca. 800 B.C.). During the period of Roman rule, four different types of ard were in use in the Balkans, and each was employed there in one district or another at least until the mid-twentieth century.

In the Sava and Morava basins and in northwestern Bulgaria, an instrument was used that possessed characteristics of both ard and plow. The implement in question was symmetrical. But like a plow, it was furnished with a moldboard *(daska)*. It therefore could plow unsymmetrically. In other words, it functioned like the plow in pushing the earth to one side but like the ard in that it did not turn the soil over.

Debated by scholars for a century or more, the origin of the plow is nevertheless open to less dispute than that of the ard. A growing body of evidence supports the thesis that the iron-rich alpine regions, notably Rhaetia, were where the plow and plowshare first came into use, perhaps around 400 B.C., concurrently with the invention of the iron horseshoe by the alpine Celts. By the first century A.D., the plow was widely known in the northern Roman provinces. It was soon transmitted by the Romanized Celts to their Germanic neighbors.

The South Slavs may have acquired the plow in several different periods and from at least three different donors: the Celto-Illyrians, the Germanic peoples (including perhaps the Goths), and Byzantium. But the Balkan plow zone was confined, until the middle of the nineteenth century, to a few lake, river, and coastal basins in the south and east and to the Pannonian regions in the north, extending occasionally south of the Sava and Danube rivers.[4]

After 1830, the plow penetrated into the peninsula from north, south, east, and west. Its expansion was based in large measure on the importation of modern agricultural machinery from Hungary or western and Germanic Europe. Poor roads and inadequate vehicles, however, impeded the delivery of heavy machines to districts beyond the main routes of commerce.

Thus, as late as 1882, when the Serbian government granted a subsidy to the firm of Vasić and Maksimović to enable it to found a factory at Kraljevo for the manufacture of farm machines, Serbia customarily imported each year no more than four hundred or five hundred plows of modern make.[5] Nowhere in the Balkans did modern machines come quickly into use.

Almost everywhere, however, the growth of a cereal economy led after 1830 to a rapid contraction in the per capita distribution of horses, bovines, sheep, goats, mules, and asses. The per capita distribution of old sources of energy—animal power in particular—declined before the adoption of new energy sources.[6] Moreover, even old types of plow and ard were few in number. In 1866, for example, there were in the principality of Serbia only 50,142 instruments called plow *(plug)* and 35,635 known as araire *(ralo)*, no more than 7 plowing instruments as compared to 10.5 carts and wagons per 100 inhabitants.[7]

Animal and Rotary Power

Known in Sumer since the beginning of the fourth millennium, where it was used in processional celebrations of the sun (thus as a prayer wheel), the wheeled vehicle was diffused to Europe during the third and second millennium B.C. from two directions: from Asia Minor to the Aegean, thence northward, and from across the steppes of southeastern Europe to Pannonia and the northern Balkans.[8] It reached the Danubian basin and the Balkans before it got to any other part of Europe beyond the steppes.[9]

The vehicle arriving in the highlands of the south was two-wheeled, whereas both two- and four-wheeled (and even six-wheeled) vehicles were introduced from the steppes. Both presumably were of the pole or perch type. In other words, draft animals were hitched to the cart by means of a pole extending forward from the middle of the axletree.

The function of the two-wheeled country cart that reached Greece in antiquity was primarily religious or ceremonial. It was used in wedding, funeral, and other religious processions. It was also used for local travel.[10] If used to transport goods, it probably again served a local purpose except among the peoples of the steppes, whose way of life was oriented toward long-distance travel. In the latter case, the four-wheeled wagon, which was a habitat as well as a means of transport, played a more important role than the two-wheeled cart.

Even in the transport of bulky goods, as if to reinforce a choice that may have been made with due regard for geography, a preference continued to be given in much of Greece to vehicles that played an important role in Greek religious and ceremonial life. Thus, in 1591, the only carts that the Venetian Lorenzo Bernardo encountered between Genizzè (Yenidje-Vardar) and Salonika were carts with two block wheels. Drawn by water buffaloes, the carts had a carriage in the shape of a vat for crushing grapes (a ceremonial occasion).[11]

Between 1400 and 1800, the Balkans only marginally promoted the use of wheeled vehicles, presumably because of the region's superiority in the number of domesticated animals per capita and because the Ottoman command economy therefore may have had no need for more vehicles.

For four millennia the four-wheeled vehicle prevailed only in the region north of the Danube and Sava. South of these rivers and east of the Morava and Vardar basins lay a mixed zone in which the two-wheeled cart prevailed but in which the four-wheeled wagon appeared in fertile lowland areas. The latter vehicle was also occasionally present as far west as the Drina River, but the area between the Morava in the east and the province of Hercegovina in the west was essentially a zone of the two-wheeled cart. West of Serbia, there were almost no four-wheeled vehicles until 1850. In the Dinaric provinces of Hercegovina and Montenegro, as in the Peloponnesus, carts of any kind were rare until the mid-nineteenth century.

A serious obstacle to the diffusion of the four-wheeled vehicle to highland areas was that it required a longer carriage. Moreover, the front wheels of a four-wheeled vehicle were not placed on a pivot. Lacking a pivot, they could not make sharp turns. Four-wheeled vehicles thus were impractical for narrow roads with sharp turns and constantly changing gradients.

In most of the Balkans, the prevailing carts continued to resemble their ancient prototypes until the middle or end of the nineteenth century. Along the northern fringes, however, a few vehicles of a new type appeared during the seventeenth and eighteenth centuries. The new vehicle was the Hungarian *kocsi*, named after the village of Kocs in the vicinity of Buda (one of the twin cities later forming Budapest), where craftsmen manufactured coaches at least as early as the first decades of the sixteenth century.

But coaches may have been invented earlier. For the ambassador of the king of Hungary and Bohemia, relates Johann Beckmann, presented the king of France in 1457 with a gift that aroused much amazement in Paris: a vehicle "branlant et moult riche" that may have had a suspension carriage. In this context, it may be worth noting that the common name for a covered vehicle in Germany in the time of Charles V was "Hungarian carriage" and that the usual German term for coach was *kotzschi* or *gutschi*, presumably derived from *kocsi*. The Hungarian *kocsi* of the time was a coach drawn by three horses running abreast of each other and able to carry, in addition to the driver, four passengers and their baggage.[12] It spread alike to Germany and the southern Pannonian areas.

Ottoman sources of the mid-seventeenth century refer to the use in the districts lying between the Sava and Drava rivers of a *serem araba* or "Syrmian vehicle," which may have been either a *kocsi* or a covered wagon with springs.

The Serbs of Niš county continued to call this type of vehicle a *srem* until the beginning of the twentieth century. By 1800, moreover, the Serbians of the forests (Šumadija) discerned in the marshy Mačva lowlands just south of the Sava a vehicle to which they gave the name "Mačva coach" *(mačvanska kočija)*. A few such coaches may have been in use in the Mačva district earlier in the century.[13]

Sensing the superiority of central European over Spanish and Italian roads and vehicles, Philip II of Spain issued an order that the roads between Ascoli and the province of Apulia be repaired and improved to facilitate the delivery of grains to their destination (Naples), *"como se hace en Alemania y otras partes—* as is done in Germany and other parts."[14] One of these other parts was the Pannonian basin, which was politically Ottoman during the greater part of the sixteenth and seventeenth centuries. In other words, the portion of the Ottoman Empire directly facing Germany (or Austria) was precisely the portion with the best vehicles. It also may have been the zone from which, before its conquest by the Turks, at least one new type of vehicle had spread to Germany itself. The Ottoman Empire consequently may have felt no urgent need to continue doing in Pannonia what was being done without let or hindrance in Germany.

But why were the *kocsi* and *serem araba* not widely diffused to the Balkans proper, south of the Sava and Danube, until very late? The answer may lie in the fact that the Balkans were endowed with a road system, inherited from Rome, that was more than suitable for all but the most extraordinary purposes. It had straight, unswerving tracks of heavy flagstone two and a half or three feet wide, appropriate for a post-horse—the Roman *veredus*—in single file. From this Roman term for "saddle horse," presumably of Celtic origin, may have been derived the later name among the Serbs, borrowed perhaps from the Romance-speaking Vlachs (at least partly Romanized Volcae or Celts) for a two-wheeled cart, *vrdelj* or *vrndulj*, which was known to the Ottoman Turks as a *domuz araba* or "pig cart." From *veredarius*, the term for "horse-riding courier" or "herald," probably was derived the Slavic term for the Vardar River, the Axios of the Greeks.[15]

To the right and left of the flagstones of the military or "imperial" road between Istanbul and Belgrade, the earth was beaten down by herds, soldiers, and ordinary foot travelers to form a path the total width of which was thirty feet or more.[16] It was adequately maintained during the sixteenth century. Central Europe, on the other hand, possessed a less important heritage of Roman roads. It therefore began to build paved roads suitable for haulage in the Middle Ages. As an Asian state, on the other hand, the Ottoman Empire continued to be persuaded by the evidence—convincing in Asia itself almost until 1900—that the camel, dromedary, horse, and mule were a superior mode of transport to the wheeled vehicle except for conveying bulk commodities over short distances.[17]

The Byzantine Empire, the medieval Balkan states,[18] and the Ottoman Empire could be largely content with the interregional roads they inherited because they probably held an advantage in draft-animal power not only over western and central Europe but over the western Mediterranean as well. I refer to the camel, Asiatic buffalo, mule, and donkey. In mountainous regions, even the best vehicles were of doubtful value until the advent of motor transport. The donkey was present there in large numbers. Its very name—*gomari* in Greek and *magare* or *magarac* in South Slavic—signifies "beast of burden." In addition, early in the Middle Ages, the Asiatic water buffalo was introduced into Byzantium and Bulgaria and later spread to the southern Serbian lands.

With the advent of the Ottoman Turks, more water buffaloes entered the Balkans. They were present in Thrace, Dobrudja, and Macedonia until the mid-twentieth century. Between 1500 and 1850, they had been both more numerous and spread out over a larger territory, including Epirus, Thessaly, many parts of Bulgaria, Kosovo, and Serbia.

Less numerous than the water buffalo but important nonetheless after the Ottoman conquest was the camel. Camels provisioned the armies of Suleiman (Süleyman) the Magnificent during the siege of Vienna in 1529. Camel caravans regularly visited Buda so long as it remained under Ottoman control, and camel caravans came regularly to Belgrade as late as 1848 and sporadically until the evacuation of the city by the Turks in 1867.[19]

The use of mules as draft animals may also have increased in the Balkans during the sixteenth century, as throughout the Mediterranean. At the same time, Pannonia and the northern Balkans retained a reputation in western Europe as a source of horses, especially for reconnaissance cavalry.[20]

There thus may have been several different periods during which the use of carts in Asia Minor and the Balkans may have receded—first in the fifth and fourth centuries B.C., as the use of horses and mules became more common; then through the diffusion of the camel; and finally, in the sixteenth century, with the yet greater use of mules as draft animals.

A historian of the horse and of antique and medieval technology, Lefebvre des Noëttes contrasts the material civilization of Byzantium and the medieval West. In the ninth and tenth centuries, western Europe adopted the iron horseshoe (for this invention of the Celts may not have been widely diffused under Roman rule), the file arrangement for carriage horses, and the shoulder collar for the horse. (The latter had been known to the Chinese since the second century and to eastern Europeans at least as early as the eighth.) Together, the three innovations allowed a horse to draw heavier loads and transport goods more rapidly over longer distances. Along with the improved roads of a later period, they helped create an incentive for the ultimate construction in western and central Europe of better carts and carriages. Similar innovations were made in ninth-century Byzantium: the iron horseshoe and an improved breastband for the horse. But not until the close of the fifteenth century, according to Lefebvre des Noëttes, did the Greeks adopt the shoulder collar, even though their neighbors, the Serbs, had employed it since the thirteenth century. Furthermore, he maintains, Byzantium did not apply the iron shoe to oxen, and although Byzantine carts were lengthened in the tenth century to give more elasticity to the perch and thus soften the effect of jolting, the weights that a horse or an ox could pull were not augmented by the change. The normal draft power of a pair of oxen remained at or below half a ton in addition to the weight of a cart.[21]

One may question Lefebvre des Noëttes's reasoning on several grounds. In the first place, he himself acknowledges that Byzantium did achieve certain improvements. Second, his data are derived largely from medieval art. But while western European, Serbian, and provincial Greek art was open to "naturalism," the Byzantine art that was subject to Lefebvre des Noëttes's scrutiny, essentially the art of Constantinople, manifested a certain formality. The art of Constantinople consequently may have refrained from depicting the horse with a modern collar even if such a collar was employed. Finally, Byzantium and the other Balkan states probably enjoyed a numerical superiority in draft animals to compensate for their technological inferiority in vehicles, if there really was such an inferiority.

It is a mistake in any case to conclude that the medieval Balkan states fell because of technological backwardness. On the other hand, the Ottoman Empire was triumphant in the fifteenth and sixteenth centuries partly because its total technological equipment was not significantly inferior to that of western Europe, particularly if compensating factors are taken into account, such as a probable superiority in animal power. The latter factor ceased to be compensating to the same degree after 1600, however, and ceased to be a compensating factor at all after 1700. By that time, European technology was in fact vastly superior.

On the testimony of François René de Chateaubriand, the noise of carriages and carts, the peel of church bells, and the pounding of the blacksmith's hammer were still absent in 1806 from the sounds of the city space of Istanbul,[22] in sharp contrast to Paris and other European cities for which the smithy had become the equivalent of "the garage of today."[23] Instead, porters abounded in Istanbul, and one did not hear the soft tread of people clad in slippers.

William Turner similarly observed of Istanbul in 1812:

> Amid the novelties that strike the European on his arrival, nothing surprises him more than the silence that pervades so large a capital. He hears no noise of carts or carriages rattling through the streets, for there are no wheeled vehicles in the city, except a very few painted carts—called *arabahs*—drawn by buffaloes, in which women occasionally take the air in the suburbs, and which go only a foot's pace. The only sounds he hears by day, are the cries of bread, fruits, sweetmeats, or sherbet, carried on a large wooden tray on the head of an itinerant vender, and at intervals the barking of dogs disturbed by the foot of the passenger.[24]

There were few carriages and hardly the sound of a hammer in this civilization —this complex of audiographic signs (revelations and reverberations)—in which the iron nail was used scantily, although several important places in the Ottoman Empire, including Bulgarian Samokov and Gabrovo, made knives, horseshoes, nails, plowshares, pickaxes, and other iron commodities.[25] As late as the mid-twentieth century, despite important changes during the previous century and a half, Ottoman towns continued to be "dominated by a contrast between the noisy bazaar and the silence of the residential districts, where one [heard] only the cries and games of children" (and sometimes of packs of dogs and, in earlier times, of the town crier)—the noise of people and animals, not of machines and machine-made things. They continued to differ from the cities and ports of the Greek islands. Even the most animated of the Turkish towns—the Turkish Aegean ports—hardly compared to the Greek Aegean towns, generators of "an orgy of light and noise."[26] The gasoline-driven automobile to some extent undid these differences between 1950 and 1990.

As in classical Antiquity, toward the end of the nineteenth century, Hellenism became again, within the confines of the Ottoman Empire, "an agent of light, an illuminating power." Having served for more than a century as distributors of sugar and coffee, Greeks became distributors of petroleum and of the petroleum tin can (often containing the petroleum of Batum)—the *teneke*, from which the possessors made lamps, plates, flowerpots, sprinklers, buckets, and washbasins.[27]

An increase in the per capita cubic consumption of petroleum (light and energy) and in the distribution ratio of tin cans, illustrative as prized material objects of a per capita increase of "material density," may not always have promoted the cause of Hellenism understood narrowly. It did serve the cause of "modernity," understood as a craving for goods and world mastery.[28] It was part of the same structural set, in the words of the waterman John Tyler, as the craving in England, already in the seventeenth century, to "runne on Wheeles."

As against Tyler's "rattling, rowling, rumbling" English urban space-time,[29] much of the space-time of Istanbul was, according to Chateaubriand, one of "continual silence." Apart from the *araba*, which was primarily used by towns-women, and a few suspension carriages, few vehicles existed in the Ottoman Empire, most of them less splendidly adorned than the townswomen's *arabas*. In Albania, there was a vehicle known as a *kotschi* and another, presumably a suspension carriage, called a *karrotza*. These names suggest two or three different routes of diffusion of material culture, the first southward from Hungary or Trieste to Albania, the second *[carrozza]* eastward from across the sea [Italy] or via the Sava valley to Belgrade and thence southward to Albania.[30] Both types of vehicles were rare. Indeed, during the Napoleonic era, in the extensive south-western territories governed by Ali Pasha of Janina, only Ali Pasha, his sons, and their wives were authorized to make use of a *carrozza*.[31]

Usually drawn by oxen or buffaloes but sometimes by horses, particularly as one neared the Danube, vehicles were rare south of the Danube until after 1830. By the late 1840s, however, "vehicles of every form" had begun to "circulate in the streets and on the promenades" of Istanbul.[32] A similar trend was evident in other Ottoman cities. The continuation of that process was facilitated by the widening, straightening, and paving of the main city streets.

In Istanbul, the changes were also the product of the doubling, between 1836 and 1846, in the number of European (non-Ottoman) residents and of the zeal of the newcomers in opening hotels, fashion and perfume boutiques, furniture and hardware stores, and pastry shops, particularly in the mainly Greek and European suburb of Pera, in order to gratify the needs of the growing European colony and promote in this manner a consumer economy.

But the *tastes* of the indigenous elites were also changing.[33] The cigarette began to dethrone the chibouk. In the bazaars, the textiles of Damascus, Aleppo, and Bursa gave way to English and Swiss linens and cotton prints. The Stambouliot demand for the European products was part of a larger complex, including a growing demand—in response to a new *taste*—for carriages, watches, clocks, opera glasses, and pianos.[34]

Crucial to the assertion of new tastes and acceptance of new techniques was the subtle alteration of the structures of an old *dromocracy* (later defined in detail) —a modification of route organization to meet the demands of the world market and the commands of the territorial states through whose political will the capitalist world-market economy functioned. Geography and history, however, made change more difficult in some areas than in others.

Until the middle of the nineteenth century, for example, the use of wheeled vehicles was absent altogether west or southwest of the line Banjaluka-Zvornik-Užice-Višegrad and east of the Adriatic coastal plain of Konavle (Canali) south of Ragusa (Dubrovnik).[35] In the Konavle area, on the other hand, wheeled vehicles may have been known for hundreds or thousands of years. One may infer this from the probable Slavic etymology of Konavle—*kolo* for wheel and *nav* (perhaps related to Latin *navis*) for vessel, both for one serving a practical purpose and for the burial vessel used to carry the dead to the other or nether world. Emperor Constantine Porphyrogenitus may not have known this. He does relate, however, that the name Kanali meant *hamaxia* or "waggon-load."[36]

East of Konavle and particularly as one approached the watershed just beyond Trebinje (Travunia, Terbounia), in Hercegovina (Hlm, Hum), sleds rather than wheeled vehicles were used both for carrying goods and for funeral and wedding rites.[37] Konavle thus might be regarded as the country of vessels on wheels, while pre-1860 Hercegovina would be the country of the sled, with the horse, mule, and donkey complementing the local vehicle in both areas.

Well suited for drawing loads over grass, snow, and rocky tablelands, sleds were in common use not only in Bosnia and Hercegovina but in the mountain zones of Bulgaria. Immediately to the east of the Zvornik-Užice-Višegrad line, however, lay a narrow zone in which prevailed a short, light, narrow, usually low cart with two disklike wheels, the *vrdelj* (from Latin *birotae*) or *domuz araba*. It is unclear how this cart resembled, or differed from, the small two-wheeled *sousta* of southern and western Greece or the two-wheeled *kolesnik* of medieval Serbia.[38]

Along the Sava and Danube rivers and eastward from the Morava basin to the Black Sea, with interruptions in the mountain zones, lay a region in which there were both two-wheeled and four-wheeled vehicles. A wagon with four well-rounded and often spoked wheels prevailed in Thrace. In general use in south-western Macedonia and Thessaly, drawn by oxen or water buffaloes, was a two-wheeled cart raised high on two solid spokeless or block wheels. Until the early decades of the twentieth century, the "only indigenous vehicle for land transportation" in the lowlands of Albania was "a horribly creaking springless cart with two wheels nearly six and a half feet in diameter,"[39] so made to cope with the proverbial mud of the plains. In Epirus, around Arta, on the other hand, the carts in circulation in 1731 were short and of weak construction, consisting merely of three planks set upon an axletree and moved by two very small block wheels without springs. As in other southern and eastern Balkan regions, they were drawn by water buffaloes.[40]

North of the Danube and Sava rivers, wheeled vehicles had been more numerous for centuries. It may be appropriate, therefore, to divide southeastern Europe between 1600 and 1850 in terms of three urban transportation models—Istanbul, Bucharest, and Vienna—each reflecting a specific rural mode of transportation.

A former English consul to Turkey, William Eton, observed at the end of the eighteenth century: "The sultan has a coach or carriage, exactly of the shape of a hearse in England, but without any springs; it was, when I saw it, drawn by six mules. The pole was of an enormous thickness, as well as every other part. I enquired the reason; the answer was, that if the pole, the axletree, &c. broke, the man who made it would lose his head. The sultan never uses a carriage as any kind of state; it is only in excursions into the country that it follows him." The noise of carriages and carts was rare in Istanbul. On the other hand, wrote Eton, the people of Moldavia and Wallachia constructed "waggons for carrying merchandize on very just principles of mechanics."[41]

Similarly, the "first thing that struck" the Reverend Robert Walsh, former chaplain of the British embassy to the Porte, upon his arrival in Bucharest in the 1820s, was "the number of brilliant carriages rolling in all directions, or standing at the doors," in such stark contrast, however, to "the rude and miserable little machines for the public," not too different from the carts of the eastern Balkan regions south of the Danube, if more numerous and often larger. Even the "gaudy carriages" of the boyars, imported primarily from the archduchy of Austria and from Saxony and Bohemia, fell to pieces "in a year or two." To supply new carriages was "a constant expense." They were made, in effect, "merely for show," conspicuous consumption. As Walsh advanced from Wallachia into Hungary and Austria, the roads improved "considerably." The numerous carriages along the approaches to Vienna presented "a strong contrast" to the approaches to Istanbul. Vehicles like the brewers' drays, "drawn by numerous Flanders horses, with glittering harness covered with bright brass plates," here served not only a private but a public function.[42]

Figure 3.1. **Vehicle Distribution in the Balkans and Adjacent Regions, 1850**

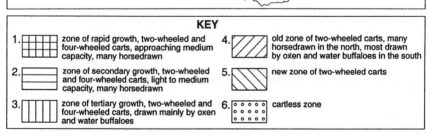

The Balkan and immediately neighboring regions divided around 1850, as shown on the map of vehicle distribution (Figure 3.1), into several broad zones of traffic:

(1) a zone of rapid growth of two- and four-wheeled vehicles of medium capacity in Serbia;

(2) a zone of secondary growth of light-to-medium capacity vehicles in Danubian Bulgaria;

(3) a zone of tertiary growth of two- and four-wheeled vehicles, drawn mainly by oxen and water buffaloes, in the southeastern Balkans and northern and

western Anatolia, where the number of carts per capita was lower than in Serbia or Danubian Bulgaria;

(4) an old zone of two-wheeled carts immediately to the west of the three previous zones;

(5) a new zone of two-wheeled carts in the northwest (Bosnia);

(6) a cartless territory in Hercegovina and adjacent lands including Montenegro, and in a not fully charted region of the Morea or Peloponnesus;[43]

(7) an old zone of great carts north of the Danube, in Wallachia and Moldavia, where the carts bore nevertheless a strong resemblance to those of Danubian Bulgaria and of the southeastern Balkan zone; and

(8) a northwestern Danubian zone, in which the carts, wagons, and carriages were both larger and of a highly improved type.

Except in the cartless territories—and perhaps in the coastal plains, where carts may have been more numerous than in the cis-Danubian interior regions—the number of carts per capita tended to increase as one moved from south to north. The per capita distribution was also generally greater to the east of the Vardar and southern Morava valleys than to the west. Finally, by 1850, the zone in which some four-wheeled vehicles were in use had been extended to Užice, and carts had begun to be introduced in the once almost cartless region lying to the west of Užice and Zvornik.[44]

After 1830 or 1860, there was a general increase in the number of carts, in the size and variety of vehicles, and in the quality of their construction. The country south of the Sava and Danube in which the most notable progress was made was Serbia. Arriving at the Austrian frontier town of Semlin (Zemun) in 1835 and gazing at the fortress of the Serbian river town of Belgrade (still containing a Turkish garrison), the British traveler Alexander William Kinglake thought that he "had come, as it were, to the end of this wheel-going Europe" and was about to be introduced to "the Splendour and Havoc of The East."[45] Despite the mix of admiration and condescension, Kinglake closely resembled "the last of the eighteenth century travellers in the Levant." He was without the "superior attitude" toward the East of many nineteenth-century European travelers.[46]

Until 1830, an ordinary cartweight (kola) usually was defined in Serbia—there were regional variations—as two horseweights or 200 okas (256 kg.). From 1855, it more usually was set at 400 okas, as against a somewhat heavier cartweight in Vojvodina to the north and a somewhat lighter one of 300 okas in Turkish Niš to the south. The customary commercial cartweight (kiridžijska kola) rose from 600 okas in the 1840s to about 900 okas in the 1860s. The carrying capacity of Serbian carts thus probably increased by 50 percent between 1830 and 1870; it may have even doubled. The change was made possible by the development of the blacksmith's and wheelwright's crafts.[47] Even so, the carrying capacity of such improved carts and wagons was only twice as great as that of the vehicles of the public post in the late Roman or early Byzantine empire, which stood at 200 pounds for the light two-wheeled carts *(birotae)* drawn by three mules; 1,000 pounds for the four-wheeled wagon *(raedae)* drawn by eight mules in summer and ten in winter; and 1,500 pounds for the heavier (four-wheeled?) vehicle drawn by two pairs of oxen.[48]

Austrian intelligence reports place the number of carts in 1784 at 3,000 in the Požarevac area, half of them horse-drawn; 1,200 in the Kragujevac area; 1,000 each in the Belgrade (excluding the city) and Jagodina areas; 950 in the Požega district; 700 in the Smederevo district; 500 in Krajina Negotin; 300 in the Rudnik district; 250 in Krajina Kladovo; and 200 each in the Aleksinac, Ćuprija, and Ražanj districts, all ox-drawn. If one allows for the carts of Belgrade and of the remaining districts of the pashalik of Belgrade/Smederevo (Valjevo, Zvornik, Šabac, and Bijeljina), one may attribute to the province a total of 12,000–13,000 carts, with a probable total carrying capacity of 3,000 metric tons. More than half the carts were located along the Danube and a sixth each along the Morava, along the Sava, and in the rest of Serbia.

The census of 1866 showed the presence in the principality of Serbia, corresponding in large measure to the former pashalik of Belgrade/Smederevo, of 14,360 horse-drawn and 112,791 ox-drawn carts, or about 12 horse-drawn and 93 ox-drawn carts per population of 1,000.[49] There was thus a tenfold absolute and an almost threefold per capita increase in the number of carts in the country between 1784 and 1866, as well as an increase in circulation and velocity. In terms of carrying capacity, the absolute increase may have been almost twenty-fold—from 3,000 to almost 60,000 metric tons—while the per capita increase was fourfold or fivefold.

By way of comparison, the Austrian port city of Trieste at the head of the Adriatic, with an estimated population of 28,000 in 1802, had access, in 1804, to 70,000 carts, a third of which had a carrying capacity of three tons each,[50] consequently a haulage capacity of well over 100,000 metric tons for the overland movement of exports and imports at any one time. Around 1800, therefore, the cart capacity of Trieste was at least thirty-three times as great as that of the pashalik of Belgrade/Smederevo. On a per capita basis, it was well over three hundred times as great.

The number of carts present in 1784 in the neighboring Vidin and Niš areas was estimated at 2,000 and 1,000 respectively, many of the carts in the Vidin area being horse-drawn and the few horse-drawn carts in the Niš area being confined to the city itself.[51] Since there were many fewer carts immediately to the west of Serbia and since the number of carts both per capita and per square kilometer in the rest of the Balkans proper did not exceed, and even fell below, the Serbian ratio, the total number of carts south of the Sava-Danube region probably stood, in 1784, at 100,000–200,000: 1 cart to 35–70 persons or 1 cart to 2.2–4.4 square kilometers. In the world's industrial societies of 1970, there were in use for transportation alone at least twenty wheels per capita (perhaps 700 times as many per capita as were present in the Balkans around

1800) and an additional eighty wheels for use in industry and in the home.[52]

The increase in the number and size of Balkan carts required an improvement of roads. The improvement of roads spurred an increase in the number, size, quality, and circulation of goods-carrying vehicles.

In mid-1858, Serbia possessed 194.75 "Turkish hours" (722, 866, or 935 km., depending on how a "Turkish hour" is calculated) of paved roads *(chemins ferrés)*. By the beginning of 1883, the road network in the departments that had formed part of Serbia before the territorial annexations of 1878 included 647.6 kilometers of national roads (roads linking the departmental capitals to the national capital), 1,952.9 kilometers of departmental roads (roads linking district capitals to a departmental capital), and 814 kilometers of vicinal roads (roads linking communes to a district capital or market town)—in all, 3,414.5 kilometers, four to five times the road network in existence twenty-five years earlier.[53]

Vicinal roads were designed to give the inhabitants of one or more rural communes access to a market town. Their achievement was far short of the success in building national and departmental roads. The ratio of vicinal to national roads was barely more than 1:1 as against a ratio in France, in 1871, of 10:1, 5:1, or 3:1, depending on the usability of the vicinal roads under various seasonal and weather conditions.[54]

Ottoman official sources estimated the extent of roads suitable for travel by cart in Bosnia-Hercegovina in 1870 (A.H. 1286) at 456.75 "Turkish hours" (1,694, 2,031, or 2,192 km.): 140 hours in the sanjak of Banjaluka, 103 in Zvornik sanjak, 101 in Sarajevo sanjak, 73.5 in Hercegovina, 66 in Bihać sanjak, 57 in Travnik sanjak, and 16.25 in the sanjak of Novi Pazar.[55] Austro-Hungarian occupational authorities, on the other hand, estimated the road length suitable for wheeled traffic in Bosnia-Hercegovina (without the Novi Pazar sanjak), in 1878, at only 900 kilometers, and the extent of first-class, second-class, and third-class roads, in 1880, at 1,542.8 kilometers.[56]

The road network of Serbia in 1875 or 1880 thus was almost or more than twice as extensive as that of Bosnia-Hercegovina, while the road network suitable for wheeled traffic was three times as great, even though, at that time, Serbia was a smaller albeit more densely populated country. As early as 1863 or earlier, some roads in the Bosnian lowlands had been widened to allow the passage of carts going in opposite directions. Most roads in the province, however, did not permit movement by more than one narrow cart moving in either direction.[57]

In Hercegovina, where the road building began in 1864, 20 leagues (80 km.) of road were completed by the end of 1866. One of these roads ran from Stolac to Mostar (6 leagues), continuing thence to Metković (8 leagues). At the end of 1866 only two-thirds of the route between Mostar and Sarajevo was suitable for travel by cart, and only portions of the Bileće-Trebinje-Dubrovnik and Mostar-Nevesinje-Gacko-Nikšić routes were ready for use in 1867. Soon after the completion of the Mostar-Metković road in 1866, the Mostar branch of a Sarajevo haulage firm imported six carts and a "voiture de luxe" from Trieste for use on that road.[58] As late as 1879, however, there were only forty horse-drawn vehicles in all of Hercegovina, and the Ljubuški district had only two ox-drawn and no horse-drawn carts.[59]

Most of the carts then in use in Bosnia and Hercegovina had a short narrow train and two block wheels, each about two feet in diameter. No nail entered their making, and they were never greased. Too small to carry much of a load, they were so poorly built that sixteen oxen were needed to pull them over rough or muddy terrain.[60]

The major road-building effort in Bosnia-Hercegovina was the work of the Austro-Hungarian administration, especially after the adoption by the Austro-Hungarian General Ministry of Finance (in charge of Bosnian affairs), in 1883, of a ten-year road construction program. Between 1878 and the end of 1891, 1,965 kilometers of new roads were laid out in the province.[61]

An "excellent carriage road" existed between Bileće (Bilek, Bilechia), Trebinje, and Dubrovnik as early as the 1870s or 1880s, but there was no carriage road between Bileće and Gacko until after 1890. In the 1880s, maintained a counselor in the Austro-Hungarian Foreign Office, the "only representatives of civilization" between Gacko and the fertile Bileće tableland, and in much of the rest of Hercegovina, were "the fortified camps of our troops lying at a day's march from one another. The whole way of life, and therefore also all means of travelling, [were] here still medieval. We rode for five consecutive days, and were sometimes eleven hours in the saddle."[62]

Nor until the 1890s did a good carriage road run from Trebinje to the fertile but heretofore "lawless" mountain valley of Lastva, whose development the government encouraged by forming model vineyards, orchards, and tobacco farms. The military post-carriage road between Gacko and Bileće was built at that time. By 1906, the military post provided daily service between Bileće and Trebinje and mail exchange three times a week between Gacko and Bileće.[63]

The penetration of carriage roads to Bosnia and Hercegovina was two phases behind their introduction in Serbia, each phase requiring some twenty years. In many Bosnian and Hercegovinian districts, national carriage roads were built during the 1860s and early 1870s while the province was still under Ottoman rule. The building of departmental carriage roads was achieved only during the 1880s and 1890s. The building of vicinal carriage roads had to await the twentieth century.

In the southern and eastern Balkan regions, road improvement came later than in Serbia but earlier than in Bosnia. It was pursued with vigor, as in Bosnia, only after 1860. In 1840, the only newly paved Ottoman roads included a portion of the Kačanik-Üsküb route and the route between Istanbul and the plateau northeast of Büyük-Çekmece.[64] In 1843, however, the Ottoman governor in Belgrade, Hafiz Pasha, a Circassian "gentleman in air and manner, with a grey beard" and a taste for geography and maps, perhaps under the influence of Serbian and neighboring Habsburg achievements, "wittily reversed the proverb *'El rafyk söm el taryk'* (companionship makes secure roads) by saying *'el taryk söm el rafyk'* (good roads increase passenger traffic)."[65]

The new mentality, however, was still a rare phenomenon. As late as 1846, when the environs of Varna, Burgas, Balçik, Mesembria, and Anchialos were filled with wretched carts drawn by "magnifiques" water buffaloes, arriving twice a year—in the spring and autumn—from a distance sometimes of fifty or sixty leagues, the roads of the Bulgarian Black Sea region had not yet begun to be improved. Carts destined for Balçik sometimes had to wait forty-eight hours outside the town because the road was too narrow to allow travel in double file. Moreover, upon the advent of the late autumn rains, the roads became impracticable. Transport costs in the dry season might raise the price of grains by 40 percent. In the wet season, they caused the price of wheat, the region's main export commodity, to double.[66]

Not until after 1860 was the transportation system of Thrace and Bulgaria improved significantly. The main improvement took the form of railroad building, starting with the line from Constanţa (Köstence) on the Black Sea to Cernavodă on the Danube and continuing with the line from Varna on the Black Sea to Rusçuk (Ruse) on the Danube. The two lines were built respectively in the 1850s and 1860s to facilitate Wallachian and Bulgarian grain exports at times when the port of Galaţi was closed by ice, to avoid the hazards of the numerous secondary arms of the Danube in their northward meandering through the marshlands lying between Cernavodă and Brăila, and to shorten the distance between the Danube and the Mediterranean.

In the early 1870s, when the Bosnian Banjaluka-Novi line was put into operation, construction began of a railway linking the Aegean coast to the Balkan interior and of another joining it to the Bosporus—the Salonika-Üsküb-Mitrovica and the Istanbul-Edirne-Sarembey-Dedeagaç lines.[67] With a terminus on the Bosporus or on the Black or Aegean seas, such lines were mainly in the interest of the world-market economy, especially British commerce.

Railroad building inland from the Black and Aegean seas was complemented in 1863–64 by the construction of a paved route—*une route empierrée*—between Niš and Vidin on the Danube,[68] and in 1864 and following years by a general effort by the governor of the Danube *vilayet*, Midhat Pasha, to build and improve roads—the Rusçuk-Biala-Tŭrnovo road, the Niš to Biala road, roads from Rusçuk to Pleven, Orhanie, Araba-Konak, and Sofia, and the Razgrad-Shumen-Provadiya-Varna road. Along each side of this last road, saplings were planted as embellishments but also to induce milder temperatures and to make the roadway recognizable when buried under snow. Midhat Pasha also sponsored the building of a school in Rusçuk for poor children and waifs who were taught various trades by foreign instructors—chiefly typesetting and the making of finely decorated carriages and phaetons. Some of these carriages were sold to buyers in Bucharest who previously had bought their vehicles in Austria, Saxony, and Bohemia.[69]

The improvements were confined, however, to roads of commercial significance. The roads of the Bulgarian interior, on the other hand, were "in the most deplorable state" as late as 1866 and, according to the French consul in Belgrade, "quite inferior to those of Serbia."[70]

In Greece, communication was mainly by sea. Until 1832, no road was practicable by cart (the Ionian Islands, where good roads had been built under Venetian rule, were not yet annexed to Greece), and between 1828 and 1852, only 168 kilometers of roads were built there.[71] One such road ran from the cereal-growing Arcadian plain of Tripolitsa to the ports of Argos and Nafplion. Writing in 1861, the British historian George Finlay addressed the problem: "The traveller finds post-horses and khans on every great road in the Ottoman Empire; while in Greece he will find neither post-horses nor inns on any road in the kingdom. With all the pageantry of a pompous court at Athens, there is not a good cart-road between any two large towns in Greece. He who would send his furniture from Athens to Sparta, to Delphi, or to the baths of Hypaté, must convey it from the sea-side on the backs of mules."[72] The mutation of vehicles and roads in the Ottoman Empire and Balkan successor states, a process initiated several hundred years after its inception in western Europe, was nonetheless the most important technological change made in the area since the end of the Neolithic era. Almost a precondition for other changes, it was made in response to the institutional and politico-ideological demands of a world world-economy.

As the production, transportation, and political space systems of the northern and western territories of the Ottoman Empire were reordered between 1830 and 1870 or 1880, there was an increase in middle-distance land traffic (50–200 km.) and in access to markets beyond the fifty-kilometer radius at which, under then prevailing conditions, transportation costs for cereals usually became prohibitive. Foundations thus were laid for the formation of regional, territorial, or "national" markets. The building of vicinal roads to assure integrated national markets, however, was delayed until a later time.

Metallurgy

Let us retrace our steps to see how a further modification of the Neolithic culture occurred through the invention of metallurgy and the diffusion of techniques for fashioning ornamentations, tools, and weapons of metal. As in the Near East, the first metal so employed was copper, apparently in the fourth millennium by the peoples of the pre-Cucuteni, Boian, Vinča A, and Tisza cultures. Some of the copper objects of these cultures were imports. Others were probably made by metallurgical artisans and prospectors of unknown origin—perhaps from the Caucasus—who came to exploit the copper resources of the Carpatho-Transylvanian Alps and later of the Balkan, Rhodope, and Dinaric mountain chains. The Neolithic peoples of the Balkans may have acquired copper objects from the metallurgists through gift exchange and subsequently made use of them as symbols of social distinction and for the purpose of facilitating ceremonial and other forms of gift exchange. Early copper products, including massive hatchet coins, were of minor practical value as tools or weapons.

The Neolithic cultures lacked efficient metal tools and weapons until the invention of bronze, a harder metal, through the fusion of tin, antimony, or arsenic and native copper or reduced copper ores. Around 2000 B.C., several centuries after bronze tools and weapons began to be known in the Caucasus and Near East, a bronze technology spread to the Balkans from three directions: from Minoan Crete and Anatolia to the southern Balkan periphery and from the northeast to the Danube and northern Balkan regions. The bearers of the bronze culture were two groups of nomadic peoples known respectively as the chalice pottery folk and the red ochre or corded pottery folk. The origins of the chalice pottery people, who installed themselves in the Pannonian plain and adjacent mountain regions, are obscure. The red ochre and corded pottery folk seem to have come from the vast steppes of southeastern Europe and the Caucasus-Mesopotamian frontier. In addition to their bronze technology, they brought with them the ox-drawn cart and the horse, which had been domesticated along the confines of Mesopotamia a millennium or so earlier.

The diffusion of a yet newer metallurgical technique, iron manufacture, was similarly tridirectional. Thraco-Cimmerian horsemen ushered it into the northeastern zone (Moldavia and Wallachia) during the tenth century B.C., at approximately the same time as its entry into the Aegean area, whence it ultimately expanded into the southern and central Balkan regions. In the northwest (Dalmatia and Bosnia), iron objects, notably pins, pendants, brooches, bracelets, and razors, appeared shortly before 800 B.C. as imports from Italy. Soon thereafter, local iron manufactures were developed there, as in the south and northeast.

By the fifth century B.C., six great metallurgical regions had emerged in the Old World: Armenia and the Caucasus, the frontier territories of the Iranian plateau, central Asia, the territories of the Indian Ocean, northern Africa, and Europe's alpine regions, including the Dinaric, Balkan, and Transylvanian Alps. One consequence of this occurrence was the formation of states that attempted to extend their conquests to one or more of the metallurgical regions, following up conquest by opening new roads, improving the old ones, and controlling the road networks that converged on the territories in question. These territories were situated not only at the peripheries of empire but in mountainous districts of difficult access. Their products, however, were necessary to the achievement of one of the goals of empire—a linkage between one of the main objects of politics (to control the supplies of gold and silver) and one of the main objects of economy (to obtain access to timber as well as copper, bronze, iron, and other minerals, not only for the production of objects of ostentation but also for the manufacture of objects of utility). The number of empires or great territorial states thus ultimately tended to equal or only slightly surpass the number of metallurgical regions.[73]

One of the great states was the Roman Empire. The attraction of copper, iron, lead, silver, and gold drew the Romans deeper into the Balkan peninsula from the second century B.C. onward. The process of imperial expansion was complex, however. Periodically, Rome would pursue a policy of excluding the "barbarians" instead of conquering, "civilizing," and using them to suit their own ends. The "barbarians," however, refused to be excluded. Therefore, as the Romans unearthed new sources of wealth after each undertaking against "barbarism," they pressed forward beyond the Danube.

The booty in objects of gold and silver accruing to Emperor Trajan from the conquest of Dacia (Transylvania) at the opening of the second century A.D., in addition to fifty thousand prisoners of war (to be put on the market as slaves) and arms, plate, and herds, may have amounted to 165,500 kilograms of gold (perhaps twenty times the annual gold production of Bosnia during the same period) and 331,000 kilograms of silver. These treasures allowed him to remedy temporarily the precarious condition of Roman finances.[74]

The Gothic, Hunnic, Avaro-Slavic, and Bulgar invasions of the fourth to the seventh century discouraged the operation of some Balkan mines. Other mining activity ceased or diminished as a result of the spread of epidemics and decline of population in the eastern Mediterranean during the second half of the sixth century.

One of the decisive factors behind the iconoclasm of Byzantium during the seventh and eighth centuries, apart from theological controversy and questions of cultural identity, may have been the loss of minerals to the triumphant Arabs in Asia and to the conquering Slavs in the Balkans, whence the need of Byzantine emperors to salvage the gold and silver of the holy ikons and their consequent determination to wage a systematic campaign against the use of images in religious worship.[75]

But mining was never wholly interrupted in the Balkans.[76] Before the end of the twelfth century, new incentives inspired a more systematic mining of gold, silver, and other metals.[77] The growth of population and European economic expansion in the eleventh, twelfth, and thirteenth centuries stimulated mining activity in Bohemia, Hungary, Transylvania, Carinthia, Carniola, and the Germanies. The city-state of Venice became the chief intermediary in the exchange of the silver of Europe's northern alpine regions for the slaves and furs of Tana, in the Crimea, and of New Sarai and Astrakhan. As such exchanges dwindled after 1300, partly as a result of the incursions on the middle Volga River of pirates from Great Novgorod, Venice shifted its focus to Alexandria, where it exchanged the silver of the alpine regions for the pepper and other spices of the Indies and for the gold of the Sudan.

The decline of the Astrakhan–New Sarai–Tana route of commerce also served as a stimulus to the trade of Italian merchants who bought spices in Trebizond (Trabzon), Beirut, and Alexandria, some of them for resale in Moldavia, Wallachia, Transylvania, and Hungary. From Brăila at the mouth of the Danube, the Trebizond/Trabzon trade route continued to Cimpulung and the

Figure 3.2. **Europe's Main Latitudinal Route of Commerce, ca. 1500: Skirting the Balkans Proper**

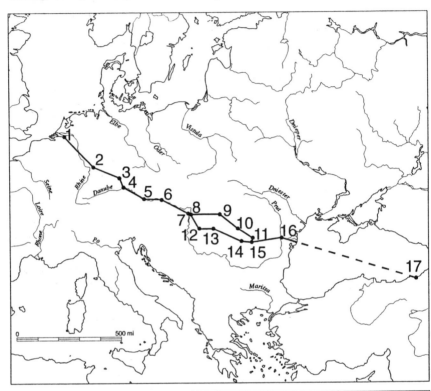

KEY		
1 Antwerp	7 Buda	13 Arad
2 Frankfurt	8 Pest	14 Hermannstadt (Sibiu)
3 Nürnberg	9 Oradea	15 Cîmpulung
4 Regensburg	10 Clausenburg (Cluj)	16 Brăila
5 Linz	11 Cronstadt (Braşov)	17 Trabzon
6 Vienna	12 Szeged	

Transylvanian mining and trading towns of Cronstadt (Braşov, Brassó), Sighişoara (Schässburg), Mediaş (Mediasch), Cluj (Clausenburg), and Oradea (Grosswardein, Nagyvárad). It proceeded thence to Ofen (Buda). An alternative route went from Clausenburg to Buda by way of Hermannstadt (Sibiu, Nagyszeben), Arad, and Szeged. These two routes were in fact an extension of the primary European latitudinal commercial route leading from Buda to Vienna, Linz, Regensburg, Nürnberg, and Antwerp. The north-south routes linking the North Sea and Baltic with the Adriatic and Mediterranean converged with the latitudinal route at Nürnberg[78] (see Figure 3.2).

The growing demand for silver and the growth of European commerce and craft production stimulated in turn a revival of the silver and other mines and the use of new mining techniques in Serbia and Bosnia. The first mine explicitly mentioned in medieval Serbian documents is that of Brskovo, which was put into operation in the 1250s by Saxon miners from Transylvania or Hungary. In Bosnia, mining as an activity of specialists resumed around 1330.

Silver mining grew in Macedonia, Serbia, western Bulgaria, and Bosnia during the fourteenth and fifteenth centuries. Upon the decline of the central European silver mines during the Hundred Years' and Hussite wars, Balkan silver became a yet more desired commodity in Ragusa (Dubrovnik), Venice, Alexandria, and Florence and in the cities of southern Italy and Sicily.

At the moment of Europe's greatest need for the silver of Macedonia, Serbia, and Bosnia, however, the mines of these provinces fell one after another into the hands of the Ottoman Turks. Ottoman rulers and commanders consciously pursued a brilliant three-step program of conquering the roads leading to the gold, silver, lead, copper, and iron mines of the medieval Balkan states, then seizing the mines themselves, and finally reducing the centers of political opposition after they had been deprived of the economic basis of their power. Following the seizure of the mines of Kratovo in northern Macedonia at the close of the fourteenth century, further Ottoman expansion was temporarily halted by Tamerlane's victory in 1402 at Ankara. A decade later, however, the Ottoman commander Evrenos initiated a plan, subsequently pursued by his son Ishakbeg and his grandson Isabeg, to acquire the site of the most important silver mines in all of Europe: Novo Brdo. Finally, in 1454 and 1455, Mehmed the Conqueror's troops captured not only Novo Brdo but a series of other Serbian mining sites: Rudnik, Plana, Zaplanina, Trepča, and Janjevo.[79] The despot (title of the ruler) of Serbia sadly informed the king of Hungary that the loss of Novo Brdo, "the nerve center of war on account of its mines," was tantamount to the loss of the country's very "head" (caput patriae et ob mineras nervus belli). A few years later the Turks occupied most of the Bosnian mining sites, including Srebr(e)nica (literally, Silver Town), which had temporarily fallen into Turkish hands already in 1440.[80]

Several of the Balkan mines declined during the second half of the fifteenth and early part of the sixteenth century. For example, the yearly revenues accruing to the state (or to the personal treasury of the sovereign) from the mines of Novo Brdo fell from more than 200,000 gold ducats in 1432 to 120,000 in 1520 and 40,000 in 1661.[81] On the whole, however, the Turks maintained silver production at a high level. In compensation for the decline of Novo Brdo and certain other mining centers, they pushed the exploitation of the silver mines of Siderocapsa, presumably the former Chrysitis of Philip of Macedon.[82] Located in the Chalcidice peninsula in the district later known as "the mining communities" (Mademochoria), the mines of Siderocapsa rapidly extended operations after 1530. Achieving a high level of production during the 1540s, they brought in monthly revenues to the Ottoman state of 9,000 to 30,000 ducats, or more than 200,000 ducats annually. Upon his visit to Siderocapsa in 1547 at the order of his king, François I, relates the mineralogist Pierre Belon du Mans, the six thousand miners and prospectors working in the area—mostly persons he identified as Bulgarians (while specifically affirming that Serbs lived in the neighboring villages) but including some Greeks and Jews—employed Spanish, recently introduced there by Jews expelled from Spain, as the language of trade. The technical vocabulary of the miners, on the other hand, was a Slavicized form of Saxon. Some of them may have been descendants of the Saxon immigrants who had gone to Serbia, Bosnia, northern Macedonia, and Bulgaria during the thirteenth and fourteenth centuries. An unidentified Christian Armenian had taught the miners to separate gold from silver and lead with aquafortis (nitric acid). In other respects their mining technology was central European.[83]

A century earlier, Cardinal Bessarion, a Greek scholar from Trebizond who favored the idea of union between the Roman Catholic and Orthodox churches, had tried to persuade Constantine Palaeologus, despot of the autonomous Byzantine province of Morea (Peloponnesus), to duplicate the technological strides then being made in Italy. In particular, Bessarion admired the technique of smelting by means of water-driven "leather bellows which are distended and relaxed untouched by any hand, and separate the metal from the useless and earthy matter that may be present."[84]

Noted in France as early as 1340 (but apparently employed there earlier) and adopted widely in Italy before or during Bessarion's time, water-driven leather bellows were in use at Siderocapsa at the time of Belon's visit. How the technique had developed there is unclear. It may have been part of the heritage of the Slavo-Saxons. Leather bellows themselves, however, are an innovation traditionally credited (albeit invented earlier) to the Scythian philosopher Anacharsis, contemporary of Solon.[85]

The Siderocapsa bellows were operated by eight-spoked waterwheels turned by the water of seven mountain streams beside which were erected the five hundred or more charcoal blast furnaces of the miners. The heat created in the furnaces by the bellows was sufficient to melt and refine metals so well that they did not require subsequent hammering. One consequence of the process was the production of cast iron on a larger scale.

On the other hand, iron-casting techniques may have reached the Balkans from two directions: not only from western Europe by way of the north but also by way of the south and east through the agency of Turkic and Indic peoples, such as the Gipsies. The Chinese may have produced cast iron as early as the second century B.C., during the reign of Emperor Wu. Several centuries later, the Sarmatians, who overran the southeastern European steppe from the east, were known to employ corselets of cast iron as part of their armament, and cast-iron manufacturing techniques probably quickly spread from them to the neighboring Turkic peoples.

The term for cast iron in Russian and Bulgarian is *chugun*, derived perhaps from the Osmanli *çöygen* or from some other Turkic variant for cast iron.[86] The period during which eastern cast-iron manufacturing techniques were assimilated in the Balkans, however, is uncertain—in the fourteenth century? earlier? or later? William Eton believed, probably on the basis of insufficient evidence, that cast-iron techniques were unknown to the Ottoman Turks in the eighteenth century or had been discovered only recently—by "an Arabian, at Constantinople," whose cast iron, "when it came out of the mould, was as malleable as hammered iron," but whose techniques had not yet been transmitted to other Ottoman artisans.[87]

As a unit, the Balkans were not technologically backward in the fifteenth century and were not to become so until the closing decades of the sixteenth century. Balkan mining was as important during the 1540s and 1550s as it had been a century earlier. Slow between 1580 and 1640 (there may even have been a minor recovery during the reign of Murad IV, 1623–40), the decline was precipitous thereafter. The annual mining revenues of the Ottoman Empire, which were mostly of Balkan origin, fell from 600,000 ducats in 1546 to 500,000 ducats in 1590 and 100,000 by the early eighteenth century.[88]

The arrival in Europe after the mid-sixteenth century of enormous quantities of cheaply produced American silver made unprofitable the continued extraction of undiminished quantities of silver from the mines of central Europe (revived between 1460 and 1540). The Germanies consequently lost their role of leadership in heavy industry. As German and other central European investments were diverted to agriculture, landlords augmented the labor required of peasant cultivators in order to create farm export surpluses. There emerged in the eastern portions of central Europe in this manner what is known as the "second serfdom."

The advent of cheap American silver produced a similar effect in the Balkans. To compete with the Indian slave labor of the Hispano-American mines, the Ottomans resorted to the use of forced labor in their own enterprises. The latter practice, however, induced skilled miners to run away and even become leaders of insurrection. With the decline of the material foundations of Balkan heavy industry, a "second serfdom" made strides in the Balkans, as in central Europe. Since other factors also played a key role in its emergence, however, we shall return to this subject in the chapter on the Balkan economy.

A new revival of Balkan mining began around the middle of the nineteenth century. In the long interval of industrial stagnation and contraction, tales of lost or buried treasures and of forgotten sites of precious mines had been widely disseminated.[89] Count Čedomilj Mijatović, a Serbian minister of foreign affairs, finance, and commerce and envoy extraordinary and minister plenipotentiary to the courts of St. James, Istanbul, Bucharest, and the Hague, offers the following explanation for the credibility of such tales:

Serbia was, in the thirteenth, fourteenth and fifteenth centuries, one of the few gold- and silver-producing countries of Europe. Her aristocracy, possessing large estates, became, in those centuries very rich. When the Turkish invasion took place, and the Serbian noblesse fled to save their lives from the conqueror's sword, they could not carry away the gold and silver which had been through generations accumulating in their castles. Hoping they would return again, they hid their treasures or buried them in their castles or in the neighbourhood. Circumstances did not allow them to return, but ere they died they communicated, orally or in writing, the secret of their buried treasures to their heirs. The consequence was that after Serbia became autonomous almost every year people arrived in Belgrade from all parts of the world for permits to search for the treasures of their ancestors. I remember that, in the course of only one year, I gave, as Minister of Finance, fifty such permissions. The Serbs have a special word to designate these treasures. They do not call them generally "the treasure" *(blago),* but *ostave,* which means "something that has been left." [90]

The tradition of hunting for buried treasure was yet stronger during the first half of the nineteenth century. A Serbian writer born in 1820 remembered that when he was a child visitors used to come from afar with descriptions of places where treasure was supposedly buried. A man who claimed to be a descendant of the medieval hero Miloš Obilić even afirmed that he had returned from America in quest of the heritage left to him by his ancestors. Hidden treasures were sought in particular around the ruins of Kulič fortress near the junction of the Danube and Morava and in the vicinity of Mount Avala. A song current in the 1830s reflects the mood of the time:

> Four youths bestirred themselves,
> All four one to another alike,
> To dig for treasure on Mount Avala. [91]

Serbs commonly believed, moreover, that Greeks were better informed about the location of lost treasures, and itinerant Greek vendors were not averse to selling maps and "ancient letters" showing their supposed location. [92] With or without such maps and letters, hundreds of persons set forth each year in search of precious "relics." The common wisdom of the Timok valley was that upon finding a hoard, one should make a sacrifice in order to obtain release from the curse of death. [93] Other wisdom held that the search for treasure should follow a prescribed ritual to prevent the trove from being transformed into coal or from being swallowed up again by the earth. [94]

Stories of buried treasure and prescriptions for how to find it were a worldwide phenomenon. [95] One of the great interpreters of capitalism, Werner Sombart, contends indeed that one of the historical antecedents, perhaps even a precondition, of capitalism was the belief in enrichment by magical means, more precisely, the reality of an "epoch of the accumulation of treasures." [96] Such an epoch lasted in western Europe until the end of the seventeenth century. In the Balkans, it lasted until after the mid-nineteenth century, when hunters of metallic "relics" began to yield to engineers, agents of the introduction to the Balkans of the new era of steam.

Costs of War

Advances in military and civil technology alike have been greatest in those parts of the world in which population density and/or the circulation of goods, information, and opinions reach high levels. With each advance, however, military technology becomes costlier, necessitating the diversion of resources from those who produce goods to those who produce war. The use of bronze and iron weapons drove states on to obtain control of the mines at which such resources were to be had and to effect a partial diversion of the metals from ceremonial and economic to military purposes.

Government administration was costly. To cover such costs, two avenues of action existed—imposing tribute levies (often after a costly war) and securing access to silver, gold, and other mines. But as the mines in Europe from which metals could be obtained on the basis of known techniques diminished after A.D. 300, war technology was linked to a pastoral-agricultural economy characterized by an abundance of cattle, from which was derived the word for "fief." To equip a heavily armed knight, writes Lynn White, may have "cost about twenty oxen, or the plough-teams of at least ten peasant families." In addition, the knight's squire had to be clothed, fed, and armed.[97] That could not have been done without the new, wheeled, horse-drawn moldboard plow that penetrated and turned over the deep, wet, heavy soils of northern Europe but that only a few cultivator families could afford.[98]

In Byzantium, war technology at first took another direction. Fleeing the Arab invasion of Syria shortly after the mid-seventh century, a certain Kallinikos brought knowledge to Constantinople of how to make "marine fire," or what came to be known in western Europe as "Greek fire," an invention made perhaps as early as A.D. 500. "Greek fire" comprised a mix of various inflammable substances: saltpeter, sulphur, naphtha, and pitch; sulphur, tartar, nitre, and petroleum; or a pound of sulphur, two pounds of charcoal, and six pounds of nitre. In its first two forms (there were also other combinations), it usually was placed in an earthen pot, set afire, and projected by means of a sling that was operated by a war engine known in western Europe as a trebuchet. The fire caused by the projectile could be put out only by urine, vinegar, or sand. In the third form, the pounded contents were placed in a long narrow cartridge, which presumably was then catapulted.[99]

In its early form, Greek fire bore no resemblance to later gunpowder firearms and artillery. In its later forms, it was a prelude to the cannon, whose use—however inefficient for a century—dates back to the early decades of the fourteenth century. In 1363, Ragusa began to make its own guns. In 1373, their use spread to Serbia.[100]

Improvements in artillery between 1450 and 1550 made it difficult for small states to sustain the costs of such innovations. As one of the largest states in the world, the Ottoman Empire benefited from the change. After 1550, however, the European and Mediterranean states concentrated on building fortifications, most of which were situated along the seacoasts and land frontiers. But there were drawbacks to territorial vastness as well as smallness. An extensive territorial perimeter required a heavy investment in defenses, for fortified places had to be established at more or less regular intervals along the sea and land margins.

Great size also made it difficult to govern distant provinces, where local notables, such as the *ayan* of the Ottoman Empire and provincial governors and local commanders *(ağas)* were primarily preoccupied by provincial, local, or personal interests. Like the European states, the Ottoman Empire augmented its tax levies. By the end of the sixteenth century, however, the taxes reaching the coffers of the central government fell to a low level. A good proportion of the levies was channeled to tax farmers, notables, and local commanders.

Faced with this problem, the Ottoman government had to make a choice that also confronted other vast states, namely, Spain, China, and the Mughal Empire. In all four cases, the landed interests prevailed over the numerically smaller group of advocates of offensive naval power. The function of the navies of these states consequently became primarily defensive.

After entering the Indian Ocean with their ships in 1517, the Turks took Aden in 1538 and Basra at the close of 1546. The inadequacy of timber supplies, however, soon obliged the Ottoman government to withdraw from the Indian Ocean to the Red Sea.

In the Mediterranean, where the Turks already were a naval power, they quickly rebuilt a navy after their defeat at Lepanto in 1571. They forced Venice to yield Cyprus in 1573. In 1574, they organized a great armada and compelled Spain to give up Tunis in the costliest battle of the sixteenth century. But Tunis lay fifteen hundred kilometers west of Istanbul. The Ottoman gun parks and naval stations in the Aegean and eastern Mediterranean were unable to supply Ottoman ships regularly in the western Mediterranean. In practice, therefore, the Ottoman government allowed Tunis and Algiers to develop as autonomous political entities as early as the 1580s.

To all intents and purposes, the Ottoman Empire thereafter limited its zone of naval operations to the Black, Aegean, and Ionian seas. It did so because it was confronted in the 1590s and early 1600s by a land war on two distant fronts—with the Habsburg monarchy in the north and west and with Persia in the east. Moreover, even though the South Slav *uskoks*—alternately pirates, corsairs, and local heroes—came under the stricter control of Austria after 1620, a new source of coastal hit-raid-and-run or guerrilla tactics appeared, much closer to the Ottoman capital: daring river-pirate Cossacks who pillaged not only the Black Sea coasts but also the more sheltered Bosporus.

Faced with such problems, the Ottoman Empire made a new choice. It reduced its navy by 1640 to a fourth or fifth of its size in the 1570s. Its navy was yet weaker in 1730. To have maintained a navy at the 1570 level—a navy capable of large-scale offensive operations—would have required the diversion to naval purposes of 15–30 percent of the customary revenues of the Ottoman state.[101]

The Ottoman state could have attempted to augment its revenues. In that case, however, it would have had to transform itself from a polity founded on tributary and command principles into what Joseph A. Schumpeter called a "tax state" *(Steuerstaat)*,[102] a state with a more open economy, more closely linked to its rural sectors by exchange than by command.

That solution collided with the interests of powerful groups. It was not taken until after 1830. By that time, because so many changes had to be made so quickly, it may have been too late to save the empire as a territorial unit. By 1830, five different portions of the Ottomon Empire—Greece, Egypt, Serbia, Wallachia, and Moldavia—had obtained special status. Greece had even won nominal independence.

Ottoman efforts to create a "tax state" were made with some success after 1830. They were unequal, however, to the force of nationalism or aspirations on the part of a growing portion of the "political classes," educated youth, and intelligentsias of the non-Turkish Balkan and Egyptian—and later Asian— ethnicities to create states that corresponded with the maximum territorial extent of each ethnic group. This last goal created other conflicts.

Industrial Devolution and Transactional Modes

Every society has its own particular combination of ways of reallocating land, labor, goods, capital, services, and rights of use, its own combination of transactional modes. The four such modes that have been developed by human societies are reciprocity, redistribution, linear market exchange, and territorial market economy. In varying degree, the first three types have existed for thousands of years. Of the four modes, reciprocity may be the oldest. Probably having biological foundations, it is also found among nonhuman animals, especially "intelligent, closely integrated species."[103] Redistribution is a newer mode, evolving simultaneously from the practice of reciprocity and from its violation but growing in particular out of religion and the organization of power. Newer yet is linear exchange, which exists only in human societies and has been practiced in some parts of the world for four or five thousand years.

The underlying relationship expressed by the reciprocal and redistributional modes is one of social obligation. But while the social obligation of reciprocity extends to kin and "friends," the social obligation of redistribution operates on the basis of religious or political affiliation or dependence.[104] Linear market exchange has been the product of interaction between reason of state and the acquisitive passion of private interests.

The newest transactional mode is territorial market economy. Only several centuries old anywhere and of posterior development in most places, it was threatened after the late 1920s in the Soviet Union and after the late 1940s in the Balkans by the transformation of the old redistributional mode into a command mode of a centralized planned economy, intent on controlling and determining both investment and production.

Territorial market economy is the product of the extension of linear market exchange to a level at which a precarious balance of private interests is realized and maintained by means of political intervention in favor of different particular interests. It is not firmly in place, however, until the precarious balance of private interests has been transformed into "a strong *web* of interdependent relationships," allowing a market increasingly responsive to supply and demand and a redefinition of the relationship between economy and reason of state.[105]

Reciprocity is of two basic types—generalized and balanced. Generalized reciprocity is the reciprocity of kin, of the male and female members and of young and old of the same household, of real and potential matrimonial allies, and of companions in combat. For one of the parties to the transaction, namely, the young, generalized reciprocity is of the deferred type almost by definition. It is also more altruistic than balanced reciprocity, which is founded on the principle of *quid pro quo*, requiring the almost immediate return of a gift for a gift and, almost invariably, of a gift of the same general value in the prevailing prestige hierarchy.

Some transactions, however, are characterized by variations in the exchange obligation in accordance with the status, power, or advantage and interest of each party. Known to sociologists and anthropologists as "negative reciprocity," this mode of exchange embraces the principle of giving to more powerful, more prestigious, or more egotistical groups, a thing or service of greater value than the thing or service returned.[106] It thus embodies the tendency of reciprocity, generalized and balanced alike, to become redistribution.

Kinship distance, spatial distance, and political distance alter the nature of reciprocity. Reciprocity is thus generalized at the level of household and lineage. Tending to become balanced at the level of the village, it assumes negative reciprocal or strong redistributive aspects at tribal, intertribal, and state levels.[107]

How important reciprocity was in the Balkans is one of the subjects of the next chapter. My present concern is to examine the relationship between communications technology and the Ottoman command economy or system of redistribution.

The guiding tenet of Ottoman political-economic life was what Karl Polanyi called "centricity," under which control patterns were defined not by autonomous markets but mainly by administration and political decision.[108] Identified by Sir John Hicks as "command economy" and by others as "Oriental despotism," "Asiatic mode of production," and "tributary economy,"[109] Ottoman centricity was a transactional mode "with state control over the supply of basic cereals and raw materials for crafts."[110] It was able to function in that manner by the fact that, as a "gunpowder empire" (or protection-producing political enterprise with monopoly rights to powder and shot within its own wide territorial limits), it was able to command domestic support and had the power to crush domestic rebellion.[111]

The attribute of command and of tribute exaction to a command economy requires making a distinction between tributes and taxes. Only two main services accrue to the payers of tribute—protection against the payment of tribute to some other political force and the organization of routes and authority markets. On the other hand, many more services may be expected in return for the payment of taxes, including the entitlement of taxpayers to participate in the political process of making decisions and thus partly reconciling the principle of centricity with the exogenous principles of eccentricity, autonomy, representation, and democracy.[112]

The relationship between the Ottoman command economy and mining, agriculture, sylviculture, and stock raising was reproduced in at least five different ways: by the payment of tithes *(öşr)* to timariots or *sipahis*, who in turn were obligated to provide the state, during the ordinary fighting season of the year, with a prescribed number of armed horsemen (or to perform some other designated service); by the farming out *(iltizam)* of the right to various revenues (including salt, copper, iron, and other mining revenues), which in 1695 was placed on a lifetime basis *(malikâne);* by the issuance of government patents giving privileged buyers temporary rights of exclusivity to certain sylvicultural, agricultural, and pastoral products; by the forced contribution to the state of labor, capital, or land (in the economist's sense); and by the exaction from non-Muslim males of a head or capitation tax *(cizye)* that had to be paid in cash.

To pay the head tax, Christian peasants normally had to sell their product in town—presumably the town to whose administrative decisions they were subject. If they lacked a "surplus" in some year—not at all an unusual occurrence— they had to borrow money, or goods with which to obtain money, at usurious rates of interest. If they possessed the necessary "surplus," they had to market their goods when all other peasants were offering them for sale for the same reason, thus at a time when prices tended to be depressed.

As for the privileged buyers, they were commissioned to buy certain staples at low prices set by the government. By an easy abuse of authority, they often bought them at yet lower prices. In the latter part of the seventeenth and in the eighteenth century, several categories of ordinary forced purchases were current. In the vassal Danubian principalities of Wallachia and Moldavia, purveyors known as *kapanlis* were authorized to obtain specific quantities of cheese, butter, honey, beeswax, tallow, and smoked beef and mutton at prices set by the government for delivery to the imperial palace, to the Ottoman armed forces, and to the *kapan* or wholesale food market of Istanbul. In the same principalities and in Rumelia or Ottoman core territories in Europe, authorized and sometimes coerced buyers known as *celeps*—many of them wealthy sheepmen—were charged with buying specific quantities of sheep (occasionally also cattle and dairy products), similarly for delivery to the capital or army. The total contribution of each district was determined by the government. Purchases of sheep by other buyers were forbidden—although violations of the law may have been frequent—until the *celeps* had effected their purchases in the early spring. Furthermore, from the Black Sea coasts of Bulgaria, Wallachia, and Moldavia, from the Aegean coasts of Thrace, Macedonia, Thessaly, and Morea, and from several Mediterranean districts in Asia Minor, government purchasing agents known as *iştiracis* regularly bought during the seventeenth and eighteenth centuries almost one-twelfth of the wheat production at a low, government-set price. The *iştira* or forced wheat purchase was transported to Istanbul. There a portion was conveyed to public storage granaries, another portion was redistributed to the army, and a third quantity was resold by the government, usually much above the purchase price and cost of transportation.

The *kapanlis*, *celeps*, and *iştiracis* enjoyed the right, or at least took advantage of their authority, to buy a designated quantity or proportion of the same staple(s) for private gain at the same low government price. In the case of wheat, the amount was set by the government at 10 percent of the authorized *iştira* collection.[113]

Hardly an item of rural production and labor entering into it was not subject to some form of monopoly right, some technique by means of which its consumption was prevented from entering a market economy. Included among such items were timber, transport labor, the labor products (nails) of the villages of the Asian Black Sea shores, and the resin production of the mastic evergreens of Chios, which was used as chewing gum by the ladies of the imperial seraglio and prized both as an oral refreshener and as a whitening and cleaning dental agent.[114]

Being off limits to foreign merchants, who were usually obliged to buy and sell in the authorized sea and land ports of trade, the Ottoman domestic market was organized almost wholly in the context of a command economy that protected the staples rights of its constituent administrative territories or subordinate central places once the staples rights of Istanbul and the army and navy had been assured. The privileged subordinate administrative cities, however, tended to subvert the command economy of Istanbul or highest-order central place in two ways—by striving to gain autonomy and by their propensity for the expensive imports of long-distance trade with other political and cultural systems. In the course of the eighteenth century, the Ottoman command economy yielded to the pressures of the previously dependent European "peripheral economy" of long-distance and international trade and the market mechanisms of the mixed market and command world-economy of the European states.

The circulatory system of Ottoman command mobilization was essentially a *dromocracy*,[115] a system of management of sea lanes and land routes designed to assure a regular flow of troops, messages, and officials and their retinues from the capital to the provinces (and back), and of tributes and staples from the provinces to the capital and provincial centers of command. Command routes also served as routes of commerce. Their primary function, however, was to serve the command economy. It was not their function to articulate a web of commercial relations independent of command.

A *dromocracy* does not produce a circulatory and territorial system favorable to market economy. The partial shift after 1600, and especially after 1700, of the function of command from one center—Istanbul—to many provincial centers had two consequences. On the one hand, it led to disinvestment in route management by the central government. On the other, it promoted the development of an economy of market places—but not of a market economy.[116]

In the maritime sphere of the Ottoman *dromocracy*, one result was a decline in the size of the Ottoman navy and the virtual absence of maritime technological improvements until the second half of the eighteenth century. A second result was the appearance of rival provincial merchant marines, each associated with a particular city and/or ethnic-religious group—Tripoli, Tunis, and Algiers in North Africa since the 1580s and, by 1750, a Muslim Albanian merchant marine at Dulcigno and an Orthodox Greco-Albanian merchant marine at Hydra, Spetsai, and Psara.

The Balkan merchant marines reflected the conflicting politics and ideology (religion) of rival quasi city-states. They were also a response to the increasing readiness on the part of urban-based "landlords" (revenue farmers) to export their grains to western Mediterranean ports. Thus they were an expression of the desire of Ottoman "landlords" to contest the continued application of central command mobilization to their own particular surpluses.[117]

Neither the central command economy nor the provincial command economies were prone to make the necessary investments in social overhead to improve land routes for general use. There was no need for this. For peasants required few items apart from salt that could not be obtained locally, and the *dromocratic* system of Ottoman land routes, extending from Buda (until 1683) and Belgrade to Erzurum fulfilled the needs of the cities.

Technology and Politics

Under the disarray of the Ottoman command economy, Balkan industry faltered, succumbing to the onslaught of European technology (and society, economy, and ideology). One of the first sectors to feel the impact of British superiority was the Ottoman cotton industry, which was forced into competition with the most "progressive" sector of English production. In the last few decades of the eighteenth century, cotton yarn manufactures had metamorphosed minuscule Thessalian

Ambelakia into a hamlet with the prosperous air of "a borough of Holland." By 1801, however, residents of Ambelakia complained to the British traveler Edward Daniel Clarke that they had begun to "feel the effect of the preference given to English cotton thread in the German markets." Clarke further observed that the grievance was aimed against "the improvement adopted in Great Britain of spinning cotton thread in mills, by means of engines that are worked by steam, which has caused such a considerable reduction in its price;—all the thread made at Ambelakia being spun by manual labour."[118]

After the Napoleonic wars the Ambelakiot cotton industry deteriorated rapidly. Having lost its former German markets, Ambelakia sank again into oblivion. In adjacent Tyrnavos,[119] the number of handloom establishments for the weaving of muslins declined from 2,000 in 1812 to 200 in 1830. In Albanian Scutari (Shkodër), the number of handlooms fell from 600 in 1812 to 40 in 1821. Between the Napoleonic era and 1847, the number of silk looms in Bursa declined from 1,000 to 75. In Istanbul and Üsküdar, the number of cloth-producing looms fell from 2,750 in the 1830s to 25 in 1868; the number of brocade looms fell from 350 to 4; and the number of upholstery silk looms from 60 to 8.[120]

The demise of the old crafts extended from the westernmost to the easternmost districts of the Ottoman Empire. It was part of a pattern of decline common alike to eastern Europe and almost the whole of Asia—indeed, to all countries unable or unwilling to challenge the ideology of capitalism and European state power.

One Balkan area in which textile manufactures, especially coarse woolens (aba), prospered after 1830, however, was Bulgaria, a great sheep-raising and wool-producing land geographically closer to Istanbul than the other Balkan territories of Turkey. Unlike Serbia and Greece, it had refrained from large-scale political rebellion. Ottoman officials therefore readily entrusted governmental orders for woolen cloth and military uniforms to wool merchants in Bulgaria.

The Bulgarian wool merchants functioned as Verleger, putting out their wool to be woven into cloth by Bulgarian peasants. After the wool was woven, the cloth was returned to the wool merchants, who used it to make the uniforms for which they had orders. Inspired by the regularity of the official demand for their products, several wool merchants established modern textile mills. The first woolen factory, founded in Sliven in 1834, was followed by others in Plovdiv (Philippopolis), Stara Zagora, Gabrovo, Samokov, Kotel, and other communities. New industry thus may have compensated for the decline of old crafts in at least some parts of Bulgaria.[121]

The continued inclusion of Bulgaria (until 1878) within the political and economic confines of the still territorially vast Ottoman Empire—in other words, the absence of revolution and political autonomy—aided the development of a modest Bulgarian textile industry. The Serbian revolution, on the other hand, provoked a further impairment of the long-deteriorating Serbian urban economy by causing skilled labor, capital, and capitalists to leave the area.

Other deterrents to Serbian industrial development were the abundance of fuel wood, which removed any incentive for developing other types of fuel; the ample supply of meat and other foods, ample at least in terms of the prevailing style of life; and the wealth of land in proportion to the total population of the country. Shortages of fuel wood and land began to be felt around 1860, but attempts to industrialize encountered serious obstacles because they coincided with a local economic crisis that started in the late 1860s and merged with the world-wide economic crisis of 1873–96. But as population density increased four times between 1815 and the end of the century, as forests declined to a third of their former size, and as the per capita distribution of meat and milk animals and beasts of burden fell sharply between 1859 and 1905, a need arose for industrialization.

Industrialization, however, had to await the creation of a social foundation that would allow the pursuit of an industrial policy: law and order; the founding of primary, secondary, and higher schools; the improvement of roads; the establishment of pharmacies and hospitals; and the inauguration of relatively efficient agencies for the collection, evaluation, and dissemination of economic data. An industrialization policy also required the prior creation of an economic foundation: monetary and fiscal facilities, and public utilities. In Greece, a national bank was founded in 1841. In Serbia, on the other hand, the formation of stable banking institutions was delayed until the 1870s or 1880s.[122]

The achievement of adequate social and economic foundations was itself contingent upon the development of town life, that is, centers of concentration of diverse talents. But as late as 1866, Serbia possessed only one town (Belgrade) with a population of more than 25,000 (25,178, according to the census of that year) and only four others with more than 5,000. The situation was essentially the same in 1874. Only after the 1870s was a dependable urban base laid that would favor the establishment of industry.[123] Until 1880, Serbian capitalists reinvested their profits in commerce, land, and occasionally in institutions with a social purpose, such as schools.

The principality of Serbia thus had only a single factory in 1847: a small glassworks near Jagodina (for a time after World War II called Svetozarevo, after Svetozar Marković), founded by the Serbian minister of foreign affairs, Avram Petronijević. Brought from Liège in 1849, the first steam engine was not put into operation until the 1850s. As late as 1888, apart from its smelting establishments in the mines, a number of sawmills operated by hydraulic wheels, several flour mills, and its munitions and armaments works, Serbia possessed only 12 factories: 7 breweries, 1 distillery, 1 wax factory, 1 "fine soap" factory, 1 glass factory, and 1 textile mill (the Woolens Factory founded in 1882 at Paraćin by the Moravian Jews, the Münch brothers). As late as 1898, only 17 Serbian enterprises made use of steam power. In 1908, the number was still only 78.[124]

Many Serbians had at first been hostile to steam power, not because of a repugnance to technological innovation but out of fear that the diffusion of steam would further undermine the ability of existing industry (mostly crafts, many of recent origin) to compete with the more highly industrialized countries of the world. Prince Miloš was opposed to the deepening of the Iron Gate (Danubian gorge at the Serbo-Romanian frontier) and hostile to the introduction of steam navigation on the Danube on the ground that such action would hurt or destroy Serbian commerce and industry. At the time, Serbian, Greek, and other Balkan boats and barges were able to negotiate the Iron Gate with relative ease. If steam navigation were introduced or the Iron Gate were deepened, virtually all the advantages would accrue to territorially larger, economically more viable, and technologically more advanced Austria (and Hungary).

Following the Serbian revolution, the ownership of boats operating along the Serbian and lower Danube shifted from predominantly Turkish into Greek, Jewish, and Serbian hands. The ports of Belgrade, Vidin, and Rusçuk (Ruse) were rapidly transformed into shipbuilding centers that made small seagoing vessels with an initial maximum displacement of 128 tons, usually without precise plan or symmetry but commercially adequate. Between 1832 and 1834, the entrepreneur Nikola Kefala built at the request of the Serbian government, in the yards of Smederevo, a brig (the *Srbija*) with a displacement of 250 tons. Employing German, Turkish, Serbian, Greek, and perhaps English craftsmen, Kefala built other boats on commission from the government. By 1834, about 200 small Serbian craft were engaged in transporting cereals, skins, salt (on boats known as *solarice*), and timber (on boats known as *drvarice*)—100 of them operating from the newly established tiny port town of Milanovac, 40 of them from Šabac, and 30 each from Belgrade and Smederevo, plying along the Sava and Danube, going sometimes to Istanbul. Shipbuilding continued to flourish, and in 1840–42 the brothers German(os) of Belgrade built a seagoing ship (the *Prince Michael*) at Brza Palanka (the only Serbian river port below the Iron Gate) with a displacement of 384 metric tons.[125]

But hardly had the program of building a Serbian merchant marine got under way than it was confronted with the competition of steam. In 1831, the Austrian government granted the newly created Danube Steamship Navigation Company (Donau-Dampfschiffahrts-Gesellschaft, hereafter referred to as DSNC) an eighty-year monopoly of navigation on the Danube on condition that it extend its activities to the lower Danube and Black Sea. Putting a first steamboat into operation along the course between Belgrade and the Iron Gate in 1834, the DSNC added a second in 1836. In 1844, a DSNC steamboat inaugurated service on the Serbian Sava, and in 1847 four DSNC steamboats were charged with passenger and freight service along the lower Danube. When, soon thereafter, Serbia announced its intention to open its own steamship service, DSNC competition, seconded by the Hungarian Society of River and Maritime Navigation, quickly nullified its aim. By mid-century there was no longer a Serbian merchant marine.[126] Serbia failed to reestablish a viable river navigation company until 1893. In 1908, its river navigation was limited to the activity of eight boats and forty-six tugs.[127]

In the grotesquely unequal struggle for markets and commercial supremacy, an adequate Serbian merchant marine could not be built unless Serbia ceased to be economically subservient, notably, by ceasing to be a landlocked state. Thus, when the Polish émigré statesman Prince Adam Czartoryski and his Paris-centered Polish Agency counseled Serbian "Constitutionalist" leaders *(Ustavobranitelji)* in 1843 to embrace a program of expansion to the Adriatic, the Serbian minister, Ilija Garašanin, took heed. In the following year, he prepared a secret project *(Načertanije)*, whose main goal was to make the Serbian economy independent of Austria. Other goals, and the means to the realization of the previous one, were the acquisition of an Adriatic port, the construction of a good road linking Belgrade to this port, the procurement of international guarantees of freedom of trade along the designated road, and, as soon as feasible, the direct annexation to Serbia both of this road and of adjacent territories. Beyond these aims lay the vision of a South Slavic state stretching from the Adriatic to the Black Sea.[128]

But Serbia was weak. Garašanin's project had to be postponed. At the turn of the century, however, following the redoubling of Austrian efforts to thwart Serbian economic independence by frustrating a Serbo-Bulgarian customs union, imposing a virtual embargo on Serbian pigs, and annexing Bosnia-Hercegovina, the Serbian bourgeoisie and intelligentsia openly espoused a policy of expansion to the sea.[129] On the eve of World War I, the British minister to Belgrade complained to his government that the Serbians were "quite off their heads" in their "visions of blue seas and Servian ships in the offing bringing home the wealth of the Indies."[130]

Frustrating Serbian navigation on the Danube, Austrian steam removed the possibility of any other strong Balkan merchant marine on the river. By 1854, the DSNC was operating 7 steamboats and 29 tugs on the lower Danube (between the Iron Gate and Sulina); by 1864 this number grew to 29 steamboats and 102 tugs. At the close of 1863, the company owned a total of 130 steamboats, with a displacement of 12,268 tons, and 492 barges, with a displacement of 98,176 tons.[131]

Simultaneously, Austrian shipping penetrated the Black Sea from Trieste by means of the Austrian Lloyd Lines, which inaugurated regular service in 1839 between the mouth of the Danube and the Black Sea ports of Odessa and Trebizond. In 1846, 6 Austrian ships visited the Bulgarian port of Varna, as against 79 Turkish, 70 Greek, and 28 Russian ships. In 1849, it was 81 Austrian as against 76 Turkish, 49 Greek, 52 Russian, and 8 British ships. In 1851, 116 Austrian ships arrived at Varna. French and Russian companies failed to establish regular service on the lower Danube until the 1880s.[132]

Far freer in the commercial sphere because of its situation amid a relatively open sea was Greece. Between the mid-eighteenth century and 1855, the Greek merchant marine grew dramatically. In 1763, with a primary basis in the cereal and timber trade, the Muslim-Albanian merchant marine (principally the ships of

Table 3.1

Greco-Albanian Merchant Marine, 1750–1806

Year	Number of Ships	Average Metric Tonnage Capacity	Total Metric Tonnage Capacity
1750	150	60	9,000
1780	300	60	18,000
1787	400	100	40,000
1806	500	150	75,000
1813	615	150–200	92,250–123,000

Dulcigno and Durazzo) numbered 200–250 ships, with a possible capacity of 50,000 tons. But between 1750 and 1806 a Greco-Albanian merchant marine (a merchant marine of Greeks and Albanians of the Greek Orthodox faith) first equaled and then surpassed it.

Around 1750, no more than 150 Greek sailing boats with a home port in the Aegean (thus without the merchant marines of the Greeks of the Ionian Islands, the Bosporus, and the Black Sea) may have been available for interregional trade. Several factors operated to promote the growth of this merchant marine, including the disinclination of the French government to protect the coastal trade of its own small Mediterranean ports. Another element was Balkan poverty and internecine war, as a result of which Muslim Albanians forced Greeks and Orthodox Albanians to move southward to Attica, the Peloponnesus, and some of the small Greek islands. The soil resources of the small islands could not meet the needs of an even slightly growing population. To survive, many islanders had to seek part-time employment elsewhere—in Istanbul or Izmir (Smyrna), for example. Piracy and the carrying trade were alternative occupations, which became lucrative when one European warring state drove off the maritime craft of a fellow warring state, as during the Seven Years' War (1756–63). By the time peace came, the carriers had an established clientele, which they were able to augment by their readiness to accept a small profit margin.

Reinterpreting the available documentary evidence, I offer in Table 3.1 above, a "guesstimate" of the growth of the Greco-Albanian merchant marine. The islands that made the greatest contribution to this growth were Hydra, Spetsai, and Psara, which in the early part of the century had been sparsely populated and possessed few ships until the middle of the eighteenth century. Hydra's share then rose to a hundred ships or more in 1780, with a possible total tonnage capacity of 6,000. It stood, in 1787, at 83 large and 50 small ships, with a total capacity of 15,000 tons. In 1796, Hydra had 84 large and 41 small ships. In 1806, the figure stood at 73 large ships and 30 small craft, with a tonnage capacity for the large ships alone of 15,000. In 1813, it equipped 120 ships, while Spetsai and Psara each equipped 60, with a possible tonnage capacity for

Hydra of more than 24,000 tons and somewhat under 24,000 for the other two islands.

F.C.H.L. Pouqueville's estimate of a Greco-Albanian merchant marine of 615 ships in 1813 probably is correct, but his estimate of a tonnage capacity of 153,580 tons is almost certainly too high.[133] One may surmise a Greco-Albanian merchant marine equal in strength to the Muslim-Albanian merchant marine before 1806 (if, as we suppose, the strength of that marine did not vary much from the level attained in 1763). Yet another reason may thus be added to the long list of reasons for the Greek revolution of 1821: a struggle for power between two groups of port towns—the Muslim-Albanian ports, with Durazzo and Dulcigno at the head of the list, and the Orthodox-Greco-Albanian ports, with Hydra, Spetsai, and Psara as sources of inspiration. As of 1813, both groups of port towns were confronted by an economic crisis that had both a political foundation (the end of the Napoleonic wars and the revival of the shipping activity of the former warring states, with a consequent reduction in their own carrying activity) and a cosmic foundation in the short-term climatic disorders of 1813–18.

The shipping capacity of the merchant marine of the new Greek state rose from 75,000 metric tons in 1834 (five years after the conclusion of the war of Greek independence)—the level it had attained in 1806—to 111,000 tons in 1840, 147,000 tons in 1844 (probably greater than but certainly equal to the 1813 level), and 297,000 tons in 1855.

Between 1855 and the early 1890s, on the other hand, the Greeks were slow to adopt the steamship, partly because of the unavailability of diaspora capital to the Greek state merchant marine until the 1880s. At the same time, the stiff competition of British, French, Italian, and Austrian steamships impeded an increase in the number and tonnage of Greek sailing ships. Greece's tonnage in sailing ships and motor boats was only 260,000 in 1856 and 254,000 in 1875. After rising to 263,000 in 1860, 324,000 in 1866, and a high of 399,000 in 1870, it fell to 254,000 in 1875, rose to 259,000 in 1885, and then fell to 246,000 in 1895, 145,000 in 1901, and 107,000 in 1915. Greece's steamship tonnage was only 150 in 1860, 5,360 in 1870, and 8,241 in 1875. Similarly, the building of sailing ships on the Croatian Littoral reached a peak in 1855—41 ships with a total capacity of 17,472 tons.[134]

The shift from a merchant marine in which the sailing ship prevailed to one in which the steamship won favor occurred in Greece only after 1895. The investment of diaspora capital by Greeks in London and Istanbul and at the lower Danube allowed an increase in the number of steamships from 107 in 1895 to 343 in 1911 and 475 in 1915. The steamship carrying capacity grew during the same years from 145,000 to 388,000 and 894,000 tons. War losses brought down the total steamship tonnage capacity to 291,000 at the end of World War I. By 1927, however, Greece had 504 steamships with a total capacity of 1,111,050 tons, compared to Yugoslavia's share of 144 steamships with a total capacity of

245,698 tons, Romania's share of 39 steamships with a carrying capacity of 71,185 tons, and Bulgaria's share of 5 steamships with a carrying capacity of 6,300 tons.[135]

The diffusion of steam as a source of energy hurt small commodity production. Detrimental to local shipbuilding and craft production, steam's advent was not always welcome. The building of railroads met with opposition partly because of peasant fears that, indirectly if not directly, it would be chiefly financed by the peasantry. Many persons in Serbia and Bulgaria believed that a preferable approach would have been to enable peasants to acquire yet better carts and wagons and to build the vicinal roads that would have allowed them to take their goods to market during all seasons of the year. Another common view was that industrially backward states should concentrate on the improvement of industrial production for domestic consumption, not on international transportation, which was of chief advantage to the economically most highly developed European states.

Balkan railroads remained financially passive for the first two decades of their existence. The principal articles transported thereby—agricultural goods destined for foreign markets—were available only during three months of the year. During the remainder of the year, railroad traffic was confined largely to passengers and mail. Moreover, the new Balkan states were not free to determine the direction of the railways but had to agree to compromise solutions amenable to the political or industrial Great Powers. Austria-Hungary thus thwarted Serbian preferences for a railway from Belgrade to an Adriatic port not under Austro-Hungarian rule, notably, Bar (Antivari), Ulcinj (Dulcigno), Durrës (Durazzo), or Shën Gjin (St. John of Medua). Even the Ottoman Empire was reduced to a position of humiliating inferiority vis-à-vis the steam-power states. Henry Noel Brailsford vividly describes the kind of railroads the Great Powers and European financial interests imposed upon the Balkans:

It seemed as though the line had laid itself across the countryside in the track of some writhing serpent. It curled in sinuous folds, it described enormous arcs, it bent and doubled so that a passing train resembled nothing so much as a kitten in pursuit of its own tail. Yet the country was a vast level plain. . . . And oddly enough this railway did not seem to serve any visible town. Indeed, a plausible theory of its gyrations and its undulations might have been that it was desperately trying to dodge the towns. Stations, indeed, there were, but they were at every conceivable distance from the centres of population—one, two, or even five miles away. The explanation was [that the private company which had built and owned the line had insisted upon and obtained] a kilometric guarantee. In order to induce the European financiers—who all the while were bribing and competing to obtain the favour—to perform the onerous work of "opening up Turkey," the Government agreed to guarantee the fortunate company an assured profit, reckoned at so much on every mile or kilometre of rails. . . . In order to make certain that the Turkish Government will pay this annual tribute, the tithes of the luckless provinces through which it passes are mortgaged. Be the season good or bad, whether famine rages or massacre decimates, and whatever the deficit in Constantinople itself may be, so much of the tithes of grain are annually set aside, a first charge on the whole amount, to assure the punctual payment of this debt. And, further, since the financiers know only too well how corrupt Turkish officials are, the collection of this mortgaged revenue is placed in the hands of some European official responsible ultimately to the great Powers.[136]

Railway building began in Slovenia between 1846 and 1857. In the Balkans proper, the first railroad was the Cernavodă-Constanţa line in the Ottoman (now partly Romanian) province of Dobrudja (Dobrogea), built by an English company shortly after the Crimean War. In Croatia, the first railways date back to the early 1860s; in the major European provinces of the Ottoman Empire and in Greece and Romania, to the late 1860s; in Serbia, to the 1880s; in Albania proper, there was no railroad until 1947.

Railroad building was accompanied by numerous financial irregularities, the most notorious of which may have been the bribery of high personages in the Serbian government and members of the Serbian National Assembly by various financial groups desirous of winning the contract for the construction of the Belgrade-to-Niš railway, which was initially given to the publicly French but covertly Austrian Union Générale, the bankruptcy of which was announced in February 1882. The irregularities, however, were essentially a characteristic of European rather than specifically Balkan society. They should be set in the framework of the Panama and other scandals characterizing the 1880s and 1890s as an era of *trasformismo*, attuned to political expediency and commercial and financial opportunism.

By 1913, at great cost to the Balkan peoples, there were in the peninsula over 8,200 kilometers of rail. In the early 1920s, the railway density per 1,000 square kilometers of territory varied regionally as follows: Albania, 0; Greece, 21.9 kilometers; Bosnia-Hercegovina, 24.5; Bulgaria, 27.7; Serbia and Serbian Macedonia, 28.5; Wallachia and Moldavia, 31.5; Croatia, 52.8; Transylvania, 54.8; Slovenia, 69; Bukovina, 70.5; Bačka, 101.8. By comparison, there was a density of 13 kilometers of rail in the Russian Empire, 67 in Italy, 97 in France and the Netherlands, 123 in Germany, and 370 in Belgium. In Greece and Bosnia-Hercegovina, the density should be reduced considerably since much of the track was narrow gauge. Moreover, the rolling stock available to the Balkan countries was quantitatively and qualitatively inferior to the stock of the countries of western and central Europe.[137]

Capitalism and Communism: Six Industrializing Experiments

After 1880, the governments of Romania, Serbia, Bulgaria, and Greece, and the Austro-Hungarian administration of Bosnia-Hercegovina all pursued policies of industrialization that were closely linked to but inadequately coordinated with the program of railway construction. All efforts at industrialization met with some success, but in no case was there an industrial takeoff—or establishment of a self-sustaining industrial economy.

When the Balkan states tried to imitate the post-1880 European pattern of industrialization by setting up protective tariffs, the highly industrialized countries set impediments in their way by trying to preserve intact the provisions of the Congress of Berlin (1878), which denied Serbia, Bulgaria, and Romania the right to establish protective tariffs. The aim of the Great Powers was to retain their extraterritorial rights. In the centuries of its greatness, the Ottoman Empire had freely extended such rights, known as capitulations, to one European country after another. In the eighteenth century, the Great Powers took advantage of these rights to prevent the improvement of Ottoman manufactures. In the nineteenth, they obliged the new Balkan states to submit to similar terms. The economic provisions of the Congress of Berlin represented a continuation of a policy designed to maintain the Balkans as a reservoir of raw materials for the European industrial states.

By capturing the world market for industrial goods, especially cotton textiles, Britain became the primary industrial state in the world. In 1814, British manufacturers exported 32 yards of cotton cloth for every 24 consumed at home; by 1850, the ratio was 39 to 24.[138] The countries of western and central Europe duplicated the British example.

The last in Europe to industrialize or institute a modern technology, the Balkan states could not compete in the world market with the steam-power and multipower states. At the same time, thwarted until the very last years of the century—and in the case of Greece as late as 1910—in their aspirations to protect domestic industry, they could not rapidly create a home market for their new industrial products.

In Romania, industrialization was somewhat easier than in the other Balkan countries, partly because, as the chief exporters of Balkan grains, Romanian landowners accumulated greater amounts of capital than their counterparts in the other Balkan states. Second, Romanian petroleum production, rising from 1,118 tons in 1860 to 15,000 tons in 1880, 53,000–54,000 tons in 1890, 250,000 tons in 1900, 1,352,000 tons in 1910, 1.8 million tons in 1913, and, after the disturbances of war, to 1.5 million tons in 1923, 4.3 million tons in 1928, 7.4 million tons in 1933, and 8.4 million tons in 1935, drew foreign capital into the country. In 1928, Romania held sixth place—after the United States, Russia, Venezuela, Mexico, and Persia (Iran)—among the world's petroleum producers.[139] Despite its greater attractiveness to foreign investors, however, Romania similarly failed to achieve an industrial takeoff.

Prerequisite to an industrial takeoff is economic growth, which one may define as an increase in the real per capita labor product. Such growth can be achieved by improving the average quality of labor, by using labor resources more efficiently, and by investing in machinery and other capital goods. In the pursuit of that goal, government as promoter and businessmen as entrepreneurs should be free from outside coercion.

Aware of the diverse ways in which they and their governments were dominated from outside, the most intelligent and sensitive members of the middle elements of Balkan society systematically denounced their condition of inferiority. In Romania, the unsatisfactory relationship between the technologically, politically, and economically dominating European powers and the dominated Balkan states was defined with particular cogency by the Romanian historian Alexander D. Xenopol, who, a year after the Congress of Berlin, bitterly censured western Europe for monopolizing the work of industry, which he described as ennobling, better recompensed, and (so he believed) energy saving, and for relegating the rude, heavy, fatiguing, demeaning, even feral work of unmechanized agriculture —not unlike that of beasts of burden—to the peoples of the rest of the world, among them the Romanians and other peoples of eastern Europe.[140]

While some Balkan merchants such as those of Varna were hostile to industrialization, a large segment of the Romanian, Greek, Serbian, and Bulgarian bourgeoisies welcomed it. Following early attempts to promote putting-out and/or to revive or institute craft production, industrialization based upon steam power was undertaken during the last three decades preceding World War I. That effort was resumed during the 1920s and again after the deep economic crisis of the early 1930s. In the interwar era, however, and especially during the 1930s, the Balkan bourgeoisies were less confident, less exuberant, less self-reliant than on the eve of World War I. One reason for the change in mentality may have been the great loss of manpower during the war, especially by Serbia, of persons in the prime of life, whose talents were never discovered. Many survivors, on the other hand, were fearful of the consequences of rapid industrialization, notably, proletarian revolution.

An idea therefore advanced by some bourgeois leaders, especially in Yugoslavia, successor state to the former Serbia, was that, before a large industrial proletariat developed, a powerful homogeneous bourgeoisie should be created, one untroubled by differences of religion, dialect, or provincial origin.[141]

A second bourgeois group, most vociferous in the territories of former Austria-Hungary, regretted the breakup of the Dual Monarchy and the subdivision of large estates. Following the example of the Croatian economist Otto Frangeš, they yearned to reintegrate southeastern Europe into a Middle European "great-space" economy *(Grossraumwirtschaft)*.[142] But this yearning may have been tantamount to a social and cultural death wish, for the only Middle European great-space economy then in the offing was the "co-prosperity sphere" of expanding Nazi Germany, in which the Balkan states were welcome only as subservient satellites.

Under the intellectual leadership of the Romanian economist Mihail Manoilescu, a third bourgeois group developed an anti-Ricardian theory dividing the world into economically advanced and economically retarded countries.

Manoilescu contended, in effect, that, technologically backward countries could raise their low labor productivity only if they embraced protectionism. Manifesting another aspect of the fear and despondency of the Balkan bourgeoisies, however, Manoilescu also maintained that protectionism would allow a technologically backward state to industrialize effectively only if it eliminated the threats of class struggle and proletarian revolution. The only way to do this would be to organize society on a vertical basis into corporate status groups, with conflicts between vertical units to be held in check by an authoritarian state.[143]

The alternating bourgeois sentiments of overconfidence, or indifference to public opinion, and of deep anxiety, culminating in bourgeois subservience to the most technologically advanced and most neurotic state in Europe, Nazi Germany, or in flight to western Europe, North Africa, and the Americas, alienated many people from the bourgeois leadership. Left leaderless or with leaders they did not trust, a significant minority in Yugoslavia and Greece transferred its allegiance during World War II to a set of leaders who espoused a communist ideology and directed movements of national liberation. In Greece and the Serb-inhabited parts of Yugoslavia, anticommunist movements of national liberation were also formed. In the Balkan provinces in which the bourgeoisies and official and landowning elements identified their interests with German, Italian, or native fascism, or with the principle of a German or Italian great-space economy, a new communist leadership came to power partly as the result of a Churchill-Stalin "percentage agreement" that provided for the establishment—at the close of the war against Nazi Germany—of a preponderance of Soviet influence in Romania (90 percent Soviet influence, 10 percent western influence) and Bulgaria (75 percent Soviet, 25 percent western), of a balance between Soviet and western influence in Hungary and Yugoslavia (50–50), and of a preponderance of western influence in Greece (10 percent Soviet, 90 percent western).[144]

The terms of the Churchill-Stalin agreement were in keeping with traditional Russian policies. Ever since the reign of Catherine II, Russian governments had thought primarily in terms of the division of the Balkans into three spheres of influence—a zone of Russian influence in the east, a zone of the maritime powers in the south and extreme west, and a central European or joint sphere of influence in the central and nonmaritime western portions.[145] Since at the time of the Churchill-Stalin agreement, Britain and the Soviet Union were jointly engaged in a life-and-death struggle against Germany, the customary provisions for a zone of central European (Austrian, German) influence had to yield to the equally old idea of a joint sphere of influence.

As a consequence of the Soviet-British agreement, Britain and the United States were able to pursue in Greece, where a substantial segment of the population then sympathized with communism, policies that would lead to the defeat of the communists in the Greek civil war of 1946–48. In Romania and Bulgaria, on the other hand, native communists dependent on the USSR succeeded in extending their authority. In Yugoslavia, after the anticommunist guerrilla leader Draža

Mihailović was hunted down, tried, and executed, victory went to the native communism of the war leader Josip Broz Tito and, after the split between Tito and the Kominform and the Soviet Union in 1948, to the ideology of "different roads to socialism."

Albania presents a special problem. There, communist leaders rose to ascendancy with the aid of Yugoslav communism, but after the open ideological and political break between Yugoslav and Soviet communism, they oriented their domestic and foreign policies around the Soviet example. In the later ideological and political dispute between Soviet and Chinese communism, Albania was in the Chinese camp, which at some levels was also joined by Romania.

By 1960, after pursuing industrial policies with different psychological foundations and economic principles but purportedly with common social goals, Romania and Yugoslavia seemed to be at the point of an industrial takeoff. Bulgaria was in close pursuit, while backward Albania also was making progress. Greece made great forward strides under bourgeois leadership.

From a level of less than 2 million tons just before World War II, Bulgaria increased its production of lignite by the early 1960s to 20 million tons. It also brought under irrigation a sixth of its cultivated surface, an important achievement from the perspective of laying a solid agricultural foundation for further industrial development. It greatly expanded its hydroelectric production. In 1958, its steel production stood at 211,000 tons, compared to 6,000 in 1938.

During the same period, Romania increased its steel production from 284,000 to 934,000 tons. Between 1938 and 1962, it doubled its petroleum and lignite production, increased its production of natural gas tenfold, and raised its production of coal to 5 million tons, twelve times the prewar figure.

In Yugoslavia, steel production rose from 230,000 tons in 1938 to 1.1 million tons in 1958 and 1.5 million tons in the mid-1960s. By that time, it was also extracting 25 million tons of lignite (as against an average 4.7 million tons between 1926 and 1931), 1.5 million tons of petroleum, and 1.2 million tons of bauxite. From 460 million kilowatt hours in 1929 and 503 million in 1935, it raised its hydroelectric production to 10 billion kilowatt hours.[146] Yet more to the point, the average yearly increase in national product between 1950 and 1965 was about 13 percent, compared to an annual demographic growth of 1.3 percent. The average annual increase in per capita national product was thus about 10 percent. Similar growth rates were attained in Romania and Bulgaria. Figure 3.3 illustrates Balkan industry and industrial resource foundations around 1990.

Between 1830 and 1990, the major Balkan states—Bulgaria/Turkey, Greece, Romania, and Serbia/Yugoslavia—made six attempts at industrialization under different psychological and sociopolitical conditions. The role of government grew successively more important during the first five attempts. The first four attempts were made under bourgeois leadership. The fifth attempt was made in all the Balkan states except Greece (and Turkey, essentially an Asian state) under state direction.

Figure 3.3. **Industry and Natural Resource Foundations of Balkan Industry, 1990**

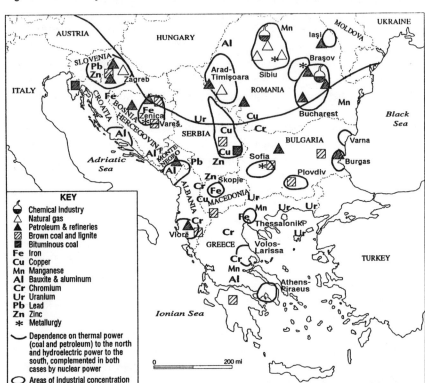

The first attempt was basically designed to revive or develop craft production. The psychology of the bourgeois leadership of the second attempt, between the 1880s and 1914, was steeped in optimism and positivism. That of the third attempt, following World War I, and of the fourth, between 1935 and 1941, following the world economic crisis of 1929, was one of uncertainty, mixed feelings, dependence, pessimism. Then came the second great war of the century, out of whose embers and chaos emerged a new communist leadership with faith in communism and in their own abilities at social engineering, almost an act of hubris.

The pursuit in the communist states after 1950, if not already in 1948, of "different roads to socialism" (the fifth attempt at industrialization) presaged difficulties to come. But not until the mid-1960s, probably in response to objective world conditions, namely, the economic successes of capitalism, did idealism mixed in Romania with an obdurate nonchalance toward human suffering yield to uncertainty, pessimism, and empiricism. Such would be the psychological conditions under which would be pursued the sixth attempt at industrialization.

The sixth experience occasionally offered the prospect of a possible convergence between capitalism and communism. The obverse of the dialectic, however, was the gathering in the West of a strong current of antagonism against the egalitarian ideas of the French and communist revolutions alike, often motivated by the consumerist expectations of a culture of desire.[147]

From the close of World War II to the end of 1963, the United States poured into Greece more than $3 billion in aid, more aid per capita during that period than to any other country in the world. Despite this assistance, the annual growth rate in Greece was only 6.5 percent between 1950 and 1956 and 5.5 percent between 1956 and 1962, or about half the growth rate in the communist states. The chief reason for this difference may be that, during its own fifth attempt at industrialization, Greece concentrated upon improving consumption—satisfying desires. Funds for investment in capital goods were thus limited.

Partly to drive it closer to an industrial takeoff, the countries of western Europe admitted Greece to associate membership in the customs union of the Common Market in November 1962, allowing it to dismantle its protective tariffs slowly while pursuing—in its sixth phase of industrial development—a policy of encouraging business consolidations, welcoming foreign capital, and eliminating marginal enterprise.

United States and western European aid in money, raw materials, food, arms, and credits to Yugoslavia in the decade after that country's break with Joseph Stalin enabled the Yugoslavs to preserve their political independence of the Soviet Union and to pursue the fifth effort at industrialization—only to be subverted, between 1989 and 1993, at the close of its sixth unsuccessful industrializing attempt, as much by outside intervention as by internal dissension and by the vaunted triumph of world capitalism.

That triumph may be of short duration. Convinced in 1830, for example, that the French Revolution or struggle between groups with the traditions and remembrances and hopes of the *ancien régime* and the *classe moyenne* had come to an end, Alexis de Tocqueville reversed himself in 1848, contending that the revolution could not end in the foreseeable future. It had a basis in a European cultural proclivity of long date for mobility *(mobilité)*. Without observing that Europe ran on wheels, Tocqueville stressed the mobility of its institutions and ideas, its constitution as a mobile *(mouvante)* society, "stirred up *[remuée]* by seven great revolutions in less than sixty years [1789–1848], not to mention a multitude of commotions *[ébranlements]* of secondary importance," all of which together were one revolution of long duration (a permanent revolution?).[148] Is it not possible that the communist revolutions may be similarly tenacious?

A second point to bear in mind as a new millennium looms before us is that many of the events of today are mere noise. In the long term, they may affect the future much less than some quieter continuities and changes. If collapse is the destiny of communism, that may also be the destiny of capitalism. For communism (or Marxism) and capitalism alike aspire to economic growth without end. Given this predilection, capitalism combats nature, refusing to make allowances for regional and social inequalities. Despite a similar promethean predilection, communism, on the contrary, desires to make such corrections. It cannot do so, however, because of its continuing bias against land and its undervaluation of nature—of nature as it has been, is, and is constantly worked over or remade.

Notes

1. Mauss, *Oeuvres*, III, 252; Cazeneuve, "Technical Methods in the Prehistoric Age," pp. 104–9, 119–20; Cazeneuve, *Sociologie de Marcel Mauss*, pp. 25–27.

2. Papaioannou, "Nature and History in the Greek Conception of the Cosmos," pp. 1–27; Agard, *The Greek Mind*, pp. 64–65.

3. Jardé *Les Céréales dans l'Antiquité grecque*, pp. 20–21.

4. On the early history of the ard and plow in the Balkans and rest of the world, see Haudricourt and Jean-Brunhes Delamarre, *L'Homme et la charrue à travers le monde;* Curwen and Hatt, *Plough and Pasture;* Branimir Bratanič, "Some Similarities between Ards," pp. 221–28; Haberlandt, "Zur Systematik der Pflugforschung und Entwicklungs-geschichte des Pfluges," pp. 28–34, 76–79; Nopcsa, "Zur Genese der primitiven Pflug-typen," pp. 234–42; Vakarelski, "Iz veshtestvenata kultura na Bŭlgarite," pp. 55–109, 130–65; Hobhouse, *A Journey through Albania,* p. 140; Niederle, *Manuel de l'Antiquité slave,* II, 188, 190, 194.

5. Great Britain, Parliament, *Sessional Papers*, LXXXII (1883), Sidney Lockock's Report.

6. See chapter 8.

7. Vučo, *Privredna istorija Srbije*, p. 182.

8. Deffontaines, "Notes sur la répartition des types de voiture," pp. 169–85; Piggott, *The Earliest Wheeled Transport*, pp. 14–15, 32; Cazeneuve, "Technical Methods in the Prehistoric Age," pp. 116–17.

9. Anati, *Camonica Valley*, pp. 146–47.

10. Lorimer, "The Country Cart of Ancient Greece," pp. 132–51.

11. Bernardo, *Viaggio a Costantinopoli*, p. 32.

12. Beckmann, *A History of Inventions, Discoveries, and Origins*, pp. 68–82, esp. pp. 77–78.

13. Kostić, "Domaće životinje kao transportna sredstva u srpskim zemljama za turskog vremena," pp. 79–80; Trojanović, "Naše kiridžije," pp. 63–65; Popović, *Srbija i Beograd od Požarevačkog do Beogradskog mira,* pp. 94–95.

14. Braudel, *La Méditerranée*, I, 260.

15. Grégoire, "Deux étymologies," pp. 268–69; Renouard, "Information et transmission des nouvelles," p. 104; Kostić, "Domaće životinje kao transportna sredstva u srpskim zemljama za turskog vremena," p. 81; Karadžić, *Danica;* pp. 52–53; Bergier, *Histoire des grands chemins de l'Empire romain*, pp. 600–604.

16. Braudel, *La Méditerranée*, I, 260.

17. McNeill, "The Eccentricity of Wheels," pp. 1111–26; Bulliet, *The Camel and the Wheel*, pp. 16–27, 217, 226–28.

18. On roads and road management in the Middle Ages, see Jireček, *Die Hand-elsstrassen und Bergwerke von Serbien und Bosnien;* Škrivanić, "Mreža puteva prema Svetostefanskoj . . . povelji," pp. 387–97.

19. Trojanović, "Naše kiridžije," pp. 1–154.

20. Braudel, *La Méditerranée*, I, 259–61, 367–68.

21. Lefebvre des Noëttes, *L'Attelage*.

22. Chateaubriand, *Itinéraire de Paris à Jérusalem*, I, 186–87.

23. Braudel, *Civilisation matérielle et capitalisme*, I, 270.

24. Turner, *Journal of a Tour in the Levant*, I, 82.

25. Mikhov, *Contribution à l'histoire du commerce bulgare*, I, 123–24.

26. Planhol, *The World of Islam*, pp. 1–2.

27. Bérard, *La Turquie et l'hellénisme contemporain*, pp. 53–54.

28. For the concept of "material density," see Durkheim, *Les Règles de la méthode sociologique*, pp. 112–14.

29. Cited in Nef, *Western Civilization since the Renaissance*, p. 82.

30. Chateaubriand, *Itinéraire de Paris à Jérusalem*, p. 187; Boué, *La Turquie d'Europe*, III, 86–87.

31. Cerfberr de Medelsheim, *Mémoires sur la Grèce et l'Albanie*, pp. 184, 352.

32. Hommaire de Hell, *Voyage en Turquie et en Perse*, Vol. I, pt. 1, p. 116.

33. For a general treatment of the subject of tastes, see Bourdieu, *La Distinction*.

34. Hommaire de Hell, *Voyage en Turquie et en Perse*, Vol. I, pt. 1, pp. 110–15.

35. Boué, *La Turquie d'Europe*, III, 87; Schmidt, "Napoléon et les routes balkaniques," p. 340.

36. Constantine Porphyrogenitus, *De Administrando Imperio*, pp. 144–45, 162–63.

37. Niederle, *Manuel de l'Antiquité slave*, II, 49–51, 253–54.

38. Boué, *La Turquie d'Europe*, III, 87; Karadžić, *Danica*, pp. 52–53; Evelpidi, *Les États balkaniques*, pp. 156–57.

39. Lowie, *An Introduction to Cultural Anthropology*, p. 516.

40. AN, MAR, D^3 9, document No. 4, memoir by the carpenter Lartier, December 23, 1731.

41. Eton, *A Survey of the Turkish Empire*, p. 214.

42. Walsh, *Narrative of a Journey from Constantinople to England*, pp. 132–33, 250–51.

43. Sion, "Quelques Problèmes de transports dans l'Antiquité," p. 630.

44. Djordjević, *Srbija pre sto godina*, pp. 8–10.

45. Kinglake, *Kinglake's Eothen*, p. 7. In Greek, *eothen* means "from the early dawn" or "from the east."

46. Hogarth, "Introduction," ibid., p. xii.

47. Vlajinac, *Rečnik naših starih mera u toku vekova*, III, 431–43 *(Kola)*, 456–58 *(Konj)*, IV, 904 *(Taljige);* Trojanović, "Naše kiridžije," pp. 63–65; Af. Étr., CC, Belgrade, IV, letter from Botmiliau, Belgrade, January 17, 1865; Kuželj, *Zur Entwicklung der Handwerkerfrage im gegenwärtigen Serbien*, pp. 38–41.

48. Hendy, *Studies in the Byzantine Monetary Economy*, pp. 602–5.

49. Vučo, *Privredna istorija Srbije*, p. 182, for 1866.

50. Babudieri, "Maritime Commerce of the Habsburg Empire," p. 225.

51. For the estimates of the number of carts in the pashalik of Belgrade and in the neighboring Vidin and Niš districts, see Pantelić, "Vojno-geografski opisi Srbije pred Kočinu Krajinu," pp. 1–144.

52. Walters, *Ecology, Food and Civilisation*, p. 184.

53. Boué, *La Turquie d'Europe*, III, 47–48; Af. Étr., CC, Belgrade, II, fol. 372, Dozon, Belgrade, August 20, 1858; ibid., III, fol. 316, Botmiliau, Belgrade, December 22, 1864; ibid., VI, fols. 379–82, Richemont, Belgrade, December 20, 1884.

54. Weber, *Peasants into Frenchmen*, p. 203.

55. Af. Étr., CPC, Sérajevo, X, fol. 19, Statistique de la province Bosnie-Herzégovine, travail dressé par l'autorité locale en 1286 (1870), annexed to the letter of Charles de Vienne, February 3, 1875.

56. Sugar, *Industrialization of Bosnia-Hercegovina*, pp. 71–73, 86.

57. Vlajinac, *Rečnik naših starih mera u toku vekova*, III, 440–41 *(Kola)*.

58. Af. Étr., CC, Turquie, Mostar, I, fols. 31–37, Vice-Consul Louis Moreau, mémoire commercial annuel pour 1866; ibid., fols. 103–4, L. Moreau, mémoire commercial pour l'année 1867.

59. Trojanović, "Naše kiridžije," p. 64.

60. Ebinger, *Studien über Bosnien und die Herzegovina*, p. 25.

61. Sugar, *Industrialization of Bosnia-Hercegovina*, pp. 71–73, 86.

62. Asbóth, *An Official Tour through Bosnia and Herzegovina*, pp. 352–53, 392–93.

63. Holbach, *Bosnia and Herzegovina*, pp. 224–26.

64. Boué, *La Turquie d'Europe*, III, 51–52.

65. Paton, *Servia*, pp. 56–58.

66. Hommaire de Hell, *Voyage en Turquie*, I, 157, 165–66, 182, 184–85, 216–19.

67. Jensen and Rosegger, "British Railway Building along the Lower Danube," pp. 105–28; Jensen and Rosegger, "Transferring Technology to a Peripheral Economy"; Sugar, *Industrialization of Bosnia-Hercegovina*, pp. 71, 75.

68. Af. Étr., CC, Belgrade, III, Botmiliau, February 6, 1864.

69. Pinto, "Bulgaria," pp. 231–32.

70. Af. Étr., CC, Belgrade, IV, fol. 194, Botmiliau, March 26, 1866. On the desolation of the routes between Istanbul and Adrianople (Edirne) and between Gallipoli and Adrianople, see ibid., CPC, Turquie: Andrinople, Sérajevo, Janina, Philippopolis, Vol. I, fols. 133–35, Tissot, October 8, 1860.

71. Mouzelis, *Modern Greece*, p. 15; Evelpidi, *Les États balkaniques*, p. 154 n.

72. Finlay, "The Euthanasia of the Ottoman Empire," pp. 577, 588.

73. Lombard, *Les Métaux dans l'ancien monde*, pp. 9–44, and the maps "Les Empires entre la steppe et la mer" (p. 57) and "Le Monde musulman et le problème de l'or" (end map).

74. Carcopino, "Un Retour à l'impérialisme," pp. 73–86; Tenney et al., eds., *An Economic Survey of Ancient Rome*, V, 65 n. 13.

75. Lombard, "Les Bases monétaires d'une suprématie économique," pp. 146–60.

76. Davies, *Roman Mines in Europe*, on mines in Illyria (pp. 182–97), in Dacia (pp. 198–208), in Moesia (pp. 209–25), in Macedonia and Thrace (pp. 226–38), and in Greece (pp. 239–68).

77. Vryonis, Jr., "The Question of the Byzantine Mines," pp. 1–17.

78. Schneider et al., eds., *Wirtschaftskräfte und Wirtschaftswege*, Vol. I, articles by Małowist, pp. 15–29; Krekić, pp. 413–29; Lane, pp. 431–40; Pach, pp. 522–29; Goldenberg, pp. 549–56; Hirschmann, pp. 557–80; and Bergier, pp. 581–602. See also the review by Stoianovich in *Journal of Economic History*.

79. Kovačević, "Dans la Serbie et la Bosnie médiévales," pp. 248–58; Kovačević, "O Janjevu u doba srednjovekovne srpske države," pp. 121–26.

80. Mehlan, "Über die Bedeutung der mittelalterlichen Bergbaukolonien," pp. 400–401.

81. Radovanović, "Novo Brdo," pp. 170–173; Jireček, *Istorija Srba*, I, 431–32; Mehlan, "Über die Bedeutung der mittelalterlichen Bergbaukolonien," pp. 383–404.

82. Delaunay, *L'Aventureuse existence de Pierre Belon du Mans*, pp. 32–33.

83. Belon du Mans, *Les Observations de plvsievrs singvlarritez et choses memorables*, pp. 45–46; Jacob, *An Historical Inquiry into the Production and Consumption of the Precious Metals*, I, 239.

84. Keller, "A Byzantine Admirer of 'Western' Progress," p. 346.

85. See Beckmann, *A History of Inventions, Discoveries, and Origins*, I, 63–68, on leather bellows and the improved wooden bellows.

86. Haudricourt, "Ce que peuvent nous apprendre les mots voyageurs," pp. 26–27.

87. Eton, *A Survey of the Turkish Empire*, pp. 216, 227–28.

88. Mehlan, "Über die Bedeutung der mittelalterlichen Bergbaukolonien," pp. 383–404; Elezović, "Tarapana (Darb-Hane) u Novom Brdu," pp. 115–26; "Soetbeer, Edelmetall-Produktion," p. 37. For a comparison of Ottoman, Spanish, Venetian, and French state revenues, see Stoianovich, *Between East and West*, I, 19–21.

89. Cerfberr de Medelsheim, *Mémoires sur la Grèce et l'Albanie*, pp. 237–38.

90. Mijatovich, *The Memoirs of a Balkan Diplomatist*, pp. 182–88.

91. Sreten L. Popović, *Putovanje po novoj Srbiji*, p. 26, my translation.

92. Tomasic, *Personality and Culture in Eastern European Politics*, pp. 87–88.

93. Stanojević, "Iz narodnog života na Timoku," p. 67.

94. Petrović, *Život i običaji narodni u Gruži*, p. 349.

95. Frazer, *The Golden Bough*, pp. 816–18; Krappe, *The Science of Folk-Lore*, p. 83.

96. Sombart, *Le Bourgeois*, pp. 34, 51.

97. White, Jr., *Medieval Technology and Social Change*, pp. 28–29.

98. For the suggestion, see Fox, *History in Geographic Perspective*, p. 43.

99. Lindsay, *Byzantium into Europe*, pp. 429–30; Heichelheim, "Man's Role in Changing the Face of the Earth in Classical Antiquity," pp. 318–59; Lot, *L'Art militaire at les armes au Moyen âge*, II, 465; Théodoridès, "La Science byzantine," pp. 490–502.

100. Škrivanić, *Oružje u srednjovekovnoj Srbiji, Bosni i Dubrovniku*, pp. 201–5.

101. Stoianovich, "L'Espace maritime segmentaire de l'Empire ottoman," pp. 203–18; Stoianovich, "Russian Domination in the Balkans," pp. 199–200; Braudel, *La Méditerranée*, II, 164–212, 366–430; McNeill, *The Pursuit of Power*, pp. 1–10, 91–95, 102–14; Cipolla, *Guns, Sails, and Empires*, pp. 101–3; Hess, "The Evolution of the Ottoman Seaborne Empire," pp. 1892–1919; Hess, *The Forgotten Frontier;* Anderson, *Naval Wars in the Levant*, pp. 37–45; Guilmartin, Jr., *Gunpowder and Galleys;* Kortepeter, *Ottoman Imperialism during the Reformation;* Rycaut, *The History of the Turkish Empire*, pp. 6–7; Mantran, *Istanbul dans la seconde moitié du XVIIe siècle*, pp. 83–85; Bracewell, *The Uskoks of Senj*.

102. Schumpeter, "The Crisis of the Tax State," pp. 5–38.

103. Barash, *Sociobiology and Behavior*, p. 95.

104. Dalton, "Primitive, Archaic, and Modern Economies," pp. 3–4.

105. Hirschman, *The Passions and the Interests*, pp. 32–33, 42–48, 51–52.

106. Gouldner, "The Norm of Reciprocity," pp. 171–72.

107. Sahlins, *Tribesmen*, p. 85; Barash, *Sociobiology and Behavior*, p. 316.

108. Polanyi, *The Great Transformation*, p. 48; Rotstein, "Karl Polanyi's Concept of Non-Market Trade," pp. 117–26.

109. Hicks, *A Theory of Economic History*, pp. 9–24; Stoianovich, *French Historical Method*, pp. 144–49.

110. Mardin and Zartman, "Ottoman Turkey and the Maghreb in the 19th and 20th Centuries," p. 63.

111. McNeill, "The Ottoman Empire in World History," pp. 374–85. On protection production, see Lane, "Economic Consequences of Organized Violence," pp. 401–10; Lane, "The Role of Governments in Economic Growth," pp. 8–17.

112. Schumpeter, "The Crisis of the Tax State," pp. 5–38.

113. Sugar, *Southeastern Europe under Ottoman Rule,* pp. 124–26; Raicevich, *Osservazioni storiche naturali, e politiche intorno,* pp. 120–21; Svoronos, *Le Commerce de Salonique*, pp. 45–52, 379, 398–99; Stoianovich, "Land Tenure and Related Sectors of the Balkan Economy," pp. 398–411; Cvetkova, "Le Service des 'Celep' et le ravitaillement en bétail," pp.145–72; Cvetkova, "Les *Celep* et leur rôle dans la vie économique des Balkans," pp. 172–92; Gücer, "Le Problème d'approvisionnement d'Istanbul," pp. 153–62; Gücer, "Le Commerce intérieur des céréales dans l'Empire ottoman," pp. 163–88; Todorov, *Balkanskiiat grad,* pp. 80–99; Alexandrescu-Dersca, "Contribution à l'étude de

l'approvisionnement en blé de Constantinople," pp. 13–37; Mouradgea d'Ohsson, *Tableau général de l'Empire ottoman*, Vol. IV, pt. 1, pp. 222–25; Wallerstein, Decadeli, and Kasaba, "The Incorporation of the Ottoman Empire into the World-Economy"; Genç, "A Comparative Study of the Life Term Tax Farming Data and the Volume of Commercial and Industrial Activities in the Ottoman Empire," pp. 245–48. The average *iştira* contribution of the Macedonian territorial jurisdictions of Salonika, Volo(s), and Orphano(s) amounted in the late eighteenth century to 260,000 *kile* of wheat out of a total average production of 3,120,000 *kile*. *Istira* and other exports from these territories were about 1,200,000 *kile*, leaving for domestic consumption of an estimated population of 500,000 persons only 1,920,000 *kile* of wheat, plus 960,000 *kile* of maize and barley, or (at 22 *okas* to a *kile* and 1.28 kg. to an *oka*), an average per capita cereal consumption of 333 grams. Cf. Beaujour, *Tableau du commerce de la Grèce*, I, 118–23.

114. AN, MAR, B⁷ 481, memoir on Ottoman vessels and galleys, 1688; BN, Département des Manuscrits, Fonds Français 7176, "État des places fortes que les princes mahométans possèdent sur la côte de la mer Méditerranée," Vol. I, fol. 39, undated manuscript pertaining to the period after 1687; Tavernier, *Les Six voyages de Jean Tavernier*, I, 350.

115. Ancel, *Géographie des frontières*, pp. 32, 58–61; Spiridonakis, *Essays on the Historical Geography of the Greek World*, p. 60; for command mobilization along a specific route system, the Via Egnatia, see Stoianovich, "Routes as Sources of Information."

116. For a distinction between a market economy and an economy of markets, see Stoianovich, "Before and After 1789: A Cantonal Markets Economy."

117. Stoianovich, "L'Espace maritime segmentaire de l'Empire ottoman," pp. 203–18.

118. Clarke, *Travels in Various Countries of Europe, Asia, and Africa*, pt. II, sec. 3, Vol. IV, pp. 281–87. See also Stoianovich, "The Conquering Balkan Orthodox Merchant," p. 257.

119. Andréadès, "L'Administration financière de la Grèce," pp. 154–55. Andréadès gives the name of the town as Tournovo. This may be either Thessalian Tyrnavos or Bulgarian Tŭrnovo, where there were silk manufactures. It is probably the former, since Thessaly and Macedonia, rather than Bulgaria, were the important areas of cotton cultivation.

120. Sarç, "Ottoman Industrial Policy," pp. 50–54.

121. Todorov, "La Révolution industrielle en Europe occidentale et les provinces balkaniques de l'Empire ottoman," pp. 140–62; Todorov, *Balkanskiiat grad*, pp. 267–94.

122. Evelpidi, *Les États balkaniques*, pp. 316–34; Borchgrave, *La Serbie administrative, économique et commerciale*, pp. 61–72.

123. See Serbia, Ministarstvo Finansije, *Državopis Srbije*, Vols. IX–XVI, for further demographic data; see ibid., XIII, 34, 36, 106, 108, 110, for the population of Serbian towns in 1866.

124. Af. Étr., CC, Belgrade, Vols. I–VIII (1838–89); Vučo, *Privredna istorija Srbije*, pp. 247–51; Vučo, *Privredna istorija naroda FNRJ do Prvog svetskog rata*, pp. 211–12, 224, 228–29; Janković, *O političkim strankama u Srbiji XIX veka*, pp. 140–41, 172; Vivian, *Servia, the Poor Man's Paradise*, pp. 115–16; Borchgrave, *La Serbie administrative, économique et commerciale*, pp. 180–89. For the development of manufactures in the other Balkan states, see Wilhelmy, *Hochbulgarien, Sofia*, p. 113; Rothschild, *The Communist Party of Bulgaria*, p. 5; Dicey, *The Peasant State*, p. 195; Spulber, "The Role of the State in Economic Growth in Eastern Europe," pp. 255–86.

125. Protić, *Razvitak industrije i promet dobara u Srbiji za vreme prve vlade Kneza Miloša*, pp. 34, 79–82; Bois-le-Comte de Rigni (Rigny), "Srbija u godini 1834," pp. 1–64; Milenković, *Ekonomska istorija Beograda do Svetskog rata*, pp. 67–68, 95.

126. Borchgrave, *La Serbie administrative, économique et commerciale*, pp. 79–86; Jensen and Rosegger, "The Danube and Black Sea Railway."

127. Yankovitch, "Le Problème de notre navigation fluviale," pp. 268–77; Vučo, *Privredna istorija Srbije*, p. 224.

128. Kukiel, *Czartoryski and European Unity*, pp. 245–48; Stranjaković, "Kako je postalo Garašaninovo 'Načertanije,'" pp. 3–12; Stoianovich, *Between East and West*, IV, chapter on "The Pattern of Serbian Intellectual Evolution, 1830–1880."

129. Cvijić, "Izlazak Srbije na Jadransko More"; Stoianovich, *Between East and West*, IV, chapter on "The 'Rationalization' of a Small Space-Economy: Serbia and the Great Powers, 1881–1914."

130. Gooch and Temperley, eds., *British Documents on the Origins of the War*, Vol. IX, pt. 2, p. 234, No. 313, letter dated Belgrade, November 30, 1912.

131. Af. Étr., CC, Belgrade, IV, fol. 61, Botmiliau, May 31, 1865.

132. Paskaleva, "Les Relations commerciales des contrées bulgares," pp. 268–73.

133. AN, AÉ, B^1 470, Brousset, March 1, 1763; AN, AÉ, B^1 906, Guy de Villeneuve, August 4, 1780; AN, MAR, B^4 272, fol. 96–97, le chevalier de Ligondès, May 30, 1786; Stadtmüller, *Geschichte Südosteuropas*, p. 363; Leon, "The Greek Merchant Marine," pp. 31–44; Pouqueville, *Voyage de la Grèce*, VI, 305–10.

134. Štampar, "Borba jedrenjača s parobrodima u hrvatskom Primorju," p. 59.

135. Héritier, *La Grèce*, pp. 91–94; Evelpidi, *Les États balkaniques*, pp. 182–84; Svoronos, *Histoire de la Grèce moderne*, p. 73; Papathanassopoulos, "The State and the Greek Commercial Fleet," pp. 179, 182.

136. Brailsford, *The War of Steel and Gold*, pp. 83–85.

137. Evelpidi, *Les États balkaniques*, pp. 157–64; Marcovitch, "Création et développement des chemins de fer dans le Royaume de Serbie," pp. 151–64; Parliament (Great Britain), *Sessional Papers*, LXXXVII (1884). See also Mijatovich, *The Memoirs of a Balkan Diplomatist*, pp. 18–23, 34–35, 254–60; Bouvier, *Le Krach de l'Union Générale*, pp. 7–8, 11, 24, 27, 31, 36, 39, 69–70, 76–102, 280; Borchgrave, *La Serbie administrative, économique et commerciale*, pp. 87–89, 93–97; Milenković, *Istorija gradjenja železnica i železnička politika kod nas*, pp. 11, 16–18, 27–33, 36–37, 45, 47, 53–54, 60–68; Mirković, *Ekonomska historija Jugoslavije*, pp. 286–87.

138. I have misplaced the reference to the precise source of the statement. The following works corroborate the general thrust of my argument: Landes, *The Unbound Prometheus*, pp. 41–42, 138–39; Mathias, *The First Industrial Nation*, pp. 104, 250, 466; Schlote, *British Overseas Trade from 1700 to the 1930s*, pp. 50, 152–54.

139. Evelpidi, *Les Etats balkaniques*, pp. 240–41; Royal Institute of International Affairs, Information Department, *The Balkan States*, I, p. 16.

140. For Alexander D. Xenopol's views, see Roberts, *Rumania*, p. 335.

141. Stoianovich, *Between East and West*, III, chapter on "The Social Foundations of Balkan Politics, 1750–1941."

142. Frangeš, "Die Donaustaaten Südosteuropas und der deutsche Grosswirtschaftsraum," pp. 284–316; Frangeš, "L'Industrialisation des pays agricoles du Sud-est de l'Europe," pp. 27–77; Frangeš, "Die treibenden Kräfte der wirtschaftlichen Strukturwandlungen in Jugoslawien," pp. 309–38.

143. Manoilescu, "Arbeitsproduktivität und Aussenhandel," pp. 13–43; Brinkmann, "Mihail Manoïlesco und die klassische Aussenhandelstheorie," pp. 273–86.

144. Barker, *British Policy in South-East Europe*, pp. 140–47.

145. Stoianovich, *Between East and West*, IV, chapter on "Russian Domination in the Balkans."

146. For several of the pre-1940 statistics, see the Royal Institute of International Affairs, *The Balkan States*, I, 16, 18, 154.

147. Birken, *Consuming Desire*, pp. 22–39.

148. Tocqueville, *Souvenirs*, pp. 39, 47, 112–18, 124, my translation.

4 SOCIETY

A society is a group of communities with a common network of interdependent systems for the management of social strains and solidarities. Every society has its own way of organizing interpersonal and intergroup relationships so that the members of the society are in regular, if generally indirect, communication with each other at several different levels of life—religion, art, play, production, consumption, education, and exchange. In addition, every society has its own set of social structures.

Social structure refers not to the particular parts of a society, or to the role-players, but to the wholes that remain much the same for decades and even centuries in spite of the fact that the players constantly change. Class structure, patterns of consumption, patterns of exchange, and other structural complexes identify functional rather than organizational aspects of society. Behind the functions or social structures, and woven into them, are a society's fundamental values. Ordinarily, therefore, structural change is taboo.

Societies, however, always remain in a precarious equilibrium. Fields of structural solidarity, they are also fields of structural strain and stress. For, at a potential level, they allow the existence of variant social structures. Under certain conditions, a struggle may ensue between the defenders of the dominant structures and the role-players who identify with the variant patterns. When several structures change simultaneously, the change is said to be a revolution.

Structural change and ethnic change are the themes of the present chapter. After dealing with the problem of ethnic change or almost total transformation of roles and partial transformation of structures, especially linguistic, we shall examine the Balkans as a general field of structural solidarities and tensions.

Ethnogenesis

Speakers of various Indo-European or proto-Indo-European languages, as well as representatives of earlier non-Indo-European linguistic groups, may have been present in the Balkans since at least the fourth millennium B.C. The ethnic or linguistic affiliation of the inhabitants can be identified with limited assurance, however, only since 2000 B.C. At that time, the main ethnic or linguistic groups in the peninsula were the Istrians, Liburnians, Dalmatians, and Illyrians in the west; Pannonians, related perhaps to the Illyrians, in the north; Daco-Mysians, Thracians, and Phrygians or Armeno-Phrygians in the east; and Greeks, Macedonians, and Pelasgians (who a thousand years earlier may have spoken a common language) in the southern maritime fringes. All these peoples spoke Indo-European languages. The Pelasgians apparently were related to the Lydians, Carians, and Lycians of western Anatolia (speakers of the Hittite-Luwian group of Indo-European languages). They may have been the creators of the so-called Dimini culture of Thessaly.

Several scholars, among them Gustav Kossinnas, V. Gordon Childe, and Marija Gimbutas, have suggested an affinity between Indo-European speech and certain forms of material culture—a close interdependence among social forms, ways of thought, language, and material culture, notably the making of corded pottery, the use of the battle-ax and of carts and wagons, the possession of a common word for "wheel," the combined practice of horse breeding (a male occupation) and soil cultivation (mainly women's work as hoe farming), knowledge of metallurgy, and the custom of tumulus *(kurgan, mogila, maghoula, gomila)* burials.[1] Gimbutas further suggests that the "whimsical, imaginative" cultures of what she calls "Old Europe"—that is, the Balkan cultures prior to 4000 B.C., with their strong emphasis on what modernity perceives as aesthetics —were not Indo-European.[2] Sociologically patriarchal in contrast to the psychologically matriarchal Neolithic cultures of the preceding four millennia, the later cultures were the product of speakers of Indo-European languages. The presumable "homeland" of these peoples ("homeland" only in the sense of the place of their first known appearance) was the area at the junction of forest and steppe north of the Caucasus and Black Sea, where hunting and farming converged to develop into pastoralism.

A partial reconciliation may be possible, however, between the Gimbutas and the Renfrew thesis. Colin Renfrew holds, in effect, that small groups of Indo-European populations from Anatolia introduced farming into the Balkans. Once such small groups arrived, knowledge of farming practices was probably diffused by short-distance movements of new small groups ever northward every twenty years or so as the population of a given settlement of farmers exceeded the level authorized by the existing farming technology. At the end of the Paleolithic era the population of the Near East (principally Anatolia, Iran, Iraq, Egypt, and the Arabian peninsula) did not exceed 50,000 to 100,000. Encompassing a much smaller area with a similar population of food gatherers and hunters and an endowment of natural resources capable of supporting a density of one person to ten square kilometers, the Balkans south of the Danube and Sava valleys may have had a population at that time of 22,000 to 25,000. The fishing resources of the Balkan lakes, rivers, and adjacent seas may even have made possible a population of 50,000 to 100,000. If, excessively perhaps, one further attributes to an early farming culture a population density of three to five persons per square kilometer,[3] one may estimate the total Balkan population around 4,000 B.C. at 1.3–1.5 to 2.2–2.5 million.

Promoting the introduction of new forms of material culture, new techniques, new forms of social organization, and modified forms of religious belief, the growth of farming stimulated the growth and transformation of language. The languages and cultural anthropology of the Balkan populations of the fifth millennium, before the widespread diffusion to the Danube of Indo-Europeans from the northeast, thus may have differed considerably from the languages spoken before the Neolithic era. On the other hand, since the practice of farming and stock raising—albeit in different proportions—characterized both the first group of Balkan agriculturalists and the later Danubian "battle-ax" and "corded ware" cultures, their respective languages probably had a greater functional resemblance than the languages of the first Balkan farmers and their hunter-gatherer predecessors. The new mode of production (a mix of agriculture and stock raising) and new level of population density thus may explain the submergence of the non-Indo-European local idioms.

Indo-European linguistic groups—Illyrians, Achaeans, Dorians, and Thracians—are more easily identifiable during the second millennium B.C. The Achaean and Dorian Greeks ultimately settled in the southernmost areas, where they mingled with or dispersed the former Pelasgians. In the eighth century B.C., on the other hand, a population of diverse linguistic affiliation and ethnic origin known as the Scythians or Saka overran the territories of the Thraco-Phrygian Cimmerians north of the Black Sea. The Scythians subsequently also occupied the region between the Black Sea and Pannonia, where they may have mingled with the Getae (sometimes confused with the Goths).

Between the eighth and fifth century B.C., the Greeks arrived at the idea of Delphi as the ὀμφαλος γῆς (navel of the earth) and of directional extremes (east, west, north, south). But if an ideal center and extremes exist, the nature of places and peoples may vary with the distance from the center.[4] This conception gave rise to the view implicit in the history of Herodotus (book 4 in particular) of a succession of barbarian rings around civilization, each more barbarian as it was further removed from the city cultures, especially as one moved north of the city cultures of the Greeks—farmers, nomads, hunters, and man-eaters. But as Owen Lattimore has shown and as may be inferred from Herodotus and Euripides, civilization and barbarism, or city cultures and cultures marked by the rarity or absence of cities, represent interdependent rather than independent lines of development. Tempted "by the material culture of civilization," barbarians either entered the service of the city cultures or attacked them. Partly in retaliation and partly to satisfy their desire for gold, silver, tin, and amber, cities extended their geographic-political framework into the barbarian world even as the barbarians moved peacefully or with arms into the political-geographic framework of the world of city cultures. But as one "barbary" was domesticated, a new "barbary" took its place.[5]

To set the process in a Chinese and Braudelian mode of thought, one might say that the encounter with a succession of barbarians would continue until all the barbarians were at least partly "cooked," that is "domesticated," prone to act within a system of city cultures even if only as "internal barbarians." If one embraced a yet more Lévi-Straussian mode of thought, one might say that human language always tends to distinguish between two categories of beings, things, and actions: beings, things, and actions perceived as nature, and beings, things, and actions perceived as culture. From that point of view, there will always be barbarians. One person or human group always will always perceive another as too raw or as cooked to excess.[6]

Around or before the mid-fifth century B.C., the Illyrian Neuri, identified by some Soviet scholars as possible ancestors of the Slavs, migrated from the mountains of the northeastern Adriatic to an area beyond the Danube and north of the Getae. Shortly after 400 B.C. began an era of yet other ethnic formations, heralded by the southward penetration of the Celts to the Drava, Sava, and middle Danube. Between 380 and 360 B.C., the Celts moved into the Morava valley, where they mingled with the Daco-Mysians (related to the Getae) and drove a wedge between the Illyrians and Thracians. In addition, they forced the remaining Illyrians of the northern Adriatic to withdraw southward to the mouth of the Narenta (Neretva). In the next century, Celtic groups pushed southward from the Danube and Sava into Thrace, Macedonia, and Asia Minor. Following cultural and biological intermingling, some Illyrians and Thracians were transformed into Celto-Illyrians and Celto-Thracians. At about the same time an Iranian population known as the Sarmatians affirmed its hegemony over the territories previously dominated by the Scythians.

Carried out between the latter part of the third century B.C. and the opening of the second century A.D., the Roman conquest of the Balkans added to the ethnic complexities. Among the last areas to come under Roman rule (A.D. 101–7) and among the first to be abandoned (A.D. 270–75) was Dacia. Today, however, after Wallachia and Moldavia, linguistically the most Romanized of all the southeastern European provinces is Dacia, or modern Transylvania. We shall therefore turn to the seductive question of how its Romanization may have occurred.

At the close of the fifth century A.D., the Balkans formed two urban linguistic zones, divided by what has come to be known as the Jireček line (so named after the Czech medievalist, Constantin Josef Jireček): a Roman zone in the north and west and a Greek zone in the south and east, lying somewhat east of the line along which the Roman Empire was separated in A.D. 395 into a western territory and an eastern territory. The zone of Romanization, however, comprised two noncontiguous blocs: a coastal Adriatic zone, in which the population spoke a southern Italic language known as "Roman" or "Dalmatian," and a Danubian zone, in which the inhabitants may have spoken an idiom or idioms replete with "Balkanisms," including the use of the suffix -ul(a), -ulj, -elj, which may be derived from Thracian -ala, -ila, -ula.

In the mountainous interior between the two blocs of Romanization lay a zone of lightly Romanized Illyrians. Intervening between the Romanized middle and lower Danube and the more or less Hellenized south lay a highly mixed zone: Thracian Besses in the district of Tatar Pazardzhik, Thracian Sapes (from whom the Shopi may be descended, unless they are the descendants, as scholars also have suggested, of one of eight Pecheneg tribes known to Emperor Constantine VII Porphyrogenitus as Tsopon) who settled in the territory between Kratovo and Sofia, Celto-Illyrian Scordisci and Daco-Mysians between the county of Srem (Syrmium) north of the Sava and west of the Danube and the district of Sardica (or Serdica, modern Sofia) to the southeast, Thracian Paeonians to the east of the middle Vardar, and Celto-Thracians or Celto-Mysians in the district of Philippopolis. One may infer the presence in the last region of Thracians, Celts, or Daco-Mysians, or of all three groups, from the fact that the Slavs who later settled there derived their own name for Philippopolis—Plovdiv and Plovdin —directly from the Thracian or Daco-Mysian Pulpudeva or from the Thraco-Mysian, with a modified form of the Celtic ending *-dun(um).

The towns of the northern and western Black Sea littoral and some of the rural dwellers of the southeastern Balkan interior were Hellenized. Everywhere, at least superficially, the soldiery was Romanized. After defeating the Sarmatians, however, groups of Goths entered Dacia from the north, forcing the Romans to withdraw. Some Goths subsequently moved into the Roman Empire, occupying part of what later became Croatia (the Gacka *banovina* of the Croatian Littoral), northeastern Albania, the area that the Serbs later would know as the Gothic Plain (Gacko Polje), the Dobrudja, and the region between the Balkan (Haemus) foothills and Danubian Nikopol, where Gothic continued to be spoken until the ninth century.

Along with Dacians and Getae, Germanic Gepids and Goths, and Sarmatians, the inhabitants of Dacia also included the Carps, a Carpathian people that successfully resisted Romanization. Other ethnic elements present in fifth-century Dacia and Pannonia included many tribes of Slavs, who had long resided in areas under Gothic or Sarmatian rule. In the 440s, the Huns invaded the region and moved southward to occupy Singidunum (Belgrade), Naissus (Niš), and Sardica (Sofia), penetrating eastward into Thrace and westward into Illyria. To the east, in Bessarabia, present also in the fifth century were some ten to twenty thousand Turkic Bulgars.

But after the departure of the Roman legions in the third century, were any people left in Dacia who spoke a Romance dialect? Romanian and Hungarian scholars have long been divided in their answers to this question. The general Hungarian view is that few speakers of a Romance tongue, or none at all, remained, for no existent records mention their presence until the eleventh and twelfth centuries. The general Romanian version is that Romance-speaking populations—Daco-Romans—never ceased to exist in some districts of the country. The archaeological evidence of Romanian scholars suggests that some

Romanized groups continued to be found in Dacia—namely, at Alba Iulia—into the fifth century.[7]

The question then arises as to the fate of such groups between the sixth and eleventh or twelfth centuries, when records again show the presence of speakers of a Romance language in the former Dacia, known henceforth as Transylvania, Erdely (Ardeal), or Siebenbürgen. To answer this beguiling question, one must first turn to the advent of the Slavs into the Balkans proper, south of the Danube and Sava valleys.

The movement of Slavs from north of the Carpathians to the left banks of the middle Danube and Sava rivers was a long process, beginning perhaps in the first or second and continuing into the fifth and sixth centuries. The first mention in the extant literature of the names "Slav" and "Serb" occurs in Ptolemy's *Geography* (second century A.D.), which situates a people called Soubeni (Slovenes) in a vague area north of the Black Sea that was also inhabited by the Sarmatian Alans. Ptolemy likewise identified a people called Serboi in that part of Sarmatia lying between the northeastern foothills of the Keraunian (Caucasus?) mountains and the river Ra (Volga). Two second- and third-century Greek inscriptions further identify a people or rather person called Xoroathos or Xorouathos (Croat) at the lower Don.

The areas with which these populations were associated, however, may have been territories in which they once had lived rather than areas they then inhabited. Moreover, segments of a given population may have remained in place while other segments moved elsewhere. Peoples identified by the same name thus could be and have been found in widely separate areas.

A possibly Slavic people situated by Pliny the Elder in his *Naturalis Historiae* (first century A.D.) and by Tacitus in his *Germania* (second century A.D.), between Germania to the west of the Vistula and Sarmatia to the east, was the Venedi (whose name in revised form reappears as Venice, Vendée, Wend, Viatka, and Viatichi), with whom some scholars associate a population identified in the fifth century as the Antes or Antae.[8] A word of caution may be necessary here, however, for language shifts among populations that continue to call themselves by the same name are not at all impossible, especially in preliterate cultures.

Scholars have suggested that the names "Slav" and "Slovene" derive from the Slavic terms for "word" *(slovo)* or "glory" *(slava)* or from a hypothetical Indo-European root for "clean" or "pure" *(*k'leu-)*. Paradoxically and in illustration of ethnic prejudice, the English term "slovenly" means just the opposite. The name "Venedi" may be derived from a hypothetical Indo-European root *(*vent-)* meaning "great." A derivation has also been suggested from Indo-European *wen-*, with the meaning of English "win" and "want" (and of the name of the Roman goddess Venus). The name "Serb" has been derived from a word *(ser,* pl. *ser-b)* in a Caucasian language (related to Karp?) meaning "man" and "people" or from an Indo-European root *(*ser-, *serv-)* meaning "guard" or "protect" (as applied, in particular, to herds or flocks of domesticated animals). Finally, the name

"Croat" (Hrvat) has been derived from a Paleo-European root in the plural *(kar-p)* meaning "stones," from Iranian *churava* for "people" or *hu + urvatha* for "one who has friends," from a hypothetical Sarmatian **xarv-*, or from the name of a Bulgarian war leader with an Iranian name, Kouvrat, who supposedly led the migration of the Croats into Pannonian and Illyrian Croatia.[9]

By the early part of the sixth century, Slavs settled south of the Danube in the Timok and Morava valleys. Other Slavs made incursions from Pannonia, Dacia, and territories yet further east deep into Thessaly, Epirus, Illyricum, and Thrace. In the latter part of the sixth and first quarter of the seventh century, Slavs from Pannonia entered Dalmatia and Istria, and Slavs and Mongol or Turkic Avars jointly organized numerous attacks against the maritime cities of the Adriatic, Aegean, and Pontus Euxinus. As attested to by toponyms, their settlements were numerous along the middle courses of middle-sized rivers, such as the Morava, Struma, and Vardar, but rare in northeastern Bulgaria and eastern Thrace. They even settled in the Peloponnesus, where, in much reduced numbers, they remained until they were forcibly removed by the Turks in the fifteenth century. Their entry into the Balkans proper may have been facilitated by a pandemic that considerably reduced the population of the Byzantine towns, including its soldiery. ⌈JUSTINIAN PLAGUE⌉

Arnold J. Toynbee cites a passage from the annals of Theophylactus Simocatta concerning the contact, in A.D. 591, between the Slavs and the Eastern Roman Empire:

> Three men of Slav race without weapons or military equipment were captured by the Imperial Body-Guard. Their only baggage consisted of harps, and they carried nothing else with them.... They carried harps because they were not trained to bear arms. Their country [on the boundary of "the Western Ocean" or Baltic] was ignorant of iron, and this accounted for their peaceful and harmonious life.... They were a people among whom war was unheard-of; and it was only natural there should be a bucolic note in their musical technique.

Toynbee then goes on to conclude that Slavic history begins only after the Avars compelled the Slavs to fight for and beside them.[10] In A.D. 584, however, John of Ephesus reported that the Slavs were capable of waging war more effectively than the Romans. The "Miracles of St. Demetrius," or accounts of the first and second sieges of Salonika by the Slavs at the end of the sixth and opening of the seventh century, further relate that the Slavs possessed arms of a kind that "no man of our era has ever seen, or has ever known their names."[11] Several centuries earlier the Slavs may have been poorly armed. But by the latter half of the sixth century, having come into contact with Gothic, Sarmatian, Roman, and Hunnic as well as Avar arms, they were no longer the "unarmed folk" (ἔθνη ἄοπλα) of Constantine Porphyrogenitus or the "weaponless" folk *(armis despecti)* of Jordanes.

Upon the advent of the Slavs deep into the southernmost parts of the Balkan peninsula, some of the Romanized populations of the right-bank Danube and Daco-Mysians may have fled to mountain retreats—presumably to the very areas in which tenth-, eleventh-, or twelfth-century and later documents situate them: the Balkan, Rhodope, Dinaric, and Pindus mountain systems. Perhaps some groups fled northward to the Transylvanian Alps. The Dalmatian Latini locked themselves in their island and coastal fortresses. The Greeks found refuge in the Aegean and Pontic cities and in a few interior cities such as Sardica. Formerly living at a great distance from each other, Danubian Romans and Adriatic Latini (speakers of southern Italic) now became neighbors. In language and way of life, however, distinctions were perpetuated. For the Latini, the Danubian Romans in their new Dinaric mountain homes were Nigri Latini, Maurovalachi, or Morlaks: Black Vlachs.

Along the Dinaric chain the Morlaks ultimately occupied a series of mountain pastures from Kotor (Cattaro) in the south to Senj (Segna) in the north. A complex of Dinaric Valachiae (countries of Romanized populations)—covered the region east of the Adriatic coast: Hlm or Hum (from Vlach *culme*,[12] derived from Latin *culmen*, for "hill"), or part of the region later known as Hercegovina; Old Valachia (Stari Vlah), in the mountain corridor that divided Bosnia-Hercegovina and Montenegro from Serbia and was itself separated into two halves by the caravan route that ran southeastward between Foča and Novi-pazar;[13] Romanija to the east of Sarajevo; Mount Cicarija (so-called after a speech habit of the Vlachs) in Istria; and numerous Morlak cantons *(katuni)* in the central and northern mountain regions inland from the Adriatic of the Latini, whose Italic language largely disappeared by the end of the seventeenth century, yielding to Slavic and Venetian Italian. The last speaker of that tongue died on the island of Krk (Veglia) in 1898.[14]

Apart from the western Valachiae emerged three other groups of Valachiae—southern, eastern, and northeastern. The southern Valachiae included an Upper Valachia in Epirus; a Valachia Major in Thessaly; a Valachia Minor in Aetolia and Acarnania; and a Valachia (Vlachorynchinoi, a name suggesting a mingling of Vlachs or speakers of a Romance language and the Slavic or Avaro-Slavic tribe known to the Greeks as Rynchinoi, after an unidentified river) in southern Macedonia, probably between the lower Vardar and the lower Struma (Strymon). The eastern group included Balkan and Rhodope Valachiae and a group of Valachiae stretching from the Dobrudja to Anchialos on the Black Sea. The fourth or northern group of Valachiae included a White Valachia (Muntenia, Wallachia) on the left-bank lower Danube; a Black Valachia (Moldavia or Bogdania) from the Carpathians to the Prut River; a Valachia Minor (often known as Oltenia) to the west of Black Valachia; Valachiae projecting from the Carpathians into Transylvania; and a Valachia Minor (Mala Vlaška) in western Slavonia between the Ilova River to the northwest and the Psunj Woods to the southeast.[15]

The four geographic groups may have comprised several different components and mixes of Romanization: Celtic, Illyrian, Daco-Mysian, Thracian, and Gothic. The name "Vlach" itself may come from the name of a partly Romanized Celtic population, the Volcae. One group of Volcae had migrated from the middle Danube to Languedoc (between the Rhone and Toulouse). The rest had stayed in place, perhaps in the valley of the Oulkos (medieval Volka, contemporary Vuka) or moved eastward or southeastward.[16] The Slavs themselves associate the name "Volka" with their own word for "wolf,"[17] suggesting in turn the possible earlier presence in the area of a Romanized Dacian population. For the earlier name of the Dacians was Daoi, probably meaning "wolves" and suggesting a totemic relationship between Dacians and wolves. In effect, a portion of the Dacian youth may have been organized as a martial brotherhood whose ritual name was Wolves. That name was later extended to the whole population of western Dacia, while their kin in the Black Sea area continued to be known as Getae.[18]

At least since the late Middle Ages, Germanic, Slavic, and Greek populations alike have applied the term "Vlach" or a variant thereof (Welsh, Walloon, Vlah, Vlachos) to Romanized populations in their own midst but sometimes to other populations who adopted a similar way of life, namely, pastoralism. Around 1900, the total number of ethnic Vlachs south of the Danube and Sava rivers may have been no more than five hundred thousand.[19] If one may assume that the total number of ethnic Vlachs declined after 1830 or 1850, as a result both of the decline of pastoralism and of the further assimilation of many Vlachs by Greeks, Serbs, Croats, Muslim Bosnians, Albanians, and Bulgarians, and if one further assumes that birth and death rates were not significantly altered among the Vlachs between 1830 and 1900 (an assumption one may not make for the agricultural populations of the Balkans), one may conclude that Vlachs were numerically yet stronger before 1830. Between 1550 and 1700 (a period of rapid pastoral expansion) among the Serbs and during the eighteenth century (a period of rapid commercialization of the economy of the southern group of Vlachs in particular) among the Greeks, on the other hand, pastoralization probably more than compensated for assimilation. Almost 10 percent of the cis-Danubian Balkan population (see chapter 8) thus may have been Vlach between 1550 and the end of the seventeenth century. As the process of assimilation between Bulgarians and Vlachs may have begun as early as the twelfth century, the number of Balkan Vlachs in proportion to other Balkan ethnicities may have been yet greater in 1500, in 1200, and in earlier centuries.

What little information exists on the Vlach way of life before 1500 suggests that they played an important role in the transport services of medieval princes and bishops and in providing the agricultural, urban, and political economies with carrying services and auxiliary defense, as well as supplying them with goods of pastoral production (wool, skins, cheese, meat). An occupation with which they were associated in the medieval "Serbian lands" was that of *kelator* (or *ćelator*), wrongly linked to the function of *cellarius*.[20] It is more likely that, probably deriving from Greek κέλλω,[21] the term meant (sheep or cattle) driver while also embracing other activities in which men of that occupation might be expected to engage.

The number of Vlachs in any given place probably varied with the season, which may be one of the reasons why travelers and administrators sometimes fail to associate them with a particular territory. That kind of association was unlikely until permanent structures replaced their tents and huts of branches, mud, and straw. They did not build such structures until the sixteenth and especially seventeenth, eighteenth, and nineteenth centuries. It is not impossible that territories from which they may have departed, such as Dacia and Daco-Mysia (the right-bank Danube from the Morava valley of Serbia—or even from the Sava valley—almost to the Black Sea), were also territories to which they sometimes may have returned, perhaps even seasonally. Between 1500 and 1800, however, they may also have transformed a customary earlier short-distance and perhaps irregular transhumance into a long-distance and regular one.

Varying degrees of Romanization were achieved in the Balkans during the two to five centuries of Roman rule. The least degree of Romanization logically could be expected in two areas—among the Greeks, who were able to compete more effectively than the other Balkan ethnicities with the rival Roman urban culture, and in zones of difficult communication, especially the Dinaric and Pindus mountain chains.

On the basis of medieval inscriptions and coinage, Jireček postulated that the line of division between the zone of Roman influence to the west and north and the zone of Greek influence to the south and east extended roughly from the Adriatic port of Lesh (Alessio) across Albania to just north of Scupi (Skoplje, Skopje). Running therefrom south of Niš and north of Pirot to the Haemus mountains,[22] the line then swerved eastward toward the Black Sea.

The inclusion on the Latin side of the line of only a portion of what today is northern Albania (a portion that even now, despite seventeenth-century conversions to Islam, is largely Roman Catholic), despite the fact that, at the end of the nineteenth century, a quarter of the Albanian vocabulary was of Latin origin, some of it through the later filter of Venice, suggests that northern and southern Albanians may be of different ethnic origins. Albanians themselves acknowledge that fact by distinguishing between the Ghegs of the north and the Tosks of the south. Physical and cultural anthropology, including studies of different modes of dress and idiom, confirm that distinction.

An interesting fact in this connection is that in the Gruža district of central Serbia a common derisive name for the people of the countryside as late as the first half of the twentieth century was *geak, gedža,* or *gegula*.[23] The term may contain the meaning of "Gheg," which itself may stem from the Greek word for earth, with an occasional addition of the Vlach or Thracian suffix *-ula*. I infer therefrom that a stratum of partly Romanized populations of Thracian, Daco-

Table 4.1

Linguistic Affinities

Latin	Romanian	Arumanian	Albanian	Meaning
caballum	cal		kal	horse
cubitum	cot		kut	elbow
lucta	luptă	luftă	luftë	struggle

Source: Georgiev, "The Earliest Ethnological Situation of the Balkan Peninsula."

Mysian, and Illyrian origin remained in place or soon returned (seasonally or permanently) to their previous habitat following the Avaro-Slav invasions of the sixth and seventh centuries. Indeed, a southward migration of partly Romanized populations from the hills west and east of the Morava may have occurred during the tenth and eleventh centuries, accounting for the advent to Macedonia of the Megleno-Vlachs.

A further consequence of migratory movements may have been the joining of partly Romanized Illyrian and partly Romanized Daco-Mysian elements to form the Gheg population of northern Albania. Partly Romanized Daco-Mysians and Thracians may have joined partly Romanized Pelasgian remnants to form the Tosk population of southern Albania.

A strong mix of Daco-Mysians from Mysia (Moesia) Inferior and Dardania (parts of present-day Serbia and Bulgaria) contributed to the formation not only of Albanian ethnicity but of the southern Balkan group of Vlachs. The difference between the two was that the Albanian language was lightly Romanized, while the southern Vlach (Arumanian) language was Romanized more profoundly. But as Vladimir I. Georgiev has shown, the most ancient Latin loan words in Albanian and Arumanian are of Balkan-Latin—not of southern Italic-Latin (as in the old Romance language of Dalmatia)—origin. They thus have an affinity with Latin loan words in Romanian (that is, with the language of the northeastern Vlachs), as may be seen from the examples in Table 4.1 above. The low number of *ancient* Greek loan words in Albanian suggests that most of the ancestors of the Albanians of today probably entered the region from elsewhere. Their employment of a marine terminology of diverse origin suggests that they were not originally a coastal people.[24]

The southward movement of Vlachs was accompanied or followed by a northward movement at the same time and in the succeeding centuries. As a result, Vlachs accounted for 24 percent of the population of Transylvania in the early part of the sixteenth century and a third of the population in the mid-seventeenth century.[25] The proportion rose thereafter to higher levels as peasants fled from Wallachia and Moldavia to escape increasing labor dues and other servitudes.

Sclaviniae and Mixobarbara

Large as may have been the Valachiae, still larger were the Sclaviniae or settlements of Slavs. The Vlachs occupied the high country, land of refugees fleeing from foreign invaders or state authority. The Slavs settled the plains and middle and lower courses of rivers. The relationship between Vlachs and Slavs exposes, indeed, a principle of human development, a kind of law of history: conquerors occupy easily exploitable resources, rebels withdraw to seemingly less hospitable lands, which offer them at least the advantage of preserving their freedom. The un-Romanized Carps were thus mountaineers, the Romanized Dacians were plainsmen. Following the Slavic invasions, the Romanized plainsmen were forced into the mountains and the Slavs occupied the plains. As a result of the Ottoman conquest, many Slav peasants abandoned the plains to join the Vlach folk of the mountains, and the plains came into the possession of Turks and Muslim Albanians. When, during the sixteenth and seventeenth centuries, Serb and western Vlach pastoralists, both of the Orthodox faith, abandoned Ottoman territories to serve as defenders of the Croatian Military Frontier against the Turks, the common name of the Croats for Serbs and Vlachs alike was "Vlah."

Between the ninth and fifteenth centuries, the southernmost Sclaviniae, notably those of the Peloponnesus, were largely eliminated as a result of the Byzantine policy of recolonizing these territories with Greeks from southern Italy and of the population transfer policies of the Ottoman Empire. To prevent the triumph of the principle of ethnicity or—from a Lévi-Straussian perspective—of nature as opposed to culture, Byzantium settled Armenians, Turks, and Monophysite Syrians in Macedonia and Thrace.[26] Ottoman and Habsburg governments pursued similar strategies.

Partly as a result of the policies of empire and even more as a consequence of unlike rates of cultural evolution and of the long succession of migrations and invasions, peoples of ambivalent cultural identity came to inhabit certain Balkan areas. Perceiving their presence in Epirus, Acarnania, and Aetolia even in Antiquity, Euripides called them Mixobarbaroi.

Mixobarbaroi were semibarbarians or rural folk without an autonomous city culture of their own or without an imperial, ecumenical, or missionary religion, but acculturated through their contacts with peoples such as the Greeks or Romans, who did possess a city culture. Mixobarbaroi were also Greeks (or members of some other urban culture) who adopted some of the habits of the "nature" peoples without a developed urban culture.[27] In medieval Anatolia, mixovarvaroi were often persons of mixed parentage, one parent having an urban or settled-farming heritage and the other a patrimony of nomadism or transhumance. They also included persons whose religious identity fluctuated as they became the dependents of a lord of one faith (Christian) or the other (Muslim).[28] In some Balkan districts, they were people with a floating sense of ethnic and/or religious consciousness, identifying—or identified by others—first with one ethnicity, then with another, and sometimes with several ethnicities. A Greek chronicle from the monastery of Panteleimon on Lake Janina thus describes a certain Vonko, who conquered Arta in 1400, as a "Servalvanitovoulgarovlachos," a Serbo-Albanian-Bulgarian-Vlach.[29]

In diluted form, Mixobarbara, or lands of Mixobarbaroi, continue to exist in the Balkans to the present. Macedonia and the Dobrudja long provided particularly striking examples of such provinces.

To the previous ethnic changes, moreover, one should add the entry into the peninsula of large numbers of Turkic peoples. During the second half of the fifth century, Turkic Bulgars from the Don and Volga settled along the left bank of the lower Danube, arriving at the invitation of Byzantium, which needed their aid against the Goths. After accepting Avar rule for almost a century and then coming under pressure from the steppic Turkic state of Khazaria, some ten to twenty thousand Bulgars crossed the Danube in A.D. 679 to settle in the "crazy thicket" (Deli Orman) district of the Dobrudja,[30] then occupied by Severian Slavs (a mix of Slavs and Slavicized formerly Turkic-speaking Huns). Seizing Sardica in A.D. 809, the Bulgars proceeded to create a Bulgarian Empire, the language of which became increasingly Slavic, particularly after the translation of the Scriptures into the Slavic dialect of southern Macedonia (from which the other Slavic languages then presumably differed little) and the conversion of the Bulgarian *khakan* and his subjects to Christianity during the second half of the ninth century.

Numerically more important than the Turkic Bulgars were other Turkic peoples who surged forward from the steppes of southeastern Europe and from Anatolia: Pechenegs, Cumanians, Tartars (Tatars), and Ottoman Turks. In the ninth century, the Pechenegs dwelled in the steppes east of the Dnieper. In the 890s, however, the Bulgarian state sought their alliance to cope with a concerted attack from the south by Byzantium and from the north by the Magyars, a Finno-Ugrian people that then occupied an area between the Dnieper and the lower Danube. Upon losing their pastures to the Pechenegs while they were in Bulgaria, the Magyars had to seek new pastures. They found them in Pannonia (present-day Hungary and adjacent lands). Later, under pressure from the Turkic Cumanians, the Pechenegs withdrew to the Dobrudja. To prevent a resurgence of the Slavs of Bulgaria, whose territories had reverted to Byzantine control at the beginning of the eleventh century, Byzantium allowed some Pecheneg groups to occupy the area around Adrianople and Philippopolis. To separate the Slavs of the western from those of the eastern areas, it allowed another Pecheneg group to move into the region that now forms eastern Serbia and western Bulgaria.

Probably numerically the most significant of the pre-Ottoman Turkic groups, the Cumanians established their political authority over a territory extending from the lightly wooded sandy soils between the Danube and the Tisza in the west to the lower Danube in the south and the Dnieper in the east. Cumanians also sought pastures south of the Danube, notably in the Byzantine province of

Paristrion around Varna and in northern Macedonia (Kumanovo). In Transylvania, they were Magyarized through contact with the Finno-Ugrian Magyars of Hungary and by their conversion to Roman Catholicism. In Wallachia and Moldavia, they were Romanized. In Bulgaria and Macedonia, they were Slavicized or Romanized. Cumanians also played a key role in the forging of Romanian and Vlacho-Bulgarian states.

The great Mongol invasion of 1241 and repeated subsequent Tatar incursions, first under Mongol and later under Ottoman sponsorship or on their own initiative, brought yet other Turkic elements to the eastern Balkans, especially to Moldavia, the Dobrudja, Macedonia, and eastern Bulgaria. Politically and religiously most important, however, was the last group of Turkic invaders to penetrate the Balkans—the Muslim Ottoman Turks.

Between Turkey and "Germany"

Ottoman Turks settled in the plains and river basins of the eastern and central Balkans and in the towns of the entire peninsula. Many Slavs abandoned the lowlands to settle in the uplands, where they Slavicized the Vlachs but adopted their pastoral habits. Slavs and Slavicized Vlachs also migrated to Dalmatia, with a resultant rapid recession of the Romanic Dalmatian dialect before various Serbo-Croatian idioms. In the sixteenth century, Italian was the language of commerce in Venetian Dalmatia and in Ragusa, but the language of the hearth was predominantly Slavic. The language of literature was both Slavic and Italian. By the end of the seventeenth century, Latini and Morlaks alike were more or less completely Slavicized.

In Wallachia and Moldavia, the Ottoman conquest indirectly aided the process of Romanian state development if not of Romanization. The weakening of the Slavic states gave the Romanians an opportunity to strengthen their own recently constituted political entities with the aid of Serbian and Bulgarian scholars and administrators who fled Ottoman rule after the fall of the Bulgarian and Serbian states. On the other hand, some degree of Slavicization occurred in the Wallachian and Moldavian principalities at the level of elites both before and after they became Ottoman tributaries. A process of Hellenization then followed, particularly after the office of hospodar or Ottoman farmer-general fell, during the latter part of the seventeenth century, into the hands of men of wealth in Istanbul/Constantinople known as Phanariots. At lower social levels, the process of Romanization continued unbroken.

As a consequence of Ottoman rule, by the end of the seventeenth century, a fifth and perhaps nearly a third of the population of the eastern Balkan areas was ethnically or linguistically Turkic. In the western areas, the number probably did not exceed 10 percent. Thus, while the Slavic character of the western and the Romanic character of the trans-Danubian eastern territories were affirmed and the linguistic Hellenism of the southern maritime zone was not challenged until the great Albanian incursions of the eighteenth century, the ethnic future of the eastern and southern inland regions was a big question mark. Would they ultimately become singularly Hellenic, Turkic, Albanian, Slavic, or Romanic? Would they retain their conglomerate character?

In the northwestern and north central areas, the Germanic ethnic element grew rapidly after the Austro-Turkish war of 1683–99. Throughout the same period the Saxons of Transylvania retained their identity as a separate nation, reaffirmed by their sixteenth-century conversion to Lutheranism. In the eighteenth century, the Habsburg monarchy welcomed the settlement of Roman Catholic colonists from the Rhineland and other sections of Germany and from Lorraine and Italy in the provinces taken from the Turks (Hungary, Transylvania, the Banat, Syrmium, and Slavonia). The monarchy had two reasons for encouraging this colonization—to use the new inhabitants as a lever and bulwark against the rebellious Magyar nobility (many of them Calvinist) and dissident Lutheran Saxons and to repopulate the devastated plains, often with dire consequences for the early colonists, as briefly underlined an eighteenth-century German song:

> Der Erst hat den Tod/Death to the First,
> Der Zweite hat die Not/Want to the Second,
> Der Dritte erst hat Brot/Bread only to the Third.[31]

In the nineteenth century, Germanization proceeded apace in Dalmatia. After 1878, it was extended to Bosnia-Hercegovina, which the Turks had been forced to evacuate and place under an Austro-Hungarian administration. In Hungary, on the other hand, the Magyar minority succeeded in becoming a majority by assimilating Germans, Slavs, Jews, and other ethnic groups.

Physical Types

Ethnicity and nationality do not constitute race. On the basis of available fragmentary information, every Balkan ethnic group comprised several different physical types even prior to its entry into the Balkan peninsula. Even territorially small Montenegro, traditionally (but only since the latter part of the nineteenth century) noted for its so-called Dinaric race, the very existence of which physical anthropology now questions, manifests considerable racial diversity. In fact, at the close of the nineteenth century one discerned three Montenegrin physical types: a relatively short, brown-haired, dark-skinned, and either blue- or tawny-eyed inhabitant of Old Montenegro; a taller, more thickset, auburn-haired, blue- or gray-eyed inhabitant of the Brda or northeastern mountain districts; and a very tall solidly built type with long legs and a relatively short body and blond hair (but sometimes very dark hair and skin) in the North Border area.

There was a great difference between the height of men and that of women.

The average height of Montenegrin women tended to be under 5 feet 3 inches and the average height of men 5 feet 10 inches (177 centimeters) in the period between World Wars I and II (as against 173 centimeters twenty to fifty years earlier). The main reasons for this difference were that women were overworked, underfed, and often not given an opportunity to reach their full stature. It was common practice, for example, to marry girls when they were ten to fifteen years of age and thus oblige them to become mothers of two, three, or four infants before they were twenty.

The greatest mean stature among males before World War I was attained along the shores of the eastern Adriatic and especially in the Dinaric and Pindus mountain ranges. A mean height of 175–176 centimeters prevailed in Herce-govina, 175 centimeters among the Sphakiots (descendants of the Dorians?) at the western end of the south side of Crete, 174 centimeters in the Bosnian district of Sarajevo and Adriatic district of Makarska, 173–174 centimeters in the north-ern (some but not all of the Gheg) districts of Albania, 173 centimeters in the Adriatic district of the Neretva, 172 centimeters in the Bihać and Banjaluka districts of Bosnia, and 171 centimeters in the Adriatic districts of Sinj and Split, compared to an average height of 170 centimeters in the Adriatic district of Kotor, 169 centimeters in the Adriatic districts of Zadar, Šibenik, and Dubrov-nik, and 166–170 centimeters nearly everywhere else (but 171.5 centimeters among students of the Sofia Military Academy in 1906) north of the Aegean during the late nineteenth and early twentieth century. Deviations from the mean naturally prevailed in all geographic areas.

Prehistoric, early historic, and medieval human skulls discovered in Balkan tombs and cemeteries indicate a greater dolichocephaly or narrow-headedness and a less marked condition of brachycephaly or broad-headedness than in mod-ern times. The conclusion is inescapable nonetheless that subracial diversity has prevailed in the Balkans for many millennia. Evidence from the necropolis (cem-etery) of prehistoric Glasinac, northeast of Sarajevo, indicates that 24 percent of the prehistoric population of that region may have been brachycephalic and 76 percent dolichocephalic and mesocephalic (possessing an intermediate relation-ship between head length and breadth). The cephalic-index distribution in con-temporary Bosnia is almost the reverse of the prehistoric Glasinac situation. The latter is paralleled, however, in Bulgaria, where 23 percent of the population is brachycephalic and 77 percent dolichocephalic and mesocephalic, and in Serbia, where 30 percent is brachycephalic and 70 percent dolichocephalic and mesoce-phalic. In fact, however, western Serbia, western Macedonia, and western Greece are primarily brachycephalic and mesocephalic. Eastern Serbia, eastern Macedonia, and eastern Greece are predominantly dolichocephalic (index of 75 and less) and mesocephalic (index of 75.1–80). The highest level of brachyceph-aly (a mean of 90.8, the highest recorded mean in Europe) occurred in the Tosk Albanian Gjinokastër (Argyrókastron) district, where the mean height was 164 centimeters (perhaps the lowest in the Balkans), compared to a mean height in

Figure 4.1. **Probable Distribution of Mean Male Stature and Mean Cephalic Index in the Balkan Peninsula, ca. 1880–1920**

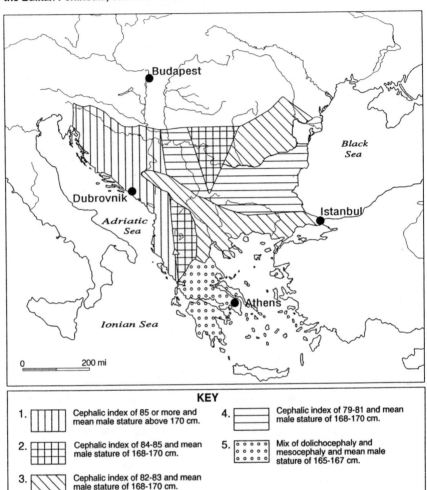

KEY

1. Cephalic index of 85 or more and mean male stature above 170 cm.

2. Cephalic index of 84-85 and mean male stature of 168-170 cm.

3. Cephalic index of 82-83 and mean male stature of 168-170 cm.

4. Cephalic index of 79-81 and mean male stature of 168-170 cm.

5. Mix of dolichocephaly and mesocephaly and mean male stature of 165-167 cm.

Sources: Based on data in Pittard, *Les Peuples des Balkans,* pp. 95, 105, 109–10, 129, 131, 136, 153–54, 160, 185–87, 205, 239–43, 274–77, 281, 562, 572–73 and maps on pp. 564–84; *Les Races et l'histoire,* pp. 313, 321–22, 334–42, 347–48, 352–55, 365–66, 371–73; Pittard, *Race and Culture,* pp. 246–61, 278–98; Coon, *The Races of Europe,* pp.184–85, 199–200, 585, 588–92, 597, 602–5, 608–10, 614–21. The presentation deviates from Pittard's maps in regard to the northeastern regions.

north central Albania of 167 centimeters and in the Albanian regions adjacent to Montenegro of 173–174 centimeters.[32]

Every Balkan nationality is a complex mixture of Caucasian physical types. As shown in Figure 4.1, the territories of brachycephaly and great height virtually coincide (except in the Gjinokastër district), occupying the westernmost (Adriatic, Dinaric, and Pindus) regions. They are succeeded in the southeast interior by a zone of brachycephaly and medium height, which, after an interruption, continues northward across eastern Serbia and western Bulgaria into the Banat and Transylvania. A further zone extending from the central to the southeastern Balkans and resumed in Wallachia and Moldavia is characterized by subbrachycephaly and medium height. A north central and eastern zone of dolichocephaly-mesocephaly and medium stature and a southern zone of dolichocephaly-mesocephaly and short-to-medium stature complete the picture.

This kind of distribution suggests that the western mountain zone was a region of repeated flight from a succession of invaders in which natural selection allowed only highly resistant human physical specimens (by and large, males who were tall and of solid build) to survive and perpetuate a progeny. As for the high incidence of brachycephaly in the western regions, the explanations are both complex and uncertain. It may have a partial genetic basis. It also may be characteristic both of mountain and of urbanized populations, the product perhaps of the selective advantage of a spherical over an oblong brain container as peoples must compete more effectively under either difficult physical or difficult man-made conditions. In no sense confined to the Balkans, the tendency toward an increasing mesocephaly and brachycephaly has also been observed in western and central Europe, in Asia, and among the pre-Columbian populations of the Americas. Some scholars maintain while others deny that marked brachycephaly is the product of cradling, as practiced for example in Albania and Montenegro, where an infant was strapped in a horizontal cradle to its mother's back while the mother walked about and worked, causing a flattening of the occipital region of the infant's head.[33]

Further possible (but not necessary) inferences that one may draw from the map in Figure 4.1 are that there may have been a migration (or migrations) of peoples from a northern area 2 to a southwestern area 2 and from a northeastern area 3 to a southern area 3, and that the dispersion may have been provoked by other invading populations from the north—Slavs, Slavicized Iranians, and/or other groups—that entered respectively into areas 4, 3, and 2.

The current language and dialect distribution more or less corresponds to the data in Figure 4.2.

Semiotics of Religion

The current religious distribution, no less complex than the linguistic distribution, corresponds to the data in Figure 4.3.

Christianity spread into the region between the first and fifteenth centuries. Rivalry between Rome and Constantinople (Byzantium) resulted, however, in the formation of two religious zones, Roman Catholic in the north and west and Orthodox in the south and east, with a mix between the two. Islam was diffused by conquest and conversion between the fourteenth and eighteenth centuries. It spread in particular to areas of late development of an institutionalized Christian

138

Figure 4.2. Language Areas, 1990

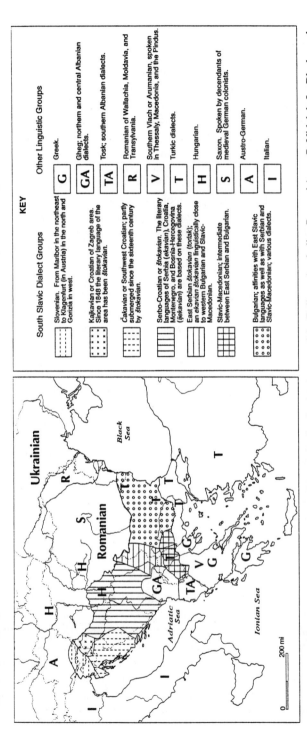

KEY

South Slavic Dialect Groups

Slovenian. From Maribor in the northeast to Klagenfurt (in Austria) in the north and Gorizia in west.

Kajkavian or Croatian of Zagreb area. Since 1848 the literary language of the area has been *štokavian*.

Čakavian or Southwest Croatian; partly submerged since the sixteenth century by *štokavian*.

Serbo-Croatian or *štokavian*. The literary languages of Serbia (*ekavian*), Croatia, Montenegro, and Bosnia-Hercegovina (*ijekavian*) are based on these dialects.

East Serbian *štokavian* (*torlak*); an *ekavian štokavian* linguistically close to western Bulgarian and Slavic-Macedonian.

Slavic-Macedonian; intermediate between East Serbian and Bulgarian.

Bulgarian; affinities with East Slavic languages as well as with Serbian and Slavic-Macedonian; various dialects.

Other Linguistic Groups

G   Greek.

GA   Gheg; northern and central Albanian dialects.

TA   Tosk; southern Albanian dialects.

R   Romanian of Wallachia, Moldavia, and Transylvania.

V   Southern Vlach or Arumanian, spoken in Thessaly, Macedonia, and the Pindus.

T   Turkic dialects.

H   Hungarian.

S   Saxon. Spoken by descendants of medieval German colonists.

A   Austro-German.

I   Italian.

Note: For similar but more detailed versions of linguistic distribution in part of the Balkans (excluding Rumania), see P. Vidal de La Blache and L. Gallois, eds., *Géographie universelle*, VII; *Méditerranée*, Part 2 (in fact, the second volume of tome VII), section on "Pays balkaniques," by Y. Chataigneau and Jules Sion (Paris: Armand Colin, 1934), p. 405; Werner Markert, ed., *Osteuropa-Handbuch: Jugoslawien* (Köln/Graz: Böhlau-Verlag, 1954), map II (between pp. 32 and 33). Our map of language areas is also partly based on Pavle Ivić, *Die serbokroatischen Dialekte: Ihre Struktur und Entwicklung. I. Allgemeines und die štokavische Dialekt-gruppe*, Slavistic Printings and Reprintings, XVIII, C. H. van Schooneveld, ed. ('s-Gravenhage: Mouton, 1958); Oskar Schmieder, *Die alte Welt: Anatolien und die Mittelmeerländer Europas*, 2 vols. (Kiel: Verlag Schmidt & Klaunig, 1969), II, 269; George W. Hoffman, "The Evolution of the Ethnographic Map of Yugoslavia: A Historical Geographic Interpretation," in Francis W. Carter, ed., *An Historical Geography of the Balkans*, (London, New York, San Francisco: Academic Press, [1977]), pp. 436–99.

Figure 4.3. **Religious Distribution, 1990**

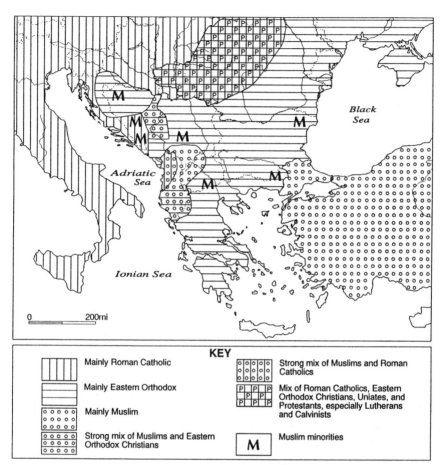

Black
Sea

Adriatic
Sea

Ionian Sea

0   200mi

KEY

Mainly Roman Catholic	Strong mix of Muslims and Roman Catholics
Mainly Eastern Orthodox	Mix of Roman Catholics, Eastern Orthodox Christians, Uniates, and Protestants, especially Lutherans and Calvinists
Mainly Muslim	Muslim minorities
Strong mix of Muslims and Eastern Orthodox Christians	

Source: For similar but more detailed versions of religious distribution in part of the Balkans (excluding Romania), see Vidal de La Blache and Gallois, eds. *Géographie universelle*, Vol. VII; *Méditerranée*, Pt. 2, p. 404; März, *Jugoslawien*, p. 19; Markert, ed., *Osteuropa-Handbuch: Jugoslawien*, map VIII (between pp. 177 and 178).

church; to areas of heterodoxy and heresy, thus to the Mithraic Danube, to Paulician Rhodope Bulgaria, to Bogomil Macedonia, and to Bosnia and Hercegovina. It found adherents among soldiers and among pastoral populations of many mountain regions, as in Albania. It also found root along the major routes of communication, in places along critical provincial frontiers, and in the towns and cities of the Ottoman Empire. As in the rest of Europe, Protestant communities sprang up along the northern Balkan periphery during the sixteenth and seventeenth centuries. Slovenian Protestants were checked in their aspirations to convert all Orthodox, Catholic, and Muslim South Slavs to their creed. However, many Transylvanian nobles espoused Calvinism. The Saxons of the province embraced Lutheranism. Unitarians also made some headway in Transylvania and Hungary.

At the end of the sixteenth century and during the seventeenth and eigthteenth centuries, Uniate Catholicism made some advances, recovering some of the earlier losses to Protestantism and Orthodoxy. Judaic communities were already present in Hellenistic Greece and in some of the towns of Byzantium. Hungarian, Iberian, and Italian Jews emigrated to Ottoman ports and to towns of political or commercial importance toward the end of the fifteenth and during the sixteenth century. Ukrainian (or Polish and Lithuanian) Jews settled in Moldavia, Wallachia, and Hungary between the close of the seventeenth and end of the nineteenth century. Nazi Germany exterminated tens of thousands of Balkan Jews. Most Romanian Jews emigrated to Israel after World War II.

Ethnicity itself was revised through the diffusion to the Balkans of the so-called ecumenical or universal religions, notably, Christianity and Islam. Let us see how this occurred.

Christianity spread during two main periods—between the first century and the end of the fifth century and between the ninth century and mid-fifteenth century. In the eastern or southeastern Balkan cities and neighboring districts—with the exception of Attica, a stronghold of paganism—Christianization may have been complete by the end of the fifth century. In isolated rural districts of that region and in the territories east of Dalmatia and coastal Albania and north of the Jireček line, Christianity was similarly diffused during the first period but mainly on a noninstitutional basis, through the actions of informal missionaries and self-appointed or community-appointed priests, protopopes,[34] and what the Slavs of later centuries called *djeds* (grandfathers, elders). That informal basis was maintained throughout this area until the latter part of the ninth century. In Bosnia, Christianity continued to have a noninstitutional foundation until the end of the thirteenth century. As a result, important elements of Mithraism, shamanism, and other aspects of paganism were incorporated into the religious beliefs and practices of nominally Christian populations.

The second effort at Christianization came after the spread of Islam and the compromise between iconoclasm and its opponents. It was stimulated, however, by the spread of Christianity from west to east, impelling a prince of Moravia to call for Byzantine missionaries. The prince's main motive may have been to combat the growing authority of the Frankish princes of the West.

Byzantium had just failed in its attempt to bring Christianity to the Khazars north of the Caucasus. Two brothers involved in that missionary effort, Constantine and Methodius, sons of an imperial official in Thessaloniki, thereupon undertook the project of translating the Gospels into Slavonic. They thus welcomed the opportunity to undertake a mission to the Slavs of Moravia, where they arrived in A.D. 863.

Having translated the Gospels into Slavonic, probably as spoken in the vicinity of Thessaloniki, by means of a new script called Glagolitic that was unlike either Latin or Greek, the brothers met with some success, only to anger the Franks. Summoned by the pope to Rome, under whose ecclesiastical jurisdiction Moravia fell, they made a plausible defense of their undertaking. Soon after taking monastic vows in Rome, however, Constantine (renamed Cyril) died. Appointed bishop of Syrmium by the pope, Methodius returned to Moravia. A pro-Frankish faction ordered his arrest, however, and banned the use of the Slavonic liturgy. Following his release and death, his fellow missionaries were expelled from Moravia, only to be welcomed by Bulgaria, where they arrived in 886 with translations of religious texts into Slavonic in the Glagolitic script.

There was already a Greek bishop in the Bulgar capital of Pliska. Khan Boris, however, wanted to establish an autonomous Bulgarian patriarchate in order to form a clergy that would be both grateful to him and serve as a bureaucracy, thus reducing his need to rely on a rebellious Bulgar nobility. Failing to obtain satisfaction from the ecumenical patriarch of Constantinople, he requested missionaries from both Rome and the Franks. The pope appointed a bishop to assume the direction of a Bulgarian church but refused to comply with the Bulgarian request for an archbishop.

These events of the 860s and 870s coincided with a doctrinal dispute over whether the Spirit descended from God alone or from both God and the Son (Filioque), as was maintained by Rome,[35] with a dispute over ecclesiastical practices, and with a power struggle between the papacy and the patriarchate of Constantinople. At a church council held in Constantinople, the eastern bishops refused to sanction the pope's condemnation of the deposed patriarch Photius. The patriarchate of Constantinople subsequently placed Bulgaria under the nominal ecclesiastical jurisdiction of Constantinople. In practice, it allowed considerable autonomy to churchmen.

The welcome extended by the Bulgarian ruler to the fellow missionaries of Methodius was designed to strengthen that autonomy by the formation of a Slavic priesthood. It also aimed to reaffirm Christianity in Macedonia, where it had lapsed in most regions upon the advent of the Slavs. St. Clement in particular established a religious school at Ohrid, where Boris's successor, Tsar Symeon, appointed him bishop, the first bishop of the Slavic rite. Modeled upon the Greek, the writing that Clement adopted and diffused is known as Cyrillic. In modified form, it is still the writing of the eastern Slavs and nominally Orthodox southern Slavs. The more difficult Glagolitic script, on the other hand, had a more restricted spatial and temporal success.

Before Symeon became tsar, his brother and the great nobles of Bulgaria had attempted to uproot Christianity. They had failed. On the other hand, paganism, magical rites, and other practices at variance with the teachings of the church continued to flourish. A distinction may be made between popular beliefs and practices and formal heresy. The two converged, however, through the action of preachers who were never recognized by the ecclesiastical hierarchy. These preachers presumably had conceptual roots in the pre-episcopal Christian religious tradition of the non-Greek Romance population of the Balkans, altered by and combined with Mithraism and Thracian, Pelasgian, Daco-Mysian, Gothic, Cumanian, and Slavic magical and religious practices.

Formal heresy was represented by the Messalians, by Syrian and Armenian Monophysites, by the Paulicians and adoptionists, and by dualists. Opposed to marriage and playing down the importance of rite, the Messalians stressed the importance of prayer. Comprising Armenians who had been transferred by Byzantium from Asia Minor to the vicinity of Philippopolis so they could be watched and used in defense of the empire's western frontier, the Paulicians may have been dualists. It is more likely, however, that they were adoptionists, believing that Christ had achieved divinity only after baptism. Dualists distinguished between the principle of evil, darkness, and matter, on the one hand, and goodness, light, and spirit, on the other. Rejecting the Old Testament God, creator of matter, and associating material objects and acts—crosses, ikons, churches, and sex—with evil, they embraced the Son as the symbol of Spirit.

All these heresies were centered in and around the cities and ports of Byzantium and onetime Byzantium. Medieval sources generally associate Balkan dualism, by which may have been meant almost any heterodoxy or heresy, mainly with two territories—Bulgaria and eastern Thrace. In its more restricted sense, dualism spread from Byzantium to Italy, Provence, and Languedoc (as the Albigensian, Patarene, or Cathari heresy).

Who the Bogomils were, on the other hand, is yet more controversial. The movement may have obtained its name from a certain tenth-century *pop* (father) Bogomil. But *pop* Bogomil may have been one of many preachers "dear to God" *(Bogu mili)*, whose preaching centered in Macedonia.[36] Later evidence suggests that one of the centers of "Bogomilism" was arid Mount Babuna southwest of Prilep (more famous for its association in poetry and legend with Kraljević Marko), whence the identification of the movement in mid-fourteenth-century Serbia as the "Babuna word."[37]

There may have been, indeed, a multiplicity of popular *babuna* discourses centered in particular in mountain retreats and isolated districts, where the talk or discourse of episcopal and abbatial authority was not or could not be heard; where it was misunderstood; where Christian beliefs and practices commingled with shamanism *(vlhovstvo)*; where some of the preachers may have been individuals disinherited of the first function (prayer, sacrifice, and divination) by the new priesthood;[38] and/or where *Bog* (God) just as well could have been Veles the protector of livestock or the Slavic pagan all-God or giver God, *Dabog*.

In 1185, for example, Emperor Isaac II Angelus levied a new tax on the flocks of the Bulgarians, Vlachs, and Cumanians who usually wintered in the Byzantine duchy of Paristrion (situated between the Danube and the Black Sea in the vicinity of Anchialos). Despite vigorous protests, the emperor refused to withdraw the tax. The humiliated emissaries of the pastoral populations, the brothers Peter and Ivan Asen, thereupon built a chapel at Tŭrnovo dedicated to St. Demetrius, the patron saint of Thessaloniki. According to Nicetas Choniates, they invited to the inauguration "many men and women possessed of demons." In frenzied dance, eyes squinting and bloodshot, the celebrants flagellated themselves with iron rods, concluding the ceremony with the prophecy that St. Demetrius would lead the Bulgarians (farmers) and Vlachs (herdsmen) in a movement of liberation from foreign (Byzantine) domination. Prior to the inauguration, Slavic refugees from Macedonia had propagated the belief in the healing powers of St. Demetrius and voiced his millennialist resolve to abandon the Greeks in order to settle among the Slavs as their horseman savior and liberator. St. Demetrius was thus given the attributes of the sun god and cavalier hero, Mithras.[39]

Can there be any doubt that the flagellant dancers were shamans—shamans in a Christian chapel? More than six hundred years later, one still found instances in the Balkans of shamanistic practices. At the Bektashi *tekke* (Muslim monastery) of the resort of Alicouli, for example, the well-to-do Muslim summer visitors from the provincial Thessalian town of Larissa had occasion to see the dervishes strike their breasts with slabs of stone as they rhythmically danced about and finally bit into a red-hot iron.[40]

Self-castigation by means of iron rods in the Vlach-Bulgarian-Cumanian case and of slabs of stone and a red-hot iron in the Bektashi case no doubt served, like the nineteenth-century ceremonial dances of Yakut shamans in a costume with sleeves of elongated strips of narrow metal, as a rite of purification designed to drive away evil spirits.[41] In the Bulgarian case, the conjunction of shamanism and Christian millennialism provided the rebels with a ritually sanctified ideology that they used to create, between 1185 and 1188, a new Bulgarian state.[42]

As for the conflict between Rome and Byzantine Orthodoxy, it had several other repercussions. In Moravia, the Glagolitic script was scrapped. In the mid-eleventh century, a synod of high churchmen of the Adriatic towns condemned the wearing of beards by priests (as practiced by the Orthodox) and declared heretical the Slavonic Glagolitic liturgy, which had continued to be employed in Istria and parts of northern Dalmatia. In 1074, a Latin church council in Split confirmed the foregoing acts,[43] symbolizing the ascendancy of the Cluniac reform movement, source of inspiration of the crusades and of the hardening of the developing schism between Rome and Constantinople.

The fascination of Venice, of other Italian cities, of the Normans, and of French and German knights with the wealth of Constantinople, Thessaloniki, the Holy Land, Islam, and the Aegean and Black Sea ports intensified the conflict between the Christian East and West, culminating in the so-called Fourth Crusade. In 1202, Venice persuaded an army of crusaders to seize the port city of Zara (Zadar), then under the authority of the king of Hungary, and transfer it to

Venice in payment for the cost of transportation by ship to the Holy Land. Conspiring further with a claimant to the Byzantine throne, Venice dangled before the crusaders the promise of more loot. It thus persuaded them to postpone their armed pilgrimage to the Holy Land and set sail instead for Constantinople to drive out the reigning emperor. When the division of the spoils fell short of the crusaders' expectations, they seized the loot they coveted, massacred the local population, appointed a Latin emperor of their own, and divided up the Byzantine territories among the crusade's participants. In theory, one-fourth of Constantinople and three-eighths of the former empire—in fact, almost all the important ports, along with a trade monopoly in every port—fell to Venice. One-fourth of Constantinople and the new "empire" were ceded to the Latin emperor. The remaining lands were allocated as fiefs to the more powerful crusaders.

The Latin Empire also declared the union of the eastern church with Rome. In 1208, however, representatives of the Orthodox clergy moved the site of the ecumenical patriarchate from Constantinople to Nicaea (today, Iznik). A dispute then ensued between the Greek "empire" at Nicaea and the rival archbishopric of Ohrid, chief ecclesiastical support of the despotate of Epirus.

Prior to the misnamed Fourth Crusade, the youngest son of the Grand Župan of Rascia (the medieval name of the largest of the Serbian lands) had become a monk, assuming the name of Sava and departing for the Orthodox monastic complex of Mount Athos. Obtaining authorization from the emperor of Byzantium to repair and renovate the abandoned monastery of Khilandari (known to the Serbs as Hilandar), Sava transformed it into a center of learning for the Serbs. A few years after the Fourth Crusade, to transport the body of his dead father (who, after abdicating to become a monk, had also retired to Mount Athos) to his native land, but also to express his displeasure (as that of most of the Athonite monks) at the forced union with the Latin church, he returned to his country, where he became abbot of Studenica. In 1217, perhaps to express his displeasure at his brother's acceptance of the title of king from a papal envoy, he returned to Hilandar. In 1219, upon a visit to the ecumenical patriarch at Nicaea to solicit the creation of a Serbian archbishopric, he himself was named archbishop of an autocephalous Serbian church. From the point of view of Nicaea, an autocephalous Serbian church served the purpose of weakening the authority of the ambitious archbishopric of Ohrid.

In 1235, Bulgaria similarly recognized the ecumenical patriarch of Nicaea, who in turn raised the status of the bishop of Tŭrnovo to that of patriarch. In this manner, Bulgaria, too, acquired an autocephalous Orthodox church.[44]

At this conjuncture, Hungary responded to a papal appeal for a crusade against the "heretics" of Bosnia, who may have grown in number as they were driven out of Rascia (by the Orthodox) and Dalmatia (by the Roman Catholics). Often identified as dualists and Bogomils, the "heretics" of Bosnia may have been little other than wandering monks and djeds with a poor understanding of theology and without the control of an ecclesiastical hierarchy. Their followers probably had an even poorer understanding of Christian doctrine, embracing beliefs that were essentially pagan.

Established in Bosnia toward the middle of the thirteenth century was what was known as the Bosnian church, headed by a *djed* and a council of twelve and served by monk missionaries known as *krstjani (krščani)* or "adherents of the cross." A pagan no less than a Christian symbol, the cross was a symbolic tree of life. As a "Greek cross" in form, with four equal arms or spokes, sometimes constituted as a wheel, it represented the sun, a Mithraic symbol. It was so shown in the tattoo patterns of Bosnian Catholics and Muslims as late as the twentieth century.[45] Some of the *krstjani* resided in small monasteries *(hiže)*, others were wanderers *(gosti)*. Like the Orthodox, the Bosnian church employed the Slavic liturgy. How its "theology" differed from that of either the Latin or Orthodox church is difficult to ascertain. Its practices, however, were acceptable to neither. Its lack of a strong territorial organization may have served the interests of the great nobility of Bosnia and Hlm (Hum, the later Hercegovina).

Finally, in the 1340s, a Franciscan mission was established in Bosnia. Roman Catholicism won over a substantial number of Bosnians, however, only after 1430. The weak attachment of most Bosnians to any religious doctrine, along with the privileges accompanying conversion to Islam, may have persuaded many Bosnian men (the women often retained their old faith, although the faith of the father was passed on to the children), toward the end of the fifteenth and early decades of the sixteenth century, to embrace the *tekke* or warrior-missionary Islam of the dervish "men's societies" of the conquering Ottoman Turks. The major exceptions to this rule were eastern Hercegovina, where Orthodoxy prevailed, and the western districts of Bosnia and Hercegovina, where Catholicism made headway. Conversion to Islam thus tended to occur in central Bosnia, where the authority of the Bosnian church had prevailed, and in frontier districts that had been a bone of contention between the Latin church and Serbian Orthodoxy or between Serbian Orthodoxy and the Bosnian church.[46]

Conversion to Islam among the Orthodox of the Balkans, on the other hand, was rare, partly because Orthodoxy was more highly institutionalized than the Bosnian church but also because, by embracing hesychasm, it had become almost a "people's church."[47] Hesychasm simultaneously rejected the neo-Platonic rationalism of the Latin church and the dualist rejection of the things of this world, emphasizing instead the possibility of improving life in this world.

Communicated to the Greek and Slavic monks of Mount Athos around 1300 by Gregory Sinaita of Mount Sinai and further propagated by Gregory Palamas (ca. 1296–1356), hesychasm held that everyone who is mystically enlightened may capture the rays of the Divine Light. God is accessible not through pure reason but through the edification of the heart. He is to be reached by expelling all other thoughts, which may be achieved by concentrating on and repeating in prayer the name of Jesus.[48]

Like Sufi Islam and Indian asceticism, hesychasm made use of breathing techniques to achieve perfect tranquillity. Repeating the divine name without cease, its adherents attained what in Islam was known as the *dhikr* of the heart by the practice of the *dhikr* of the tongue.[49]

In 1351, an Orthodox ecclesiastical synod recognized the orthodoxy of Gregory Palamas. A few years later Palamas was proclaimed a saint, vindicating the principle that some degree of divine energy is present everywhere and in everything and everyone. The Orthodox could therefore carry on disputations with Islam instead of submitting to, or embracing, the ghazis, *akhis* (members of mystic fraternities and craft organizations), and dervishes, vanguard of the Ottoman conquests of the fourteenth and fifteenth centuries, who welcomed both pantheism and the idea of the ubiquity of God and eternity of divine energies. Nominally Orthodox peasants who sometimes turned against their secular lords no longer had an equally compelling reason to turn against the church.

In Bosnia, on the other hand, 54 percent of the population was Muslim by 1530.[50] By the end of the sixteenth or beginning of the seventeenth century, three-quarters of the population was nominally Muslim. But by 1655 the proportion fell to two-thirds. By 1800, it did not exceed 50 percent. By the mid-nineteenth century, it may have been no more than 40 percent.

Two facts explain the change—a continuing immigration into the province of Orthodox Serbs and a continuing emigration of Roman Catholics, and a possible declining fertility among the Muslims as the result of the spread of venereal disease. In 1808, the population of Bosnia and Hercegovina (including the sanjak of Novi Pazar and the district of Zvornik) numbered 1.25 million to 1.3 million, divided along religious lines as follows: 600,000 Muslims, or 46–48 percent of the population; 500,000 Orthodox, or 39–40 percent of the population; and 120,000 Catholics, or 9.6 percent of the population. In 1655, on the other hand, Roman Catholics may have constituted 17 percent of the population, and they may have been more numerous in the sixteenth century.[51] The decline in the proportion of Roman Catholics between 1655 and 1808 was the result of conversion to Islam and of a continuing westward and northward emigration into Venetian and Habsburg territories.

The Orthodox population of Bosnia and Hercegovina in the sixteenth century may not have exceeded 10 percent. Two centuries later, the Orthodox were proportionately four times as strong. The Roman Catholic element expanded rapidly after the Austro-Hungarian occupation of the province in 1878, mainly by immigration from the west and north.

The religious experience of the Balkans confirms the hypothesis that mountain areas constitute zones of separatism, dividing one mountain group from another and pastoral from farming cultures. As the case of Bosnia and Hercegovina so poignantly shows, mountain areas appear both as zones of religious particularism—interpreted by neighboring farming and city cultures as heresy—and as zones of fragile alignment with a succession of agricultural and/or city cultures. As the case of the mountain regions of Albania and even of parts of

Rhodope Bulgaria may illustrate, on the other hand, massive nominal conversions to Islam did not have to occur immediately upon the Ottoman conquest. They were postponed in many cases to another turbulent era, 1650–1830.[52]

Macrosociety: Tripartition and Estates States

In social and territorial organization no less than in mode of thought, Indo-European societies in particular, the European cultures in general, and even other, especially neighboring, peoples of the world have embraced the triad. The triad existed in the Neolithic symbolism of the bird and snake goddess (three holes or notches in a vase or a vertical line dividing a V sign).[53] The triadic orientation is present in the human conception of mother, father, and child as a long-term or lasting relationship. It is evident in the presence in the religious beliefs of ancient Egypt and Babylonia, and of the Indo-European peoples, of triads of gods;[54] in the Christian idea of the Trinity; in the contribution of the equilateral triangle to the development of ancient Greek philosophy;[55] in the medieval western European notion of *sacerdotum* as the privilege of Rome, *studium* as the privilege of France, and *imperium* as the duty of Germany;[56] in Plato's distinction between three human traits (a rational, reflective, integrative disposition; an irrational or appetitive disposition; and a pugnacious disposition), variably present in individuals;[57] in Giambattista Vico's conception of three ages (age of the gods, age of heroes, age of the people); in G.W.F. Hegel's conception of the dialectic (thesis, antithesis, synthesis); in the temporal categories of historians (ancient, medieval, modern); in Auguste Comte's three stages of history (theological, metaphysical, and positivist); in Gabriel Tarde's three processes of cultural evolution (invention, imitation, and opposition); in V.I. Lenin's identification of the three components of Marxism as German philosophy, English political economy, and French socialism; in the Bauhaus conception of an aesthetic of the "triadic ballet" (the achievement of a dynamic equilibrium by the resolution of the conflict between monism or egoism and dualism); in Pitirim Sorokin's three-phased rhythm of cultural predilection (ideational, idealistic, and sensate); and in Fernand Braudel's three categories of historical mobility and stability (events, conjunctures, and structures).[58]

In Sanskrit, the word for "order" or "estate" is *varna*, meaning "color."[59] It may be worth noting, therefore, that many peoples have used color to denote simultaneously a particular segment of associated populations, its location or position in reference to the other associated peoples, its specialization in one of three primary functions (propitiation, war, and production), and/or its appropriate position as part of an army of related or associated armed peoples in movement with their families and baggage trains (*corios*, pl., *corii*, in Celtic; *Herr* in German).[60]

The chief colors of reference were white, red, and black. The following peoples, for example, were divided into at least two groups, white and black:

Sarmatians, Bulgars, Khazars, Tatars, Ugri, and Cumanians. To the Romanians themselves or to their neighbors, all or parts of Transylvania, Muntenia, and Wallachia were known as White Valachia, while all or parts of Moldavia (also called Bogdania) and Wallachia were known as Black Valachia. Among the Albanians, central Albania or the Mirditë country was known as the country of the "black" people, perhaps because of the black capes worn by adult males. Farther north, the Ghegs called themselves the people of the "red banner."[61] Murkier is the precise connection between the red vests of the Muslim Ghegs (sometimes sporting the favorite Muslim green) and the black vests of the Roman Catholic Ghegs.[62]

Among Romanians and Albanians, the colors may have lost their directional significance. In the case of the "Russian lands," on the other hand, the terms white, red, and black, when their use is first recorded, may have meant, respectively, east, south, and north. "White Russia" was the Russia of the upper Dnieper, "Red Russia" was the Russia of Brest-Litovsk and Halicz or Galicia, while "Black Russia" was the Russia athwart the upper Neman basin north of the Pripet marshes, corresponding to what today is "White Russia" or Belarus.[63] Similarly, among the ancient Greeks, the three seas were the Aegean or White Sea (east), the ἐρυθρά Θάλασσα or Red Sea (south), and the Πόντος ἄξεινος (from Iranian axšaena, meaning "dark") or Black Sea.[64]

Colors sometimes signified a function. White, for example, was associated with a population whose primary function was sacrifice and prayer, red with the function of war, and black (or green) with production, the soil, and reproduction. Thus in ancient Rome, the three original circus factions—albati, russati, and uirides—identified respectively the "whites" or priestly people, the "reds" or warrior people, and the "greens" or freemen, that is, the common people with civic rights.[65] In the "Russian lands," the term chern (chernye liudi) identified the "black people," members of the third function, charged with production and the payment of taxes or tributes.[66]

Colors among the populations that we know today as South Slavs may also have had a functional significance. Their directional or locational significance, however, is more certain.

During or before the second century B.C., the Slovenes may have inhabited an area north of the Black Sea. The Croats may have occupied a region along the lower Don, and the Serbs an area yet farther east along the lower Volga. Soon afterward, they presumably migrated to the Carpathians, perhaps in a succession of moves. All three groups may or may not have been Slavic speaking before that migration. Having lived in close proximity with, and probably under the rule of, Sarmatians in the first area of settlement with which one may identify them, they lived in close proximity with Goths as well as Sarmatians in their next area of settlement.

A White Croatia was thus formed along the upper reaches of the San and Dniester rivers and a Black Croatia to the northwest, centering on the upper reaches of the Oder. Theoretically, a Red Croatia should have existed to the south of the other two Croatias. While there is no written reference to such a region, soon after the migration of the Slavs south of the Carpathians and Pannonia during the sixth and seventh centuries, both a Red and White Croatia are identified in the new areas of settlement.

The new White Croatia—Croatia Alba—stretched from Vinodol in the north to Delminium (Duvno) in the south, perhaps even to the Neretva River. South of this White Croatia lay Croatia Rubea, a narrow strip of territory extending to the Bay of Kotor, in the southern districts of which Serbian tribes also settled. There is no specific mention of a Black Croatia in the new areas of settlement. Logically, however, it comprised Pannonian Croatia.

One group of Serbs (known today as Lusatian Sorbs) occupied an area along the Elbe (Laba) or between the Elbe and the Oder (Odra) to the northwest of the earliest known Black Croatia. To the south of Black Croatia lived a Slavic population known as Moravians. We know furthermore that the name of Emperor Constantine VII Porphyrogenitus for the Serbs of the Balkan peninsula was "White Serbs," ἄσπροι Σέρβοι. Their color designation suggests that, in their previous area of longtime settlement, they may have occupied a territory to the east of the other (hypothetical Black and Red) Serbs. Pursuing this logic, one may conjecture that their previous area of settlement lay somewhere south of the habitat of the Lusatian Sorbs, west of old Black Croatia, and west or south of the Moravians.

All three (if, in fact, there were three) Croat and especially Serb "color" units may not have participated in the migratory movements into the Balkans. As for the movement of individual Slavic tribes, it is virtually certain that many of them split into at least two groups. One group of Moravians, who may or may not have been Serbs, remained more or less in place. Another group settled south of the Danube along the right bank of the middle reaches of the Morava. One group of Obodriti migrated northward to the right bank of the Elbe at the Baltic. Another group settled west of the Moravians in what today is Serbia. One group of Slovenes moved into the Drava valley. Another group moved northward, settling ultimately in the vicinity of Novgorod. One group of Berziti moved northward to Brest Litovsk, while another group, known today as the Brsjaci, entered western Macedonia. One group of Draguviti or Dregovichi moved northward from Dacia into the Pripet marshes. Another group moved southward to the middle Vardar. One group of Smoleni (Smiljani) ultimately settled in the vicnity of Smolensk. Another group turned southward to settle along the east bank of the lower Struma (Strymon). One group of Severians moved northward to settle along the left bank of the middle Dnieper. Another group moved southward into the Deli Orman district of northeastern Bulgaria (see Figure 4.4).[67]

Many questions remain regarding Serbs and Croats alike. Did the Serbs move south of the Danube around the middle of the sixth century (or even earlier)

Figure 4.4. **The Bifurcated Slavic Migrations, Sixth to Ninth Century**

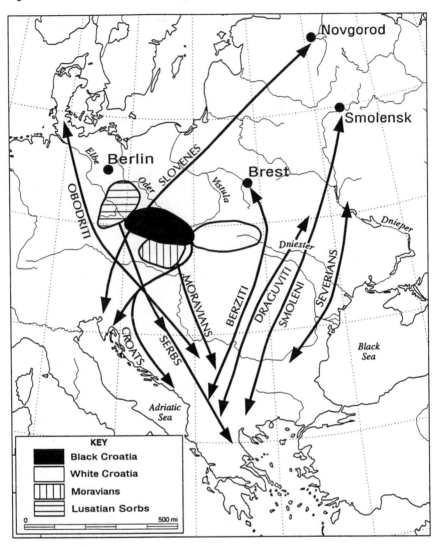

together with the Moravians and the Obodriti? Is the term "Moravian" a tribal name or just a geographic name applied to the Serbs who emigrated from the Morava valley northwest of Pannonia to settle in the Balkans along the right-bank Danube tributary to which they gave the name of the river that previously had been their home? Or did the Serbs separate into small groups, each settling in a different place, some along the Morava and its tributaries and others elsewhere? Toponymic evidence suggests that some of them settled as far south as

Epirus and Thessaly and as far east as eastern Thrace. Other toponymic evidence suggests that some groups of Croats similarly settled in eastern Thrace, while others made their homes in Attica, Argolis, and even Crete. In the 620s, according to the much-disputed statements of Constantine Porphyrogenitus, Emperor Heraclitus persuaded some of the Serb inhabitants of the district of Servia (renamed Serfidje under the Ottoman Turks) to move north (presumably to the tributaries of the Morava) to wage war against the Avars.

In a more general framework, the tripartite ideology of the Indo-European peoples entailed a division of society into three orders, estates, or *bioi:* makers of sacrifices and/or specialists in production for the general good; protectors; and producers for the good of individual communities and families. In Aryan India, the three orders were respectively the *brâhmana, kshatriya,* and *vaiçya.* In Rome, they were the *flamines, milites,* and *quirites,* or the three tribes of the Ramnes (cult experts), Luceres (warriors), and Titienses (herdsmen).[68] In pre-seventh-century ancient Greece, they may have comprised the demiurges (workers for the public good, especially persons whose crafts were associated with fire—potters and smiths, for example—and the production of metal goods symbolic of spiritual and military power); the aristocrats *(eupatridai, aristoi)* and horse breeders; and the rural smallholders who owned a plot of land *(kleros)* and had the right to be represented in a civic assembly.[69] Among the pagan Scandinavians, the three functions were that of *godi* (demiurge), that of *jarl* (earl), and that of *karl* (free farmer).

By the seventh century B.C., the status of the Greek demiurges declined as they included an increasing number of social categories (product of a division of labor) and also grew in number.[70] Moreover, as a result of the conquest of other peoples and of internal social differentiation, a fourth way of life was added to the previous three, that of dependents or inferior folk: the *çûdra,* or human cattle of the Indian system, the clients of Rome, the *penestai* of Thessaly, the helots of Sparta, and the thralls of Scandinavia. The earlier ternary divisions may in turn have been revisions of the tripartition common in hunting societies—adult male hunters, food-gathering and child-nurturing women, and shamans and supervisory elders.[71]

The Balkan Slavs also distinguished among three functions and possessed at first three corresponding orders. However, they, too, developed a system of four estates. In late medieval Serbia, the four estates comprised the priest's cap *(popova kapa),* the great protectors *(vlastele,* cognate of Irish *flaith)* and professional soldiery *(voin),* the free farmers *(sebri),* and the serfs or persons of low birth. The word *sebri* (sing., *sebar),* deriving from the Common Slavic **sem-b,* gave rise in Russia to the word for "family." It exists in Greek, Albanian, and Magyar, respectively, as σέμπρος, *sember,* and *cimbora.*[72]

The *sebri* were the families of a village community with local cultivation rights within a larger territorial/personal complex of clan land known as a *župa.* They constituted the population with rights of use to the village commons known as the *văs*, from which were derived the words *vsak* and *ysi*.[73] As probable cognates of Sanskrit *vaiçya*, these words—translated today as "everyone" and "all"—literally meant "member" and "members with a right to the use of the commons."

Persons of low birth were variously known as *meropsi*, *pareques*, *villeins (villani* or *posadnici)*, or *kmeti*. At the limits of a *župa* lay a territory known as *krajište*, a borderland to which nonagricultural or pastoral populations presumably had access. Beyond a complex of several *župe*, as between the Neretva and Cetina rivers, sometimes lay a borderland known as *krajina*, the reserve of *vlah* populations or breeders of livestock.[74]

Distinctions between Serb farmers (known until the end of the fourteenth century as *sebri)* and Vlachs may have begun to break down before the fourteenth century. After the mid-fourteenth century, as Slav farmers moved from the lowlands to the uplands, the process of mingling was accelerated. Distinctions persisted, however, until the close of the sixteenth century. After having served during the fourteenth and fifteenth centuries as the protectors of caravans, some of the the Vlachs entered the service of the Ottoman Turks as *voynuks* or *martolosi* (in Greek areas, *armatoloi)*—that is, as the Christian rural police of the main Balkan routes or as mercenary defenders of the western Ottoman frontiers. Registered as herdsmen, other Vlachs paid a low tax rate per household. This privilege moved many of them to form large or extended households. Slavs were drawn to the Vlach way of life by the advantages it then offered.

As privileges were restricted toward the end of the sixteenth century, some Vlachs converted to Islam.[75] Most of them, however, retained their nominal Christian faith. In either case, they were Slavicized as the Slavs were pastoralized. Other Vlachs, Slavicized Vlachs, and Serbs fled to Dalmatia or the Croatian Military Frontier, often to exercise similar occupations. In areas of Greek settlement, a like process was evident, with Hellenization occurring at a later time—for the most part during the eighteenth and nineteenth centuries.[76]

In neighboring Dalmatia, five distinct status groups emerged: clergy (successors to the pre-Christian Roman *flamines)*, patricians *(sjor* or *vlastela)*, citizens or bourgeois, plebs *(puk)*, and *coloni* or *contadini*. The last status group was made up mainly of peasants contractually bound to render a fixed portion of their produce to their lords in return for military and other forms of protection.[77]

As among the Serbs, there were in the Greek portions of the peninsula four basic ways of life during the later Middle Ages. The medieval history of Wallachia and Moldavia is more obscure. It is virtually certain, however, that they at first recognized three estates: clergy, boyars, and free communal small landholders known as *moşneni* or *răzăşi*. A fourth status of Wallacho-Moldavian client peasants or villeins *(vecini* or *rumâni)* has been documented only since the fifteenth century.[78]

Late medieval and postmedieval Balkan society was basically divided into four orders. However, it was also more complex. In the polyethnic fourteenth-century state of Emperor Stephen Dušan, for example, there were, in addition to the four functional divisions, four specially recognized ethnic orders: Vlachs, Albanians, Saxons, and Latins. A fifth ethnic order of Greeks or Romans (the designation applied to subjects of the Byzantine Empire) ultimately might have emerged if Serbian imperial enterprise had been less ephemeral. There was a tendency in the medieval Serbian lands to set up the kind of estates system that evolved in Transylvania, where society continued to be divided into three privileged ethnic estates—Magyars, Saxons, and Szeklers (the last group occupying the valleys of the Olt and Mureş or Maros rivers)—until 1863, despite an attempt during the second half of the eighteenth century to reform, perhaps even abolish, the system.

Contrary to common belief, however, the estates society was not an immobile social system. Efforts were exerted in the Serbian lands to prevent intermarriage between Vlachs and *sebri*. These efforts had to be made, however, because intermingling between the two groups probably did occur. The legal obstacle may have slowed down the process, but there is no reason to suppose that it stopped intermingling altogether. While the principle of kinship was a deterrent to social mobility, another principle of the estates society—adoption or initiation—facilitated some degree of movement from one estate into another.

Certain groups without a direct connection to any of the functional or ethnic estates also emerged. Among these was the *svobodnik*, a former serf or slave who obtained personal freedom but was not admitted into the estate of *sebri* because he lacked a hereditary right of usufruct to a plot of land. Another was the *sokalnik*, a very numerous social category the exact duties of which scholars dispute. *Sokalniks* may have been temple or state butchers, cooks, bakers, or masons (builders of hearths); judicial officers like the medieval English sokemen; or lower officials charged with the collection of the tithe in grains and enjoying judicial powers in matters relating to their function. Such "public workers" were recruited in part from among the younger sons of Orthodox priests.[79] In addition, there was a group of underground demiurges—public workers expelled from the estate of official propitiators after the conversion of the South Slavs to Orthodox Christianity: magicians, poisoners, heretics, and shamans or practitioners of *vlhovstvo*.

The term *vlh (volh, vlŭh)* may be related to Scandinavian *volva* and Russian *volkhva*. It may have been communicated to the Vlachs and Slavs by the Goths, whose own name gave rise to one of the other names in Serbian and Croatian for a prophet or shaman: *gatar*. It may even have been associated with Vlach (Vlah) ethnicity, perhaps because shamanistic ritual healing dances were so common among the Vlachs, vestigially even in the early decades of the twentieth century, and because, in the Middle Ages, there were few Christian priests in the Vlach *katuns* or pastoral cantons.[80]

The first three estates—propitiation, protection, and production—initially enjoyed almost equal esteem. During the thirteenth and especially fourteenth and fifteenth centuries, however, the third estate of free smallholders underwent considerable social differentiation. Some members improved their condition. Others lost their land or freedom. The order itself was pushed into a position of inferiority.

In declining Byzantium, the transfer of commercial franchises to Venice and Genoa deprived the state of revenues with which to remunerate its bureaucracy. To compensate its officials the government had to raise taxes. Many members of the free peasantry were thus impoverished. In dire need of loans and protection against extortionist tax collectors and pitiless mercenaries, many free farmers submitted to the authority of powerful lords who promised to satisfy their needs. Formerly free peasants bound themselves and their descendants to provide their superiors each year with a designated quantity of labor, as well as a portion of their crop. In turn, many lords succeeded in transforming their *pronoia* or conditional properties into hereditary lands.

A similar evolution toward the formation of great holdings and the transformation of benefices into hereditary properties occurred in the Slavic areas. Here, however, one other reason explained the new trend, notably, population growth —at least until the mid-fourteenth century. As the rural population grew, the size of the plots of land available to the peasantry diminished. As in Byzantium, powerful lords took advantage of their power to hasten the process.

The expansion of mining and growth of towns in the Slavic areas led to the rise of native artisans and merchants, side by side with the artisans and great merchants of foreign extraction—Saxons, Latini (mostly Ragusans), and Greeks. The new "middle elements" were still weak, however, and were quickly deprived of the one institution that might have become an instrument of their eventual ascendancy—an assembly of the *sebri* or third estate.

The Law Code of Stephen Dušan and the Serbian ecclesiastical and noble estates encouraged the rise and growth of market places, made corvée obligations uniform throughout the realm, subjected the emperor himself to the provisions of the law, and authorized assemblies of the priest's cap and *vlastele* (medieval form of the plural). But it forbade an assembly of *sebri* (freemen), and particularly their assembly as an estate, under threat to organizers and participants of the loss of both ears (hence, of all reason) and of the branding of the cheeks (thus, of the permanent tarnishing of the face).[81]

Instituted in 1349 by an assembly of the first two estates, the provisions of the Law Code regarding the *sebri* were a regional reflection of a general European seigniorial reaction that culminated in the Hundred Years' War. The war to which we allude was not simply the war between France and England but the complex strife of Catholic against Catholic, Christian against Muslim, Orthodox against Catholic, Hussite against Imperial and Catholic, Taborite against Utraquist, Poland and Lithuania against the Teutonic Order, Ottoman against the kingdom of Hungary and the fragments of the empires of Byzantium and of Stephen Dušan, Muscovite against Tatar and Novgorodian, Venice and Milan against

Genoa, Tamerlane against Bayezid, Denmark against the Hanse, one feudal lord against another, mercenary against peasant, peasant against lord.

In the Balkans, a crucial aspect of this conflict was the attempt on the part of lords, patricians, or aristocrats to transform themselves into a largely closed estate, ally with powerful foreign merchants, seize the land and revenues of the peasantry, and curb the aspirations of native "middle elements," regardless of whether these were a potentially rising group, as in the Slavic portions of the Balkans, or a seemingly declining group, as in the Greek areas. In 1341 and 1342, the middle elements of Adrianople and Salonika (Thessaloniki) and the peasantry of Didymotichon took up arms against the aristocrats and absentee landlords. In Salonika, a faction known as the Zealots seized power between 1342 and 1349 and proceeded to confiscate the properties of magnates, churches, and monasteries. Transferring a portion to the poor, it also made use of the newly available funds to repair the walls of the city and create a people's army. It even promised to open careers to talent and wealth.

Partly as a result of a split between the middle elements and the poor and of divergences among the middle elements themselves, the aristocrats soon prevailed again. Similar conflicts in the Adriatic towns of Cattaro (Kotor) and Antivari (Bar) also culminated in victory for the patricians or nobility. That triumph was sealed by the transformation of the Antivari general assembly of elders into a grand council and of the general assembly of Cattaro into a senate.[82]

Explanations abound for the relative ease with which the Ottoman Turks spread across the Balkans during the second half of the fourteenth and in the fifteenth century. The foregoing transformation of Balkan society into a field of strain, stress, and strife was one important factor in their initial expansion (as well as in their later conquest of Hungary). But however welcome Ottoman rule may have been at first to an unknown number of peasants and middle elements, it did not lead to an abolition of status differences. Instead, the already modified system of estates was altered again to suit Ottoman requirements.

On the basis of Ottoman social theory, derived in part from the Arabs, Ottoman society was a vertically structured social order of four pillars or estates: men of the faith and law ('ulemâ), men of the sword ('asker), merchants and craftsmen (tüccar), and raya or husbandmen. One also may conceive it, however, as a society of six estates (excluding slaves, who were not legally persons): the 'ulemâ or Muslim institution; the 'asker or ruling institution, many of whose members engaged in trade and thus were closely associated with the new "third estate" of non-Muslim businessmen; the fourth estate of the privileged raya or auxiliary 'asker of Orthodox Christians; the pseudoestate of the oppressed raya; and the collection of estates of self-governing foreign communities (and their Ottoman protégés) who were eventually protected by international agreements.

In fact, the Ottoman social order was even more complex, assuming two forms, religious and functional. In terms of the religious form, it was ostensibly divided into four officially autonomous communities called millets: Muslims,

Orthodox Christians, Jews, and Gregorian (Monophysite) Armenians. But the Muslims were further subdivided into two broad religious groups, the heretical Ši'a and the "orthodox" Sunni, the latter subdivided into a multitude of brotherhoods of varying orthodoxy. Although the Orthodox Christians were all theoretically subject to the ecumenical patriarch of Constantinople, they were separated in some periods into two self-governing churches (Greek and Serbian), each enjoying jurisdiction over different combinations of ethnic groups and subcultures. Jews constituted four main religious groups until the second half of the seventeenth century, when some of the adherents of the sect of Shabbethai Zevi, following the example of their leader, espoused Islam while retaining a portion of their Judaic heritage. The Armenian *millet* embraced not only Monophysites but Roman Catholics, Nestorians, and Jacobites. The latter churches, however, sometimes obtained charters that set them apart from the Armenian group. In actuality, therefore, the total number of Ottoman religious groups was closer to three or four times the official number.

In terms of function, Ottoman society was organized into a pseudo-order of men of the faith and law, separated into as many tangible orders as there were *millets;* an order of the sword, separated into a military and ruling estate of dominant Muslims and an auxiliary order of dependent but privileged Orthodox Christians; and a business order of Jews, Orthodox Christians, Gregorian Armenians, and converts or descendants of converts to Islam, whose members derived a sense of communion through the frequent exercise of a common craft in a common guild with a common patron saint or prophet. To these one must add the pariah *raya* of Orthodox Christian peasants and the privileged foreign communities.[83]

The frame of reference of the dependent Balkan populations was similarly "social condition" or status. The Greeks of Ottoman Athens, for example, acknowledged four main social statuses. First in the order of ranks stood the archons or notability, who, according to tradition real or invented, were the descendants of the Greek tribes of ancient Athens and, in the seventeenth century, numbered just over sixty families, among them the Charkokondyles (Chalkokondyles), the Benizeloi, and the Palaiologoi. The right to flowing locks and long beards and to the aristocratic name of Alexander was reserved to members of these families. Second in the order of ranks stood the *noikokyraioi* or homeowners. The third rank was made up of the *pazaritai* or shopkeepers and tradesmen who were organized into a number of guilds. On the last Sunday in February of each year, the *noikokyraioi* and the *pazaritai* gathered outside the church of St. Panteleimon to elect a council of elders *(demogerontes)*, which was charged with the administration of the Orthodox Greeks of the town. The Ottoman *kadi* of the city had to ratify the election. Fourth and last in the order of ranks stood the *zotarides* or garden cultivators and beekeepers of the suburbs.[84]

The English physician Henry Holland, who traveled widely in Greece during 1812 and 1813, appropriately observed that "family antiquity and connections" carried "a good deal of weight" among the Greeks and procured respect "independently of mere wealth." Greeks thus took care to address an archon as *Eugenestatos* (Noble Sir) or *Entimotatos* (Honorable Sir), a physician as *Exochotatos* (Excellent Sir), and a teacher as *Sophologiotatos* (Most Learned Sir). Nor did they neglect to observe all other expected forms of usage and dress.[85]

The system of estates and social "conditions" was grossly imperfect. In practice and theory alike, "ritually correct rebellion" was permissible but punishable if unsuccessful. Ritually correct rebellion was rebellion in which the object was to transfer power from one group of individuals to another in order to correct flaws in the management of the existing estates structures or of government and the economy. Rebellion ceased to be ritually correct if the aim widened to include revolution, that is, if the goal of the rebels became the abolition of the existing system.

Ritually correct rebellions against the sultan or very arbiter of the system, the ghazi (warrior of the Faith) of ghazis and padishah, thus occurred repeatedly. Quarrels or disagreements between the estates were indeed normal, and the state was often absorbed with the problem of resolving such conflicts. These rebellions and rivalries did not constitute a threat to the basic purposes of the existing social structure; often, in fact, their aim was to reaffirm those purposes. Nevertheless, by the close of the eighteenth century, there had come into being a real threat to the Ottoman system of maintaining stability and even to the very principle of estates society.

An important element in the transformation was the European Enlightenment —as manifested in particular in the Habsburg monarchy—and the French Revolution. In 1779, for example, in the second edition of his *Satir iliti divji čovik* (The Satyr or the Wild/Demonic Man), published in Osijek (Slavonia), Matija Antun Reljković not only affirmed the existence in the world's societies since the time of Noah of three orders—prayer men or makers of sacrifices, food providers, and protectors *(tri reda—moleći, hraneći i braneći)*—but eulogized the estate of food providers.[86] On July 4, 1781, the decree of Concivilität of Joseph II granted equal rights of citizenship to the inhabitants of the Fundus Regius (Braşov, Sibiu, and Bistriţa districts), thus extending to the Romanians of the region political equality with the previously privileged Saxons. Later in the same year, the Habsburg monarch issued an edict of toleration allowing Orthodox Romanians to build and maintain their own churches and schools in communities with at least a hundred Orthodox Romanian families. The emancipation decree of 1785, made in response to the peasant revolt of 1784,[87] extended complete personal freedom to the peasants of the region (without freeing them from labor and other dues). Following the constitutional crisis (in the midst of a war with Turkey) of 1790–92, however, the old privileges of the three "nations" or estates—Magyars, Szeklers, and Saxons—were restored.[88]

It is doubtful that the foregoing events went unnoticed in the neighboring Ottoman territories. Indeed, in a letter on how to establish order and enlightenment in the rebel Ottoman province of Serbia, Dositej Obradović focused on the importance of a proper organization of the three functions: prayer, war, and work.[89]

Both in a later portion of this chapter and in subsequent chapters, we shall have occasion to return to the subject of the Enlightenment and French Revolution. We now propose, however, to take a brief, systematic look at the Balkan microsociety and its relationships to the macrosociety.

Kinship, Clanship, and Men's and Women's Societies

One result of medieval social differentiation and the development of state officialdoms in the Slavic areas of the Balkans had been a decline in the importance of distant kinship relations and a weakening of clans as effective political, economic, and religious units. In other words, the decline of family solidarity, which had started in Mycenaean Greece (second millennium) and had spread ever more widely through the Balkan peninsula during the Roman era, gained a new momentum. Ottoman rule accelerated the process in some regions in regard to Muslim families. It slowed it down, halted, or reversed it in the case of most Christians.

The sense of family solidarity probably was weakened among many Balkan Muslims by the very fact of their recent apostasy or abandonment of one faith and civilization for another. Often motivated by the desire to preserve old or acquire new wealth and privilege or by the need for a new identity on the part of some of the conquered populations, especially those that had been resettled in regions distant from their old homes and families, the conversions generally constituted a significant break with some of the more recent old traditions. In particular, their sense of kinship suffered as a result of the very nature of Ottoman military life, which was divided into a campaigning season (from St. George's Day to St. Demetrius's Day) and a billeting season, with different wives and concubines in different camps and billets.

Count Ferrières-Sauveboeuf describes the events that occurred after the grand vizier encamped his army, in 1788, near the gates of Sofia to prepare an offensive against Austria:

> Nothing created a greater stir in this city than the betrothals of the Janissaries to the young local [supposedly Muslim] beauties, who apparently thought that the army would never again quit their territory. Nearly all the young ladies got married and spent their honeymoon quite pleasantly. The latter was succeeded, however, by a general abandonment and the most complete widowhood. As the Vizier left Sofia to pitch camp near Niš, it was not without difficulty that the belles were turned away, for they missed the Janissaries too exceedingly not to want to follow them. I saw a group of them being brought back in carts, but since they had disobeyed orders they were now threatened, in the event of a repetition of the offense, with a not very delicate ceremony commonly practiced in Turkey: the authorities would slip a cat into their ordinarily ample bloomers; and this poor beast, flogged without mercy, would hardly show claws of velvet.[90]

A sentiment of some degree of family solidarity doubtless was not altogether wanting among Muslims, especially among men of wealth and influence. A German-Imperial (Austrian) ambassadorial report of 1779 thus observed that Ottoman luminaries were "very careful in their marriage alliances," while consulting "only their taste in choosing concubines."[91] Another indication that Muslim families were not invariably seasonal and occasional affairs is the popularity of the practice of transforming properties into special pious (vakf) holdings. The transfer entailed the donation of a property to a mosque or some other religious establishment, but very commonly the donation was made with the proviso that the descendants of the author of the testament should continue to receive a portion of the revenues derived from the property until the family was extinct. In this way, much private property was rescued from state confiscation. If Muslims had failed altogether to perceive a sense of family responsibility, it is unlikely they would have felt a need to resort to such practices.

By and large, however, we are forced to agree with the British ambassador to the Porte, Henry Grenville, that the institutions of polygamy and concubinage were unsuitable as instruments of family solidarity.[92] Since they were frequently abandoned when they were no longer wanted, wives and concubines of Muslim men often had recourse to abortion, infanticide, and other birth control measures. A typical well-to-do Muslim family thus might be said to have consisted of one man, several women, but relatively few children in proportion to the total number of adults. The comments of a French consul on Muslim sexual habits in general, and particularly on the practices of Moreot women of Muslim faith during the latter part of the eighteenth century, provide both a description and an analysis:

> Although they are often Greeks themselves, unlike the latter they rarely have a large number of children. This may be explained, on the one hand, by the institution of polygamy and, on the other, by the frightful art of abortion, which is familiar to them. Nowhere have the effects of abortion been so harmful [as among the Turks], nor so solemnly consecrated. Avowed publicly in the family of the Sultan, who condemns his sisters and nieces to sterility, these horrible means of depopulation pass on to the different strata of society. When suspected of infidelity, the wives of a Turk do not hesitate to commit the crime. They even resort to it, and without remorse, with the sole object of conserving their attractiveness and protecting the beauty that gives them an empire over their rivals, with whom they never cease to be at war.[93]

Added to abortion and infanticide were the ravages of venereal disease, all of which resulted by the eighteenth century in a low rate of fertility for Muslims in many Balkan areas. Islam was also more permissive toward the practice of coïtus interruptus.[94] A ceiling upon Muslim demographic growth was further imposed by the presence in the Ottoman Empire at the opening of the nineteenth century of perhaps as many as a million eunuchs.[95] The population balance thus shifted in favor of the Orthodox Christians in certain heretofore predominantly Muslim provinces such as Bosnia-Hercegovina.

Liberal and conservative eighteenth- and early nineteenth-century European thinkers alike saw a correlation between what they called Asiatic or Oriental despotism and the practice of polygamy. Anne-Robert-Jacques Turgot, for example, affirmed that political despotism tended to result in the subservience of women. Polygamy in turn had a basis in "the inequality of corporal forces."[96] The *vicomte* Louis de Bonald explicitly defined polygamy as "domestic despotism," arising wherever there was "political despotism, as in Turkey, China, Persia, etc."[97]

Like Muslims in general, Muslim Bosnians placed less emphasis on agnatic and fictive kinship than either the Orthodox Serbs (and other Slavic and Greek Orthodox populations) or the Roman Catholic Croats.[98] The trend among Christians, on the other hand, was not only toward a strengthening of the extended family—a trend almost equally prevalent among Bosnian Muslims—but also toward an extension of kinship and quasi-kinship relations. Broadly speaking, Christian rural-familial relationships developed along two lines, one confined to the western mountain areas of Hercegovina, Montenegro, northern Albania, Epirus, and Mani (in the Morea),[99] while the other, somewhat less predisposed to kinship and household extension, prevailed in the rest of the Balkans. In the western regions, a household generally comprised more than just a husband, wife, and children. Often it would include several brothers, their respective wives and children, and, if still alive, the father and mother of the brothers. The size of households varied greatly. Some South Slavic household units numbered more than a hundred persons. Others were quite small. Between 1600 and 1800, however, the average number of persons in a rural household of the western South Slavic regions was 10 or more.[100] Thereafter, extended families became less common. In the Serbian district of Gruža, household size declined from 9 persons in 1844 to 6.2 in 1905, 5.9 in 1910, and 5.5 in 1931. In Croatia, it declined from 8.4 members in 1857 to 4.9 in 1910 and 4.4 in 1953.[101]

Generally known in Serbian areas as a *kuća*, a household was a group of persons closely related by birth or admitted by adoption. All members were destined to engage eventually in production for the entire group, and they regarded land and cattle as the common property of the group. The household was thus a corporate organization, aiming to perpetuate itself and its properties beyond the lifetime of any existing set of members, although it was sometimes dissolved by war, famine, epidemics, or quarrels. Aware of the economic aspects of the *kuća* or Serbian household, eighteenth-century Austrian observers defined it as a *Wirth*—an economic *(oikonomic)* enterprise.

Above and beyond the household were the autonomous villages and federations of rural communes,[102] similarly organized on a corporate basis. Many members of such units were related by kinship, but the territorial units themselves were kinship organizations only vestigially. Kinship, however, was important to the Christian peasantry as a source of support and protection against hostile families and aggressors. It also assured the peasant of an adequate labor power—through the institution of ritualized (work to the rhythm of song, a ritual washing of hands, prayer or sacrifice, and a banquet—originally a common sacrificial meal—concluded by singing and dancing) mutual aid *(moba, bedba)* among kin and "friends" to assure the completion of certain tasks that otherwise might have remained undone.[103]

Family affiliation was asymmetrically bilateral, with relationships in the masculine line—"kin through blood"—being counted to the sixth, seventh, or eighth degree, and sometimes beyond, and kinship through the female line—"kin through milk"—only to the second or third degree.[104] In the greater part of the Balkans, therefore, kinship—as distinct from the household—was a personal rather than permanent corporate institution, for the kin of one age cohort was not exactly the same as the kin of another. Moreover, in highly urbanized districts, and notably in the plains and maritime districts of the south and southeast, kinship relations were not as extensive as among most of the Slavs or among the Greeks of the highlands. Regions along routes of trade and imperial communication, such as the Vardar-Morava axis, often valued kinship quite as much as the inhabitants of the high mountains. In their "women's songs," however, they owned to the fact that conformity to the kinship code was sometimes unduly onerous, as it also may have been among mountain populations:

> An innocent lamb hath no sin,
> A pretty maiden hath no kin.[105]

In terms of immediately and easily perceptible phenomena, patriarchy characterized the Balkan cultures. But at a deeper if not the deepest level (that is, not at the level at which hunting and gathering were the prevalent ways of life), as I interpret and revise Yvonne Castellan, still manifest in early nineteenth-century Serbian society of the Morava valley were vestiges of a "matriarchal" order—the order of the Balkan First Europe. Such conservation of a distant past was reflected in particular by close brother-sister and mother-son relationships and by the idealization in the extended South Slavic family of equality among brothers, resulting in the weakening of the authority of particular biological fathers.[106]

The presence of a submerged "matriarchy" in some parts of the Balkans, as in many other parts of the world, also is suggested by the persistence of women's quasi-secret societies, which probably originated in the early Neolithic era, being linked with certain feminine crafts—in the Balkan context, with spinning and weaving. Traditionally nocturnal work performed far from the gaze of the sun, under the auspices of the moon and the spinners of time and fate, spinning often was carried on at a gathering of women and adolescent girls that was known to many Serbs as a *prelo* (spinning vigil). It was held in the open air or at a succession of homes. At the gathering, the older women—literally, the spinsters

—taught the girls the art of spinning and sang ritual or "women's songs." At the open-air gatherings, they sometimes engaged in (erotic?) dances.

In some parts of the world, as in Japan, writes Mircea Eliade, "one can still discern the mythological memory of a lasting tension, and even a conflict, between the secret societies of young women and the societies of men, the *Männerbände*. The men and their gods, during the night, attack the spinsters, break their shuttles and weaving-tackle."[107] Something of that sort may also have happened at Serbian evening gatherings of spinners, resulting sometimes in premarital sex or in fights between rival young males. In 1833 and 1834, therefore, Prince Miloš of Serbia forbade, in the department of Požarevac and the Danube-Timok command, the holding of spinning vigils in the open air and the attendance of males at women's spinning gatherings.[108]

Exogamy—the prohibition of marriage between members of a given group— was the rule between kin throughout the Balkans. In most areas, however, there was no specifically exogamous corporate entity apart from the household into which one was born or initiated. Exceptionally, in the southwestern mountain provinces from Mani in the south to Hercegovina in the north, clanship and phratries prevailed.[109] The number of corporate kinship units here rose to three (phratry, family [*rod* or *vamilija*], and household or *kuća*) if exogamy was confined to the phratry or subclan, and to four if it extended to the clan. In those cases where the clan was endogamous, or favorable to clan inbreeding, it served to regulate the flow of marriageable girls from one phratry into another and thus tended to inspire among member phratries a sense of solidarity against intruders.

Some form of this kind of biosocial arrangement was not new to the Balkans. But twice at least the peninsula had experienced detribalization, once in Roman times (in Greece, however, during or before the eighth century B.C.) and again during the Middle Ages,[110] before the ruin of clan and tribal structures during the nineteenth and twentieth centuries. Even in the Roman era, when the clan structure was under attack, the Celto-Illyrians of Pannonia were divided into *civitates,* or territorial centers of public administration, and each *civitas* was subdivided into several *pagi,* or constituent rural districts with vestiges of a clan structure. Although generally described as a territorial unit, the *pagus* was essentially a group of families who practiced exogamy and a common agrarian cult and traced their origins to a common ancestor, mythical or real. Similar arrangements later were instituted in Dacia.[111]

The ethnic or pre-Roman foundation of the *pagus* probably bore some resemblance to the Sanskrit *sapa*, Germanic *Zippe*, and early South Slavic *župa*, a cluster of families with a common place of assembly and/or with some lands and resources to which they possessed rights in common. Repeating the experience of the *pagus*, the Serbian *župa*, too, was territorialized, much like the *comitatus* or county in Pannonia and western Europe.

Under Ottoman rule, the kinship organization of the southwestern Balkans comprised three fundamental units: households, which were hereditary members

Figure 4.5. **Family and Clan Structure**

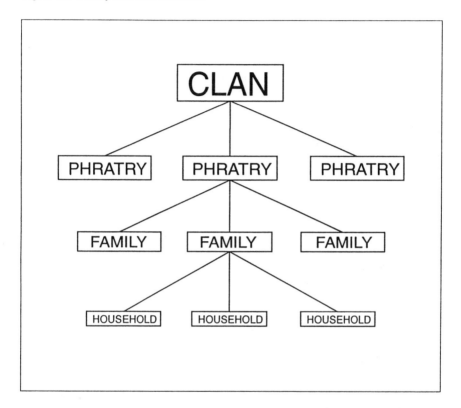

of a given phratry, and two or more phratries, which together constituted either an exogamous or endogamous clan. The Vasojevići clan *(pleme)* distinguished between a small phratry *(trbuščić)* of two to four families and a large phratry *(trbuh)* of more than four families.[112] Translatable as "belly," the word *trbuh* may be derived in fact from an Indo-European root meaning "to clear" (for example, a space in a forest), from which also may be derived the word "tribe."[113]

Diagrammatically, kinship organization among Montenegrins and Albanians (but with a different nomenclature among Albanians), and to some degree in eastern Hercegovina, assumed the form shown in Figure 4.5. In a modified form, this organization penetrated northeastward into Serbia, where, side by side with the institution of household and personal kinship appeared phratries practicing exogamy but lacking a clan structure.

The strengthening of the rural Christian family during the Ottoman era was accompanied by the strengthening and extension of various forms of initiatory and contractual kinship associations:

1. Godfatherhood relationships sanctioned but not defined solely by a church ceremony, implying indeed a relationship and obligations of exchange not just between individuals but between two groups.[114]

2. The institution of the haircutting godfather *(šišani kum* or *striženi kum)* or the father-son relationship established through the pagan ceremony of the first haircut.[115] In ancient Greece, this ceremony was part of the festival of enrollment into a phratry (the *apatouria)* or group having the same "father." The performers of the rites, however, were women. Later patriarchal both in form and content, it was known in Byzantium as *trichokouria.*[116]

3. Foster brother or foster sister *(pobratimstvo, posestrimstvo, adelfopoias, aderfopoitoi, bratimoi)* relationships, which were opposed by the Orthodox church during the Byzantine era but to which priests gave wide sanction during the Ottoman era.[117]

4. Brother-of-the-cross affiliations *(stavroderfoi)*, especially among the Greeks, whereby, upon the performance of a special initiatory ceremony by an Orthodox priest, two or more persons became brothers-of-the-cross and acquired rights of inheritance to each other's property.

5. Relationships of friendship *(prijateljstvo)* between families not related by kinship, thus kith or potential kith (among the Greeks, *sympetheroi).*[118] For whoever is not of one's kin, phratry, or clan, normally is an enemy or potential enemy unless designated as a friend. As in other human societies, marriage served the function of "masking hostility" between two groups of potential enemies.[119]

6. *Tselingas, tseligas,* or *čelnik* associations of shepherds, often bound by kinship or quasi-kinship, as well as by economic ties, for a temporary period.[120]

7. The expansion during the eighteenth century of Greek, Vlach, Serb, Macedonian, and Bulgarian merchant *companiae (kumpanije),* and of Greek or Greco-Albanian associations of seamen *(syntrofonaftai).*

One other form of association expanded during the latter centuries of Ottoman rule: the men's society or band. In classical Greece, men's societies had assumed the form of clubs or *thiasoi,* associations with a basis in initiation rather than kinship.[121] In an earlier form, however, men's societies may have reflected, in effect, a determination on the part of a portion of youth to reject toil, agriculture, herding, and kin and opt instead either in favor of the life of the shaman who draws closer to the wilderness (forest or desert) and lore of nature, or of the life of the hunter and aesthetic of the body (an evolution that may have prompted the formation in classical Greece of gymnasia). Another course in the evolution of men's clubs was the formation, as among the Spartans, of gangs (κρυπτεία) whose mission was the murder of peasants (helots) who shirked their work tasks or showed too much spirit.[122] Informally and on an irregular basis, Muslim bands in the Ottoman Balkans similarly organized forays to hunt down objectionable Christians—*lov 'na kaure.*[123] Other men's societies or bands exacted booty from ξένοι, merchant-adventurer *gosti,* or subject populations.

Among farming populations, men's societies had a basis not only in rebellion against agriculture but also in protest against the submission of farming communities to the city cultures. Thus, while Greeks under Ottoman rule distinguished between kin, kith, and outsiders *(dikoi, sympetheroi,* and *xenoi)*,[124] their male members also divided into two main power groups—the gerontocracy, who valued above all else family honor and integrity, and the youth, who were responsible for protecting and avenging the honor of all family members, especially sisters, but whose predilection for action and self-assertion could lead them to prefer the life of braves—association with a band of *pallikaria.*[125]

Members of men's societies might return to their families and communities in the autumn, when the plowing, planting, and harvesting were over for the year. Thus, among the Celts, bands known as *fiana* lived with the clans from Samain (All Souls' Day, November 1) to Beltane (May Day). After Beltane they would resume their life of hunting and banditry.[126] With a minor variation in the terminal dates of their activities, the Balkan *hajduks, haiduts,* or *klephts* behaved in like manner. They shared their booty with farmers and herdsmen and disposed of their own share with the aid of receivers. Their law, however, was the custom of the band, not the tradition of the ruling elders (gerontocracy) of the clan, household, or community.

The members of such men's societies were not ordinary thieves and cutthroats. In essence, they symbolized a variant value pattern that the gerontocracy frequently allowed as a means of diverting hostility from parents, household, kinfolk, community, and clan to other objects and as a vicarious expression of their own hostility to the same objects. One may concur with the Serbian historian Slobodan Jovanović that men's societies of this kind (bonding or banding to engage in banditry)—*hajdučija*—were a manifestation of an "atavistic rebellion," if one defines atavistic rebellion as rebellion in which the aim of the rebels is to bring down the newer (agricultural, urban, political, or imperial) and restore the older (pre-agricultural, pre-urban, or pre-imperial) culture. It is altogether tendentious, however, to view the existence of such men's societies as evidence of "the anarchistic traits of the people."[127] The people lived in communities, clans, and many diverse kinds of associations, including bands, all of which had their own law.

Under Ottoman rule, two forms of band or band action prevailed. One type was what to the Greeks was known as the "tame klephts," who usually collaborated with the political authorities. The "wild klephts" *(klephtes sauvages)*, on the other hand, without being revolutionary, were opposed to the existing local order of things or took advantage of the local order for their own personal or family benefit. In fact, a band could be "wild" or "tame"—"cooked" or "raw," to set the polarity in a Lévi-Straussian culture-nature framework—depending on the occasion.[128]

A third category of band was that of the so-called *kirjalis,* who operated in the Rhodope Mountains and then spread to other areas during the latter part of the eighteenth and early part of the nineteenth century.[129] While often opposed to existing political authority, the *kirjalis* committed acts of brigandage indiscriminately. They did not intend to return to a community on St. Demetrius's Day except as predators.

These three types of men's societies are in part ideal constructs. In practice, the same band behaved in various ways. The differences among the three categories, especially between the unregistered *hajduk* (in Hungary, there were registered *hajduks;* in Senj, registered *uskoks;* in the Ukraine, registered Cossacks) or wild klepht and the *kirjali,* were nevertheless important. Whereas the bands of wild klephts were generally made up of discontented rural youths, often from distinguished well-to-do families, the *kirjalis* were recruited in large measure from urban and semiurban sources and from the riffraff and most deprived sectors of society: demobilized soldiers, "bachelors" and propertyless menservants or farmhands *(momci),* and the "houseless," "barefoot," and "naked."[130] Moreover, the wild klephts were almost wholly Christians. The *kirjalis* constituted a highly mixed group: Christians, Muslims, Turks, Albanians, Bulgarians, Bosnians.

Recruited from among floaters and vagabonds, *kirjalis* often obtained employment as security guards and were charged by their employers with carrying out raids against the domains of neighboring lords and with preventing or crushing retaliatory raids. When one employer did not suit them, they sought another, journeying from Albania to Bosnia, from Bosnia to Serbia and Bulgaria, from Bulgaria to Macedonia and Thessaly, into the Morea, and back to Albania. Numerous in quiet times, they doubled and trebled in number during and after a war.

As early as 1502 and throughout the era of Ottoman rule, there were also bands of three or four to ten or fifteen men—drawn from among *derbend* guards, village provisioners for travelers, and muleteers—who, upon appropriate occasions, constituted themselves as robber bands. Such bands not only robbed but sometimes murdered their guests or merchant employers.

Common sites of banditry were the Kačanik gorge (between Serbia and Montenegro), the defile of Rogožna between Novi Pazar and Višegrad, and the defile of German near Vranje. Acts of brigandage were also frequent in the districts of Philippopolis, Serres, and Strumica, on the Danube and Kolubara rivers or along their banks, in areas near fair sites, and along the route between Thessaloniki and Üsküb (often ravaged by brigands of the Clementine or Klementi mountains).

One of two Englishmen who traveled from Dubrovnik to Istanbul in 1589 relates that on May 27 they passed by Novi Pazar "but went not into the towne for our genysary [janissary] says that yt was a thevyshe plac and that many robbaryes and murthers had byne comytted ther. The XXIXth we past by Nyza [Niš] but left the toun for the like causes."[131]

In 1613, according to Ragusan reports, the imperial route between Niš and Istanbul regorged with bandits and cadavers. In 1623, the Ragusan envoys traveling to Toplica were accompanied by an armed escort of a hundred soldiers to protect them against banditry. Journeying by land from the Adriatic coast across the Balkans to Egypt in 1634, Henry Blount was struck by the prevalence of banditry along the route between Valjevo and Belgrade, between Belgrade and Sofia, and, indeed throughout Turkey, where, "especially in places desert there are many Mountainers, or Outlawes, like the wild Irish, who live upon spoyle, and are not held members of the State, but enemies, and used accordingly." Along the imperial route running through the brushwood of the Rhodope mountain region, there were stations of guards, who, "by reason of the frequent robberies there committed, doe by little *Drums* give the inhabitants [or rather travelers] warning of all suspicious passengers." Blount relates the tactics of his group on the road between Valjevo and Belgrade:

> . . . being to passe a wood neere the *Christian* countrey, doubting [in the sense of thinking] it to bee (as confines are) full of Thieves, we divided our *Caravan* of sixscore Horse into two parts; halfe with the Persons, and Goods of lest esteeme, wee sent a day before the rest, that so the thieves having a booty, might be gone before we came; which happened accordingly; they were robbed; one thiefe, and two of ours slaine; some hundred *dollars* worth of good lost: The next day we passed, and found sixteen Thieves, in a narrow passage, before whom, wee set a good guard of *Harquebuze*, and *Pistols*, till the weaker sort passed by: so in three dayes, we came safe to *Belgrade*.[132]

Traveling from Belgrade to Adrianople in the early spring of 1717 to join her husband the English ambassador to the Porte, Lady Mary Wortley Montagu wrote that "the desart Woods of Servia are the common refuge of Theeves who rob 50 in a company, [so] that we had need of all our Guards to secure us, and the villages so poor that only force could extract from them necessary provisions. Indeed, the Janizarys had no mercy on their poverty, killing all the poultry and sheep they could find, without asking whom they belong'd to, while the wretched owners durst not put in their claim for fear of being beaten. Lambs just fall'n, Geese and Turkeys big with Egg: all masacre'd without distinction."[133]

In 1783, a group of violent Muslim Albanians was expelled from Scutari (Shkodër), Prizren, and Vučitrn. Settling in Karanovac and Trstenik, they drove out the older inhabitants and seized their properties. Soon thereafter, they dispersed an official Ottoman convoy that was carrying money from Istanbul to Novi Pazar.[134] Such groups were predecessors of the *kirjalis*, who soon formed bands of a hundred or even a thousand or more persons. Their appearance was a sign not only of a continuing banditry without well-defined social goals but of the breakdown in Rumelia of the authority of the Ottoman central government.

The *hajduks* and wild klephts, on the other hand, ultimately became an instrument of new forms of social cohesion. To set the problem in perspective, let us backtrack. By 1573, according to Stephan Gerlach, chaplain of the Habsburg legation to Istanbul, Serbian and Bulgarian peasants of the districts between Niš and Sofia were already in the habit of singing *hajduk* songs or *Räyber Lieder* while wending homeward from their fields.[135] As the Ottoman government withdrew one privilege after another from the auxiliary *'asker* of Orthodox Christians *(martolosi, voynuks)*, the latter shifted their support to Austria, Venice, and Russia, manned the military frontiers of Venice and the Habsburg monarchy, and readily furnished the *hajduk* bands with fresh contingents of fighters. Along the Ottoman frontiers with the Christian states, by the close of the eighteenth century, 10 percent or more of the rural Christian population, or a third of the Christian male youth, may at least occasionally have been members of wild outlaw bands.

The *hajduks* and wild klephts were not nationalists. In spite of themselves, however, they were "nation"-oriented in that their conception of the community —every forest and every mountain, and every village and hamlet that sheltered them in winter—was broader than that of the leaders of the clans, villages, and rural confederations. Although they did not plan a national revolution, they were vulnerable to the incipient national ideology of some of the secular-oriented merchants and intellectuals of their own faith and ethnicity who grew in number during the eighteenth century and entered into frequent contact with central Europe or with Russia and the Italian states.

From Re-Volution to Revolution

In Serbia of the Morava valley or pashalik of Belgrade, where an intelligentsia was virtually nonexistent at the end of the eighteenth century, Serbs from Austrian Vojvodina filled the need for secretaries and teachers during the Serbian wars of independence (1804–14 and 1815, or even 1788–1815). A Serbian intelligentsia, however, was not the catalyst of the national and social revolution, and even the potentially "nation"-oriented *hajduks* might have failed to take advantage of the opportunity to create an autonomous Serbian state during the Napoleonic era if the people had lacked a millenarian outlook. Millenarism, the belief in the coming of a messiah or liberating ancestor or god, with a vestigial basis in the notion of the dead as an age cohort with whom one may communicate, was not, of course, confined to Serbians. The conception of the dead as a participant age cohort had also been known to the Celts,[136] and millennialism forms part of the history not only of Greeks, Vlachs, Bulgarians, Turks, and Balkan (and other) Jews, but of many other of the world's peoples. The Serbian millenarian spirit, however, rose to a high pitch during the second half of the eighteenth century—almost concurrently with the French Revolution, albeit independently of it.

Many millenarian visions spread among the Serbs after the middle of the fifteenth century. During the last two decades of the sixteenth century, when millenarism was rampant among almost every people of the Ottoman Empire,[137] Serbians looked forward to the messianic return of St. Sava—historically the thirteenth-century princely founder of a Serbian archbishopric but mythically an ancestral hero or archetype. In the 1590s, along with other Balkan peoples, they rose in rebellion against Ottoman rule while the Turks were at war with the Germanic-Roman Empire (Austria) and the princes of Transylvania, Wallachia, and Moldavia and with the Cossacks of the Ukrainian steppe. To put down the insurrection, the Turks ordered a *jihad*, or holy war: the cult of Mohammed against the cult of St. Sava. Removing what were supposedly the bones of St. Sava from the monastery of Mileševo, the Turks set fire to them in Belgrade. Even this, however, was insufficient to stifle forever popular belief in Sava's messianic return.

Serbian and Macedonian balladry also envisioned the return of another culture hero, Kraljević Marko—historically, a fourteenth-century Serbian vassal of the Turks, who, from a poetic standpoint, was a grand figure with the moral traits and character of Digenis Akritas and Dionysos. Legend held that Marko had temporarily withdrawn from earthly life to slumber and "bide his time" in some secret cavern—symbol of the Earth Mother—or in a cave near his Macedonian fortress of Prilep, or on a secret isle. But when "the time strikes" for Serbian renewal, he will rise and lead the Serbs and other Slavs and Christians against the Turks and drive them "across the blue sea" whence they came.

To those beliefs were added many others during the eighteenth century, and certain natural occurrences—namely, the comets of 1781, 1797, and 1807; the eclipse of the moon on January 14, 1804, and the eclipse of the sun two weeks later on January 30; and the thunderstorm on January 14 (the Eve of St. Sava's), 1801—were interpreted as portents of liberation and renovation to be achieved by war, epidemic, and rebellion.[138]

Finally, in the eighteenth century—or around the middle of the seventeenth, when Mediterranean and European Jews were being stirred by visions of Shabbethai Zevi—an "old man" of the Vasojević clan, a prophet by the name of Stanj, foretold the advent of a Serbian messiah, and for two centuries Serbians eagerly repeated his prophecy:

> From below the point where the Lim discharges into the [Drina, the Drina into the Sava, and the Sava into the] Danube [and presumably from the bowels of the earth and empire of the dead] will appear a dark man—*crni čovjek*—who will reveal himself as the king in moccasins. Until his coming there will be much evil, but he will liberate many Serbians. . . . The liberated then will live well, and the Mist Cap *(Crnokapa)* and Mist God *(Crnogaća)* will show up in our midst. Increasingly, the Turks will disappear from the face of the earth.[139]

Thus, on the eve of the Serbian social and national revolution—regardless of whether one accepts the traditional date of 1804 or prefers to trace its beginning to the Austro-Turkish war of 1788–91—there prevailed in Serbia what Vittorio Lanternari, in his analysis of dominated societies, calls a "premonitory religious movement of revival and transformation."[140] The messianic cult of liberation took the form of a fantasy of the sleeping god, hero, or king who would awaken at the proper moment. Wearing perhaps a protective "mist cap(e)" to make himself invisible to his enemies, a replica of the "dogskin" bonnet of the Greek god of death or of the *tarnkappe* of the nebulous, nightmarish, underworld heroes and elves of Teutonic mythology, he would free his people and allow them to revert to the mythical "golden age."

Ever present at a latent or covert level, millennialist expectations rose to the surface in the era of the Enlightenment, French Revolution, and Napoleonic wars. At some other time, Serbian chiliast visions probably would have suffered the dismal fate—from a short-term point of view—of many past millenarian movements. If Serbia had not been looking forward to a messianic liberation, however, Enlightenment and Revolution may have had no immediate ideological or social consequences. But as the Serbian goal of re-volution, a return to the "golden age," synchronized with the revolution in France, with the larger social and economic revolution that was taking place throughout the West, and with the stirrings of the 1780s and 1790s among the Serbs, Croats, Magyars, and Romanians of Hungary,[141] the impossible became an imagined reality.

In the Romanian principalities and South Slavic provinces north and northwest of Serbia, and among the Greeks of Constantinople, Chios, Smyrna, Kydoniai, Janina, Ambelakia, Tyrnavos, Tripolitsa ("a large walled city," residence of the pasha of the Morea, with a population in 1812 of perhaps fifteen thousand, a third or fourth of them Turks),[142] Corfu, Bucharest, and Iaşi, millenarian sentiments yielded at least superficially to the mental structure of the Enlightenment as the chief psychological and ideological agent of revolution. "People" in Jules Michelet's sense were, of course, everywhere potentially of a millenarian outlook, but in the foregoing areas were found certain social categories and institutions that were absent in Serbia or present only in protonuclear form, whose partial function it was to "disenchant," that is, unveil a new "magic": native urban and semiurban merchants, a Christian "nobility of the robe," middle and higher schools, some private libraries, a considerable number of physicians trained in Italian or other European universities, a growing public of literate "middle elements," and, in the 1790s, a few private theaters.

The most numerous Balkan intelligentsia, both ecclesiastical and secular, existed among the Greeks, the Balkan people with the longest heritage of literacy and bureaucracy. Around the middle of the eighteenth century, Greek ecclesiastical scholars were divided into two groups: "grammarians," who sought refuge in Aristotle and grammar; and "mathematicists," who found consolation in the science of Nicholaus Copernicus, Isaac Newton, René Descartes, John Locke, and Tycho Brahe. Several patriarchs of the time denounced their "foolish wisdom."[143]

There also grew during the second half of the eighteenth century a secular intelligentsia of Phanariot "gentlemen scholars" and heterogeneous "middle elements." The Phanariots were educated wealthy Greeks, often of mercantile origin, who succeeded in winning appointment to high posts in the Ottoman government and in becoming lay administrators of the Greek Orthodox church and aspirants to the governorships of Wallachia and Moldavia.[144] They constituted in fact a "nobility of the robe."

The middle elements comprised secretaries in the service of the Phanariot "nobility of the robe," merchants who were often self-educated, and merchants' sons who were educated in western universities. Typical of these merchants' sons were the Drosos youths of Ambelakia. After studying at Leipzig and Jena, the Drosos young men returned to organize a little theater in their community. Adamantios Korais, the son of a prominent Smyrniot merchant, tried his hand at merchantry. Failing in that venture, he went on to study medicine at Montpellier, and finally chose a literary and political-pamphleteering career in Paris. It was his aim to convert fellow Greeks to the cause of the European Enlightenment and "liberal" aspects of the French Revolution.

In 1805, Korais turned to the publication of a *Hellenic Library*, which comprised at the time of his death twenty-six copiously annotated volumes of the works of the ancient Greek philosopers, poets, and other thinkers. He was able to execute the project thanks to a wealthy Greek merchant, Sosimas (or Zosimas), who guaranteed him a yearly salary, paid for the publication, and took charge of the distribution of the books. Sosimas found a market for the books in Paris, London, Vienna, Moscow, Trieste, Livorno, the Greek islands, the Peloponnesus, the cities of Asia Minor and Rumelia, and among the Greeks of Wallachia and Moldavia. When the arrangement with Sosimas broke down, other Greek merchants, especially merchants from the island of Chios, provided Korais with funds for the publication and distribution of his books.

In 1812, the Sosimas or Zosimas family, "one of the greatest and most wealthy of the modern Greek families," included at least four brothers, one resident in Janina (Ioannina), two in Italy, and a fourth in Russia. It magnificently exemplified the Greek mercantile diaspora. "I have learnt," wrote Dr. Henry Holland, "that the sums they annually transmit to Ioannina, in the form of books, of funds for the school, and of other literary benefactions, do not fall short of 20,000 piastres." Indeed, Ioannina was then "a sort of mart for books, which are brought hither from the continent when printed; and from this point diffused over other parts of Greece. At the *dogana* [customs house] of Arta I have seen numerous packages of books on their way to Ioannina, and in the city itself there are several shops, which have long been known for their extensive dealings in this branch of business." The home of the Ioannina merchant Ioannes Melas thus had "a small library, neatly furnished, provided with a piano-forte, and a good collection of books." Melas even possessed a copy of "a modern Greek translation of Laplace's *Système du monde*."[145]

The merchant philanthropists who diffused to Greek diaspora and Greek homeland communities the works of European literature, and who made possible the publication and diffusion of the works of Korais and other Greek writers, typified a group—the mercantile bourgeoisie—that had strong links with the economically and politically dominant cities, merchants, and states of Europe.

Looking at the world from a different geographic, political, economic, and cultural perspective, they identified with and developed territorial and political imaginaries (simultaneously national and European) at great variance with the provincial and intraimperial spatial conceptions of the privileged but dependent Greek provincial primates.[146]

In regard to the conceptualization of territory, the Serbian revolution, too, despite its partial foundations in millennialism, began, as I have explained elsewhere in greater detail, "as a struggle of newly prospering but threatened [Serbian] little-county and peasant interests against the blocked economy and aggressive redistributive ideology of [Ottoman Muslim] urban and great-county notables." Like other empires of old type, I repeat, the Ottoman Empire was organized territorially on the basis of "center-periphery relations," requiring "state control of the routes between cities." That kind of organization entailed "a large degree of household and village autonomy and some (but a highly variable) degree of provincial and great-county autonomy, especially for distant lands, so long as the inhabitants paid their taxes and did not rebel against the legitimate political authority."[147] Caught in a balancing act in the conflict between the great-county (but also urban and Muslim) and little-county (and specifically rural and Christian) interests, the empire had to make a choice. But by siding with the great-county interests, it provoked the leaders of the Serbian peasant insurrection to embrace in part a yet different ideology of territorial or spatial organization. The new national ideology was propagated in embryonic form by Serb merchants, officers, and intellectuals from the Habsburg Sava-Kupa basin, from Hungary and the middle Danube, from Srem county and the Banat, and from the Croatian Military Frontier.

In similar fashion, the movement for a common South Slavic literary language was centered, during the second third of the nineteenth century, in a city of the Croatian Military Frontier, Karlovac (Carlstadt), then both commercially and culturally more important than Zagreb (Agram). Karlovac merchants with stock in the navigation company Sloga (Accord) promoted steam navigation on the Sava and Danube. A Karlovac grain merchant, Josip Šipuš, wrote a book in support of South Slav (Yugoslav) union.[148] As the new ideology matured, it called for the creation, in my own words, of "a nation state that would function as a national market in an essentially commercial rather than redistributive world economy."[149]

An example of an exceptional secretary in the temporary employ of the Phanariot "nobility of the robe" was the Thessalian poet Rhigas Pheraios. After serving as secretary to a Wallachian boyar, rising to the rank of governor of Little Wallachia, and moving in Bucharest in so-called Jacobin boyar and *bonjuristi (bonjouristes)* circles, he departed for Vienna. In 1796, he formed a revolutionary club with the object of transforming the Ottoman Empire into a pseudo-Jacobin republic. He then left Vienna for Trieste to join the bey of Mani, Zanettos Gregorakis, who had sought Napoleon's support to undertake the liberation of Greece. Betrayed by a fellow Greek, Rhigas and seventeen fellow conspirators were apprehended by the Austrian police. Turned over with seven of the plotters to the Turks, Rhigas and his fellow prisoners were duly strangled in a Belgrade prison in 1798.[150]

As a group, merchants, secretaries, sons of merchants, and Phanariots preferred reform to revolution, and many were perfectly ready to continue to accept the *ancien régime*, particularly after 1789, when the official church took a strong stand against westernism and modernism and threatened deviation with anathema.[151] However, an important segment of the secular intelligentsia and merchants doing business with Russia and the West was favorably disposed toward organization in revolutionary clubs. Several such clubs, called hetairies, were formed during the French Revolutionary and Napoleonic era.

Certain Greeks in the Macedonian community of Kozani took pride in being known as Gallophrones ("people who think in the French manner"). Some of the islanders of Samos rejoiced in the name of *carmagnoles* (the name of a costume worn by French revolutionists, of songs they sang, and of a dance they danced). In 1797, French and Venetian troops occupied Corfu and other islands of the Ionian group. Soon after the occupation, General Gentili—a Corsican, an "islander," in the overly optimistic words of his fellow-Corsican superior Napoleon, "accustomed to the management of islanders"[152]—dispatched a delegation headed by a native of Patras, Adjutant General Roze, to determine the true intentions of his new neighbor, Ali Pasha of Janina (Ioannina), governor of Epirus and Thessaly.

Ali Pasha provided a magnificent reception. Adorning his turban with a tricolor cockade, he proclaimed that he had been converted to the religion of the Supreme Being. To prove his friendship, he offered Roze as wife the prettiest girl of the palace, rumored to be one of Ali's daughters. An Orthodox wedding followed at which Albanian soldiers and an Orthodox bishop danced the *carmagnole*. In honor of the occasion, the French delegation released an aerostatic balloon.[153]

A year later, the French distributed four thousand tricolor cockades to the peasants of Lower Albania in an effort to win their support. At the same time, they attempted to divert the attention of the Turks from Napoleon's invasion of Syria and Egypt to the revolt of Osman Pasha Pasvanoğlu in the Vidin region of Bulgaria. Ali Pasha, however, attacked the French token forces that had been dispatched to the mainland coast opposite the Ionian Islands. Prevailing on Roze to attend a meeting, he obtained from him the local French order of battle and then sent him as prisoner to Istanbul.[154]

Finally, in 1814, a secret revolutionary society known as the Philike Hetairia was founded in Odessa, a Russian port on the Black Sea that was opened only in 1794 but quickly transformed into a great grain emporium with a swarming population of Serbs, Greeks, Bulgarians, Italians, Jews, Russians, and Turks.[155] Odessa was a nucleus of political intrigue and radical conspiracy. It linked

Russia to the Mediterranean spirit and élan of the Italian revolutionary group, the Carbonari, just as St. Petersburg joined it to the philosophy, ideology, and industry of western and central Europe.

The ostensible purpose of the Philike Hetairia was the promotion of Greek culture, but its chief goal was the creation either of a Greek nation-state or of a neo-Byzantine empire. Of the 452 men officially enrolled in this club in 1819, 153 were merchants and shippers, 60 were notables, 36 were fighting men, 24 were priests, 23 were officials or secretaries, 22 were teachers and students, 10 were doctors, 4 were lawyers, and 16 were members of miscellaneous professions. The professions of the remaining 104 persons are unknown. Thus, of the 348 persons whose professions we do know, 44 percent were engaged in trade, 41 percent were members of the bureaucracy and intelligentsia, and 10 percent were fighting men joining a new kind of men's society.

The Philike Hetairia contacted other revolutionary or quasi-revolutionary groups, namely, the associates of the Serbian rebel leader Karageorge (Karadjordje) Petrović, the Kishinev branch of the revolutionary Russian Decembrists, the Phanariot Russian officer Alexander Ypsilanti, and the Romanian *moşnean* (freeman) and ex-Russian officer Tudor Vladimirescu. After 1819, however, it admitted to membership, and even to positions of leadership, conservatives who embraced the objective of a national or Christian-Balkan state. Entertaining the project of a general Balkan insurrection,[156] it hoped to reproduce the kind of situation that had threatened in 1807 and 1808, when peasant disturbances broke out in the Banat and other Habsburg territories and the Ottoman Empire had to face the blows of Russia in the northeast, Serbia in the north center, and Montenegro in the west. In those years, moreover, there had been klephtic attempts to join forces with the Serbian rebels and insurrections in Thessaly and Macedonia— most important among them, the revolt of 1808 by the *armatoloi* and peasants of Thessaly, led by the priest klepht *Papa* Evthymio Vlachavas and his brother Theodore.[157]

This had been the turbulent era of what Bosnian Muslims called the *vampir*, the vampire empire and frame of mind born of the murder of the *ancien régime*, namely, the French Revolution and Empire of Napoleon.[158] Master of Corfu, Dalmatia, Ragusa, and the Bay of Kotor, Napoleon united the last three in 1809 to the Croatian Military Frontier and to Trieste, Istria, Carinthia, and Carniola, under the name of the French Illyrian Provinces.

A general Balkan revolution failed to materialize in 1821, however, as it had failed in 1807. Miloš Obrenović of Serbia, leader of the Serbian insurrection of 1815 and organizer of a new semiautonomous Serbian state, refused to join the movement. The heterogeneous Balkan bands under the command of Ypsilanti found little support among the peasantry of Moldavia. Because of his imperviousness to their grievances against the seigniorial regime, the peasantry of Wallachia also withdrew its support from Vladimirescu.

But revolution did come to the Morea or Peloponnesus and to neighboring

Greek areas. The Greeks fought the Turks from 1821 to 1829, engaging simulta-
neously in bitter internecine strife. Muslim Albanian troops in the employ of
Mehmed Ali of Egypt intervened against them, but they received moral, finan-
cial, and volunteer-fighter aid from liberals in the western European countries.
They eventually received additional aid in the form of joint French, British, and
Russian naval action against the Ottoman fleet and of a Russian invasion of
Moldavia, Wallachia, and Bulgaria. Of the European countries and provinces in
which insurrection occurred during the 1820s—Wallachia, Moldavia, Greece,
Italy, Spain, and Russia—Greece was the only one that could lay claim to a
partly successful political and social revolution.

In one manner or another, however, all Balkan provinces felt the consequences of a half-century of revolution extending from 1788 to 1833. In the
Ottoman Empire itself, the threat of revolution made imperative the reforms
collectively known as the Tanzimat (1826–76). To Wallachia and Moldavia it
brought, under Russian sponsorship, a charter known as the Organic Statutes,
and it deprived the Ottoman Empire of the right to preempt the raw materials of
these provinces. To Serbia revolution brought autonomy; to Greece, nominal
independence. Finally, Bulgaria opened itself to the modern world, or to such
outside influences as were acceptable to the various sectors of Bulgarian society.

A new generation of Bulgarians, nourished intellectually in the middle and
higher schools and in the liberal and radical circles of Russia, Greece, Serbia,
and Wallachia, espoused the cause of modern nationalism and social revolution. Even conservatives became nationalists, supporting the idea of a Turco-
Bulgarian dual state (like the Austro-Hungarian dual state set up in 1867). Moreover, they led a movement that culminated in 1870 in the emancipation of the
Bulgarian church from the patriarchate of Constantinople. Actual political autonomy was won in 1878 through a combination of peasant rebellions (in Bosnia-
Hercegovina and Macedonia, as well as Bulgaria), cooperation between *haiduts*
and liberal and radical revolutionaries, and, most important of all, Russian
intervention.

The evaluation of the Serbian revolution by the nineteenth-century liberal
folklorist, lexicographer, and man of letters Vuk Karadžić, and by the socialist
Svetozar Marković, is almost equally applicable to the Greek and Bulgarian. In
all three countries, the revolutions were national and social, involving, in the
words of Marković, the "eradication of an entire unproductive class of people,
who lived a completely different life, spoke a different language, worshiped
another faith, and regarded the Serbian [and the Greek and Bulgarian] people as
its property."[159] One may contest the view that the Turks and other Ottoman
Muslims were an "unproductive class." On the other hand, we unreservedly
agree that the revolutions undermined the preexisting estates structures. Although a new social order guaranteeing the security of property and based upon
the principles of equality before the law, freedom of contract, and social mobility
through free political and economic competition had to be fought for and won

over and over again, many institutions resembling those that had been introduced only very recently in western Europe itself—written constitutions, political parties with a variety of ideologies (liberalism, nationalism, progressivism, populism, utopian socialism, Marxism, and peasantism), and educational facilities for an increasingly larger public—were rapidly brought into being.

Theory of Nationality

During and after the Napoleonic wars, a series of autonomous or nominally independent Balkan states arose along the Danube (Serbia, Wallachia and Moldavia united as Romania, and Bulgaria) or on the sea (Greece); Montenegro already enjoyed a considerable degree of autonomy. This increase in the number of self-governing states immediately raised the question of which would be victor, the revolutionary principle of nationality as represented by the new states or the principle of empire as embodied in the Habsburg, Ottoman, and Russian monarchies. In the long run (1804–1920), the empires collapsed and, with the creation between 1912 and 1920 of a Serb-Croat-Slovene state (Yugoslavia), an enlarged Romania, a slightly enlarged (but disaffected) Bulgaria, and a nominally independent Albania, the theory of nationality triumphed.

The period since 1920 has been typically an era of striving to mold a homogeneous nationality or a cluster of mutually compatible subnationalities. Threatened by and accommodating themselves to German and Italian fascism and developing authoritarianisms of their own during the interwar and World War II periods, the Balkan states almost foundered in the sea of nationality conflict.

In the hope of solving the national question, they pursued the following policies during one or both of the postwar periods:

1. Subdivision of large estates, resulting in the expropriation of Germans and Magyars in Romania and Yugoslavia and of Turks in Bulgaria, Greece, and Yugoslavia.

2. Nationalization of enterprises known to have collaborated with the enemy during World War II.

3. Exchange of populations, involving more than 2 million persons during the first postwar period, with Greeks going from Turkey and Bulgaria to Greece, Macedonian Slavs from Greece to Bulgaria, and Turks from Bulgaria and Greece to Turkey.

4. "Voluntary" expatriation of minority ethnic and religious groups to the countries of their choice.

5. Expulsion after World War II of a large portion of the German minority from Yugoslavia and Romania and the Turkish minority from Bulgaria.

6. Establishment of limitations upon the movements of populations engaging in transhumance or seasonal migrations, thus facilitating their assimilation with the settled folk.

7. Adoption of other assimilationist policies, including the nonenforcement of minority "rights" and the maintenance of educational facilities and employment opportunities for minority nationalities and ethnicities at a reduced level.

8. Promotion by Romania after World War II of policies designed to encourage the emigration of Jews (to Israel) and Gipsies.

9. Genocide, as practiced by Turkey against the Armenians of Asia Minor before and during World War I and by the Croats and Muslims of Croatia (including Bosnia and Hercegovina) against the Serbs and by the Germans against Jews, Gipsies, and Slovenians during World War II, and "ethnic cleansing" (expulsion from settlement areas where they were not wanted) by the Serbs, Croats, and Muslims of Croatia and Bosnia and Hercegovina of each other during the Yugoslav civil war of the 1990s.

In all the Balkan countries, 75 to 90 percent of the population was composed, between 1950 and 1990, of a dominant nationality or of several theoretically co-dominant subnational groups. In Yugoslavia, where the principle of subnationality was operative, the subnationalities (called nations or peoples) comprised Serbs, Montenegrins, Croats, Slovenes, Muslims (an identity officially recognized in the 1960s for Serbo-Croat-speaking Bosnians and Hercegovinians of the Muslim faith), Macedonian Slavs, and Yugoslavs (South Slavs who, instead of identifying with one of the subnationalities preferred the designation Yugoslav). In Romanian Transylvania, in the Ruse, Shumen, and Varna districts of Bulgaria, in Greek and Bulgarian Thrace, and in Yugoslav Macedonia and Vojvodina, the minority nationalities are large, and in Yugoslavia's Kosmet (Kosovo-Metohija) or Kosovo region, the Albanians continue to constitute an overwhelming majority. The maze of ethnic enclaves already existent in Antiquity but much complicated by the migrations of peoples and the resettlement policies of empires and other states was simplified between 1850 and 1950. The subsequent failure to maintain a viable system of socialist states has led, however, to a revival of ethnic and national strife, culminating in 1991 in civil war and the dismemberment of Yugoslavia.

The Balkan national and social revolutions alike remain an unfinished affair. From one point of view, this is not a great indictment. Even the French Revolution remained an "unfinished revolution" until the 1880s, perhaps even until the 1930s. By identifying the Balkan revolutions since 1788 as "unfinished revolutions," we mean that they did not fully institute the social structures that might have enabled them to perpetuate a stable new social system: a group of "middle elements" sufficiently large, homogeneous, and independent as to be able to manage the abnormal social strains created by three world wars (the French Revolution, World War I and World War II), a succession of major world economic crises, communist revolution, fascist counterrevolution, Yugoslav (1941–46, 1990s) and Greek (1946–48) civil wars, technological backwardness, cold war, demographic restructuring, conflict between a multiplicity of cultural and political traditions, and since 1989–91 a revolution or counterrevolution that may take unforseen directions.

The task of achieving "disalienation" or removing the condition of estrange-ment between the various sectors of society and generalizing, intensifying, so-cializing, or "completing" revolution, giving it a new élan or taking it along new directions, ultimately fell, after 1941 or 1944, to communist leadership in Yugo-slavia, Bulgaria, Romania, and Albania. In 1949, it reverted to bourgeois leader-ship in Greece.

After the Greek civil war of 1946–48 between communists and anti-communists, and the subsequent interlude of tight police control, came eight years of political stability (1955–63) under Constantine Karamanlis of the "free enterprise" Radical Union. The continuing divisions in Greek society led in 1967 to the seizure of power by a military junta. The dictatorship of the "colonels" was brought down in 1974, following the failure of the coup against the govern-ment of Makarios of Cyprus, which provoked a Turkish invasion of the northern part of the island.

Since that time Greece has moved toward the goal of completing its demo-cratic "revolution." It began the process in 1974 by holding a referendum on the monarchy (rejected in favor of a republic), by legitimizing the Communist party, and by recognizing demotic Greek as the only national language. Two parties won the allegiance of a large body of Greeks, the "New Democracy" of Constan-tine Karamanlis, and the new PASOK or Panhellenic Socialist Movement of Andreas Papandreou. "New Democracy" embraced the ideology of "European-ism," with the object of obtaining complete integration with the European Eco-nomic Community. At its formation in 1974, on the other hand, PASOK expressed its opposition to "a Europe that is more and more dominated by multinational monopolies."[160]

Since the demise of the Soviet Union and the Yugoslav civil war, the question of whether there can be a European Community—or whether there should be one—unless it alters its present basis in money and the ideology of economic growth—has become yet more crucial. It obliges us to ascertain the relationships between culture, modes of production, economic systems, and society. It forces us to confront the question of unequal factor endowments within regions, na-tions, and cultural systems.

Notes

1. For a critique, see Renfrew, *Archaeology and Language*, pp. 15–21.
2. Gimbutas, *The Goddesses and Gods of Old Europe,* pp. 9, 238; Gimbutas, *The Slavs*, pp. 17–19.
3. Renfrew, *Archaeology and Language*, pp. 125, 148–50; Hassan, *Demographic Ar-chaeology*, pp. 8, 39, 196–97, 221, 234, 254, 259.
4. Myres, "An Attempt to Reconstruct the Maps Used by Herodotus," pp. 606–31; Hartog, *The Mirror of Herodotus*, pp. 14–22.
5. Lattimore, "La Civilisation, mère de barbarie?" pp. 95–108. For a similar but modi-fied view, see René Grousset, "La Civilisation à travers l'histoire," pp. 61–111.

6. Braudel, *Civilisation matérielle, économie et capitalisme,* III, 29–30; Lévi-Strauss, *Mythologiques,* I, 36.

7. Condurachi, *Archéologie roumaine au XXe siècle,* p. 82; Condurachi and Daicoviciu, *Romania,* pp. 179–83.

8. Plinius Secundus, C. *Naturalis Historiae,* VI, I, 345 (Book IV, sec. 97); Tacitus, *Tacitus on Britain and Germany,* pp. 139–40; Gimbutas, *The Slavs,* pp. 58, 60; Črnja, *Kulturna historija Hrvatske,* pp. 72–73.

9. Gimbutas, *The Slavs,* pp. 58–61; Hauptmann, "Seobe Hrvata i Srba," p. 53; Šufflay, *Srbi i Arbanasi,* pp. 111–12; Martinet, *Des Steppes aux océans,* p. 112; Grégoire, "L'Origine et le nom des Croates et des Serbes," pp. 88–118.

10. Toynbee, *A Study of History,* II, 318.

11. Škrivanić, *Oružje u srednjovekovnoj Srbiji, Bosni i Dubrovniku,* p. 204.

12. Xénopol, *Une énigme historique,* p. 93.

13. For a map of Stari Vlah, caravan routes, and directions of transhumance in the region between Dubrovnik and Mostar in the west and Belgrade, Niš, and Skopje in the east, see Roglić, "The Geographical Setting of Medieval Dubrovnik," p. 149.

14. Winnifrith, *The Vlachs,* p. 28.

15. For Mala Vlaška in Slavonia, see Karger, *Die Entwicklung der Siedlungen im westlichen Slawonien,* p. 64.

16. Martinet, *Des Steppes aux océans,* pp. 27–28.

17. Niederle, *Manuel de l'Antiquité slave,* I, 56.

18. Eliade, *Zalmoxis, the Vanishing God,* pp. 1–2, 12–14.

19. Wace and M. S. Thompson, *The Nomads of the Balkans,* p. 10.

20. Novaković, "Selo," p. 54.

21. Liddell and Scott, comps., *A Greek-English Lexicon,* I, 936–37 (κέλης [courser], κέλλω, and κελεύω [drive on, urge]); Buck, *Dictionary of Selected Synonyms in the Principal Indo-European Languages,* pp. 712–13; Chantraine, *Dictionnaire étymologique de la langue grecque,* I, 512–13 (κελεύω).

22. Jireček, "Albanien in der Vergangenheit," I, 66. See also Winnifrith, *The Vlachs,* pp. 49–50 and map 10 (endpaper map), where the author draws the Jireček line too far south.

23. Petrović, *Život i običaji narodni u Gruži,* p. 502.

24. Georgiev, "The Earliest Ethnological Situation of the Balkan Peninsula," pp. 50–65; Commission Nationale de la République Populaire d'Albanie, "Note sur les Illyriens," pp. 955–58; Fine, Jr., *The Early Medieval Balkans,* pp. 10–11.

25. Haraszti, *Origin of the Rumanians,* pp. 70–71.

26. Charanis, "The Transfer of Population as a Policy in the Byzantine Empire," pp. 140–54.

27. Hall, *Inventing the Barbarian,* p. 178; Hettich, *A Study in Ancient Nationalism,* pp. 45–54; Tăpkova-Zaimova, "L'Idée byzantine de l'unité du monde et l'État bulgare," pp. 296.

28. Vryonis, Jr., "Nomadization and Islamization in Asia Minor," p. 59.

29. Šufflay, *Srbi i Arbanasi,* p. 69; Popović, *O Cincarima,* p. 27.

30. Babinger, "Deli-Orman," pp. 202–3.

31. Quoted in Paikert, *The Danube Swabians,* pp. 26–27.

32. Pittard, *Les Peuples des Balkans,* pp. 95, 105, 109–10, 129, 131, 136, 153–54, 160, 185–87, 205, 239–43, 274–77, 281, 562, 572–73; Pittard, *Les Races et l'histoire,* pp. 313, 321–22, 334–42, 347–48, 352–55, 365–66, 371–73; Pittard, *Race and Culture,* pp. 246–61, 278–98; Coon, *The Races of Europe,* pp. 184–85, 199–200, 585, 588–92, 597, 602–5, 608–10, 614–21.

33. Coon, *The Races of Europe,* pp. 10–11; Coon, *The Living Races of Man,* pp. 64–65, 74, 304; Coon, *Racial Adaptations,* pp. 88–89, 116–23; Tildesley, "The Albanians

of the North and South," pp. 21–29; Biometric Laboratory Staff, "Discussion of Miss M. L. Tildesley's Measurements of the Northern and Southern Albanians," pp. 29–42.

34. For suggestions along this line, see Iorga, *Le Caractère commun des institutions du Sud-est de l'Europe*, pp. 110–19.

35. On the difference between Latin and Orthodox conceptions of the Trinity, see Geanakoplos, "The Council of Florence", pp. 84–111. See also Dvornik, *Byzantine Missions among the Slavs*.

36. Fine, Jr., *The Early Medieval Balkans*, pp. 113–35, 141–42, 171–79; Browning, *Byzantium and Bulgaria*, pp. 153–69.

37. Novaković, *Zakonik Stefana Dušana cara srpskog, 1349 i 1354*, pp. 67, 198; Niederle, *Manuel de l'Antiquité slave*, II, 142–43.

38. Novaković, *Zakonik Stefana Dušana cara srpskog 1349 i 1354*, pp. 23, 67, 84, 197–98, 212–13; Katić, *Medicina kod Srba u srednjem veku*, p. 17; Obolensky, "Bogomilism in the Byzantine Empire," p. 290; Obolensky, *The Bogomils*, pp. 164–67.

39. Bekker, ed., *Nicetae Choniatae Historiae*, p. 485; Jireček, *Geschichte der Bulgaren*, pp. 225–26; Arnaudov, *Studii vŭrkhu bŭlgarskite obredi i legendi*, pt. 1–2, pp. 92–96, 105–8; Zlatarski, *Istoriia na bŭlgarskata dŭrzhava prez srednite vekove*, Vol. II, Pt. 1, pp. 413–14; Bănescu, *Un Problème d'histoire médiévale*, pp. 8–9; Wolff, "The Second Bulgarian Empire," pp. 182–83; Barišić, *Čuda Dimitrija Solunskog kao istoriski izvori*, pp. 41–45, 68, 72 n.; Uspenskii, *Obrazovanie Vtorago Bolgarskago Tsarstva*, pp. 126–27, 222; Picard, "Nouvelles observations sur diverses représentations du héros cavalier des Balkans"; Vermaseren, *Mithras*, pp. 27–32, 67–75, 90–94, 129–42.

40. Pouqueville, *Voyage dans la Grèce*, III, 61–62, 288 n. 1.

41. Harva, *Les Représentations religieuses des peuples altaïques*, pp. 343–49.

42. Fine, Jr., *The Late Medieval Balkans*, pp. 10–15.

43. Fine, Jr., *The Early Medieval Balkans*, pp. 280–81.

44. Fine, Jr., *The Late Medieval Balkans*, pp. 38–49, 60–63, 78–81, 106–8, 115–19, 130–31, 143–49.

45. Durham, *Some Tribal Origins, Laws, and Customs*, pp. 102–11, 118–24, 129; Wenzel, "Bosnian and Herzegovinian Tombstones," pp. 107–8 n. 19.

46. Fine, Jr., *The Late Medieval Balkans*, pp. 279–85, 481–87. For an excellent, more detailed study of religion in Bosnia and Hercegovina, see Fine, Jr., *The Bosnian Church*, pp. 9–39. On Islam, see Von Grunebaum, "Islamic Studies and Cultural Research," p. 14; Kissling, "The Sociological and Educational Role of the Dervish Orders in the Ottoman Empire," pp. 23–35.

47. Francès, "La Féodalité et les villes byzantines," p. 93.

48. Palamas, *Grégoire Palamas*, ed. Meyendorff, pp. 184, 196, 202, 282–85, 334; Meyendorff, *St. Grégoire Palamas et la mystique orthodoxe*, p. 64.

49. Gardet, "Un Problème de mystique comparée."

50. Vryonis, Jr., "Religious Changes and Patterns in the Balkans," p. 169.

51. Solovjev, "Nestanak bogomilstva i islamizacija Bosne," pp. 63–72; Chaumette des Fossés, *Voyage en Bosnie*, pp. 31–45.

52. Burns, "The Circum-Alpine Culture Area," pp. 152–54; Planhol, *The World of Islam*, pp. 82–86; Skendi, "Religion in Albania during the Ottoman Rule," pp. 311–27.

53. Gimbutas, *The Goddesses and Gods of Old Europe*, p. 137.

54. Soper, *The Religions of Mankind*, pp. 58, 67.

55. Adams, *Mont-Saint-Michel and Chartres*, p. 298.

56. Curtius, *The Civilization of France*, p. 149.

57. Plato, *The Republic*.

58. Cowell, *History, Civilization, and Culture*, pp. 224–25; Schlemmer, "Warum triadisch?" p. 16.

59. Dumézil, *L'Idéologie tripartite des Indo-Européens*, p. 7.

60. Martinet, *Des Steppes aux océans*, p. 27.

61. Pouqueville, *Voyage dans la Grèce*, III, 397–98; Macartney, *The Magyars in the Ninth Century*, pp. 174–76.

62. Cerfberr de Medelsheim, *Mémoires sur la Grèce et l'Albanie*, pp. 382–83.

63. Ludat, "Farbenzeichnungen in Völkernamen," pp. 138–55; Fennel, *Ivan the Great of Moscow*, pp. 8–9.

64. Ludat, "Farbenzeichnungen in Völkernamen," pp. 151–52.

65. Dumézil, *L'Idéologie tripartite des Indo-Européens*, pp. 26–27, 50.

66. Grekov, *Krestiane na Rusi s drevneishikh vremen do XVII veka*, pp. 529–30, 635–36, 638; Pipes, *Russia under the Old Regime*, pp. 47–48, 100–105; Raeff, *Understanding Imperial Russia*, p. 7.

67. Portal, *Les Slaves*, p. 17; Kosminskii and Levandovskii, eds., *Atlas istorii srednikh vekov*, pp. 5, 12, 13; Šufflay, *Srbi i Arbanasi*, pp. 107–8; Nikitin et al., eds., *Istoriia Iuzhnykh i Zapadnykh Slavian*, map "Slaviane na Balkanskom poluostrove"; Guldescu, *History of Medieval Croatia*, pp. 68–88, 111, 115–16, 193–95, 245–47; Toynbee, *Constantine Porphyrogenitus and His World*, "The Slavonic-Speaking Peoples," (end map).

68. Dumézil, *L'Idéologie tripartite des Indo-Européens*, pp. 5–8. See also Benveniste, *Le Vocabulaire des institutions indo-européennes*, I, 279–92. For a critique of the theory of an ideology and sociology of tripartition, see Renfrew, *Archaeology and Language*, pp. 250–62.

69. Thomson, *Studies in Ancient Greek Society*, I, 355, 359, 363–64; Hopper, *Trade and Industry in Classical Greece*, p. 63; Kitto, *The Greeks*, pp. 40–41; Mireaux, *Daily Life in the Time of Homer*, p. 106; Dumézil, "Métiers et classes fonctionnelles chez divers peuples," pp. 716–24.

70. Mireaux, *Daily Life in the Time of Homer*, pp. 148–50, 165–69.

71. Thomson, *Studies in Ancient Greek Society*, I, 45.

72. Gasparini, "La 'Verv' e i 'Sjabry," pp. 12–14; Iorga, *Le Caractère commun des institutions du Sud-est de l'Europe*.

73. I have drawn this conclusion after a careful reading of the following: Koledarov, "Place-Name Classification in the Central Part of the Balkan Peninsula in the Middle Ages," and my comment on p. 288; Krauss, "Aux temps anciens," pp. 183–84.

74. Dinić, *Srpske zemlje u srednjem veku*, p. 213; Krauss, "Aux temps anciens," pp. 179–84.

75. Wenzel, "Bosnian and Herzegovinian Tombstones," p. 119.

76. Werner, "Yürüken und Wlachen"; Sučević, "Razvitak 'vlaških prava' u Varaždinskom Generalatu," pp. 33–70. See also chapter 8.

77. Marinović, "Prilog poznavanju dubrovačkih bratovština," pp. 233–45; Stoianovich, *Between East and West*, III, chapter on "Raguse—Société sans imprimerie."

78. Roberts, *Political Problems of an Agrarian State*, pp. 7–8; Stahl, *Traditional Romanian Village Communities*, pp. 217–18; Chirot, *Social Change in a Peripheral Society*, pp. 24–25, 74–78, 97–98.

79. Bloch, *La Société féodale*, p. 136; Novaković, *Zakonik Stefana Dušana Cara srpskog 1349 i 1354*, pp. 82, 211; Novaković, "Djuvendija," pp. 175–81; Radojković, *O Sokalnicima*, pp. 63–95, 106–8, 138–43; Vlajinac, *Die agrar-rechtlichen Verhältnisse des mittelalterlichen Serbiens*, pp. 143–50, 157–58.

80. Kemp, *Healing Ritual*, pp. 157, 183–84; Mirković, *Ekonomska historija Jugoslavije*, p. 138. For a description of a *katun* as a "tribal domain" or "special governmental region," see Wenzel, "Bosnian and Herzegovinian Tombstones," p. 116. For an interesting, partly autobiographical study of the *katun*, see Vucinich, *A Study in Social Survival*.

81. Novaković, *Zakonik Stefana Dušana cara srpskog 1349 i 1354*, p. 56.

82. Rački, "Nutarnje stanje Hrvatske prije XII stoljeća"; Francès, "La Féodalité et les villes byzantines," p. 93; Charanis, "Internal Strife in Byzantium during the Fourteenth Century," pp. 208–30; Jireček, *La Civilisation serbe au Moyen âge*, pp. 24–26; Antoljak, *Bune pučana i seljaka u Hrvatskoj*, pp. 16–18.

83. The paragraphs on Ottoman estates follow closely a section in Stoianovich, "Factors in the Decline of Ottoman Society," pp. 623–25. See also Stoianovich, "The Social Foundations of Balkan Politics," pp. 298–303.

84. Miller, "Greece under the Turks," pp. 658–59.

85. Holland, *Travels in the Ionian Isles, Albania, Thessaly, Macedonia*, pp. 153, 165.

86. Reljković, *Satir iliti divji čovik*, pp. 152–55.

87. Verdery, *Transylvanian Villagers*, pp. 98–106.

88. Hitchins, "Samuel Clain and the Rumanian Enlightenment," pp. 665–66.

89. Radojčić, "Dositejevo pismo o uredjenju i prosvećenju Srbije," p. 26.

90. Ferrières-Sauveboeuf, *Mémoires historiques, politiques et géographiques*, II, 253, my translation.

91. Stoianovich, "The Social Foundations of Balkan Politics," p. 301.

92. Grenville, *Observations sur l'état actuel de l'Empire ottoman*, p. 71. Grenville served as ambassador to Turkey between 1762 and 1765.

93. Pouqueville, *Voyage en Morée, à Constantinople, en Albanie*, I, 265, translated in Stoianovich, "Factors in the Decline of Ottoman Society," p. 630. On polygamy and Ottoman Muslim women in the eighteenth century, see also Eton, *A Survey of the Turkish Empire*, pp. 242–44. On male and female homosexuality and the practice and punishment of adultery and fornication in the Ottoman Empire, see Cerfberr de Medelsheim, *Mémoires sur la Grèce et l'Albanie*, pp. 252–57.

94. Bousquet, "L'Islam et la limitation volontaire des naissances," pp. 121–28.

95. Bouthol, *Biologie sociale*, pp. 69–71.

96. Turgot, "Plan de deux discours sur l'histoire universelle."

97. Bonald, "Du Divorce," pp. 175.

98. Lockwood, "Bride Theft and Social Maneuverability in Western Bosnia," pp. 255–56.

99. On kinship, socioeconomic organization, the extended family, and gender roles among the Saracatsans, Greek-speaking groups of pastoralists about whose origins there is much controversy but who probably embraced pastoralism during the fourteenth and fifteenth centuries, see Kavadias, *Pasteurs-nomades méditerranéens*, pp. 123–75.

100. For a detailed analysis of historical and spatial variations in household size, see Stoianovich, *Between East and West*, II, 133–46.

101. Halpern, "The Zadruga," pp. 83–97; Petrović, *Život i običaji narodni u Gruži*, p. 185; Bićanić, "Occupational Heterogeneity of Peasant Families," p. 82.

102. Stahl, *Traditional Romanian Village Communities*, pp. 24–27.

103. On *moba* or *bedba*, see Schneeweis, *Serbokroatische Volkskunde*, I, 153, 181–82; Mijatović, *Servia and the Servians*, p. 242; Petrović, *Život i običaji narodni u Gruži*, p. 196. For a more complete treatment, see Vlajinac, *Moba i pozajmica*.

104. Petrović, *Život i običaji narodni u Gruži*, pp. 192–93.

105. Quoted in Milićević, *Kraljevina Srbija*, pp. 262–63, my translation. For Slav-Macedonian and Serbian variants, see Milićević, *Kneževina Srbija*, II, 858; Cvijić, *La Péninsule balkanique*, p. 391. See also Djordjević, "Uzimanje u rodu u našem narodu," pp. 331–39.

106. Castellan, *La Culture serbe au seuil de l'Indépendance*, pp. 53–54, 62–66, 70, 78, 81–82, 87, 111–12, 138, 140–41.

107. Eliade, *Myths, Dreams, and Mysteries*, pp. 211–12.

108. Djordjević, *Gradja za srpske narodne običaje iz vremena prve vlade Kneza Miloša*, pp. 458–59.

109. For the phratry in preclassical Greece, see Thomson, *Studies in Ancient Greek Society*, I, 58–59, 71–72, 104–8.

110. Šobajić, "Povodom dvaju najnovijih priloga proučavanju plemena u staroj Hercegovini," pp. 257–78.

111. Oliva, *Pannonia*, pp. 145–48; Condurachi and Daicoviciu, *Romania*, p. 127.

112. Trojanović, "Manners and Customs," pp. 174–76; Dučić, *Život i običaji plemena Kuči*, p. 127.

113. Hubert, *The Greatness and Decline of the Celts*, pp. 189, 211; Flatrès, "Historical Geography of Western France," p. 321.

114. Hammel, *Alternative Social Structures*, pp. 43–93.

115. Grbić, *Srpski narodni običaji iz sreza Boljevačkog*, pp. 114–16, 136–38; Kemp, *Healing Ritual*, pp. 83–84; Hammel, *Alternative Social Structures*, pp. 8–9.

116. On the haircutting ceremony in Byzantium, see Gavazzi, "Das Kulturerbe der Südslaven im Lichte der Völkerkunde," pp. 71–72. For at least one way of representing kinship in Byzantium, see Patlagean, "Une représentation byzantine de la parenté et ses origines occidentales," pp. 59–81. For initiatory haircutting ceremonies among the ancient Greeks, see Harrison, *Themis*, pp. 378, 441, 498–500.

117. Kemp, *Healing Ritual*, pp. 85–88.

118. Erdeljanović, *Etnološka gradja o Šumadincima*, pp. 137–38; Campbell, "The Kindred in a Greek Mountain Community," p. 77; Schneeweis, *Serbokroatische Volkskunde*, I, 176–77; Hammel, *Alternative Social Structures*, p. 28.

119. Devereux, "Considérations ethnopsychanalytiques sur la notion de parenté," p. 237; Heusch, "Introduction à une ritologie générale," p. 218.

120. Campbell, "The Kindred in a Greek Mountain Community," pp. 79–80; Campbell, *Honour, Family, and Patronage*, p. 41; Kavadias, *Pasteurs nomades méditerranéens*, pp. 175–83, for the *tseli(n)gas* associations among the Saracatsans; Stahl, *Household, Village, and Village Confederation*, p. 163.

121. Berr, *En marge de l'histoire universelle*, p. 170; Myres, *Geographical History in Greek Lands*, pp. 205–7.

122. Toynbee, *A Study of History*, III, pp. 65–66.

123. Popović, *O Hajducima*, I, 66.

124. Campbell, "The Kindred in a Greek Mountain Community," p. 77; Campbell, *Honour, Family, and Patronage*, p. 38.

125. For the persistence of the concept of *pallikari* into the twentieth century, see Campbell, *Honour, Family, and Patronage*, pp. 182–83, 278–81.

126. Sjoestedt, *Dieux et héros des Celtes*, pp. 109–21.

127. Jovanović, *Iz naše istorije i književnosti*, pp. 16–17.

128. Pouqueville, *Voyage de la Grèce*, IV, 245; Edmonds, "Introductory and Historical Sketch of the Klephts," p. 10; Spandonidis, "Le Clefte," pp. 3–17.

129. Wilhelmy, *Hochbulgarien*, I, 120–22; Pouqueville, *Voyage de la Grèce*, III, 68, 280–89, where the author refers to the *kirjalis* or Rumeliot marauders as "Haidouts Kersales."

130. Popović, *O Hajducima*, II, 125–43.

131. Wood, ed., *Mr. Harrie Cavendish*, p. 14.

132. Blount, *A Briefe Relation of a Iourney*, pp. 8–18.

133. Lady Mary (Pierrepont) Wortley Montagu, to the abbé Conti, Adrianople, 1 April [O.S.] 1717, in *The Complete Letters*, I, 316.

134. For further details on banditry in the Balkans between 1500 and 1800, see Braudel, "Misère et banditisme," pp. 129–42; Elezović, *Turski spomenici*, pp. 337–47;

Karadžić, *Danica*; Mittesser, "Militairische Beschreibung," pp. 57–102, in Pantelić, "Vojno-geografski opisi Srbije."

135. Gerlach, ed., *Stephan Gerlach dess Aeltern Tage-Buch;* Matković, "Putovanje po Balkanskom poluotoku XVI vieka," pp. 50–51.

136. Varagnac, *Civilisation traditionnelle et genres de vie*, pp. 212–19; Wenzel, "The Dioscuri in the Balkans," pp. 369–75.

137. On millennialism in the Balkans and Asia Minor, see Stoianovich, *Between East and West*, IV, chapter on "Prospective: Third and Fourth Levels of History." On millennialism (but not identified as such) among the Vlachs or Vlacho-Serbs and Croats of the Dinaric and Adriatic regions toward the close of the sixteenth century, see Bracewell, *The Uskoks of Senj*, pp. 24, 72–73, 216.

138. Janković, *Astronomija u predanjima*, pp. 114–16.

139. Čajkanović, *O srpskom vrhovnom bogu*, p. 116, my translation. For a fuller discussion of Stanj and other Serbian augurs but at a lower analytical level, see Milićević, *Život Srba seljaka*, pp. 76–86. The quotation comes from Čajkanović and differs slightly from the statements which Milićević's informants attributed to Stanj. Čajkanović situates Stanj in the eighteenth century, whereas Milićević leads us to believe that he was a seventeenth-century figure. On millennialism among the South Slavs and for a justification of the translation of *Crnokapa* and *Crnogaća*, see Stoianovich, *Between East and West*, IV, chapter on "Les Structures millénaristes sud-slaves aux XVIIe et XVIIIe siècles."

140. Lanternari, *The Religions of the Oppressed*, p. 3.

141. Benda, "Les Jacobins hongrois," pp. 38–60; d'Eszláry, "Les Jacobins hongrois," pp. 291–307; Godechot, *La Grande Nation*, I, 123, 187–89; Kostić, "Nekoliko idejnih odraza Francuske Revolucije," pp. 5–20; Palmer, *The Age of the Democratic Revolution*, I, 245, 388–96; McNeill, *Europe's Steppe Frontier*, pp. 218–20.

142. Holland, *Travels in the Ionian Isles, Albania, Thessaly, Macedonia*, p. 428.

143. Demos, "The Neo-Hellenic Enlightenment," pp. 523–41; Svoronos, *Histoire de la Grèce moderne*, pp. 30–33.

144. Gottwald, "Phanariotische Studien," pp. 1–58.

145. Holland, *Travels in the Ionian Isles, Albania, Thessaly, Macedonia*, pp. 148–52, 167.

146. Stephen Chaconas, *Adamantios Korais*, pp. 34–44. Richard Clogg may disagree with some of my conclusions, but I have learned much from his "The Greek Mercantile Bourgeoisie," pp. 85–110.

147. Stoianovich, "The Segmentary State and *La Grande Nation*," pp. 279, 259, for the quotations in the order of their appearance.

148. Blanc, *La Croatie occidentale*, pp. 276–77.

149. Stoianovich, "The Segmentary State and *La Grande Nation*," p. 279.

150. Godechot, *La Grande Nation*, I, 198–200; Lebel, *La France et les Principautés danubiennes*, pp. 301–2; Dascalakis, *Rhigas Velestinlis*.

151. For a variety of interesting recent interpretations of the Serbian, Greek, and Balkan revolutions, see Stavrianos, "Antecedents to the Balkan Revolutions of the Nineteenth Century," pp. 335–48; Stavrianos, "The Influence of the West on the Balkans," pp. 184–226; Karal, "La Transformation de la Turquie," pp. 426–45; Lewis, "The Impact of the French Revolution on Turkey," pp. 105–25; Vucinich, "Marxian Interpretations of the First Serbian Revolution," pp. 3–14; Vucinich, ed., *The First Serbian Uprising;* Djordjević, *Révolutions nationales des peuples balkaniques;* Djordjević and Fischer-Galati, *The Balkan Revolutionary Tradition;* Paxton, "Nationalism and Revolution," pp. 337–62; Sadat, "Rumeli Ayanlari," pp. 346–63; Banac, "The Role of Vojvodina in Karadjordje's Revolution," pp. 31–61.

152. Rodocanachi, *Bonaparte et les Îles Ioniennes*, pp. 34–36.

153. Rodocanachi, "Les Îles Ioniennes pendant l'occupation française," pp. 601–2.

154. Olivier, *Voyage dans l'Empire othoman, l'Égypte et la Perse*, I, 199–205; Lebel, *La France et les Principautés danubiennes*, pp. 79–82; Boppe, *L'Albanie et Napoléon*, p. 13; Rodocanachi, *Bonaparte et les Îles Ioniennes*, pp. 90–93, 100–102, 105–15.

155. Stoianovich, "Russian Domination in the Balkans," pp. 216–18; Stoianovich, "The Conquering Balkan Orthodox Merchant," pp. 288–89; Herlihy, "Russian Grain and Mediterranean Markets." See also Topping, "Greek Historical Writing," pp. 157–73.

156. Stoianovich, "The Conquering Balkan Orthodox Merchant," p. 308; Crawley, "John Capodistrias and the Greeks before 1821," pp. 162–82; Capodistrias, "Aperçu de ma carrière."

157. Bagally, *The Klephtic Ballads in Relation to Greek History*, pp. 78–92.

158. Šamić, "Un Consul français en Bosnie," p. 73.

159. Quote in McClellan, *Svetozar Marković*, pp. 184–85.

160. Constas, "Greek Foreign Policy Objectives," p. 37.

5 ECONOMY

The primary economic difference between archaic and modern (or precapitalist and capitalist) societies may appear to be the lack of a market in the archaic society. In fact, however, archaic societies were not without markets. A more important distinction was the absence of conditions conducive to the elaboration of a clear concept of economic value.

Number and Economic Value

The diffusion of a concept of economic value required a relatively highly developed notion of number. Even in Aristotle's Greece, however, there existed a primitive tribe that could not count beyond the number four.[1] The use in ancient Greek, Old Slavonic, and modern Serbo-Croatian of one form of expression for two, three, and four items of a given thing, but of a different plural form to refer to more than four items, suggests that counting may have occurred in two steps; first up to the number four, probably early in human history, and later beyond that number. The presence in the Indo-European languages of common cognate terms for one hundred may further indicate that some of the speakers of these languages at least were able to count up to nine hundred ninety-nine before the Indo-European dispersions of the fourth, third, and second millennia. They may have even been able to count in the thousands simply by associating the idea of a thousand with the term ten hundred, as did the Goths and Slavs. As for the Greeks, even before 500 B.C., they had devised symbols in their alphabetic notations for numbers up to 99,999,999. In the third century B.C., they conceived yet bigger numbers.[2]

Finally, in the late Middle Ages, the symbol for zero reached the Balkans by way of the Arabs. The use of Arabic numbers was not generalized in the Balkans, however, until the nineteenth century. Even today, among the Greeks, the letters of the alphabet continue to play the role of numbers for some purposes.

Numerical conceptualization by itself does not guarantee the existence of a clear concept of economic (or exchange, as against use) value, whether explained in terms of labor, utility, scarcity, supply and demand (equilibrium), or of varying attitudes toward these phenomena. Movement toward such a discovery, or invention, required the prior elaboration of a larger complex of structures that together would favor such an occurrence: the diffusion of writing, especially improved forms of written communication; the development of the three main transportation containers (sleds, wheeled vehicles, and boats, comprising in fact one basic invention adapted to three environments—grass- and snow-covered land, firm ground, and water); and the diffusion of the idea of money, culminating in the development of coinage.

A continuing obstacle to the conception and diffusion of the concept of economic value, however, stemmed from the very nature of prehistoric and premodern markets—their purpose, the kinds of goods that circulated therein, and the particular traits of the market traders. As a system of goods exchange, premodern markets would seem to have had an economic basis. Their function, however, was broader than that of the modern market. They provided a setting not only for the exchange of goods but also for the holding of games and for entertainment, feasts, and religious worship, and for the formation of alliances.

In the actual exchange of goods, premodern markets were also at a disadvantage because "priced goods" did not exist in them or were few in number, or because the traders in the premodern markets lacked good information on the basis of which to move toward the formation, at a given time and place, of what the Physiocrats later called a "common price." Among the Greeks, the concept of price arose only after coins were put into general use during the seventh and sixth centuries B.C. Long after that, however, they continued to regard many items as "free goods," destined to circulate without hindrance among members of the same family or clan, or as "ceremonial goods," reserved for exchange with outside groups.

One of the earliest forms of money among the Slavs was linen cloth *(platno)*. Flax *(plat)* itself, however, may have been a commodity of exchange. In any event, the words for these objects gave rise to the Slavic and Serbo-Croatian terms for "payment" *(plata)* and "to pay" *(platiti)*. In the tenth century, the Slavs of Franconia paid certain imposts in linen cloth. It is doubtful, however, that even a blurred conception of economic value existed among most Slavs before that time. Indeed, linen cloth was used primarily for making ceremonial gifts, a role that it continued to play among the Balkan Slavs (as among many other peoples) until the twentieth century. In ceremonies of diplomatic exchange, moreover, Byzantium had been in the habit of presenting the Pechenegs with gifts of purple cloth, or *blattia*, a word derived from the Latin for "purple." The Pechenegs, however, may have associated the word with the Slavic term for "linen cloth" or "ceremonial gift."[3]

In the fifth century B.C., relates Herodotus, the Carthaginians carried on trade

> with a race of men who live[d] in a part of Libya [the name then applied to a vast area of northern Africa] beyond the Pillars of Hercules [Gibraltar and Jebel Musa]. On reaching this country, they [would] unload their goods, ar-

range them tidily along the beach, and then, returning to their boats, [they would] raise a smoke. Seeing the smoke, the natives [would] come down to the beach, place on the ground a certain quantity of gold in exchange for the goods, and go off again to a distance. The Carthaginians then [would] come ashore and take a look at the gold; and if they [thought] it represent[ed] a fair price for their wares, they [would] collect it and go away; if, on the other hand, it seem[ed] too little, they [would] go back aboard and wait, and the natives [would] come and add to the gold until they [were] satisfied.[4]

If the Carthaginians took the gold, the other traders were authorized to return to the site to take away the goods brought by the Carthaginians.

One of the purposes of such *silent trade*, in the course of which the two groups of trading populations never or seldom entered into physical contact with each other, was to avoid disputes and armed conflict. As late as the 1760s, a modified version of such silent trade continued to be practiced along the southern Black Sea coast to the east of Trebizond (Trabzon). The British ambassador to Istanbul, Henry Grenville, describes the transaction of the boats that came to obtain the coastal-forest boxwood of which the Turks made many of their utensils:

> The vessels anchor at some distance from the coasts, for the inhabitants are great brigands. They place on the shore a large tinned copper plate (used by the peoples of the Levant as a table) containing gun barrels, gunlocks, sabre blades, knives, and small copper plates and other items of hardware conforming to the taste of these peoples. They then depart and give a signal with a cannon shot. The inhabitants then come, readily reach an agreement, authorizing the felling of a certain number of trees. There is nothing to fear thereupon, and they never take goods if the transaction falls through. If, on the other hand, a boat remains at anchor near the coast, it has to be on its guard lest it be pillaged at night during a calm or at the onset of contrary winds.[5]

I have found no documentary evidence to suggest the practice of silent trade in the Balkans during the last two thousand years, whether among the Greeks or among other Balkan peoples. In Homeric poetry, on the other hand, the same word, *prexis*, was used both for action or enterprise and for trade, which generally took the form of piracy, barter, or gift exchange.[6]

The Aegean was one of the first areas of the world outside the Near East to which the notion of price penetrated. Priced goods continued to be relatively few in number, however, in the rural areas of the inland and more isolated portions of the Balkans until the middle of the nineteenth century. In western Serbia, it was shameful and derogating—*sramota*—to sell locally produced foods ("free goods") or "ceremonial goods," such as towels, stockings, or shirts. Such goods played an important role as items of exchange, but they were not for sale.

Among the few food products whose sale the western Serbs allowed were cattle and salt, which enjoyed that privilege because they both served as a means of exchange—that is, as money—for goods that were not locally available and because cattle were not food so long as they were on the hoof.[8] On Tuesdays or when the moon was "empty," on the other hand, the sale of goods, particularly cattle, was taboo.[9]

Throughout the Balkans, sales and exchanges on a large scale were customarily confined to seasonal fairs. One of the most famous of such fairs during the Byzantine era, and still in existence today, was the autumnal fair of Salonika, which was held during the feast of St. Demetrius. A Cappadocian traveler, Timarion, describes the international stamp of the visitors to the fair during the first half of the twelfth century: "Not only do the natives of the country flock together to it in great numbers, but multitudes also come from all lands and of every race—Greeks, wherever they are found, the various tribes of Mysians [Moesians, or inhabitants of eastern Serbia and northern Bulgaria] who dwell on our borders as far as the Ister [Danube] and Scythia, Campanians and other Italians, Iberians, Lusitanians, and Transalpine Celts."[10]

First mentioned in the Homeric hymns, fairs were places of exchange.[11] Primarily, however, they were a time of ritual, festivity, and panegyric and a place for the formation of alliances. In Antiquity, the exchange of goods at the religious festivals of Olympia, Delphi, Corinth, and Delos, old examples of fairs, was important but incidental to the religious, social, and political function of the celebrations. As late as 1858, in their effort to bring down the authoritarian regime of Prince Alexander Karadjordjević, the first generation of Serbian liberals sought allies mainly at monastic fairs.[12] The persistent socioreligious and political function of fairs was in fact a notable vestigial characteristic of one of the basic purposes of gift exchange—to establish ties of friendship with another family or clan and placate its demons or ancestors through the exchange of objects, especially foods and ornaments. Such items were believed to be highly charged with what the ancient Greeks called *agalma*, a term translatable as "supernatural virtues."[13]

Fairs differed, however, from the earliest places of assembly at which gifts were ritually exchanged between neighboring groups, for they were open to professional traders as well. They were places of exchange honoring the principles of kinship, clanship, and "friendship," or alliance, but they were also increasingly inclined to embrace the principle of the business contract—whether the individual contract between two professional traders or the mixed contract between a professional trader and a clan or family.

The growth of fairs signified the appearance of a more objective conception of economic value. The communication of economic and other information became easier as more fairs were held and as the exchange of goods at the fairs grew. Fair development was slow, however, intensifying in the Balkans only after 1300, but especially between 1650 and 1875. There were, south of the Danube and Sava rivers, only about 50 fairs in 1300, rising to 60 to a 100 in 1400 and remaining at that level until 1600. By 1800, the number stood at

200–400; by 1875, it was about 1,000. Thus, in 1600, there may have been twice as many fairs as in 1300. By 1800, there were twice to four times as many as in 1600, the result in all probability of the upsurge of pastoralism and consequent need for stock fairs. By 1875, there were more than twice or even five times as many fairs as in 1800 and twenty times as many as in 1300.

Until well into the nineteenth century, on the other hand, merchants usually had to travel in armed caravans. The primary function of the Balkan fair thus became economic only during the last main phase of fair development, that is, between the mid-eighteenth and mid-nineteenth century, partly in response to the growing utilization of the more important fairs by western European merchants and their intermediaries.[14] One wonders, nonetheless, whether a conception of economic value may have been furthered in earlier times by other means, namely, by the growth in the number and activity of professional traders.

In conjunction with the adoption of a phonetic alphabet—albeit at first in many variant forms—and the development of numerous urban polities, maritime navigation, and coinage, professional traders emerged in the maritime regions, becoming especially important after 700 B.C. To fulfill their professional function, such traders had to be relatively well informed concerning supply and demand. Being so informed, they could imagine the existence of price differences from place to place for the same good and a price level for each good in each place at a given moment. Being aware that different societies put a different value on the same object, they dealt in goods that allowed them to realize a profit.

In the central, western, and northern Balkans, however, clanship and kinship prevailed as strong principles of association at least until the second century A.D. and were revived in the sixth and seventh and again in the fifteenth, sixteenth, and seventeenth centuries. A full development of the concept of economic value consequently was delayed. Moreover, Greek law itself failed to distinguish between a community of persons (a company) brought together to practice a common cult or eat at a common table and an association of businessmen.

Precisely how or how much the character of associations of traders changed during the first half of the Byzantine era is uncertain. In the later medieval centuries, however, when Venetian, Genoese, and Ragusan merchants captured the international trade of Byzantium or of the former Byzantine territories, there arose, beside the traders' associations, which for centuries had been *de facto* partnerships, the institution of the *commenda* or *société en commandite*. This was a more formal business association, organized customarily for a period of three or four years. It generally included two or three members, one of them an active partner with full liability and the others with limited liability—liable only to the extent of their capital investment. There is no evidence to substantiate the existence of this form of business organization among the Greeks of Antiquity.[15]

Nor were the Greek and Roman economies of Antiquity sufficiently "rationalized" to require double-entry (debit and credit entries in separate columns) bookkeeping. The elaboration of double-entry bookkeeping was also hindered by the fact that neither the Greek acrophonic nor the Greek alphabetic nor the Roman numeral system of numerical notation recognized the principle of place value.[16] In the second half of the fifteenth century, on the other hand, the Ragusan Benedetto Cotrugli's *Della mercatura e del mercante perfetto* (1458) distinguished between the rational business practices—*mercatura*—of the "perfect" or accomplished merchant, who knew his markets and how to take advantage of differences in value (price) that arose from differences in location, distance, mode of locomotion, and time, and the business practices—*mercanzia*—of the petty trader, who dealt in smaller quantities and usually was less well informed.[17] This distinction was followed by the diffusion to the Balkans of double-entry bookkeeping, whose practice, however limited, was reinforced in the sixteenth century by the migration to Balkan towns of almost a hundred thousand Spanish, Italian, and North African Jews,[18] representing the relocation of a "mobilized diaspora" skilled in the communication of goods, numbers, messages, and health or disease (through the practice of medicine and pharmacy).[19]

By the middle of the sixteenth century or by the 1590s, however, despite some progress over the previous century, the interior Balkan regions were among the economically least well developed in geographic Europe. One indicator of that underdevelopment was the low cost of food and the high cost of money, or the division of Europe, as one may infer from the observations of the learned English gentleman and prolific traveler, Fynes Moryson, into a core area including the lower Rhine, the lower and middle Po, and perhaps—marginally at least—the lower and middle Seine, in which food was dear and money was relatively cheap, and around this core a succession of peripheries in which the opposite fact was increasingly true, at least when there was no famine. In the core area, or within the space enclosed by the innermost isobar, the average price of a given quantity of locally produced foods was x. Within the area of the second isobar, it was $0.7x$, declining to $0.4x$ at the third isobar and $0.3x$ at the fourth isobar, which extended to the middle Vistula, or continental Poland, than which "No countrey in Europe [west of the Vistula] affordes victuals at a lower rate"[20] (see Figure 5.1).

Prices of victuals probably fell to a yet lower level as one moved from Germanic Europe and northern Italy into the Balkan interior. At the same time, nowhere did greater extremes prevail in the cost of victuals than in the ordinarily low-price zones. Prices rose there to extreme levels in times of dearth largely because their continental or eccentric location made carriage to them both more difficult and dearer. As one moved from the Balkan interior toward the Mediterranean, prices rose again. In the western Mediterranean, cereal prices—if not the price of victuals in general—were often higher than in what, toward the end of the sixteenth century, became the new core.

Closer to the price levels alike prevalent in the commercialized economies of the western Mediterranean and the new European core than to the price levels

Figure 5.1. **Food Costs of a Traveler (Fynes Moryson), 1590s: The New Core Economy and the Half-Closed Economies of Eastern Europe and the Balkans, Which Were Poorly Joined to the Monetary Economy of the Core**

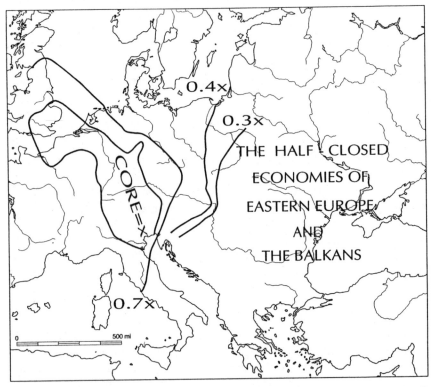

Source: Moryson, *An Itinerary Containing His Ten Yeeres Travell*, I, 148–50, 421; II, 82–83, 114; III, 464–83; IV, 46, 70, 72, 95, 140–41.

of the Balkan interior, price levels in the eastern Adriatic, Aegean, and eastern Mediterranean maritime zones were still marked by the cheapness of foods in terms of silver coin—or by the dearness of silver coin. A 1682 memoir on French commerce in Cyprus thus relates that 300 pounds *(livres pesant)* of wheat could be obtained for an *écu*. An ox could be had for an *écu* and a half and would have been even cheaper but for the fact that it had been drawn partly into a money economy by the use of Cypriot bovines to make hams for export to Malta and Marseille that were "better than those of Bayonne and Mainz." A turkey of 20–25 pounds cost only 12–15 *sols*. A bottle of fine muscatel red or white wine cost only 2 *sols*.[21]

Fynes Moryson explained the geographic price variations as follows: "And in truth, my selfe having in Poland and Ireland, found a strange cheapnesse of all such necessaries, in respect they want, and so more esteeme Silver, this observation makes me of an opinion much contrary to the vulgar, that there is no more certaine signe of a flourishing and rich commonwealth, then [sic] the deare price of these things (excepting the yeeres of famine), nor any greater argument of a poore and weake State, then the cheape price of them."[22]

The living costs of travelers (food and lodging in particular) tend to reflect local prices, the quality of goods and services, the variety of available products, and market conditions. Such costs—and even food costs alone—may be regarded as the value of a basket of diverse items. They may also reflect a traveler's ways of "experiencing" another country or region. In general, nonetheless, they are better indicators of price conditions than the price of a single item such as wheat or meat.

Wholesale wheat prices (in silver) between the 1440s and the 1540s show an even sharper division of the world into price zones. But if one examines the shifts in core-European and western Mediterranean wheat prices between the 1440s and 1740s over fifty-year periods, one may observe two main changes. First, the zone of highest prices shifted from the northwestern Mediterranean—between Naples and Udine in the east and Valencia in the west—to the Rhine and Thames and, marginally, to the lower and middle Seine, while the zone of lowest wheat prices shifted from the north and east to the east. Second, the zonal differences in wheat prices ultimately become less sharp.[23]

The rise in wheat prices in western Europe during the sixteenth century, especially after 1550 or 1560 and yet more after 1580, created a demand for Ottoman wheat. But as the export price of wheat in Ottoman Mediterranean ports reached European levels around 1600, European demand was curtailed and the price of Ottoman wheat in maritime export markets fell again below the western Mediterranean and northern European levels.

A convergence between European and western Mediterranean prices may have been already under way during the second half of the eighteenth century. Cereal prices in the Ottoman Empire and its European successor states, however, continued to be lower than in western Europe until the closing decades of the nineteenth century.[24] But between 1800 and 1819, the price of bread in Rumelia expressed in silver rose by more than 250 percent,[25] providing a foretaste of things to come.

Nongenerative Cities and Command Economy

The poor enmeshment of the Balkan continental territories with a monetary economy, or their constitution as "closed" or half-closed" economies or *oikonomies* (units of household management), was not simply the result of their relative isolation by reason of their position and distance from the centers of an articulated economy. It was also the consequence of the affirmation of the Ottoman Empire during the sixteenth, seventeenth, and eighteenth centuries as a command economy.

In a command economy, prices have a political origin. The Ottoman command economy was, of course, not immutable. Even though weakened after the 1730s, however, it was not dismantled until the treaty of Adrianople (1829), following Russian intervention against Turkey during the Greek revolution of 1821. A British traveler, William Turner, describes that economy during the last years of its existence (in the Napoleonic and immediately post-Napoleonic era), especially as it functioned in, and in reference to, Istanbul (Constantinople) during the exceptionally cold winter and plague of 1812–13:

> The Porte [Ottoman government], with its usual short-sighted policy, thought to lighten the evil [of the scarcity of food supplies, especially grains] by fixing a maximum of prices, which it prohibited the dealers in provisions from exceeding, by the severest punishments; frequently by the infliction of death. In consequence of this, the limited supply accumulated in the city, instead of being brought to market, was carefully concealed. The starving populace resorted to tumultuous meetings and robbery. The streets after dusk were so unsafe, that the Porte ordered that no subject of the Sultan, under penalty of being arrested by the patrole, and recommended that no European, should walk in them without a lantern (a common precaution in Turkish cities in times of disturbance), and scarce a night passed in which numerous burglaries were not committed. These excesses could only be controlled by a sanguinary police, and the number of executions was frightfully great. In a circumscribed walk about Pera [the suburb in which Greeks and Franks or Europeans were concentrated] at this time, I counted one morning sixteen decapitated bodies lying in the streets. The provision of food for Constantinople is so mismanaged, that a continuance of bad weather is sure to entail a scarcity on the city, by preventing the arrival of supplies from the Archipelago [Aegean]; and indeed any hostile power which should station a force at the mouth of the Dardanelles, to prevent the passage of vessels up the Hellespont, would in a few weeks reduce the Porte to accept any terms they thought fit to impose. The environs of the city consist of hills destitute of trees, and totally uncultivated; for who would risk the fruits of his labour in the neighbourhood of a turbulent soldiery, and a weak government subject to such frequent disturbances?
>
> The supply of corn [grains] for the capital is monopolized by the government, to whom all the farmers and proprietors of land throughout the empire [in practice, however, mainly in the maritime provinces] are compelled, if required, to sell their corn at a low rate. Four piastres a kilo [*kile*, an Ottoman measure of weight] is the settled price, which, having been fixed long ago, is, under the daily increasing depreciation of Turkish money, extremely below its value. It is fetched away in vessels hired by the government, who, after having increased its quantity by adulteration, sell it to the people at a profit of at least 100 per cent. But the high prices paid for corn throughout the Mediterranean, and especially in Malta during the occupation of the [Iberian] Peninsula by our troops, proved so irresistible an inducement to a contraband disposal of it, that the supply of Constantinople became precarious and scanty, and the city was in consequence disturbed by frequent tumults; the avoidance of which is generally such an object to the Porte, that their policy has always been rather to

starve the provinces, than risk an increase of the price of this article in Constantinople. The evil consequences of their short-sighted policy are every day becoming more apparent, and within a few years the prices of meat and of all the necessaries of life have been more than doubled in most parts of Turkey.[26]

Committed to a policy of urbanization after 1470 and especially after 1520, and confronted by the problems of a vast territorial state, the Ottoman government instituted a system of command-economic relationships that were designed to favor the capital, its provincial cities, its armed forces and centers of administration, the pastoral populations that complemented its war arm, and Muslims and other partisans of the imperial enterprise. It did this by embracing the principle of "centricity," which entailed the adoption not of the control patterns of autonomous markets but those of a highest-order central place (Istanbul) and, in a hierarchical relationship with the central place and with each other, of a set of lower levels of territorial administration.

Ottoman cities performed exchange functions. The hegemonic Ottoman mode of production, however, was redistribution. As a result, there was an increasing diversion of resources from the direct producers of crops (peasants) to landlords, to cities, to the raisers of sheep, and to the state. As the Ottoman urban system became more urban during the sixteenth, seventeenth, and eighteenth centuries, therefore, it became more "nongenerative" or "parasitic," with an ever greater imbalance of wealth between towns and cultivators.

The latter dénouement was partly the product of the northward shift of the center of international trade between 1580 and 1650—away from the Mediterranean. It was also the consequence of the command-economic system itself, which tended to turn most towns into centers of consumption and places of residence of rentiers.

Deprived increasingly of a large part of their production by extraeconomic means, the countryside could not emerge as a demand market for urban products. Urban craft production stagnated, and urban notables *(ayans)* and rural commanders *(ağas)* to whom rural surpluses were made available by devolution became increasingly committed to the export of such goods (especially grains, cotton, wool, silk, tobacco, and olive oil) to European markets and to the import of European manufactured goods. The Ottoman economy was thus peripheralized between 1730 and 1830, to be further enmeshed subsequently in the world-market economy as a dependent territorial unit of supply and demand.[27]

Ottoman cities were nongenerative in one further but related respect. They were unable to institute a "civil society." In the words of Şerif Mardin, they could not "generate that drive for independence which in the West won them rights of autonomous jurisdiction. Any such drive would have been frustrated by the stream of directives emanating from the Sultan, in particular by the orders constantly uprooting and resettling people, orders backed by force."[28]

When provincial notables did succeed in weakening the controls of the central command economy, the Ottoman cities became externally dependent. As they themselves became increasingly dependent on the geographically peripheral but economically and politically hegemonic world-economy of capitalism, they acted too slowly and without sufficient determination to undo the peripheralization of the surrounding countryside. However, they did confirm and diffuse the idea of economic value.

One of the institutions associated with the affirmation of capitalism as a hegemonic world-economy during the nineteenth and twentieth centuries is the corporation or limited liability company. Even the commercially backward principality of Serbia adopted a commercial code in 1860 that duplicated the provisions of the Napoleonic *Code de commerce* of 1807. The Serbian code recognized three basic types of business association: the simple or public partnership with unlimited liability *(iavnyi ortakluk);* the mixed partnership, or *société en commandite (mešovityi* or *komanditnyi ortakluk);* and the *société anonyme (anonimno* or *bezimeno društvo),* or limited liability company, in which each owner was liable only to the extent of his share as an investor in the business.[29]

Aided by improved business organization and practices, by the growth of cities and the creation of more rapid means of transportation and communication, by the development of the Balkan states as tax states, by changes in social structure, and by the recognition of private property in land, the concept of economic value—without displacing the concept of use value—entered at last into the *outillage mental* of the Balkan peoples. The process by which this occurred is elucidated in the next chapter.

Freedom and Slavery

An old deterrent to the diffusion of a clear concept of economic value was the low representation of intermediate social categories. Thus, if one visualizes a status scale for the societies of classical and late Antiquity, with free status represented at one end and slave status at the other, one will discover that most people were clustered at the two ends of the scale.[30] Although certain social categories combined some of the freeman's characteristics with some of the slave's, in most cases one was either free and a person or unfree and an unperson.

Slavery reached a high level of development in the Old World as several conditions were met—as some areas of sedentary settlement that were organized as city cultures acquired the skills and technology that allowed them to undertake periodic raids into politically less well organized neighboring territories; as slave traders emerged, ready to engage in the buying and selling of slaves during periods of peace and immediately after a successful war, when a large supply of war prisoners became available; and as political units of tribute-gathering nomads arose to undertake slave raids both against the same politically weak territories and against the more distant *polit*-ical (that is, city-culture) territories, with the slave traders acting as intermediaries between the slave-supplying nomadic societies and the slave-demanding sedentary polities. A further condition for the flourishing of slavery was the presence of cities of a preindustrial and non-generative type, that is, with a relatively low division of labor and predisposed to discourage the development of a well-to-do peasantry.

The foregoing conditions prevailed in parts of the Balkans and in large parts of southeastern Europe and the Caucasus for about twenty-five hundred years—from the seventh century B.C. to the mid-nineteenth century. In classical Antiquity, the chief eastern European and northeastern Mediterranean slave markets prevailed near the northern and eastern boundaries of the Greek world—at such places as Ephesus in Asia Minor, at Chios (still a center of the slave trade in the early part of the nineteenth century), at Pagasae in Thessaly, in the Black Sea ports, and at the Greek sanctuary fairs, as at Delos, where, in the first century B.C., ten thousand slaves were sometimes sold in one day. To prevent mass escapes, the congregation in one place of a large number of slaves of the same ethnicity was discouraged.[31]

The price of a slave varied with their sex, age, and presumed health and physical attributes, and with religion, ethnicity, race, and culture. It also varied periodically in response to variations in supply. Upon the organization of increasingly strong political states in eastern Europe during and after the ninth and tenth centuries, it became increasingly difficult or costly to deprive them of their sources of labor. A reinforcing event in the decline of eastern Europe as a source of labor supply for western Europe was the formation in western Europe, during the eleventh and twelfth centuries, of generative cities, which allowed immigrant peasants to obtain freedom, forcing rural lords who could not expect new supplies of slaves to temper the conditions of slavery, thereby transforming slaves into serfs and, in the process, sometimes causing the condition of some free peasants to worsen.[32]

One should distinguish nonetheless among eastern, western, and southern or Mediterranean Europe. In Mediterranean Europe, cities were closer to the sources of labor supply—the east and/or the south. They also had a greater concentration of wealth. As a result, even though their demand for slaves slackened for a time, it soon resumed as a demand for domestic servants. As late as the eighteenth century, the number of domestic servants black and white—many of them technically slaves—in major Italian and Spanish cities may have accounted for 3 to 10 percent of the population. Livorno and Malta served as the major intermediaries between the supply and demand markets.[33]

The teachings of Christianity may also have played a role in the decline of slavery in Europe as more than an ancillary mode of production. Christianity discouraged the taking of Christian slaves unless they were heretics, and it may have fostered an improvement in the social status of slaves. The slave trade persisted nonetheless along the frontiers between Catholic Europe, the fringe worlds of heresy and paganism, and the Muslim and Orthodox worlds.

In 1388, Ragusa (Dubrovnik) forbade the buying and selling of Serbs and

Albanians—often for export to Sicily and Apulia—in the slave markets of the Adriatic. In 1413, however, it had to repeat the order. In 1416, Ragusa's Great Council called such traffic *turpis mercantia*, a "shameful commerce," and threatened to tax perpetrators with a six-month prison term and a heavy fine. In 1455, the Venetian Senate similarly forbade the sale in Venice of South Slavic and Albanian slaves. The mouth of the Neretva, the Bay of Kotor (Bocche di Cattaro, Boka Kotorska), and the hinterland of Dubrovnik (consequently, Trebinje) nonetheless continued to draw slaves—most of them probably young girls—from the interior mountain lands, who were either sold into slavery by their own families, as in Georgia, or were the victims of capture by roaming *raptores hominum*.[34]

The slave trade from East to West was nonetheless considerably less significant in 1400 than in 1200, partly perhaps because of a sharp increase in the price of slaves as the demand for domestic urban servants grew in the Mediterranean and as slaves were diverted eastward by the Mongol conquests. In Venice and Genoa, the price of a slave doubled between 1200 and 1400. Between 1400 and 1500, as an increasing number of slaves was retained by the Ottoman Turks, the price of slaves in the Italian cities rose by 60 percent. In Ragusa, the price of slaves from Bosnia grew three times between 1280 and 1300 and four to five times between 1300 and 1400. In the Venetian colony of Crete, during the fourteenth century, the price of a female slave rose fivefold; that of a male slave, tenfold. In the Genoese colony of Chios, slave prices trebled during the fifteenth century. In the sixteenth century, the price of a slave may have been about the same in Istanbul and in Naples—35 ducats in Naples during the first half of the century, 34 ducats in Istanbul in 1576 for a thirteen- or fourteen-year-old girl *"médiocrement belle"* from Hungary.[35]

In the Venetian colony of Tana, on the other hand, the price of female slaves fell by 1400 to one-third or one-half the 1360 level. The price for young male slaves, who had been more expensive than females in 1360, fell below the level for a female slave. The apparent aberration may have had a basis in the development of new desires or tastes, leading to a recentering of routes during and after the 1340s as African gold found its way from Alexandria to Venice and as Venice and Ragusa became centers of redistribution to the Orient of the silver of the mines of Serbia, Bosnia, Bohemia, and the neighboring alpine lands, in return for pepper and other spices from the Indies that were obtained in Beirut and Alexandria. Less silver thereupon went to Tana, especially since the routes from Tana to New Sarai and Astrakhan became less secure as pirates from Novgorod the Great appeared on the middle Volga to obstruct the southward movement of chattels.

The land route from New Sarai to Tana and the sea route between Tana and Venice thereupon yielded in importance to the sea routes between Venice and Alexandria, Venice and Brăila (at the mouth of the Danube), Alexandria or Beirut and Brăila, and Trebizond and Brăila. From Brăila, the route continued by land to Cîmpulung. Traversing Transylvania and Hungary, thus skirting the Balkans proper, it continued to Buda and Vienna.

This was, indeed, the less commercialized eastern branch of the great European latitudinal route Vienna-Linz-Regensburg-Nürnberg-Frankfurt-Antwerp (see Figure 3.2, page 88). The "geometric centre" of European economic life before 1500 and during the first half of the sixteenth century,[36] Nürnberg was the link between Venice and Antwerp. From it radiated Europe's main routes of continental commerce in silver, spices, sugar, Mediterranean fruits, dyes, alum, cloth, silks, wool, furs, and leather goods.[37] As the price of slaves grew and the supply of slaves in proportion to total population diminished in western Europe and the Balkans alike between 1100 and 1400, the status of many freemen deteriorated and the intermediate categories between freeman and slave grew in number. In compensation for the inadequate supply of slaves, the clerical estate and the estate of great protectors augmented their levies of compulsory labor, reducing many freemen to a condition of dependency.

The Ottoman conquest of the Balkans, however, partially restored the previous form of freedom-slavery continuum, with most persons being either free or slaves. In any event, slavery and the slave trade acquired a new importance in the Balkans during the fifteenth and sixteenth centuries.

At the height of Ottoman power in the mid-sixteenth century, an average of 40,000 slaves per year may have been introduced into the Ottoman Empire—20,000 from Africa,[38] 10,000 as European (Hungarian, Croatian, Serbian, Romanian, German, Italian, and other) prisoners of war, and the remainder by war, slave (and cattle) raids, and purchase in the Caucasus and East Slavic lands and by the *devşirme*, or tribute in Christian children.

A polychronic vision may help one to understand how the treatment of populations in earlier centuries may have unforseen future consequences. Between 1991 and 1993, upon the partition of Yugoslavia and resulting civil war, Croats, Serbs, and Muslim Bosnians all pursued policies of population transfers, forcing populations to move out of one area into another. These policies, variously known as "ethnic cleansing" or "ethnic shifting," were in part the painful consequence of a long human heritage of population transfers. They were the culmination in particular of the population policies of Rome, Byzantium (the second Rome), and the Ottoman Empire, all of which repeated what earlier empires had done. Byzantium, for example, resettled Scythians, Slavs, Armenians, Syrian Jacobites, Pechenegs, Turks, and other ethnic and ethno-religious groups in order to limit civil strife, stifle heresy, or promote production. The Ottoman Empire (a kind of "third Rome," a term applied also to Moscow but in a different sense) followed the tradition for five centuries, often more brutally. Between 1804 and 1878, upon winning autonomy, Serbia, Greece, and Bulgaria retaliated.

The Balkan wars of 1912 and 1913, the Great War of 1914–18, and the subsequent war between Greece and Turkey were accompanied and/or followed by population expulsions and exchanges. Following the Second Balkan War, for example, 100,000 Romanians were moved from the southern Dobrudja (in Bulgaria) to Romania and 60,000 Bulgarians from the northern Dobrudja

(Dobrogea, in Romania) to Bulgaria. Between 1921 and 1928, 1,190,000 Greeks and Greek Orthodox populations were forced to evacuate Bulgaria and Turkish Asia Minor and Eastern Thrace to be resettled in Greece. During the same period, 388,000 Turks and other Muslims were transferred from Greece and 60,000 from Romania and the Balkans proper to Turkey. Between 1918 and 1928, 250,000 refugees (including 96,000 Slavs) left Greece, Romania, and Turkey to resettle in Bulgaria, while 46,000 refugees from Bulgaria were resettled in Greece. Between 1912 and 1930, 240,000 Turks left Bulgaria for Turkey after a yet greater flight of Turks following the liberation of Bulgaria from Ottoman rule. Between 1931 and 1939, 100,000 Turks and other Muslims from Bulgaria and 40,000 from Romania and Yugoslavia departed for Turkey. During and immediately after World War II, 94,000 Germans were expelled from Bessarabia, 44,000 from Bukovina, and more than 300,000 from Vojvodina. Similarly, 200,000 Romanians fled from northern Transylvania (transferred to Hungary) to Romania. A few years later, a similar number of Hungarians fled from Transylvania (returned to Romania) to resettle in Hungary. In 1950 and 1951, 150,000 Turks and Gipsies were forcibly evacuated from Bulgaria to Turkey. During World War II, 185,000 Jews were deported from Bessarabia and Bukovina to Trans-Dnistria (a region between the Dniester and Bug rivers), where 155,000 perished under conditions almost as horrible as in the German death camps. More than 62,000 Greek Jews, or three-quarters of Greece's Jewish population, were deported or lost their lives. In addition, some 17,000 Jews were deported to death camps from the Axis-controlled territories of the former Yugoslavia, while thousands of other Yugoslav Jews, along with at least several hundred thousand Croatian and Bosnian Serbs, were victims of the genocide of the puppet state of Croatia.[39] In the forty-year period after 1912, even without the deportations of the Jews, more than 3 million people were more or less forcibly resettled from one Balkan or onetime Ottoman area to a different Balkan or non-Balkan area, mainly to counteract the historic Germanic colonization from the north and west and Turkish colonization from the south and east.

Such ethnic revisions were not new. Nor have they been confined to the Balkans and Asia—unless Poland, Czechoslovakia, and Germany are in the Balkans or Asia. In the Balkans, they have been a constant factor since the fifteenth century, mainly a product of Ottoman population policies and of deferred counteraction to these policies.

Between the 1450s and 1550s the Ottoman Empire may have seized in its Balkan campaigns and wars against Hungary and the Habsburgs a million prisoner-of-war slaves: 100,000 upon its conquest of Bosnia in 1463, 70,000 during its campaigns against Croatia between 1462 and 1520, an additional 70,000 from Croatia in 1556,[40] and the rest in its campaigns in the Peloponnesus and against Serbia, Hungary, the Habsburg dominions, and the Italian states. Europe's average annual human tribute to the Ottoman Empire, without the contributions of the East Slavs and of the peoples of the Caucasus, may thus have numbered 10,000 persons.

According to Emanuel Sarkisyanz, the slave trade (and presumably the capture of slaves in war and in periodic razzias) may have brought down the population of Georgia from 8 million (perhaps too high) in the twelfth century to less than 1 million in the eighteenth.[41] He may exaggerate. The phenomenon to which he alludes, however, was not negligible.

In their valuable analyses of the *devşirme* institution, V.L. Ménage and Peter F. Sugar show that the tribute levies of male Christian children and youths between 1400 and 1600 may have amounted to 200,000, thus an annual average of 1,000 persons. In addition to the authorized or "official" tribute, there was an untold "unofficial" tribute of young males for the needs, pleasures, and desires of the tribute collectors or recruiters.[42] The one estimate I have found of a *devşirme* levy, that of Stephan Gerlach, sets the levy (perhaps from several districts of Anatolia as well as the Balkans) that was concluded in January 1574—excluding the "unofficial" tribute—at 8,000 young males.[43]

Applied not generally but differentially, such levies shifted periodically from one area to another.[44] They were aimed against Christians but were particularly harsh in the Serbian and Croatian frontier territories. By law or in practice, some localities, regions, and ethnic or ethnoreligious and occupational groups were excluded from the levies. The exemptions included the Christian Greeks of the Aegean islands, the principalities of Wallachia and Moldavia, married men, cities, guards of the passes and of military and caravan routes (*voynuk* communities), mining populations, breeder families of hunting falcons, and ethnic and perhaps occupational Vlachs (thus pastoral communities). At first exempt from the tribute, Armenians later were included in some of the levies.

In Bosnia and Hercegovina, conversion to Islam may have been a small price to pay for escape from the *devşirme*. Some Muslim families strove to have a son taken by the recruiters so that he might have the opportunity to go to school and advance professionally, economically, or socially by becoming a janissary or member of the court cavalry, or even by rising sometimes to a high position at the court or in the imperial administration.

According to Benedikt Kuripešić, the interpreter in the embassy enjoined in 1530 by Ferdinand of Austria to negotiate peace with the Turks, the incidence of the recruitment—presumably both the "official" and "unofficial" *devşirme*—may have been every third, fourth, or fifth male child or youth in the district or region to which it was applied,[45] at least in Bosnia and Hercegovina. The boys and youths selected were supposedly strong, healthy, and of sound mind. Fynes Moryson, who, according to his Eurocentric biographer, "resolved to write an account of Europe, to make, in fact, a sociological survey of the civilised world" as it was at the close of the sixteenth century,[46] described the *devşirme* as "the Tributory Children of Christian Subiects gathered euery fifth yeare or oftner if occasion requires, and carried farr from their parents while they are going to be brought vpp in the Turkish religion and military exercises."[47]

If the riposte to that practice by some Christian Serbs and Croats was conversion, that of others was to organize themselves into extended households, which would be both better able to defend themselves and better able to survive the loss of a child, and to have their male children marry at an early age, often in their early teens. In a small household of two adults and one grown-up unmarried son of thirteen, fourteen, or fifteen years of age, the loss of that son meant the loss of full labor power just as it was becoming available. It was not only a painful loss but a calamity. An extended household, on the other hand, was a kind of insurance policy against disaster.

Probably introduced during the second half of the fourteenth century to cope with the problem of the general rapid rise in the price of slaves, the *devşirme* may have been designed both to keep down the price of slaves and to provide the Ottoman government with an opportunity to create the labor skills and force that it needed. It was a complement to victory in warfare, a manifestation of the command economy.

As the Ottomans extended their conquests, slave labor increased correspondingly. Female slaves often became the concubines of their captors or buyers. Young male slaves were recruited for the galleys and assigned to work in the arsenal of the capital, or they were taught urban crafts. Many thousands of older prisoner-slaves were settled as agricultural workers, or *ortaks*, on private or imperial domains, with the requirement that they furnish their masters half their labor product while the latter provided the tools, livestock, seed, and land. To meet their own needs, the *ortaks* sometimes ate a portion of the seed, sold some of the livestock, and hid part of the harvest.

During the latter part of the fifteenth and first half of the sixteenth century, 110 of the 160 villages of the imperial domain in the vicinity of Istanbul were slave villages. Their inhabitants were not free to leave the land, and they were allowed to marry only other slaves who were settled on the imperial domain. If caught, runaway slaves were hanged by the feet, or after being beaten, the heels of their feet were cut open and filled with salt, and a hoop was put around their neck. As the supply of slaves diminished once again toward the end of the sixteenth century, the *ortaks* often succeeded in improving their economic and social status, becoming sharecroppers.[48] On the other hand, the pressures upon the "free" peasantry steadily increased. Thus, from the latter part of the sixteenth to the early part of the nineteenth century, the intermediate categories between the "freemen" and the slaves grew again. The *devşirme* itself may have become rare after 1640.

As the power of Austria and Russia grew, the Ottoman Empire suffered territorial losses during the seventeenth and eighteenth centuries. It could rely less and less on warfare as a means of augmenting its labor supply. Demographic decline in the Caucasus may have provoked a decline in the trade in white Mingrelian, Georgian, and Circassian slaves. Moreover, the diversion of African slaves to the Americas caused the number of black slaves available to the Otto-

Table 5.1

Wage and Grain-Price Fluctuations in Istanbul, 1550–1790

Years	Percentage of Rise in Grain Prices	Percentage of Rise in Wages of	
		Skilled Labor	Unskilled Labor
1550–1585	40–60	0	0
1585–1605	25–33	100	80
1605–1700	200–250	100	40
1700–1790	80–100	100	25–50
1550–1790	700 or more	800	350

Source: The documentation is given in Stoianovich, "Factors in the Decline of Ottoman Society."

man Empire to diminish. Thus, during the second half of the eighteenth century and until at least 1813, only five to six thousand black slaves, four-fifths of them female, reached the Ottoman Empire each year—most of them by way of the Darfur caravan and several hundred each by the Sennar caravan and the so-called Suez caravan (the last charged with Abyssinian slaves, most of them to be sold in Jedda/Iuddah).[49] By 1800, the total number of new slaves—black and white—annually available to the Ottoman Empire probably did not exceed twelve to twenty thousand,[50] half or a third as many as in the mid-sixteenth century.

A cessation to the Ottoman trade in white slaves was not decreed until October 1854. Legally abolished in 1857, the trade in black slaves continued until 1895.[51] But the persistent decline in the Ottoman slave trade since the end of the sixteenth century led to an expansion, during the seventeenth and eighteenth centuries and early part of the nineteenth century, of the intermediate categories between "freemen" and slaves, giving rise to what has been called the "second serfdom."

Prices, Wages, and the "Second Serfdom"

The "second serfdom" was aggravated by a simultaneous long-term rise in prices, caused by the flow of American silver into the eastern Mediterranean and by a growing disparity between prices and wages. This price-wage disparity came about largely because the economy could not keep up with the rapid growth of a propertyless urban and rural population, and it was further aggravated by the technological stagnation of the seventeenth century and the technological backwardness of the eighteenth.

The customary wage of an unskilled worker in the second half of the eighteenth century could purchase only half as much grain as the customary wage of the mid-sixteenth century. The fluctuations in wages and prices in the Ottoman capital between 1550 and 1790 can be seen in Table 5.1 above.

The decline in the real wages of unskilled labor persuaded many impoverished workers to place their services at the disposal of powerful lords. These lords thereupon imposed themselves on the peasantry as second landlords or overseers.

The initial and continuing trigger to the interest of Ottoman landlords and overseers in promoting a sharecropping, or *çiftlik*, agriculture was urban growth. From the point of view of the macroeconomy, sharecropping practices spread from the commercialized coastal regions inland along the arteries of communication from one enclosed or nearly enclosed valley or *polje* to the next. From a microeconomic point of view, the territories of sharecropping practices assumed the shape of scattered patches, often surrounded by extensive wasteland and fallow.

In its early forms, as I have explained elsewhere,

> a *çiftlik* enterprise was not very impressive. It often started as the pasturage ground of a family or clan that later claimed it as its own "private" or familial property, to which it could lure peasants by its stock of animals and to which it could drive them by its possession of arms. Its successful development of agriculture in lacustrine marshes and wet river valleys was mainly a product of its relatively abundant stock of tools and capital, especially in the form of cattle, with which to attract labor to labor-deficient areas. Sometimes it began as the site of a simple water mill or of a network of beehives. As an enterprise of recent colonization, it was generally the site of a new village, hence a smaller village than the traditional village of the highlands.[52]

During the second half of the sixteenth century and especially during the seventeenth century, *çiftlik* cultivation spread to Thrace, Macedonia, Thessaly, and Epirus. By 1750, it was present in northwestern Bulgaria around such towns as Vidin, Lom, and Belogradchik and also perhaps around Sofia and Rusçuk (Ruse). In Bosnia and Hercegovina, it was probably of much earlier origin, for it was widely prevalent there by 1800. Between 1750 and 1800, but especially during the 1790s, it spread to the pashalik of Smederevo-Belgrade, where it took the form of the *deveto*, or "ninth," and the exaction of corvée labor.[53]

The *çiftlik* regime strove to satisfy the food needs of the neighboring town or towns and of the provincial capital. It did not try to create a market of rural consumers. It would have been futile to do so, for until the 1830s at least there was almost no land market. But as agents of the "second serfdom" or *çiftlik* regime, landlords (often absentee landlords resident in provincial towns) and second (or false) landlords and overseers applied pressures on the government to allow the clandestine exportation of foodstuffs and raw materials to the countries of Europe.

Committed to exporting their own raw materials, the landlords opposed development of new manufactures out of fear that such manufactures might deprive them of cheap labor. European states similarly exerted pressures upon the Ottoman government to prevent it from aiding the growth of industry.

But if government could not or would not check the expansion of the "second serfdom," the Balkan and Danubian peasantries eventually did. The means toward this end were the Romanian peasant stirrings of 1784 (in Transylvania) and of 1793–1821 and the Serbian and Greek revolutions or wars of independence. Between 1830 and the 1860s, by waging a struggle against domestic as well as foreign tyranny, the Balkan peoples also succeeded in obtaining the abolition or curtailment of the estates society and recognition of the principle of equality before the law.

The problems arising after 1860 stem from the fact that equality before the law does not abolish economic inequalities. Moreover, the latter inequalities were aggravated by a population explosion that left the peasantries with less and less land as they became "more and more equal."

The Power and Rhythm of Number

The population of the Balkans, like that of most of the rest of the world, has generally been growing since the "agricultural revolution" of the early Neolithic period. In the present state of research, we can determine the average population density by the usual methods only for a late period. But since a society of hunters can hardly exist if the population exceeds one person per square kilometer, we may assume that the population density in the fifth millennium, shortly after the establishment of the first extensive network of Balkan agricultural communities, was at least one person per square kilometer, yielding a total population of half a million.

In Greece, the population density rose by 400 B.C. to 20 or 30 persons per square kilometer. In the Balkan interior, where cities were still nonexistent or in the process of initial formation, the density was lower, probably no more than 5 persons. Demographic historians further estimate the population density of the nondesert portions of the Roman Empire in A.D. 14 at 17 persons: 31 persons in the Asiatic, 27 in the African, and 10 in the European parts. The population density in the Hellenic areas of the Balkans may have fallen between 400 B.C. (but especially 200 B.C.) and A.D. 200. In the northern regions, it continued to grow. Rising again between A.D. 300 or 350 and 540, in response in particular to Christian denunciations of slavery, castration, onanism, infanticide, and contraception, the population of the Greek regions may have attained a density of 30 persons by the end of this period, as in Antiquity. But as the southern zone became overpopulated, epidemics—in particular, a little-known pandemic that spread across the Mediterranean between the sixth and eighth centuries—and famines depopulated many areas, facilitating the invasions of the Slavs from the north and the Arabs from the south and east.[54]

A century or two after the Slavic invasions, the population of the Greek areas may have taken another upward turn, lasting until the close of the eleventh or until the twelfth century. In the northern areas, the population grew between the twelfth and mid-fourteenth century.

The second half of the fifteenth century was chiefly a time of forced population transfers by the Ottoman government and of flights of people from the
immediate south and east to Dalmatia, Italy, and Hungary. The western Balkan
areas were grievously depopulated, but the population density of the eastern
areas, which generally benefited from the Ottoman resettlement policies, remained constant or went up. In the Balkans as a whole, however, the century
from 1420 to 1520 was one of population decline.

Since 1520, the population density of the area south of the Sava and Danube
has varied from approximately 12 persons per square kilometer in 1520 to 17 in
1590, 12 in 1700, and 15 in 1800. The decades between 1520 and 1590 were a
time of population expansion, as in most of Europe. In 1590 the population
density of the Balkans was about equal to that of Spain and Portugal. The density
of France was approximately 34, or twice as great; that of Italy was around 44.

During the second half of the nineteenth century the Balkan countries attained
a population density never previously equaled there. By the middle of the twentieth century, the density was two, three, or four times as great as the highest
density achieved in a given area. Table 5.2 shows how it increased.

In 1893, European creditors were accorded first rights to the revenues of the
Greek state. In 1897, the military adventure in Crete caused a further incursion
into the Greek budget. One of the consequences of the sharply increased tax
burden was a sharp increase in emigration, especially to the United States.

The emigration of Greeks from Greece to the United States grew from an
annual average of 2,238 between 1896 and 1900 to 9,992 between 1901 and
1905, 23,511 between 1906 and 1910, and 23,783 between 1911 and 1914,
falling to 13,057 between 1916 and 1920 and 8,197 between 1921 and 1925.
Immigration to the United States of Greeks from other areas, chiefly the Ottoman
Empire, rose from an annual average of 644 between 1901 and 1905 to an annual
average of 8,012 between 1906 and 1910, 9,877 between 1911 and 1915, declining to an annual average of 968 between 1916 and 1920 and 1,032 between 1921
and 1925. The total emigration of Greeks from Greece rose from 7,795 during
the five-year period from 1896 to 1900 to 49,964 during 1901–5, 116,557 during
1906–10, and 116,916 during 1911–15. High levels of emigration continued
until 1922. They are reflected in the decline in Greek population density between
1912 and 1920 even though that decline was also the result of the annexation, in
1912 and 1913, of the sparsely settled territories of Macedonia and Thrace. The
process was reversed only by the adoption by the United States of a restrictive
immigration policy and by the resettlement in Macedonia, Thrace, and Attica of
Greeks (and Turkish-speaking Orthodox Christians) from Anatolia, Istanbul, and
Bulgaria.[55]

Within a given region, population densities might be highly variable. Thus, in
1881, the density in the Othrys district of south central Thessaly was no more
than 4.9. In the Iolkos district of the Gulf of Volo(s), it stood at 365. The density
for the whole of Thessaly was then 21,[56] hardly higher and perhaps lower than in

Table 5.2

Population Density per Square Kilometer in Three Balkan Lands

Year	Serbia	Greece	Bulgaria
1718	3.0	—	—
1735	5.0	—	—
1800	10.0	—	—
1813	13.0	—	—
1821	—	19.8	—
1828	—	15.9	—
1834	18.0	—	—
1838	—	15.8	—
1840	—	17.9	—
1844	—	19.6	—
1846	24.3	—	—
1848	—	20.8	—
1853	—	21.8	—
1856	—	22.4	—
1861	—	23.1	—
1863	29.5	—	—
1864	—	23.7	—
1866	32.3	—	—
1870	—	29.0	—
1874	36.0	—	—
1879	—	33.5	—
1881	—	33.8	—
1887	—	—	32.7
1889	—	34.4	—
1890	44.3	—	—
1900	51.3	—	38.9
1907	—	41.6	—
1910	59.9	—	45.0
1912	—	43.0	—
1920	—	36.7	47.0
1940	—	—	61.7
1950	—	56.9	65.7
1953	80.0	—	—
1960	—	—	71.4
1961	86.0	64.1	—
1970	—	—	76.8
1980	—	—	80.0
1983	—	—	80.7

Sources: For Greece 1864, 1881, and 1912, see Vergopoulos, *Le Capitalisme difforme et la nouvelle question agraire,* p. 97; for other years between 1821 and 1881 in Greece, see Polyzos, *Essai sur l'émigration grecque,* p. 40; for Greece 1961, see Kayser, "La Carte de la distribution géographique de la population grecque en 1961." For further demographic details regarding Greece, see Valaoras, "A Construction of the Demographic History of Modern Greece," reviewed in J.C.C., "La Population de la Grèce depuis 1860." For Bulgaria 1887–1910, see the note by G.G., "Le développement de la population de Bugarie," on the basis of the research of D. Balevski and N. Minkov; for Bulgaria, 1900–83, see Lampe, *The Bulgarian Economy in the Twentieth Century,* p. 159. For Serbia, 1718–1813, the estimates are my own, based on the review by Stojančević of *Prilozi statističkom proučavanju Prvog srpskog ustanka NR Srbije;* and on Popović, *Srbija i Beograd od Požarevačkog do Beogradskog mira;* for the period before the Great War, see Vučo, *Privredna istorija Srbije do Prvog svetskog rata,* p. 199; for 1961 and for data on the individual republics and regions of Yugoslavia in 1948, 1953, and 1961, see Blanc, *La Yougoslavie,* p. 11.

1814 as a result of the northward emigration of the descendants of Greek converts to Islam (Koniarides) even before the transfer of Thessaly from Turkey to
Greece, as well as of the decline since 1830 of the pastoral way of life. My own
conversion of François Pouqueville's data yields an average density for mainland
Greece, in 1814, of 13 persons per square kilometer and a province-by-province
density of 4 persons in Acarnania (on the southwestern mainland coast), 9 in neighboring Aetolia and Locris to the east, 11 in Macedonia, 12 in Phocis and Livadia,
14 in Epirus, and 22 in Thessaly. The plague of 1814–15 brought down the densities
by a fifth in Epirus and by a sixth in the remaining territories, with a per capita
casualty rate five times as high among the Muslims as among the Christians.[57]

When the general density in Greece rose to 64.1 persons in 1961, the density
of its rural communes was only 37.6, compared to a rural density at that time in
Italian Calabria of 100 persons per square kilometer. A low rural density has
been a continuing "distinguishing characteristic of Greek human geography."[58]

From the close of the fifth century B.C. to the middle of the nineteenth century, the population history of the Balkans was characterized by a fairly uniform
and unsurpassable point of saturation. A certain general maximum population
density simply could not be exceeded without a fundamental change in the
existing social order and technology. The saturation point stood at 20–30 persons
per square kilometer. Only by their participation in the complex "Western Revolution" were the Balkan countries able to surpass that point.

Per capita costs for social overhead, on the other hand, vary inversely with
population density—at least until a high level of population density is achieved.
The sparser the population the costlier schooling and religious instruction become unless the inhabitants are colonists who have come with a fund of skills
and knowledge acquired elsewhere, where it was made possible by a greater
population density.[59] In Serbia, which was a *Neuland* made up mostly of settlers
from lands of low population density, the number of elementary schools, teachers, and pupils varied directly with the rising population density. Human capital
and facilities for its production grew between 1804 and 1900, as illustrated in
Table 5.3.

In 1879, there were still only 15 elementary school pupils in a population of
1,000, compared to 22 in Romania, 23 in Russia, 50 in Greece, 73 in Italy, 106 in
Spain, 109 in Austria-Hungary, 123 in Great Britain, 133 in France, and 157 in
Germany and Switzerland. In 1900 or shortly thereafter, the ratio was 51 for
Serbia, 88 for Romania, 117 for Greece, and 121 for Bulgaria. Moreover, only 3
Serbian women out of 100 were literate in 1884 and still only 7.4 out of 100 in
1900, concentrated largely in the towns.[60]

Population density alone is not a full explanation for the slower development
of social overhead in Serbia, which was more densely settled than either Greece or
Bulgaria during the second half of the nineteenth century. Other variables include
the fact that it began its political existence with a lower investment in social
overhead than Greece, Bulgaria, or Romania, and that it was a landlocked state.

Table 5.3

Elementary Schools, Teachers, and Pupils in Serbia, 1804–1900

Year	Schools			Teachers	Pupils
	Boys	Girls	Total		
1804			2		
1817			3		
1836			72		2,514
1841			137		
1844–45	213	0	233		6,201
1849	258	6	264		7,354
1859	318	22			11,478
1860–61	318	41			12,079
1863				388	13,563
1869	380	38	418		18,030
1870			441	550	23,346
1874			517	644	18,135
1880			614	817	35,939
1883			618	821	29,434
1890			713	1,344	56,592
1898			977	1,816	73,522
1900			936	1,644	102,408

Sources: Subotić, "The Serbia of Prince Miloš," p. 161; Popov, *Srbija i Rusija*, II, 441; Jovanović,*Ustavobranitelji i njihova vlada*, pp. 48–50; Ubicini, *Les Serbes de Turquie*, pp. 82–83; Spasić, "Neki podaci o osnovnim školama u Srbiji," p. 226; Jovanović, "Stanje javne nastave u Kraljevini Srbiji," pp. 126, 154; Skerlić, *Istorija nove srpske književnosti*, pp. 115–17, 344, 426.

The upward readjustment of the saturation point was achieved in some measure by hygienic improvements and the control of epidemics by the institution of relatively well regulated quarantine stations. Most of all, however, the accomplishment was the result of the systematic development of a cereal economy and of a change in eating habits: the consumption of less meat, less cheese, and more maize, wheat, and other cereals.

One pound of wheat releases three to ten times as many calories as the same quantity of meat. Pound for pound, a cereal diet thus will sustain a larger population than a meat diet. That is why the growth of a cereal economy and the adoption of a cereal diet may explain much of the Balkan population growth of the nineteenth century. The per capita cereal consumption of the Serbs of Serbia, grew by more than seven times between 1721 and 1890, while their consumption of meat was only one-third or one-fourth as great in 1905 as in 1830. The proportions are different for the other Balkan provinces. The trend, however, was similar.[61]

These changes were inspired by the recognition in the Ottoman Empire of private property; by the opening of the Black Sea and Balkan interior to world trade; by the political and social revolutions that put an end to the "second serfdom," thereby encouraging peasants to bring more land under cultivation; and by the resulting urban expansion.

Balkan urban development has occurred, in fact, in several stages, each associated with a particular area or culture: Minoan and Mycenaean cities of the Aegean during the second millennium B.C.; Greek Aegean cities after 800 B.C.; Greek colonies along the Black Sea and Adriatic Littoral during and after the seventh century B.C.; Thracian cities during the fourth century B.C.; Celtic and Roman cities along the middle Danube, Sava, Morava, and their tributaries between the third century B.C. and the fourth century A.D.; medieval cities in Serbia, Bulgaria, Bosnia, Croatia, Transylvania, Wallachia, and Moldavia during the thirteenth and fourteenth centuries; and Ottoman cities, such as Bosna Serai (Sarajevo) and Tirana, during the fifteenth and sixteenth centuries.

During the foregoing period of four millennia, few urban communities north of the Aegean had a population of more than 2,000 to 5,000. In Croatia (excluding Istria, Dalmatia, and Ragusa) and Slavonia, the three largest towns— Varaždin, Zagreb, and Karlovac—each possessed a population of less than 5,000 as late as 1787. In the Balkan portions of the Ottoman Empire itself, there were, in 1520, only three towns with more than 20,000 inhabitants—Istanbul, Salonika, and Adrianople. In 1600, there were fewer than ten such towns.[62]

The great era of urban expansion, as in the rest of the world, has been the period since 1750, and particularly since 1850. Above all, this has been a period during which cities with a population of 100,000 or more have grown. In no period of Antiquity were there simultaneously more than two such cities. In 1450, there was no Balkan city with a population of 100,000. Constantinople itself then numbered little more than 50,000. A century later, when it was also known as Istanbul, its population grew once again, soon exceeding 100,000 and rising to more than 300,000. Not until 1850, however, did a second city reach the hundred-thousand level: Bucharest (a former swampland, with a population in the 1820s of about 60,000, perhaps even 80,000, and with 366 churches, 20 monasteries, and 30 large oriental inns).[63]

By 1900, there were four such cities: Istanbul (with a population of 691,000 in 1927, 741,000 in 1935, and 844,000 in 1945), Bucharest (with a population of 1,240,000 in 1964), Athens (with a population of 14,000 in 1834, 42,000 in 1860, 65,000 in 1879, 110,000 in 1889, 167,000 in 1907, and 287,000 in 1921), and Salonika (with a population of 60,000 or more during the second half of the eighteenth century, falling to 44,000—made up of 18,000 Jews; 8,000 Mamins, or Jewish converts to Islam; 12,000 Muslims, many of them of Albanian ethnicity; and 6,000 Greeks—during and immediately after the Greek revolution, which incited the local janissaries to abuses of power, resulting in the emigration of thousands of Greeks). The population of Salonika rose to 158,000 by 1913 and to 200,00 during World War I. Declining to 172,000 in 1921, it rose to 218,000 in 1951 and 251,000 in 1961. The population of Greater Salonika grew from 301,000 in 1951 to 551,000 in 1971. Sofia, with a population in 1828 of about 46,000, joined the group of cities at the hundred-thousand level by 1910. Peripheralized by Turkey's loss in the 1870s and 1880s of Danubian Bulgaria and Eastern Rumelia and by the pull of Istanbul, Adrianople (Edirne), on the other hand, declined from a presumably higher pre-1878 population level to 60,000 in 1900. After rising to 65,000 in 1911, its population fell to 49,000 in 1920 and 20,000 in 1961.[64]

By 1920, there were seven cities at or above the hundred-thousand level, the last three to join the group being Piraeus (with a population of 11,000 in 1870, 22,000 in 1879, 34,000 in 1889, 51,000 in 1896, 75,000 in 1907, and 130,000 in 1921), Belgrade (with a population in 1838 of less than 15,000, including the Turkish garrison of 1,828, rising to 25,000 in 1866, 28,000 in 1874, 35,000 in 1884, and 54,000 in 1890),[65] and Zagreb, whose population rose to 351,000 in 1951 and 566,000 in 1971.

Between 1920 and 1940, the existing large cities continued to expand. But cities in the twenty-thousand range grew only slowly. In 1930 and 1940, there were no more than nine or ten cities with a population of 100,000 or more. The Pannonian *agrogorod* of Subotica, with rural dwellers accounting for more than a third of its population, was the latest addition.[66]

Mainly because of the slowdown in the growth of cities in the twenty-thousand range, the urban sector was unable to absorb the population surpluses of the rural areas. As early as 1890, therefore, another solution was tried, especially in the Adriatic and Aegean provinces: emigration to the New World, mostly by males.

The emigration from Greece was reflected in the decline in the ratio of males to females from a stable 99.3 to 100 between 1860 and 1890 to 98.7 in 1895, 96.0 in 1900, 92.5 in 1905, and 88.7 in 1910. In Albania, on the other hand, the Balkan land in which women were least valued except for their procreative and work functions, the ratio of males to females was still 109 to 100 in 1937 and 104 to 100 in 1945.[67]

Until almost 1890, the share in the total population of the age group 0–15 years, in Greece as in the Balkans in general, had been almost 40 percent. It thereupon began to fall in response to the declining representation of males in the total population, especially in Greece.[68] It continued to fall as a result of the diffusion of birth control practices. Between the two world wars, improved birth control practices spread even to remote Balkan villages—except perhaps among the Muslim Albanians of Albania and Kosovo.

In Albania, indeed, the age group 0–15 years fell from 36.4 percent in 1940 to 29.0 percent in 1955. It fell, however, not because of a decline in the birthrate but because of an increase in life expectancy for the age groups 15–65. In fact, the Albanian birthrate per population of 1,000 rose from 24.9 in 1931 to 40.2 in 1954. In Bulgaria, on the other hand, the birthrate fell from 39 per population of 1,000 during 1921–25 to 22.2 in 1940.[69] In interwar Yugoslavia, where the practice of repeated abortions was not uncommon in some rural districts, it dropped from 35.0 during 1921–25 to 27.4 during 1936–39.[70]

Despite these important transformations, the total population engaged in agriculture continued to grow at least until 1950, even though the ratio of persons in agriculture began to decline before or soon after the First World War. In Yugoslavia, for example, as that country was constituted territorially after World War II, the population deriving a livelihood from agriculture declined from 80 percent in 1910 (and higher earlier percentages) to 79 percent in 1921, 76 percent in 1931, 74 percent in 1941, 67–70 percent in 1948, and 61–63 percent in 1953. In absolute terms, however, it remained constant or even grew between 1910 and 1953, fluctuating from 10.2 million people in 1910 to 9.9 million in 1921, 11.0 million in 1931, 12.3 million in 1941, 10.6–11.1 million in 1948, and 10.3–10.8 million in 1953. In percentage terms, it declined to 51 percent in 1961, 38 percent in 1971, and 26 percent in 1985. In absolute terms, it dropped successively, during the same years, to 9.2–9.4, 7.8–7.9, and 6.0 million people.[71]

Behind the large agricultural population of the 1920s and 1930s lurked the problem of hidden unemployment (that is, the presence of too many people in the agricultural sector of the economy). During the interwar era, therefore, clashes between city and country sharpened.

The population of Sofia, the Bulgarian capital, grew from 154,000 in 1920 to 355,000 in 1938. Many of its residents, however, were employed in the tertiary sector and particularly in government service. By 1941, the number of public officials in Bulgaria, many of them poorly paid but holding positions that enabled them to exercise power over the less-advantaged peasantry, rose to 130,000. With their families, they numbered 650,000 persons, equal to a third of the urban population.[72] Not all peasants were poor. For the impoverished peasantry, however, cities —especially the capitals, centers of concentration of money, power, and corruption —became the enemy, doomed to feel the wrath of heaven. Bulgarian, Romanian, and Croatian demagogues and leaders of newly constituted peasant parties (undergoing *embourgeoisement* at the level of the leadership almost from the beginning) were quick to extol peasant values and laud the peasant way of life.[73]

The World-Economy of a Hegemonic Capitalism

The Balkan states thus failed to eradicate a problem inherited from the Ottoman past—a nongenerative urban system, marked by the diversion of wealth or resources from peasants to cities, to the state, and (especially in Romania) to landlords.[74] Like the Ottoman Empire itself, the new Balkan states were economically and financially dependent on the core states of the capitalist Atlantic economy. Similarly, the Balkan peasantries lacked autonomy in their relations with their own cities, states, and officialdom. Repeated land reforms were repeatedly frustrated—at least until 1950 or 1960—by a continuing rural demographic growth except in Greece,[75] where a significant portion of the rural population was either diverted to Athens, Piraeus, and Thessaloniki or drawn in larger numbers to the New World.

The Balkan bourgeoisies made important improvements. But failing to win the confidence, and neglecting to mobilize sufficiently the energies, of their peoples, they failed in their efforts to establish a viable economic order.

When the rural poverty and the generally low standard of living were compounded in the 1930s and 1940s by fascist aggrandizement and a world war, the result was revolution. That revolution was partly an article of export from the Soviet Union. In Yugoslavia, Greece, and Bulgaria, it also possessed important native foundations. In Romania and Albania, the native foundations were weaker but not altogether absent.

As a result of the rapid technological progress made between 1950 and 1970, both under postwar communism in most of the Balkan states and under the impetus of capitalism in Greece and Turkey, the number of Balkan cities with a population of 100,000 or more grew from 16 in 1950 to 31 in 1960. Of the 31, 13 were located south of the Danube and Sava, 6 in Wallachia and Moldavia, 6 in Transylvania and the Romanian Banat, and 6 in Yugoslavia north of the Danube and the Sava or along the Adriatic. In the communist states, small and middle-sized cities also expanded during this period, and new industrial towns came into being. In Greece, until a few years earlier the most highly urbanized Balkan country, there were, in 1990, still only three cities with a population of more than 100,000 (Patras moved into the hundred-thousand category in 1960, but Athens and Piraeus are now generally counted as a single metropolitan area). Athens-Piraeus, however, is the most populous metropolitan area in the Balkans. By 1980, four Balkan cities—Athens (with a population of 1,379,000 in 1951, 1,853,000 in 1961, and 2,530,000 in 1971), Bucharest (with a population of 648,000 in 1939 and twice that in 1964), Istanbul, and Sofia (with a population in 1965 of 811,000)—contained a population of more than a million each.[76] Maintained for almost five decades, the federal structure of communist Yugoslavia, with sharp competition for resources among six republican capitals and two autonomous territories that were nominally part of Serbia, prevented Belgrade from joining that group.

[handwritten margin note: EXCLUDING ISTAMBUL !]

In all the Balkan states except Albania, the peasantry today constitutes less than half the total population. Many peasants were organized into collective farms in Romania, Bulgaria, and Albania. In Yugoslavia, on the other hand, collectivization was abandoned after 1950 in favor of using the rural-urban commune (komuna) and socialist sector of society as devices to instill a socialist psychology in the peasantry. In Greece, where the forces of anticommunism prevailed at the conclusion of the civil war of 1946–48, no collectivization occurred. Everywhere, however, the process of collectivization has been reversed since 1990 in response to the call for "restructuring" that spread westward and southward from Poland and the Soviet Union to the neighboring communist states. In retrospect, the greatest change in the rural areas has not been collectivization so much as the shift of more than half the peasantry from the villages and hamlets to the cities.

Historians and others will argue for many decades over the reasons for the demise of the Soviet Union and the consequent retrenchment of communism in eastern Europe and the Balkans. From my own perspective, the problem of the communist countries was similar to that of the entire group of developing countries which succeeded in achieving a nineteenth-century form of industrialization based on coal and steel (heavy industry) but lacked the resources (capital, information, skilled labor, entrepreneurship, energy resources, etc.) with which to undertake a reorganization of the economy and society on the basis of science, technology, and the tools of the new communications revolution.[77] As the ideology of capitalism, redefined as rising (but in practice, frustrated) expectations, spread to these countries, they were forced to whittle down the cherished notion of an isolated, self-defined, sheltered world-economy. The abandonment of isolation (or insulation)—the almost complete dissolution of the Old World system of eight linked but separate world circuits (or, in the vocabulary of Fernand Braudel and Immanuel Wallerstein, "world-economies"), which extended in the thirteenth century from the Atlantic to the South China seas but over which the Atlantic circuit gained increasing authority during and after the sixteenth century[78]—forced them in turn to compete in markets and with enterprises whose object was profit maximization, for which they lacked the necessary historical socioeconomic foundations or facilitative infrastructure of long duration.

Economic competition has always had force or political power behind it. But the hegemonic capitalist states created more political barriers against the competition of the communist states than against that of states with a presumably more innocuous ideology. It would be naive to suppose, however, that politico-economic rivalry between states began only after the establishment of communist states. Let us see, therefore, whether the problem—as it relates to the Balkan states —has remained much the same or has changed over the two centuries since 1800.

The absence or scarcity of generative Balkan cities—made more generative than they had been but retaining nongenerative aspects through their very peripheralization or subordination to the capitalist world-economy—long impeded their ability to compete in the international market except in a few commodities. World trade grew from £280 million in 1800 to £380 million in 1830, £800 million in 1850, £2,800 million in the late 1870s, an average of £3,800 million during the last two decades of the century, and to more than £8,000 million by 1913. It thus grew 2.6 times between 1800 and 1850 and almost 4 times between 1850 and 1900. It doubled between 1900 and 1913. It consequently grew 10 times between 1800 and 1880 and 2.8 times between 1880 and 1913. By 1880, half the world's trade (imports plus exports) was carried on by the United Kingdom, United States, France, and Germany. As other countries took a greater interest in world trade, the share of these four states in world trade fell to 44 percent.[79]

The commerce of the Balkan states, on the other hand, grew at a less rapid rate. Serbian exports, which had been growing during the second half of the eighteenth century, hardly grew at all between 1800 and 1865, averaging 16.5 million francs during the early 1840s, 17.2 million francs annually between 1851 and 1855, 17.5 million francs annually between 1856 and 1860, and 17.6 million between 1861 and 1865. They then rose to an annual average of 29 million between 1866 and 1870, 32 million between 1871 and 1875, about 40 million between 1876 and 1880 (in view of Serbia's territorial expansion during those years, the increase was only nominal), and 85 million between 1906 and 1910.[80] If the increase due to territorial expansion and population growth is discounted, Serbian international trade barely doubled between 1840 and 1880. It doubled again between 1880 and 1910.

The combined export trade of Serbia and Greece grew by 4.9 times between 1861–65 and 1906–10. The combined export trade of Romania, Bulgaria, Serbia, and Greece grew by 2.2 times between 1881–85 and 1906–10. Between 1886 and 1910, however, during which there was no change in Bulgaria's political frontiers, Bulgaria's exports grew by only 72 percent, rising from 69.5 million to 119.3 million gold francs.[81] During the same period, world trade grew by 3.5 times. Between 1850 and 1910, it grew by almost 10 times, compared to a quadrupling for Serbia as a territory of constant territorial extent. The supposed fourteenfold increase between 1851 and 1914 in Greece's foreign trade does not factor out Greece's territorial growth (Ionian Islands, Thessaly, Epirus, Macedonia, Thrace, and Crete) during the same period.[82]

In a world perspective, the Balkan states fell behind economically even as they made improvements. In terms of per capita income, the experience of the poorer Balkan regions has been broadly similar to, if less unfortunate than, that of most of the other poor or underdeveloped countries of the world, among which, despite improvements, the ratio (presumably of per capita national income) fell from 1 for the poor states compared to 2 for the rich ones in 1800 to 1:20 in 1945 and 1:40 in 1965.[83] In 1986, the real per capita social product—a better measure than per capita national income, which exaggerates differences between poor and rich countries—in Slovenia, a non-Balkan alpine republic in nominally communist federal Yugoslavia, was five times as great as the real per capita social product in Kosovo, one of the most backward Balkan regions (in which the natural increase of population was five to six times as great as the natural increase in Slovenia), and more than twice as great as the real social product in Bosnia and Hercegovina, some portions of which were as backward as Kosovo while others were comparatively privileged.[84]

A first phase of falling behind (while moving ahead) of the Balkan states between 1800 and 1900 was followed by a second phase of falling behind (again while moving ahead) after 1950. Between 1913 and 1950, for example, the average annual percentage growth in western Europe's volume of exports was 0.1 percent, with a negative growth of –2.5 percent for Germany and a growth of 1.4 percent for Italy, 1.1 percent for France, and 0.2 percent for the United Kingdom, as against 2.3 percent for the United States, 1.8 percent for the non-

Table 5.4

Foreign Trade of the Balkan States, 1922–1930 and 1931–1935

	Average Value of Exports in Swiss Francs		Average Value of Imports in Swiss Francs	
Country	1922–1930	1931–1935	1922–1930	1931–1935
Albania	11.8	5.6	25.7	18.9
Bulgaria	213.7	132.9	232.0	115.3
Greece	376.3	197.8	731.8	347.4
Romania	814.3	501.9	773.4	379.4
Yugoslavia	594.4	298.7	625.4	279.4
Total	2,010.5	1,136.9	2,388.3	1,140.6

Sources: Royal Institute of International Affairs, *The Balkan States*, I, 73, 75, 128–31. See also Frangeš, "Die treibenden Kräfte der wirtschaftlichen Strukturwandlungen in Jugoslawien," p. 333.

European states, with a world average of 1.3 percent.[85] Between 1921 and 1930, the per capita foreign trade of Bulgaria, Greece, and Yugoslavia (in constant values) may have exceeded the 1906–10 level,[86] but the total foreign trade of the old territories of Romania (Wallachia and Moldavia) in 1934 may not have been much more than half of what they had been in 1913.[87]

The foreign trade of the Balkan states fell between 1922–30 and 1931–35, as shown in Table 5.4 above.

The average annual Balkan foreign trade from 1931 through 1935 thus was only half as great as the average annual trade from 1922 through 1930. Whatever gain may have been made between 1922 and 1930 over the prewar decade was lost between 1931 and 1935, and the loss was even greater if the calculation is made on a per capita basis. One should keep in mind, however, that the above decline was primarily an expression of money values. Expressed in metric tons, the foreign trade of Bulgaria, Greece, Romania, and Yugoslavia was modified during the same years from a yearly average of 13.4 million metric tons of exports and 5.5 million metric tons of imports to 13.5 million metric tons of exports and 4.1 million metric tons of imports, resulting in virtually no change in the export tonnage—despite a continuing demographic growth—and a 25 percent decline in the import tonnage.[88]

Hard times served as an impetus to notions of economic nationalism. In Romania, economist-politician Mihail Manoilescu propagated the idea that economic principles conducive to economic growth in economically advanced countries (free trade) do not necessarily conform to the needs of economically backward countries. Agricultural countries, he maintained, should be protectionist. Moreover, the prevailing conditions of world, European, and Romanian social disequilibrium may require an act of social engineering—the organization of society on a corporate basis. Pursuing such recommendations during the 1930s, Romania extended state economic controls, strengthened industrial and trading monopolies, and seemingly embraced the goal of corporatism.[89]

In Yugoslavia, as of the summer of 1935, the government of Milan Stojadinović (minister between June 1935 and February 1939), adopted a policy of promoting exports, raising the price of agricultural goods, lowering tariffs on railway cars and fuel in order to improve the country's transportation system, and raising purchasing power by expanding the public works program set up earlier in the year. In the fall of 1936, it reduced the debts of low-income and medium-income peasants by a half. It also promoted elastic credit and the growth of cotton and rice.[90]

None of the Balkan states, however, was able to remedy the basic economic problem of backwardness, which was further complicated by World War II. Between 1950 and 1973, moreover, there was, in terms of the expansion of world trade, a repetition of the experience of 1850 to the 1870s. That was followed for two decades, beginning in 1974, by a repetition of the 1880–1900 experience: a rapid increase in the trade volume of the industrially advanced countries of the world, followed by a continuing but less rapid growth. The combined foreign trade volume of France, Germany, Japan, the Netherlands, the United Kingdom, and the United States grew by 9.4 percent per year between 1950 and 1973 and 4.17 percent per year between 1973 and 1987.[91]

To set the problem of the differential rates of development of economically advanced and economically backward but advancing countries in a proper perspective, to understand how and why the Balkans got behind relative to the countries of advanced industry and technology, first under capitalism and then under communism, one would do well to explain first how some countries got behind while moving ahead under capitalism. I thus turn to a book by Francis Delaisi, *Les deux Europes.*

Delaisi distinguished between four main parts of the world: Europe A, Europe B, a "third Europe," and the rest of the world. West of the line Gdańsk-Cracow-Budapest, south of the line Stockholm-Bergen-Aberdeen-Glasgow, east of the line Glasgow-Bilbao, and north of the line Bilbao-Barcelona extended eastward to include Lombardy and Venetia lay Europe A. It was an area with an abundance of coal, iron, capital, and information. East of Gdańsk-Cracow-Budapest lay Europe B proper, complemented by a western Europe B in portions of the westernmost parts of geographic Europe. Europe B was the Europe of the "draft horse" and of "the old system of family economy" (Delaisi was writing in the 1920s), relying on animal power as its primary source of energy (see Figure 5.2). The "third Europe" (perhaps a misnomer but an understandable one) lay across the seas. It included the Americas, South Africa, and Australia.

Europe A was an exporter to the "third Europe" of capital, information, agricultural machines, and skilled labor. Europe B became an exporter to the "third

Figure 5.2. **The Old Europe of the Earth Culture (7000–3500 B.c.) and the New Industrial Europe (Europe A), as Represented Respectively by Marija Gimbutas and Francis Delaisi**

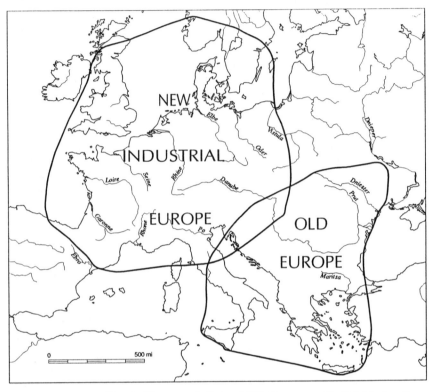

Sources: Gimbutas, *The Goddesses and Gods of Old Europe*, p. 16; Delaisi, *Les Deux Europes*, pp. 24–25.

Europe" of unskilled labor. Between 1880 and 1913, 26 million Europeans emigrated either permanently or temporarily to the "third Europe," half of them from Europe B proper and a quarter from Ireland. With the new agricultural machines, one farmer in Argentina, Canada, or the United States was able to produce as much wheat as fifty men in Europe B on land of approximately the same quality. Rails, locomotives, and railroad cars, supplied in large measure by Europe A, enabled the "third Europe" after 1870 to place its agricultural surpluses in the world market.

According to Delaisi's estimates, the export trade of the rapidly industrializing nations grew as follows between 1840 and 1913: 5.5 times for Britain, whose growth of foreign trade had begun earlier; 10 times for France; 21 times for the United States; and 26 times for Belgium. Even after the slowdown in the growth of their foreign trade between 1873 and 1913, the total foreign trade of France and the United Kingdom doubled, that of Italy almost tripled, that of Germany more than tripled, and that of the United States quadrupled.[92]

As a result of the growth of cereal production in all four of Delaisi's main divisions of the world, cereal prices tumbled. The chief victim of this convergence of circumstances was Europe B, in which a record expansion of cereal production had been made between 1830 and 1870.[93] Nor was Europe B better placed in regard to meat, wool, and leather exports, in which the advantage again lay with the land-extensive and/or capital-intensive world of the "third Europe." A continuing rise in longevity, achieved partly by the pursuit of improved health policies, therefore made it even more imperative that Europe B should export its cheap labor.

The expansion of industry in the United States, Canada, South Africa, and Australia enabled these countries to become exporters of manufactures. At the same time, the slowing down in the rate of expansion of world trade persuaded their governments to augment or establish protective tariffs and, in the case of the United States, to restrict immigration.

Unable to export as many manufactures to the "third Europe" as its industry called for, Europe A—particularly Britain, Germany, Austria, Switzerland, and Czechoslovakia—was confronted after World War I by unemployment for much of its industrial labor force. Unable to continue diverting labor from its peasant farms to the "third Europe," Europe B had to contend with the problem of an enormous hidden rural unemployment—that is, overemployment in agriculture.

Delaisi argued that the problems facing Europes A and B could be resolved if Europe A took advantage of the presence in Europe B of a hundred million small farm owners to invest in the agriculture of Europe B—to provide it, in effect, with farm machines. Pointing out that the purchases of Europe B from Europe A in 1913 amounted to $5.70 per capita, that the share of Romania in imports from Europe A was even $12.58 per capita, and that the share of Europe B in the products of Europe A was then twenty-two times as great per capita as the share of China, four times as great per capita as the share of India, and more than three times as great per capita as the share of Japan, Delaisi recommended that Europe A strengthen its bonds with Europe B.[94]

How could this have been done? To whom would the peasants of Europe B have sold their surplus production? Would the producers of farm machines in Europe A have known that the farm machines for Europe B should be small, simple, and cheap, the only kinds of machines that the peasant cultivators could have paid for and known how to use? Finally, were all parts of eastern Europe and, in terms of the particular focus of this book, all parts of the Balkans, equally suited to the promotion of an agricultural economy?

The governments of the Balkan states did not get an opportunity to answer these questions, or they reached pessimistic or negative conclusions. Instead, they attempted to improve their textile, chemical, and metallurgical manufactures, along with a few sectors of the agricultural economy.

Between 1925 and 1936, the government of Yugoslavia imported from Poland and Czechoslovakia whole textile factories with their workers in order to develop a ready-to-wear textile industry. As a result, Italian textile exports to Yugoslavia declined by 40 percent. The number of textile factories grew from 30 in 1929 to 363 in 1936. The number of persons employed in textile manufactures grew from 32,000 in 1932 to 53,000 in 1936 and 60,000 in 1937. Employment in metal and machine manufactures grew from 32,000 in 1932 to 40,000 in 1936. Between 1921 and 1938, therefore, jobs in industry grew in Yugoslavia at an average rate of 8,900 per year. Such an increase, however, was able to absorb only 9 percent of the average yearly population growth.[95] In Greece, a smaller country, the number of jobs in industry grew from an average of 5,000 per year between 1921 and 1938 to 15,000 per year between 1938 and 1951.[96]

The foreign trade policies of the Balkan states became increasingly bound after 1935 to clearing agreements with Germany by which that country became their chief trading partner. All the Balkan states except Albania (an Italian sphere of influence) were thus included in Germany's political-economic Mitteleuropean *Grossraum*, from which they obtained needed manufactures in return for performing the function of enabling Germany to obtain food supplies and raw materials that otherwise might not have been available to it under equally favorable terms.

Only Germany took advantage of Delaisi's recommendations. Even if Europe A as whole had been able to do in Europe B what he had proposed, however, the Balkan countries still may not have been able to restructure their economies. They had to start creating social infrastructures in 1830 that Europe A had been able to institute over a period of five hundred years. The countries of Europe A had achieved this by promoting "agricultural productivity," through their ability to find export markets for their raw materials converted into manufactures, and import markets for the raw materials they lacked, which they similarly converted into manufactures. Laying a stable groundwork for the implementation of industrial capitalism, this policy of "mercantile agrarianism" was precisely what the Ottoman Empire and successor Balkan states were unable to pursue until the latter part of the nineteenth century.[97]

Delaisi was unaware of what a large proportion of their meager capital the Balkan countries had to divert to costs of social overhead, such as dwellings, schools, other public buildings, roads, and bridges.[98] In Serbia, for example, the number of urban and rural shops grew by three times—from 5,511 to 17,078—between 1857 and 1886.[99] Moreover, the process of creating an appropriate social overhead has to be repeated over and over again, and the maintenance and expansion of a national patrimony become more difficult if man-made catastrophes periodically interrupt the previous process at certain intervals. Interruptions of that kind, the last one of which began in 1990, have repeatedly occurred in the Balkans during the last six hundred years.

Also missing from Delaisi's otherwise excellent analysis was the fact that the creation of a massive commercialized cereal economy in the interior regions of the Balkans occurred later than in any other region of geographic Europe, namely, between 1830 and 1870. Between 1814 and 1861, for example, the grain yield of Bessarabia grew ninefold. Between 1812–25 and 1860–68, the per capita cereal product of Bessarabia doubled, rising from 3.56 to 7.54 hectoliters. The wheat and maize exports of the Wallachian port of Galați and the Moldavian port of Brăila grew from 1.179 million hectoliters in 1837 to 4.206 million hectoliters in 1847. Russian grain exports from Black Sea and Azov ports grew from an average of 2,298 million hectoliters for 1826 to 1830 to 4,401 million hectoliters for 1841 to 1845.[100] In 1847, a year of the potato blight, an estimated 505,000 tons of grains were shipped out from the Turkish (that is, Romanian) Danube ports, 430,000 tons from the Russian Black Sea and Danube ports, and 500,000 tons from the Turkish ports south of the Danube (mostly from Bulgaria).

Then averaging, on the threshing floor in Rumelia (the eastern portions of European Turkey), one shilling three pence for an English bushel, wrote the British publicist David Urquhart, the price of grain soon began to rise, quickly almost tripling. An "outpouring" of grains commenced. "From the plains of Vienna" to the ports of the Black Sea "might be traced, along the plain, as far as eye could reach, double lines of waggons, the one arriving full, the other returning empty; night and day, week after week, month after month, this stream continued to flow, and when the price no longer permitted exportation, the granaries were still full."[101]

In neighboring Hungary, the process of developing a commercialized cereal economy began a hundred years earlier, in the 1720s, and was given sound foundations between 1770 and 1870.[102] On the other hand, at the very moment at which systematic capital investment in Balkan agriculture should have made good sense, namely in the 1870s, the fall in farm prices turned investments away from agriculture except in the highly privileged Danube basin and its main tributaries. Even in Romania, however, cereal exports plunged from 40.8 percent of the total harvest between 1911 and 1915 to 18.7 percent between 1923 and 1927. Partly—but only partly—the problem was geographic. Longer than any other European river outside of the territories of the former Russian Empire and Soviet Union (2,900 km), the Danube flows away from what, since the latter part of the sixteenth century, has been the most commercialized and industrialized part of Europe. As a result, the tonnage passing up and down the Danube south and east of Budapest on the eve of the First World War amounted to no more than 7 percent of the tonnage going up and down the Rhine. In the 1930s it did not exceed 10 percent.[103]

Also a factor in the weak showing of postwar or interwar Balkan agriculture was that it received little foreign or domestic capital. Moreover, the financial crisis of 1931–32 provoked the disinvestment of foreign capital from Balkan industry until 1934 or 1935. Foreign capital was invested in any case primarily in mining enterprise, heavy industry, and the development of energy resources (coal and petroleum).[104] By 1936, however, despite the limited sectors of the overall economy in which it was present, foreign capital represented 33.8 percent of the total capital investment in Yugoslavia.[105]

Little private domestic capital was available. Indeed, the biggest capitalist in the Balkans was the state. In Yugoslavia, the state owned and operated all radio stations and post office, telephone, and telegraph lines and offices. It also owned many forests, lumber mills, mines, spas, railroads, river boats and harbor facilities, arms and munitions factories, sugar refineries, and silk and carpet manufactures. State industrial monopolies and private domestic and foreign cartelized industries were reinforced by state promotion of cereal exports and state sales and trading monopolies in salt, matches, petroleum, alcohol, tobacco, cigarette paper, and stamp paper for legal documents. Both a cause and consequence of the relative scarcity of private capitalist (as against simply trading) enterprise, the foregoing system in variant forms also prevailed in the other Balkan states, especially Romania. Balkan merchants and industry thus depended on the state, while the state depended on foreign capital.[106]

Instead of narrowing, market forces may widen national and regional inequalities for many decades, perhaps centuries, for both capital and skilled labor—that is, human capital—prefer developed to lagging regions. Rondo Cameron thus concurs with John R. Lampe that "the principal weakness of the Serbian economy, which the banking system, or economic policy in general, was almost powerless to counteract," between 1878 and 1912, was "the shortage of human capital at the managerial or entrepreneurial level as well as throughout the labor force."[107] In fact, although Serbian economic accomplishments during the decade preceding the Balkan war of 1912 were considerable, human capital was still scarce.

Foreign banks and other foreign enterprises invested in the Balkans primarily for political reasons or for the development of mining and railroad and canal transportation and for the drainage of easily accessible fertile marshlands. In pre-1912 Serbia, foreign banks did little to promote the growth of Serbian industry, a policy to which Lampe refers as "the reluctant imperialism of foreign banks." Between 1906 and 1910, two-thirds of the investment in fixed capital for the development of Serbian industry, most of it for the manufacture of construction materials previously imported from Austria-Hungary, thus came from Serbian rather than foreign banks.[108]

What economically backward regions must achieve in order to lift their economies to the level of the economically most advanced countries is a rate of growth at least as great as that of the advanced countries in periods both of slow and rapid economic growth. But that is precisely what the Balkans were unable to accomplish either under the aegis of capitalism—from 1870 to 1914, from 1920 to 1940, and from 1950 to 1990—or, between 1950 and 1990, under the multiple Balkan forms of communism.

Comparative Advantage of an Informed
New-Model Capitalism

I have tried to explain why the attempts of the Balkan states to achieve economic parity with the world's economically highly developed states failed between 1870 and 1940 under the auspices of capitalism. Why did the attempt fail between 1950 and 1990 under the dual and rival auspices of capitalism in Greece and Turkey and of communism in Albania, Bulgaria, Romania, and Yugoslavia?

The attempt to use import substitutes in order to develop domestic industry prior to World War I was repeated by the Balkan states during the 1920s and especially during the 1960s and 1970s. In this last period, the items sought for "import-led growth" included not only capital goods but petroleum, chemicals, and special metals.[109] To obtain access to western technology, communist Romania pursued a policy of "import-led growth" as of 1967 primarily by concluding agreements with multinational or transnational capitalist enterprises. An important producer of petroleum since the 1890s—the producing regions were the Buzău and Dîmbovița valleys and the area around Bacău—and a net exporter of petroleum until 1977, Romania became thereafter a net importer.[110]

But the costs of industrialization were dear, creating a balance of payments problem. The problem was contained for a time in three main ways—by the promotion of tourism, especially to Greece, Yugoslavia, and Turkey but also to Romania and Bulgaria; by the immigrant remittances of workers from Greece, Yugoslavia, and Turkey, who were temporarily employed in Germany; and by shipping services that were provided in particular by Greece.

The external debt of the Balkan states nonetheless grew by leaps and bounds. The long-term public external debt of Greece grew from U.S. $905 million in 1970 to U.S. $3,532 million in 1979 and U.S. $12,452 million in 1985. Turkey's long-term public external debt grew during the same period from U.S. $1,854 (or U.S. $1,840) million to U.S. $10,972 million and U.S. $17,821 million. Yugoslavia's external debt rose from U.S. $941 million in 1965 to U.S. $1,198 million in 1970, U.S. $2,706 million in 1971, U.S. $21,096 million in 1981, and U.S. $32,079 million in 1985 (the 1971 to 1985 figures for Yugoslavia and the 1979 and 1985 figures for Turkey include substantial private nonguaranteed debts). Romania's public debt, on the other hand, fell from U.S. $10,000 million in 1981 to U.S. $6,977 million in 1985 and to yet lower levels in subsequent years. That result was obtained only by decreasing imports and increasing exports, especially of petrochemical products, and applying the funds obtained thereby not to technical modernization but to the repayment of the external debt—namely, through the implementation, by the government of communist dictator Nicolae Ceaușescu, of an austerity program that caused the Romanian standard of living to plummet. Debt service, on the other hand, absorbed a good portion of the revenues of Yugoslavia, Greece, and Turkey, that is, of communist and noncommunist states alike, as a result of which prices more than doubled in these states between 1970 and 1976.

They continued their upward spiral thereafter—first as a result of the increase between 1973 and 1980 in the price of petroleum, which was effected unilaterally by the Organization of Petroleum Exporting Countries (OPEC), to twenty times the 1970 level and then, even after the 1980 fall in the price of petroleum, by the continuing rise in the price of high-quality industrial goods. After 1980, therefore, Yugoslavia was no longer able to pursue a policy of import-led growth. As a result, the already acute problem of unemployment was exacerbated. The standard of living came tumbling down, intensifying the preexisting regional and ethnic antagonisms.[111]

In Yugoslavia, the ratio of exports to gross domestic product (GDP) grew from 8.3 percent in 1950 to 9.9 percent in 1955, 14.3 percent in 1960, 18.3 percent in 1965, and 21.3 percent in 1970. It then fell to 18.3 percent in 1975 and 17.5 percent in 1980, remaining at a level below 20 percent during the 1980s. The ratio of imports to GDP grew from 12.3 percent in 1950 to 13.9 percent in 1955, 17.6 percent in 1960 and 1965, and 27.3 percent in 1970. It then declined to 24.2 percent in 1975, 20.2 percent in 1980, and under 20 percent during the 1980s.

If, as some economists believe, a country with a population of 20 million to 30 million is not well integrated in a free or open world-market economy unless it attains an export-to-GDP and an import-to-GDP ratio of about 20 percent, Yugoslavia could have been so integrated only between 1966 and 1974.

In principle, such an integration is desirable. It may not be desirable for a country, however, if the hegemonic world-economy is not in fact a free or open world-economy but instead a capitalist world-economy. It may be especially nefarious when it occurs at a time of retrenchment and restructuring of the capitalist world-economy and of redefinition of the spheres of territorial hegemony. As a practical system, capitalism acts on the Ricardian principle of the comparative advantage of supposedly constant factor endowments (land, labor, and capital), as a result of which, despite brief aberrations, there is always a return to an equilibrium. In the ideology of capitalism, therefore, free trade is fair trade or tends to create it.

In practice, however, the reconstituted equilibrium of comparative advantage tends to return to the advantage of the privileged—as the privileged (among whom the rank order may change but who remain privileged as a group even though some additional units may in time join the group) were constituted in 1817 (the year in which David Ricardo advanced the principle) or as they were later reconstituted.[112] Developed countries do not seek to prevent underdeveloped countries from developing (to impede development would not be in their interest), but their half-conscious purpose at least is to prevent them from becoming equally developed. Readier than underdeveloped regions to welcome a large degree of openness and to equate free trade with fair trade, developed regions within a given country may act similarly, as the conflicts between the developed republics and regions and the underdeveloped republics and regions in Yugoslavia (that have to be explained, however, in much more complex terms) so eloquently demonstrate.

Changes have occurred in the relative position of the initial group of developed countries, but that has happened only because there were, to begin with, no great disparities in their respective factor endowments. They thus competed successfully with each other. On the other hand, as the gap between the developing but underdeveloped countries and the developed countries has widened, partly as a result of the political actions (with economic consequences) of the developed countries, it has become increasingly more difficult for the underdeveloped countries to catch up with the developed ones. The few possible exceptions to this rule, such as Singapore, Hong Kong, Taiwan, South Korea, and Kuwait, are all city or small maritime states. They have all benefited from a combination of two or three circumstances: small size (the absence of large interior regions for which they must accept political responsibility but often with the advantage—as in the case of Hong Kong and Singapore—of being able to obtain cheap labor from the interior regions for which they have no political responsibility), the possession of a scarce commodity in great demand (petroleum), and geographic situation.

Yugoslavia's "increased import-to-GDP indebtedness" or "import substitutions dependence," on the other hand, did not allow it to attain the export levels to which it aspired.[113] Among the reasons for that failure may have been inappropriate monetary policies and inadequate liberalization. A further obstacle to Yugoslav economic growth by means of a policy of import-substitutions dependence was the oil shock of 1973–74 and the resultant price inflation.

To explain the failure, however, one should also give weight to Nuno Valério's evaluation of the long-term experience of the Mediterranean countries in general: "The competition from commodities exported by the leading powers of the world economy was certainly detrimental to the growth of modern sectors, and the regulations of economic life imposed by the powers [the most highly developed and politically most powerful states], either as colonial powers or as formally equal partners, were certainly intended to promote primarily the interests of those who imposed them."[114] Other interpreters of the relationship between the northern tier of European states (in contemporary form, the dominant states of the European Community) and the Mediterranean countries in general —among them Stefan A. Musto, Susan L. Woodward, and Adamantia Pollis— reach similar conclusions. They emphasize the asymmetrical nature of the relationship.[115] I myself date the asymmetry in the Balkans at least to the period since 1500.[116]

Yugoslavia also had to pay a penalty for trying to achieve integration with the world-market capitalist economy at exactly the wrong time. Its attempts to achieve integration during the 1970s and 1980s, like Serbia's attempts and the attempts of the other Balkan states, first toward the end of the nineteenth century and before the First World War (the Great War) and then again in the 1920s and 1930s, have been out of phase with the needs of the developed capitalist economies.

The World Bank (the International Bank for Reconstruction and Development), established in 1944 in Washington, D.C., in order to fund long-term loans to the world community, has tended to promote investment in power plants, railroads, highways, and other communications and transportation facilities. Such projects enable the developed capitalist countries to export their own products and import the goods they themselves need.[117] They have not been without a political bias.

In 1974, the European Economic Community embraced a policy of ceilings or quotas on imports from nonmember countries. In particular, it placed restrictions on the importation of such agricultural products as beef, veal, wine, brandy, and fruits, which formed an important part of Yugoslavia's exports to Greece and Germany, forcing Yugoslavia to seek other outlets for these products in the so-called Third World and in the countries of eastern Europe, neither of which could provide it with most of the goods that were required for the development of its industry. Yugoslavia therefore continued to import the latter commodities from western Europe, allowing its foreign trade deficit to continue to grow.[118]

The practices of the European Community, which was officially inaugurated in 1992, currently offer no better promise for nonmembers. European countries that are not well developed or insufficiently integrated with European, especially German, banks are threatened by the prospect of nonadmission, that is, continuing discrimination.

The basic reasons for the economic disorder in all the countries of eastern Europe—from the Soviet Union to Yugoslavia, from the Polish Baltic to the Greek Aegean, under every form of communism but also in the capitalist "new democracy" of Greece—have a foundation, as I have already indicated, in the changes that have occurred in world trade. World trade expanded greatly between 1950 and 1973 but thereafter entered a more difficult period of expansion. The greatest expansion, moreover, occurred in the trade with each other of the technologically most advanced states. The goods involved in the expansion were primarily manufactures, whose share in world trade grew from about 43 percent during the fifty-year period before 1939 to 55 percent in 1962. The most important manufactures in world trade were capital goods (which in the second or slower phase of expansion also included communications technology) and, less important, new chemical products, especially plastic materials.

The capital goods in question were by and large products of an acceleration in "the pace of technological advance." Only the technologically most advanced countries of the world could afford the research and innovation costs without which the new capital goods could not be made. By and large, only the technologically most advanced states could afford to buy many such goods from each other.[119]

With the slowdown in the expansion of world trade after 1973, the decline in the ability of the advanced countries to buy and sell was paralleled by a yet greater decline in the ability of the developing but underdeveloped countries to buy and sell—now relatively more underdeveloped than ever because of the change in the nature of the most desirable capital goods. The latter difficulty was compounded by the fact that the technologically most developed states—by and large, the advanced capitalist states—sometimes withheld "critical" capital goods and other "critical" products from countries that did not have "critical" products to return or from countries of whose politics they disapproved. So much for "market economy," the name by which capitalism is so often passed off.

In 1953, a defender of the idea of European unity, the economist André Philip, hoping to avert in the future the kind of world economic or politico-economic crisis that had beset Europe and the world between 1914 and 1949, envisioned "the union of Europe" as a "vital" prelude and complement to the construction of "a viable international market." He imagined it not as "a new economic and political bloc" that would "suscitate a regional nationalism as dangerous and historically outdated as the old local nationalisms" but as "the solution to the problems that engulf and surpass" Europe. Rejecting the notion of state sovereignty, he defined a nation as no more than "a transitory historical reality."[120]

The notion of sovereignty is, of course, a legal fiction. As for states, they have evolved over the centuries in form, size, and content. As for nation-states, they have hardly existed for more than the last two hundred years. One should not be surprised, therefore, at the resurgence and explosions of nationalism during the 1980s and 1990s. People who have developed a sense of nationhood but have lost their state or have never had the opportunity to build a so-called nation-state of their own want to do what others have done, and as in the past they sometimes want to do it even though it may be at the expense of the others, or even at their own expense.

In the long term, the nation-state may be a transitory historical phenomenon. But it may have a life for some time yet. What may now be in the process of formation, however, is a new system of international and transnational relations (not just one state or coalition of states but a combination of political, economic, and other interests, including regional blocs). The possible emergence of such a system is no guarantee, however, that all older types of state will disappear, including the state in which there is a close approximation of political and ethnic frontiers.

To paraphrase Paul R. Brass, competition for valued economic and political opportunities and resources, an important aspect of the conflict among Serbs, Croats, and Bosnian Muslims in Yugoslavia,[121] produces rival conceptions of the best way to organize space and the human and other animate and inanimate populations to be included within that space. Such competition exists alike within states and between states.

On the basis of his observation and analysis of economic relations in the Habsburg Monarchy, Otto Bauer concluded that the drummer for capitalism is the law of unequal development of peoples and regions. Able to attract more capital precisely because it is more developed, a highly developed region also draws skilled labor.[122] Possessing both capital and skilled labor (human capital), it can obtain the raw materials or natural resources it needs more cheaply than regions or states that have the natural resources but lack the necessary capital and labor skills. As the processes of development and growth continue, the gap between the developed and underdeveloped regions widens. The very emergence of developed regions culminates in the formation of less-developed regions and manifestation of unequal rates of development.

In those parts of the world in which both plants and animals were domesticated, differences between developed and underdeveloped regions were real but minor. These differences widened during the sixteenth century and widened further after 1800. Around each developed region there thus arose, to use the terminology of Immanuel Wallerstein, a less-developed peripheral region. Beyond that periphery lay yet more underdeveloped zones.

In the world-economy that arose in Europe, all three regions—core, periphery, and semiperiphery[123]—related in different ways and in unequal degrees to a central or core money market,[124] which, partly through its association with political institutions that by and large defended its cause, was in fact as much a command economy as the more explicitly political old-style command economies. The new-style command economy was directed, however, by what the classical economists called an "invisible hand," that is, the market—albeit not without the guidance of the political institutions with which money and commerce were allied.

It was perhaps natural that peripheries and semiperipheries should want to duplicate the technological achievements of the successful core—that is, the North Atlantic or circum-oceanic territories. But no model is permanently useful, and a given model of economic or technological development may not be appropriate for all regions or cultures. Unfortunately, the only model available to Europe B and to the so-called Third World was the nineteenth-century model of Europe A and the model of the Soviet Union—coal, iron, and electrification (an abbreviated model of the United States), with Marx and despotism thrown in.

Since 1950 and especially since 1970, however, the circum-oceanic capitalist states have developed a new model, in the functioning of which the most important factor may be reliable and comparable information quickly obtained and diffused. Modified versions of that model may be suited to many other parts of the world, including the Balkans.

As I show in the final chapter, an insufficient concern for agriculture has been a virtual constant in the Balkans from 1600 (and earlier yet) to 1830 and from the 1870s to 1990.[125] Between 1920 and 1940, the annual industrial growth rate in Romania and Bulgaria was respectively three and four times the European average, but improvements in agriculture were so slow that the general economy of the Balkan states continued to fall behind even when the industrial growth rate in the economically and technologically more advanced countries of Europe was very low. The great decline in Greece, between 1950 and 1970, in the proportion of the population engaged in agriculture was not accompanied by a significant increase of capital investment in agriculture. In communist Yugoslavia, fixed capital investments in agriculture between 1952 and 1982 amounted to only 7.7 percent of that country's overall investment in fixed capital.[126]

The new information model for the Balkans therefore should make an ample provision for the development of a flourishing and regionally differentiated agriculture. The new model or models should be designed to fit local and regional needs, taking advantage both of thorough information and of the originality of which the Balkan peoples are capable. Finally, and this is a theme that I shall later stress again, the Balkan peoples, like the peoples of the world in general, must strive to develop cultures, economies, and societies with a basis in sound ecological and anthropological principles—essentially, principles of conservation and expansion of the imagination, so much at odds with the means and goals of expanding material appetites and of an endless, self-destructive economic growth.

Notes

1. Gerschel, "La Conquête du nombre"; Liebel, "History and the Limitations of Scientific Method."

2. Ste.-Croix, "Greek and Roman Accounting," pp. 54–55.

3. Niederle, *Manuel de l'antiquité slave*, II, 62, 260–61; Miller, *Imperial Constantinople*, p. 58; Stoianovich, *Between East and West*, III, 5.

4. Herodotus, *The Histories*, p. 307.

5. Grenville, *Observations sur l'état actuel de l'Empire ottoman*, p. 53.

6. Bolkestein, *Economic Life in Greece's Golden Age*, p. 104; Hopper, *Trade and Industry in Classical Greece*, pp. 195–96.

7. On the general distinction among the three types of goods (priced, free, and ceremonial), see Hoselitz, "The Market Matrix," p. 219.

8. Kostić, "Postanak i razvitak 'čaršije' (primer 'čaršije' Bajine Bašte)," pp. 132–33.

9. Protić, "Neki običaji oko kupovine, prodaje i trampe," XI, 21; XII, 40–60.

10. Timarion, quoted in Tozer, "Byzantine Satire," pp. 244–45.

11. Vryonis, "The Byzantine Legacy in Folk Life and Tradition in the Balkans," p. 136.

12. Grujić, *Zapisi*, I, 22–28, 53, 147.

13. Vernant, "Du Mythe à la raison," p. 200.

14. Stoianovich, *Between East and West*, II, 109–13; Sevin, *Lettres sur Constantinople*, p. 108. See also Allix, "The Geography of Fairs."

15. Bolkestein, *Economic Life in Greece's Golden Age*, p. 122.

16. Ste.-Croix, "Greek and Roman Accounting."

17. Braudel, *Civilisation matérielle, économie et capitalisme*, II, pp. 332, 511–13.

18. Stoianovich, *Between East and West*, II, 10–13.

19. Armstrong, "Mobilized and Proletarian Diasporas"; Armstrong, *Nations before Nationalism*, pp. 206–13.

20. Moryson, *An Itinerary Containing His Ten Yeeres Travell*, I, 148–50, 421; II, 82–83, 114; III, 464–83 (valuable pages on transportation and travel costs); IV, 46, 140–41, 72, 95.

21. AN, AÉ B^III 234, mémoire sur l'état du négoce des François et des autres nations européennes en Levant (1682).

22. Moryson, *An Itinerary Containing His Ten Yeeres Travell*, IV, 70. See also Mączak, "Travel Expenses and Living Costs in Sixteenth Century Europe"; Mączak, "Un Voyageur témoin des prix européens," pp. 327–36, esp. price data on p. 330 and map on p. 336; Mączak, "Progress and Underdevelopment in the Ages of Renaissance and Baroque Man," p. 92. Moryson's statement is also cited and further analyzed by Braudel, *Civilization and Capitalism*, II, 171–72. Braudel (III, 40) provides additional data on the decline in the price of foodstuffs as one journeyed from the core area eastward (but also westward) across Europe.

23. Braudel, *Civilization and Capitalism*, III, 40, 293; Braudel and Spooner, "Prices in Europe from 1450 to 1750," pp. 395–400.

24. Berov, "Changes in Price Conditions in Trade between Turkey and Europe."

25. Pouqueville, *Voyage dans la Grèce*, III, 443–44.

26. Turner, *Journal of a Tour in the Levant*, I, 79–81.

27. Stoianovich, "Cities, Capital Accumulation, and the Ottoman Command Economy," forthcoming. On the general nature of nongenerative cities, see Hoselitz, "Generative and Parasitic Cities"; Bairoch, "Urbanization and the Economy in Preindustrial Societies."

28. Mardin, "Power, Civil Society and Culture in the Ottoman Empire," p. 265.

29. DA, PO, 1/51, copy of the Commercial Code. See also Mijatović, *Izvod iz političke ekonomike*, p. 107.

30. Finley, "Between Slavery and Freedom"; Dockès, *Medieval Slavery and Liberation*, pp. 105–6.

31. Bolkestein, *Economic Life in Greece's Golden Age*, pp. 77–80, 88–89, 95–96, 101–2.

32. On the decline of slavery and the slave trade in Europe north of the Loire valley (but excluding England, where war between Celts and Saxons resulted in giving the word "wealth," which is of Celtic origin, the sense of "slave," just as among the Slavs there was a confusion between the word for "slave" and the word for "merchandise," both having *rob-* as their root) and west of the Rhine or Verdun as early as the ninth or tenth century, and in Hungary by the end of the thirteenth, see Bloch, "Comment et pourquoi finit l'esclavage antique"; Rutkowski, "Medieval Agrarian Society in Its Prime," pp. 405–6; Lopez, "The Trade of Medieval Europe: The South," pp. 261–62, 271–72; Maricq, "Notes sur les Slaves dans le Péloponnèse"; Verlinden, "Le Franc Samo"; Origo, "The Domestic Enemy."

33. Mathiex, "Trafic et prix de l'homme en Méditerranée."

34. Jireček, *Istorija Srba*, pp. 188–89; Vinaver, "Trgovina bosanskim robljem," pp. 125–47; Villari, *The Republic of Ragusa*, p. 279.

35. Heyd, *Histoire du commerce du Levant au Moyen-âge*, II, pp. 316, 558–63; Verlinden, "La Colonie vénitienne de Tana," pp. 1–25; Verlinden, "La Crète," p. 699; Lombard, "Caffa et la fin de la route mongole," pp. 100–103; Vinaver, "Trgovina bosanskim robljem," pp. 125–47; Lopez, "Market Expansion," pp. 445–64; Braudel, *La Méditerranée*, II, 92–94; Nicolay, *Les Navigations, peregrinations et voyages faicts en la Tvrqvie*, bk. II, Chap. xxiii, p. 114.

36. Braudel, *Civilization and Capitalism*, II, 188–89.

37. Schneider, et al., eds., *Wirtschaftskräfte und Wirtschaftswege*, Vol. I: Małowist, "Saraï la Nouvelle," Krekić, "Venetian Merchants in the Balkan Hinterland"; Lane, "The Venetian Galleys to Alexandria"; Pach, "Zur Geschichte des levantinischen Pfefferhandels"; Goldenberg, "Peter Hallers Darlehen an Nürnberg"; Hirschmann, "Kunz Horn (+1517), ein Nürnberger Grosshändler und Frühkapitalist"; Bergier, "De Nuremberg à Genève"; Vol. II: Westermann, "Zur künftigen Erforschung der Frankfurter Messen des 16. und frühen 17. Jahrhunderts."

38. Turner, *Journal of a Tour in the Levant*, II, 366 n.

39. Kulischer, *Europe on the Move*, pp. 150, 153; Lampe, *The Bulgarian Economy in the Twentieth Century*, p. 18 n. 6; Kostanick, "The Geopolitics of the Balkans," pp. 14, 28, 31, 36, 39, 41; Kitroeff, "Approaches to the Study of the Holocaust in the Balkans."

40. Zinkeisen, *Geschichte des osmanischen Reiches in Europa*, II, 117, 155–56, 206, 454–55; Filipović, "Pogled na osmanski feudalizam," p. 59.

41. Sarkisyanz, *Geschichte der orientalischen Völker Russlands bis 1917*, p. 81.

42. Ménage, "Devshirme"; Sugar, *Southeastern Europe under Ottoman Rule*, pp. 55–59. See also Wittek, "Devshirme and Shari'a."

43. Gerlach, *Stephan Gerlachs dess Aeltern Tage-Buch*, p. 34B.

44. Arnakis, "The Role of Religion in the Development of Balkan Nationalism," pp. 120–21.

45. Kuripešić, *Putopis kroz Bosnu, Srbiju, Bugarsku i Rumeliju 1530*, p. 22.

46. Hughes, "Introduction," p. iii.

47. Moryson, *Shakespeare's Europe*, pp. 11–15.

48. Barkan, "Les Formes de l'organisation du travail agricole dans l'Empire ottoman"; Barkan, "Le Servage existait-il en Turquie?"; Filipović, "Pogled na osmanski feudalizam," pp. 59–63.

49. Gibb and Bowen, *Islamic Society and the West*, Vol. I, pt. 1, pp. 304–5; Turner, *Journal of a Tour in the Levant*, II, 366 n.

50. For an estimate of twenty thousand (but with imprecision as to the period), see Mougenot, *Grand atlas historique*, p. 205.

51. Young, *Corps de droit ottoman*, II, 167–75. For further details on slavery and the slave trade in the Ottoman Empire during the nineteenth century, see Toledano, *The Ottoman Slave Trade*, pp. 8, 53, 56–57, 63, 81–82, 90, 124–25, 136, 138, 149–51.

52. Stoianovich, *Between East and West*, I, 25.

53. Cvetkova, "Changements intervenus dans la condition de la population des terres bulgares," p. 312; Gandev, "L'Apparition des rapports capitalistes"; Braudel, *La Méditerranée*, II, 67; Karadžić, *Danica*, pp. 80–81.

54. Bérard, "Problèmes démographiques dans l'histoire de la Grèce antique"; Moreau, "Les Théories démographiques dans l'Antiquité grecque"; Myres, *Geographical History in Greek Lands*, p. 203; Bolkestein, *Economic Life in Greece's Golden Age*, p. 98; Cook, *The Greeks until Alexander*, pp. 123–24; Oliva, *Pannonia and the Onset of Crisis in the Roman Empire*, pp. 127–37; Charanis, comment on the views held by Soviet Byzantinists as expressed in "Gorod i derevnia v Vizantii v IV–XII vv," p. 286; Riquet, "Christianisme et population"; Latouche, "Aspect démographique de la crise des grandes invasions"; Russell, "Late Ancient and Medieval Population."

55. Polyzos, *Essai sur l'émigration grecque*, pp. 173–96; L'Héritier, *La Grèce*, p. 37 n.; Kitroeff, "Émigration transatlantique et stratégie familiale en Grèce," pp. 244–46.

56. Sivignon, "The Demographic and Economic Evolution of Thessaly," p. 381.

57. Pouqueville, *Voyage dans la Grèce*, III, 440–41. To obtain the above densities, I have calculated the *toise*, a prerevolutionary measure of length, at 1.949 meters.

58. Kayser, "La Carte de la distribution géographique de la population grecque en 1961," p. 304.

59. Von Thünen, *Von Thünen's Isolated State*, pp. 291–94.

60. See the sources for Table 5.3, p. 209.

61. Stoianovich, "Arithmetic and Ethnography of Balkan Foods," forthcoming.

62. Stoianovich, "Cities, Capital Accumulation, and the Ottoman Command Economy," forthcoming.

63. Walsh, *Narrative of a Journey from Constantinople to England*, p. 135.

64. Mollat du Jourdan, *L'Âme des cités*, pp. 303–5; L'Héritier, *La Grèce*, pp. 38, 119;

Mikhov, *Beiträge zur Handelsgeschichte Bulgariens*, pp. 24–26; Vacalopoulos, "Commercial Development and Economic Importance of the Port of Thessaloniki," p. 302; Zedlitz-Neukirch, *Europa im Jahre 1829*, p. 341; Blanc, "La Roumanie," p. 233; Hoffman, *Regional Development Strategy in Southeast Europe*, pp. 300–301.

65. Cunibert, *Essai historique sur les révolutions de l'indépendance*, II, 477–78; Serbia, Ministarstvo Finansije, *Državopis Srbije*, IX, 142–45; XIII, 34, 36, 106, 108, 110; Serbia, Ministarstvo Narodne Privrede, *Prethodni resultati popisa stanovništva 1890*, pp. 92–95; ibid., *1895*, pp. 84–87.

66. Krallert, "Die Verstädterung in Südosteuropa."

67. Valaoras, "A Construction of the Demographic History of Modern Greece," p. 128; Skendi, *Albania*, p. 54.

68. J.C.C., "La Population de la Grèce depuis 1860," p. 891.

69. Kulischer, *Europe on the Move*, p. 151; Skendi, *Albania*, pp. 55–56.

70. Tomasevich, *Peasants, Politics, and Economic Change in Yugoslavia*, pp. 289, 332, 599.

71. Macesich, "The Yugoslav Model in Perspective," p. 2; Stipetić, "Agriculture in Yugoslavia: Problems and Prospects," p. 327.

72. Kulischer, *Europe on the Move*, p. 151.

73. Tomasic, "Ideologies and the Structure of Eastern European Society," p. 370; Graham, *Alexander of Yugoslavia*, p. 132; Roucek, *The Politics of the Balkans*, p. 124.

74. Stoianovich, "Cities, Capital Accumulation, and the Ottoman Command Economy."

75. Dertilis, "Terre, paysans et pouvoir politique."

76. Lampe, *The Bulgarian Economy in the Twentieth Century*, p. 16, for Sofia; Blanc, "La Roumanie," p. 233, for Bucharest; Rey, *La Roumanie*, p. 98, for Romania; Hoffman, *Regional Development Strategy in Southeast Europe*, pp. 300–301, for alternative data; for Athens, see Burgel, *Athènes*, p. 15.

77. Richta et al., *Civilization at the Crossroads*, pp. 24, 36.

78. Abu-Lughod, *Before European Hegemony*, pp. 340, 352–73, and map on p. 34 of "the eight circuits of the thirteenth-century world system."

79. Ashworth, *A Short History of the International Economy since 1850*, pp. 17, 183, 206, 208, 210–11, 218; Damianov, "French Commerce with the Bulgarian Territories," p. 26.

80. Af. Étr., CC, Belgrade, I, fol. 138 (for 1840); fol. 216, A. de Codrika, Belgrade, February 3, 1842 (for 1841); I, fol. 393, Adolphe Durand de Saint-André, Belgrade, May 14, 1847 (for 1843 and 1844); II, fol. 524, memoir by consul general Tastu, Belgrade, November 1862 (for 1850–59); IV, fols. 80–89, Botmiliau, Belgrade, July 11, 1865 (for 1861–62, 1862–63); fol 71–403, Engelhardt to the marquis de La Valette and the *états de commerce* (for 1863–64 and 1864–65); Lampe and Jackson, *Balkan Economic History*, p. 165.

81. Lampe and Jackson, *Balkan Economic History*, p.165.

82. Petrakis, "Economic Fluctuations in Greece," pp. 32–38.

83. Macesich, *Economic Nationalism and Stability*, pp. 71–72.

84. Lydall, *Yugoslavia in Crisis*, pp. 188–89; Krejci, "Ethnic Problems in Europe," p. 152.

85. Maddison, *Economic Growth in the West*, p. 166.

86. Lampe and Jackson, *Balkan Economic History*, p. 343.

87. Spulber, "Changes in the Economic Structures of the Balkans," p. 359.

88. Royal Institute of International Affairs, *The Balkan States*, I, 73, 75, 128–31.

89. Roberts, *Rumania: Political Problems of an Agrarian State*, pp. 192–98; Manoïlesco, "Arbeitsproduktivität und Aussenhandel"; Brinkmann, "Mihail Manoïlesco

und die klassische Aussenhandelstheorie"; Janos, "Modernization and Decay in Historical Perspective," pp. 103–5; Schmitter, "Reflections on Mihail Manoilescu."

90. Markert, ed., *Osteuropa-Handbuch: Jugoslawien*, pp. 217, 219.

91. Maddison, *Dynamic Forces in Capitalist Development*, pp. 74–76, 108–11, 147–48, 154.

92. Delaisi, *Political Myths and Economic Realities*, p. 102 n.

93. Stoianovich, "Russian Domination in the Balkans," pp. 216–21.

94. Delaisi, *Les Deux Europes*, esp. pp. 127–28, 134, 138–39, 196.

95. März, *Jugoslawien*, pp. 120–22, 150–54; Wagemann, *Der neue Balkan*, pp. 84–85; Mišić, "Industrija Jugoslavije do Drugog svetskog rata," p. 267; Frangeš, "Die treibenden Kräfte der wirtschaftlichen Strukturwandlungen in Jugoslawien," p. 324; Markert, ed., *Osteuropa-Handbuch: Jugoslawien*, p. 219.

96. Koty, "Greece," p. 340.

97. Fei and Ranis, "Economic Development in Historical Perspective."

98. [Bloch], review of Wilhelmy, *Hochbulgarien*.

99. Af. Étr., CC, Belgrade, II, fols. 472–73, "Statistique de la Principauté de Serbie," extrait abrégé de la brochure serbe publiée à Belgrade à la fin de 1858, sous le titre de *Predlog Narodnoj Skupštini*, par Vladimir Jakšić, professeur de statistique et finances au Lycée de Belgrade, joined to the letter of Auguste Dozon, Belgrade, July 23, 1861; Belgrade, VII, fol. 178, report of the first secretary of the French legation at Belgrade, Baron Méneval, joined to the letter of René Millet, March 23, 1888.

100. Stoianovich, "Russian Domination in the Balkans," pp. 217–19.

101. Urquhart, *Progress of Russia*, pp. 358, 401–2.

102. Good, "Modern Economic Growth in the Habsburg Monarchy," pp. 214, 216–20.

103. Ogilvie, *Europe and Its Borderlands*, pp. 214–15, for comparative tonnage on the Rhine and Danube; Janos, "Modernization and Decay in Historical Perspective," pp. 97, 103, on the Romanian economy.

104. Frangeš, "Die treibenden Kräfte der wirtschaftlichen Struktwrwandlungen in Jugoslawien," p. 325.

105. Markert, ed., *Osteuropa-Handbuch: Jugoslawien*, pp. 219–21; März, *Jugoslawien*, pp. 124–25; Tenenbaum, *National Socialism vs. International Capitalism*, pp. 75–76.

106. Jovanović, "Les Classes moyennes chez les Slaves du Sud," pp. 237–41; Wagemann, *Der neue Balkan*, pp. 52–56; Stoianovich, "The Social Foundations of Balkan Politics," pp. 336–37.

107. Lampe, "Serbia, 1878–1912"; Cameron, *Banking and Economic Development*, pp. 20–21.

108. Lampe, "Serbia, 1878–1912," pp. 155, 159.

109. Lampe, *The Bulgarian Economy in the Twentieth Century*, pp. 179–80, 188.

110. Turnock, "The Industrial Development of Romania," p. 325; Smith, "Is There a Romanian Economic Crisis?"

111. Gianaris, *Greece and Turkey*, pp. 144–46; Sjöberg and Wyzan, "The Balkan States," p. 4; Teodorescu, "The Future of a Failure," pp. 70–71; Bartlett, "Economic Change in Yugoslavia," p. 33; Havrylyshyn, "Yugoslavia," p. 264; Rosecrance, *The Rise of the Trading State*, pp. 9–13; Woodward, "Political Changes in the European Mediterranean Arena, p. 188.

112. Ricardo, *The Principles of Political Economy and Taxation*, pp. 77–93; Braudel, *Civilization and Capitalism*, III, 48; Edwards, *The Fragmented World*, pp. 293–96, 305–7. For a modification of the Ricardian views, brought more closely in line with the consumerist and potentially transnationalist conceptions of the marginalist school of economics, see Heckscher, "The Effect of Foreign Trade on the Distribution of Income"; Ohlin, "The Theory of Trade"; Flam and Flanders, "Introduction."

113. Havrylyshyn, "Yugoslavia," pp. 183, 206–9, 286, 326–32.

114. Valério, "Some Remarks about Growth and Stagnation in the Mediterranean World," p. 131.

115. Musto, "The European Community in Search of a New Mediterranean Policy"; Woodward, "Political Changes in the European Mediterranean Arena"; Pollis, "The Southern European Semiperiphery and the European Community." On the asymmetry of relations between regions of unequal development as seen from an ethnographic perspective, see Nash, "Ethnographic Aspects of the World Capitalist System."

116. Stoianovich, "Europe and the Balkans."

117. Sutton, "Development Ideology," pp. 51–55; Helleiner, *International Economic Disorder*, pp. 34–35; Edwards, *The Fragmented World*, pp. 170–75.

118. Singleton, "Objectives and Methods of Economic Policies in Yugoslavia."

119. Shonfield, *Modern Capitalism*, pp. 23–26, 35–36, 41–48.

120. Philip, *L'Europe unie*, pp. 3, 355.

121. Brass, "Ethnic Groups and Nationalities," p. 30.

122. Bourque, *L'État capitaliste et la question allemande*, pp. 245–46.

123. For the concepts of core, periphery, and semiperiphery, see Wallerstein, *The Modern World-System*.

124. Philip, *L'Europe unie*, pp. 12–21; Braudel, *Afterthoughts on Material Civilization and Capitalism*, pp. 78–115.

125. For a similar view of Balkan backwardness as the product of "an accumulation of historical setbacks," see Blanc, *L'Économie des Balkans*, p. 30.

126. Teichova, "Structural Change and Industrialisation in Inter-War Central-East Europe," pp. 179, 181; Mouzelis, *Modern Greece*, p. 39; Marsenic, "Accumulation and Investment in the Yugoslav Economy," p. 94.

6 PERSONALITY AND CULTURE

Apart from the three value orientations described in the chapter on biotechnics and social biology, a fourth value orientation exists in the Balkans today. One may overlook that innovation if one focuses on the passions let loose by the demise of the Soviet Union, the crisis of communism, and the overt expression of latent ethnic hostilities. That fourth system of values first appeared among the Greeks during the classical era, while a few elements of the system may have come into being among the South Slavs during the later Middle Ages. But as a complex system of attitudes that could strengthen the notion of economic value and of individual as against collective responsibility, the new orientation was not fully elaborated in the Balkans until the nineteenth and twentieth centuries. Finding expression in a new conception of personality—a new identity—it had a basis in the emergence of new attitudes toward space, time, work, and leisure. Limited at first to select individuals and small groups, it spread to wider groups after 1900. As among other peoples, when threats arise to concurrent perceptions of group identities, the new orientation may lose some of its force. Fragile as it may be, however, it still remains in place, ready to recover fully when the threats to group identities are diminished or removed and when persuasive reasons can be offered for a revision or renovation of group identity.

Work and Leisure

One finds in the Balkans several different general attitudes toward work, each with its own special cultural, historical, and socioeconomic foundations. These attitudes have a basis in different ways of experiencing time. Some are more archaic than others. They also have different geographic or ecological foundations, out of which have evolved different ways of experiencing and organizing space. Along with language and religion, they may be a means of distinguishing between one ethnocultural unit and another.

Anthropologist Dorothy Demetracopoulou Lee aptly describes one of the most general contemporary Greek views of work, identifying in this manner one such possible ethnocultural unit:

Diligence is an internal attitude; it rests on self-discipline and free incentive, it includes interest and enjoyment. It does not mean a valuation of work for its own sake; it is the personal quality of diligence, not work itself, which is good. To work compulsively is to be a slave to work; and what can be worse than slavery? Even to work under the compulsion of work as a virtue is to deny oneself prized freedom; all work under pressure, such as the pressure of a time limit or the dictates of an employer, means loss of freedom.[1]

In certain respects, the modern conception of work is Hesiodic, going back to values current in Greece since 800 B.C. It is especially Hesiodic in embracing the notion that work is not *ipso facto* a virtue but acquires virtue only when it facilitates an accumulation of wealth. Wealth in turn gives an actor freedom to choose between the way of nobility and the way of wanton violence and overbearing pride.

Only in the post-Hesiodic classical era, however, did the Greeks modify and refine Hesiod's notions. The new ingredient embodied a new respect for the kind of trade that resulted in the acquisition of wealth and, through wealth, the freedom of the landed aristocrat. On the other hand, the cultivation of land that failed to bring wealth might be regarded as dishonorable.

In terms of their own ethic, many Greeks had to lead a dishonorable way of life. But their object was to flee that way of life whenever possible. Except for a few persons, however, that moment did not come until the mid-eighteenth century. Since that time the Greek aversion toward cultivating land has led to an increasingly persistent flight from the farm to the shop.

By the time of Napoleon, wrote John Cam Hobhouse, the Greeks were "all traders in some degree. In the district of Athens, as well as in that of Livadia, and many parts of the Morea, the cultivation of the earth [was] left to the [Orthodox] Albanian colonists, and every Greek [had] either a shop or was employed in wholesale dealings."[2] Bulgarians, Vlachs, and Greeks from the island of Zante later supplemented the farm labor of the Albanians, whereas "the grand object" of most Greeks of the new kingdom was "a place under Government, some authority with a little stipend, to enable them to live in idleness." If they were "of a more adventurous disposition," they tried their hand at revolution or took to the highway—"anything but work."[3]

A form of work that they did not disdain was what a Belgian observer of Greek society and culture, Edmond About, called *l'activité de l'esprit* (entrepreneurial spirit). Regarding the work of the cultivator as lowly, they were ambitious to become shopkeepers or traders, but not so much out of a sheer desire to gain wealth, maintained About, as "for the pleasure of selling."[4] They aspired to demonstrate ingenuity in the acquisition of wealth.

A few decades earlier, in an essay on Machiavelli (1827), Thomas Babington Macaulay had distinguished between the "courage" culture of "rude" and "barbarian" peoples and the "ingenuity" culture of "the polished Italians" of the *quattrocento*, "enriched by commerce, governed by law, and passionately attached to literature," doing everything "by superiority of intelligence. Their very wars, more pacific than the peace of their neighbors, required rather civil than military qualifications. Hence, while courage was the point of honor in other countries, ingenuity became the point of honor in Italy."[5]

In Greece, too, side by side with what Gerhard Gesemann called *humanitas heroica*, there emerged over the centuries another personality type, the *Erwerbsmensch* or "acquisitive man."[6] Valuing ingenuity more than courage, the "acquisitive man" was imbued with positive attitudes toward acquisition, as in the heroic or courage culture, and with negative attitudes toward manual labor, again as in the courage culture. By the mid-twentieth century, the predilection for ingenuity in the acquisition of wealth was a distinctive characteristic of Greek culture. William H. McNeill further observes:

> The [Greek] disdain for manual labor [was] perhaps part of a more general social scheme of values which [put] the rentier at or near the top of the social pyramid. To own land or buildings that [would] produce an income without personal effort [was] for most Greeks the pinnacle of ambition; and those who [fell] short of this ideal but still [managed] to escape the necessity of manual work sometimes [allowed] the nail of the little finger on one hand to grow long as public proof of their privileged status.[7]

To this explanation one should add another. Since Homeric and Hesiodic times, Greeks have distinguished between the honorable and demeaning on the basis of whether an activity allows or forbids play and struggle, or *agon*. The honorable is the agonal. But there can be free play and struggle only between approximate equals. There cannot be a real game between a guardian and a child, a freeman and a slave, a lord and a serf, a conqueror and the conquered. One ought to distinguish, therefore, between work that is agonal or competitive and work as an involuntary obligation; between work as a game and as leisure, based on the rhythm of one's culture, as distinct from the manner of work that imposes a rhythm of its own.[8]

In Hesiod, labor that neither originates in freedom nor results in wealth and ultimately in aristocracy *(arete)* is *ponos*—painful, burdensome toil. To work in the sense of *ponein* is to do work in the German sense of *arbeiten*—to do work that neither enriches nor uplifts, serving only to maintain a person in indigence (*penia* in Greek, *Armut* in German). *Ponos* demeans, voluntary works—*erga*—dignify. They dignify because they are freely given.[9]

In later times and until the end of the nineteenth century, therefore, one of the most honorable forms of work, among Greeks and other Balkanites alike, was mutual aid—the *daneike ergasia* of the Theban countryside, the *xelassi* of the Koroni (Coron) district of the Peloponnesus and of Epirus,[10] the *moba* of the Serbs, and even the *clacă* of the Wallacho-Moldavians before their lords changed it into compulsory labor during the seventeenth and eighteenth centuries.

A tacit understanding prevails that the family of a donor of such aid has a future claim to the labor of the recipient family. At the moment of the giving, however, the labor is voluntary. It is also ennobling because it is agonal, taking the form of a contest among the donors to accomplish the greatest amount of work. Thus, at their *mobas*, or gatherings of ritualized agonal mutual aid,[11] Serbians of the Morava sang ritual songs. One of the most frequent of such songs celebrated a contest between Marko Kraljević (Dionysos) and the Maid of the Morava (Persephone or Demeter), wherein victory accrued to the Maid:

> Marko gathered two hundred and two sheaves,
> The Morava Maid reaped three hundred and three.

According to one version of the song, she did this by deceit. In another version, the Maid reaped 304 sheaves. Other songs relate that Marko (clearly Dionysos) prevailed over the Morava Maid (Moravka) in a drinking contest by imbibing 303 glasses of wine to the Morava Maid's mere 204.[12]

A second term used in classical Greece to denote honorable work was *ascholia*. Ascholia embodied a readiness to forgo present leisure *(schole)* or freedom, "primarily freedom from political activity,"[13] in order to win greater freedom and leisure in the future. Literally, however, the term signifies "unleisure," much like Latin *negotium* (from *nec* and *otium*), from which one obtains English "negotiation" and French *négoce*. Unleisure was honorable, however, only if the wealth so acquired was diverted in part to socially or politically desirable ends. It was honorable and a true creator of liberty only if it resulted in part in philanthropy. This view of the purpose of *ascholia* was incorporated into the teachings of Orthodox Christianity.[14]

In the latter half of the eighteenth century, a self-unfrocked but pious Serbian monk from the Banat, Dositej Obradović (1742–1811), a patriot, an admirer of the ancient Greeks, and an advocate of the Enlightenment, issued a clear statement of the essence of *ascholia* without employing the term itself:

> Such is the law of the trader's profession. Whoever buys, is glad to buy cheap; and whoever sells, strives to sell dear. To acquire goods and money by honest trade and toil [in the original, the last term is *trud*, which we define below] depends on the one hand upon a man's capacity, and on the other upon the circumstances in which he finds himself. Wherever extensive trading is carried on, there a capable man can acquire money, and therein consists his capacity; but it is a virtue to employ for good ends what one has acquired, protecting the weak from the strong, aiding the wretched, freeing honorable families from poverty, furthering the advance of knowledge among one's own people.[15]

Noting a close relationship between consumption and what later would be called "economic growth," Obradović embraced a secular outlook with a mix of "rising expectations." Delighting in 1783 in the conclusion to "the time of weeping and lamentation, hunger and wailing; in a word, of the Lenten fast, when the haricot is king and its sister the lentil [or duckweed] and peas and cabbage govern the earth," he burst into a frenzy of didactic poetry, confusing the present with an expected future:

> Now is a time golden and joyous,
> No more is food prohibited to us!
> Evangelical freedom doth now reign,
> O golden epoch! o delectable times!

The word "capital" (for resources that were not "land" or "labor") entered the literary discourse of the Greeks, Romanians, and Serbs of the Habsburg monarchy almost simultaneously. The Hellenized Vlach Dimitrios Darvar(is) of the prominent well-to-do Darvar family, who wrote in Serbian as well as Greek, introduced the term *(to kapitali)* in a letter from a friend to a novice merchant, which he included in his dictionary of the Greek language published in Vienna in 1785. But the first person to introduce the terms "national pride" *(nacionalni ponos)*, "capital" *(kapital)*, and "nation" *(nacija)* into Serbian literature (without the "j," a letter adopted only after the nineteenth-century reform of the Serbian orthography), respectively in 1784, 1788, and in a letter dated Leipzig, January 1, 1789, was the Hellenophile Obradović, who was appointed director of schools in 1806 by the rebel government of Serbia.[16]

Austrian sources called Obradović a "hypocrite," a "pseudo-philosopher," and "a regular Tartuffe." They also identified him as "the Serbian idol." Recognized by Serbs as the "philosopher" or "Serbian Socrates," he was the founder of Serbia's first Velika Škola, a higher school named after—if not altogether following the model of—the French revolutionary and Napoleonic *grandes écoles*.[17]

The South Slavs possess many terms to denote various conditions of work. The word *delo* contains the root *dha-*, meaning to "do," "set," "place," or "apportion." Corresponding to Greek *ergon* (pl., *erga*), it refers to a thing done or to an appropriate share of something done. Containing the root *sar- (sal-)*, in which presides the sense of running or dispatching, *posao* refers to the exercise of a function. Formed from the root *tar-*, meaning to "draw," "push," "carry," "raise," or "transport," *trud* contains the sense of painful work dutifully or devotedly performed because it is self-imposed or imposed by one's own group. Containing the sense of striking, pressing, or oppressing, the root *ma-* serves to give the word *mŭka* (or *muka*) the meaning of labor or torture of a patiently endured martyrdom.[18] Confined to the northwest (essentially the area of the Croatian *kajkavski* dialect), *teg*, *tegota*, or *tegoba* contains the sense of heavy, onerous labor.[19]

At least four other words denote unfree, painful, compulsory, or difficult labor. Two *(ponos* and *angarija)* are taken directly from the Greek; one *(kuluk)* comes from Turkish; a fourth *(rabota)* is of Slavic origin. Derived from the specific form *arbh-* (like German *Arbeit* and Latin *laborare*) of the primitive root *ar-*, *rabota* obtained the sense not only of doing but of a painful doing, probably through the use of slaves as farm laborers, later transformed into serfs. This last word is the most common term for work among the Bulgarians and Macedonian Slavs and among many Serbians of the Morava. It occurs, too, in Croatia and in the western South Slavic regions. Among the Romanians of Wallachia and Moldavia, the terms for compulsory, heavy, and unfree labor are yet more numerous: *angaria* and *rabot; povoz* and *slujbe; munci, lucru,* and ultimately, *clacǎ.*[20]

In the specific form of *ardh-*, the root *ar-* also gave rise in the *štokavski* dialects of the Serbs and southwestern Croats to another word for "work": *rad, raditi.*[21] Hardly used at all in the early Old Slavonic literature except in the sense of "to care for" (but perhaps more common in the spoken language),[22] the word came to be employed more generally in some of the *štokavski* dialects during the latter part of the Middle Ages. It did not enter into the dialect of Zagreb until the eighteenth century.

Probably related etymologically to *rod,* meaning "birth," and to Latin *ars (artis)* or English and French "art," the word was used to describe the initiation or performance of good works, the endowment or administration of a church, or employment in some higher capacity at a princely court.[23] Later it was applied to many other activities that did not constitute wearisome toil or involuntary labor. In Ragusa, in addition to the meaning associated with the administration of an ecclesiastical or princely estate, noun *(rad)* and verb *(raditi)* acquired the sense of a business transaction *(negotium)* by a citizen or anyone not subject to corvée or the ignoble task of furnishing unrecompensed labor to a lord.[24]

Rad may contain a slight sense of pain. It emphasizes, however, the joy of creation, innovation, or management. Since there can be no joy in doing what is not voluntary, it was not applied at first to hard manual labor. With the gradual abolition of labor obligations on private estates, the fortune of *rad* was assured. As work began to acquire a new dignity, *rad* became in the new principality of Serbia the commonest expression for "work."

Unsparing of their own lives, Montenegrin men were disinclined to save money except for the purpose of purchasing arms and garnishing their mounts. Until the latter part of the nineteenth century, the main form of work acceptable to them was *nadžiranje,* the noble task of an overseer or shepherd of men.[25] Other work was relegated to women, beasts of burden like their mules and asses.

In the new principality of Serbia, as late as 1844, according to a British traveler and later consul to Dubrovnik, the inhabitants were "haughty, warlike, and somewhat indolent," with a revulsion for most of the mechanical and manual arts and "very lazy in agricultural operations." Unlike the Bulgarian, who readily performed the "more humble and laborious services," the Serbian resembled "the Scottish Highlander." Hospitable and "brave in battle," and with "little aptitude for trade," he manifested "a certain low cunning in the prosecution of his material interests."[26] Reluctant to accept the habits that had penetrated into the towns and preserving "the extremely severe economy and frugality" of former times, the peasant of Serbia hoarded his wealth, impeding the growth of a market economy until after 1850.[27]

Acknowledging a slow movement toward the rationalization of a work ethic among a portion of the peasantry of Serbia by 1864, another Briton said of the Serb in general that he was "averse to labour, impatient, careless, and, though quick at learning, . . . troublesome to teach. Especially he [differed] from the Bulgarian in this, that *nothing can be got out of him by oppression*. The Croatian peasant was, the Dalmatian Morlack and the Bosnian rayah still are, the laziest, sulkiest, most intractable, most implacable of mortals. Such merchants as succeed in Bosnia come *not* out of the crushed Christians in that province, but from the insurgent districts of Herzegovina."[28]

In a similar vein, the Serbian statesman Ilija Garašanin ascribed the lack of a widespread spirit of rebellion among the Bulgarians in the 1840s to the fact that work had become among them a tradition.[29] An apparently bourgeois-inspired nineteenth-century Bulgarian "folk" tale on "the share of each nation" relates, indeed, that on the occasion of the distribution of gifts to the world's peoples, God granted lordship and the power of property to the Turks, the power of invention and imagination to the French, intrigue and negotiation to the Greeks, arithmetic to the Jews, misery to the Gipsies, and hard work—*rabota*—to the Bulgarians.[30]

The attitude toward work, however, was not uniform in all Bulgarian areas. Where the geographic setting presented a challenge and stimulus, as in many mountainous areas, the need for work often gave rise to ingenuity. Where the work was imposed by other men, as in the plains, the result was often submission. In 1880, a Belgian consul general explained thus the enterprise of the inhabitants of the Sredna Gora ("Middle Mountain") and the towns of Elena, Tŭrnovo, Gabrovo, and Tryavna: "The area is mountainous and its people are therefore more industrious. . . . They have had to find in their own enterprise what the soil, more ungrateful than that of the plain, refused to give them." [31]

The Bulgarian poet-revolutionary Liuben Karavelov similarly explained the emergence of his own mountain community, Koprivshtitsa, as a center of commercial activity: "Requiring tenacious toil and ample irrigation, its arid land did not permit people to sink into drowsy Asiatic indolence but constantly spurred them to combat and the show of energy, making them into enterprising profit makers and thinking beings."[32]

Additional support for the main thrust of such arguments is present in the fact that the Aegean islands, which acquired commercial importance after 1750, were "but a few miles in circumference, with a surface so rocky as scarcely to yield the common vegetables and even without any other water than that collected in cisterns."[33] Agricultural barrenness and geographic isolation inspired commercial and industrial activity by keeping away greedy lords, discouraging the spread of a feudal authority or seigniorial economy. The activity of the mountain communities may also have stemmed from the lower incidence of plague and malaria in the highlands than in the plains.

The impact of every mountain is not exactly the same. Whether a geographic region produces one effect or another depends, moreover, on the culture and society of its inhabitants. To attribute rigidly a single cluster of attitudes to each ethnic group is also misleading. Attitudes associated with *rabota* are not uniquely Bulgarian. They are proper in fact to Serbs, Bulgarians, and Macedonian Slavs of the Morava, Maritsa, and Vardar valleys. They also extend from Old Serbia deep into Bosnia.

The spirit of enterprise present in the Sredna Gora since the latter part of the eighteenth century was a special manifestation of a more general pattern of attitudes and social organization that characterized a large area surrounding and projecting into the zone of *rabota* culture. Generally designated as *pečalba*, this pattern was intricately woven, in different colors, into the culture of Hercegovina, Old Serbia, Macedonia, southern Albania, Epirus, and Thessaly, and of the Bulgarian Sredna Gora and Bosnian Lika, as well as of Gorski Kotar and Primorje, or the region between northern Bosnia and the Adriatic.

Pečalba denoted two essential qualities, deriving perhaps from a double etymology: an attitude of patient endurance and a readiness to undertake a multitude of diverse tasks in order to accumulate a small sum of money, primarily for the needs of one's family. It involved a periodic migration in order to bring one's labor or carry one's (or someone else's) goods to a market where there was a demand for such "commodities." Although many *pečalbars* came from the zone of *rabota* culture, *pečalba* differed from *rabota* in entailing a self-imposition of hard work as a means of escaping hard labor imposed by others. It consequently possessed a greater degree of voluntariness.

An integral part of all the attitudes toward work was either the notion that work is not an end or the idea that there is a proper and improper time for work. Orthodox Balkan Slavs thus celebrated about 120 religious and state holidays and 60 to 90 votive days,[34] during which some or most kinds of work were considered taboo. Workless days in the Greek zone of *ascholia* culture were almost as numerous. Integrated with the old attitudes toward work was thus the notion that work and leisure are complementary.

During the nineteenth century, however, a scheme of values emphasizing the virtue of production found expression in the region immediately south of the Sava and Danube on the basis, in part, of work attitudes diffused from Syrmium and the polyethnic Banat. Such attitudes slowly extended farther southward, converging and mingling with the *pečalba* and *rabota* cultures. A similar scheme penetrated to the maritime regions by way of the sea.[35] The diffusion of modern European values into the Balkans, however, was in fact an example of historical convergence, for the new valuation was an import for which there was a certain demand.

Under the influence of the European Enlightenment, as interpreted by

Obradović and other early Balkan exponents of the rationalization of work, a body of opinion hostile to beggary emerged. Many medieval values, including tolerance and even respect for beggary by Muslim and Orthodox Christian alike, persisted until the mid-nineteenth century.[36] After 1850 or 1860, however, beggary became less respectable among the Greeks and Slavs, being confined thereafter to Gipsies. In the succeeding decades, certain members of the Turkish intelligentsia—among them Namik Kemal and Ahmed Midhat Efendi—similarly condemned laziness and sloth, urging sustained effort, diligence, and self-help—in short, "love of work."[37]

Among the first to take concrete measures to encourage positive values toward production were Serbian political leaders. Miloš Obrenović, for example, issued an order in 1820 aiming to promote the immigration of industrious *(radni)* colonists. In the following year, he ordered the local notables to encourage the sowing of potatoes in their districts. In 1837, a Serbian general assembly established the institution of *ekonom*, an appointed official whose task was to advise district subprefects on the best ways of achieving a more rational pattern of production. Miloš thereupon issued instructions to the rural police to see that peasants performed the right tasks at the right time. In particular, they were to refrain from distilling brandy when they should be harvesting.

In the 1840s, the Constitutionalists or Progressists continued to promote the immigration of colonists from the north (chiefly Vojvodina) to compensate for the influx of immigrants from the southwest (Hercegovina and Montenegro) who lacked a work ethic favorable to agricultural production.[38] The Serbian policy of acquiring tillers of the soil in Hungary compelled Prince Klemens von Metternich to write on July 16, 1847:

> Ever since [it] has come to be persuaded that profits can be derived from agriculture, [the government of] Serbia has been more inclined to promote the cultivation of the soil. According to reports from the Royal-Imperial Consulate in Belgrade, it is attempting each year to put under cultivation stretches of land previously given over exclusively to cattle raising or forest life. In view of the fact that the natives have not yet decided to put their hand to the plow, [the government is pursuing a policy of making] welcome all immigrants who are ready to turn their energies to agriculture.[39]

After 1860, an entire Serbian literature developed around the theme of the value of work. In his *Précis of Political Economy*, published in 1867, the future Progressist Serbian minister and diplomat Čedomilj Mijatović defended work as an inspiring and refreshing source of individuality and civilization. Individuality and civilization, he held, knowingly or unknowingly embracing or borrowing an idea that one usually attributes to François Guizot, are two aspects of a single idea, *obrazovanost* (analogous to German *Bildung*). *Obrazovanost* exemplifies a social order in which the culture itself is defined by the recognition of the individual as the basic elementary unit of social organization. More precisely,

Mijatović was prone to define personhood not only in a juridical sense but also as the mark of a free, independent, conscious, and responsible unit of social and cultural action. That definition reflected a choice made by some Greeks between the second century B.C. and the fourth century A.D. and by elite groups in western Europe during the second half of the eighteenth century.[40]

Insistent on the complementary nature of "order and freedom" *(red i sloboda)*, Mijatović wrote: "By working man grows morally stronger. Through his labor he lifts himself above nature and conquers it, and by this conquest, or discovery and elaboration of its laws, he becomes more independent of it, more autonomous, more of an individual, endowed with ever greater means for a yet greater strengthening of his individuality. Civilization has developed most highly in those parts of the earth where man has been most obliged to work."[41]

In his provocative *Serbia in the East*, published in 1872, the young socialist Svetozar Marković, seeking to orient Serbian society around the goal of production (as against trade), denounced the prevalent view among bureaucrats and petty bourgeois of the shamefulness of manual work. The ethnographer and political leader Milan Djuro Milićević concluded the introduction to his *Kneževina Srbija* (1876) with the didactic verse: "Knowledge is enlightenment, will is might. Let us learn, let us work day and night!" Twenty-five years later, he was more convinced than ever of the virtue of work: "Work *(rad)* is life, while idleness *(nerad)* is virtual death."[42]

In 1874, at a session of the Serbian National Assembly, Milićević voiced some misgivings, however, about positive laws that paid no heed to custom, reiterating a view that Dositej Obradović had voiced a century earlier:[43]

> What generally happens among people after the patriarchal [stage of] life is that they begin to institute positive law. But these positive laws, these institutions for the development of state life, often fail to correspond to the character and [way of] life of the nation, to the [kind of] life that preceded such laws and institutions. . . . Between the needs of the land and nation, on the one hand, and the content or tone of the laws, on the other, there can easily be a discordance. It is quite possible that the needs include many more questions than can be resolved by the laws. In that case, the laws are unsatisfactory and inadequate. They therefore should be extended, completed, provided with what may be missing. . . . [Law] is a fortress against lawlessness. . . , [but it should not prevent the people from saying what they want and desire].[44]

The last two decades of the nineteenth century in the new Balkan states were, in fact, a period of canonization of positivism with its triple slogan of progress, order, and modernism, defined in the Balkans as "European culture." A Serbian counterpart to the Latin American *científico* was the Progressist Vladan Djordjević. In the opinion of his friend Čedomilj Mijatović, Djordjević was "one of the most brilliant men" in the Serbia of his time—"a poet, a novelist, a clever physician and surgeon (winning the German Iron Cross for services rendered to the wounded in 1870), an eloquent debater, organiser of the State Sanitary Service." Mijatović defined the authoritarian government of Djordjević (1897–1900) as a regime of "Order and Work" *(Red i Rad)*.[45] An exponent of "progressive culture" *(napredna kultura)*, he defined it in 1869 in positivist terms as a culture in which "harmony" prevails between the interests of the state and the interests of its subjects.

Delineating the function of the state as the promotion of the production and circulation of "those goods that guarantee the existence and development of every person in every aspect (moral, intellectual, political, economic, religious) of human life, and consequently the development of every aspect of the whole society," Mijatović defended the right of the state to tax as "the indispensable condition for the existence and development of each individual." He subjected that right to the proviso that the state use its authority to promote the amelioration of private economic interests.[46]

At about the same time, Silvije S. Kranjčević (1865–1908), a Croat from Senj who was known to his fellow students at the Collegium Germanico-Hungaricum in Rome as the *Seeräuber* (pirate) because of his attachment to the freebooter *uskok* traditions of his native Senj and who spent the latter part of his life in Austro-Hungarian Bosnia-Hercegovina, made use of poetry to defend the role of the state as a promoter of work in preference to its function as the promoter of war:

> War detachments, nicely ranged man to man,
> Would that they were worthy diggers!
> Battle cannon, squandered iron,
> Would that they were worthy plowmen![47]

In the Niš districts annexed to Serbia only since 1878, nonpositivist conceptions of work continued to prevail during the 1880s and 1890s. A certain *baba* or "old woman" Mitra thwarted the efforts of the government to eradicate "superstition" and instill a positivist work ethic. In a vision or dream, St. Friday (Sveta Petka) had warned her that if people worked on Fridays—in accordance with the new work ethic and in violation of the old—she would send hail, drought, and disease and bring ruin to them and their crops. Rumors of the vision spread from village to village. Most villages and village priests decided to be idle on Fridays, prevent violations of the taboo by members of their own communities, and turn back outsiders who attempted to move their carts across their territories to go to work.[48] Only a few villages and individuals failed to respond to the appeal to tradition.

Many years passed before the government succeeded in diffusing the new work ethic to the southern districts. The problem did not stem, however, from the indolence of the people. It arose from the fact that their craving for material goods was limited to a few items and from their association of work with the prior performance of certain rites that were not easily compatible with the new cultural demands. Not insignificantly, it was reinforced by the fact that culture is a language and that the language of the old culture was replete with a vocabulary that called for avoiding certain kinds of work on certain days: *svetkovanje* (sanctifying), *slavljenje* (glorifying), *pirovanje* (banqueting, "symposium making" in the ancient Greek sense; among Muslims, the *pir* was usually a celebration of the patron of a confraternity),[49] *nedeljovanje* (keeping Sunday, literally the "no-work day"), *praznovanje* (keeping a holy day, literally an "empty day"), *petkovanje* (keeping Friday), and *odmoravanje* (resting). To the foregoing one should add thirty to forty days during which some specific forms of work were forbidden to women, the practice in some districts of beginning no new tasks on Tuesdays, the avoidance of plowing on a succession of seven "green Thursdays" following Easter so that the crops would not be spoiled by hail (an agent or instrument of the onetime pagan god Perun, who corresponded to the Germanic Thor), and other beliefs.[50]

Under the partial inspiration of the Serbian geographer Jovan Cvijić,[51] efforts to institutionalize the new ethic became more systematic and were pursued with great diligence in the decade before World War I. Thus, in 1911, the Executive Committee of the Serbian Society of National Defense (Narodna Odbrana), a group wrongly accused of provoking war with Austria in 1914, published a pamphlet in which it expressed its views on how to achieve Serbian national unification. The greatest need was to "transplant into our social order completely new methods of developing the work of private initiative." The theme of the pamphlet was "the value of work on a small scale," the need to replace "big talk" with "modest small tasks" or "practical effort." "Small work" performed on a regular basis by everyone, implied the committee, was infinitely more important than gigantic strides by a few individuals, for "every great work is built of a number of smaller ones," as "the more civilized peoples of the world," especially the Germans and Czechs, "have long recognized."[52]

Diffusion of the new work ethic continued after World War I. The sociologist and agrarian leader Dragoljub Jovanović emphasized the "heroism of work."[53] The engineer Miodrag Novaković hailed the work ethic but criticized Taylorism. Coined after the American efficiency engineer, Frederick Winslow Taylor (1856–1915), Taylorism aimed at the "rationalization" of industry and business management, in part through the introduction of standard "time and motion" practices. Like other critics, Novaković maintained that Taylorism put too much stress on labor tempo, thereby threatening discord between management and labor. Holding that the greatest capital in the world is human labor, he concluded that attempts to raise the tempo of industrial labor would fail to ensure a higher labor productivity unless the purchasing power of workers was also increased. A science of "psychotechnics" properly understood requires that an occupation give the worker personal satisfaction and that the employer provide him with an incentive to work productively.[54]

Until after World War II, such pleas went largely unheard. In agriculture, on the other hand, where the work ethic had been fostered by various elites since 1820, it was almost completely integrated into the beliefs and practices of the peasantry of Serbia by the 1950s,[55] thus before communism had much effect on people's behavior.

In Romania, Bulgaria, and Greece, the details were different. All Balkan countries, however, participated in the same general movement, the development of a new work ethic adaptable to either a capitalist or a socialist society. Socialism continued a process that had started with the diffusion of bourgeois values. The slowness of the process is characteristic of nearly all fundamental change. It may also have had a basis in the reluctance of capitalism—at least until the mutation of a large territory into a relatively integrated national market—to recognize that work and leisure are complementary, and in capitalism's conception of time as chronometric and continuous, in its equation of time and money.

Time and Space

A Yugoslav philosopher, Vladimir Dvorniković, distinguished between the time system of a space-dominated people *(Raumvolk* or *narod prostora)* and that of a time-oriented people *(Zeitvolk* or *narod vremena)*, between the time system of "historic" and that of "unhistoric" peoples. He interpreted the Yugoslav past, and inferentially the past of all the Balkan peoples and of mankind in general, as an unremitting struggle of space-dominated people to nullify the compulsions of space or nature and become a time-oriented people.[56]

The French geographer, Pierre George, maintains that both a space-dominated people and a time-oriented people may have a time system that is exact and demanding. Each of these systems, however, is based upon a different set of values. They are exact and demanding in different ways. George even contends that the time system of nature (rural) peoples is more demanding than that of culture (urban) peoples: "The rhythms of the earth are not as flexible as those of the factory."[57] George and Dvorniković both reject the distinction made by Melville J. Herskovits between the "imprecise and relaxed" time system of societies in which man submits to nature—or, as Émile Durkheim and Marcel Mauss might have said,[58] in which he identifies closely with his totem or *numen*—and the "exact and demanding" time system of societies that refuse to submit to nature.[59]

Herskovits's distinction requires revision. But the terms "historic" and "unhistoric" are also misused. In some ways more useful albeit not fully satisfactory may be the Bergsonian vision of anthropologist Claude Lévi-Strauss, who has proposed the term "cold societies" for societies that ignore or annul history as an agent of change and "hot societies" for those that internalize historical experience in order to mobilize and bring it to their aid whenever the need may arise.[60]

Accordingly, the "hottest" Balkan society before the mid-nineteenth century was the Greek. Greeks were the inventors of historical writing, and Greek society preserved its historical tradition almost intact during the Byzantine and Ottoman eras. Among the South Slavs, on the other hand, historical scholarship emerged only in the fourteenth and fifteenth centuries, and the Ottoman conquest interrupted further progress in that direction.

The notions of time and space of the non-Greeks of the peninsula were medieval Christian or resembled those of the preclassical Greeks. Most Greeks held analogous views, and there were fighters in the Greek revolution of 1821 who had never heard of the hero Achilles.[61] Moreover, familiarity with culture heroes and an ability to trace kinship for six, nine, or ten generations, as was common among Albanian Ghegs and Montenegrins, are far from being equivalent to the possession of a sense of historical time. They are rather manifestations of a kinship time.

For all the Balkan peasantries, time was a perpetual return of the seasons, of night and day, and of life and death. It was fate, an inexorable necessity. Conscious of the demands of time, peasants were also close to a timeless world, the way of life before the rise of farming and cities, a world in which time went unregulated, in which "the roosters [did] not crow."[62] Although generally ready to submit to nature, they were prone to rebel when too many demands of human origin were imposed upon them. Their object was then re-volution, a "golden age," an abolition of time.

The "golden age" of the peasant was an earthly society. The "golden age" of the monk—or at least of some monks—was the "heavenly kingdom." This "golden age" similarly represented an abolition of time but achieved through work, meditation, and prayer and concerned with a wholly different "space." Preoccupied with the hereafter and devoted to the regular observance of liturgy, medieval Orthodox monasteries were freer of the time of nature but voluntarily yielded to an ecclesiastical time of hours (ὥρα, čas) announced by the blows of a hammer against a plate of copper or iron or against a wooden board.[63] For pious Christian and Muslim alike, time was a moment of prayer.

A distinctly bourgeois time was late in coming not because of the absence of a large bourgeoisie but because bourgeois time was closely related to the time of religion. This connection had also been true in the West until the fourteenth century. In the Balkans, however, the spread of Hesychasm and Islam acted to delay the laicization of time.

Serving to call people to work, remind them of their civic duties, and diffuse a secular conception of time, public clocks were erected in the Balkans only long after they had been set up in western and central Europe. The Huguenot, Philippe du Fresne-Canaye, who traversed the Balkans in 1573, maintains that the first public clock in any Ottoman-Balkan town was the clock of the wooden bell tower of Skoplje (Skopje, Üsküb), which was brought there from Croato-Hungarian Siget (Szigetvár) shortly after the Ottoman invasion of that Pannonian town in 1566. Sounding the hours "in the French manner," the clock could be heard by the entire city, and "in all of Turkey," added Philippe du Fresne-Canaye, there was "no other public clock, despite the liking and great esteem of the

Turks for clocks."[64] An English traveler described the monument in 1669 as "a Tower of wood with a Clock and Bell."[65]

In 1670, there were thirty-four clockmakers and engravers under French protection in Istanbul. Eleven of them were there with their families. Many of them were from Geneva or Lyon. Three of the thirty-four were Catholics, one had converted to Islam, and the rest were presumably Protestants. A French observer further remarked of the Turks of Istanbul in the 1680s that they "esteem clockwork very much but . . . lack workers who understand it." [66]

The obstacle to the introduction of public clocks in the Ottoman Empire, according to the Imperial ambassador to the Porte, Ogier Ghiselin de Busbecq, was the belief of the muezzins—who daily summoned the Muslim faithful to prayer by a long loud chant from the pinnacles of their minarets—that their authority would thereby be impaired.[67] The first observation of François René de Chateaubriand upon his arrival in Istanbul in 1806 more than two centuries later was thus appropriate. "No bells were to be heard" *(il n'y a point de cloches)*.[68]

The second public clock in the Ottoman Balkans (outside the Peloponnesus and Aegean islands, where Italian influences may have favored the introduction of public clocks in a few places) may have been that of the clock tower of Philippopolis, present there since before 1623 and followed, before 1714, by a public clock at Drama. A fourth public clock appeared in Varna around 1775,[69] presumably after the Russo-Turkish war of 1768–74. A clock was also present in Kladovo (Fethislam) before 1784 and, according to Louis-François Ferrières-Sauveboeuf, yet another public clock sounded the hours from the public square of Bazargic (Bazarcik, Tatar Pazardzhik) at least as early as the 1780s.[70]

On his way to England from India and Burma by way of Persia and the Ottoman dominions, James Edward Alexander entered Bulgaria in 1826, passing successively through the towns of Karnobat (Karnabad), Shumla (Shumen), and Rusçuk (Ruse). "The towns through which we passed," he wrote, "were particularly clean and neat, with large clocks on the minarets."[71] The Reverend Robert Walsh, chaplain to the embassy in Istanbul of Lord Strangford, passed through Shumla soon thereafter, confirming the presence "at this point at which all the roads leading from the Danube concentrate," of "an extraordinary novelty in a Turkish town—a large town clock; it tells the hours by a bell which is heard all over the city, and regulates the time of the inhabitants, instead of the muezzims [sic] crying the hour from the minarets." He explained how it got to Shumla:

> This extraordinary innovation, and approximation to European manners, was introduced some years ago [thus probably soon after 1812] by a basha, who had been a prisoner in Russia: he there acquired a taste for bells; and on his return brought with him a striking clock, which he erected in Shumla. The improvement, however, has not yet proceeded beyond this northern frontier. I have never seen or heard of any other town-clock in the Turkish dominions except at Athens, presented by Lord Elgin [Thomas Bruce, seventh earl of Elgin, who was envoy extraordinary to Istanbul during 1799 and 1800 and

removed from Athens the celebrated sculptures known as the Elgin Marbles] as some remuneration for the dilapidation of the Parthenon.[72]

Before the end of the 1830s, the new church in Belgrade and the church of Topčider (outside Belgrade) also had a public clock. In Bulgaria, according to geographer Ami Boué, "each city, each bourg, and even large villages like Bania (at the foot of the Rhodope [in the Gorna Dzhumaia district])," had their clock and clock tower, usually four stories *(trois étages)* high and without bells except in the larger cities. A public clock was present, too, by that time in Albanian Tirana, Preschja (Preshjë), and Kruë, and in Macedonian Ohrid.[73] By mid-century, Gabrovo, Niš, Leskovac, and tiny Hercegovinian Nevesinje, the last hardly numbering a thousand inhabitants, similarly had public clocks.[74] As late as 1868, on the other hand, there was no public clock in Montenegro.[75]

The century after 1775 was the era of the diffusion to the Balkans of the public clock. The era of diffusion of the pocket watch began somewhat earlier. By 1790, when the annual watch production of London amounted to 130,000 watches, of which 80,000 were for export,[76] Ottoman watch imports from England amounted to almost 14,000, twice as many as in 1740. Of that total, 400 dozen watches went to Smyrna (Izmir), 300 dozen to Istanbul, 250 dozen to Egypt, 150 dozen to Syria, 30 dozen to Salonika, and 30 dozen to the Morea. The watchmaker George Prior provided two-fifths of the English watch exports to Turkey. A further fifth was of Benjamin Barber's manufacture. Prior and Barber alike used the name George Charles (shown on the dial) for their poorer watches. Another fifth was the work of Périgal, more elegant but less solid than the Prior and Barber watches, and of watchmakers who sold their wares under the name of the no longer existent clock manufactory of Markwick and Markham. After England, the most important exporter of watches to the Ottoman Empire was Geneva, followed by France.

The preference for English watches, of which only one out of twenty was of gold, had a basis in the concern of Ottoman consumers for solidity, not for the running mechanism of the watch. Custom and fashion alike dictated that watches for the Levant be composed of at least two cases. The need of the Turkish buyer for a watch that did not run the risk of being crushed by the pistols at his belt was a yet more overwhelming argument for solidity. Furnished with a Turkish dial, the thick broad English watches, usually composed of three cases, two inner cases of silver and an outer case of shell, met the expectations of the largest number of Ottoman consumers.[77]

By the 1830s, many Balkan watchmakers were Ottoman subjects, some of them of the Muslim faith. The skills of most of these artisans were limited. A Greek in Adrianople, however, could make alarm clocks. In Salonika, there was a grocer-clockmaker and a clockmaker jack-of-all-trades who repaired watches, spectacles, and umbrellas.[78]

Even at that late date, therefore, the temporal sensibility of the Balkan peoples was barely greater than that of François Rabelais's Friar John.[79] Between 1400 and 1800, indeed, Europe's three Mediterranean peninsulas manifested three distinct perceptions of time and space: a simultaneously strong temporal or historical perspective and a strong spatial, optical, and cartographic perspective in Italy;[80] an intense spatial perspective but a less well developed sense of chronometric time in the Iberian peninsula, lulling Spain into being content with vessels slower than those of their Dutch and English rivals;[81] and not much of either a new temporal or a new spatial perspective in the Ottoman dominions.

In England, on the other hand, a generalized chronometric perspective gave clockmakers of that country an opportunity to devise machines for textile manufactures on the basis of clockwork principles,[82] thus laying part of the basis—complemented by the continuing development of a strong spatial perspective—for England's emergence as the world's "first industrial nation." The French consul to Salonika, who provided the data on the Ottoman consumption of English watches, thus aptly concluded that "wherever civilization exists"—that is, wherever there is a culture with an appreciation of order and economic growth—"time is a precious article, and its value renders the instrument necessary that portions it out."[83]

The scarcity of public clocks in the Balkans until after 1800 was as nothing, however, compared to the inadequacy of illumination or the means of reducing the distinction between the order of day and the chaos of night. Past human efforts at illumination had been largely limited to special occasions, generally religious festivals and times of great rejoicing, and may have grown out of earlier fire festivals. By the fifth century, however, there were at least two Roman cities—Syrian Antioch and Edessa—in which streets were regularly lighted at night with oil lamps.

Efforts then flagged. In 1524, however, the occupants of houses fronting certain streets in Paris were ordered to keep lights burning in their windows. In 1558, large vases filled with pitch, resin, or some other combustible—and later lanterns—were set up at street corners. Paris may have attained thereby the level of lighting practiced in pre-Ottoman Cairo, where a burning light had to be kept in the street at night by every fourth or fifth house. The perfection of street lighting in Paris was an accomplishment only of the period after 1667.[84] In Istanbul, by contrast, there was still no system of regular illumination at the end of the eighteenth century, although for the feast of Ramadan and other special occasions streets were brightened at night by the light of a red fire kindled by the burning of pinewood or tarred rags in irons raised high on pikes.[85]

During the latter half of the nineteenth century, however, the Greeks emerged again as agents of visualism, bearers of oil from the petroleum fields of the Caucasus. The oil of the Caucasus was inferior to the oil of Romania, the best in the world for lamps and consequently reserved to the markets of Europe. Victor Bérard was nevertheless correct in describing modern Hellenism as an agent of light, an illuminating power. It suffices to spend one day in Greece in order to know what place the petroleum of Batum and the tin cans—the *tenekes*—that contain it hold there. The number and the size of the lamps is the first luxury of the Greeks. During its life or after its death, full or empty, the *teneke* is the furniture, the instrument *par excellence:* buckets, basins, lamps, plates, watering-cans, everything comes from the *teneke*.

In Turkey, one might estimate the influence of Hellenism by each region's cubic consumption of petroleum. The Muslim and un-Hellenized Christian go to sleep with the sun or smoke and converse in obscurity; at the evening meal, in order to see themselves and show their guests the common plate into which the entire company fraternally plunges its fingers, they kindle only some small bits of wood if they are poor, or, when they are rich, great fires of resinous wood. Hellenism makes its appearance with the bringing of the *teneke*, as it formerly carried from Corinth and Athens terra cotta, lamps, goblets, and amphorae.[86]

A yet stronger influence than Hellenism was the formerly barbarian world, modern Europe. In 1857, under western European inspiration, Belgrade established a street-lighting system. However partially, the obscurity of the night was forced to yield before the light of sixty lanterns set up at public expense and about a hundred more that wine shops and innkeepers were required to display. In the 1880s, this smallest of the Balkan capitals, Montenegrin Cetinje excepted, began to study the lighting system of Vienna and Berlin and soon established modern gas and electric lighting along with other municipal utilities.[87]

By the turn of the century, according to a Cairo newspaper, the capitals of Greece, Serbia, Bulgaria, and Romania had been "illumined by the light of civilization." They had acquired "straight and wide streets, public squares, theatres, museums, zoological and botanical gardens, electric light, tramways," while the great European and Asiatic cities of the shrinking Ottoman Empire—Istanbul, Adrianople (Edirne), Bursa, Damascus, Aleppo, and Bagdad—had shamefully sunk into "darkness and ignorance."[88] More precisely, they had postponed to a later day their effort to moderate the distinction between day and night.

The search for the *white world* (enlightenment) had in fact never been totally abandoned, and in the eighteenth century and early part of the nineteenth century it was resumed with more vigor than ever. The Serbian archpriest Matija Nenadović reveals his sentiments in 1804 upon embarking with his fellow envoys to seek out Russia, bearer of the old light of Orthodoxy and new light of the Enlightenment:

> In the name of God we departed and when we sat down in the boat and set off, I said: "Columbus and his company set forth thus on the blue sea to find America and acquaint her with Europe. Today we have set forth on the pacific Danube [shortly, he would discover, not so pacific] to find Russia and acquaint Serbia with Russia, of whose location we know nothing but of whose existence we have heard in song."

But raised for the most part in the dark world of the Šumadija forests, Nenadović lacked the visualism to appreciate in detail the magnificence of Moscow:

> When one has never before seen so many houses in one heap, will not one marvel in such a spacious town at whatever one sees first: the old imperial Kremlin, the churches, the wondrous palaces and shops? A child born and raised there may in its old age relate something about Moscow. Someone like me, virtually brought up in the mountain, who leaves a dark room at maturity to gaze at the [glittering] white world *(beli svet)* . . . sees only a fantasmagoria until he begins to rub his eyes.[89]

The Balkan peoples became increasingly space oriented, conscious of space, thinking increasingly in terms of reorganizing it or regretting the particular reorganization that was being made. Villages became more compact, forests disappeared or grew thinner, roads were built, and after the roads, railroads.

This transformation of spatial horizons led to a change in temporal ones, and vice versa. Mijatović observed that transportation improvements produce a saving of time. The saving of time results in turn in the saving of capital, including human capital or skilled, imaginative labor. The improvement of roads and transport may also produce population shifts as goods are transferred more rapidly and with greater certainty from the places of production to where they are needed, thus encouraging the growth of cities. "Intellectual and material capital" *(intelektualni i materijalni kapital)* is thus "the means by which man exerts his influence upon nature. It is the instrument with which he evokes, regulates, and dominates the forces of nature."[90]

Even in such otherwise relatively isolated provincial towns as Bosnian Višegrad on the Drina, the advent of the railroad caused an acceleration in the rhythms of social time, stimulating a quickening of events, a craving for an everyday fare of sensations and exciting news,[91] the *Reizsamkeit* of Karl Lamprecht.[92]

By the end of the century, the idea that "time is money" (for Paul Valéry,[93] the paragon of baseness)—attributed to Benjamin Franklin but actually older—began to be voiced. There was, on the other hand, some resistance to the notion of punctuality, and even as late as the mid-twentieth century, Greeks who were punctual were derisively called "Englishmen."[94] The number of "Englishmen," however, grew considerably in the Balkans after 1900.

Whether capitalist or socialist, the new culture of the Balkans has not totally destroyed the old. In many respects, the old ways are more significant because they lie deep and rise to the surface in times of crisis. But the new ways are also a factor to contend with, and one day the new ways will become old and familiar.

Individuality

Some of the new ways have in fact a relatively long history. For example, the ideal of a large portion of the elite groups of classical Greece was *sophrosyne*, a term initially signifying "sound midriff" that after the seventh century B.C., acquired the sense of "sound reason."[95] Many Greeks preferred the Dionysian ideal of excess and rapture, but forever thereafter "sound reason" would remain as the goal of some Greeks. It was an especially vital force during the classical period of its first emergence, during the European Enlightenment, and during the era of positivism. As an Apollonian value, *sophrosyne* represented a striving for order and harmony—the Greek term was *eunomie*—or for moderation and the middle way, the elimination of *dysnomie*.[96]

Among the other peoples of the Balkans, the first persistent call to *sophrosyne* came during the second half of the eighteenth century, and one of its earliest South Slavic exponents was Dositej Obradović. Before fully discerning the European Enlightenment and becoming himself a minor European *philosophe*, Obradović discovered Hellenism by going from the writings of the church fathers to those of the classical and preclassical era. From the Greeks, along with other ideas, he borrowed the notion of *sophrosyne*, which he translated into Serbian as *zdrav razum* (literally, "sound reason").[97] Here commenced, among the South Slavs of Orthodox faith, an option in favor of the Apollonian (and Hesiodic) value of measure and order as against the Dionysian ideal of frenzy and ecstasy. Other advocates of the Enlightenment, along with the exponents of positivism, continued the task of taking Serbians, Bulgarians, Bosnians, Montenegrins, Greeks, Romanians, and lastly Albanians along a path that was supposed to end in *eunomie* but has also engendered discord.[98]

The process of creating order is an interminable dialectic. Each order leads to a new disorder, each harmony to a new discord. One of the consequences of enlightenment, order, progress, and European culture was the diffusion of the idea of land as private property. This idea may have been common among the Greeks since before the eighth century B.C., but it was relatively weak in the rest of the Balkans and was weakened to some degree even among the Greeks during the Byzantine and Ottoman eras. In the late Byzantine and late Ottoman eras, however, the idea of private ownership of land was reaffirmed, and benefices and other conditional properties were transformed into private property.

The "second serfdom" represents among other things a diversion of property from peasant families who regarded it as "ancestral"—that is, as belonging to a particular family rather than to a particular individual—to usurpers who regarded it as "theirs"—that is, as belonging to a particular individual. But legal recognition of the main aim of the agents of the "second serfdom"—to transform the properties that they or their ancestors had stolen into private property—came late, in the era of reforms collectively known as the Tanzimat, 1826–76.

In Romania, the greatest spur to a further evolution of the notion of land as private property was the agrarian reform of 1864, which abolished corvée and allowed peasants to buy the land on which they worked, generally below the current market value. This was another consequence of the Enlightenment, of the Russian example, and of the threat of social upheaval.

Along with the idea of private real property, the concept of "natural rights" also won adherents. Thus, according to the manifesto of January 1, 1822 (O.S.), of the Greek National Assembly of Epidauros, the object of the Greek revolution was to reaffirm, if only in discourse, the rights of honor, private property, and individual liberty, without negating local and other privileges or rights of the notables and "captains" *(kapetanioi)*. Centralization had to be delayed until the 1830s and 1840s, as in Serbia, where the Civil Code of 1844 recognized land as private property (although placing some restrictions on its sale or transfer). Declaring "every man" to be entitled by "natural right" to "equality before the law," the Civil Code was part of a process initiated several years earlier by the Constitutionalists to create a government of law. The goal of the Constitutionalists was to institute a system of government under which the old local autonomies, associated with superstition, backwardness, and active or passive resistance to government, were replaced by natural-rights principles of individual responsibility and equality before the law. A set of common laws, they believed, should replace the plethora of local customs. Through its courts and territorial organization of prefects and subprefects, it would be the function of such a government to see that the bias in favor of the individual, the state, and private property was regularly observed. The old social order of local privileges and special rights would thus yield to the idea of a great society or nation-state with no autonomous intermediate bodies between the individual and the state unless the government recognized their activity as one of public utility.[99]

The Serbian Civil Code authorized the fission of the extended family into smaller family units and the subdivision of its land into smaller plots. In spite of homestead laws, government policies similarly favored the unrestricted sale and disposal of land. Under these circumstances, the notion of mine and thine slowly evolved. Thus, in an 1856 article, ethnographer M.Dj. Milićević relates how his grandfather, who had migrated to Serbia from the unfree south, one day gathered together all his sons, grandsons, and older nephews to tell them that the family should separate, exculpating them of all blame for the exigencies of the time that were making of Serbians, as we have shown, a *Zeitvolk* or historical people: "No one wants the division, my children, but I. More than any of you I regret that what was hitherto called *ours* will henceforth be called *ours* and *yours* and *theirs*, but it is better to separate now than when you too are of my age." The grandfather was then eighty-five. Unlike the grandfather, the preadolescent children could not easily accommodate to the new mentality. After having been raised under one set of values, they were told to operate according to another. There was nothing unusual about their response. Unlike adolescents and young persons in their twenties—who, in a changing society, often emerge as "nihilists" —children are essentially conservatives. They display this in their games, often reservoirs of the values of a bygone age, of an archaic mentality. Milićević comments appropriately on the problem: "Accustomed to obey the old man in all things, they [the adults] separated. But their children were long unable to distinguish between one house and another and therefore always spent the day or night wherever day or dusk came upon them. They say that all sometimes started to cry vigorously when they were told: 'Come, everyone to his own house; this is not your house.' "[100]

All divisions were not so pacific as in the family of Milićević. Often there were quarrels. Sometimes disputes were taken to a court of law. However a division was achieved, the result was largely the same despite the games of children: a favoring of the idea of private and personal property, a transformation of attitudes toward space. Such a change may have been promoted in particular by women (as opposed to children), whose demands for consumers' goods grew faster than the readiness of heads of joint households to fulfill them.[101]

The extension of private property, however, did not allow an equally facile expansion of individuality. The consequence of that extension was an overvaluation both of what Jovan Bošković called "market-place value" *(caršiska vrednost)* and of social (or socialist) realism—an emphasis on the primacy of matter and the quasi-repudiation of individual free will, as in the writings of Svetozar Marković and especially Pera Todorović.[102]

On the other hand, emphasizing the autonomous or semiautonomous character of genius and aesthetic imagination and expression, Matija Ban, a political conservative,[103] contended that, in the theater as in life, one must reach the mind through the heart. A decade later, in 1884, while admitting that natural dramatic talent can be improved with practice, Djordje Maletić affirmed that practice cannot create a talent that does not already exist. He lauded the role of the theater, however, as defender of a people's national language (as one of the means, in my view, of diffusing to a large area the dialect of a small area), as an awakener of a national identity, and as a school for "everything that is good, beautiful, and lofty."[104]

Jovan Bošković, a literature teacher in the seventh or highest grade of the Belgrade Gymnasium and professor of Slavic philology at the Velika Škola, formulated a theory of "the real and ideal [in combination] as the movers of people's works." Cultural choices, he maintained, occur in cycles, with waves of idealism of varying duration and intensity succeeding waves of realism but with contrary tendencies present in nearly every epoch. Thus, despite its materialist manifestations, Europe's eighteenth century was essentially idealist. Calling itself materialist, the nineteenth century did not renounce its quest of the ideal.[105]

The orientation toward a "market-place value" of things, Bošković believed, awakened a lust for luxury and possession. The latter desire promoted in turn the diffusion of the railroad and steam engine, which then served to promote the two ideals of the equality of states and of a unified humanity. The ideal of a unified humanity had to yield, however, to the idea of nationalism or self-determination of peoples, which in practice opened the possibility of the oppression of one people, nation, or ethnic group by another.

No nation in Europe since the time of the Romans, Bošković affirmed, had been a greater oppressor of other peoples than the Germans. For a time, the

Germans had been cosmopolitan idealists. Now, however, they were pressuring Italy and threatening France. After having swallowed up the Polabians and Baltic Slavs and reduced the Lusatian Sorbs, they were striving to Germanize the Czechs, Poles, Ruthenians, Slovenians, and other South Slavs. In Germany, "Everything now is *deutsch, deutsch, deutsch*, even culture."

Given the Slavic predilection for decentralization (localism, provincialism) and German, Magyar, Turkish, and even Russian oppression of Slavic ethnic groups, the political goal of the Serbs should be, said Bošković, to form a confederation of Serbs and Bulgarians, a "southern Scandinavia" of two autonomous states with a common foreign policy, committed to combat aggression whether from Europe or Asia. The ultimate goal, however, was a "higher human nobility," to be realized by the recurrent dialectic between the ideal and real and the successive but transitory triumph of each. In the past, such triumphs lasted for centuries. That period, he explained, has now been shortened to a quarter of a century or even a decade. The time may even come when the ideal and real can be harmonized.

Harmonization, Bošković continued, does not mean perfection. Nothing in the world can be perfect. Through the persons who act upon them, ideas may culminate in ideals. But they have a basis in objective forms, acts, and events. Persons who aspire to an ideal seek in turn to give it form, which by definition is imperfect. But just as some forms are farther removed from perfection—order, unity, purity, simplicity, truth—than others, so some ideas and ideals are farther removed from perfection than other ideas and ideals. While embracing a well-defined world view, Bošković discouraged students from parroting remarks without understanding them.[106]

Representing a later generation of Serbian thinkers was the philosopher Božidar Knežević (1862–1905), an admirer of Thomas Babington Macaulay, Auguste Comte, and Friedrich Nietzsche. In his two-volume *Principles of History* (1898–1901), Knežević observed that men (he did not intend to be gender-specific) may be separated into two categories, the "higher man" *(viši čovek)* and the "lower men" *(niži ljudi)*. The "higher man" possesses sufficient resources to rise to abstraction and achieve autonomy. "Lower men" are prisoners of their senses and of the concrete and particular. They are complete only in society. Knežević acknowledged that the abstract is born of the concrete and that every great social goal should be formulated in terms of the needs and interests of the people. But innovation and abstraction are the work of higher men, whose blossoming society strives to prevent even though they are necessary to it if society itself is to bloom—that is, move away from tribal hatreds and nation-state systems toward the goal of a common humanity.[107] But "things develop . . . in the same order in which they become necessary." As a result, there is a progression from the more necessary to the less necessary, from the satisfaction of the needs of the body (the lower man) to the satisfaction of the needs of the mind (the higher man), from the simple to the complex, from the highly stable and relatively unchanging to the highly fragile and unstable.[108]

The very fact that a Knežević could write in this manner in 1898 and that, in 1899, a Romanian disciple of Karl Lamprecht, Alexander D. Xenopol, could publish his important *Principes fondamentaux de l'histoire*, confirms the appearance or reappearance of the "higher man" in Balkan history. Devoting an entire chapter to "the constant factors in history," Xenopol identified them as biology, geography, and cultural conservatism or the law of reaction against action. "Every modification of intellectual continuity," he wrote, "provokes a movement of reaction which tends to preserve the acquisitions of continuity."[109]

For the first time in many centuries, since about 1860 but especially since the 1890s, "higher men" appeared on the Balkan scene. As they appeared, they rebelled against what the playwright Radoje Domanović called the "dead sea" of public opinion.[110] Custom and public opinion (*svet*, in the ancient Greek sense of φήμη) direct, meddle, make it difficult to rise above or fall below what Branislav Nušić called the "level line" of the crowd, "petty milieu," and everyday event.[111] They forbid the I—this new factor, the I-factor—to ring out.

The Spaniards called the "higher men" of their own country the "generation of '98." But common opinion notwithstanding, the Spanish-American War was only incidental to their rise. The generation of the 1890s was a European, not a narrowly national, phenomenon.[112] To the extent that this generation existed also in the Balkans, we may say that the Balkans—this "First Europe" and former "Asia in Europe"—were again *of* Europe as well as in it.

In the Balkans, as in central Europe, the generation of the 1890s and prewar decade is sometimes called "modernist." But some of its members rose above the quarrel separating the "young" from the "old," the modernists from the traditionalists, the symbolists from the realists, or the partisans of science from the advocates of art and aesthetics. No one bridged the gap between the two groups more brilliantly, "opening all the windows to Europe,"[113] than the Serbian essayist and literary critic Bogdan Popović (1863–1914), especially in two essays entitled "On the Cultivation of Taste" and "Literary Leaves," published respectively in 1896 and 1901.

In the first essay, Popović urged teachers to strive to develop in students an "independence of judgment" with a basis in facts that each individual is able to find for himself through the prior elaboration of a milieu conducive to discovery. Independence of judgment does not necessarily result in correctness of judgment, but its practice under appropriate conditions will promote a more frequent expression of correct and sound judgments. Moreover, held Popović, one cannot know man—"Know thyself," said the ancient Greeks—without knowing oneself: "A man will come to know himself if he learns, on every occasion, to be *conscious of what is happening within him*. There must be in him two men, one who will act, suffer, and live, a second who will observe and examine the first. This undoubling *(deduplovanje)*, this self-uncoupling aiming at self-understanding— *dédoublement*, as the French call it—is the key to our entire moral life."[114]

In his second essay, Popović drew again on psychology and invoked the principle of the economical use of energy in defense of the use of foreign models:

> From the psychology of creativity, it is well-known that every production is basically a reproduction; that every creation is more or less a new combination of attitudes and conceptions existing in the spirit previously, and without which neither the simplest image nor thing could be imagined. . . .
>
> It is, indeed, only too clear that we should be very poor economists *(ekonomi)* if we refused to profit from what others have achieved before us in a misguided zeal to repeat every experience and error, to begin anew the entire process of evolution.

Borrowings, Popović continued, will never be made at the expense of autonomous creation. Cultural imitation and innovation are complementary rather than contradictory:

> For original spirits, for spirits that have something of their own to tell, there is never a danger that foreign models will turn them into foreigners. The *"race" will always manifest itself in the person who is original*, precisely because he creates from his own special fund of resources; such an artist will always be national. Where originality is lacking, there is generally nothing anyhow, with or without models.[115]

In 1881, on the other hand, Xenopol had simply argued that the only alternative to the adoption of the western model of development was stagnation or retrogression:

> The entire progress of our nation [Romania] has taken place in a sense opposite to that taken by other peoples; instead of developing from below upward *[de jos in sus]*, civilization has come to us from above downward *[de sus in jos]*. Thus we have a constitution that must teach us freedom, instead of the exercise of freedom giving birth to a constitutional compact; thus we have railroads before we have covered roads. . . . From this it ensues that we must develop industry on the basis of the latest results that Western nations have attained, through large-scale industry.[116]

The innovation of new values was accompanied by the diffusion of a new vocabulary. Employed by Dositej Obradović before the end of the eighteenth century, the word *persona* was still rarely used by the Serbs of Serbia as late as the 1880s. Equally foreign-sounding *individua* also had to be explained to Serbian theater audiences of that time. Borrowed from Czech or Russian, on the other hand, the Slavic term *osoba* for "person" or "self" was more easily domesticated in the course of the nineteenth century.[117]

The old Balkan values and personality types did not disappear with the appearance of new values and a new vocabulary. Indeed, in modified form, they continue to dominate. But there was also by the 1890s a new reality—a new type of personality added to the older types. To understand the Balkans of the last hundred years, of the 1890s to the 1990s, one must bring together all these types and be ready for all kinds of combinations and confusions in a setting marked by foreign wars, civil wars, and experiments with, and struggles against, communism. One of the functions of Part Two of this book will be to clarify that experience as an evolution of a multiplicity of temporal rhythms—long and deep, middling and oscillating, quick and short.

Notes

1. Lee, "View of the Self in Greek Culture," pp. 150–52.
2. Hobhouse, *A Journey through Albania*, I, 510.
3. Spencer, *Travels in European Turkey in 1850*, II, 232, 235.
4. About, *La Grèce contemporaine*, p. 64.
5. Macaulay, "Machiavelli," p. 87. For the use of the concepts "courage culture" and "ingenuity culture" to explain the process of "modernizing" in Turkey, see Lerner, *The Passing of Traditional Society*, pp. 133–34, 152.
6. Gesemann, *Heroische Lebensform*, p. 35.
7. McNeill, *Greece*, pp. 18–19.
8. Mauss, *Manuel d'ethnographie*, pp. 89–91.
9. Solmsen, *Hesiod and Aeschylus*, pp. 83, 87; Arendt, *The Human Condition*, pp. 48, 80–81. In Serbian, the word *ponos* has several different meanings—not only burdensome work but also pride, dignity, behavior or demeanor (whether honorable, rude or stubborn, or ostentatious), and excessive pride or hubris. Cf. JAZU, *Rječnik hrvatskoga ili srpskoga jezika*, X, 754–56, *(ponos, ponosan,* and *ponosit).*
10. Sanders, *Rainbow in the Rock*, p. 269.
11. Vlajinac, *Moba i pozajmica*, pp. 20–24.
12. Bušetić, *Srpske narodne pesme i igre s melodijama iz Levča*, p. 82; Grbić, *Srpski narodni običaji iz sreza Boljevačkog*, p. 265; Mijatović and Bušetić, "Tehnički radovi Srba seljaka u Levču i Temniću," pp. 110–13; Petrović, *Život i običaji narodni u Gruži*, p. 391.
13. Arendt, *The Human Condition*, pp. 14–15, esp. p. 14 n. 10. See also Aristotle, *Aristotle's Politics and Poetics*, p. 208; Pieper, *Leisure the Basis of Culture*, pp. 26, 56; de Grazia, *Of Time, Work, and Leisure*, pp. 12, 14, 21.
14. Constantelos, "Philanthropia as an Imperial Virtue in the Byzantine Empire."
15. Obradović, *The Life and Adventures of Dimitrije Obradović*, p. 170.
16. Clogg, "The Greek Mercantile Bourgeoisie," p. 97; Obradović, *The Life and Adventures of Dimitrije Obradović*, p. 131; Obradović, *Dela Dositeja Obradovića*, pp. 3, 61, 82, 93, 110, my translation.
17. Obradović, *The Life and Adventures of Dimitrije Obradović*, pp. 42, 62; Kostić, *Dositej Obradović u istoriskoj perspektivi*, pp. 258–61; Pribić, "Dositej Obradović," pp. 41–49.
18. Daničić, *Korijeni*, pp. 87, 97–99, 107–8, 152–55, 216–18.
19. JAZU, *Rječnik hrvatskoga ili srpskoga jezika*, XII, 865, *(rad).*
20. On the growth of labor obligations among the Romanians, see Ştefănescu, Mioc, and Chircă, "L'Évolution de la rente féodale en travail"; Chirot, *Social Change in a Peripheral Society*, pp. 74–78, 97–98; H.H. Stahl, *Traditional Romanian Village Communities*, pp. 168–209; Roberts, *Rumania: Political Problems of an Agrarian State*, pp. 7–9; Emerit, *Les Paysans roumains*, pp. 34–38; Evans, *The Agrarian Revolution in Roumania*, p. 20.
21. Daničić, *Korijeni*, pp. 20–23. On the roots *ar-* and *dha-*, see also Benveniste, *Le*

Vocabulaire des institutions indo-européennes, I, 81; II, 100–101.

22. Leskien, *Handbuch der altbulgarischen (altkirchenslawischen) Sprache*, p. 225.

23. Meillet, *Etudes sur l'étymologie*, II, 461–503, "Index des mots vieux slaves"; Daničić, *Rječnik iz književnih starina srpskih*, III, 9; JAZU, *Rječnik hrvatskoga ili srpskoga jezika*, IV, 285 *(izraditi)*.

24. A Slaveno-Italo-Latin dictionary published in Ragusa in 1806 attributed the following meanings to the verb: *attendere, operare, cercare, procurare, trattare, dare operam, incumbere, vacare, operari, agere, efficere, facere, curare, tractare.* See Stulli, *Rjecsoslòxje slovinsko-italiansko-latinsko,* under the words in question.

25. Gesemann, *Heroische Lebensform,* pp. 100–101. On Montenegrin attitudes toward work, see also Cvijić, "Des migrations dans les pays yougoslaves," pp. 11–13.

26. Paton, *Servia,* pp. 232, 265.

27. Af. Étr., CC, Belgrade, II, fols. 106–7, Théodore Goepp, March 9, 1850; II, fols. 464–66, Auguste Dozon, July 23, 1861.

28. MacKenzie, *Notes on the South Slavonic Countries,* pp. 39, 63.

29. See Dvorniković, *Karakterologija Jugoslovena,* p. 663.

30. Schischmanoff, trans., *Légendes religieuses bulgares,* pp. 284–87.

31. Mikhov, ed., *Contribution à l'histoire du commerce bulgare,* I, 129, my translation.

32. Karavelov, *Bolgary starogo vremeni,* p. 3, my translation.

33. Holland, *Travels in the Ionian Isles, Albania, Thessaly, Macedonia,* p. 424.

34. Frangeš, "Die treibenden Kräfte der wirtschaftlichen Strukturwandlungen in Jugoslawien," p. 316.

35. Karić, *Srbija,* pp. 224–25; Dvorniković, *Karakterologija Jugoslovena,* pp. 663–68; Cvijić, "O naučnom radu," I, 37–38; Cvijić, *La Péninsule balkanique,* pp. 390–91.

36. Čajkanović, *Studije iz religije i folklora,* pp. 12–22.

37. Mardin, "The Mind of the Turkish Reformer," pp. 432–33. See also Mardin, *The Genesis of Young Ottoman Thought,* on the ideas of Ottoman reformers.

38. Novaković, "Srbija u godini 1834," p. 20; Jovanović, *Svetozar Marković,* p. 24; DA, PO, XXXVIII/238, prefect of Jagodina to Stevča Mihailović, September 25 (O.S.), 1837; Petrović and Petrović, *Gradja za istoriju Kraljevine Srbije,* I, 332, 355–57.

39. Šurmin, "Dokumenti o Srbiji od 1842–1848," pp. 57–58, my translation.

40. Mauss, "Une catégorie de l'esprit humain," pp. 331–62.

41. Mijatović, *Izvod iz politične ekonomike,* pp. 10, 238, 47–48, my translation.

42. Milićević, *Kneževina Srbija,* I. xiii; Milićević, *Dodatak pomeniku od 1888,* p. 88, my translation.

43. Obradović, *The Life and Adventures of Dimitrije Obradović,* pp. 180–81.

44. Serbia, Narodna Skupština, *Stenografske beleške o sednicama Narodne Skupštine držane u Beogradu 1874/5 godine,* I, 163–64.

45. Mijatović, *The Memoirs of a Balkan Diplomatist,* pp. 107–8, 172.

46. Mijatović, *Izvod iz politične ekonomike,* p. 130; Mijatović, *Nauka o državnom gazdinstvu ili nauka o financiji,* pp. 2, 52–54, my translation.

47. Silvije S. Kranjčević, quoted in Dvorniković, *Karakterologija Jugoslovena,* p. 668, my translation. For a biographical sketch of Kranjčević, see Kadić, *The Tradition of Freedom in Croatian Literature,* pp. 166–215.

48. Milićević, *Kraljevina Srbija,* pp. 157–58.

49. Schneeweis, *Serbokroatische Volkskunde,* I, 75; Niederle, *Manuel de l'antiquité slave,* II, 37, 39, 53; Hony, *A Turkish-English Dictionary,* p. 289 *(pir).*

50. Dvorniković, *Karakterologija Jugoslovena,* p. 657; Lotić, *Prilozi o ekonomskom stanju u Ugarskoj i u našem narodu,* p. 70; Milićevic, *Život Srba seljaka,* p. 112; Janković, *Astronomija u predanjima,* p. 162.

51. Cvijić, "O nacionalnom radu"; Cvijić, "O naučnom radu."

52. "Nationalism in Action: Program of the Society of National Defense *[Narodna Odbrana]* (1911)," in Anderson, Pincetl, Jr., and Ziegler, eds., *Europe in the Nineteenth Century*, II, 319, 326–27.

53. Jovanović, *Kult rada*, pp. 9, 30, 58–62.

54. Novaković, *Racionalizacija*, pp. 66–67, 88–89, 173–202.

55. Halpern, *A Serbian Village*, p. 293; Halpern, "The Economies of Lao and Serb Peasants," p. 168.

56. Dvorniković, *Karakterologija Jugoslovena*, pp. 251–52.

57. George, "Le Travail au village," p. 119.

58. Durkheim and Mauss, "De quelque formes primitives de classification," p. 4.

59. Herskovits, "Economic Change and Cultural Dynamics."

60. Lévi-Strauss, "Le temps retrouvé," p. 1421.

61. Spandonidis, "Le Clefte," p. 9.

62. Čajkanović, *Studije iz religije i folklora*, p. 37.

63. Jireček, *La Civilisation serbe au Moyen âge*, pp. 87–88; Fresne-Canaye, *Le Voyage du Levant de Philippe du Fresne-Canaye*, pp. 29–30.

64. Ibid., p. 34, my translation.

65. Brown[e], *A Brief Account of Some Travels*, p. 48.

66. AN, AÉ, B¹ 376, Constantinople, Correspondance consulaire, 1637–1675, fols. 72–73, March 5, 1670; Bibliothèque Nationale (Paris), Fonds Français 7176, t. Ier (Constantinople), "Estat des places que les princes mahométans possèdent sur les côtes de la mer Méditerranée," p. 22, my translation.

67. Busbecq, *The Life and Letters of Ogier Ghiselin de Busbecq*, I, 100–102, 255, 291.

68. Chateaubriand, *Itinéraire de Paris à Jérusalem*, I, 187.

69. Lechevalier, *Voyage de la Propontide et du Pont-Euxin*, II, 372, cited by Mikhov, *Contribution à l'histoire du commerce de la Turquie et de la Bulgarie*, VI, 56; Tafel, *De Via Militari Romanorum Egnatia*, p. xxxiii.

70. Tafel, *De Via Militari Romanorum Egnatia*, p. xxxiii; Pantelić, "Vojno-geografski opisi Srbije pred Kočinu Krajinu," p. 47; Ferrières-Sauveboeuf, *Mémoires historiques, politiques et géographiques*, II, 253.

71. Alexander, *Travels from India to England*, p. 247, cited by Mikhov, *Contribution à l'histoire du commerce de la Turquie et de la Bulgarie*, VI, 130.

72. Walsh, *Narrative of a Journey from Constantinople to England*, pp. 105–6.

73. Boué, *La Turquie d'Europe*, II, 315, my translation; IV, 545; Boué, *Recueil d'itinéraires dans la Turquie d'Europe*, II, 10, 12, 13; Stojančević, *Miloš Obrenović i njegovo doba*, p. 336, for a picture of the Topčider church (built in 1834) and its clock.

74. Boué, *Recueil d'itinéraires dans la Turquie d'Europe*, I, 32, 60, 80; II, 208.

75. Boulongne, *Le Monténégro*, p. 43.

76. Cipolla, *Clocks and Culture*, pp. 75, 149.

77. Beaujour, *A View of the Commerce of Greece*, pp. 240–46.

78. Boué, *La Turquie d'Europe*, III, 81–82.

79. Rabelais, *The Histories of Gargantua and Pantagruel*, pp. 128–29, 150.

80. Abbagnano, "Italian Renaissance Humanism," pp. 267–82.

81. Freyre, "On the Iberian Concept of Time." A Canadian scholar, Harold A. Innis, affirms: "The character of the medium of communication tends to create a bias in civilization favourable to an overemphasis on the time concept or on the space concept and only at rare intervals are the biases offset by the influence of another medium and stability achieved." *The Bias of Communication*, p. 64.

82. Musson and Robinson, "The Origins of Engineering in Lancashire," p. 221.

83. Beaujour, *A View of the Commerce of Greece*, pp. 244–45.

84. Beckmann, *A History of Inventions, Discoveries, and Origins*, II, 172–85. For street lighting in Cairo, see Stripling, *The Ottoman Turks and the Arabs*, p. 20. See also Stavrianos, ed., *The Epic of Modern Man*, p. 33.

85. Mouradgea d'Ohsson, *Tableau général de l'Empire othoman*, IV, 241–42.

86. Bérard, *La Turquie et l'hellénisme contemporain*, pp. 53–54, my translation. Bérard writes *dénéke*.

87. Af. Étr., CC, Belgrade, II (1848–62), VI (1881–85), VII (1885–89).

88. Vambéry, *Western Culture in Eastern Lands*, pp. 343–44, cited by Stavrianos, "The Influence of the West on the Balkans," p. 212.

89. Nenadović, *Memoari*, pp. 155–56, 171, my translation.

90. Mijatović, *Izvod iz politične ekonomike*, pp. 132, 91–92, my translation.

91. Andrić, *The Bridge on the Drina*, p. 292.

92. Lamprecht, *Zur jüngsten deutschen Vergangenheit*, II, 59–60, 389, 465. See also Lamprecht, *What Is History?*

93. Valéry, *Tel quel*, II, 37.

94. Lee, "View of the Self in Greek Culture," p. 153.

95. Liddell and Scott, comps., *A Greek-English Dictionary*, II, 1750, 1751, 1954, (σώς, σωφροσύνη, φρήν)

96. Jaeger, *Paideia*, I, 70.

97. Obradović, "Sovjeti zdravago razuma," in *Dela Dositeja Obradovića*, pp. 95–131.

98. On the ancient Greek concept of *eunomie*, see Jaeger, *Paideia*, I, 70; Solmsen, *Hesiod and Aeschylus*, pp. 108–9, 116–17, 121.

99. Gordon, *History of the Greek Revolution*, I, 323–25; Djordjevic, *Révolutions nationales des peuples balkaniques*, pp. 68–77; Tomasevich, *Peasants, Politics, and Economic Change in Yugoslavia*, p. 200; Jovanović, *Ustavobranitelji*, p. 11; Marcovitch, "Two Anniversaries of Serbian Law," pp. 270–71; Čubrilović, *Istorija političke misli*, pp. 149–50. For text of the Civil Code, see Haus-, Hof- und Staatsarchiv (Wien) Staatenabteilung, Serbien VII, "Zakonik gradjanski za kniažestvo srbsko."

100. Milićević, "Pregled zadružnog stanja Srba seljaka," p. 157, Milićević's italics, my translation.

101. Malet, *En Serbie*, p. 31.

102. Stoianovich, "The Pattern of Serbian Intellectual Evolution," pp. 264–69.

103. DA, PO, kutija 35, red. br. 170, Matija Ban to Dr. Pacek, Belgrade, February 7 (O.S.), 1859.

104. [Maletić], *Gradja za istoriju srpskog narodnog pozorišta u Beogradu*, pp. 453, 814, 822, 998.

105. Quotations from Jovan Bošković here and in the following paragraphs from DA, PO, kutija 62, red. br. 23, "O realnom i idealnom kao pokretačima ljudskih dela," Književnost iz zaostavštine Jovana Boškovića; "Estetika," Beograd, 14/12 1862. Prepisa K. Petrović, pravnik II god., Knjiž. iz zaostavštine Jovana Boškovića.

106. Marković, "Kako su nas vaspitali" (1868), *Celokupna dela*, VIII, p. 34.

107. Knežević, *Misli*; Atanasijević, *Penseurs yougoslaves*, pp. 136–83; Tomashevich, "Božidar Knežević."

108. Knežević, *History, the Anatomy of Time*, pp. 160–61, 199–200, quotation on p. 143.

109. Xenopol, *La Théorie de l'histoire*, pp. 164–209, my translation. The definition of the law of reaction against action occurs on page 189.

110. Domanović, "Mrtvo more," in *Odabrane pripovetke*, pp. 149–73.

111. Jaeger, *Paideia*, I, 58–59; Nušić, foreword to his play "Gospodja Ministarka," in *Sabrana dela*, I, 7–11.

112. Stoianovich, *French Historical Method*, pp. 64–65.

113. Slijepčević, "Jovan Dučić," pp. 148–57.

114. Popović, *Ogledi iz književnosti i umetnosti*, pp. 14–15, 36, 43–44, my translation.

115. Ibid., pp. 77, 81–82, 83–85, my translation, Popović's italics.

116. Xenopol, quoted in Montias, "Notes on the Romanian Debate on Sheltered Industrialization," p. 60.

117. JAZU, *Rječnik hrvatskoga ili srpskoga jezika*, IX, 237 *(osoba)*, 796 *(persona)*; Nušić, "Narodni Poslanik," in *Sabrana dela*, XII, 44, 63.

PART TWO

7 THE LIBERTIES AND CONSTRAINTS OF CULTURE

"We carry in our heads images of other groups, and we bring those images into all our relationships," wrote R.M. MacIver.[1] Such "mental images" and "imaginative conceptions" affect the group-diffused "images" of the action "preferences" and "goals" of our own groups,[2] formed partly in reaction to the "group images" that other groups form of us.

Freedom from Barbarity, Local and Universal

A nation is also an "imagined community" created, conserved, and modified in response to specific historical circumstances.[3] In the Balkans, the conception of nations as "imagined communities" was the product of two partly overlapping phases of historical experience—a positivist enlightenment phase and a romantic phase. In the enlightenment vision, the nation was conceived as a means to "freedom from barbarity."[4] Barbarity itself was defined as localism, provincialism, parochialism, feudalism, and tyranny, or what in western Europe was sometimes called oriental or Asiatic despotism. Like feudalism, oriental despotism let localism thrive.

The imagined space of a given nation during the enlightenment phase was extensive. The territory of the Greek nation thus could include the former areas of Byzantine rule in the Balkans and Asia Minor. The territory of the Serbian or Serbo-Bulgarian nation (as imagined by Serbs in eighteenth-century Hungary) could extend from the Adriatic to the Black Sea and from Hungary to the Aegean.

In this southeastern European enlightenment phase, the links between the concept of nation and the concept of religion were strong. Thus neither Greeks nor western Europeans had any problem regarding the Balkan Slavs as Greeks, and Hungarian Serbs could easily create an imaginary union of Serbs and Bulgars, for most Serbs and Bulgars (like most Greeks) were of the same Orthodox faith and possessed almost the same sacred literary language. In the Habsburg monarchy, this way of thinking culminated in the portrayal of Hungary by a

267

Viennese lawyer, Johann Csaplovics, as "a little Europe," in which nationhood did not preclude ethnic diversity and ethnic diversity did not exclude nationhood.[5]

Remaking Time, Territory, and Mind

To comprehend the transition from the first phase to the second, there is no better text than Constantin-François Chasseboeuf de Volney. On the eve of and during the French Revolution, contemplating the ruins of former empires and civilizations of the Near and Middle East, which he knew intimately, Volney wondered whether the same fate might not befall Europe, including his own country, France.

Two centuries later we contemplate the failed economies and weakening, dismemberment, reterritorialization, and collapse of the Soviet Union and some of the states of eastern and southeastern Europe. We are forced to reflect upon the growing economic power of Japan and the new European Community (called European Union), the possible domination of the latter by a reunited Germany, the threat and reality of a declining standard of material life, and the unreadiness to deal effectively with the man-made disequilibria of the earth's ecosystems.[6]

A comparatist by inclination, Volney recollected his own country's fields,

> so richly cultivated; its roads, so admirably executed; its towns, inhabited by an immense multitude; its ships scattered over every ocean; its ports filled with the produce of either India; and comparing the activity of its commerce, the extent of its navigation, the magnificence of its buildings, the arts and industry of its inhabitants, with all that Egypt and Syria could formerly boast of a similar nature, I pleased myself with the idea that I had found in modern Europe the past splendour of Asia: but the charm of my reverie was presently dissolved by the last step of the comparison. Reflecting that if the places before me had once exhibited this animated picture: who, said I to myself, can assure me that their present desolation will not one day be the lot of our own country?[7]

Volney might have reached the conclusion of a mystical medieval missionary dervish, Jalal al-Din Rumi, who pursued his mission in Anatolia and about whom is recounted the following anecdote:

> There is a well known story that the sheikh Salah al-Din one day hired some Turkish workmen to build the walls of his garden. "Effendi Salah al-Din, said the Master [Rumi], you must hire Greek workmen for this construction. It is for the work of demolition that Turkish workmen must be hired. For the construction of the world is special to the Greeks, and the demolition of this same world is reserved to the Turks. When God created the universe, he first made the carefree infidels. He gave them a long life and considerable force in such a fashion . . . that in the manner of paid workmen they constructed the earthly world. They erected numerous cities and mountain fortresses . . . so

that after centuries these constructions serve as models to the men of recent times. But divine predestination has disposed of affairs in such a way that little by little the constructions became ruins. He created the people of the Turks in order to demolish, without respect or pity, all the constructions which they see. They have done this and are still doing it. They shall continue to do it day in and day out until the day of the Resurrection."[8]

Rationalist Volney asked, on the other hand, Can God be responsible for the ruins of states, empires, and civilizations? Rejecting that possibility, he argued that the creator had "established a regular order of causes and effects, of principles and consequences, which, under an appearance of chance, governs the universe, and maintains the equilibrium of the world." Endowed by the creator with "the faculty of perception," frail man responds to "every action injurious to his life" with "a sensation of pain and evil" and to "every favourable action" with "a sensation of pleasure and good." But the "self-love" of some men turned into unbridled desire and "love of accumulation," resulting in the exploitation of the weak by the strong. When founded on intemperance and ignorance, self-love "tends to the dissolution of society." Government thus became necessary, not the kind of government that promotes self-love only in those who possess it to the greatest degree, but the kind that tempers self-love. Temperate government, however, may then reawaken cupidity by the industry it favors. Industry creates affluence, which in turn arouses cupidity—the cupidity of barbarians, who govern on the basis of distinctions between conquerors and conquered. Such a misanthropic system of government encourages the formation of "misanthropic systems of religion," founded one and the other on the principle of despotism.[9]

Will should not be confused with freedom. As "the power to choose and deliberate," wrote a contemporary with whom Volney would probably have concurred, freedom depends upon knowledge and, in particular, on the presence of a social order conducive to the circulation of information, along with individuals favorably disposed toward reflection and reason.[10] The *"evils of society,"* on the other hand, continued Volney, *"flow from* IGNORANCE *and* INORDINATE DESIRE." Consequently, *"men will never cease to be tormented till they shall become intelligent and wise; till they shall practice the art of justice, founded on a knowledge of the various relations in which they stand, and the laws of their own organization."* Fortunately, "within the last three centuries especially, the light of knowledge has been perceptibly advanced," manners have become milder, "the spirit of estrangement" among peoples has been attenuated, parochialism has been reined in. In Europe, despotism has become enlightened.

By redefining their ecumene as Europe rather than Latin or western (Protestant and Catholic) Christendom, Enlightenment thinkers—now with a capital "E" to emphasize the connection between an era and a way of thought—gave the mediator elites of eastern Europe an opportunity to envision their own ultimate inclusion in a common European home.

But enlightenment was incomplete. In 1788, the government of France threw its diplomatic support to Ottoman Turkey, the enemy of enlightenment, in the war of Russia and Austria against that country. Nevertheless, wrote Volney, even if European despots,

> with timid and mysterious jealousy, have interdicted all knowledge of their administration, all rivalship for the direction of affairs, the passions of mankind, excluded from the political career, have fixed upon the arts and the science of nature; the sphere of ideas has enlarged on every side; man, devoted to abstract studies, has better understood his place in the system of nature, and his social relations; principles have been more fully discussed, objects more accurately discerned, knowledge more widely diffused, individuals made more capable, manners more sociable, life more benevolent and pleasing; the species at large, particularly in certain countries, have been evidently gainers; nor can this improvement fail to proceed, since its two principal obstacles, those which have hitherto rendered it so slow, and frequently retrograde, the difficulty of transmitting ideas from age to age, and communicating them rapidly from man to man, have been removed.
>
> With the people of antiquity, every canton and every city, having a language peculiar to itself, stood aloof from the rest, and the result was favorable to ignorance and anarchy; they had no communication of ideas, no participation of discoveries, no harmony of interests or of will, no unity of action or conduct. Beside, the only means of diffusing and transmitting ideas being that of speech, fugitive and limited, and that of writing slow of execution, expensive, and acquired by few, there resulted an extreme difficulty as to instruction in the first instance, the loss of advantages one generation might derive from the experience of another, instability, retrogradation of science, and one unvaried scene of chaos and childhood.
>
> On the contrary, in the modern world, and particularly in Europe, great nations having allied themselves by a sort of universal language, the firm of opinion has been placed upon a broad basis; the minds of men have sympathised, their hearts have enlarged: we have seen agreement in thinking and concord in acting; in fine, that sacred art, that memorable gift of celestial genius, the press, furnished a means of communicating, of diffusing at one instance any idea to millions of the species, and of giving it a permanence which all the power of tyrants has been able neither to suspend nor suppress.

Volney might have ended up with a cyclical theory of history. Such a history would have argued that driven by self-love, man creates order. Order promotes affluence. Affluence stimulates cupidity. Cupidity creates in turn the disorder of tyranny or despotism, which, too, may be undone, renewing the process we have described. But, contended Volney, the diffusion of the printing press, resulting in the diffusion of information and formation of public opinion, has given mankind an opportunity to escape the fate of perpetual rise and fall, an eternal return. Being ever better informed, men will "cease to be dupes of inordinate desire" and form thereupon a new kind of "human organization." That organization will be based on the principle that "in the order of nature all men are equal." But just as freedom requires equality, so equality requires freedom. For equality can be an equality of abjection or subjection. To escape abjection and subjection, one must be free. At the same time, men must be equal so that cupidity may not prevail.[11]

Customs, Laws, and Gods

Picking up on the theme of the ruin of empires and civilizations, a twentieth-century thinker, Ernest Gellner, contends that the ruin of empires was not necessarily a great disaster. The societal units of which they were constituted could have survived "as well, or nearly as well, or indeed better, if the totality [had] remained fragmented," except perhaps in several of the world's major river valleys, where extensive irrigation systems had been instituted.[12]

In the immediate post-Napoleonic era, a French historian concerned with the problem of the decline and fall of classical Greece and Byzantium, Alphonse Rabbe, issued a new warning against the "illusion of human pride" that nations and states are imperishable. "The surface of the globe," he wrote, is "covered with the débris" of ancient peoples. "The life of nations has its term, for everything has an end in this world below. Nations die naturally when not brought down by revolution, conquest, or civil war. But they also cease to be in another and more common way—by the loss of the institutions that made them great and prosperous and by the alteration of the genius [the nation's representation of itself] that makes a population what it is and not another." What is lost on such occasions is "the most precious" element of nationality: patriotism or, in terms of the discourse of the closing decades of the twentieth century, the sense of national identity. "For the fatherland does not lie wholly in the soil; it finds its main expression in its customs, laws, and gods."[13]

Customs, laws, and gods have been defined historically, however, less by nations and states than by more archaic territorial and cultural entities, units to which have been applied such terms as *comitatus*, *megye* or *vármegye*, *župa* or *županija* (cognate of *Sippe*, *Zippe*, "sib"?), *territorio*, *pays*, *contado*, *knežina*, *kotar*, *srez*, *Gau*, "district," "barony," or "county."[14] One may think of early fourteenth-century Macedonia, for example, as a country of Eastern Orthodox faith. But upon stopping at the Macedonian town of Strumica to celebrate Easter in 1325 or 1326, the anti-Hesychast scholar Nicephorus Gregoras recorded his dismay: "We celebrated divine Passover there, sadly and not as we have been accustomed from the beginning, but celebrate it we did nonetheless. [The people of Strumica, on the other hand, a wild folk] regard all religious practice and harmonious music of sacred hymns as nonsense."[15]

In eighteenth-century Albania, three main religions prevailed—Greek Orthodoxy, Latin Christianity, and Islam (both Shi'a/Şi'a, and Sunni). But Lady Mary Wortley Montagu, wife of the English ambassador to the Porte, wrote of the Albanian religious practices: "These people, living between Christians and

Mahometans, and not being skill'd in controversie, declare that they are utterly unable to judge which Religion is best; but to be certain of not entirely rejecting the Truth, they very prudently follow both, and go to the Mosque on Fridays and the Church on Sundays, saying for their excuse, that at the day of Judgment they are sure of protection from the True Prophet, but which that is they are not able to determine in this World."[16]

The presence of such syncretic folk religions may have played a role in inspiring the Ecumenical Patriarchate of Constantinople and the Phanariots—Greek grammarians, secretaries, Ottoman Christian undersecretaries of state, bankers, and businessmen—to join forces in order to bring the European provinces of the Ottoman Empire to (universal) reason. One manifestation of that reason was the placing of the archbishopric of Ohrid and patriarchate of Peć under the authority of Greek prelates and the direct jurisdiction of the patriarchate of Constantinople.

Regional variation—local customs, laws, and gods—also prevailed among Roman Catholics. During the insurrection of 1875 and 1876 in Bosnia-Hercegovina, for example, Roman Catholics and Orthodox Serbs alike rebelled in the sanjaks of Hercegovina and Travnik. Catholics under the jurisdiction of the diocese of Dubrovnik, occupying the left bank of the Neretva, joined the rebellion. Catholics of the right bank, under the authority of the bishop of Mostar and the influence of the Franciscan order, did not stir. In the sanjak of Banjaluka north of Travnik, the Catholics of Gradiška joined the Muslims against the Orthodox Serb rebels. In March 1876, however, many Banjaluka Catholics returned to their farms. In areas where the Catholics were not numerous, they made common cause with the Muslims.[17]

"The Catholic priest" of Bosnia, wrote an observer of the insurrection, "pretends to possess a supernatural power. The Orthodox do not accord to their priests or popes what they attribute to the Franciscans, who sell amulets and talismans against the evil eye and infernal spirits."[18] The supposed Marian apparitions of the 1980s at Medjugorje occurred in this area of Franciscan influence on the right bank of the Neretva.[19]

Clan vendettas were also common in the area, surfacing in particular during periods of acute crisis, as during World War II, when the (Orthodox) Serb minority of Medjugorje was the victim of clan warfare with an overlay of Ustaša genocide—that is, of local conflict exacerbated by the ongoing European and world conflict. The vendettas persisted until 1957 but then calmed down as the "ancestors" of the rival clans withdrew underground, becoming again *podzemni* (literally, "underground people"), in response to the performance of reconciliation rituals locally known as *slavas*.[20] The evidence for what happened after 1991 is not yet in. One may formulate, however, a possible hypothesis. As the crisis of the Yugoslav state was complicated by the greater crisis of states, societies, economies, and cultures at a world level, the *podzemni* may have left their subterranean homes to lead their respective families in a war against the traditional enemy clans, whether Orthodox Serb, Catholic Croat, or Muslim.

A mix of pagan, Orthodox, Catholic, and Muslim practices has prevailed in western Hercegovina since the fifteenth century. A tendency has also prevailed in each of the three institutionalized religions, however, to cleanse themselves of their respective impurities, an extremely difficult task. Let us address in particular a few of the problems that have confronted the Catholic diocese of Mostar and its parish of Medjugorje, one of the centers of Franciscan missionary activity since the fourteenth century. Competition between the bishopric of Mostar and its secular clergy, more or less controlled by Rome, and the Franciscans, closer to the traditions of the people, has persisted over the centuries. Present in the struggle for clienteles, however, were two other rivals: local lords, princes, or the state; and local visionaries and shamans, who curried favor with the Franciscans but who could also divert loyalties from the three other groups. In principle, the diocesan or episcopal authority and the authority of the state both grew, especially during the nineteenth and twentieth centuries.

As in other areas, the inhabitants of Medjugorje had their own holy mountain, whose powers they personalized, calling it Gromovnik, the Thunderer. As the authority of both the bishop and the Franciscans grew, the name of the mountain was depaganized, being changed to Šipovac in description of the local flora. After World War II, following the victory of the Partisans of Marshal Josip Broz Tito, it was personalized again, being renamed Titovac. A more populist name of a possible earlier origin, however, prevailed after 1981. The mountain was repersonalized, becoming Križevac, the Crusader.

In the early summer of 1981, four boys and two girls of the parish reported having had a vision in which appeared the Gospa or Virgin Mary with a message that they should purify the church. The visions recurred, as they may have done to earlier seers of the region. The incidents seem to have been accidental. In fact, they were the product of a developing alliance of convenience, initiated in the 1960s, between the state authorities of the republic of Bosnia and Hercegovina and the bishop of Mostar. This alliance was advantageous to the state since it could more easily maintain surveillance over the urban or *polis*-based diocese than over the ruralized Franciscan order. It was advantageous to the bishop of Mostar since it allowed him to establish his own priests in many parishes in which there previously had been only Franciscans. The readiness of the people and Franciscans of Medjugorje to embrace the seers may have come as a reaction against the expanding power of the city and state. It may even have been part of a world phenomenon, defined by what may be called the crisis of the state or overexpansion of state authority and resurgence of localism, provincialism, "tribalism," and populist fundamentalism.

The Franciscans of Medjugorje seized the opportunity of the visions of their young seers to organize local prayer groups whose members were known as *križevci* (crusaders). Pilgrims began to come regularly to hear and touch the seers and see the site where the visions had supposedly occurred. Within a single decade, the total number of visiting pilgrims and domestic and foreign tourists grew to ten million. As tourism advanced, the active seers were reduced to three and then only two of the original number, but several new young visionaries appeared. The seers also made incursions into the zone of action of the Franciscans, obtaining direct control of some of the prayer groups, engaging increasingly in the healing activities of shamans, previously a specialty of the Franciscan order. At the same time, they made contacts with two tourist agencies and local boarding houses, exposing themselves and the whole parish to an intense low-level commercialization,[21] drawing the local culture more deeply into the cash nexus of the world-economy of capitalism.

How the closer association between local cultures, such as the local culture of Medjugorje, and world capitalism affected the outbreak of the Yugoslav civil war in 1991 is not yet clear. What is probable, on the other hand, is that the varying quantitative and qualitative increase in connections or sociocultural contacts between individual local cultures and the capitalist world led to a sharpening of perceptions of regional differences, as different ethnic (Serbs, Croats, Muslims) and professional groups, diversely distributed territorially as they were, arrived at divergent conclusions regarding how they would benefit from or be hurt by various ties with the outside world.[22] To deal with the Yugoslav civil war, one may ultimately have to raise questions not only about nationalism, international rivalries, the fall of communism, and the world world-economy, but about how these factors were enmeshed with individual local cultures, shamanism and prayer groups, and millennialist expectations of returning or avenging savior ancestors.

Neither Universal nor Parochial

What has occurred was unforeseen. It was not supposed to happen, just as in the Napoleonic and immediate post-Napoleonic era there occurred what in E/enlightenment thought had been almost unthinkable. The critical event in this earlier era was an idea voiced by the Serbian lexicologist, Vuk Stefanović Karadžić: Write as you speak, speak as you write. To this credo, Karadžić joined a plea for the security of "life, property, and honor" and for the union of freedom and knowledge.[23] On the other hand, in the idea that, both as an individual and as a people, one becomes free only by knowing and that one gets to know well only by speaking, reading, and writing in one's own tongue, not in an antiquated ecclesiastical tongue, Metropolitan Stefan Stratimirović of Sremski Karlovci perceived a threat to the monopoly of the clergy. Convinced that this last innovation would be the prelude to a more open, less ordered, society, clerico-bourgeois conservatives resisted the call to give up a modified Church Slavonic or Hellenistic Greek written language in favor of a spoken popular idiom.[24] For Serbian ecclesiastics in Hungary, the spoken language of the people was a "cowherd's tongue" *(govedarski jezik).*[25]

In the whole of Europe—and despite what some scholars have said, not excluding France—the idea of the nation was merged with the idea of language. The E/enlightenment ideal did not have general literacy as its goal. But that was the ultimate goal of the romantics, of whom Karadžić, in daily touch with the Germanic milieu of Vienna, was but one representative. Schools and armies were to become the instruments for the creation of the imagined nations by teachers and officers who were taught to speak and write, and then taught their own pupils and soldiers to speak and write, in a uniform manner—sometimes not exactly as they had spoken in their homes.

The Enlightenment ideal of a state that was neither too small nor too large and was not tyrannical survived. The vehicle of that ideal, however, was a number of small states—Greece, Serbia, Montenegro, Wallachia, and Moldavia—which often aspired to expand to each other's frontiers and annex territories of the three neighboring empires or monster states—Turkey, Austria, and Russia. All these states grew in size during the nineteenth century. In 1878, a new state emerged—Bulgaria. Bulgaria also grew in size. Its political elites and spinners of words and makers of political imaginaries similarly started with the enlightenment ideal of a Bulgarian state stretching from the Danube to the Aegean Sea and from the Aegean to the Adriatic.

Without destroying or weakening one or more of the others, none of these states could fully concretize its imaginary ideal. Thus the partial concretization of the imaginary of a Bulgarian state, in combination with the development of a modern Bulgarian literary language distinct from the Church Slavonic of Serbian or Bulgarian recension, as from the modern Serbian literary language, made virtually impossible the realization of a Serbo-Bulgarian state.

During the 1830s and 1840s, Croatian romantics proposed the adoption of a unitary Croatian literary language to replace the parochial Croatian literary language in the *kaj*-idiom *(ekavski-kajkavski)* of Zagreb, Varaždin, Križevci, and the Croatian Zagorje, which bore a close resemblance to Slovenian, and the language in the *ča*-idiom *(ikavski-čakavski)* of Istria, of the Dalmatian islands, of Zadar (ancient Liburnia), of the Croatian Littoral, of parts of Slavonia, and of Dubrovnik's first printing press (but not of Dubrovnik itself),[26] an idiom to which Slavonian Calvinists had given literary expression in three different scripts—Latin, Glagolitic, and Cyrillic. The choice of the romantics fell upon the *što*-idiom of Dubrovnik (Ragusa) and Hercegovina, which differed little from the speech of the Serbs.

Adopted as the official literary language of Croatia in 1850, the new unitary literary language retained the Latin script. The Serbs and Montenegrins, on the other hand, preserved their Cyrillic script, albeit ultimately slightly revised—Latinized, objected critics. In 1868, the Serbian government adopted the western or (i)jekavian variant of the štokavian speech; basically, the new literary language of Croatia and the literary and spoken language of Montenegro. Most of the Serbs of Serbia and parts of Hungarian Vojvodina, however, spoke and increasingly wrote in a dialect known to linguists as ckavian-štokavian *(ekavski-*

štokavski), which, in Serbia, quickly submerged the (i)jekavian literary form.[27]

The new Slavic literary languages made increasingly remote the possibility of a Serbo-Bulgarian union, although such an imagined community received some political support as late as 1905 and, in the form of a projected Yugoslav-Bulgarian union, as late as 1948. Moreover, partly as a consequence of the shift from one Serbian literary language to another, the number of Serbian schools dropped from 94 in the Ottoman vilayet of Kosovo and from 59 in the vilayets of Monastir and Salonika in 1875, to no more than 69 in the combined vilayets in 1879. In 1889, the number fell to 19, all in the vilayet of Kosovo.[28] The relative density of speech or written speech traffic between Serbia and Macedonia thus declined to the advantage of Bulgaria and Greece, both of which sent to Macedonia an increasing number of teachers, starting in the case of not yet autonomous Bulgaria as early as the Crimean War.[29]

The literary languages of all the Balkan peoples were altered in some fundamental manner—at the unofficial level until the second half of the twentieth century in the Greek case and at the official level in every other case. Under the influence of Lutheranism and Calvinism, and then of Uniate seminarians, the Romanians of Transylvania abandoned the Cyrillic script and purged Romanian of much of its Slavic, Greek, and Turkish vocabulary. During the first half of the nineteenth century, the Romanians of Wallachia and Moldavia followed the Transylvanian example.

Under the impetus of Calvinist and other Protestant thought, the seventeenth-century patriarch of Constantinople, Cyril Loukaris, allowed the translation of the New Testament from Byzantine into demotic Greek. The yearning for purity and universalism, however, prevented many Greeks from accepting the spoken language—local by definition and suffused with foreign elements—as their written vehicle. Until the latter part of the nineteenth century, demotic Greek competed under adverse conditions with *katharevousa*, the "pure" language, as one may infer from the etymology.[30]

As for the Albanians, they lacked a common alphabet until the twentieth century. Few in number, literate Albanians employed three, four, or even five different scripts (Arabic, Greek, Latin, and even Glagolitic and Cyrillic), several variants of the Latin alphabet, and even mixed alphabets. Finally, at a congress held in Elbasan in September 1909, the participants opted in favor of the dialect of Elbasan, midway between the language of the Ghegs to the north and of the Tosks to the south. Partly because Latin presses may have been cheaper or easier to obtain, but mainly in order to emphasize the difference between Greeks and Albanians, and Serbs and Bulgarians and Albanians, the Latin script prevailed.[31]

Pure and Impure

People often define a culture on the basis of distance from a given point, in terms of attitudes toward north and south and east and west, and in terms of perfection and imperfection. But everyone does not define perfect and imperfect (or pure and impure) in the same way. For some persons and groups, the concept of perfection is Platonic, identifiable with a small space. For others, it may be neo-Aristotelian, partaking of the spatial visions of the Enlightenment but capable, by its aspiration for territorial expansion, of becoming Alexandrian.

Aristotle himself affirmed that a state should be neither too small nor too large. He did not define the appropriate size, however, by specific dimensions. The right size was variable, designed to include as many people as could be supported by its resources and production, by its ability to obtain goods that it lacked without reducing its citizens to demeaning commercial activity or becoming economically or politically dependent on some other state, and by its ability to communicate governmental decisions to its citizens on a daily basis. In Aristotle's own time, these criteria favored a small state.

By the 1830s, on the other hand, the innovation of the telegraph enabled the governments of western Europe to communicate their decisions on a daily basis over an area of 400,000 square kilometers,[32] roughly equal in area to all the Balkan territories under Ottoman rule lying south of the Danube and Sava rivers. By the term "neo-Aristotelian," therefore, I have in mind the reinterpretation of Aristotle that could be made by reference to the new technology that also penetrated into the Balkans during the second half of the nineteenth century.

In post-1914 Greece, a division thus occurred between the Venizelist (neo-Aristotelian) vision of "the inextricable link between internal reforms and territorial expansion" and the Royalist (Platonic) view in favor of the pursuit of authoritarian rule at home and, for the time being at least, peace with other states, namely Germany.[33]

One may also portray the Greek experience since 1789 as an "interplay between two basic sociopolitical orientations and cultures," a western European and a southeastern European–Middle Eastern model. In one form of the western European model, a heterochthonous Greek elite (Greeks born outside Greece proper) sought to institute in the new Greek state a relatively highly structured model of bureaucratic and military organization. Pitted against that model was a "folk-heroic" cultural model with a preference for local autonomy and "a more decentralized and autonomous military organization."[34] Among the Serbs, a similar division existed between the Serbians of Serbia (most of them actually recent immigrants or the descendants of recent immigrants) and the transriparian Serbs (prečani), most of them from across (preko) the Sava (many of them descendants of Serbs from Old Serbia and Macedonia and a few from across the Drina).

In the eyes of some nineteenth- and twentieth-century Greek thinkers, Greece has always been part of Europe. According to others, Greece and Europe were two different things. The most common image of Greek identity, however, was some mix of the two ideas, with a shift in stress with each change in circumstance. One thus might say that Greeks had a double or even multiple identity. In that identity were present two dimensions, Hellenic and Rhomaic (Romeic). The

Rhomaic outlook was likely to be an eastern identity. But it could be western, and it might be either local or imperial. The Hellenic outlook was likely to be western. In that event, however, it might assume one of two different forms. One form was the image of classical Greece as modern Europe's model. The second form was the image of modern Europe as the model for the new Greece. To complicate matters, one might disagree over the definition of Europe (to include or not to include Russia?) or the East (to include or not to include Russia, the Slavs, or Islam?). Without this last complication, identity could become for the same Greek under different circumstances a matter of three different poles or six different orientations: East/West, local/universal, self (Greece as the old Europe and model for modern Europe)/other (modern Europe as the model for the new Greece).[35]

For Platonists and neo-Aristotelians alike, but especially for neo-Aristotelians, the favored partial outside models varied. For some persons and groups they were the north and west; for others, the north and east (Russia); for yet others, as for Ion Dragoumis and Athanasios Souliotes-Nicolaides,[36] the south and east (Turkey, a new Byzantium, or the colonial empire of an expanding *Mitteleuropa*). For nearly everyone, however, a desirable north or south, or a desirable east or west, could become an undesirable or extreme north, south, east, or west.

A similar conflict and confusion of outlooks prevailed among the Romanians. The oldest Romanian ideology, going back to Moldavian chroniclers but reinforced by the arguments of the Uniate Romanian thinkers of Transylvania, was Latinism or a sense of identity with Roman antiquity, achievement, and power. Against, but sometimes fused with, the Latinizing neo-Aristotelian current emerged a neo-Aristotelian current emphasizing the Byzantine and Orthodox— Greek, Russian, and Serbian—affinities of the Romanians. By the middle of the nineteenth century arose a third current. Emphasizing neither Latin-western nor Byzantine-eastern affinities, it focused rather on the Dacian origins of the Romanians. This third current was Platonic in the sense of stressing its separateness from both the Latin-western and Greek-Slavic-eastern ecumene in favor of the increasingly powerful nationalist and populist idea of "indigenous" origins. It was neo-Aristotelian in its conception of a Dacia much more extensive and powerful than the Dacia subjugated by the Romans. Linking the Dacian culture with what was "protochronic," natural, original, and organic, and with permanence, it regarded whatever was Roman, Greek, Slavic, eastern, cosmopolitan, foreign, or "synchronic" as artificial and perishable, a product of temporary historical mishap.[37]

The idea of a pure or true ethnicity, culture, or language—authentic even though of mixed origin—was also common, however, among members of the Balkan cultures no less than among foreign observers. Andrew Archibald Paton thus distinguished in 1862 between the Morlak, whom he called "the Servian of the Adriatic," and "the Servian proper." The Servian (that is, Serbian) proper "burns for modern civilization and advancement," while the Morlak "has still a rooted antipathy to modern European usages."[38] The Morlaks inhabited territories far to the west of Serbia. Their ideal was local, not European. For many Serbian Serbs, on the other hand, a European model was not unattractive.

North of the middle Danube and stretching eastward to Oltenia lies the territory of the Banat of Temesvar (Temesvár, Timisoara)—a territory of Magyar villages in the north, Serbian villages in the west, exclusively Roman Catholic German colonies (from the eighteenth century until the end of World War II) in the south and east, a few Bulgarian settlements, and several other small ethnic groups, nearly all spread out over a settlement foundation of Daco-Romans (Romanians). In its post-1720 form, it was the product of Habsburg mercantilism and *Populationistik*—the drainage of Danubian marshes by skilled Dutch colonists, deforestation, the promotion of cereal cultivation, and the formation of checkerboard towns on the model of Mannheim, Karlsruhe, and Erlangen.[39]

"From 1718 to 1779," wrote Paton,

> the Banat was an integral part of the Austrian Empire, and in that period the aspect of the duchy was completely altered from that of a desolate Turkish Pashalik to that of a flourishing and prosperous European province. Millions were expended by the Cabinet of Vienna in cutting the great navigable canal that connects Temesvar with the confluence of the Theiss [Tisza] and the Danube, in draining the marshes, settling German colonies on the reclaimed lands, in rebuilding Temesvar (the capital) in the truly pompous style of Louis Quatorze, then the favourite passion of Charles VI. Owing to this *interregnum* of an improving European government between 1718 and 1779, or a period of sixty years, the Banat has not the least resemblance to the interior of Hungary; and if a stranger were to have his eyes bandaged, he would suppose that he had been carried back towards the centre of Europe, instead of being nearer the Turkish frontier.[40]

The fact that Timişoara was one of the few hearths of revolution in Romania in December 1989 may represent no anomaly. Located considerably to the east of Croatia, portions of the Banat probably have been culturally more "western" than many parts of Croatia.

TRUE!

European images of the Balkan peoples and cultures—of this "other" that was both a Europe and a non-Europe and sometimes an anti-Europe—depended on the image of the beholder of his or her own culture and specific attitudes toward folk, nature, spontaneity, efficiency, and organization. A few Europeans admired the poetry, mystery, or piety of Islam. Most European observers, however, drew a sharp contrast between Europe as the repository of the values of industry, probity, discipline, science, and technological achievement, and the archaisms of the Balkan cultures.

German and Austrian travelers to the Balkans during the war years 1912–18 described the Romanians as half-French, half-oriental. The Montenegrins and Albanians were a "nature" or "robber folk." Most observers admired the penchant of the Bulgarians for method, work, and discipline, likening them to the Prussians, Swabians, or Japanese. The Turks were portrayed as gentlemen, a master folk, Asiatic barbarians, nomads, or tyrants. The joyfulness, capriciousness, and lightheartedness of the Serbs of Serbia reminded travelers of the French and of Rhinelanders.[41]

Under the impact of the Yugoslav civil war of the 1990s, however, three French scholars of Croat origin published documents dating back to the Serbian uprising against Ottoman misrule in the Napoleonic era with the object of showing a continuing Serbian predilection for "ethnic cleansing." The "ethnic cleansing" of the civil wars of the 1990s was not an aberration. It was rather, in their view, an intrinsic part of two centuries of Serbian politics, ideology, popular poetry, and belles-lettres.[42] By a similar tendentious use of documents, one could probably prove much the same thing about any people that has been involved in a long struggle to form a political state or preserve its political life. As for the specific "ethnic cleansing" in the civil war of the 1990s—whether as the humiliation of another group's women by rape, as mass killings, or as the expulsion of a particular ethnic group from certain communities, districts, or regions—it is a practice in which all three contestants (Serbs, Croats, and Bosnian Muslims) have engaged. The practice must not be condoned. On the other hand, it may be expected to occur when civil authority breaks down and the transition from one political authority to another has not been completed.

The object of "ethnic cleansing"—*etničko čišćenje*—is a supposedly "pure" society. Derived from the word *čist* meaning "clean" or "pure," related in turn to *čast* or "honor," *etničko čišćenje* brings us back to the old honor-shame orientation of the Balkan (but also of other) cultures. What is shameful is what may harm or has already harmed the community. A community that has been harmed —or some members of the community acting on its behalf—retaliates by harming any person or group that it associates with the shame and harm done to its own community. Archaic human or social values are thus revived, and "ethnic cleansing" becomes popular, in the consciousness, not the act of the perpetrators but rather an act that others have perpetrated against them. In an address to the factory workers of a small town in the spring of 1987, the president of Serbia, Slobodan Milošević, thus castigated the continuing violence (often rape) by Albanians against Serbs in the province of Kosovo: "With every assaulted Serbian child a stain falls on every Albanian who has not prevented such a shameful thing." John B. Allcock has aptly identified this populist reaction as "the language of traditional Balkan values—the collective responsibility of kin for the defence of moral values, and shared responsibility for the avoidance of shame."[43]

Cultural Mobilization by Generation

A culture reads like a film. It is filled with recurring images of things, people, and action, and with things over which other things are said and done, including the trivial and quotidian,[44] which are sometimes no less political than some of the things that make a big noise. Everyone who comes into contact with a culture, stranger and native alike, reads it, sees it, and responds to it. Everyone, however, does not read, see, hear, taste, smell, sense, and understand it in the same way.

Speech traffic is an insufficient criterion of the meaning of a culture. The only sufficient criterion is the collective criterion of a whole culture—the mass of accumulated information "in the form of representations distributed through a population, as well as in artifacts and event structures that can be 'read.' " New "readings," new representations, are possible, for no cultural system is wholly closed. Such readings may also be counterfactual but nonetheless real, creating new facts by the very fact of their having been imagined. A new text may assume many different forms. It may include, among other things, "resistance to increase of scale" or the expression of a preference for Platonic over neo-Aristotelian solutions.[45]

New cultural readings are made in part in response to the increased effectiveness of communication in time and across space, culminating in the production of a succession of generational cohorts at intervals of two or three decades. Age cohorts have existed since time immemorial. They are simply groups of people falling into specific age categories as a result of which they are expected to behave in specific ways. When they move into a different age category, other modes of behavior are expected of them. The generation or generational cohort, on the other hand, is a relatively new phenomenon. Identifiable by special temporal, spatial, social, and thematic referents, it retains a more or less permanent character based not upon the specific age of its members but on a crucial common experience during late adolescence and early adulthood. The members of a generation act as cultural mediators and mobilizers. In the smaller cultures, they give a national form to "cultural flows" from other and especially from the more dynamic or culturally and politically more powerful cores of a new world system of cultural intercommunication. Without necessarily reaching uniform conclusions, they generally raise similar questions.[46] Constituted for the first time during a period of growing European male ascendancy (1760–1860), the membership of the early Balkan generations was almost exclusively male.

The earliest evidence of the later coming of generations among the Balkan peoples may have been the response of the émigré Greek thinker, Adamantios Korais, in 1798, to a pamphlet attributed to Patriarch Anthinos of Jerusalem that may have been the work of Ecumenical Patriarch Gregory V. Under the suitably expressive title *Paternal Teaching*, the patriarchal missive aimed to mobilize Orthodoxy against Napoleon and the French Revolution. Entitled no less appropriately *Fraternal Teaching*, the counterpamphlet, had as its object a countermobilization.[47]

Under the term "mobilization," Karl W. Deutsch subsumes the social, economic, and technological kinetics by which a population is organized "for relatively more intensive communication."[48] But mobilization cannot be effected without mobilizers, and the critical mobilizers—the mobilizers who direct a population toward new means and goals—are new generational cohorts with links to the young and young movements even though some of their gurus may not be so young.[49]

A product in part of the emergence of a succession of generational cohorts, nationalist movements have also been likened to "children's crusades."[50] That may not be an inaccurate representation if by children one means persons in their teens and twenties—marginal persons in quest of (a new?) identity, who rebel against parents, especially fathers, and against intruders upon their own sentiments of territoriality. The rebels find security with new gurus, becoming their own fathers or finding surrogate fathers to provide them with a new system of beliefs.

The young guru of the linguistic reform of the 1830s and 1840s in Croatia, as a result of which the Croats gave up their literary languages in the *kaj*-idiom of Zagreb and *ča*-idiom of Rijeka (Fiume) for a third literary language, *štokavski*, was Ljudevit Gaj, son of Julijana Schmidt, whose German father had immigrated to Croatia in the 1770s when she was a child, and of Johann Gay (perhaps of a family originally from Gayerstein), a German immigrant to Croatia from Hungarian Slovakia. Even as a child, growing up in the romantic era of "sensibility," Ljudevit Gaj felt the *štokavski* dialect to be more beautiful than the *kajkavski*. Upon later visiting Karlovac, a center of Habsburg Serb commercial enterprise in the territories of the Croatian Military Frontier, he was moved by the "vigorous language" of "the core of *our Croat and Serb nation*."[51]

Never wholly resolved, Croatia's first identity crisis of the 1830s and 1840s, known as the "Illyrian" movement (hence, mobilization), has been followed by a succession of further identity crises and spatio-political orientations—pro-"Illyrian" (that is neo-Aristotelian or pro-Yugoslav) followed by anti-"Illyrian" (that is Platonic or anti-Yugoslav). Since 1840, Croatia may have experienced six such conjunctures. All but the first have been little investigated as generational reactions to changing social, political, and economic conjunctures—generational responses to modifications in the workings of the world world-economy and its multiple political containers.

A signifying event of the emergence of a second Croat generation was the formation in 1861 by Ante Starčević and Eugen Kvaternik of a so-called Party of Right(s), for which Serbs were but "old" Croats.[52] From that point of view, the orientation of the Party of Rights was neo-Aristotelian.

As a defender of the particular state rights of Croatia, however, the group also embraced a Platonic world view. As an exponent of privilege and an opponent of liberty and equality, it reflected the post-1848 reaction against the ideas of the Enlightenment and French Revolution. By 1885, perhaps earlier, even a former exponent of the Illyrian idea, Bishop Josip Juraj Strossmayer, who had tried without avail to persuade the papacy to authorize the use in Croatia of the

Glagolitic in place of the Latin liturgy, embraced a view not unlike that of the Party of Rights by distinguishing between (presumably good) Croatian "western-ness" and (presumably bad) Serbian "easternness."[53]

Generational movements also emerged among the other Balkan peoples, earliest of all among the Greeks. Corresponding to the first Croat generation both in time of occurrence and in its predilection for a neo-Aristotelian, perhaps even Alexandrian, view of space—for the *Megali* Idea—was a Greek generation to which the Greek political leader Ioannis Kolettes gave voice on January 15, 1844: "The kingdom of Greece is not Greece. It is but the smallest and poorest part of Greece. Greece includes not only the kingdom but also the inhabitants of Ioannina, Thessaloniki, Seres, Adrianople, Constantinople, Trebizond, Crete, and Samos, and every land of Greek history or of the Greek people."[54]

Corresponding in time to what I have identified as the second Croat generation was a Greek generation, neither quite Platonic nor (after Britain's cession to Greece of the Ionian Islands in the early 1860s) aggressively neo-Aristotelian, which was instrumental in forming philosophical societies known as *syllogoi*, among them the Hellenic Literary Society of Constantinople (founded in 1861) and the Association for the Propagation of Greek Letters (founded in Athens in 1869). Each of these "national" clubs possessed branch associations in the smaller cities of Greece and Turkey. In 1878, there were some twenty such *syllogoi* in Istanbul.

By 1890, however, arose yet another generation of educated Greek youth subscribing to other ways of attaining their national goals. The discourse of the previous generation was not abandoned, but the new generation organized for *action*. By 1892, it was not uncommon to regard the old form of organization, defined primarily by discourse, as *syllogomania*.[55]

A third South Slav generational structure, on the upbeat and favorable to the Yugoslav idea like that of the first and fifth generations, similarly was formed during the 1890s. A critical event in its affirmation was the founding in Serbia, in 1901, of the *Srpski Književni Glasnik* (Serbian Literary Herald) by Bogdan Popović (literary critic and professor of literature at the new University of Belgrade), Slobodan Jovanović (literary critic and historian), and Jovan Skerlić (literary critic, historian, and orator).

Of critical importance was the fact that the founders of *Srpski Književni Glasnik* had completed their formal education in France and were advocates of French revolutionary ideas of liberty and self-determination and opponents of medieval or Germanic ideas of privilege or liberties, hence, dissymmetry and inequality. They preferred positive law to organic or purely historical right.

In addition, Bogdan Popović was the initiator (by an article in Serbian on Pierre-Augustin Beaumarchais, published in 1889) of a literary reform that came to be known as the *beogradski stil* (Belgrade style) and which Miodrag B. Petrovich has characterized as "the French style of writing and expression." By means of the *beogradski stil*, the Serbian written language was reintegrated with the spoken popular idiom and freed "from its traditional cumbersome structure." Introduced in 1889 and institutionalized between 1901 and 1914, the "Belgrade style" represented an option in favor of brevity, simplicity, lightness, and direct-ness of expression. As such, it was an indirect critique of the Germanic heaviness and complexity so characteristic of the literary language of Zagreb. At the level of literary action during the decade preceding the Great War, the Belgrade style complemented the contemporaneous acts of Serbian political and economic lib-eration from domination by the Dual Monarchy. Some pro-Yugoslav Croats— among them Josip Smodlaka (founder in 1905 of the Croatian Democratic party) and Viktor Novak (born in the *kajkavian*-speaking Croatian Zagorje and, after the Great War, professor of Croatian history at the University of Belgrade)— accepted the Belgrade style, the *ekavski* speech, or both. The triumph of the Belgrade style and affirmation of a Serbian expression of the Yugoslav idea were the product of the emergence, between 1880 and 1900, of Belgrade as an urban core of communication or cultural mobilization. The tiny capital of Serbia be-came the center of an all-Serbian culture, with 25 newspapers in 1882 (as against 4 in all the other towns of Serbia) and 126 newspapers and magazines in 1912 (as against 71 in the other towns of Serbia).[56]

On the eve of the Balkan wars and before the start of the Great War, two main questions were raised by the Serbian and Croatian intelligentsia: Should there be a Yugoslav state? Should that state have a unitary language? In the writings and speeches of this third generation occurred a crescendo of reaction against *pravaštvo* or corporatist privilege. The reaction was not uniform, but a group of writers, including Jovan Skerlić, Aleksa Šantić, Vladimir Čerina, and Djordje Pejanović, embraced both the idea of Yugoslav unity and of a common literary language in the *štokavian-ekavian* dialect or literary language of Serbia.[57]

Then came the Great War and, at its end, the destruction of the Dual Monar-chy, the creation of a Serb-Croat-Slovene state, later renamed Yugoslavia, and rabid competition for jobs and cultural markets between the political and cultural mobilizers of the Belgrade style and *ekavski* dialect, on the one hand, and the mobilizers of the Zagreb style and western *(i)jekavski* dialect. That competition among the members of the fourth generation complemented the concurrent competition between Belgrade and Zagreb for political power and commodity and capital markets.

As a form of cultural-political competition among powerful mobilizing cities, nationalism is fundamentally an urban movement.[58] It normally represents the ideology of an interior or otherwise protected city. Offering protection to neigh-boring territories by appeals to ethnicity, religion, or other possible ties, the mobilizing political city strives to obtain taxpayers and markets. If it succeeds, it can proceed to strengthen its authority and find an outlet to the sea. Examples of interior capital cities that have so acted include Paris, Vienna, Madrid, Moscow, Warsaw, Bucharest, Sofia, Belgrade, Zagreb, and Sarajevo.

Where the process of state formation is slow and the result of centuries of give-and-take, to the eventual advantage of the populations of both the annexing or expanding state and the annexed territories, a "core area" is formed that is culturally, politically, and economically dominant. In that case, a clear hierarchical distinction may appear among the primary city or highest-order central place, the country's second city, and so on down the line, with a rank-size ordering of cities.[59]

But the territories knit together at the conclusion of World War I as the Kingdom of Serbs, Croats, and Slovenes had had a great diversity of foreign political experiences—Byzantine, Carolingian, Venetian, Ottoman, Hungarian, and Austrian. Between the two twentieth-century world wars (or were they one?), Belgrade, the capital of a nominally victorious Serbia, continued to be the focus of political power in the expanded kingdom. Zagreb, the capital of Croatia, a former enemy territory, retained much of its former strength as an economic and financial center.[60]

The wretched tale of rivalry between Yugoslavia's two cities—Belgrade and Zagreb—and later among three and more than three cities (Ljubljana, Sarajevo) culminated during World War II in the occupation of Yugoslavia by Germany, Italy, Bulgaria, Albania, and Hungary; in a civil war, with Croats and Bosnian and Albanian Muslims fighting against the Serbs; in the formation of a Croatian puppet state; in the waging by the leaders of that state of a genocidal massacre of several hundred thousand Croatian and Bosnian Serbs; and in the formation of several rival guerrilla movements and triumph in that struggle, partly as a result of political decisions by the American and British governments, of the pro-communist Partisans of Marshal Josip Broz Tito, a Croatian from the Zagorje.

At the end of World War II and the formation of a second Yugoslavia under communist rule, Zagreb recovered its status as Yugoslavia's chief economic city. Belgrade reverted to its interwar status as the main political city, the capital alike of Yugoslavia and of the republic of Serbia—but of a territorially diminished Serbia, punished for having produced the rival resistance movement of Draža Mihailović.

By the 1960s, however, Belgrade began to catch up to Zagreb in the economic realm. Having favored the notion of economic aid by the economically more developed republics (Croatia and Slovenia in particular) to the economically less developed republics of the south, it embraced the idea of giving primarily a "Danubian" orientation to economic development—an orientation, according to Croatian economists, toward a nearly closed Black Sea or limited world market in opposition to Zagreb's choice of an "Adriatic" orientation, designed to obtain access to the whole world. It also sought to realize a goal to which it had aspired since the 1840s—the development of a flourishing "political port" at Bar, in the Serb republic of Montenegro. Above all, it embraced what a Croatian economist called a "big brother" view of Serbia's role—"equal rights but greater duties" for Serbia—as the state builder and economic director.[61]

Serbs and Croats agreed in principle that the uneven apportionment of factor equipment—capital, land, labor, skills, information, and enterprise—gave a comparative advantage to one or more factors over the others. But the Croats argued that the advantage lay primarily with the factors of capital and labor skills, therefore, with an Adriatic orientation. The Serbs contended that capital and labor should be mobilized and brought to the point of immobility, that is, to the areas of concentration of raw materials, so that heavy transportation costs might be avoided. The Slovenes differed from the Croats only in emphasizing that the most-developed republic—Slovenia—should be the primary beneficiary of capital investment for its function as an all-purpose (cultural, geographic, and economic) link to Europe and its connection to the whole world by way of the Adriatic. Behind such economic views lay two distinct spatio-political orientations.[62]

The political rivalry between Belgrade and Zagreb—the two main cores of Yugoslavia—intensified as the economic capabilities of Belgrade grew, particularly as the banks of the Serbian-Yugoslav capital became, during the 1960s, the primary source of investment funds for commercial and economic development.[63] The fall from power in 1966 of Aleksandar Ranković, head of the secret police and vice-president of the federal republic, similarly had the effect of giving Serbian national aspirations an economic focus.

Croatian political leaders and the Croatian media thereupon pursued a systematic policy of mobilizing culture on behalf of a Croatian *état politique*. Culture, politics, and economics were inextricably intertwined. An increased openness in public affairs culminated in an intensification of ethnic rivalries. The government clamped down in 1972, but following the death of Tito in 1980 the media resumed their function as molders of public opinion. The ethnic quarrels became more strident.

Just as the first four generational movements were a reflection of specific economic reorientations and world-economic readjustments, so the fifth (pro-Yugoslav) and sixth (anti-Yugoslav) generational movements respectively reflected changes in the world-economy and its political containers from 1950 to 1966–73 and from 1967–74 well into the 1990s. The fifth generational and political- economic conjuncture may be discerned through the responses to the countrywide sample survey carried out in 1966 by the Yugoslav Center for Public Opinion Research. Executed with professional objectivity, the survey contained thirty-eight attitudinal statements that were designed to measure ethnic distance (readiness to marry, make friends, work and collaborate with a member of a different group) and particularism among the several South Slavic ethnic groups of Yugoslavia. The greatest ethnic distance from the other groups showed up among Slovenians, the greatest particularism among Macedonians, with the widest divergence occurring between Slovenians and Macedonians. On the other hand, there was a close convergence in the responses of the Serbs and Croats, leading one scholar to surmise that the subsequent resurgence of antagonism between the two groups was "primarily an elitist movement."[64] Another scholar concluded that the feelings of ethnic distance were stronger "among the most highly educated respondents" than among the rest of the population.[65] The fifth cultural and political-economic expression of generational difference thus was coming to an end, merging with the sixth.

Between the late 1960s and 1990, the growth of openness and expression of public opinion converged with a slowing down of the rate of expansion of both the Yugoslav and the world-economy. As a result, public opinion tended to organize, indirectly at least, around several different ethnic and territory-oriented views of the world, as projected in particular by the rival media of Yugoslavia's major urban cores (Belgrade, Zagreb, Sarajevo) and territorial subdivisions (six republics and two autonomous areas).

In March 1967, under the inspiration of Matica Hrvatska (Croatian Queen [Mother] Bee), the chief gatekeeper of Croatian literary and linguistic activity, a group of Croatian literary organizations and leading writers denounced the 1954 Novi Sad agreement at which fifth-generation Yugoslav teachers and intellectuals had identified the chief language of the country as Serbo-Croat or Croato-Serb, and agreed to create a commission to devise a common dictionary, of which a short version was published in 1960. The new view of Matica Hrvatska was that there was a separate Serb and a separate Croat language and that the only authentic language for Croatia was Croatian. Before the end of 1970, it withdrew from the collaborative project with Matica Srpska (Serb Queen [Mother] Bee) to produce a definitive dictionary of the Serbo-Croat literary language.

Between November 1970 and December 1971, the membership of Matica Hrvatska grew from 2,323 to nearly 41,000. In the spring of 1971, it organized its own weekly newspaper, *Hrvatski Tjednik*, which had a circulation by the end of the year of more than 100,000. At the same time, it fostered the appearance of specialized parallel publications, such as the *Hrvatski Gospodarski Glasnik* (Croatian Economic Herald) of the Zagreb Society of Economists. It also obtained entry into Croatia's large economic enterprises. With their physical resources and financial support it was able to expand its mobilizing activities. It undertook "head-counts" in businesses, government offices, and other establishments to prevent the overrepresentation of Serbs and other non-Croats in managerial and administrative positions. Winning the sympathy of local and republican officials, it aided the transformation of *Studentski List* from a student newspaper into a forum for Croatian nationalism. As the new coordinator of Croatia's political, economic, and cultural elites, it framed all questions in a Croat national context. In the summer of 1971, the Croatian Philological Society and Školska Knjiga (a Croatian textbook publishing house) clamored that two-thirds of all time devoted to teaching history in Croatian schools should be devoted exclusively to Croatian history. In only a slightly less nationalist and parochial tone, the Zagreb daily *Vjesnik* and Radio-Television (RTV) Zagreb followed suit.

The Croatian media thus converged upon a common goal—the mobilization of Croats in the exclusive interest of Croatian nationalism by isolating Croatia from Serbia, that part of Yugoslavia with which the greatest convergence had occurred, and thus undermining the unfinished process of making Yugoslavs out of Serbs and Croats.[66]

Sabrina P. Ramet correctly observes that the perception of a threat to one's group may "stimulate recourse to countervailing action. . . . Threat perception may, thus, be manipulated." But Ramet adds, "It seems not to have been manipulated" in the Croatian case, "at least not consciously: those nationalists who anxiously warned Croats of impending Serbianization were convinced that the threat was real."[67] No doubt they were convinced of the reality of the threat. But the Croatian media did manipulate the threat perception. As media, they were manipulators by definition—manipulators who, by their separatism, did not want to compete in a common market for language and ideas with the Serbian media.

The response of the Serbian media and mediators to Croatian cultural and political separatism, especially during the 1980s, was to reanimate Serbian nationalism, revive the idea of *jugoslovenstvo* or "Yugoslav nationality," decry the inefficiency of a system of six or even eight separate republican or quasi-republican economies, denounce the policy of applying national and republican "keys" (ethnic quotas) in the staffing of cadres and federal institutions, accuse Croatians of favoring economic policies that were designed to primitivize Serbia, advocate the separation of Dalmatia from Croatia, and raise the question not simply of *Ustaša* (Croatians who collaborated with Germany) responsibility but of a more general Croatian responsibility for the genocide of hundreds of thousands of Serbs, Gipsies, and Jews in Croatia and Bosnia-Hercegovina—with the numbers always deflated by the Croats and inflated by the Serbs—during World War II. Among the leading Serbian mediators and media in the formulation of some aspects of that response were the novelist and first president of the new (since 1992) rump Yugoslavia, Dobrica Ćosić; the dissident Marxist philosopher Mihajlo Marković, for several years a tenured professor at the University of Pennsylvania and later vice-president of Serbia's Socialist party; the linguist Pavle Ivić; the gifted caricaturist Milenko Mihajlović; Belgrade's *Književne Novine* (Literary News); and the Serbian Academy of Sciences and Arts.[68]

Marxist intellectuals bear some responsibility for the sad turn of the national question in Yugoslavia: the anti-Serbian bias of the Marxist leadership during the 1920s and 1930s, its recognition and encouragement of a separate (Slav)-Macedonian written language and nationality in the 1940s, its recognition during the 1960s and early 1970s of a separate Muslim (that is, Bosnian or Slavic Muslim) nationality, and the ideological shifts on the national question of the Slovene Marxist ideologist, Edvard Kardelj.

In 1939, under the pseudonym Sperans, Kardelj published a book entitled *Razvoj slovenskega narodnega vprašanja* in which he identified nationality as a permanent and only slowly transformable phenomenon. In 1957, he published a revised edition of the book, with an emphasis on the fluid character of language and culture. Convinced at that time that Yugoslavia was moving toward economic integration, he expressed faith in the possibility of developing a "socialist Yugoslav consciousness." But economic integration did not come. Kardelj therefore backtracked during the 1970s.[69] Not surprisingly, his changing views reflected the changing outlook of the three Yugoslav generations of the same overall period.

The six generational world views of the Yugoslav experience—duplicated in somewhat altered form among the other Balkan cultures—correspond to three interconnected stages of national and capitalist development, each with an upward economic phase and a neo-Aristotelian conception of identity and territoriality followed by a slowdown or downward economic movement and an attraction to a Platonic conception of identity and territoriality. The first generational outlook emerged concurrently with the initial joining of capitalism and the ideology of market economy, the second with the slowdown of international trade of many individual countries as more countries entered the world market. The third generational world view corresponds to an expansion and revision of capitalism, while the fourth reflects the crisis of the world world-economy and state system in which that economy functioned. The fifth generational experience corresponds to the formation of two world blocs, one led by the United States and the other by the Soviet Union, both possessing a confident ideology, both wedded to the idea of economic growth. A decline in the rate of expansion of world trade, a decline in the standard of living, a readiness to use political means to achieve frustrated economic expectations, challenges to economic growth even in the midst of a growing commitment to consumption, student and youth rebellions and gender and ethno-religious divisions, the diffusion of microelectronic technologies and transnational corporate enterprise to the disadvantage of second- and third-category states, the growing threat of ecological disaster, and the demise of the Soviet Union made up the sociopolitical and economic climate in which the sixth generation was nurtured.

With or Without a Civil Society?

Added to the problem of generations as it evolved in the context of the world world-economy was the problem of some important differences between the sociopolitical evolution of the Balkan cultures and the sociopolitical evolution of the western and central European cultures. In the 1860s, for example, Andrew Archibald Paton collated what he believed to be "the respective laws of [the three stages of] Saxon and Slaavic [sic] revolutionary development" and expression (see Table 7.1).

Despite Austria's "Germanic nucleus," observed Paton, "her destiny has been determined by the large preponderance of the Slaavic element." The "law of Slaavic ... revolutionary development," however, has impeded the "development of the spontaneous energies of the individual man."[70]

Table 7.1

Paton's Three Stages of Saxon and Slavic Political Expression

Ethnicity	First Stage	Second Stage	Third Stage
Saxon	Emancipation of towns by sovereigns as counterpoise to feudal nobles.	Emancipation of peasantry from serfdom.	Power of crown and aristocracy limited; fuller representation of third estate.
Slavic	Emancipation of towns by sovereigns as counterpoise to feudal nobles.	Comparative cessation of anarchy and consolidation of the power of the crown by the substitution of standing armies for the feudal system.	Emancipation of peasantry from serfdom by the crown in spite of the prejudices of the nobles. Aristocracy balanced by bureaucracy; subordination of all civil privileges to the scheme of military defence.

Source: Paton, *Researches on the Danube and the Adriatic*, II, 174–75. (Italicized in Paton.)

For a confirmation of, but also a corrective to, Paton's analysis, one has but to return to the preceding chapter. One should also add Henry Wickham Steed's observation that the institution "most nearly" corresponding to the Habsburg monarchy's "professed purpose" was "the Army," which was commanded and administered by an officers' staff that was "a kind of Samurai caste." The "joint army" of the Dual Monarchy, further observed Oscar Jászi,

> formed a real state within the state, the members of which—especially its officers and under-officers—breathed first of all throughout their whole life the spirit of their military colleges or their regiments and not that of their mother-nations. Indeed the fatherland of the officers' staff was the whole monarchy and not the territory of a particular nation. It was a real educational principle in the army to move the officers around from one country to another. These men who lived now in Vienna, now in Budapest, now in Prague and then in Zagreb, in Galicia, in Transylvania, in Bosnia, or in the Bocche [di Cattaro, Boka Kotorska] represented a certain spirit of internationalism confronted with the impatient and hateful nationalism of their surroundings.

Often speaking a special language, derisively identified by the literati as *arärisch deutsch* or "fiscal German," with little heed for the common rules of grammar, they "constituted something like an *anational caste*," a bulwark against the ideologies of the competing nationalities and ethnicities of the empire.[71] They constituted an obstacle to the formation of a civil society.

Paton's analysis was correct in regard to the organization of the territories of the Sava axis or fragile, contested economic core of what became Yugoslavia. These territories had existed for three centuries as three different systems of military marches—a Habsburg, a Venetian, and an Ottoman system. Paton described the Habsburg system, whose population was made up in large measure of Orthodox Serbs:

> There is no landed aristocracy in the country; the peasantry pay no rent, and scarcely any taxes, but in lieu thereof maintain a military force in proportion to each family. A house with three sons furnishes a soldier; five sons, two soldiers; and so on; nourished by the family, but receiving uniform, arms, and accoutrements from the government. The active service is from twenty to twenty-three years of age; they are then enrolled in the reserve, and the district is divided geographically into regiments instead of counties; so that it is one vast camp, every soldier being a peasant, and every peasant a soldier.[72]

How very different this Croatian Military Frontier was from the Banat! How different, too, from so-called Civil Croatia to the north, with its servile Croat peasantry, Hungarian or cosmopolitan nobility, barely two hundred landowners in possession of a quarter of the farmland, German middle elements, a flourishing bureaucracy, and tradition of a legalistic quasi-civil society, whose ultimate form was *pravaštvo*—the mobilization of law in defense of privilege and in the supposed interest of a homogeneous Croatian culture.

For complex historical reasons, eastern, southeastern, and east central Europe were slower than western Europe in producing and consolidating an effective civil society—or, to adopt Montesquieu's terminology, in producing an *état civil* to hold in check the *état politique*, whether concentrated or dispersed. In Byzantium, a "civil life" had existed but had been dependent upon the state. Later it was weakened through the dissemination of an antiurban monasticism and ascetism, especially in the form of Hesychasm.[73] In the Ottoman Balkans, the practice of ethno-religious separatism discouraged the affirmation of urban autonomy.

State development in western Europe, on the other hand, evolved "in the midst of a pre-existent civil society," which antedated industrialization by hundreds of years.[74] A civil society, maintains Frans A.M. Alting von Geusau, comprises a network of group associations that are independent of but strive to affect the instituted political power and have done so historically through the community of a shared city instead of a common ancestry. Its strength derives more from the market than from the bonds of family or local patronage.[75]

On the basis of this definition, one would have to conclude that the French Revolution, at least in one of its phases, aimed to abolish civil society, especially when it sought to promote civic virtue. By abolishing or refusing to recognize all intermediate interest and professional groups between the individual and the nation (state), it augmented the role of the primary political city (Paris), subordinating commerce to the exigencies of politics.

The notion of a "civil society" as the experience of "a shared city," however, in which many diverse groups participate in determining a common destiny, may be incomplete. To formulate the problem with greater precision, one should embrace a three-sector model of societal analysis, implicit already in Alexis de Tocqueville but which Robert Wuthnow has raised to an explicit level. The three sectors would include the state, the market, and voluntary associations, with the third sector being defined as "those activities in which neither formal coercion nor the profit-oriented exchange of goods is the dominant principle."[76] This definition, too, may have to be improved, but it has an advantage over the conceptualization of a civil society as simply a two-sectored model—that is, as one in which the "shared city" serves the purpose of restraining the political or command sector and redefining its means and goals—by its division of the notion of a shared city (understood, of course, in a plural sense) into two main parts, with an ensuing reduction of the authority of the state as an independent actor.

Let us also explore the relationship between the experience of "a shared city" and the experience in Europe of at least three categories of nation-state development, each associated with a particular area, thus with three different convergences of space and time. One space-time group of nation-states, maintains Theodor Schieder, was the product of a community of will imposed upon the state, as in England, France, Scandinavia, and the Low Countries. A second space-time group included Germany and Italy, in which political unity was a response to literary-linguistic unity but in which a civil society based upon privilege(s) preceded political unity. A third space-time group was the product of the fragmentation of four great polyethnic states—Poland, Russia, the Habsburg monarchy, and the Ottoman Empire—by power struggles; by appeals to the principles of self-determination, socialism, and linguistic unity; and by the violation of the principle of linguistic unity and constitution of smaller multinational or polyethnic states—and, in the case of the Soviet Union, of a great socialist multinational state—on the model of the polyethnic states that they helped to destroy.[77]

A more highly developed civil society exists in the first group of states, in which a relatively unhindered circulation of goods, information, and opinions has prevailed for a longer period than in the third group and parts of the second. In the second group, the alliance between civil society and privilege lasted much longer than in the first group. The third group possesses a fragmented political experience. To the extent that it has known some degree of civil society, that civil society has tended, in the regions close to Germany or Italy, to resemble the civil society of the second group of states. The southern regions of the third group of states, on the other hand, have wavered between three political models —the model of the western group of European states, the model of the middle group of European states, and the eastern model of despotism. Their experience of a European form of civil society has been brief.

The southern regions were not without a civil society but lacked a civil society of the type present in the first and second groups of states. The basis of civil society in the Balkans lay in a sharp separation of city and country, especially mountain country—in the relative freedom of the country so long as it paid the expected tributes. In the first two groups of states, city air made free. In the third group, only mountain air made free.

As exemplified by the league of the forty-four villages of Souli, the forty-six villages of the Zagora, the twenty-four villages of the Pelion, and the five villages of Metsovo, and by the privileges of such island communities as Chios, Naxos, Mykonos, Amorgos, and others,[78] a restricted rural civil life did exist in the Balkans. It was evident also in the *knežina* institution of Serbia and in the village confederations of the districts of Vrancea and Tigheciu in Moldavia.[79] As for voluntary associations, there was hardly a district in the Balkans where they did not exist, especially in the form of mutual aid.

The spatial outlook of the civil society of the Balkans, however, was local, primarily rural, and ambivalent toward the promotion of security along the arteries of commerce, which, in the Ottoman Balkans, were also the arteries of despotism (routes of war and the command economy). By that very fact, interregional and long-distance commerce could not serve as a foundation for the development of an integrated market economy. If there was a civil society in the Balkans, it was founded upon principles of kinship, friendship, and localism. It did not serve as a mediator between state and society but rather as an isolator. What had to be achieved, therefore, was a new form of civil society, one based upon principles of intercommunication.

Among the Greeks and perhaps even among the non-Greeks, the Phanariots might have become the agents of the kind of civil society that was also the propagator of what Volney had called a *grande société*, or society—in Tocquevillian terms—of many intermediaries or voluntary associations between the state as a communicator and other agents of social and cultural communication.[80] Reaching the zenith of their authority only around 1800, however, when the appropriate means of communication from district to district began to be defined as national languages, the Phanariots were unable to play that role. Soon thereafter the partition of the Ottoman Empire began in earnest.

The Greek diasporas were also well suited to playing the role of mediators. For a long time, however, even until the latter part of the nineteenth century, their primary function was not as intermediaries between a Greek or Ottoman state, on the one hand, and local Greek communities, on the other, but between two or more groups of non-Greek states and their sources of supply and objects of demand. Their focus was transnational, akin in some respects to the focus of the multinational or transnational corporate enterprises that succeeded them in the nineteenth and especially the twentieth centuries.

The creation of an appropriate type of civil society may also have been hindered in the Ottoman Balkans and successor states by the fact that a large segment of the urban upper social strata in the non-Greek areas was culturally (if not always in a narrow ethnic sense) undeniably Greek, accentuating the separation between urban and rural. In Belgrade, for example, Serbian townsmen went about with worry beads *(brojanice)* and wore a half-melon cap *(dinjara)* in the manner of the Greeks until the mid-nineteenth century. Prominent townsmen addressed each other as *kir* (or *ćir*) and their wives as *kira* (or *ćira*), from the Greek words for "sir" and "madam." Belgrade newspapers of the time usually included the rubric *Greciia* (Greece), and Greek was the language of the Christian "higher strata" of Belgrade society until about 1840. One of the best-known Belgrade cafés was the Xenodokheion tes Rossias (Russian Inn, in Greek), known in the folk idiom as Kod Rusije (At Russia's, in Serbian).[81] The customary word for painter in the Serbian principality was still *zograf*, again borrowed from the Greek.

Between 1750 and 1850, on the other hand, under the influence of immigrant Hungarian Serbs, a word for "painter" borrowed from German—*moler*—gained increasing currency. The new term reflected other changes—the spread of Baroque influences from Austria to Hungary, from Russia to the Hungarian Serbs, and from Italy to Mount Athos and thence northward to Hungary; a decline in fresco or wall painting in favor of ikon painting for the iconostasis of Orthodox churches; the diffusion of copper engraving; the introduction of paysage in church paintings; and, under the influence of the painters of Vienna, Buda, Pest, and Pressburg, the practice of making portraits of living persons.[82]

Both the foregoing groups and the Balkan promoters of the nation-state, however, were ambivalent toward, or hostile to, the principle of localism, which they often identified with anarchy.[83] They thus were led to rely upon the state as the agent of social and cultural communication and only slowly created a fragile civil society of communicating intermediaries between the state and local groups.

The tradition of local cultures, however, was strong. A product of that tradition and son of a departmental prefect, the socialist Svetozar Marković thus proposed in the early 1870s that Serbia be divided into fifty grand communes, each sufficiently small to make communication and an appreciation of local problems possible but sufficiently well provided in natural and human resources to make it economically viable.[84] Communist Yugoslavia similarly paid lip service to the idea of local government.

In revised form, the selective Balkan tradition of local autonomy joined to the practice of regular and intensive intercommunication may provide a basis for a viable civil society. A new referent of local identity, dissociated both from integralism and from the localisms of privilege, despotism, and ignorance, may arise. It may be imbued, as in Brittany,[85] with a concern both for the conservation and proper utilization of resources and with a view of the local environment as a patrimony to be protected.

The process of creating appropriate voluntary associations of communicating intermediaires was slowest in the Ottoman territories of Turkish ethnicity. The reason for that slowness was that the Ottoman state itself was for many centuries, according to Dunkwart A. Rustow, not only "an educational institution" but "essentially a military camp." The Tanzimat reforms of the half-century before 1876 may have aspired to a distinction between civil administration and military administration. They failed, however, to diminish the distinction between proper-tied persons worthy of respect and authority and persons whose primary function was production and reproduction. In republican Turkey, the valuation of "gentle-manly etiquette" persisted well into the 1960s. The prestige of officers, educa-tors, and "gentlemen employers" continued to impede the development of a civil society.[86]

At the same time, the nineteenth and twentieth centuries have been a time of encroachment by European and other states into both the market sector and the spheres of activity of the voluntary associations. The Balkan cultures now have fewer appropriate outside models as well as fewer domestic models on the basis of which to promote a viable civil society.

Rechtsstand or Gesetzstaat?

Diverted from the course of a civil society first by populism and fascism (1920s and 1930s) and then by communism, the third group of European territories has been beset since the 1960s and especially since the 1980s—following the loss of faith in the promises of communist ideology and the subsequent weakening or collapse, between 1989 and 1991, of the communist regimes and the ostensible restoration of a multiparty system—by the resurgence of parties of social integra-tion driven by the spirit of an exclusivist groupism. One of the main foyers of this spirit is Croatia, tempted apparently by the Herderian idea of an ill-defined "inner language,"[87] as by the Fichtean idea of the state as an artistic entity whose purpose is culture—the culture of enabling the individual to attain complete freedom by achieving oneness with the authentic nation and state.[88]

The goal of such states, according to Karl W. Deutsch, is the restoration of "an effective inner structure" with which to construct an "effective past" and so implement the implications of the authentic inner structure.[89] The question arises, however, whether this is an appropriate way of instituting a civil society, which by definition should embrace a distinction between the état civil and the état politique, and whose very well-being—in terms of liberal thought—requires the free circulation of opinions as well as goods?

The Croats of Yugoslavia may have felt the need for a separate state precisely because there has been no independent Croatian state since the personal union of Croatia with the kingdom of Hungary in 1102. Following the dismemberment of the first Yugoslavia in 1941, the major achievement of the satellite Ustaša Cro-atian state of Ante Pavelić was genocide. Soon after the inception of the Ustaša

MILE BUDAK : "SRBE NA VRBE"

state, the Croatian minister of education announced the policy of his government: Kill a third of the Serbian population of Croatia, expel another third, and convert the remainder to Catholicism. Mainly as the result of such policies, the proportion of Serbs in Croatia (excluding Bosnia and Hercegovina, which were also annexed to Croatia) declined from a fourth of the total population in 1910 to an eighth of the total in 1990. Before the partly forced conversions to Catholicism of the seventeenth and eighteenth centuries, the proportion of Orthodox Serbs in Croatia had probably been greater than in 1910. Forced conversions were also actively pursued during World War II by the Franciscans of Hercegovina. Particularly active in that endeavor had been the friary of Široki Brijeg.[90]

The *fin-de-siècle* "mobilizing" Croatian intelligentsia—the communications specialists who systematically promoted the idea of Croation separateness from Serbian culture—that broke away from Yugoslavia in the summer of 1991 to form its own independent state rejected the notion of cultural pluralism. It condemned Yugoslavia and Serbia alike for their centralizing policies, both real and imagined. It appears to be determined, however, to pursue a centralizing and integralist policy in Croatia itself, aimed in particular against the Serb minority, descendants of the Serbs and Serbicized Vlachs who fled Ottoman rule to Venetian Dalmatia or to join in the defense of Croatia and the Habsburg monarchy.

Worthy of further inquiry may be the question of the diverse regional and cultural approaches to nationalism. John Plamenatz, for example, distinguishes between a generally western and a generally eastern (east of *Mitteleuropa* but west of Russia) European nationalism. Nationalism of the "western" type typically prevails among peoples who are not culturally insecure—among whom a well-defined high culture (and, by inference, a civil society) preexists the formation of the nation-state. Nationalism of the "eastern" type, on the contrary, requires the creation of a state as a prelude to the elaboration of an authentic culture.[91] The "concentration of power" in its political institutions subsequently obstructs the "division of power" that a civil society implies.[92]

All the Balkan peoples are associated with the "eastern" type of nationalism. But Croat mobilizers and mobilizers in the former Habsburg territories in general are often repelled by association with the culturally and economically "backward" or racially "inferior" Balkan peoples. They yearn for cultural reintegration with *Mitteleuropa*. Prone to a nationalism of the so-called eastern type but with a Fichtean stress during the interwar era and during World War II, they have again been attracted to it as they have been increasingly exposed to a world world-economy that raises expectations, promising sometimes more than it can deliver.

Having a basis in German interwar propaganda but later given an outwardly more objectified form by some geographers of the English-speaking world, a further foundation for the distinction between a "western" and an "eastern" type of nationalism, is the perception that a system of Atlantic cultures in the western regions of Europe is succeeded in the east by a "Shatter Zone" including Poland, Czechoslovakia, Hungary, Romania, and Yugoslavia. That Shatter Zone, writes

Gordon East, is "a zone of transition, on grounds alike of physical, vegetational and cultural geography, between oceanic Europe and the European approaches to northern Asia." The cultural geography of the Shatter Zone identifies it as a zone of dispute between the authority of the two churches, Roman Catholic and Eastern Orthodox, into which Protestantism, Judaism, and the Ottoman Turks and Islam have driven wedges and in which they have established enclaves[93] (see Figure 4.3 on page 139).

The essential thrust of many exponents of the idea of a Shatter Zone, however, is to separate it into its constituent parts—or into such constituent parts as do not represent a potential threat to capitalist hegemony—and to reject the idea of a "common European home," divide the Orthodox Christian cultures from each other, and—when these cultures are by tradition both Slavic and Orthodox—exclude them from the European Community in order to prevent them from becoming sources of criticism of capitalism's new order. Consciously or unconsciously embracing some elements of the foregoing views, the western media have misleadingly portrayed Muslim-dominated polyethnic Bosnia and Hercegovina as an area lying "in the heart of Europe" that must be preserved from what they have unilaterally defined as Serbian aggression and intransigence. One of the arguments that they employed against the continued existence of Yugoslavia, on the other hand, was that it was a Serbian-dominated polyethnic state. Polyethnic states are thus good or bad, depending not upon whether some ethnic group dominates but rather upon which particular ethnic group dominates.

To set the problem in historical perspective, let us return to the decade just before World War I. The leader of the later Croatian Peasant party, Stjepan Radić, proposed at that time that the Hungarians and Danubian Slavs of the Habsburg monarchy, chiefly the Croats and Czechs, take advantage of the religious ties of the Muslim Slavs of Bosnia-Hercegovina to convert Asia Minor into their own colonial area.[94] The vehicle of Radić's ideas, his *Moderna kolonizacija i Slaveni*, was published under the auspices of Matica Hrvatska, the same society that in the late 1960s called for a Croatian literary language distinct from Serbian.

The object of populist Stjepan Radić, who distrusted what he regarded as the unprogressive Orthodox Slavs, was to give Croatia, the Slovenes, and the Czechs an opportunity to join the "global system" of his time, with the Bosnian Muslims acting in the Muslim world as compradors for the commercial interests of the Hungarians and Catholic Danubian Slavs. In much the same manner, the rejuvenated "capitalist system" of the period since 1950, and even more since the demise of the Soviet Union, has resorted to the myth of moral or "civilized" versus amoral or "pariah" states—the last term applied specifically to Serbia—as a means of deflecting "opposition to its hegemonic control of the global system" by dividing the world into good (democratic) states, ready to embrace the ideology and culture of consumerism and transnational corporatism, and recalcitrant bad states.[95]

As the Soviet Union first ceased to be "the evil empire" and then ceased to be altogether between 1989 and 1991, the media, serving as the corporate and political agents of the capitalist system, joined by liberal and nominally radical allies with little comprehension of what was happening, desperately needed an enemy upon whom to deflect criticism of their intentional confusion of capitalism and market economy in order to continue to promote the goals of a consumer society. They found a convenient enemy in Serbia and Yugoslavia. Serbia was a far more convenient enemy than Iran or Iraq, for Iran and Iraq are Muslim states, and Islam had protectors in the United Nations. Islam was also protected by the presence in France, as of 1990, of a Muslim population at least half as great as the total Muslim population (Bosnian, Albanian, and Turkish) of Bosnia, Hercegovina, Kosovo, the Sanjak, and Macedonia and by the presence of Islam in the United States. On the other hand, the countries with an Orthodox Christian tradition and with attachments on the part of a portion of their populations to the ideas alike of the French and Russian revolutions were left without a counterweight to the hegemonic system once France acknowledged the authority of German money and industry and the Soviet Union fell apart. The country in the worst position was Serbia. Its traditions were simultaneously Orthodox, Slavic, communist, and both pro-Russian and pro-French. A *transfer* of feelings of hate thus could be made from the defunct Soviet Union to Serbia, such a much more convenient enemy—a small country then without allies.

Apart from Germany and Austria (that other Germany) in the north and Turkey in the south, whose government is eager to take advantage of local divisions and weaknesses in Cyprus, Albania, Thrace, Macedonia, Kosovo, and Bosnia and Hercegovina in order to recover its centuries-old hegemony in the Balkans and eastern Mediterranean, yet another partisan of the reterritorialization of the Shatter Zone—already reterritorialized during 1991 and 1992 by the breakup of the Soviet Union, Yugoslavia, and Czechoslovakia and the creation of the states of Croatia, Slovenia, the Czech Republic, Slovakia, Moldova, and Macedonia (and further north and east, the Baltic states, Belarus, Ukraine, and the embattled Caucasian and Central Asian republics)—is Hungary, the second half of the former Dual Monarchy. The vice-president of the ruling Hungarian Democratic Forum, István Csurka, thus reacted to the foregoing events by declaring Hungary's need for "living space," consequently, for the return to Hungary of portions of Slovakia, Romania (Transylvania), and Serbia (Vojvodina), in which Hungarian minorities reside. Gheorghe Funar, the Romanian mayor of Transylvanian Cluy (Clausenburg) and presidential candidate in the Romanian elections of September 1992, proposed on the contrary, though in a similarly purist, integralist, and populist vein, that restrictions be imposed on the freedoms of the Hungarian minority in Transylvania.[96]

Let us examine the question of an enemy or enemies, however, from a philosophical-historical perspective. Since the latter part of the 1960s, there has been a revival in Germany of thought that at first sight is Fichtean. Its essential thrust, however, is a return to an estates order of things, in harmony with a new order of unlimited corporate capitalism and consumer culture, to be put into place by appropriately resolving the questions of cultural homogeneity and heterogenity and of friends and foes. I refer to the thought of the German constitutional jurist, Carl Schmitt.

In 1927, Carl Schmitt said of "the total state" that it "potentially embraces every domain. This results in the identity of state and society. In such a state, therefore, everything is at least potentially political, and in referring to the state it is no longer possible to assert for it a specifically political characteristic." Schmitt's view represented a reaction against the conception of Benjamin Constant and Auguste Comte that war (the *état politique*) had lost its usefulness and would yield to an organization of society on the basis of exchange and industry (an *état civil*).[97] Taking a contrary position, Schmitt denied that what others have called a civil society had been effectively instituted in Europe. On the contrary, the distinction between state and society had been dissolved as a result of the French and European revolutions of 1789 and 1848. The organization of society on an estates basis, as a *Rechtsstand*, had been abolished. In its place had been instituted a *Gesetzstaat*, or state governed by the principle of positive law. Such a state constantly replaces old laws with new ones. It may invade every sphere of activity. It does not like to distinguish between public and private.[98]

As the *Gesetzstaat* prevailed, argued Schmitt in post-Hitlerian Germany, the threat to democracy has grown. "Democracy" can thrive only in societies with a homogeneous culture—in societies with a state on the model of the city and with cities on the model of the individual house or human nest, the elementary protective or friendly space.[99] By its very association with the *Gesetzstaat*, democracy promotes heterogeneity. Its fundamental basis is the principle of equality before the law. Its aim is to create what Lucian W. Pye has called "patterns of trust."[100] It promotes, in fact, distrust; the division of persons and groups into two sharply differentiated categories: friends and enemies. It tends, indeed, to identify both external and internal opponents as foes or "absolute" enemies.[101]

The world's states therefore should be reconstituted territorially in conformity with the principle of cultural homogeneity. The interventionist state of heterogeneous citizens needs to be replaced by a state with a basis in the historical and cultural particularities of a homogeneous people and amenable to corporative principles. Capital would be similarly subject to these principles. It would be freed, however, of identification with any single state even though it might be more closely bound to one of several competing associated or federated territorial units *(Grossraüme)*.[102]

Seeming to diverge from Johann Gottlieb Fichte through his critique of the interventionist state, Schmitt in fact returned to Fichte by his aesthetic and ethic of cultural homogeneity. His thought converged, too, with the view prevalent among German thinkers that nature abhors mixture and that the best cultures are those that do not defy nature as they themselves define it.[103] Schmitt's complex theory is adaptable, however, to the demands of capitalism and consumer culture.

The Croatian cultural mobilizers of the sixth generation and their Slovenian contemporaries, and even their ethnic adversaries, perhaps have found partial inspiration for their actions in contemporary German or *Mitteleuropean* sources, including Herderian and Fichtean thought. Commendable as a scholarly endeavor, the active participation of Slovenes and Croats in the Alpen-Adria and Pannonian organizations of *Mitteleuropean* writers gave them an opportunity to emphasize the psychic and cultural distance separating them from the Balkan Serbs.[104] It may also have provided them with direct or indirect access to Schmittian thought.

One of the main sources of inspiration for Serbian political thinkers since the middle of the nineteenth century, on the other hand, has been the very idea that Carl Schmitt has decried—the *Gesetzstaat*, of which the classic Serbian defense occurs in the work of Slobodan Jovanović, *O državi: Osnovi jedne pravne teorije.* The contrasting approaches of the Serbs and Croats of the sixth generation to the ideas of statehood and nationhood may thus emanate not only from their different territorial situations and different ways of conceptualizing territory but from two basically different sources of inspiration—a simultaneously folk and aristocratic German source, with an emphasis upon privilege or corporate and historic rights but amenable to the needs of a capitalist and consumerist culture, and prevalent among the Croats, and a French Jacobin source, with emphasis on equality before the law, especially evident among the Serbs of Serbia.

The closing decades of the twentieth century have been a challenge not only for communism but also for the ideas of the French Revolution. The resurgence of Germany as the dominant European economic and political power has underscored the decline of France both as a source of cultural inspiration and as a pillar of political authority.

Permanent "Narcissism of Minor Differences"

Even a century and a half before Carl Schmitt, Immanuel Kant had discerned "the unsocial sociability of men . . . , their propensity to enter into society, bound together by a mutual opposition which constantly threatens to break up the society." Civil wars and wars between states, he contended, had similar psychological foundations. All wars and revolutions are "so many attempts (not in the intention of man, but in the intention of Nature) to establish new relations among states, and through the destruction or at least dismemberment of all of them to create new political bodies, which again, either internally or externally, cannot maintain themselves and which must thus suffer like revolutions" until there is such an "exact definition of freedom" that everyone is free to oppose so long as the opposition is "consistent with the freedom of others."[105]

Sigmund Freud, too, emphasized the centrality of friend-enemy relationships, stemming from the human "inclination to aggression, which . . . disturbs our relations with our neighbour and which forces civilization into such a high expenditure [of energy]. In consequence of this primary mutual hostility of human beings, civilized society is perpetually threatened with disintegration." At the same time, the inclination to aggression tends "to bind together a considerable number of people in love, so long as there are other people left over to receive the manifestations of their aggressiveness." Indeed, "it is precisely communities with adjoining territories, and related to each other in other ways as well, who are engaged in constant feuds and in ridiculing each other—like the Spaniards and Portuguese, for instance, the North Germans and South Germans, the English and Scotch, and so on." Freud defined the essence of such relationships as "the narcissism of minor differences." The latter sentiment encourages the pursuit of aggression as a means of affirming the cohesion of one imagined group against another.[106]

The historian Fernand Braudel has embraced a view similar to that of Kant and Freud. Every nation, maintained Braudel in a posthumous work devoted to the subject of ethnic and national *identity*, is a house divided. Even France, and especially France, is a house divided, both despite and because of its thousand-year investment in forging a still fragile national unity. Every nation, Braudel believed, both thrives on and, from time to time, is ripped apart by, local, regional, ethno-religious, social, political, and economic differences and disparities and by differences in the hierarchical ordering of temporal and spatial priorities.[107] If even one of Europe's oldest political states is not free of divisions, how much less free from such challenges must be new states with a diversity of political and ethno-religious traditions, states such as Yugoslavia and Romania!

The question of nationhood and statehood can be resolved only in the context of a theoretical conceptualization that goes much beyond Yugoslavia and the Balkans to include the whole of Europe and, indeed, the entire world. What kind of territorial and political organization, one must ask, is appropriate to the performance of particular functions? What kind of territorial and administrative hierarchy should there be for each? Education, communication, defense, local security, banking enterprise, transport (sea, air, river, and land), microelectronic technology, basic industries, agriculture, health, environment, sport, leisure, and the coordination of functions may each require different kinds of hierarchies, different territorial arrangements, and either the abolition of the idea of sovereignty or the adoption of an idea of sovereignty that varies in accordance with each function. In other words, the very idea of the nation-state, and of the state itself, may have to be subjected to deep questioning. If it is retained, the functions to which individual state authority may be applied may have to be reduced. Egalitarian and centralist Jacobin conceptions may be more appropriate in some spheres of action, federalist and particularist conceptions in others. As a unique general principle, neither approach may be desirable.[108]

Fetish, *Mythomoteur*, and the Media

Attachment to a nation-state as the politically organized territory of and for a particular ethnic group or groups is a recent phenomenon, barely more than two centuries old. But if one subscribes to the view of philosopher Božidar Knežević that the newest institutions tend to be the shortest lived, one may also understand how difficult it is to distinguish between a new institution at its peak strength and the beginning of the decline and transformation or disappearance of that institution.

National identity and feeling have grown in strength. But however strong, national feeling may also be superficial, less deep than local and family or clan feeling except among those individuals and groups whose well-being directly depends on the existence of a particular nation-state and the propagation of a particular national identity. National feeling thus constantly has to be reinforced. One of the functions both of the print media and electronic media has been to achieve that reinforcement.

An influential propagator of a distinctive Romanian culture and nation with Thracian or Thraco-Dacian antecedents, the poet philosopher Lucian Blaga (1895–1961), took upon himself the task of showing that Romanians feel and perceive the world about them differently from both their eastern Slavic neighbors and their fellow Saxon inhabitants of Transylvania. The Saxon perception of space, he explained, was one of infinite ascension or vertical infinity. It gave rise among them to the idea of an unlimited human freedom. It produced in them a propensity to master space. Their way of conceiving nature, man, and the world was the product of the western "matrix space," whence the Saxons had immigrated to Transylvania eight centuries earlier. The perception of space among the eastern Slavs, on the other hand, was one of a horizontal infinity. One may be inclined to agree with Blaga if one recalls the Russian longing, as depicted by Nikolai V. Gogol in his novel *Dead Souls*, to escape the constraints of space: "Russia! Russia! . . . Thou art wretched, disjointed, and comfortless . . . , yet an incomprehensible secret force draws me to thee . . . and my thought is numb before thy vast expanse. What forsooth does this boundless space presage? Does it not foretell that here in thee will be born an idea as infinite as thyself? . . . And that thou too, o Russia, will then dash on like a fleeting troika that nothing can overtake, the road asmoke, the bridges rumbling, beneath [thy wheels]!"[109]

The spirit of Romanian culture was different. It was *mioritic*. Reflected in the rhythm of Romanian melody (the *doïna*) and the theme of the little ewe *(miorița)* in popular poetry, affirmed Blaga, it was the product of the successive rise and fall of the hills and valleys of a rural folk with traditions of a transhumant pastoralism, moving from the verdant hills of their summer Transylvanian pastures to the lower valleys and even to the lonely plains of their winter sojourn in Wallachia, and then returning to their original point of departure.[110]

Whether such interpretations possess a sound basis is not the point. The essential thing is rather the use of space and name fetishes—an example of the latter is the Greek objection to the recognition of the former Yugoslav republic of Macedonia at least partly on the ground of an exclusive Greek right to the name Macedonia—as a means of affirming or reaffirming ethno-cultural distinctions and producing and reproducing a particular national or cultural identity. At first sight innocuous, the myth of a *mioritic* culture may easily be used to reinforce another myth, namely, the myth that, as the supposed descendants of the Daco-Romans, the Romanians are the rightful occupants of Transylvania and should not be confused with the Scythian, Turkic, Slavic, and other populations of the Eurasian steppe.

Another important space-time fetish is the myth of Kosovo, which has become part of the multifaceted *mythomoteur* or "constitutive myth" of Serb, not just Serbian, national identity.[111] The myth has a basis in the epic cycle of Kosovo, which originated not after the first battle of Kosovo against the Turks in 1389 but after the second and, in terms of the consequences, more important battle of 1448, but before 1530. The originator of the epic may have been a wandering professional poet or even a half-scholar, perhaps a storyteller or poet-singer from Dubrovnik or Dalmatia who was familiar with the western or French epic tradition.

Until the mid-eighteenth century, indeed, the Kosovo epic cycle may have been limited locally to the western Serbian regions and may have entered the popular culture of Serbia itself only at that late date.[112] Albert B. Lord has even suggested that "without nationalism the epic tradition of the Balkans" may have died out before the end of the nineteenth century, that nationalism may have given it "a longer lease on life by providing new subjects and giving it a respectability in the new era of education."[113]

The myth of Kosovo, however, is more than just the Kosovo epic cycle. A more important aspect of that myth, propagated during the eighteenth and especially the nineteenth century by Orthodox clerics and lay teachers, was the portrayal of Kosovo as a holy land—the chief territory of Serbia's medieval monasteries and site of the battle of Kosovo. In the myth, Kosovo became a place and time of mourning for the defeat by the Turks, in 1389, of Serbia's feudal armies. Kosovo was also identified as the land from which, in 1690, tens of thousands of Serbs (along with some Catholic Albanians and other Balkan Christian populations) had to flee with the Habsburg armies to escape the wrath of the Turks for their aid to Turkey's enemies. Kosovo thereafter became a land of encroachment by Albanian pastoralists, who after their conversion to Islam seized the properties and farmlands of the Serbs. Periodically the Serbs fled from Kosovo and adjoining districts to the security of the northern lands.

In 1912, following the victories of the Serbian, Greek, Montenegrin, and Bulgarian armies against the Turks, Serbia annexed Kosovo and northern Macedonia. Relations between the Serbs and Kosovars (or Kosovo Albanians) did not improve. Periodically, especially during and immediately after World Wars I and II, they deteriorated. Kosovo Serbs continued to emigrate northward. Pastoral

Albanians from Albania continued to come to occupy the former Serbian farm-lands. The Albanian element of Kosovo also grew after the early 1920s as a result of the rise of the Albanian birth rate to the highest level of any European population.

During World War II, Kosovo was annexed to the Italian satellite state of Albania. Upon the formation of a second Yugoslavia toward the end of World War II, the government of Tito made Kosovo and Metohija (Kosmet) into an autonomous region, partly with the purpose of punishing pro-Mihailović Serbia but also with the object of achieving a Balkan communist (con)federation in which were to be included Trieste, Albania, Bulgaria, and perhaps Greece (or Greek Macedonia), under the leadership of Tito's Yugoslavia.

The latter goal diverged, however, from Joseph Stalin's own goal of a monocentric Soviet empire. It also persuaded the American government, in March 1947, after Britain's decision to depart from Greece, to announce the Truman Doctrine of aid to Greece (in its civil war against communism) and of containment of the Soviet empire. Formed in September 1947 to resist the Marshall Plan for European economic recovery, the Soviet-sponsored Cominform soon decided that the methods and objectives of the Yugoslav communists were not only an obstacle to Soviet ideas of a unitary leadership but might even provoke a premature conflict with the West (the United States and its allies) and in the wrong area. On June 28 (anniversary of the 1389 battle of Kosovo and of the ill-fated provocative visit of Franz Ferdinand to Sarajevo in 1914), 1948, it anathemized the Yugoslav communist leadership and expelled Yugoslavia from membership.

One consequence of the discord between Yugoslavia and the Soviet Union was the strengthening of Serbian control in Kosmet. But following the fall of Aleksandar Ranković, and especially between 1974 and 1986, the Kosovar communist leadership of Kosovo systematically favored the local Albanians just as the pre-1966 leadership had favored the region's Serbs. At the same time, the newly formed University of Priština served the function of forming an intellectual proletariat of Albanian cultural mobilizers whose practical expectations could not be fulfilled.[114]

Following the revulsion of the Serbs of the region and of Serbs in Serbia proper and in Vojvodina against the Kosovar practices, the six-hundredth anniversary of the battle of Kosovo was honored by a pilgrimage to the region by bus of hundreds of thousands of Serbs from all parts of Yugoslavia.[115] The Croatian and especially Slovenian media systematically deplored and harshly denounced the Serbian efforts to bring Kosovo under direct Serbian control. In retaliation, the Serbian government boycotted Slovenian products.

To distance itself further from Serbia, the republic of Slovenia introduced a multiparty political system, as a result of which—in the elections of 1990—victory went to the DEMOS, a coalition favoring independence and the world-market economy. The Serbs, on the other hand, celebrated the tricentennial of the flight of their forebears from the beleaguered south.

The Albanians hold a different view of Kosovo. Constituting a minority of 14 percent in the republic of Serbia (concentrated in but not exclusive to the Kosovo region) and of more than a fifth of the population of the republic of Macedonia,[116] they maintain that the ancestors of the Albanians were the original inhabitants of the territory or, at least, that they settled there before the Serbs or Slavs. In point of fact, when Albanians first settled in the territory is not at all certain. It is unlikely, however, that they constituted the major ethnic group in the area until the latter part of the eighteenth century or even later.

Even though separated by religion (Orthodox Serbs and Montenegrins; Muslim Kosovars; Catholic, Muslim, and—in southern Albania—Orthodox Albanians), the two populations have much in common, including some degree of common ancestry and many common ethnic practices. Two different "myths" nonetheless divide the Serbs and Kosovars and the Serbs (and Montenegrins) and Albanians.

The historian is free to overlook neither myth. Myth may be old or new, and it may undergo many revisions. But, as William H. McNeill has remarked, it

> lies at the basis of human society. That is because myths are general statements about nations and other human in-groups, that are believed to be true and then acted on whenever circumstances suggest or require common response. This is mankind's substitute for instinct. It is the unique and characteristic human way of acting together. A people without a full quiver of relevant agreed-upon statements, accepted in advance through education or less formalized acculturation, soon finds itself in deep trouble, for, in the absence of believable myths, coherent public action becomes very difficult to improvise or sustain.[117]

On the other hand, contends Sabrina P. Ramet, "Psychologists have recognized that people with serious unresolved problems tend to rehash the past, and to read yesterday's meanings into today's events. When an entire society is locked in the past, such obsessive behavior is a sure sign of deep and pervasive unresolved problems at a mass psychological level."[118]

This is too simplistic a view of the problem. Precisely because they are believable to their respective groups as they are revised, the myths of collectivities have authorized violence in the past and may authorize new violence in the future. But they also have a cathartic function. Conflicts arise not because people have different collective myths but because one people belittles, disrespects, and disparages the myth of another. In the case of Yugoslavia, the internal discords became sharper as Slovenia and Croatia disparaged the Kosovo myth of the Serbs. Yugoslavia's domestic media—its republic-based electronic media in particular—bear a great responsibility for exacerbating the conflict and producing civil war. Perhaps without intending to support the foregoing argument, the editor of *Vreme*, an independent Belgrade weekly that has been critical of the Serbian Socialist party (former League of Communists) and its leadership, has even spoken of the civil war in Yugoslavia as "an artificial war ... , produced by [domestic] television."[119]

Equally insensitive to the *mythomoteurs* of the Balkan and southeastern European cultures, and especially to the Serbian *mythomoteur*, have been the European and American media. An ostensibly anachronistic myth of self-sacrifice and honor like the myth of Kosovo can have little appeal for the consumer cultures of transnational corporate capitalism—of which the more powerful and influential media constitute an intrinsic part.[120]

The European and American media alike have also been increasingly convinced that to sell their product they must titillate or make people laugh or shock or anger them. They must not tax their minds with abstract ideas or complex data. The onetime "emancipating role of the media" has been eroded as they have been "subordinated to the establishment" and become "part of a mechanism by which the establishment's conception of society" has been "imposed upon and internalised by all social strata."[121]

Careful by and large not to strain people's minds with the complexities of the Yugoslav civil war, the American media have neglected historical and theoretical analysis alike. Ready to deplore and denounce abuses of "human rights" and to castigate, even demonize, Serbia and the Krajina and Bosnian Serbs, and sensitive to the destruction of Catholic and Muslim monuments, they have been less ready to deal with abuses of the "human rights" of the Serbs and far less sensitive to the destruction of Orthodox monuments.

A New Order

In 1980, there were in the world about two hundred states, in which were spoken at least 8,000 languages or an average of forty languages per state.[122] In Yugoslavia, where violent civil war broke out, first in Slovenia and especially Croatia in 1991 and then in Bosnia and Hercegovina in 1992, well over 99 percent of the people spoke as their native language or language of first choice one of no more than twenty different languages or dialects, thus half as many languages as in the average state.

The number of languages in customary use in a state is an indicator but not a precise measure of the likelihood of cultural conflict. The special character of the problem of culture, ethnicity, and nationality in the Balkans arises in part from the fact that the diffusion of a "codified high culture" followed instead of preceding the formation of states. For the purpose of state formation, a new national codified high culture had to replace the old clerical or bourgeois-clerical codified culture.[123] The problem was further entangled in the case of Yugoslavia by the fact that the territorial unit in the forefront of state formation was Serbia. Precisely because of their three literary traditions *(kaj, ča, što)*, two of which they abandoned, Croatian intellectuals, on the other hand, took pride in the idea of their cultural superiority. They could not stomach the fact that a supposedly culturally superior Croatia had been reduced to political dependence on a supposedly culturally inferior Serbia.

A process that began as "decentralization" *(deetatizacija)* during the early 1960s became a process of state-unmaking during the 1980s.[124] The Yugoslav federal constitution of 1974 transformed Yugoslavia into a kind of eighteenth-century Poland, whose fate had been dismemberment. The deputies of the six constituent republics and two autonomous regions obtained veto power over the laws of the bicameral legislature, and a collective presidency assured executive impotence in regard to controversial territorial matters.

Dissident ethnic diasporas have played a role of considerable importance in the reterritorialization of states. The anti-Yugoslav Croatian nationalist movement, for example, was not confined to rhetoric and the media. Emigrant Croats organized the Croatian National Resistance (Hrvatski Narodni Otpor) with the aim of destroying Yugoslavia. Its headquarters were located successively in Spain, Australia, and Germany, countries with a large Croatian emigration. They also established guerrilla training camps in Austria and Germany, and Croatian émigrés in Canada and Australia provided the separatist movement with money and mercenaries. In October 1990, Croatia obtained from Hungary 10,000 Kalashnikov assault rifles for the war its government expected to wage against the federal army of Yugoslavia.[125] Thus, after more than two decades of subversive activity, aided by the resurgence after 1960 of separatist movements as a major global phenomenon,[126] Croatian nationalists succeeded in their goal of dismembering the second Yugoslavia.

In the summer of 1990, the Serbs of Knin—a district taken by Venice from the Turks during the 1680s—and of the territories of the former Habsburg (Croatian) Military Frontier decided to resist the centralizing policies of Croatia, just as, during the 1920s and 1930s, Croatia had opposed the centralizing policies of interwar Yugoslavia. Despite the Croatian government's use of special police to disarm them and suppress their autonomist demands, these Serbs organized an unofficial referendum. By this act, they made known their overwhelming preference for autonomy—in reality, for a civil polity in which neither Croats nor Serbs would be able to monopolize cultural and political organizations, for a distinction between state and culture, for cultural pluralism rather than cultural integration, for the existence of competing intermediate groups between the individual and the state or nation. The Croatian government declared the referendum illegal. In riposte, on October 1, 1990, the Serbs of Croatia proclaimed autonomy for counties with a preponderantly Serb population.

On June 25, 1991, Croatia and Slovenia seceded from Yugoslavia. After an unsuccessful initial venture to force Slovenia to abandon its project of independence, and submitting to pressure from the European Community, Yugoslavia withdrew its military forces from Slovenia. The conflict with Croatia, on the other hand, was transformed into a bitter civil war.[127]

The precise role in this occurrence of the Federal Republic of Germany and of its banks, business ventures, and other special groups, and of the countries immediately to the north of Yugoslavia, remains to be determined, but it is no secret that the countries most actively urging the recognition of an independent Croatia, Slovenia, and Bosnia-Hercegovina were Germany and its allies of World Wars I and II. On the cover of an issue of the Belgrade journal *Intervju* (December 13, 1991), there thus appeared a caricature of the German foreign minister, Hans-Dietrich Genscher, as a venom-injecting Dracula.[128] On December 15, the Security Council of the United Nations avoided a confrontation with Germany only by yielding to that country's plans and the plans of its foreign minister to recognize Slovenia and Croatia as independent states, underscoring thereby France's weakness and "Germany's growing power in the 12-nation European Community."[129] The Yugoslav government reacted to the subsequent recognition of the two states by Germany and the European Community with a memorandum to the secretary general of the United Nations condemning that action: "It is noteworthy that the very countries which were Yugoslavia's enemies and occupying forces, most of them so in both world wars . . . have been in the forefront and the states that have supported secession in an absolutely impermissible manner and they are the ones which are in various ways endeavouring to present territorial claims to particular parts of Yugoslavia."[130]

BBC correspondent Misha Glenny affirmed that by allowing Germany to recognize Croatia unconditionally, "Western diplomacy bears considerable responsibility" for the spread of civil war, during the spring of 1992, to Bosnia and Hercegovina. "Not only did German recognition of Croatia provoke the war in Bosnia," wrote Glenny, but it also "provided no solution for dealing with the status of the several hundred thousand Serbs who live in Croatia."[131]

One of the few scholars who may have correctly understood the Yugoslav problem, Professor Karl Kaser of Karl-Franzens Universität in Graz, has explained, in effect, why the dissolution of Yugoslavia, however it may have suited various actors on the world stage, was unlikely to bring peace to the people of the area: "It's no solution to form six completely independent states. There would never be peace in that case! Minorities are spread all over the country. It ought to be possible to create a loose federation. Yugoslavia came together after World War II despite bad interwar experiences; it's possible for such a thing to happen again."[132]

An official cessation of hostilities between Croatia and the Serbs of Croatia, concluded at the beginning of 1992, resulted in an agreement to establish three United Nations Protected Areas—eastern Slavonia, western Slavonia, and Krajina Knin—in the contested territories of Croatia, in which was deployed a United Nations force of fourteen thousand troops whose task it was to defuse the conflict without intervening against either the Croats or the Serbs. As for the cruel civil war in Bosnia and Hercegovina, which provoked an even greater "voluntary" and forced movement or shifting of populations than the conflict in Croatia, it goes on. As of this writing (March 1994), however, the prospects of an eventual precarious peace have improved as the result of several factors. First, NATO made more credible its threat to bomb Bosnian Serb positions if the Serbs did not cease their mortar or artillery attacks on Sarajevo. Second, Russia reemerged as a major player in Balkan politics by sending 400 troops to join the UN forces in Bosnia, a move welcomed by the Serbs. Third, negotiations brokered by the United States between the Bosnian Croats and Muslims and American negotiations with the government of Croatia resulted in two agreements in March 1994 to create a confederation within a confederation: a system of autonomous Croat and Muslim cantons in confederation with Bosnia and Hercegovina, and Bosnia and Hercegovina (still with undetermined boundaries) in confederation with the state of Croatia. The two confederations were to have joint ministers of foreign affairs, national defense, and commerce. This solution may represent an attempt to reconcile the principles of territoriality and market enlargement. It is also a throwback to the compromises of the Habsburg Dual Monarchy—to the way in which Hungary was bound to Austria in 1867, Croatia to Hungary in 1868, and Bosnia-Herzegovina (then with a hypen and a "z") to Hungary and Austria in 1878.

The Balkan question remains unresolved and has become more complicated than ever, partly because the Balkans are a crossroads of cultures and civilizations that almost everyone wants to cross or prevent someone else from crossing. The Croato-Muslim confederation of confederations may not work. Could it give rise, on the other hand, to a network of confederations, including the rump third Yugoslavia, formed by Serbia and Montenegro in April 1992, and the Serbs of Bosnia, Hercegovina, and the Krajina, and perhaps the other Balkan states and peoples, all part of a new European Community, a grand confederation of states with possibly reduced powers (but the question of the state is also complex) and peoples with increased powers—but also with an increased responsibility? Is Europe up to the task?

The fate of Europe—whether it will continue to rely on the American-inspired NATO alliance (whose highest political body, the North Atlantic Council, must nonetheless agree unanimously to the undertaking of military action), whether it will allow Germany and German-dominated transnational corporations to run the European show, or whether it will revise its whole conception of the proper nature of the European Community, rejecting the idea of its fundamental basis in money, consumption, and continuing economic growth (the fundamentalism of capitalism) in favor of a Europe of three basic groups of cultures (Romance, Germanic, and Slavic, and/or Roman Catholic, Protestant, and Orthodox), all three with pagan, classical Greek, and Judaic underpinnings—hinges upon Yugoslavia and the Balkans, or rather upon how Europe relates to its third part, the first Europe. By rejecting the third part, which was alienated from Europe first by the schism between the Roman and Greek churches and then by the Ottoman conquest and intrusion of Islam but was then gradually restored to Europe during the nineteenth and twentieth centuries, albeit again divided from it politically and ideologically by communism, Europe may seal its own destiny. The failure of fusion between the first Europe (the Balkans) and the new Europe may mean that there will be no Europe at all but only capitalism.

The new Europe or European Community and the Yugoslav civil war may both turn out to be part of the process of revising the world state system to correspond to the revision, starting around 1950 but intensifying between 1968–73 and 1989, of the world world-economy. Conflicts within and between states have been a regular historical constant. Normally, however, such struggles are kept within bounds so that the state system itself is not seriously disturbed. Every hundred years or so, however, state systems themselves come under attack as some new dominant groups of states attempt to establish a "new order." Between periods of two different kinds of state systems occurs a period of major disturbance.

A state system may be defined, indeed, as an autonomous "world-economy" or group of political units between which exchanges at the political, economic, and cultural-ideological levels are normal.[133] Prior to 1500, many different types of state systems existed. Each was a world-economy, but none was a global world-economy. The first global world-economy, defined by Carl Schmitt as a "global linear" world-economy,[134] arose shortly after 1500. It was the exchange system of the states and territories of western Europe, with lines of extension by sea and river route in particular and by a few land routes to a limited number of "ports of trade" in Africa, Asia, and the Americas, with little penetration into the interior regions except in the Americas,[135] where the catastrophic decline of the native populations and the fragility or nonexistence of political states allowed some degree of penetration.

A world world-economy in depth was not created until after 1830 or 1840. The first long phase in the creation of a world world-economy in depth between 1840 and 1913 was followed by a long setback, of which the major symptoms were the Great War, the dismantling of empires, communist revolution in Russia and neighboring areas of Eurasia, economic depression, the constitution of diverse forms of interventionist states, and World War II. After 1950 the global world-economy in depth received a new impetus. Its growth, indeed, played an important role in the demise of Soviet communism and the dissolution of the Soviet Union between 1989 and 1991.

The period of formation and great expansion of the first world world-economy was also the period of formation of national economies, which existed prior to 1830 in only a few countries—England, the Netherlands, and Japan. National economy was a way of activating the circulation of goods, services, capital, land (as property), and labor, so that they reached and departed from small communities as well as large ones and local isolation ceased to be possible.

The circulation or communication of goods could not be activated, however, without the mobilization of information. The activation of the circulation of information culminated in the admission as mediators of discourse of individuals whose language and orientation were usually secular and popular and who believed in the desirability of forming states whose territories would extend to all areas in which their own idiom of discourse prevailed or could prevail.

The formation of national markets for goods and for discourse was part of the same process, and the two activities were no less part of the process of creating a world world-economy in depth. The nation-state, further maintained the proponents of a national market for goods and discourse, much like Friedrich List, should be sufficiently large, with access to the sea if possible, and with a large enough population and variety and quantity of resources to make it politically and economically viable. Their object thus was not a ministate that would stay within the boundaries of a given idiom but rather a state from which a particular idiom could be diffused to neighboring regions. *Kleinstaaterei* or the formation of ministates was not the goal of the mobilizers of a national economy, national culture, or nation state. What has come to be known as "balkanization," a term generally applied in criticism or derision, was not what they wanted but what the great powers or more powerful states would allow and what also resulted from the conflicting national goals of the rival Balkan and southeast European cultural and national mobilizers.[136]

The purpose of the nation-state system was to encourage competition between states. But the same state system was also an obstacle to competition because of the unequal distribution among states of power and resources. Political-military alliances and wars were customary ways of correcting such inequalities. At the end of major wars, on the other hand, occurring every century, power generally shifted to the leading state in the victorious struggle, or another war might ensue (as after World War I) if no leading state emerged.[137]

Increasingly since 1950, as the transnational corporation, albeit in no sense a new phenomenon, became the main institutional wheel of economic action, the transnationalization of politics, of the economy, and of the media was accelerated and intensified. One consequence of this evolution has been a growth in the number of states, partly as a result of the disparagement, in the countries of concentration of transnational enterprise, of some national ideologies, such as the ideology of *jugoslovenstvo*, which has been identified for several decades at least with the ideas of separate roads to socialism and of a socialist market economy, to the advantage of those territories—such as Croatia and Slovenia, defined as two networks of politicized financial and commercial cities—that have been or desire to be enmeshed more fully with transnational capitalist enterprise and illustrate the role of certain urbanisms in the promotion of "substate" nationalism.[138] An alternative course is a temporary alliance of convenience between the fundamentalism of capitalism and certain momentarily friendly populist fundamentalisms (Bosnian Islam, for example, as preached in the "Islamic Declaration" of Alija Izetbegović and his Muslim Party for Democratic Action)[139] against certain other, perhaps irrationally exorcised, populist fundamentalisms (such as that of the Serbian Republic of Bosnia or of the myth and ethic of Kosovo).

"Territoriality," of course, is the "nemesis" even of "global power," for military intervention in distant territories may sap both the moral authority and the financial, industrial, and other resources of a chief sponsor of territorial intervention.[140] In September 1993, therefore, the American president's national security adviser, Anthony Lake, defined the basic American strategy as having passed from "containment," or a continuing territoriality or political isolation of the Soviet Union, to "enlargement," by which he meant the expansion of the market for the goods and messages of the capitalist world-economy.[141] Despite the hoped-for new strategy, however, the global capitalist network, under the leadership of the politically most powerful member of that network, currently the United States, may be unable to avoid local wars or some degree of temporary territorial intervention. Such wars, however, may provoke divisions among the members of the global network and an ultimate shift of political and economic leadership alike to a new center of political and economic authority.

Under the impact of the enmeshment of transnational corporate capitalism and an electronic communications technology, the "great society" envisioned in the late eighteenth and nineteenth centuries has culminated on the one hand in the globalization of the economy but, on the other, in the fragmentation, deconstruction, *émiettement* of society. One of the repercussions of this occurrence has been a resurgence, during the second half of the twentieth century, of criminality and fear and of a "grey" or informal economy that escapes the control of the state—almost as it is supposed to as the economy increasingly determines political action rather than the other way around. Some persons therefore contend that there is a crisis of the state, and there is. But this reality does not mean that the state will disappear in any immediate future. What is more likely is that a few states will grow more powerful as other states grow weaker and territorially smaller.[142]

Such might be the scenario for the world of tomorrow if that world continues to act on the basis of yesterday's principles. Alternative solutions remain, however. One solution would entail the organization of Europe as a cultural, economic, and ecological system or autonomous world-region that would bring eastern and western Europe together, including Slavic and Orthodox Europe and especially the Balkans—that first Europe.

Such a world-region, however, may have to reject the idea that there are no alternatives to continuing economic growth. As Björn Hettne, director of the Peace and Development Research Institute at Gothenburg University, has noted, "the era of sustained economic growth" may have come to an end in western Europe in the 1970s. In any case, the question arises whether the old "European model of development" can be resumed in the future.[143]

The constitution of Europe as a world-region of cultural as well as material goods should not necessitate the dismantling of established nation-states. It should serve instead to promote the mobilization of culture at all territorial levels as a means not only of providing people with a sense of identity but also as a means of maintaining cultural spontaneity and diversity, without which cultural creativity may be much weakened.

Finally, unless the world's cultures effectively mobilize all categories and sources of knowledge and understanding, per capita resources may be expected to diminish as the world's population continues to grow. With this perspective in mind, let us move on to the relationship between the changing distribution in the Balkans of "populations" of all kinds—people, animals, plants, things—and the ability of the earth to replenish itself. Let us address the problem of ecology, a problem just as important as, and in some respects more important than, the problem of culture.

Notes

1. MacIver, "Group Images and Group Realities," pp. 3–9. For an approach to this subject from the point of view of a geographer, see Wright, "Terrae Incognitae."
2. Deutsch, *Nationalism and Social Communication*, p. 159.
3. Anderson, *Imagined Communities*, p. 15.
4. Duțu, "Assimilations and Continuity in Romanian Culture," p. 42.
5. Sozan, *The History of Hungarian Ethnography*, p. 62. See also Hofer, "Construction of the 'Folk Cultural Heritage.' "
6. On the possible connections between the political and economic decline of states, see Olson, *The Rise and Decline of Nations*.
7. Volney, *The Ruins*, p. 7.
8. Vryonis, Jr., "Nomadization and Islamization in Asia Minor," pp. 70–71, citing and translating Eflaki, *Les Saints des derviches tourneurs*, II, 208–9.
9. Volney, *The Ruins*, pp. 20, 25–26, 28, 41.
10. Isnard, *Observations sur le principe qui a produit les révolutions*, pp. 4–5; Isnard, *Catéchisme social*, pp. 21–23, 37–39 for the quotation.
11. Volney, *The Ruins*, pp. 61–62, 76. Italics as in the original.
12. Gellner, "Scale and Nation," pp. 133–34.
13. Rabbe, "Introduction," pp. 1–2.
14. Arensberg, "The Old World Peoples," p. 82.
15. Grégoras, *Correspondance de Nicéphore Grégoras*, p. 40.
16. Mary (Pierrepont) Wortley Montagu, to the abbé Conti, Adrianople, April 1, [O.S.], 1717, in Montagu, *The Complete Letters of Lady Mary Wortley Montagu*, I, 319.
17. Af. Étr., CPC, Turquie: Sérajévo (Sarajevo), XI (Duplicata), fol. 21, dépêche adressée à l'Ambassade de France à Constantinople; Turquie: Mostar, II, fols. 275, 289, 310, letters or telegrams, September 9, 10, October 1, 1875, from the vice-consul at Mostar, Auguste Dozon; Turquie: Sérajévo, X, letter of September 25, 1875, from Charles de Vienne; Turquie: Bosna-Séraï (Sarajevo), III, fol. 147, letter of March 13, 1876, from Charles de Vienne.
18. Yriarte, *Bosnie et Herzégovine*, p. 241.
19. See Banac, "Universalist Religions in a Multinational Society," on the revival of religion.
20. Bax, "The Saints of Gomila," pp. 19–27.
21. Bax, "How the Mountain Became Sacred"; "Patronage in a Holy Place"; "The Seers of Medjugorje."
22. Ferguson, "Explaining War," pp. 31, 51–52; Whitehead and Ferguson, "Deceptive Stereotypes about 'Tribal Warfare,' " p. A48.
23. Vuk Stefanović Karadžić, to Prince Miloš, Zemun, April 12, 1832, in Karadžić, *Pisma*, pp. 161–82.

24. Kitromilides, "The Enlightenment East and West," pp. 56, 59.

25. Unbegaun, *Les Débuts de la langue littéraire chez les Serbes*, p. 73–74.

26. Stoianovich, "Raguse—Société sans imprimerie," pp. 68–73.

27. Lencek, "The Enlightenment's Interest in Languages and the National Revival of the South Slavs." See also Jelavich, "Nationalism as Reflected in the Textbooks," p. 16; Jelavich, "Serbian Nationalism and the Croats," p. 32.

28. Marcuse, *Serbien und die Revolutionsbewegung in Makedonien*, p. 18.

29. Vasiljević, *Prosvetne i političke prilike u južnim srpskim oblastima u XIX v.*, pp. 181–84; *Une confédération orientale*, p. 143. According to this last work, the number of Greek schools in territories under Turkish rule increased from 111 in 1877 to 339 in 1887 and 973 in 1905.

30. Herzfeld, *Anthropology through the Looking-Glass*, pp. 52, 54, 114–15.

31. See in particular Faensen, *Die albanische Nationalbewegung*.

32. Barthélemy Saint-Hilaire, *Politique d'Aristote*, II, 26–35. See also Veremis, "From the National State to the Stateless Nation," pp. 136, 141; Kitromilides, "Imagined Communities," p. 165.

33. Andreopoulos, "Liberalism and the Formation of the Nation-State," p. 214.

34. Kourvetaris, "Greek Armed Forces and Society in the Nineteenth Century."

35. Herzfeld, *Ours Once More*, p. 21. For the adherence of some Greek intellectuals to a Hellenic outlook since the Middle Ages, see Vryonis, Jr., "Introductory Remarks on Byzantine Intellectuals and Humanism."

36. Veremis, "From the National State to the Stateless Nation," pp. 141–44.

37. See Verdery, *National Ideology under Socialism*, pp. 31–41, 47–54, for a brilliant statement of Romanian orientations, complemented by the earlier study of Hitchins, *"Gîndirea,"* and the contemporaneous study of Dion, "L'Identité ethnique en Roumanie."

38. Paton, *Researches on the Danube and the Adriatic*, I, 340.

39. Hildebrandt, "Die Stadt in Südosteuropa," pp. 160–61; Stadtmüller, *Geschichte Südosteuropas*, pp. 320–22; Jordan, *Die kaiserliche Wirtschaftspolitik*.

40. Paton, *Researches on the Danube and the Adriatic*, II, 30–31.

41. Golczewski, *Der Balkan in deutschen und österreichischen Reise- und Erlebnisberichten*.

42. Grmek, Gjidara, and Šimac, *Le Nettoyage ethnique*, pp. 9–53.

43. Allcock, "In Praise of Chauvinism," p. 219, for Milošević's declaration and Allcock's interpretation.

44. Drakulić, *How We Survived Communism and Even Laughed*, pp. xi–xvii.

45. Schwartz, "The Size and Shape of a Culture," pp. 241, 244, 247.

46. Löfgren, "The Nationalization of Culture," pp. 17, 21.

47. Kitromilides, "'Imagined Communities,'" pp. 179–80; Pantazopoulos, "Human Liberties in the Pre-Revolutionary Greek Community System," p. 15.

48. Deutsch, *Nationalism and Social Communication*, p. 126.

49. I stressed the importance of generations in my article, "The Pattern of Serbian Intellectual Evolution." The literature on generations is immense. For readers who are interested in the subject, I recommend in particular two recent books: Spitzer, *The French Generation of 1820*, and Strauss and Howe, *Generations*, which extends the history of American generations over a much longer period than would be valid in the Balkans. Strauss and Howe conceptualize the formation of American generations as a repetition of four-part generational cycles.

50. Smith, *Theories of Nationalism*, pp. 28, 33.

51. Despalatović, *Ljudevit Gaj and the Illyrian Movement*, pp. 28–34, my italics.

52. Jelavich, *History of the Balkans*, I, 318–19.

53. Ramet, "From Strossmayer to Stepinac."

54. Ioannis Kolettes, quoted in Driault and Lhéritier, *Histoire diplomatique de la Grèce*, II, 252–53.

55. Clogg, "The Byzantine Legacy in the Modern Greek World," pp. 270–71; Kitromilides, " 'Imagined Communities,' " p. 172; Eliot, *Turkey in Europe*, p. 302.

56. Petrovich, "*Srpski Književni Glasnik* and the Yugoslav Idea," p. 142 for the data on newspapers and magazines and for the quotations.

57. Novak, *Antologija jugoslovenske misli i narodnog jedinstva*, pp. 653–702.

58. Smith, *Theories of Nationalism*, p. 134.

59. Zipf, *National Disunity*, pp. 10–11, 33, 36–37, 49; Vining, "A Description of Certain Spatial Aspects of an Economic System"; Stoianovich, "Cities, Capital Accumulation, and the Ottoman Command Economy," forthcoming.

60. Fisher, *Yugoslavia*, pp. 50–60.

61. Bićanić, *Economic Policy in Socialist Yugoslavia*, pp. 200–202.

62. Rusinow, *The Yugoslav Experiment*, pp. 123–37; Ramet, *Nationalism and Federalism in Yugoslavia*, pp. 86–87; Deutsch, *Nationalism and Social Communication*, p. 49, where, without reference to the quarrel between Zagreb and Belgrade, Deutsch argues in favor of the mobilization of capital and labor.

63. Rusinow, *The Yugoslav Experiment*, pp. 206–7.

64. Bertsch, *Nation-Building in Yugoslavia*, pp. 35–36; Bertsch, *Values and Community in Multi-National Yugoslavia*, pp. 52–53, 82–83, 108–9.

65. Burg, *Conflict and Cohesion in Socialist Yugoslavia*, pp. 45–46.

66. Ibid., pp. 120–25; Burks, "Nationalism and Communism in Yugoslavia"; Schöpflin, "The Ideology of Croatian Nationalism," pp. 133–44. For further important details but generally with a Croatian slant, see Ramet, *Nationalism and Federalism in Yugoslavia*, pp. 101–11, 121.

67. Ramet, *Nationalism and Federalism in Yugoslavia*, p. 101.

68. Burg, *Conflict and Cohesion in Socialist Yugoslavia*, pp. 100–101; Doder, "Belgrade Professor [Mihajlo Marković]." For an interesting, persuasive, but slanted view by an American scholar of Croat origin who contends that but for communism "there would have been no postwar Yugoslav state," see Banac, "The Fearful Asymmetry of War," p. 168. See also an unofficial but slanted "white book" with a Croatian bias by three French scholars of Croat origin—Grmek, Gjidara, and Šimac, *Le Nettoyage ethnique*, pp. 231–69, 291–95.

69. Rogel, "Edward Kardelj's Nationality Theory and Yugoslav Socialism"; Ramet, *Nationalism and Federalism*, pp. 50–54, 63. See also the Bibliography of this volume under Kardelj, Edvard.

70. Paton, *Researches on the Danube and the Adriatic*, II, 174–75.

71. Steed, *The Hapsburg Monarchy*, pp. 60, 62; Jászi, *The Dissolution of the Habsburg Monarchy*, p. 144. See also Kautsky, "The Politics of Traditional Aristocratic Empires and Their Legacy"; Deák, *Beyond Nationalism*.

72. Paton, *Researches on the Danube and the Adriatic*, I, 381–82.

73. Patlagean, "Ancienne hagiographie byzantine et histoire sociale."

74. Hall, *Powers and Liberties*, pp. 137, 159, 164, 190.

75. Alting von Geusau, "Europe 1992 East and West"; "The Spirit of 1989." See also Schöpflin, "The Political Traditions of Eastern Europe," pp. 61–69.

76. Wuthnow, "The Voluntary Sector," p. 7.

77. Schieder, "Typologie und Erscheinungsformen des Nationalstaats in Europa."

78. Hadjimihali, "Aspects de l'organisation économique des Grecs dans l'Empire ottoman," p. 266; Vacalopoulos, *The Greek Nation, 1453–1669*, pp. 187–210.

79. Stahl, *Traditional Romanian Village Communities*, pp. 15, 25–27, 38, 144; Chirot, *Social Change in a Peripheral Society*, pp. 20–23.

80. Volney, *The Ruins*, pp. 62–65.

81. Jakšić, address to the Srpsko Učeno Društvo, pp. 316–18; Popović, *O Cincarima*, pp. 164–75, 273, 333–34; Af. Étr., CC, Belgrade, II, fol. 7, Limpérani, February 4, 1848; II, fols. 52–57, report by Gauthier on the state of Serbian commerce in 1848; III, fol. 132, Botmiliau, September 26, 1863.

82. Kolarić, "Modernazacija srpskog slikarstva u razdoblju zografa i molera."

83. Janković, "O programima i borbama za lokalne samouprave u Srbiji XIX veka."

84. Marković, "Naše udruživanje," *Celokupna dela*, III, 10, 23–26, 45.

85. Segalen, "Breton Identity."

86. Rustow, "Turkey," pp. 196–97; see also Mardin, "Power, Civil Society and Culture in the Ottoman Empire."

87. Smith, *The Ethnic Origins of Nations*, p. 171.

88. See Kedourie, *Nationalism*, pp. 38–50, 53–54, 82–83, on Johann Gottlieb Fichte's conceptions. For a further examination of the evolution of Fichte's thought, see Hertz, *Nationality in History and Politics*, pp. 336–44.

89. Deutsch, *Nationalism and Social Communication*, p. 75.

90. Alexander, "Croatia," pp. 31, 53–55, 62 n. 1.

91. Plamenatz, "Two Types of Nationalism," pp. 27, 32–33; Gellner, "Ethnicity, Culture, Class, and Power," pp. 272–73.

92. Schöpflin, "The Political Traditions of Eastern Europe," p. 61.

93. East, "The Concept and Political Status of the Shatter Zone," pp. 8, 12.

94. Radić, *Moderna kolonizacija i Slaveni*, pp. 220–21, 255–58.

95. Sklair, *Sociology of the Global System*, pp. 24, 42, 52–53.

96. Glenny, "Bosnia: The Last Chance," p. 8; Baker, "Global Multiculturalism and the American Experiment," p. 50.

97. Schmitt, *The Concept of the Political*, esp. pp. 74–76.

98. Piccone and Ulmen, "Schmitt's 'Testament' "; Schmitt, "The Plight of European Jurisprudence."

99. Bollnow, *Mensch und Raum*, pp. 132–33, 137.

100. Pye, "Political Culture and Political Development," p. 22.

101. Schwab, "Enemy or Foe"; Ulmen, "Return of the Foe."

102. Piccone and Ulmen, "Schmitt's 'Testament,' " pp. 12–13, 28.

103. Buruma, "Outsiders," pp. 18–19.

104. Matvejević, "Central Europe Seen from the East of Europe," p. 185; Judt, "The Rediscovery of Central Europe," pp. 43–44; Ash, "Mitteleuropa?" p. 4.

105. Kant, "Idea for a Universal History from a Cosmopolitan Point of View," pp. 15–23.

106. Freud, *Civilization and Its Discontents*, pp. 58–61.

107. Braudel, *The Identity of France*, I, 119–20; Braudel, *L'Identité de la France*, I, 103–4.

108. For additional thoughts on this subject, see Taylor and House, *Political Geography*, esp. following articles: Becker, "The State Crisis and the Region"; Johnston, "The Political Geography of Electoral Geography"; Bruun, "Future of the Nation-State System"; see also Hoffmann, "Delusions of World Order."

109. Gogol, *Dead Souls*, in *Sobranie sochinenii*, V, 229–30, 258, my translation, cited first in my study "Russian Domination in the Balkans," p. 198.

110. Horia, "Roumanie," pp. 1068, 1077–83, 1089; Dion, "L'Identité ethnique en Roumanie," pp. 259–60; Hitchins, "Gîndirea," pp. 157–66.

111. On the function of the *mythomoteur*, see Armstrong, *Nations before Nationalism*, pp. 9, 51, 65, 69–75, 81–90, 129–67, 198, 238–39, 280, 283–84, 296–97.

112. Banašević, "Le Cycle de Kosovo et les chansons de geste."

113. Lord, "Nationalism and the Muses in Balkan Slavic Literature," pp. 270–71.
114. Krulic, "Deux sociétés civiles, plusieurs nations," pp. 35–36.
115. Ibid., pp. 36–37; Ramet, "Kosovo and the Limits of Yugoslav Socialist Patriotism."
116. Pavlowitch, *The Improbable Survivor*, p. 74.
117. McNeill, "The Care and Repair of Public Myth," pp. 23–24.
118. Ramet, *Nationalism and Federalism in Yugoslavia*, p. 254.
119. "Quiet Voices from the Balkans," *New Yorker*, March 15, 1993, pp. 4, 6.
120. Greider, *Who Will Tell the People?* pp. 15, 48–52, 187–88, 288–89, 294, 297–302, 328–31; Seligman, "Those Who Own the Papers Also Own This Land."
121. Brenner, *Capitalism, Competition, and Economic Crisis*, pp. 47, 167.
122. Gellner, *Nations and Nationalism*, p. 48.
123. Ibid., p. 49.
124. Rusinow, *The Yugoslav Experiment*, p. 126.
125. Clissold, "Croat Separatism"; Kaldor, "Yugoslavia and the New Nationalism," p. 110.
126. Morin, "De la culturanalyse à la politique culturelle."
127. Ramet, *Nationalism and Federalism in Yugoslavia*, pp. 252–69.
128. Banac, "The Fearful Asymmetry of War," p. 174 n. 155.
129. Lewis, "U.N. Yields to Plans by Germany to Recognize Yugoslav Republics."
130. Yugoslavia, "Memorandum of the Government of Yugoslavia on the Yugoslav Crisis," pp. 81–82.
131. Glenny, "Bosnia: The Last Chance." Glenny is the author of *The Fall of Yugoslavia: The Third Balkan War* (New York: Penguin, 1993). For an analysis of the responsibility of the German government, the Bavarian Christian Social Union, and the Vatican in fueling civil war in Yugoslavia by their support of Catholic Croatia and Slovenia, and of the presence in France of a covert opposition to the German policies in its diplomatic corps, its army, and in certain unspecified political circles, see Là Gorce, "Les Divergences franco-allemandes mises a nu."
132. Kaser, in "Karl Kaser on Austria and the Crisis in Yugoslavia."
133. Braudel, *Civilization and Capitalism*, pp. 21–29.
134. Ulmen, "American Imperialism and International Law," p. 48.
135. Polanyi, "Ports of Trade in Early Societies"; Polanyi, "The Economy as Instituted Process."
136. Hobsbawm, *Nations and Nationalism since 1780*, pp. 30–31.
137. Bruun, "Future of the Nation-State System"; Modelski, "The Long Cycle of Global Politics."
138. Murphy, "Urbanism and the Diffusion of Substate Nationalist Ideas in Western Europe."
139. Ramet, "The Breakup of Yugoslavia," p. 103.
140. Modelski, "The Long Cycle of Global Politics," pp. 229–30.
141. Decornoy, "La Chevauchée américaine pour la direction du monde."
142. Stoianovich, "Social History of the *Annales* Paradigm," pp. 38–42; Minc, *Le Nouveau Moyen âge*, pp. 68–92, 139.
143. Hettne, "Europe and the Crisis."

8 THE INTERACTING POPULATION SYSTEMS

This study began with a statement of the relationship between the earth and Balkan man and woman. It may be appropriate to return to that subject—now, however, with an emphasis not on past perceptions of the relationship between the earth and man but on how that relationship may be in need of rethinking. The previous chapter raised the question of the liberties and constraints of culture, how a specific culture or group of cultures—namely, the Balkan cultures—has simultaneously promoted and hindered the emergence of "higher men." To probe more deeply into this matter, we shall adopt what Warren Susman called an "ecological approach."[1] We shall reexamine the ways in which changes in culture, society, technology, the organization of territory, mentality, the economy, and the world at large have altered the ways in which the Balkan cultures and societies have functioned, now function, and should function in order to survive.

Theater of the Gods

A hunting or gathering ground or fishing site, a village or city, a low or high human population density—each of these different ways of organizing man's relationship with the environment alters the environment. Neither plants nor animals nor people live outside a territorial context. But every territorial context with a human component acquires meaning through a common experience of change and of ways of organizing people and making and enforcing decisions. Common experiences promote the affirmation of feelings of identity among succeeding population cohorts. The territory of a people is the milieu in which bodies and minds are housed, clothed, and fed physiologically, intellectually, and spiritually in ways that allow them to affirm their identity once they are aware of an *other* way of housing, clothing, and feeding.[2]

Among the Greeks of classical Antiquity, two views of nature prevailed, both of which stood in the way of envisioning the earth as a closed system. According to one view, observes J. Donald Hughes, nature was "the theatre of the gods." As such it was "sacred." Regarding it as sacred, one was not free to regard it "*qua*

318

nature." It was rather a cosmic order, the source alike of utility and beauty, in which man may participate but which one should not disturb. In a second view, nature was "the theatre of reason." Its purpose was to serve man as intelligent man himself saw fit. From this view one could draw optimistic conclusions. A more common consequence, however, was to view man as a tragic figure. Able to contemplate nature, man nonetheless strays from the principles of a natural equilibrium. A third view, with no ostensible influence upon ancient Greek culture, was that of Theophrastes, a student of Aristotle, who believed that nature had its own purpose, retaining its own autonomy even while interrelating with and including man in its realm.[3]

Until the eleventh century the view of nature as God's theater prevailed in the western (Roman Catholic) and eastern (Byzantine Orthodox) churches alike. Thereafter, however, under the impact of the Cluniac and other changes in the western church, nature began to be regarded in the West as an earthly theater in which the individual was free to choose between right and wrong.[4] Instead of remaining a tragic Sisyphus, man could henceforth be a Prometheus.

As a result, favored also by the cultural and social transformations alluded to in the previous chapter, western Europeans made the technological changes and acted upon nature in ways that allowed them to catch up with the Muslim world by 1600 and with China by 1750 or 1800. Much less pronounced and more fragmented, a similar movement was initiated in the Balkans. After the fourteenth century, however, despite several later attempts at innovation, the western European model failed to find support there until the end of the eighteenth century. Even as late as the mid-nineteenth century, in his *Luča mikrokozma* (Beam of the Microcosm), the Montenegrin poet-prince-bishop Petar Petrović Njegoš continued to argue that man is free to alter the form and content of things but not to meddle with the equilibrium of the cosmic order.[5]

In England, however, T.R. Malthus had embraced an environmental theory. Instead of viewing the earth as being made up of numerous distinct compartments or separate systems, he portrayed it as a single interdependent virtually closed system in which a change in human and other "populations" in one part of the earth ultimately will have an impact on "populations" in other areas.[6] The technological achievements and short-term thinking of the nineteenth century, however, induced Europeans to neglect the broad significance of that theory. Non-Europeans and the Balkan peoples followed their example.

The *Translatio* of Rationalization

People's ideas represent one aspect of reality. To accede to a more complete reality, one must include an examination of the system of continuing and changing biotic and environmental relationships among men, plants, animals, the things that men and women make, and the earth on which human beings, things, and *others* of every kind coexist, and to whose transformations they may all owe their presence.

A temporarily successful manipulation of environmental relationships in western Europe—a disturbance of ecological, semiotic, and other equilibria—may have been the product of "rationalization," which requires a shift from the conception of religion as belief, rite, and a means of collective salvation for believers toward a balance between reason and belief, an emphasis on individual responsibility, a propensity to regard achievement as a possible and even probable reflection of God's grace, and a consequent ability on the part of individuals to accumulate wealth without fear of confiscation either by church or by state.[7]

As a result of the weakness of the early medieval European states, according to Max Weber, craft production was concentrated in the towns, identifiable by their separation from the countryside by city walls and by their ability to shield their commerce from excessive control by government. When, in later centuries, the western European states succeeded in transforming themselves into what Joseph Schumpeter called tax states,[8] many cities and provinces retained some of their privileges. Sovereignty later was withdrawn from the prince and transferred in theory to the nation or people and in practice to landowners, possessors of capital, and communications specialists. In either case, goes the argument, as expounded in the previous chapter, western Europe (including *Mitteleuropa*) was able to create and maintain a civil society.

Lacking a city of the European medieval type, contend Max Weber and Otto Brunner, most of the other cities of the world were of the "ancient" or "oriental" type. Unlike the medieval European city, the "ancient" type was without suburbs and inseparable from its rural continuum. It was a center of politics much more than of commerce and industry—an association of warriors and consumers. The "oriental" city was a city of the dependent type, subject to a central authority and defined by its hierarchical position in relation to other cities.[9]

While not without value, the Weberian urban ideal types may nevertheless be misleading. How useful is the categorization of Chinese, Indian, Muslim, and even Russian, eastern European, and Balkan cities under the single rubric "oriental"? Typology may help the observer to distinguish between the self and the *other:* in the present case, between the western or European city and other cities, portrayed as cities of another time (ancient) or of another space (not-Europe, the Orient). However useful, a typology of two or three entities results in the loss of important variables when a multitude of *others* exists. A yet more negative result from a dualist conceptualization, or an idolization of "us" and "them," western and oriental, may be needless misunderstanding.

A question one should ask in attempting to define the Balkan cultures as a group of environments past and present is how that group of environments resembles or differs from standard representations of it by non-Balkanite Europeans who think of themselves as western. The Weberian and Brunnerian views are not untypical of *Mitteleuropean* conceptions of the cultures and peoples lying to the east of the areas of onetime Germanic settlement or colonization. Such conceptions may be readily adopted by other thinkers and writers because of the well-warranted high regard for Max Weber among English, American, and French social scientists and historians, especially for his contribution to an appreciation of religion and the processes of rationalization and for his conceptualization of an alternative to Marxism. In France, at least from the time of the student rebellion of May 1968 to the 1990s, Max Weber has been for many historians, social scientists, and culturologists, especially for open or covert critics of Fernand Braudel's geohistory and material culture, the "father of us all— *notre père à nous tous*."[10]

The idea that the Europe of geographers does not coincide with the Europe of history and culture, however, is older and independent of Weberian influence. In the early decades of the twentieth century, for example, R.W. Seton-Watson, a British historian of Scottish ancestry (who sometimes wrote under the pseudonym Scotus Viator) and specialist in the history of the South Slavs, was convinced that the Croats of the Habsburg monarchy were better suited (like the English in relation to the Scots?) for the task of government than the Serbs even though there was not then and had not been since 1102 an independent Croatian state and the Serbs of Serbia had governed themselves for the last fifty to one hundred years. The Serbs in his view represented an "eastern culture." Serbia thus might be assimilated into a triune Habsburg state of Germans, Magyars, and South (and other) Slavs, with the Croats in a dominant and the Serbs in a dependent political position. In 1911, Seton-Watson wrote that "the triumph of the Pan-Serb idea would mean the triumph of Eastern over Western culture." At best, the Serbs were "noble savages" (like the Highlanders of Scotland?). Upon meeting his first Serbs from Serbia in 1913 with the Serbian army in Macedonia, he conceded that many of the officers were "not only good soldiers but highly civilized and intelligent Europeans." But even after World War I, in which Serbia had been the first victim of aggression and had suffered heavier losses of human life per capita than any other country, Seton-Watson continued to believe that the appropriate political center of a South Slavic state was Croatia, not Serbia. The customary British term at that time for "Serbian" was "Servian," which Britons inaccurately derived from the Latin term for "serf" *(servus)*. Writing for the London *Times* from Vienna after the military coup that resulted in the assassination of King Alexander Obrenović and Queen Draga, the British publicist Henry Wickham Steed equated Belgrade, Serbia's modest capital, to a "Central Asian Khanate, not a European city." By inference or by direct statement, a common view in British journalism was that neither the Serbs nor "any of the [other] Balkan races" was "a civilized people."[11] American public officials and the American media repeatedly voiced a similar view of the Serbs during the Yugoslav civil strife of the 1990s.

Eager to escape the narrow confines of a small landlocked state, Serbian leaders had committed themselves as early as the 1840s to the project of obtaining an outlet to the Adriatic. Austro-Hungarian and British spatio-economic and political conceptions, however, were inimical to such a solution. In 1912, the

British minister to Belgrade, Sir Ralph Paget, represented Serbian maritime aspirations as sheer "folly." He informed his government that the Serbians were "quite off their heads" in their "visions of blue seas and Servian ships in the offing bringing home the wealth of the Indies." As a result of the "Anglo-Austrian campaign of intimidation" against Serbia, according to the minister of France to Belgrade, Serbian leaders were disgusted with "England" and regarded Paget as "more Austrian than the Austrians and more Germanic than the Germans."[12] During the civil war of the 1990s, the attitude toward Serbia and Yugoslavia of the United States government and of the German-dominated European Community —despite differences between the two—was not appreciably friendlier.

The West's mistrust of the Balkans has a long history, going back at least to the year 1000 as the schism between Eastern Orthodoxy and Roman Catholicism became ever more difficult to resolve following the introduction in the cultures and societies of the Roman Catholic West of certain fundamental changes, including the development of specifically Roman Catholic ritual, dogmas, theology, and church organization, and of a specifically western (Gothic) architecture; the partial diversion of internal dissension toward distant frontiers by means of wars of conversion, plunder, and capital accumulation known as crusades; and a growing receptivity to science, new techniques, fashion, individuality, and faith through reason. Ultimately, especially after the Fourth Crusade against Zara (Zadar) on the Adriatic and against Byzantium, some members of the Orthodox cultures of the Balkans were ready to believe that submission to the Muslim Turks could not be worse than submission to the West, from which they could expect little aid in any case because of the West's internal dissensions.

Upon the outbreak of war between Venice and the Turks in 1570, Gregorio Malaxa, a Moreot (Peloponnesian) noble who had obtained Candiot (Cretan) nobility in 1566, submitted a number of memoirs to the Venetian Council of Ten explaining why the Greeks in turn distrusted the Latins. The "first and most important" reason, he wrote, was that there was no nation in the world "so ardent in the cause of religion" as the Greeks, who consequently prefer to be subjects of the Turks than to submit to the Latins. For the Turks "allow them to live in their own way." The Latins, on the other hand, have never understood, or empathized with, the Greeks (that is, the Orthodox), aspiring always to force them to alter their ways. The Greeks have also refrained from going over to the Latins in the past out of fear that the latter eventually would abandon them to the vengeance of the "iron and fire" of the Turks. Recently, however, some Turks had put aside the former strategy of tolerance. Instead, according to Malaxa, they resorted to despoiling Orthodox churches, altars, and holy writ, and cruelly persecuted Orthodox monks to force them to reveal the location of their treasures. As a result, the Greeks probably were well disposed to join the Latins against the Turks if only they could be sure that Venice would not leave them in the lurch and the Latins agreed to respect Greek (Orthodox) rights, rites, customs, and beliefs.[13]

On the basis of such evidence, Fernand Braudel concluded that a living distinctive Greek or Hellenic (or Rhomaic) civilization still survived in the latter part of the sixteenth century. Proof of its survival was the refusal of the Greeks and the Eastern Orthodox to abandon their religious practices.[14]

Venice's Morea expedition during the summer and early fall of 1572 was too short lived to inspire a Greek insurrection. When other occasions for rebellions or jacqueries occurred in the Balkans, namely, between 1592 and 1612, 1683 and 1699, and 1792 and 1814, among the Greeks, Montenegrins, and Serbs, the insurgent Orthodox populations discovered to their dismay that they could trust neither the pope nor Venice, neither the Holy Roman Empire (Germany-Austria) nor Napoleonic France. *RUSSIA NEITHER !!!*

The orientalization of the Balkans under Ottoman rule reinforced the old distrust. Coming under the authority of another people, religion, and state, the Balkan societies and cultures received the stamp of the conquering society and culture. Life in key Balkan communities and the modes of communication and social and cultural organization were subjected to a rite of *translatio* or culture transfer. They were henceforth to be "spoken," idealized, or "read" in a different way.[15]

Spoken or read in a different way between the mid-fifteenth century and 1800, the Balkans were almost wholly orientalized, especially at the level of the urban cultures. Even before 1800 but especially after 1815, however, a new *translatio* began to find Balkan adherents, a *translatio* that we shall call "rationalization." Under Protestant influence, a modest degree of rationalization entered the Orthodox church itself toward the middle of the seventeenth century. The process continued in the eighteenth century under Roman Catholic influence. The stronger rationalizing strain of secular inspiration reached the Balkan populations only toward the end of the eighteenth and during the nineteenth century. Disillusionments with Europe or the West did not thereupon come to an end, but the process of rationalization continued to gain momentum. Many Europeans, on the other hand, continued to regard the Balkans as a crude Orient until the end of the nineteenth century and thereafter.

The crucial "event" in making rationalization acceptable to an increasing number of Balkanites was its manifestation in secular form under the name of the Enlightenment. For secularism provided Balkan merchants and intellectuals of the Eastern Orthodox faith with an opportunity to identify with Europe at the level of everyday life. In the course of the nineteenth and twentieth centuries, more and more ordinary Balkanites followed suit. As a result, the Balkan peoples put at least a foot in the door of the common European home.

By 1953, under communist rule, the process of rationalization in Yugoslavia was stronger among that country's populations of Orthodox tradition than among Roman Catholics of the interior regions. It was weakest among Yugoslavia's Muslims. The number of persons of each faith per religious leader—one priest to 2,900 Orthodox adherents, one priest to 2,000 Roman Catholics, and one imam, muezzin, or *müderris* to 900 Muslims—probably reflects that fact. The Yugoslav

ORTHODOX JUST BECAME LESS RELIGIOUS !!!

republics with the highest proportion of persons with a negative or indifferent attitude toward religion were Montenegro, Serbia, and Macedonia, in that order—in other words, the republics in which Orthodoxy was most strongly represented.[16]

The Margins as the Cores

Within the Roman Catholic church the movement toward rationalization has grown over a period of ten centuries. But among its adherents there are geohistoric zones of weak or strong proclivity to reason (or rationalizing) and faith alike. In particular, a fundamentalist Catholic zone of resistance to rationalism has existed in the western regions of Bosnia and Hercegovina and a fundamentalist Muslim zone in the eastern regions. Between the two and to the south and east of the Muslim zone, on the other hand, lies an Orthodox zone that, while affected by the two fundamentalisms, has been readier during the last century or more to reach an accommodation with reason. BECOME ATHEISTIC!

Within the three zones, factors of geography, history, religion, and vestigial social structures combine and reinforce each other to produce intense segmented small-group identities or competing sociopolitical fields of segmentation and contestation—rival small groups that define themselves and *others* on the basis of differing religious beliefs and practices, diverse territorial or clan origins, variations in speech habits, and clashing material interests that are often aggravated by the scarcity of resources.

Segmented orbits lack an ordered or hierarchical system of territorial loyalties.[17] When nationalism develops in such territories, of which Bosnia and Hercegovina, the former Dalmatian *krajine*, and the onetime Habsburg borderlands known as the Vojna Krajina (Military Frontier) are good examples, the primary loyalty may shift to one of several different states (Serbia, Croatia, Bosnia, Yugoslavia, Austria, Hungary, Venice, Italy, Turkey). The new national or state identities, however, often are little more than a veil or disguise for local, clan, religious, and provincial differences and cleavages.

Such segmented groups both differ from and greatly resemble each other. The descriptions made in the eighteenth century by the abbé Alberto Fortis of the Orthodox Morlaks (Serbs, perhaps partly of Vlach origin) of Venetian Dalmatia, and of the Roman Catholics of the Adriatic district of Poljica, stress the differences—a social regime of scarcity of material goods and a rough equality among some of the Morlaks, a system of distinctive privileges among the inhabitants of Poljica:

> A Morlack in easy circumstances has no other bed than a coarse blanket made of goats hair, and of Turkish manufacture; very few of the richest people in the country have such a piece of luxurious furniture as a bed after our fashion; and there are not many who have so much as a bedstead; which however, when

they happen to get made in their rough manner, they sleep in, between two great blankets, without sheets, or any other bedding. The greatest part of the inhabitants, content themselves with the bare ground, wrapt in the usual blanket, and only sometimes a little straw under it. But in summer they chuse to sleep in the air. . . . Their household furniture consists of few, and simple articles. . . . [They] have seldom any other houses but cottages covered with straw. . . . The animals inhabit the same cottage, divided from the masters, by a slight partition made of twigs, and plaistered with clay, and the dung of cattle.

In the middle of the Morlak cottage stood a fireplace. Smoke found its way out from the fireplace through the door,

there being rarely any other aperture. Hence every thing within these wretched habitations is varnished with black, and loathsome with smoke; not excepting the milk, which forms a great part of their sustenance, and of which they are very liberal to strangers. Their cloaths, persons, and every thing in short, contract the same smokey smell. The whole family sits round this fire place, in the cold season; and, when they have supped, lay themselves down to sleep in the same place where they sat at supper; for, in every cottage, they have not even benches to sit, and to lie upon. They burn butter instead of oil, in their lamps; but for the most part they use pieces of cleft fir, in lieu of candles.[18]

Comprising a population of about 15,000, the district of Poljica then included three main ethnic groups, each constituted as an order or estate—twenty families who claimed to be descended from the Hungarian nobility, a larger number descended from the nobility of Bosnia, and "the commonalty of peasants." Each year, on St. George's Day, the three estates met at a local plain to choose new magistrates. The village deputies of the common people then proceeded to elect new subordinate counts or village chiefs of Bosnian nobility or to reinstate their current chiefs. Elected by the inferior Bosnian counts or village chiefs, the great count or *veliki knez* always had to be a member of the Hungarian nobility. Because there was usually more than one candidate, however, the election seldom occurred without violence. The ratification of an election in which there was more than one candidate thus required that a partisan of the count-elect seize the box containing the district privileges and run a gauntlet, while the other members of the diet pursued him with stones, knives, and firearms. If the runner safely reached home base with the box of privileges, the election of the designated count was confirmed. Since the territory was a Venetian frontier district, the assembly also elected a new district captain.[19]

The Balkan segmented groups also resembled each other. From Sichelburg (Žumberak) west of Agram (Zagreb) southward across Dalmatia, Bosnia, Hercegovina, Montenegro, the Albanian highlands, Epirus, southwestern Macedonia, and Thessaly, and in the Moreot subpeninsula of Mani—in lands of Serbian, Croatian, Vlach, Albanian, and Greek ethnicity—and eastward from Zengg (Segna, Senj) on the Adriatic across the lands lying between the Drava and Sava rivers to the confluence of the Danube and the Sava and beyond, there was constituted during the fifteenth, sixteenth, and early seventeenth centuries, in territories under Venetian, Hungarian, Austrian, and Ottoman rule, a series of not always contiguous frontier districts under the command of elected, appointed, and sometimes virtually hereditary border lords usually known as captains or "wardukes" (*voivodes*). WARLORDS

The organization of Ottoman military frontier districts in Bosnia may date back to the founding, after the conquest of Vrhbosna in 1435, of the *krajište* (outlying district) of that name, perhaps on a modified model of the eastern military frontiers of Byzantium. The organization of the western frontiers of Hercegovina and Bosnia as a network of frontier and communications security dates back, however, only to the second half of the sixteenth century, with the establishment along the frontiers with Venice, Austria, and the former territories of Hungary, probably on the basis of Venetian and Hungarian models, of at least 5 "captaincies" or *kapetanije*, each under the command of a "captain" *(kapudan, kapetan, capitaneus)*. By the 1680s, the number of *kapetanije*, in Bosnia proper, in Hercegovina, and in the territories north of the Sava grew to 29. Upon the loss of the northern territories to Austria, the number was reduced, in 1699, to 12. By 1716, however, 25 territories in Bosnia and Hercegovina were organized as captaincies. The number fell in 1718, at the end of another war with Austria, to 23. It then grew successively to 34 by 1737, 36 by 1753, 38 by 1801, and 39 from 1802 to 1835, when the institution was abolished.[20] Invested in office by imperial *berat* (warrant of dignity of privilege), the captains—all Muslims in contrast to the Orthodox Christian *armatoloi* (armatoles, or border warriors) of the Greek and Greco-Vlach regions—soon acquired extensive properties and made their offices virtually hereditary in the family or clan line, much like the Greco-Vlach *armatoloi*. MARTOLOZI

In 1537, according to an unverified tradition, perhaps after a territorial re-organization of the Ottoman empire's western frontiers, Epirus and Aetolia-Acarnania, Thessaly, and Macedonia southwest of the Axios River were each divided into five *armatoliks*. Attempts in 1627 and 1699 to replace the Christian armatoles with Muslim garrisons were opposed and had to be abandoned. In 1721, however, the possibly new *armatoliks* of northeastern Macedonia were abolished. They were retained, however, west of the Axios (Vardar). On the eve of the abolition of the institution in 1821, there were ten *armatoliks* or district captaincies in Thessaly and Livadia, four in Aetolia, Acarnania, and Epirus, and three in southwestern Macedonia.[21]

In the Greek and Greco-Vlach districts, the district captains were commissioned by the provincial governor in the presence of Christian notables. Responsible for the defense of his district against external aggression and for the maintenance of internal order, a captain was expected to provide the wages of a designated number of *armatoloi*, whom he divided into companies and distributed among the cantons under his command. He raised funds for this purpose and for his own self-aggrandizement by his function as a tax farmer, with the right to levy taxes for the upkeep of the *armatolik*, supervise the collection of state taxes, and collect tolls from merchants, peddlers, woodcutters, musicians, and seasonal workers. Known in Mani as *bey*, the district captain also charged illegal fees when called upon to settle disputes. He complemented his official duties by engaging in sheep raising, farming, and commerce.[22]

Exercising similar rights, the Muslim captains of Hercegovina enjoyed similar opportunities for the accumulation of private capital by abuses of their public charge, especially in policing travel. On the route between Kliški Ključ and Sarajevo via Mostar, for example, after first facing the threat of freebooting marchmen known as *uskoks* (jumpers to and fro between borders of a contested sea and land), merchants had to traverse two captaincies. At each crossing of a territorial jurisdiction, a legal and extralegal shift of capital was made from mercantile to political ends. As a consequence, mercantile traffic sagged. Captains and their subordinates responded by expropriating local lands and property rights.[23]

Similar forms of warlordships arose earlier or later across the entire area extending from the Carpathians eastward to the Don and the Caucasus, including the Ukraine (literally, "borderland" or "borderlands"), which acknowledged the nominal authority of Poland, Russia, the Ottoman Empire, Transylvania, Wallachia, Moldavia, or the khanate of Crimea.[24]

In the Ukraine, the border warriors were known as Cossacks. In the western Slavic provinces of the Ottoman Empire, they at first were known as *martolosi* (armed men). In the Greek and Greco-Vlach provinces, they were called *armatoloi* or armatoles (a term with the same etymology). In the northern territories subjected to Austrian rule in 1522, they were known as border men *(Grenzer, graničari, krajišnici)*. Along the Venetian and Austrian coastlands, they were called *uskoks*. In Hungary and Transylvania, they were known as haiduks (from Magyar *hajdu*, pl. *hajduk*), from which was created in Serbian and Bulgarian one of the customary terms for outlaw (*haidut* in Bulgarian).

Known to the Venetians, to the Slavs of the western regions, and to the Greeks as captaincies or *armatoliks*, the frontier districts were not always well knit together because of local rivalries. Between 1522 and mid-century, however, Austria organized a unified border command comprising three major territorial units—Krabatische Gränitz (Croatian Borderland), Windische Gränitz (Slavonian Borderland), and Meer Gränitz (Maritime Borderland).

Most of the border warriors in these borderlands were Serbs or Vlachs (from the Slavicized western regions of the Ottoman Empire), almost exclusively of the Eastern Orthodox faith. In return for stipulated military services, the Orthodox soldier colonists (*kmetovi*, from *comes*, pl. *comites*) obtained family allotments of land, were allowed to choose their own magistrates, and were freed of feudal obligations to the Croatian and Hungarian nobility. Confirmed by the imperial Statuta Valachorum of 1630, their privileges were later restricted.

After the Fifteen Years' War of 1592–1606 with Turkey, Austria used the soldiery of the Military Frontier as much for the promotion of Habsburg dynastic interests as for frontier defense.[25] During the 1670s, moreover, the Society of Jesus promoted the conversion of the Orthodox military colonists to the Uniate church. Applied in particular in the Varaždin Generalcy of Slavonia, the attempt to convert the Orthodox was applied more generally after 1690. In Hercegovina, the protagonists of conversion—of the Orthodox, not of Muslims—to the Catholic faith were the Franciscans.

The dissolution of the Slavonian Generalcy toward the middle of the eighteenth century began the process of the dismantling of the border system. During the Napoleonic wars, the western Austrian borderlands (the territories of the Carlstadt and Banal or Viceregal regiments) were ceded to Napoleon, who made them part of France's Illyrian Provinces. Some members of the frontier population were seduced by French revolutionary propaganda. Other elements directly or indirectly aided the Serbian war of independence against the Turks (1804–14).[26]

At the time of the restoration, the lost provinces were returned to Austria. The Habsburg Military Frontier then stretched from the Adriatic eastward to include an area in Transylvania. Organized into nineteen regiments, each made up of twelve companies, the authority of the reduced territories of the Military Frontier extended, in 1825, over an area of 37,500 square kilometers and a population of 1,130,000. A regimental company exercised authority over two hundred to five hundred households of soldier colonists. Each household head *(gospodar, Hauswirth)* was directly responsible to a company first or second lieutenant of economic administration, who was in charge of forest conservation, tolls, and corvée labor. In the Carlstadt and Banal regiments, the policing of routes and markets and the collection of customs duties was entrusted to a much-feared frontier police known as *Serressaner* (literally, "braves"), who were recruited from a hundred or two hundred of the most notable and wealthiest families in the territory of each regiment. The Military Frontier was thus organized as a command economy in which there was little or no room for a civil society.[27] The compromise of 1868 between Hungary and Croatia, however, laid the groundwork for the abolition of the Military Frontier in 1881 as a sop to Croatian nationalism.

A Wild Space

The problem of the borderlands can be fully grasped only if one views it from a yet longer historical perspective. However difficult, unusual, or even unseemly it may appear to many members of a *monochronic* culture such as the American to focus on more than one well-defined time,[28] our focus must continue to be polychronic. To understand the quintessentially polychronic Balkan cultures, we must embrace a multitude of times and questions.

Let us turn, therefore, to the world of Charlemagne and his successors. It was a world studded with marchlands, known as *marches* in France's western regions and *Mark* in what became Germany (including the designations Marchfield for what later became Vienna and *Ostmark* for Austria or portions thereof). These lands were administered by march counts, margraves, and *marquis*. The intervening territories between England and Wales and between England and Scotland similarly were known as the Marches (from Anglo-Saxon *mearc*). The commanders of these marches were called lords marchers.

A march marked a land of low population density, a land of forest and brush, a wild space of game and wild gamesmen, of banditry, paganism, heresy, and barbarian ways.[29] It was also, or soon would become, a zone marking off two opposing civilizations or ways of universalizing and particularizing—intervening territories, for example, between eastern (Greek) and western (Latin) Christendom or between Christendom and Islam.

Around the year 1000, such a zone marked off Byzantium and Eastern Orthodoxy from Islam and the Arabic world. The continuing tension and communication —at the level of war, religion, and sex—between these two worlds is the subject of the famous ballad of the two-blood (Greek and Arabic, Christian and Muslim) border lord in Asia Minor, Digenis Akritas.[30] The lord's name is derived from the word ἄκρον, meaning "margin" or "border" like its probable Slavic cognates *kraj, krajište,* and *krajina,* and its American namesake—Akron, Ohio.

In the Serbian ballad known as "Stephen Dušan's Wedding," which the outlaw patriot Tešan Podrugović recounted to Vuk Karadžić in 1815, again about intermarriage or sexual communion—the exchange of women across cultural frontiers—the message was clear: "The Latins are deceivers, that is known."[31] In the 1990s, no less than in the fourteenth and fifteenth centuries and as in 1815, the message sent and received by many Serbs—despite a two-century-old movement toward reason—was much the same. The Latins—Dalmatians, Croats, and other Roman Catholics—and western Europeans in general have been no less lax in initiating and reciprocating such messages of distrust.

In the marchlands, at the margins or frontiers of a civilization or system of city cultures, or in areas lying between two systems of civilization, lived men who were formerly known as ἄγριοι or *homines agrestes.*[32] The winged Ottoman *delis* clad in animal skins and imbued with the fury of the *berserkr* of Germanic mythology provide but one example of the type. Such wild men living in a wild country were the remnant representatives of a heroic culture, defenders of the *egoismo* of one cultural system against another. Among the Greeks of the eighteenth and early nineteenth century, one group of such men was known as ἄγριοι, κλέφται or "wild klephts," in contradistinction to the *armatoloi,* who were called ἥμεροι κλέφται or "tame klephts" even though they often turned ἄγριοι.[33] And much like Hesiod, Metropolitan Stevan Stratimirović distinguished between the man of mild manners or *čelovek* and the "wild man" or *diviač*.[34] In medieval Germany, to cite an example from outside the Balkans, the institution of the *Landstaat* signified the triumph, over the wild (or "raw") wood of the castle town and land that, to use the language of Claude Lévi-Strauss, the castle town had tamed or "cooked."[35]

Precisely because the "wild men" abound in particular in peripheral areas, at the margins of a system of cultures, many members of one cultural system identify a neighboring system of cultures with the negative—that is, wild—qualities of the marginal groups even though they may ascribe positive qualities to their own wilderness or wildness or to unknown far-off wildernesses.[36] The "idea of the Wild Man," argues Hayden White, has been "progressively despatialized," to be redefined as "the repressed content of *both* civilized *and* primitive humanity."[37] It has not been despatialized everywhere, however, and it may be despatialized nowhere except superficially. In times of crisis, wildness becomes again a space, a territory, a people (Los Angeles, Newark, Watts), and it even may be partly misidentified as Serbia.

That is precisely how the United States government, American media, and European Community responded to the Yugoslav civil war of the 1990s in the territories of the former Habsburg Military Frontier, of the former Venetian *craine*, of the Krajina of eastern Bosnia, and of the former captaincies of Bosnia and Hercegovina. They attributed qualities to the ideological core (Serbia) that were more appropriate to the western margins or territories lying between Serbia and Croatia proper (the other main ideological core, with which they identified with greater ease) and that were just as prevalent—if not more so—among the Muslims of Bosnia and Hercegovina as among the Serbs and Croats of the same province.

In heroic poetry, the "paradigmatic deed" of a hero is to slay a dragon or monster who symbolizes primal chaos. In war, which represents a kind of hunt, the enemy may be perceived as a beast or being "both non-human and charged with demonic or totemic power."[38] In an armed confrontation between two rival cultures, the killing of members of the other culture, who by their alien practices and rites have shown their nonhuman nature, may be perceived as the equivalent of the killing of a primal monster. Its design may be to bring disorder to an end. But when the attempt to create or restore order brings more disorder, the other side perceives the enemy as a "withholding enemy," an enemy who deprives it of its physiological, psychological, and resource needs.

In the Yugoslav civil war of the 1990s, as during the internecine war between Serbs and Croats in substantially the same territories of Croatia and Bosnia-Hercegovina (then technically part of Croatia) during the Second World War, both conceptions of the enemy were common. Also common was the mutual conception of the enemy as the "enemy of God" or of reason. In the eyes of many Croats and Muslim Slavs, the Serbs and the Yugoslav army were also perceived as an "offensive" or ruthless expansionist enemy. From the point of view of local (by tradition, Orthodox) Serbs—that is, of Serbs in the republics other than Serbia and especially of Serbs in the territories of the former Military Frontier and in Bosnia and Hercegovina—and of the remaining partisans of a confederate, federal, or united Yugoslavia, the Croats and Muslims were an "oppressive/betraying enemy," the old "invisible [or not so invisible] enemy within."[39]

To what extent the enemy was for the other side or sides a "heroic enemy" is unclear. On the other hand, asked during the siege of Sarajevo what the fighting between the Bosnian Serbs and the Bosnian Muslims was about, the Muslim commander of a Bosnian militia unit at the Jezero Hospital in Sarajevo, Djordje Krčum, is reported to have replied: "It's about civilization. It's not an ethnic war, it's a war of ordinary people against primitive men who want to carry us back to tribalism."[40]

Note the polarities: "ordinary people" versus "primitive men," "civilization" versus "tribalism." Note, too, that, in the view of the speaker, the war was "not an ethnic war," a statement by which he intended to refute the more likely case that all sides—Serbs, Croats, and Muslims—were victims of their respective tribalisms.

Cities, Stock Raising, and Transhumance

The Balkan cultures may lack "shared goals and actions."[41] They constitute nonetheless a historical community of related cultures through the very fact of the local, kinship, and friendship foundations of their loyalties and of the foundations of these values themselves in a common remembered historical experience of pastoralism, especially in the form of transhumance. That mode of life is no longer ascendant. In modified form, however, the values derived therefrom and from a yet older way of life have survived the material culture.

Between 1500 and 1850, the Balkan cultures comprised a network of distinctive but interdependent ecosystems of transhumance. In its full form, that network was the product of the establishment of a single political state—the Ottoman Empire—throughout most of the Balkans. However, without two other factors—a suitable geography and a political culture specifically favorable to stock raising—transhumance probably would not have had the importance it did until the deterritorialization of the Ottoman command economy and formation of small Balkan states.

The populations of the maritime portions of the Balkans have specialized for thousands of years in the cultivation of products that one may define—in terms of their collective importance—as constituent elements of a Mediterranean cultural-ecosystemic complex. The mark of that cultural-ecosystemic complex was the cultivation in nearby areas of wheat, barley, the vine, and the olive tree. Because of the climatic difference engendered by the mountains that line the northern Mediterranean coasts, olive trees usually cannot thrive more than ten to twenty kilometers beyond the sea itself. At the same time, the proximity of the sea and mountain—two different environments, each with its own seasonal attributes—has stimulated the development of sheep and goat raising.

The food and clothing needs and tastes of a growing urban population, under the pressure of certain other demographic factors and forms of economic organization, further required the expansion or introduction of the practice of transhumance, that is, the keeping of large flocks of sheep for which summer pastures were available in the cooler mountain interior and winter pastures were to be had near the sea. Joined by pathways of transhumance, the two areas of pasturage sometimes were a hundred, two hundred, or three hundred kilometers distant from each other.

Transhumance assumed two basic forms. In one case, called "inverse transhumance," the settled or permanent community was in the highland (Dinaric, Pindus, Rhodope, Balkan, Carpathian) interior. Serving as a permanent summer residence, it often comprised an upper village and a lower village, with transhumance to a lowland or maritime region in winter. In the other case, which some twentieth-century geographers call "normal," the settled community was in the lowlands or near the sea. It also served as a winter retreat for the livestock.

Normal transhumance was practiced by the populations that were oriented toward the Adriatic side of the Dinaric Mountains but who moved their flocks and herds toward the mountain interior in the spring to escape the summer drought. Inverse transhumance, more important in terms of numbers than normal transhumance, was practiced by the South Slavs, Vlachs, and Albanians or Arnauts who inhabited the Pannonian side of the Dinaric Mountains, all the way from Mount Velebit in the north to Scutari (Shkodër) in the south, with movement from the highlands toward the Morava and Sava valleys in the fall and later from the Morava and Sava back to the mountain in order to escape the deep snows of the Pannonian winter.

Paradoxically, normal transhumance was probably the product both of a chronologically earlier (in late Antiquity or the early Middle Ages) contraction of the urban division of labor (in regions close to the sea) and of a later (eighteenth- and early nineteenth-century) manifestation of a more intense commercialization, requiring settlement near the markets of demand (thus near the sea or at other nodes of communication). Inverse transhumance, on the other hand, expanded greatly under the impetus of the Ottoman political and economic order.

Also common were variants of normal and inverse transhumance. One variant known as "double" transhumance was characterized by the formation of permanent dwellings at some point between the summer and winter pasture grounds. Such double transhumance existed in the southern Carpathians of Transylvania, whose pastoralists moved to higher regions toward the end of April, returned to their home village at the end of summer, and proceeded in the fall to the steppes of the Bărăgan or broad Wallachian plain north of the Danube, where their sheep had access to the grass germinating under the snow.

To migrate in response to famine was known in the Middle Ages among the

Serbs as *prêiti vŭ prêhranou* (literally, "to go off in search of food"). Wandering practiced in years of severe drought, known among Serbs and Croats as *posušje*, was marked by the movement of small or large human groups with their flocks of sheep and herds of cattle in search of water. In some areas, as in the Brda or High Montenegro and in eastern Hercegovina, where the agricultural crop was insufficient for the needs of an entire year, the practice of transhumance was complemented by a winter migration of individual families and parts of families and other small groups to serve as hired farmhands in the Sava region of Bosnia. A portion of the population of Popovo Polje, on the other hand, found employment during the winter in Stolac, Mostar, or the neighboring Dalmatian towns. In Crete, transhumance took the form of the movement of sheep for winter pasturage from the interior of this big island to one of the small neighboring islands.[42]

In the western Balkan (Greek, Vlach, Albanian, and South Slavic) regions, both the commercial routes and the routes of transhumance were under the control of licensed *armatoloi*, district captains, or other agents of provincial governors. These authorities collected tolls, duties, and taxes owed by the local population for the policing of the *armatolik* or captaincy against brigandage, an activity from which they themselves did not desist.[43]

Conducive to the diffusion of practices of transhumance was the further fact that limits existed on the extent to which agriculture could be practiced in the area. The Balkans were the first Europe of farmers. The areas in which agriculture could be practiced with ease south of the Danube and Sava basins, however, were confined to a few maritime plains, small river basins, and *poljes* or long narrow fertile depressions formed in the Dinaric Mountains by the sinking of the calcareous Cretaceous and Jurassic rocks and annual deposit in the depressions of new alluvial soils.

Until the nineteenth century, the narrow mountain *poljes* of the western Balkans were the customary centers of cereal cultivation. Many of the plains, on the other hand, were undrained marshlands with a low population density. Little suited to agriculture despite their soil fertility, the plains were used during the Ottoman era as an extensive grazing ground.[44] As late as the end of the nineteenth century, the plains of Durazzo, Elbasan, and Salonika were marshlands. Some members of the Elbasan population of itinerant diggers—a temporary proletarian diaspora—even had to seek seasonal employment in faraway Anatolia.[45] Indeed, in the mid-sixteenth century, while traveling along the continuation of the Via Egnatia between Thessaloniki or Siderocapsa and Istanbul, the French naturalist Pierre Belon du Mans encountered between the Maritsa River and the Ottoman capital "de grăds bendes de pauures paisans Albanois, autrement appellez Ergates, qui retournoient en leur pays"—seasonal workers (like the Lombards and Savoyards) who went each summer to hire themselves out to harvest the grains of Macedonia, Thrace, and even Anatolia.[46]

A *polje* itself, however, was not exempt from depopulation. Thus the town of Podgorica, one of the two centers of administration of the Ottoman sanjak of

Scutari (Shkodër, Skadar), had a livestock and grain market to which grain was brought from districts lying beyond the Podgorica basin. Technically a *polje*, the lake and river basin of seventeenth-century Podgorica was pastureland and a country of fisherfolk. It was sparsely settled because of the withdrawal of local peasants to the town in order to avoid the rising rents of the local landlords.[47]

A yet greater deterrent to the expansion of agriculture stemmed from the nature of the prevailing climatic characteristics since the last great Ice Age. The Mediterranean is subject to two major climatic influences, Saharan and Atlantic, the first coming from the south and the second from the west. The Saharan influence prevails between the March equinox and the September equinox, bringing clear, light, dry air, and often drought during the one season otherwise suitable for agricultural production. The Atlantic influence prevails thereafter, bringing clouds and rain. But it comes too late for the growing of crops. The northern Mediterranean and adjacent mountain lands are thus a different kind of ecosystem from the monsoon regions of Asia, where rain and warm weather come simultaneously, allowing a high level of agricultural productivity. In the Mediterranean, agricultural productivity is low except in areas of an irrigated garden cultivation.[48]

Garden cultivation was stimulated by the growth of cities and availability—but also scarcity—of water. The cultivation of rice, cotton, roses (for their essence), and tobacco spread in particular to the southern and eastern peninsular (especially Macedonia and Thrace) and Danubian regions. In parts of Hungary, including the rural area around Budapest, many of the ablest vegetable gardeners were Bulgarians whose ancestors had brought their skills northward from the garden cultures of the south.[49]

Not until the second half of the eighteenth century, however, were river, canal, and land transportation improvements or capital investments in social overhead sufficient in Habsburg Hungary to allow the movement of large quantities of cheap bulk commodities like grains (unlike sheep or cattle, which move on the hoof) over considerable distances. In the Ottoman Empire, a similar situation did not arise until after 1830.

Until that time, Ottoman administrators regarded interior regions not accessible by river navigation as areas of meat supply (moved on the hoof) and of provisions of wool, hides, and furs. Maritime regions were treated as zones of cereal supply. A desire may have existed among officials of the central government to maintain a balance between cereal needs and the need in cities for wool, hides, and furs. Many Ottoman landlords, however, favored the transhumant stockbreeders by renting rights of pasturage to them. In turn, the stockbreeders purchased cereals from the landlords for their villages before returning to their mountain homes in the fall after having disposed of their own goods (wool, wool manufactures, and live animals) in the local markets and fairs near their routes of transhumance and places of winter sojourn.

As necessary to the Ottoman state geopolitically as its defense system of the western and northern frontiers and as necessary to it economically as the practice of transhumance was a system of security along the main routes of commerce and war, especially between Adrianople and Niš, Belgrade, and (from the mid-sixteenth century to 1683) Pest; between Adrianople and Thessaloniki; between Thessaloniki and Niš; between Niš and Durrës (Durazzo); and between Üsküb and Niš on the one hand and Sarajevo and Dubrovnik on the other. Along these routes were to be found relay stations at intervals of about fifteen to forty, and exceptionally sixty, kilometers. Being part of a network of routes, cities, and control centers (*palanke/palanques* or stockades along the route Adrianople to Belgrade, *hans* or caravan stations along parts of some of the other routes), the routes were protected by the soldiers and administrators of the towns and *palanques* through which they passed or of the *hans* at which they stopped.

In the eastern Balkan regions, especially between Adrianople and Sofia, and until the latter part of the seventeenth century along the route to Belgrade, and in territories yet farther west, a rural police of *voynuk* villages complemented the task of maintaining communications security along the main routes. About halfway between two relay stations a designated *voynuk* village posted guards at several watchhouses from which movements could be observed in every direction. Upon the approach of a caravan, the guards would beat their drums to assure travelers that no bandits were lurking about. The absence of the sound of drums served as a warning of possible danger, and the *voynuk* guards presumably took more positive steps to assure the safety of the caravan.[50]

In the southern regions in particular, a local rural police of *derbend* villages was in charge of security through mountain passes. In return for their services, the *voynuk* and *derbend* villages enjoyed certain autonomies and tax exemptions.[51] By drawing to it both bandits and a sometimes disorderly soldiery, however, the system of communications security discouraged the development of agriculture around the routes, towns, and *palanques*, thereby favoring the continuing predominance of pastoralism.

Rural and Urban, People and Animals, Tamers and Tamed

In the 1520s, nomads may have formed 3.6 percent of the Balkan population, compared to 16.2 percent of the population of the western Asian province of Anadolu.[52] It is not always easy to distinguish between nomadism and transhumance. But if "pure" nomadism was of minor importance in the Balkans, the proportion of the Balkan population engaged in stock raising, transhumance, border administration and defense, and the policing of routes was much greater, probably at least five to six times as great.

South of the Sava and Danube rivers, in an area of about 440,000 square kilometers, the population may have fluctuated as follows between 1520 and 1800:

Table 8.1

Population South of the Sava and Danube Rivers, 1520–1800

Year	Rural Population	Urban Population	Total Population
1520	4,665,000–5,665,000	335,000	5 to 6 million
1580	6,400,000–7,400,000	600,000	7 to 8 million
1700	5,175,000	825,000	6 million
1800	5,800,000	1,200,000	7 million

Source: Stoianovich, "Cities, Capital Accumulation, and the Ottoman Command Economy," forthcoming.

The urban element includes market towns and *palanques* with a population of several hundred to two thousand persons. One may note further that the rural population declined from 93–94 percent in 1520 to 91–92 percent in 1580, 86 percent in 1700, and 83 percent in 1800. Some estimates, for example, place the emigration of Greeks from Macedonia between 1650 and 1850—including perhaps not only ethnic but also cultural Greeks—at 1.5 or even 2 million.[53] The population density of the territories south of the Sava and Danube thus oscillated from 11.4–13.6 persons per square kilometer in 1520 to 15.9–18.2 persons in 1580, 13.6 in 1700, and 15.9 in 1800. A more or less stabilized low population density was the product of long-term structural factors, of which wars were but one element.[54]

What the foregoing estimates conceal is that the stock raising and transhumant population rose as the urban element rose. Between 1859 and 1905, the number of sheep in Serbia per thousand inhabitants fell from 2,202 to 1,129–1,176. The number of bovines fell from 746 to 350–61, the number of goats from 452 to 159, the number of pigs from 1,637 to 322. The per capita sheep and bovine population of Serbia thus declined to one-half and the pig population to one-fifth of the 1859 level, while the goat population per capita fell to one-third of the base period.[55] During the same time span, the human population density doubled. It also doubled between 1815 and 1859. And by doubling the 1859 figures for Serbia's per capita animal population, one may obtain a presumed animal population per thousand human inhabitants, in 1815, of 4,400 sheep, 1,500 bovines, 900 goats, and 3,250 pigs.

The great extent of forest cover in pre-1815 Serbia and consequent availability of a food supply of acorns for domesticated pigs made the Serbian ratio between pigs and people much higher than the ratio in other parts of the Balkans. Contrarily, the goat ratio of Serbia was low. The ratios between people and sheep and bovines in the rest of the Balkans, however, were probably close to the Serbian ratios. If one reduces the estimated 1815 Serbian ratios for bovines, sheep, and goats by 10 percent, one may estimate the Balkan livestock population south of the Sava and Danube, in 1800 or 1815, at 27.7 million sheep, 9.5 million bovines, and 5.7 million goats.

Table 8.2

Livestock Population of Greece and Yugoslavia, 1960–1980

	Greece			Yugoslavia		
	1960	1970	1980	1960	1970	1980
Cattle	1,071,000	997,000	950,000	5,702,000	5,029,000	5,491,000
Sheep	9,353,000	7,680,000	8,000,000	10,823,000	8,974,000	7,354,000
Pigs	628,000	383,000	1,020,000	5,818,000	5,544,000	7,747,000
Horses	327,000	255,000	120,000	1,220,000	1,076,000	617,000

Source: Gianaris, *Greece and Yugoslavia*, p. 132.

This arbitrary calculation greatly understates the Balkan goat population. François Pouqueville, for example, estimated the goat population of Macedonia, Epirus, Thessaly, and the Greek lands north of Attica, in 1815, at 8,400,000; he set the sheep population of the same area at 4,800,000.[56] The total goat population of the Balkans thus may have been more than 12 million. With pigs and other domesticated animals excluding cats, dogs, and fowl, the total number of domestic animals may then have been well over eight times as great as the human population. But by 1905, there were in the same area only three such animals per capita.

Possessing a sheep population of 500,000 and a goat population of 1,500,000 in 1815 (without the numerous flocks of Ali Pasha, of his sons and grandsons, and of the *beys* and *ağas*), Epirus may have had 3 million sheep and goats in 1871, thus probably as many as in 1815. With a human population in 1871 of about 718,000, however, the ratio of sheep and goats stood at 4.18 per capita,[57] probably below the 1815 level.

By converting the other livestock to bovine units, using a conversion coefficient of 1 bovine = 2 pigs = 5 sheep = 5 goats,[58] one obtains, for 1800, a general Balkan ratio between bovine units and human population of 3:1. In 1900, the ratio was less than 1:1. In Serbia, the ratio fell from more than 4:1 in 1800 to a little over 2:1 in 1859 and less than 1:1 in 1900. The Balkan environment thus was radically transformed. The ratio between human population and domesticated animals deteriorated. The air, too, may have smelled different.

The Balkan cattle, sheep, and horse population continued to decline during the twentieth century except perhaps in Bulgaria. The fluctuation of livestock population in Greece and Yugoslavia between 1960 and 1980 can be seen in Table 8.2 above.

Other data confirm a continuing long-term downward trend in the ratio of bovine units to human population, starting perhaps around 1830 and probably continuing at least until 1980. I shall confine further observations on this subject, however, to the half-century before World War I.

In Bulgaria, the animal population per thousand inhabitants stood in 1887 at 2,179 sheep, 382 goats, 125 pigs, and 500 bovines. In 1900, it stood at only 1,874 sheep, 375 goats, 98 pigs, and 426 bovines; in 1910, at 1,999 sheep, 338 goats, 121 pigs, and 370 bovines. A drop thus occurred from 1,075 bovine units per population of 1,000 in 1887 to 925 in 1900 and 898 in 1910.[59]

In 1867, the sheep and goat population of the Plovdiv and Sliven sanjaks (Eastern Rumelia, which was not annexed to Bulgaria until 1885) of Turkey stood at 2,862,000. Under the disturbed conditions of the Russo-Turkish war of 1877–78, however, the number of sheep and goats in Eastern Rumelia declined to 1,426,000 in 1879–80. It was still no more than 1.745 million in 1881–82 and 2.28 million in 1883, still a fifth below the 1867 level.

The sheep population of Danubian Bulgaria fell from 5.01 million in 1870 to 4.27 million in 1883, a decline of 15 percent. Moreover, as a result of the entry into the world market of massive quantities of American, Argentine, and Indian cereals, as well as American and Argentine refrigerated meats, prices for Bulgarian farm products fell, and, between 1882 and 1894, cereal export values also fell. In like manner, incentives for capital investment in Balkan agriculture were curtailed. Bulgarian peasant families may have found reason to consume a larger part of their own production.

The domesticated animal population of Greece fell from 1,757 sheep, 1,284 goats, 31 pigs, and 157 bovines per thousand inhabitants in 1899 to 1,223 sheep, 910 goats, 78 pigs, and 105 bovines in 1912; it thus declined during this brief interval from 780 to 571 bovine units per thousand inhabitants.

North of the Danube, in Romania, the number of bovines per thousand inhabitants fell from 702 in 1860 to 433 in 1873 and 374 in 1911. The number of bovines per capita thus was halved between 1860 and 1910, as in Serbia. Here, as in the territories south of the Danube and Sava, the decline in the number of domesticated animals per capita was a function of the growth of population, itself an outcome of the expansion of cereal cultivation.

Forming part of the judicial district of G(h)revena and of the sanjak or generality of Serfidje (Servia), the Pindus Vlach mountain canton of Samarina possessed 81,000 sheep in 1877. In 1912, it had no more than 17,000 sheep.[60] As late as the mid-sixteenth century, Samarina may have comprised little more than the summer pastures of three or four hut encampments. Oral tradition ascribes its founding to four camp or sheep company leaders. Three more company leaders pitched camp in its vicinity by 1600. Another was drawn to the general site during the seventeenth century. The exact site of the dwellings may have shifted more than once, but Samarina continued to grow in size until 1770, after which it may have declined until the mid-nineteenth century, followed by a modest revival until 1877, when the cluster of Samarina hamlets is said to have numbered 1,200 houses, with an average of 68 sheep to a house. In 1912 it contained only 800 houses.[61]

Other Pindus Vlach communities underwent a similar experience. Most of them seem to have been formed during the sixteenth, seventeenth, or eighteenth century. Most of them likewise entered a period of decline after 1770, after the Napoleonic wars and the Greek revolution, or after 1850 and, irrevocably, after 1878. The village of Metsovo (Amintshu), for example, contained 379 houses in 1735 and perhaps 835 houses in 1880. It may have attained a maximum number of dwellings during the Napoleonic era. Avdhela, whose oldest church was not built until 1751 (or 1721), contained some 350 houses in 1912. Perivoli was founded only during the early part of the eighteenth century by the amalgamation of three hamlets. Founded at about the same time or somewhat later by the amalgamation of four hamlets, Turia contained about 50 cottages in 1800.

From four of the Pindus Vlach communities—Samarina, Smiksi, Avdhela, and Perivoli—the downhill fall and uphill spring migrations involved almost the entire population—men, women, and children—together with their sheep, horses, and other animals, and with an abundance of blankets, carpets, cushions, and kitchen utensils.[62] On October 31, 1812, while traveling on the road between Arta and Ioannina (Janina), Dr. Henry Holland encountered just such a group of nomads—made up of two "different tribes" or shepherd communities—in the vicinity of Ioannina. The temporal rhythm of their movements was the usual one in the interior regions—down the mountains with their flocks of sheep to the plains or lowlands after the feast of St. Demetrius, up the mountains from the plains after St. George's Day. Dr. Holland describes the migrating shepherd folk as

> a wandering people of the mountains of Albania, who in the summer feed their flocks in these hilly regions, and in the winter spread them over the plains in the vicinity of the gulph of Arta, and along other parts of the coast. The many large flocks of sheep we had met the day before, belonged to these people, and were preceding them to the plains. The cavalcade we now passed through was nearly two miles in length, with few interruptions. The number of horses with the emigrants might exceed a thousand; they were chiefly employed in carry-ing the moveable habitations, and the various goods of the community, which were packed with remarkable neatness and uniformity. The infants and small children were variously attached to the luggage, while the men, women, and elder children travelled for the most part on foot; a healthy and masculine race of people, but strongly marked by the wild and uncouth exterior connected with their manner of life. The greater part of the men were clad in coarse, white woollen garments; the females in the same material, but more variously coloured, and generally with some ornamented lacing about the breast. Their petticoats scarcely reached below the knee, shewing nearly the whole length of the stockings, which were made of woollen threads of different colours, red, orange, white, and yellow. Almost all the young women and children wore upon the head a sort of chaplet, composed of piastres, paras, and other silver coins, strung together, and often suspended in successive rows, so as to form something like a cap. The same coins were attached to other parts of the garments, and occasionally with some degree of taste. Two priests of the Greek church were with the emigrants, and closed the long line of their proces-sion.[63]

Most of the Vlach, Slav, Greek, and Albanian seasonal dispersions, however, were not movements of nomads but rather movements of transhumance, mainly comprising male professional specialists and apprentices. Most of the remaining population of the communities practicing transhumance stayed at their fixed abodes except in periods of crisis or disturbance. The ethnic groups among whom both transhumance and nomadism were most common were the Turkic Yürüks (literally, "migrants" or "nomads") of Rumelia (where they had been resettled from Anatolia) and the Pindus Vlachs. In the seventeenth century, the Yürüks of Rumelia are said to have numbered 1,294 *odjaks*. At thirty men to an *odjak*, they comprised 38,820 men deemed capable of fighting (plus women, children, and old men), rising in the eighteenth century to 57,000.[64] A population of territorially fragmented groups stretching from Istria in the north to Thessaly in the south, the Vlachs may once have been more numerous but numbered only half a million people in 1912.[65]

Practiced by Dinaric and Pindus highlanders, transhumance also characterized the way of life of the Carpathian highlanders. It also prevailed between the mountain interior of Thessaly and Epirus and both the Aegean coastland and shores of the shallow waters of the Gulf of Arta. It was practiced between the Rhodope and the Aegean or between the Rhodope and the lowlands lying between Adrianople and the Sea of Marmara (where the stock was fattened for the food needs of Istanbul). The Sredna Gora (Balkan Mountains) populations sought winter pastures in several different areas—in the lower Maritsa basin, along the lower Danube and in the Dobrudja steppe and marshland, and near the Black Sea in the vicinity of Burgas. As late as 1870, even after the growth of a commercial cereal economy, almost a third of the rural product of Bulgaria was derived from its livestock economy.[66]

Nongenerative Cities: A Second Look

Between 1580 and 1800 the urban population of the Ottoman Balkans doubled. The total rural population, on the other hand, may have declined by 600,000–1,600,000. These two factors in combination, namely, urban growth during a period of rural population decline—along with the withdrawal of non-Muslim populations from the lower highlands and plains to mountain retreats—required a shift from farming to stockbreeding.[67] The rising grain needs of a growing urban population were met by more stringent methods of redistribution. As a result, many rural dwellers turned to acquiring mobile stock or capital in the form of sheep or cattle to satisfy the growing urban needs for meat, leather, wool, and cheese. Such a transformation was facilitated by the fact that landlords, too, desired a friendly symbiotic relationship with the transhumant stockbreeders, for these stockbreeders filled their cereal needs, as we have seen, from the surpluses of the landlords, whose fields the flocks or herds fertilized. The intensification of such relationships probably promoted an extension of the distances between summer and winter pasturages. The latter occurrence was also encouraged by the very vastness of the Ottoman Empire.

Unaware that the foregoing situation had begun to change, the British historian George Finlay observed in 1861 that "the difficulty of the Ottoman question lies in the solution of a social problem. Can the decay of industry, and the constant diminution of the agricultural population in the Ottoman Empire, be immediately changed into activity, and a tendency to multiply and replenish the earth?" Setting the problem in a comparative historical framework, Finlay continued:

> The Ottoman Empire is not the first which has perpetuated its existence until it has exterminated the whole agricultural population by a vicious system of taxation, and which has not perished by foreign conquest until it had depopulated the country and prepared the land for colonisation by new inhabitants. The Roman emperors of the West had exterminated the population in the rural districts of Italy, Gaul, and Spain, before those provinces were repeopled by Lombards, Franks, and Goths. The emperors of the East had driven the population of Greece, Macedonia, and Thrace from the villages into the towns, before those countries were repeopled by Albanians, Sclavonians, and Bulgarians. The caliphs of Bagdat exterminated the population of Mesopotamia and Syria. The Seljouks converted Asia Minor into a declining country before its ruin was consummated by the Ottoman Turks. The Greek empire of the Paleologues existed at Constantinople for nearly two centuries in a state of moral corruption quite as degrading, and in a state of political and military weakness far more contemptible, than the Ottoman Empire now exhibits.

For the decline of agriculture under Ottoman rule (which, in fact, had been growing since 1830), Finlay provided a further explanation, writing in the historical present to emphasize the continuing nature of the process:

> The capital invested in old time in plantations, mills, water-courses, cisterns, farm-buildings, bridges, and roads, becomes annihilated, and no capital is ever saved by the landowner to repair the degradations effected by time. Abandoned villages, deserted mosques, ruined churches, and forsaken graveyards, present themselves in every district; and the traveller in the present as in past generations sees land which was recently cultivated consigned to pasturage. The burdens of taxation never diminish; but no portion of that taxation is ever employed to repair a road or a bridge.

"During the last two centuries," he continued, "the destruction of capital vested in land [namely, in crop farming as against grazing, at least in the interior as opposed to the maritime regions] throughout the East has been going on at an accelerated pace, and a corresponding diminution of the agricultural population has been the inevitable result."[68] Such disinvestment may have reached its height in fact between 1580 and 1700, but a recovery to the 1580 level probably was not realized until 1800 or 1830.

The failure to invest sufficiently in such social overhead as the maintenance of caravansaries *(hans)* is palpably evident in Ivo Andrić's historical novel, *The Bridge on the Drina*, a portrayal among other things of the state of disrepair since the eighteenth century of the *han* at the Višegrad bridge in eastern Bosnia: "Signs of decay appeared everywhere. The gutters began to crack and smell nasty, the roof to let in the rains, the doors and windows the winds, and the stables to be choked with manure and weeds. . . . Little by little travellers began to avoid spending the night in the town."[69]

The doubling of the Ottoman Balkan urban population between 1580 and 1800 during a period of decline or stagnation of the rural population led to the formation and consolidation of nongenerative cities, one aspect of which was an urban system that depended on the promotion of a livestock economy to meet town needs for food and clothing. Farmers also were prodded into pastoral occupations by the desire to flee a command economy that was becoming increasingly harsh.

The nature of the Ottoman urban system in combination with the consequent decline in rural population impeded the growth of an internal market. It also incited landlords to raise rents and increase their demands for unpaid peasant labor. Enabled thereby to acquire additional quantities of raw materials for export to Europe, Ottoman landlords obtained the means with which to augment their imports of European textile manufactures. By applying pressure upon the Ottoman state to discourage the further development of manufactures, they promoted the interests of the European states. By the end of the eighteenth century, the Ottoman economy was peripheralized.[70]

Population Thresholds and Capitalism

Let us examine the relationship between population and other factors of production from a different point of view. According to the German economist Ernst Wagemann, a new threshold of population saturation is reached as the relationships between the factors of production (land, labor, and capital) and total population in a particular territory are altered in some fundamental way. Associating European crises of overpopulation with crusades (1100), with cultural revisions such as the Renaissance and Reformation and the discoveries and explorations born of the yearning to obtain an easier access to the riches and goods of the world, and with great civil and world-system wars (1789, 1900), he sought to disprove the Malthusian notion (as non-Malthusians portrayed it) of a constant single ceiling of overpopulation. On the basis of European data, Wagemann surmised instead the existence of successive demographic thresholds of underpopulation and overpopulation, presumably as a result of social, cultural, political, or technological changes, or of an absence of such changes. The thresholds of underpopulation, he maintained, were population densities of under 10, of 30–45, and of 80–130 persons per square kilometer. The thresholds of overpopulation were densities of 10–30, 45–80, and 130–180 persons per square kilometer.[71]

Around 1600, however, the population density of France was 34, making of that country an underpopulated territory on the basis of the Wagemann proposition. But "all the known signs of life," wrote Fernand Braudel, prove that France then belonged to "the other category," the category of an overpopulated country.[72] Is this an anomaly? And what conclusion may one draw from the application of the Wagemann thresholds to the Balkan data?

On the basis of Wagemann's specific proposition, the periods of overpopulation would be 1500 to 1870 and 1910 or 1920 to 1980 or 1990 in the Balkans as a whole; 1800 to 1865 and 1890 to the 1950s in Serbia; probably 1500 to 1880 and 1910 to 1980 in Bulgaria; and 1800 to 1875 and the 1920s to the 1990s in Greece. The periods of underpopulation would be, for the Balkans as a whole, 1870 to 1920 and the period since 1980; for Serbia, probably 1600 to 1800, 1865 to 1890, and the period since the 1950s; for Greece, 1875 to the 1920s; and for Bulgaria, 1880 to 1910 and the period since about 1980. By the same criteria, the predominantly Greek areas of the Aegean and southern Balkans were at the borderline between underpopulation and overpopulation throughout the period from 1600 to 1800.

Such a scenario does not make sense. More useful, therefore, than Wagemann's thresholds of overpopulation and underpopulation expressed as the ratio of population to total area would be a relationship of which he himself was aware—namely, the relationship between the total population or the agricultural population and the total cultivated area. Such ratios may serve as indicators of the introduction or lack of introduction of new techniques of production and organization, facts that could be verified by other means.

It is doubtful that even a fifth of the Balkan land surface was under cultivation between 1500 and 1830.[73] Probably less than a tenth of the land surface was cultivated during any given year. Consequently, the Balkan land area under annual cultivation could not have exceeded 44,000 square kilometers; the arable land could not have exceeded 88,000 square kilometers. The total number of inhabitants per square kilometer of arable land thus may have hovered between a low of 57 and a high of 91, with a most frequent level of under 80 inhabitants per square kilometer of arable land. One may compare this ratio with ratios for Yugoslavia, Bulgaria, and Romania, in 1931, respectively of 141, 116, and 94 inhabitants per square kilometer of cultivated land. The ratio for Denmark, at a presumably somewhat later date, was 37 inhabitants. The wheat yield per hectare, on the other hand, was twice as great in Denmark.[74] The Balkan ratio of population to arable between 1900 and 1950 was thus probably twice as great as the prevailing Balkan ratio of the period 1500 to 1830. In fact, however, "overpopulation" has been a Balkan reality since the sixteenth century.

Until 1830, a nongenerative Ottoman urban system in alliance with pastoralism and a command economy was an obstacle to the capitalization of agriculture. Subsequently, a process that had started earlier, the peripheralization of Balkan agricultural production to European needs, inspired the holders of large farms "to regulate production by profit maximization." That, however, argues one scholar, may be "the worst thing that can happen to an overpopulated economy," for it allows an increase among a large portion of the peasant population of what, under the new economic circumstances, should be an "unwanted leisure." As in other parts of eastern Europe, capitalism was a product in the Balkans, if not of "cultural contamination,"[75] at least of the importation of a system of economic relations for which the interior Balkan regions were ill prepared. The Balkan countries were disadvantaged by the fact that they had known during the past half-millennium only an incipient autonomous "city economy." On top of this, the states of western and central Europe were economically so much more advanced that their foreign trade grew between 1830 and 1913 more than twice as fast as that of the Balkan states. Whatever economic advances may have been made in the Balkans during this period—and they did make for legitimate optimism in the short term—proved ultimately to be of a satellitic character, dependent on their ability to supply goods for which a demand existed in the advanced capitalist states.

An increasing density of "market places" characterized the Balkan economy of the period. But national markets were slow to form because of the scarcity of capital. Capital investment in agriculture was confined to farms that were close to the sea, to other navigable water systems, or to the new railroads—consequently, close to farms whose products could easily be made accessible to foreign markets.

Investments in Greece of Greek diaspora capital were minimal until the Crimean War. They then went, until about 1880, not so much into industry or agriculture as into banking, commerce, mining, and the infrastructure (hospitals, public buildings, and especially schools, with the partial aim of creating personnel capable of staffing their diaspora offices). Nondiaspora foreign capital was invested in Greece at the end of each of three different territorial and politico-ideological readjustments—after the Congress of Berlin and the transfer to Greece of Thessaly (1878, 1882), after the expulsion of Greek troops from Anatolia (1922), and after World War II and the subsequent Greek civil war and political stabilization of the area. During the first and second periods of investment, the capital was chiefly British and in the form of public loans and investments in railroads, port development, bridge construction, and social overhead. The goal of such investment was to promote world commerce. Made mainly by American companies, private capital investments in Greece after 1960 were directed toward the production of capital goods.[76]

The fundamental characteristic of capitalism is to treat everything as a commodity to be bought and sold at a price determined not just by supply and demand but also as much as possible by government subsidies and other (including tax) privileges. Capitalism promotes the treatment of commodities and services as objects to be desired and consumed as quickly, as frequently, and in as great a quantity as possible. It tends to treat nature and culture in similar fashion, namely, as tourist attractions. The sellers and buyers of tourism, of course, can destroy or wholly consume local nature and local cultures alike, for their concern is not with the preservation of natural and cultural patrimonies but with the consumption of the pleasures of which they are the mediator-producers or the customers.[77]

Tourism became in the twentieth century a major industry, often promoted to the detriment of nature and culture alike. It was drawn, moreover, to fragile environments like the Mediterranean. The annual tourist trade of Greece thus rose from several tens of thousands in the 1920s to 2 million persons in 1974, 4 million in 1977, and 9 million in 1979. In 1977, the tourist trade of Yugoslavia, Romania, and Turkey was, respectively, 5.6 million, 3.7 million, and 1.7 million persons.

A further consequence of the ideology of economic growth has been the concentration, by the 1980s, of half the population and almost half the industry of Greece in the Athens-Piraeus area. Another result was that Athens was then also "the city most affected by pollution in western [sic] Europe, followed by Nice and Milan. Thus a brown cloud of pollutants, called *nefos*, hovers over Athens for much of the summer. This cloud is a photochemical smoke, composed of nitrogen oxide, hydrocarbons, and peroxylacetyl nitrate, and sometimes is formed as low as 30 yards from the ground."[78] Airborne acid drawn to Athens between 1940 and 1990, indeed, appears to have caused a greater deterioration of the Acropolis than the wear and tear of its previous 2,500 years of existence.[79] In Istanbul, a city of less than a million people in 1950 but with almost seven million by the 1980s along with 600,000 cars and trucks, pollution was almost as great.

A Closed World-Economy in a Closed Network of Ecosystems

Whether under the Ottoman command economy or the peripheralized Balkan economies of the nineteenth and twentieth centuries, the relevant political-territorial units have had to contend with the fact that the attitudes of their human populations toward other human populations and toward production and nonhuman populations had a basis in the local interests that they intended to protect. They were not based on the conception of the earth as a closed system of intricate interrelationships among competing and reciprocating human and other populations on the one hand and scarce resources on the other.

But anthropologist Claude Lévi-Strauss objects, "The right to life, and to the free development of the living species still represented on the earth, is the only right that can be called inalienable—for the single reason that the disappearance of any species leaves us with an irreparable void in the system of creation." That principle is not "the right of man in regard to the environment" but rather "the right of the environment in regard to man."[80] It may be preferable, however, to state the case not as a matter of right but as a question of human survival as a species. A prerequisite to the survival of mankind is the survival of a large number of plant and animal species and avoidance of sudden disequilibria. But species evolution is also a matter of the creation of disequilibria. Momentary disequilibria in whose creation mankind has participated have occurred ever since man became a maker of fire, a wielder of the ax, and a manipulator of the plow. But the rate at which this process has occurred has accelerated during the last two or three centuries. In the Balkans the start of that acceleration may be traced back to about 1830.

The expansion in the Balkans, between 1500 and 1800, in the number of domestic animals was destructive of some plant life and even of some wild animal life (by the reduction of the living space of wild animals). The decline in, or stabilization of, the total number of human beings, however, may have compensated for the growth in livestock. The periods of forest destruction, on the other hand, have also been periods of population growth and agricultural expansion. The period most wasteful of Balkan forest resources was the short period between 1830 and 1900. It was comparable to the destruction of forests in France between 1600 and 1800 and earlier in England.

Situated on the Sava at the junction of the Danube and near the Tisa and Temes tributaries of that river, Belgrade enjoyed an abundance of fish—big pike and carp, sterlets, and sturgeon—until the middle of the nineteenth century. In 1852, it was still occasionally possible to acquire a sturgeon ovary of more than thirty kilograms in the Belgrade market. If the water level was low in the spring, few sturgeon penetrated beyond the rapids at Orşova, but they were available at Vidin.[81] Soon thereafter, however, as a result of the diffusion of steamboat navigation on the Danube and Sava rivers, fish became less abundant in Belgrade and at other Danube ports.[82]

The development of Balkan industry—for more than half a century as private and governmental enterprise and for about four decades under nominally communist tutelage—and the development in particular of Bulgarian agriculture have led to increased competition for scarce water between the upstream states (Albania, Bulgaria, and pre-1991 Yugoslavia), in which rivers have their source, and the downstream states (Greece and European Turkey), in which they find an outlet. Thus, the use of the water of the Mesta/Nestos for Bulgarian industrial and agricultural needs resulted, between 1975 and 1990, in a 60 percent decline in the flow of Nestos water into Greece. The growth of Balkan cities and of tourism confronts all Balkan countries with the further dilemma of how to divert water from the areas where it is plentiful to the new areas of concentration of human populations.[83]

Industrial development and the exploitation of natural resources culminated by 1990 in a major Black Sea ecological crisis, joined to a major sociopolitical and economic crisis, for which, in varying degree, communists, capitalists, and the consumer culture—the supply and demand sectors alike—were jointly re-

sponsible. Soviet, Turkish, Romanian, and Bulgarian exploitation of the resources of the Black Sea quickened to such an extent after 1950 that little fish
life was left four decades later. From a thousand tons a year in 1950, the Black
Sea sturgeon catch fell to ten tons in 1989. The number of commercial fish
species fell from twenty-six in 1970 to five in 1991. The anchovy catch of the
Turkish fishing fleet fell from 340,000 tons in 1987 to under 15,000 tons in
1989. Seals vanished from the Black Sea, and dolphins were reduced from an
estimated million in 1940 to about 200,000 in 1990. Still available were small
scad and jellyfish, the latter a consumer of the eggs and larvae of other fish.

Among the reasons for the disaster that came with a whimper were pollution
and overfishing, as during the second half of the nineteenth century but at an
accelerated pace. The environmental disruptions may have been responses to
shifts in the food chain, or they may have caused such shifts, provoking changes
in the food web or ways in which the food chains are joined together or react to
the changes in the energy-transfer processes occurring at the level of the geo-
system.[84] They may have been further complicated by a possible but not yet
clearly ascertainable climatic change.

An important factor in the equation was the Black Sea itself, into which flow
the salt waters of the Mediterranean. On the other hand, it receives relatively
little fresh water from its tributary rivers. Moreover, as a result of the diversion
of river water for dam and irrigation projects between the 1950s and 1980s, fresh
water reaching the Black Sea diminished by a fifth. For a hundred yards down, in
1990, the sea contained oxygen. Under this upper lid, however, thus affecting
nine-tenths of the sea's contents, lay a mass of hydrogen sulfide and methane in
which few living things can live, much less thrive. Caught between surging
quantities of sulfides and methane from the depths and noxious detergents, pesticides, herbicides, and fertilizers in the upper layer of water, the plant and animal
life of the Black Sea is threatened by extinction.[85]

In the Balkans as in (the rest of) Europe, oil refineries, chemical plants, and
nuclear reactors have been located near the seas or rivers. The Hungarian nuclear
power station of Paks lies near the Danube south of Budapest. The Bulgarian
nuclear power station of Kozlodui, which was set up between 1969 and 1975, is
similarly situated at the Danube halfway between Vidin and Nikopol and some
two hundred kilometers north of Sofia. At Cernavodă on the lower Romanian
Danube, the construction of a nuclear power station was started in 1972. Interrupted in 1978, the construction was resumed in 1980. A nuclear power station at
Krško, along the right bank of the Sava northwest of Zagreb, was put into
operation in 1981. Faced with the opposition of the community of Zadar, on the
other hand, the Croatian project of a nuclear power station on the Adriatic island
of Vir was abandoned in favor of one at Prevlaka (Privlaka), halfway between
Vukovar (the town subjected to the heaviest destruction of life and property in
the civil war between Serbs and Croats during 1991) on the Danube and the Sava
River to the south.

In 1991, following the departure of many of the Soviet specialists in charge of safety and operation, only two of the six Soviet-built nuclear reactors at Kozlodui —the two pressurized-water machines fully enclosed by reinforced concrete and capable of producing 1,000 megawatts each—did not present undue hazards. The threats presented by the other reactors—early Soviet pressurized-water reactors with no containment structures, each producing 400 megawatts—emanated from oil, steam, and water leaks, loose and unsealed electric cables, and valves with missing wheels. Accidents occurring before 1990 had contaminated the groundwater in the plant's vicinity.

At first Bulgaria closed only two of the defective reactors, arguing that it could not spare to give up the others since it depended on the Kozlodui operation for one-third or even two-fifths of its electrical needs. In February 1992, however, a different problem—a defective turbine outside one of the turbine buildings—temporarily caused the shutdown of electricity in the country at intervals of two hours. Toward the end of 1992, only two of the older reactors, one of which was scheduled for a seventy-five-day period of repairs, and one of the two newer reactors were still in operation. As a result, brownouts were frequent.[86]

Other damage includes the pollution of groundwater by sewage that has been treated improperly, the contamination of groundwater by the nitrates and phosphates in fertilizers, chemical and gas pollution along the Danube and its larger tributaries, overdrainage not only of the environmentally fragile Danube delta but also—since the spread of cereal cultivation—the lowering of the water table in the Hungarian Plain, the pollution of seawater along the Adriatic coasts, and general air and river pollution.[87] Coming from afar, air pollution causes salinity, which may provoke a decline in soil fertility, especially in areas with fragile soils, as in much of the Balkans. A problem partly of non-Balkan origin has thus become a Balkan problem.

Pesticides, herbicides, and fertilizers cause further soil pollution. As the soil continues to be damaged, it may fail to respond to chemical boosting. Once the rise in grain yields is thereby brought to a halt, further growth may be impeded except at further environmental and economic cost.[88]

The increase in the production of goods during the last hundred or two hundred years has resulted in the release of great quantities of thermal pollution to which the world's peoples are exposed regardless of what particular people may have created it. Some man-made goods can be recycled. Based upon current knowledge, however, the recycling of matter like the transfer of energy from producer to consumer or from one kind of consumer to another kind is only 80–90 percent effective at each step. Moreover, the recycling of goods requires a further expenditure of energy, resulting in the production of more waste (heat). But to refrain from recycling results in the depletion of desired goods for which expectations have been raised in the Balkans, as elsewhere.[89]

Such basic stocks of energy as coal and petroleum are renewable only over geologic time, and they are unevenly distributed. They are present in the Balkans, but they are insufficient or of low or mediocre quality. Even Romania, once an exporter of petroleum, no longer possesses sufficient quantities for its own use.

Meanwhile, the world has become virtually one closed system in an economic as in an ecological sense. For the conception of the earth as a closed system of materials, as suggested by the Swiss economist Jean (Johann Daniel Caspar) Herrenschwand during the 1780s[90] and made more explicit a decade later, as is well known by T.R. Malthus, was followed after 1830 by the dissolution of the old-style command economies, including the command economy of the Ottoman Empire. Then came the turn, between 1948 and 1990, of the new-style centrally planned command economies, whose dissolution may have been unknowingly prepared by the split between Stalin and Tito or the Soviet Union and Yugoslavia, for the embrace by the communist leaders of Yugoslavia of the idea of "separate roads to socialism" imperiled the idea of a closed Soviet world-system.

Susan L. Woodward explains the process that led unexpectedly and unintentionally but logically from 1948 to the death throes of Yugoslavia:

> In the Yugoslav case, balance-of-payments deficits and dangerously depleted foreign-exchange reserves were the consequence of an external shock—the economic blockade by Cominform countries in 1948–49—not of domestic prodigality. The decision to seek foreign aid within four years of the socialist revolution was not made easily, but once taken it led to a systematic decentralization of the Yugoslav economy, abandonment of development planning in favor of the market, and integration into the world economy in response to the policies dictated by the IMF [International Monetary Fund] in exchange for credit over the next 20 years (1951, 1960, and 1965 are particularly important). This dismantling of socialism has been accompanied by persistent balance-of-payments deficits, high unemployment, high inflation, and increasing inequality.[91]

Partly by its postwar claims to the resources of the eastern European countries included in its orbit, the Soviet Union achieved during the 1950s an economic growth twice as fast as that of the United States. But failing to make sufficient investments in agriculture, disadvantaged by diminishing supplies of petroleum, and addicted to a centralized system of planning that required the fixing of prices for 2 million items on the basis of information that became increasingly difficult to control as the communications revolution of the 1970s gave the edge to capitalism and the West, the Soviet economic growth rate fell to half that of the United States.[92]

Unable to maintain itself as a closed state—preserve its isolation and insulation from the capitalist world-economy—the Soviet Union was forced to choose the path of *glasnost*. The new openness in place of the old closedness led between 1989 and 1991 to Soviet acceptance of the reunification of the two Germanies, an exacerbation of the nationalities question in the Soviet Union and eastern Europe, the dissolution of the Soviet Union itself, and the fragmentation of Yugoslavia.

Ideas, however, do not operate in a vacuum. Just as the dissolution of the old-style command economies and old empires and the temporary triumph of the "new imperialism" were the product of the massive growth of world trade between 1830 and the Great War, so the dissolution of the new-style command economies or Soviet-dominated communist world system was the product in part of the great growth of world trade between 1950 and 1990. The demise of the Soviet world-system and concomitant weakening of the American economy were also the product of the heavy investment by the two power systems in the cold war. But their technological superiority, including their superiority in the technology of microelectronics, enabled the United States and its allies to put more and more of their goods on the world market. Skilled in communications, they seduced the young throughout the world by their enticing style of life and at least superficially liberating ideology.

Consumerism was absent even as a latent ideology as late as 1900 in some parts of the Balkans, such as northern Albania. In Shkodër, for example, according to anthropologist Mary E. Durham, "If your purchases [were] many," the tradesman would "kindly send out to buy a piece of common muslin in which to wrap them; for Skodra [Shkodër] [did] not supply paper, and when you ... bought a thing, conveying it away [was] your own affair. We in London," Durham adds, "are used to having paper included lavishly with the goods, but an old lady once told me that in her young days the fashionable drapers of London would lend linen wrappers to those who bought largely, and the said wrappers had to be returned next day. In this particular Skodra is not more than eighty or ninety years behind London."[93] Three or four generations later, the Croat feminist Slavenka Drakulić, daughter of a poor Partisan officer from the Croatian wilds and of a wealthy mother from the Croatian or Dalmatian core culture, would compose a tribute to the seduction of consumerism in her book, *How We Survived Communism and Even Laughed*. On the other hand, she would detect in ecology an appalling totalitarianism.[94]

The reduction of the world to a single economic system (despite many different modes of production) first as a promise or threat and then as a reality has whetted the incentive for economic growth in virtually every country of the world. In fact, however, most underdeveloped or moderately developed countries, despite such anomalies as Hong Kong, Singapore, and South Korea, are likely to fall behind in the competition with the economically highly developed countries unless capitalism is made to yield to a market economy with a basis in the principles of ecology. Conversely, they may move ahead but at the expense of countries that are already ahead or currently aspire to move ahead.

In a world defined by the mobility of goods, of capital, of land in the form of its products, and of pleasure seekers, the highly developed countries sometimes need the cheaper labor of other countries. Such other countries often want to export their own unemployed and underemployed even though they also want to avoid a "brain drain" or loss of skilled and educated persons in whom they have already made a substantial investment.

In effect, countries that accept immigrants do so mainly because of their need for certain types of labor, skilled or unskilled. During World War II, for example, Germany made use of foreign workers, many of them from eastern Europe and the overrun territories of the Soviet Union, to do work that its soldiers were not free to do. By 1944, there were almost eight million such workers in Germany. A common attitude toward these populations among the Germans was that they were *Untermenschen*—a lower breed of mankind—or even "animals." After World War II, such workers became *Gastarbeiter*, "guest workers," to be welcomed for specific work purposes and to be sent home when they were no longer needed—thus to be welcomed during the 1970s and in many cases sent home in the 1980s, when capitalism no longer required their labor. That was how not to have an unemployment problem. So long as these workers were needed, on the other hand, they contributed to German economic growth by the very fact that they spent a large proportion of their wages in Germany itself. It was a perfect way for West Germany to have its cake and eat it too.[95]

The home economies providing the *Gastarbeiter*—Turkey, Greece, and Yugoslavia—also benefited from the arrangement. During the 1970s and early 1980s, such workers numbered as many as 1.5 million Turks and 800,000 Greeks. Their respective remittances (in which were included some remittances from permanent residents) amounted to $1,375 (in 1981) and $1,400 (in 1982) per *Gastarbeiter*.[96]

Present in western and central Europe in 1990, especially in France, Germany, Italy, and Austria, were about 10 million foreigners.[97] Between 1990 and 2025, according to some projections, at least 50 million additional people may enter central and western Europe from the eastern regions of Europe and the Muslim countries of the world as a result of the destabilization of the political and socioeconomic systems of the communist world and of rapid demographic growth in the Muslim world. Together with other migratory movements to the Americas and Australia, these migrations may prove to be as important as, perhaps more important than, the migrations of 1846–1920, when more than 46 million Europeans went overseas and 10 million people left Russia, Belorussia, and the Ukraine for the Caucasus, Siberia, and Central Asia.[98]

Countries or groups of states with a population of a hundred million—not to mention a thousand million—may choose to deal with the problem of overpopulation by sacrificing a portion of their population to obtain the resources and territories that may be otherwise denied to them. Certain underdeveloped and moderately developed countries with a rapidly growing population and rising expectations such as Albania and Turkey may be inclined to transform social conflicts over who should determine how local resources should be used into national conflicts. So wasteful of the resources of the world, the so-called cold war may be metamorphosed into a series of "hot" little (but sometimes highly damaging) wars, as occurred or threatened to occur beginning in 1989 in the Baltic states, in Azerbaijan, in Armenia, in Moldova, in Ukraine (without the *the* to indicate that it now is an internationally recognized state), in Georgia, in Kazakhstan, and especially in the "old" Yugoslavia, which, however fragmented, is unlikely to cease to constitute a group of similar (albeit sometimes antagonistic) cultural units.

Let us underline furthermore a rarely mentioned fact. With 5 percent of the world's population, the United States consumes 33 percent of the processed energy and mineral resources of the world. It consumes per capita twenty-five times the processed energy and mineral resources consumed by the nonindustrial world. It is the world's biggest waster.[99] Should it also be the policeman of the world?

Who will correct the abuses of nature and culture by governments—communist and capitalist alike—by industry, and by consumers? Will the European Community, of which Greece has become a member, undertake this challenging task? One may doubt that it will do so except for limited purposes and under much public pressure, for the thinking of the Eurocrats resembles that of other bureaucrats, policy think tanks, and corporate enterprise.

The Balkan peoples and states, including the states and federation(s) or confederation(s) of states that may emerge from Yugoslavia, may thus have an opportunity to show whether they have the vision to resist both post–command economy capitalism, for which the environment may continue to be only a secondary concern as under communism, and the organization of Europe on the basis of money and cultural "homogeneity" (direct or indirect German domination) in opposition to a Europe founded on the idea of "unity through cultural diversity."

Should the Balkan peoples continue to use wasteful outside developmental models or should they initiate a model or models of their own with a basis in their own polychronic experiences and in the perceptual and conceptual abilities of their own scientists and humanists? If they choose the second course, they must also undertake the task of persuading the European Community and other peoples of Europe of the urgent need for public debate on the proper cultural foundations of the European community itself.

A European community that fulfills both general human and particular cultural needs requires the presence and equal voice therein of West, Middle, and East, of Catholic, Protestant, and Orthodox Christian, along with Judaic and Muslim traditions, so long as they all abide by the French revolutionary tradition of liberty and equality before the law and subscribe to the principle that rights entail responsibilities.

A viable, credible, autonomous European cultural community may also have to define its natural resources as the common patrimony of the whole system of European cultures. It may have to commit itself to the maintenance of a mutually beneficial equilibrium among the plant, animal, and human populations of its own geocultural system.

Such an approach will require a strict regulation of water, land, air, and energy use. As mankind improves and augments its knowledge input, the European Community and the world's other cultural-ecological communities may be able to relax these limits. Subject to the foregoing controls, market economy—without capitalism, which strives for privilege and monopoly—would be both feasible and desirable. Slow economic growth, especially for the underdeveloped and moderately developed regions, may also be pursued, especially if the production of power by means of controlled fusion, achieved on an experimental basis toward the end of 1991 by the fusion reactor station (Joint European Torus) in Oxfordshire, England—and further improved in December 1993 by the Princeton Physics Laboratory—can be made practical. If that effort succeeds, Europe, America, and the world's other societies may have at their disposal a process that, like solar power, produces little radioactive waste and frees them from dependence on virtually nonrenewable geological sources of energy.[100]

A further prerequisite to the success of a European community would be the organization of other cultural systems as similar communities. Between all such groups of cultural communities of cultural and ecological defense, freedom of trade ought to be encouraged subject to the protection of the cultural-ecological patrimony of each system or federation of cultures.

In a world that is a virtually closed economic and a closed ecological system, it is imperative not to misinterpret the demise of the Soviet system, not to impose on the rest of the world a capitalist system that is almost equally flawed. That, of course, is what is currently being done, partly because too few persons are ready to grasp the difference between capitalism and market economy, the first founded on the realities of privilege and the second on the idea of the unrestrained circulation of goods, services, information, and beliefs. Even more important than the operation of market economy at a world level and at the level of federations of regional communities of nations, however, is the safeguard of each federation's cultural-ecological patrimony, including its "aesthetic dimension."[101]

The Balkans were the first area in Europe to which farming spread; the first area, too, in which cities arose. By the separation of the Christian church into two main communities, Latin and Greek or Byzantine, then by the Ottoman conquest of the Balkans and adjacent European territories, and on a third occasion by the establishment of communist governments in all the Balkan states except Greece (where, however, there was a bitter civil war after World War II), the Balkan cultures developed along lines at variance with the directions taken in Latin, Celtic, and Germanic, and Protestant and Catholic Europe. After the mid-eighteenth century and especially after 1789, however, the peoples and cultures of the Balkans, from the Adriatic to the Black Sea, from the Pannonian plain to the Aegean, began to rejoin the European cultures, affirmed their solidarity with Europe, participated in the making of Europe II (Europe since 1789), a Europe founded on the rejection of the principle of privilege. The Balkans thus became the last group of territories to be added to the European cultures, even after Russia, which had rejoined Europe earlier—but the Europe of privilege.

Will a portion of the Balkans now be excluded from the European community? Will the institutionalized European Community (called Union) persist in its subservience to Germany, proceeding to include in Europe only Slavs of the Catholic faith and eastern Europeans who have been traditionally both anti-Russian and anticommunist? Will it have the patience and intelligence to create a dynamic creative cultural community with the active participation of the Balkan peoples? Will Europe and the Balkan peoples ultimately respond more intelligently to the demise of the second form of command economy and the resurgence of retrograde "nationalisms"—not to be confused with cultural autonomies—that parade as the hope of civilization, capitalism, and humanity?

One is tempted to despair. A more rational response would be to press for the implementation of a social order in which the need for violence—as expressed in particular by war-oriented institutions and short-term temporal perspectives—is subordinated to the need for knowing and understanding.

Notes

1. Susman, "Culture and Communications," p. 254.
2. Violich, *The Search for Cultural Identity through Urban Design.*
3. Hughes, "Ecology in Ancient Greece," pp. 116–19; Papaioannou, "Nature and History in the Greek Conception of the Cosmos"; Stoianovich, "Material Foundations of Preindustrial Civilization in the Balkans," pp. 206–8.
4. White, Jr., "The Historical Roots of Our Ecologic Crisis."
5. Banašević, "Bifon i Njegoš."
6. Boulding, *The Meaning of the Twentieth Century,* p. 143; Glacken, *Traces on the Rhodian Shore,* pp. 639, 642.
7. Bagby, *Culture and History,* pp. 175, 204–18; Furtado, *Accumulation and Development,* p. 166. On disturbances of ecological and semiotic equilibria, see McNeill, "Control and Catastrophe in Human Affairs."
8. Schumpeter, "The Crisis of the Tax State."
9. Braudel, "Sur une conception de l'histoire sociale," pp. 183–86, a critique of articles by Brunner in his *Neue Wege der Sozialgeschichte.*
10. Stoianovich, *French Historical Method,* p. 143, n. 20.
11. Seton-Watson, Steed, and other British writers, quoted in Miller, "R.W. Seton-Watson and Serbia," pp. 59–69.
12. Ralph Paget, on the "folly" of the Serbs; in Descos to Poincaré, Belgrade, November 18, 1912, in France, *Documents diplomatiques français,* IV, 496, T. No. 100; Paget on Serbian "visions of blue seas," in Gooch and Temperley, *British Documents on the Origins of the War, IX,* pt. 2, 234, No. 313, letter dated Belgrade, November 30, 1912; and in minister of France to Belgrade on the "Anglo-Austrian campaign of intimidation" quoted in Descos to Poincaré, Belgrade, December 18, 1933, in France, *Documents diplomatiques français,* V, 106, No. 88, D. No. 193.

13. Gregorio Malaxa, quoted in Lamansky, *Secrets d'État de Venise*, II, 83–89.

14. Braudel, *The Mediterranean*, II, 769–70.

15. Preziosi, "Introduction," pp. 6–8.

16. Castellan, "Éléments d'une sociologie religieuse en Yougoslavie socialiste."

17. For an analogous situation, see Peter Sahlins, *Boundaries*, pp. 110–13, 270–76.

18. Fortis, *Travels into Dalmatia*, pp. 79–81.

19. Ibid., pp. 251–53. For a brief history of Poljica, see Kadić, *Tradition of Freedom in Croatian Literature*, pp. 71–85.

20. Kreševljaković, *Kapetanije u Bosni i Hercegovini*, pp. 9, 13–21.

21. Vacalopoulos, *The Greek Nation, 1453–1669*, pp. 211–24.

22. Pouqueville, *Voyage en Morée, à Constantinople, en Albanie*, I, 198, 208; Gordon, *History of the Greek Revolution*, I, 29; AN, AÉ, B^{III} 242, "Mémoire sur la situation topographique de l'Albanie & de l'Épire, sur les productions territoriales, le commerce & l'industrie de ses habitans, & sur les meilleurs moyens d'en tirer de très bon bois, pour la construction des vaisseaux de la Marine militaire, & de la marine marchande," Pierre Dupré, former consular agent at Arta, to Talleyrand, floréal, year VIII; Koliopoulos, *Brigands with a Cause*, pp. 26–35.

23. Kreševljaković, "Kapetanije i kapetani u Bosni i Hercegovini." On the *uskoks*, see Bracewell, *The Uskoks of Senj;* Rothenberg, "Christian Insurrections in Turkish Dalmatia."

24. McNeill, *Europe's Steppe Frontier*.

25. Rothenberg, *The Austrian Military Border in Croatia*, pp. 11–12, 27–32, 48–49, 68–75, 85, 93, 105–8, 111, 124–27; Koliopoulos, "Brigandage and Irredentism in Nineteenth-Century Greece"; Gavrilović, "Obnova Slavonskih županija i njihovo razgraničavanje sa Vojnom Granicom."

26. Stoianovich, "The Segmentary State and *La Grande Nation*."

27. Blanc, *La Croatie occidentale*, pp. 120–21; Service Historique de l'Armée (Vincennes), Mémoires et Reconnaissances 1599, "Tableau général des Frontières militaires autrichiennes" and "Essai sur l'organisation des Frontières militaires, ou régiments frontières de l'Autriche, et considérations sur l'application de ce système, à un certain degré, à l'organisation des possessions françaises de l'Afrique," joined to a letter dated December 20, 1837, from A. de Terrasson, capitaine d'État major, aide de camp du Général Baron de Gazan.

28. Hall, *The Silent Language*, pp. 138–39.

29. Schmitt, "L'Histoire des marginaux," pp. 349–50.

30. Hull, trans. *Digenis Akritas, the Two-Blood Border Lord*.

31. "Stephen Dušan's Wedding," in Pennington and Levi, trans., *Marko the Prince*, with introduction and notes by Svetozar Koljević, p. 72.

32. Bartra, "Identity and Wilderness," pp. 104–8.

33. Edmonds, "Introductory and Historical Sketch of the Klephts," p. 10.

34. Radojčić, "Dositejevo pismo o uredjenju i prosvećenju Srbije," p. 26; Jaeger, *Paideia*, p. 68.

35. Mitteis, "Land und Herrschaft," pp. 48–49; Lévi-Strauss, *Mythologiques*, I, 36.

36. Tuan, *Topophilia*, pp. 104, 109–12.

37. White, *Tropics of Discourse*, pp. 150–96.

38. Chernus, "War and the Enemy in the Thought of Mircea Eliade," pp. 335–44.

39. On general types of collective enmity, see Zur, "The Love of Hating," pp. 346–49.

40. Djordje Krčum, quoted in Burns, "Hearts Heavy, Arms Light."

41. Bracewell, *The Uskoks of Senj*, pp. 228–29.

42. Müller, "Die Herdenwanderungen in Mittelmeergebiet"; Dedijer, "La Transhumance dans les pays dinariques"; Filipović, "Odlaženje na prehranu."

43. Lawless, "The Economy and Landscapes of Thessaly during Ottoman Rule"; Braudel, *The Mediterranean*, I, 56–57, 85–87.

44. Passarge, "Probleme einer Geschichtsgeographie auf landschaftskundlicher Basis," p. 273; Coulborn, *The Origin of Civilized Societies*, pp. 121–22.

45. Bérard, *La Turquie et l'hellénisme contemporain*, p. 66; Braudel, *The Mediterranean*, I, 60–63.

46. Belon du Mans, *Les Observations de plvsievrs singvlarritez et choses memorables*, p. 65.

47. Marciana (Venezia), MSS Italiani, Cl. 6, No. 176, Mariano Bolizza, "Relatione et Descrittione del Sangiacato di Scutari," account by the Venetian noble of Cattaro, 160–12, joined to his letter of May 25, 1614, to Matteo Michiele.

48. Braudel, *The Mediterranean*, I, 231–46; H. McNeill, *The Metamorphosis of Greece since World War II*, pp. 32–33.

49. Dumont, *Types of Rural Economy*, p. 483.

50. Turner, *Journal of a Tour in the Levant*, I, xvii; III, 135; "Relation uiber die Reise des Hauptmann Georg Lauterer und Unterlieutenant Franz Mihanovich, beide von Pontoniers-bataillon, von Constantinopel bis Durrazzo, nebst der Fortsetzung des letztern von Durrazzo nach Semlin, im Jahr 1783," in Pantelić, "Vojno-geografski opisi Srbije pred Kočinu Krajinu od 1783 i 1784 god.," pp. 7–26; Popović, "Trgovina i promet u Napoleonovo doba"; Tekeli, "On Institutionalized External Relations of Cities in the Ottoman Empire," pp. 54–56; Sakazov, *Bulgarische Wirtschaftsgeschichte*, pp. 220–22, 256.

51. Koliopoulos, *Brigands with a Cause*, pp. 26–35.

52. Vryonis, Jr., "Religious Changes and Patterns in the Balkans, 14th–16th Centuries," pp. 171–72.

53. Vergopoulos, *Le Capitalisme difforme et la nouvelle question agraire*, p. 64.

54. Wagstaff, "War and Settlement Desertion in the Morea."

55. Serbia, Ministarstvo Narodne Privrede, *Prethodni resultati popisa stanovništva . . . 1895*, p. xxi; Masleša, ed., *Odabrani spisi*, pp. xix, xxxix, 306; Vučo, *Privredna istorija FNRJ do Prvog svetskog rata*, p. 202; Vučo, *Privredna istorija Srbije do Prvog svetskog rata*, pp. 186–87; Mijatović, *Servia and the Servians*, p. 227; Janković, *O političkim strankama u Srbiji XIX veka*, p. 148; Lapčević, *Istorija socijalizma u Srbiji*, pp. 9–10, 20, 109.

56. Pouqueville, *Voyage dans la Grèce*, III, 450.

57. Dumont, *Le Balkan et l'Adriatique*, p. 341.

58. Based on modification of conversion unit in Tomasevich, *Peasants, Politics, and Economic Change in Yugoslavia*, p. 279.

59. The figures here and in the paragraphs that follow are from Turrill, *The Plant Life of the Balkan Peninsula*, pp. 207–8; Sakazov, *Bulgarische Wirtschaftsgeschichte*, p. 273; G.G. "Le développement de la population de Bulgarie"; Palairet, "Farm Productivity," pp. 107–9, 113, 115; L'Héritier, *La Grèce*, p. 70; Jardé, *Les Céréales dans l'Antiquité grecque*, I, 126; J.C.C., "La Population de la Grèce depuis 1860"; Evelpidi, *Les États balkaniques*, p. 217. On the Romanian economy, see Montias, "Notes on the Romanian Debate on Sheltered Industrialization"; Janos, "Modernization and Decay in Historical Perspective."

60. Wace and Thompson, *The Nomads of the Balkans*, pp. 76–77, 159.

61. The figures here and in the paragraph that follows are from ibid., pp. 2, 86, 126, 145–47, 154, 159, 173–75, 179–89, 186, 195, 208, 254.

62. Ibid., p. 175.

63. Holland, *Travels in the Ionian Isles, Albania, Thessaly, Macedonia*, pp. 90–93. See also Braudel, *The Mediterranean*, I, 100.

64. Bajraktarević, "Yürüks"; Gibb and Bowen, *Islamic Society and the West*, Vol. I, Pt. 1, pp. 250–53; Schultze Jena, *Makedonien*, p. 54. On the nomadism of the Türkmen of Anatolia, see Vryonis, Jr., "Nomadization and Islamization in Asia Minor"; Hendy, *Studies in the Byzantine Monetary Economy*, pp. 114–17.

65. Wace and Thompson, *The Nomads of the Balkans*, p. 10.

66. Palairet, "Farm Productivity," pp. 91–93; Turrill, *The Plant Life of the Balkan Peninsula*, pp. 209–10.

67. Vacalopoulos, "La Retraite des populations grecques."

68. [Finlay], "The Euthanasia of the Ottoman Empire," pp. 572, 574–75, 577–78.

69. Andrić, *The Bridge on the Drina*, p. 93.

70. Stoianovich, "Cities, Capital Accumulation, and the Ottoman Command Economy," forthcoming.

71. For a partial application of the hypothesis to the Balkans, see Wagemann *Der neue Balkan*, pp. 57–63. For a full development of the hypothesis, see Wagemann, *Die Zahl als Detektiv*, esp. pp. 50–58; and critique by Braudel, "La Démographie et les dimensions des sciences de l'homme."

72. Braudel, "La Démographie et les dimensions des sciences de l'homme," pp. 201–2.

73. Stoianovich, *Between East and West*, I, 15–38. For a century later, see Tomasevich, *Peasants, Politics, and Economic Change in Yugoslavia*, p. 279.

74. Data for the Balkan countries in Tomasevich, *Peasants, Politics, and Economic Change in Yugoslavia*, p. 317; data for Denmark in Georgescu-Roegen, "Economic Theory and Agrarian Economics," p. 12.

75. Georgescu-Roegen, "Economic Theory and Agrarian Economics," p. 33.

76. Mouzelis, *Modern Greece*, p. 28, 59, 90–91, 145; Vergopoulos, *Le Capitalisme difforme et la nouvelle question agraire*, pp. 32, 278.

77. Greenwood, "Culture by the Pound," pp. 171–85.

78. Gianaris, *Greece and Turkey*, p. 71, on pollution; on tourism and the concentration of population and industry, pp. 72–74; Gianaris, *The Economies of the Balkan Countries*, p. 119.

79. Thompson and Thompson, *Ecoshell*, p. 210.

80. Lévi-Strauss, *The View from Afar*, pp. 282–83.

81. Af. Étr., CC., Belgrade, t. II, fols. 254–55, de Ségur, Belgrade, February 24, 1853.

82. Popović, *Putovanje po Novoj Srbiji*, p. 29.

83. Vlachos, "Transboundary Water Challenges in the Balkans"; J. Margat, "L'Eau dans les pays balkaniques."

84. On geographical sphere or biosphere and food chains and food web, see Dolukhanov, *Ecology and Economy in Neolithic Eastern Europe*, pp. 4–6.

85. Simons, "For Black Sea, Slow Choking by Pollutants," a superb piece of journalism. See Thompson, "East Europe's Dark Dawn," p. 63, for the estimates of the Black Sea dolphin population.

86. Simons, "West Urges Bulgarians to Shut Reactors"; "New Problem Cripples Bulgarian Atom Plant"; Browne, "Bulgaria Must Fix Run-Down A-Plant."

87. Seers, Schaffer, and Kiljunen, eds., *Underdeveloped Europe*; Turnock, *The Human Geography of Eastern Europe;* Thompson, "East Europe's Dark Dawn," pp. 36–68; Den Hollander, "The Great Hungarian Plain."

88. Dolokhunov, *Ecology and Economy in Neolithic Eastern Europe*, p. 6.

89. Daly, "Introduction to the Steady-State Economy."

90. Herrenschwand, *De l'économie politique moderne*.

91. Woodward, "Political Changes in the European Mediterranean Arena," p. 185.

92. Heilbroner, "After Communism."

93. Durham, *Through the Lands of the Serb*, p. 101.

94. Drakulić, *How We Survived Communism and Even Laughed*, esp. pp. xi–xvii, 6,

18, 22–23, 27–30, 46–47, 63–64, 73–75, 97, 119–21, and (on ecology and on her father) 138–40.

95. Buruma, "Outsiders," p. 18.

96. Gianaris, *Greece and Turkey*, p. 75.

97. Miller, "Strangers at the Gate."

98. McNeill, *The Great Frontier*; McNeill, *Population and Politics*, p. 56; Gianaris, *Greece and Turkey*, p. 75.

99. Kevles, "Some Like It Hot."

100. Broad, "Breakthrough in Nuclear Fusion"; Browne, "Scientists at Princeton Produce World's Largest Fusion Reaction."

101. Richta *et al.*, *Civilization at the Crossroads*, pp. 189–92.

BIBLIOGRAPHY

Manuscript Sources

Archives du Ministère des Affaires Étrangères (Paris) (Af. Étr.)

Correspondance Commerciale (CC)
Belgrade, I–VIII (1838–89)
Turquie: Mostar, I (1863–72), II (1871–76), III (1875–78)
Turquie: Bosna-Séraï (Sérajevo), III (1875–78)
Correspondance Politique des Consuls (CPC)
Turquie: Andrinople, Sérajevo, Janina, Philippopolis, I (1860–61)
Turquie: Bosna-Séraï (Sérajevo), X (1875), XI (1876), XII (1877–79)

Archives Nationales (Paris) (AN)

Fonds Archives Étrangères (AÉ)
B^I 170–172, Consular correspondence, Arta, 1702–88
B^I 376–448, Consular correspondence, Constantinople, 1637 (but especially 1668) to 1790
B^I 469–473, Consular letters and reports from Coron (Koroni), 1752–91
B^I 863–865, Consular correspondence, Modon (Methoni), 1716–50
B^I 904–906, Consular correspondence from the Morea, especially from Naples de Romanie (Nafplion), 1686–1784
B^I 990–1004, Consular correspondence, Salonika (Thessaloniki), 1686–1792
B^{III} 234, Memoirs on the commerce of the Levant, 1620–84
B^{III} 242, Memoirs on the commerce and economy of the Levant, Turkey, and the Balkans, 1791–1815
Fonds Marine (MAR)
B^4 272, Policing the Mediterranean against piracy, 1786–90
B^7 322, Granger memoirs on the Aegean, Levant, and North Africa, 1733–37
B^7 481, Reports on the naval and maritime strength of Russia, Turkey, and Austria, 1688–1788
D^3 9, Memoirs on the forests and timber and other resources of Illyria, Croatia, Naxos, Epirus, and Albania, 1702–83

Bibliothèque Nationale (Paris) (BN)

Département des Manuscrits
Fonds Français 7176, "Estat des places fortes que le princes mahométans possèdent sur les côtes de la mer Méditerranée," ca. 1687–88

Mémoires et Reconnaissances 1599, "Tableau général des Frontières militaires autrichiennes" and "Essai sur l'organisation des Frontières militaires, ou régiments frontières de l'Autriche, et considérations sur l'application de ce système, à un certain degré, à l'organisation des possessions françaises de l'Afrique," joined to a letter from A. de Terrasson, capitaine d'État major, aide de camp du Général Baron de Gazan, December 20, 1837.

Državni Arhiv (Belgrade, Serbia) (DA)

Pokloni i Otkupi (Miscellaneous letters and other documents) (PO)
kut. 1, Copy of Serbia's commercial code and other documents
kut. 35, Letters on Serbian society, culture, student movements, nationalism, views of Europe, and state of mind in Serbia, especially during the 1850s, 1860s, and 1870s
kut. 38, Letters on Serbian society, especially before the mid-nineteenth century
kut. 62, Jovan Bošković on literature and aesthetics

Marciana (Venezia)

MSS Ital., Cl. 6, No. 176, "Relatione e descrittione del Sangiacato di Scutari," microfilm copy of Fernand Braudel. Account of the Venetian noble of Cattaro (Kotor), Mariano Bolizza, based upon his experiences and travels, 1604–12, joined to his letter of May 25, 1614, to Matteo Michiele. Microfilm copy belonging to Fernand Braudel.

Service Historique de l'Armée (Vincennes)

HAUS-, Hof- und Staatsarchiv (Wien)

Staatenabteilung Serbien VII: "Zakonik gradjanskii za kniažestvo srbsko" (1844).

Books, Articles, and Published Primary Sources

Abbagnano, Nicola. "Italian Renaissance Humanism," *Cahiers d'histoire mondiale, Journal of World History, Cuadernos de Historia Mundial*, VII, 2 (1963), 267–82.
About, Edmond. *La Grèce contemporaine.* Paris: L. Hachette, 1854.
Abu-Lughod, Janet L. *Before European Hegemony: The World System A.D. 1250–1350.* New York: Oxford University Press, 1989.
Academia Scientiarum et Artium Slavorum Meridionalium. *Monumenta Spectantia Historiam Slavorum Meridionalium*, Vol. VIII: Simeon Ljubić, ed., *Commissiones et Relationes Venetae*, pt. 2, *Annorum 1525–1553.* Zagrabiae, 1877.
Académie des Sciences de Bulgarie, Institut d'histoire. *Études historiques à l'occasion du XIe Congrès International des Sciences Historiques, Stockholm, août 1960.* Sofia, 1960.
Adams, Henry. *Mont-Saint-Michel and Chartres*, with an introduction by Ernest Samuels. New York: A Mentor Book—New American Library of World Literature, 1961.
Agard, Walter R. *The Greek Mind.* Princeton, Toronto, London, New York: D. Van Nostrand, 1957.
Albemarle, Earl of. *See* Keppel, George Thomas.
Alexander, J[ames] E[dward]. *Travels from India to England; Comprehending a Visit to the Burman Empire, and a Journey through Persia, Asia Minor, European Turkey, &c., in the Years 1825–26.* London: printed for Parbury, Allen, and Co., 1827.
Alexander, John. "Greeks, Italians, and the Earliest Balkan Iron Age," *Antiquity*, XXXVI (1962), 123–30.
Alexander, Stella. "Croatia: The Catholic Church and Clergy, 1919–1945," in Richard J. Wolff and Jörg K. Hoensch, eds., *Catholics, the State, and the European Radical Right, 1919–1945*, Social Science Monographs, Boulder, Colo.; Highland Lakes, N.J.:

Atlantic Research and Publications, 1987; distributed by Columbia University, New York. Pp. 31–66.

Alexandrescu-Dersca, Marie M. "Contribution à l'étude de l'approvisionnement en blé de Constantinople au XVIIIe siècle," *Studia et acta orientalia*, I (1957), 13–37.

Allcock, John B. "In Praise of Chauvinism: Rhetorics of Nationalism in Yugoslav Politics," *Third World Quarterly*, XI, 4 (October 1989), 208–22.

Allix, André. "The Geography of Fairs: Illustrated by Old-World Examples," *Geographical Review*, XII, 4 (October 1922), 532–69.

Alting von Geusau, Frans A.M. "Europe 1992 East and West," paper presented at the Second International Conference of the International Society for the Study of European Ideas, European Nationalism: Toward 1992," Leuven, Belgium, September 3–8, 1990.

———. "The Spirit of 1989: Europe on the Threshold of a New Era?" *History of European Ideas*, XV, 1–3 (August 1992), 3–14.

Anati, Emmanuel. *Camonica Valley: A Depiction of Village Life in the Alps from Neolithic Times to the Birth of Christ as Revealed by Thousands of Newly Found Rock Carvings*, translated from the French by Linda Asher. New York: Alfred A. Knopf, 1961.

———. *Palestine before the Hebrews: A History, from the Earliest Arrival of Man to the Conquest of Canaan*. New York: Alfred A. Knopf, 1963.

Ancel, Jacques. *Géographie des frontières*. Paris: Gallimard, 1938.

Anderson, Benedict. *Imagined Communities: Reflections on the Origin and Spread of Nationalism*. [London]: Verso Editions, [1983].

Anderson, Eugene N.; Pincetl, Stanley J., Jr.; and Ziegler, Donald J., eds. *Europe in the Nineteenth Century: A Documentary Analysis of Change and Conflict*, Vol. II: *1870–1914*. Indianapolis: Bobbs-Merrill Company, 1961.

Anderson, R. C. *Naval Wars in the Levant, 1550–1853*. Princeton, N.J.: Princeton University Press, 1952.

Andréadès, André. "L'Administration financière de la Grèce sous la domination turque," *Revue des études grecques*, XXIII (March–June 1910), 131–83.

Andreopoulos, George J. "Liberalism and the Formation of the Nation-State," *Journal of Modern Greek Studies*, VII (1989), 193–224.

Andrić, Ivo. *The Bridge on the Drina*, translated from the Serbo-Croat by Lovett F. Edwards. New York: Signet Book, published by the New American Library, by arrangement with the Macmillan Company, 1960; copyright by George Allen and Unwin Ltd., 1959.

Angelov, Dimitur Simeonov. *Les Balkans au Moyen âge: La Bulgarie des Bogomils aux Turcs*. London: Variorum Reprints, 1978.

Une confédération orientale comme solution de la Question d'Orient. Paris: Plon, 1905.

Antoniadis-Bibicou, Hélène. "Villages désertés en Grèce: Un Bilan provisoire," in *Villages désertés et histoire économique, XIe–XVIIIe siècle*, École Pratique des Hautes Études, VIe Section, Centre de Recherches Historiques, "Les Hommes et la Terre," XI. Paris: SEVPEN, 1965. Pp. 343–417.

Antoljak, Stjepan. *Bune pučana i seljaka u Hrvatskoj*. Zagreb: Matica Hrvatska, 1956.

Arendt, Hannah. *The Human Condition*. Chicago: University of Chicago Press, 1958.

Arensberg, Conrad M. "The Old World Peoples: The Place of European Cultures in World Ethnography," *Anthropological Quarterly*, XXXVI (1963), 75–99.

Arfeuille, seigneur d'. *See* Nicolay, Nicolas de.

Aristotle. *Aristotle's Politics and Poetics*, translated by Benjamin Jowett and Thomas Twining, with an introduction by Lincoln Diamant. Cleveland: Fine Editions Press, [1952].

Armstrong, John A. "Mobilized and Proletarian Diasporas," *American Political Science Review*, LXX (1976), 393–408.

————. *Nations before Nationalism*. Chapel Hill, N.C.: University of North Carolina Press, [1982].

Arnakis, George G. "The Role of Religion in the Development of Balkan Nationalism," in Jelavich and Jelavich, eds. *The Balkans in Transition*, pp. 115–44.

Arnaudov, Mikhail. *Studii vŭrkhu bŭlgarskite obredi i legendi*, chast I–II. Sofia: Universitetska Biblioteka, 1924.

Asbóth, J. de. *An Official Tour through Bosnia and Herzegovina, with an Account of the History, Antiquities, Agrarian Conditions, Ethnology, Folk Lore, and Social Life of the People*, authorized English ed. London: Swan Sonnenschein, 1890.

Ash, Timothy Garton. "Mitteleuropa?" *Daedalus*, CXIX (Winter 1990), 1–24.

Ashworth, William. *A Short History of the International Economy since 1850*, 2nd ed. [London]: Longmans, Green and Co., [1962].

Association Internationale d'Études du Sud-est Européen, ed. *Actes du Premier Congrès International des études balkaniques et sud-est européennes*, Vol. III: *Histoire (Ve–XVe ss.; XVe–XVIIe ss.)*. Sofia: Éditions de l'Académie Bulgare des Sciences, 1968.

Atanasijević, Ksenija. *Penseurs yougoslaves*. Belgrade: Bureau Central de Presse, 1937.

————. *See also* Knežević, Božidar.

Atanasov, Shteriu, Lt.-Gen. *Selskite vŭstaniia v Bŭlgariia kŭm kraia na XVIII. v. i nachaloto na XIX. v. i sŭzdavaneto na bŭlgarskata zemska voiska*. Sofia: Dŭrzhavno voenno izdatelstvo, 1958.

Avakumović, Ivan. *History of the Communist Party of Yugoslavia*, Vol. I. Aberdeen: Aberdeen University Press, 1964.

Aymard, André, "L'Idée de travail dans la Grèce archaïque," *Journal de psychologie normale et pathologique*, XLI (1948), 29–45.

Aymard, Maurice. *Venise, Raguse et le commerce du blé pendant la seconde moitié du XVIe siècle*. Paris: SEVPEN, 1966.

Babinger, Franz. "Deli-Orman," in *Encyclopaedia of Islam*, new ed., edited by B. Lewis, Ch. Pellat, and J. Schacht. Leiden: E. J. Brill; London: Luzac and Co., 1965. II, 202–3.

Babudieri, Fulvio. "Maritime Commerce of the Habsburg Empire: The Port of Trieste, 1789–1913," in Vacalopoulos, Svolopoulos, and Király, eds., *Southeast European Maritime Commerce*, pp. 221–44.

Bærentzen, Lars; Iatrides, John O.; and Smith, Ole L., eds., *Studies in the History of the Greek Civil War, 1945–1949*. Copenhagen: Museum Tusculanum Press, 1987.

Bagally, John Wortley. *The Klephtic Ballads in Relation to Greek History (1715–1821)*. Oxford: Basil Blackwell, 1936.

Bagby, Philip. *Culture and History: Prolegomena to the Comparative Study of Civilizations*. Berkeley and Los Angeles: University of California Press, 1963; English ed., London: Longmans, Green & Co., Ltd., 1958.

Bairoch, Paul. "Urbanization and the Economy in Preindustrial Societies: The Findings of Two Decades of Research," *Journal of European Economic History*, XVIII, 2 (Fall 1989), 239–90.

Bairoch, Paul, and Lévy-Leboyer, Maurice, eds. *Disparities in Economic Development since the Industrial Revolution*. New York: St. Martin's Press, [1981].

Bajraktarević, Fehim. "Yürüks," *Encyclopédie de l'Islam* (1936), IV, 1241–42.

Baker, Benjamin R. "Global Multiculturalism and the American Experiment," *World Policy Journal*, X, 1 (Spring 1993), 47–55.

Balevski, D. *See* G. G.

Banac, Ivo. "The Fearful Asymmetry of War: The Causes and Consequences of Yugoslavia's Demise," *Daedalus*, CXXI, 2 (Spring 1992), 141–74.

————. "Historiography of the Countries of Eastern Europe: Yugoslavia," *American Historical Review*, IIIC, 4 (October 1992), 1084–1104.

————. *The National Question in Yugoslavia: Origins, History, Politics.* Ithaca, N.Y.: Cornell University Press, [1984].

————. "Political Change and National Diversity," *Daedalus,* CXIX, 1 (Winter 1990), 141–59.

————. "The Role of Vojvodina in Karadjordje's Revolution," *Südost-Forschungen,* XI (1981), 31–61.

————. "Universalist Religions in a Multinational Society: Yugoslavia since 1966," in *Cross Currents: A Yearbook of Central European Culture,* VII (1988), 57–74.

Banašević, N. "Bifon i Njegoš," in *Zbornik u čast Bogdana Popovića.* Belgrade: Geca Kon, 1929. Pp. 121–37.

————. "Le Cycle de Kosovo et les chansons de geste," *Revue des études slaves,* VI (1926), 224–44.

Bănescu, N. *Un Problème d'histoire médiévale: Création et caractère du Second Empire Bulgare (1185).* Bucarest: Institut Roumain d'Études Byzantines, [1943].

Barash, David P. *Sociobiology and Behavior.* New York: Elsevier, 1977.

Barbu, Zevedei. *Problems of Historical Psychology.* New York: Grove Press, [1960].

Barišić, Franjo. *Čuda Dimitrija Solunskog kao istoriski izvori.* Belgrade: Srpska Akademija Nauka, 1953.

Barjaktarović, Mirko R. " 'Potka' Dušanova Zakonika," in *Zbornik Etnografskog Muzeja u Beogradu 1901–1951.* Belgrade: Naučna Knjiga, 1953. Pp. 232–33.

Barkan, Ömer Lûtfi. "Les Déportations comme méthode de peuplement et de colonisation dans l'Empire ottoman," *Revue de la Faculté des Sciences Économiques de l'université d'Istanbul,* XI (October 1949–July 1950), 67–131.

————. "Les Formes de l'organisation du travail agricole dans l'Empire ottoman," paper presented at the Centre de Recherches Historiques, Paris, February, 20, 1952.

————. "La 'Méditerranée' de Fernand Braudel vue d'Istamboul," *Annales: Économies, Sociétés, Civilisations,* IX, 2 (April–June 1954), 189–200.

————. "Le Servage existait-il en Turquie," *Annales: Économies, Sociétés, Civilisations,* XI, 1 (January–March 1956), 54–60.

Barker, Elisabeth. *British Policy in South-East Europe in the Second World War.* New York: Barnes and Noble Books, [1976].

————. *Macedonia: Its Place in Balkan Power Politics.* London: Royal Institute of International Affairs, 1950.

Barker, Sir Ernest. "Space," in Barker, Sir Ernest; Clark, Sir George; and Vaucher, P., eds. *The European Inheritance,* Vol. III. Oxford: Clarendon Press, 1954. Pp. 295–307.

Barth, Fredrik, ed. *Scale and Social Organization.* Oslo, Bergen, Tromsø: Universitetsforlaget; copyright by the Norwegian Research Council for Science and the Humanities, 1978.

Barthélemy Saint-Hilaire [or Ste.-Hilaire], Jules. *Politique d'Aristote,* 2 vols. Paris: Imprimerie Royale, 1837.

Bartlett, Will. "Economic Change in Yugoslavia: From Crisis to Reform," in Sjöberg and Wyzan, eds., *Economic Change in the Balkan States,* pp. 32–46.

Bartra, Roger. "Identity and Wilderness: Ethnography and the History of the Imaginary Primitive Group," *Ethnologia Europaea: Journal of European Ethnology,* XXI, 2 (1991), 103–23.

Bax, Mart. "How the Mountain Became Sacred: The Politics of Sacralization in a Former Yugoslav Community," *Ethnologia Europaea: Journal of European Ethnology,* XXII, 2 (1992), 115–25.

————. "Patronage in a Holy Place: Preliminary Research Notes on a 'Parallel Structure' in a Yugoslav Pilgrimage Centre," *Ethnos,* LV, 1–2 (1990), 41–55.

————. "The Saints of Gomila: Ritual and Violence in a Yugoslav Peasant Community," *Ethnologia Europaea: Journal of European Ethnology,* XXII, 1 (1992), 17–31.

―――. "The Seers of Medjugorje: Professionalization and Management Problems in a Yugoslav Pilgrimage Centre," *Ethnologia Europaea: Journal of European Ethnology*, XX, 2 (1990), 167–76.

Baxevanis, John. "Population: Internal Migration, and Urbanization in Greece," *Balkan Studies*, VI (1965), 83–98.

Beaujour, Louis-Auguste Félix, baron de. *Tableau du commerce de la Grèce, formé d'après une année moyenne depuis 1787 jusqu'en 1797*, 2 vols. Paris: Imprimerie de Carapelet, an VIII.

―――. *A View of the Commerce of Greece, Formed after an Annual Average, from 1787 to 1797*, translated from the French by Thomas Hartwell Horne. London: printed by H. L. Galabin for James Wallace, 1800.

Becker, Bertha K. "The State Crisis and the Region: Preliminary Thoughts from a Third World Perspective," in Taylor and House, eds. *Political Geography*, pp. 81–97.

Beckinsale, Monica, and Beckinsale, Robert. *Southern Europe: The Mediterranean and Alpine Lands*. London: University of London Press, [1975].

Beckmann, Johann. *A History of Inventions, Discoveries, and Origins*, translated from the German by William Johnston, 4th ed., revised and enlarged by William Francis, editor of the *Chemical Gazette*, and J. W. Griffith, licentiate of the Royal College of Physicians, 2 vols. London: Henry G. Bohn, 1846.

Bekker, Immanuel, ed. *Nicetae Choniatae Historiae*, Corpus Scriptorum Historiae Byzantiniae. Bonn: Weber, 1835.

Bell, H. I. "Philanthropia in the Papyri of the Roman Period," in *Hommages à Joseph Bidez et à Franz Cumont*. Bruxelles: Latomus, n.d. Pp. 31–37.

Belon du Mans, Pierre. *Les Observations de plvsievrs singvlarritez et choses memorables, trouuées en Grece, Asie, Iudée, Egypte, Arabie, & autres pays estranges*, redigées en trois liures. Paris: Gilles Corrozet, 1553, auec priuilege du Roy. There were also a 1553 printing with minor differences in spelling and a 1554 edition by the same publisher.

Benda, Coloman. "Les Jacobins hongrois," *Annales historiques de la Révolution française*, XXXI (January–March 1959), 38–60.

Benveniste, Émile. *Le Vocabulaire des institutions indo-européennes*, 2 vols. Paris: Les Éditions de Minuit, 1969.

Bérard, Jean. "Problèmes démographiques dans l'histoire de la Grèce antique," *Population: Revue de l'Institut National d'Études Démographiques*, II (1947), 303–12.

Bérard, Victor. *La Turquie et l'hellénisme contemporain: La Macédoine*. Paris: Félix Alcan, 1893; 6th ed., 1911.

Bergier, Jean François. "De Nuremberg à Genève: Quelques notes sur l'activité des marchands d'Allemagne aux foires de Genève autour de 1500," in Schneider, et al., eds., *Wirtschaftskräfte und Wirtschaftswege*, I, 581–602.

Bergier, Nicolas (avocat au siège présidial de Reims). *Histoire des grands chemins de l'Empire romain*. Paris: chez C. Morel, Imprimeur du Roy, 1622.

Bernardo, Lorenzo. *Viaggio a Costantinopoli di Sier Lorenzo Bernardo per l'Arresto del Bailo Sier Girolamo Lippomano Cav., 1591 Aprile*, edited by R. Deputazione Veneta Sopra gli Studi di Storia Patria. Venice, 1886.

Berov, Ljuben (Liuben). "Changes in Price Conditions in Trade between Turkey and Europe in the 16th–19th Century," *Études balkaniques*, X, 2–3 (1974), 168–78.

Berr, Henri. *En marge de l'histoire universelle*. Paris: La Renaissance du Livre, 1934.

Bertrandon de la Broquière. *Le Voyage de Bertrandon de la Broquière, écuyer tranchant et conseiller de Philippe le Bon, duc de Bourgogne*, edited by Charles Schefer. Paris: Ernest Leroux, 1892. For sections relevant to Hungary in particular, see also *Monumenta Hungariae Historica*, Diplomataria (Pest, 1859), IV, 301–23.

Bertsch, Gary K. *Nation-Building in Yugoslavia: A Study of Political Integration and Attitudinal Consensus.* Beverly Hills, Calif.; London: Sage Publications, 1971.

———. *Values and Community in Multi-National Yugoslavia.* Boulder, Colo.: *East European Quarterly,* distributed by Columbia University Press, New York, 1976.

Bićanić, Rudolf. *Economic Policy in Socialist Yugoslavia* Cambridge: University Press, 1973.

———. "Occupational Heterogeneity of Peasant Families in the Period of Accelerated Industrialization," in *Transactions of Third World Congress of Sociology,* Koninklijk Instituut voor de Tropen, Amsterdam, August 22–29, 1956, Vol. IV. *Changes in the Family.* London: International Sociological Association, 1956. Pp. 80–96.

Bierman, Irene A.; Abou-el-Haj, Rifa'at A.; and Preziosi, Donald, eds. *The Ottoman City and Its Parts: Urban Structure and Social Order.* New Rochelle, N.Y.: Aristide D. Caratzas, [1991].

Biometric Laboratory Staff. "Discussion of Miss M. L. Tildsley's Measurements on the Northern and Southern Albanians," *Biometrika,* XXV (1933), 29–42.

Birken, Lawrence. *Consuming Desire: Sexual Science and the Emergence of a Culture of Abundance, 1871–1914.* Ithaca, N.Y.: Cornell University Press, [1988].

Birnbaum, Henrik, and Vryonis, Speros, Jr., eds. *Aspects of the Balkans—Continuity and Change: Contributions to the International Balkan Conference Held at UCLA, October 23–28, 1969.* The Hague, Paris: Mouton, 1972.

Black, Cyril Edwin. *The Establishment of Constitutional Government in Bulgaria.* Princeton, N.J.: Princeton University Press, 1943.

Blanc, André. *La Croatie occidentale: Étude de géographie humaine,* Paris: Institut d'Études Slaves de l'Université de Paris, 1957.

———. *L'Économie des Balkans,* "Que sais-je?" No. 1193. Paris: Presses Universitaires de France, 1965.

———. *La Yougoslavie.* Paris: Armand Colin, 1967.

Blanc, André, avec la collaboration de I. Sandru. "La Roumanie," in Blanc, George, and Smotkine, eds., *Les Républiques socialistes d'Europe centrale,* pp. 208–58.

Blanc, André; George, Pierre; and Smotkine, Henri, eds., avec la collaboration de G. Enyedi et I. Sandru, *Les Républiques socialistes d'Europe centrale.* Paris: Presses Universitaires de France, 1967.

Bloch, Marc. "Comment et pourquoi finit l'esclavage antique," *Annales: Économies, Sociétés, Civilisations,* II (January–March 1947), 30–44, and II (April–June 1947), 161–70.

———. *La Société féodale: Les Classes et le gouvernement des hommes.* Paris: Albin Michel, 1940.

———. [M. Fougères, pseud.]. Review of Herbert Wilhelmy, *Hochbulgarien,* Vol. I: *Die ländlichen Siedlungen und die bauerliche Wirtschaft* (Kiel, 1935), in *Mélanges d'histoire sociale,* I (1942), 118–19.

Blockmans, Wim P. *See* Tilly, Charles.

Blount, Sir Henry. *A Briefe Relation of a Iourney, Lately Performed by Master Henry Blount, Gentleman, from England by the Way of Venice, into Dalmatia, Sclavonia, Bosnah, Hungary, Macedonia, Thessaly, Thrace, Rhodes and Egypt, unto Gran Cairo,* 3rd ed. London: Andrew Crooke, 1638.

Blum, Richard, and Blum, Eva, assisted by Anna Amera and Sophie Kallifatidou. *The Dangerous Hour: The Lore of Crisis and Mystery in Rural Greece.* New York: Charles Scribner's Sons, [1970].

———. *Health and Healing in Rural Greece: A Study of Three Communities.* Stanford, Calif.: Stanford University Press, 1965.

Bois-le-Comte de Rigni (Rigny), Count. "Srbija u godini 1834: Pisma grofa Boa-le-

Konta de Rinji Ministru Inostranih Dela u Parizu o tadašnjem stanju u Srbiji," edited by Stojan Novaković, in *Srpska Kraljevska Akademija, Spomenik*, XXIV (Belgrade, 1894), 1–64.

Bolkestein, Hendrik. *Economic Life in Greece's Golden Age*, revised and annotated by E. J. Jonkers. Leiden: E. J. Brill, 1958.

Bollnow, Otto Friedrich. *Mensch und Raum*. Stuttgart: W. Kohlhammer, 1963.

Bonald, Louis, vicomte de. "Du Divorce, considéré au XIXe siècle relativement à l'état domestique et à l'état public de la société," in *Oeuvres de Bonald: Essai analytique sur les lois naturelles de l'ordre social; Du Divorce considéré au XIXe siècle relativement à l'état domestique et à l'état public de société; Pensées sur divers sujets*. Paris: Librairie d'Adrien le Clere et Cie, 1847. Pp. 123–278.

Boppe, Auguste. *L'Albanie et Napoléon (1797–1814)*. Paris, 1914.

Borchgrave, Émile [Jacques Yvon Marie], baron de (ministre résident de Belgique à Belgrade). *La Serbie administrative, économique et commerciale*. Brussels: P. Weissenbruch; Belgrade: P. Tchourtchitch, 1883.

Boswell, Terry, and Sweat, Mike. "Hegemony, Long Waves, and Major Wars: A Time Series Analysis of Systemic Dynamics, 1496–1967," *International Studies Quarterly*, XXXV (1991), 123–49.

Botzaris, Notis. *Visions balkaniques dans la préparation de la Révolution grecque (1789–1821)*. Geneva: Droz; Paris: Minard, 1962.

Boué, Ami. *Recueil d'itinéraires dans la Turquie d'Europe*, 2 vols. Vienna: W. Braumüller, libraire de l'Académie Impériale des Sciences, 1854.

―――. *La Turquie d'Europe, ou Observations sur la géographie, la géologie, l'histoire naturelle, la statistique, les moeurs, les coutumes, l'archéologie, l'agriculture, l'industrie, le commerce, les gouvernements divers, le clergé, l'histoire de l'état politique de cet empire*, 4 vols. Paris: chez Arthus Bertrand, 1840.

Boulding, Kenneth E. *The Meaning of the Twentieth Century: The Great Transition*. New York: Harper and Row, copyright 1964 by Kenneth Ewart Boulding; first Colophon ed., 1965.

Boulongne, Alfred, Dr. *Le Monténégro: Le Pays et ses habitants*. Paris: Victor Rozier, 1869.

Bourdieu, Pierre. *La Distinction: Critique sociale du jugement*. Paris: Les Éditions de Minuit, 1979.

Bourque, Gilles. *L'État capitaliste et la question allemande*. Montréal: Les Presses de l'Université de Montréal, 1977.

Bousquet, G. H. "L'Islam et la limitation volontaire des naissances," *Population*, V (1950), 121–28.

Bouthol, Gaston. *Biologie sociale*, "Que sais-je?" No. 738. Paris: Presses Universitaires de France, 1957.

Bouvier, Jean. *Le Krach de l'Union Générale (1878–1885)*. Paris: Presses Universitaires de France, 1960.

Bracewell, Catherine Wendy. *The Uskoks of Senj: Piracy, Banditry, and Holy War in the Sixteenth Century Adriatic*. Ithaca, N.Y.: Cornell University Press, 1992.

Braidwood, Robert J., and Willey, Gordon R. "Conclusions and Afterthoughts," in Braidwood and Willey, *Courses Toward Urban Life*, 330–59.

―――, eds., *Courses toward Urban Life: Archeological Considerations for Some Cultural Alternates*. New York: Wenner-Gren Foundation for Anthropological Research, 1962.

―――. *Prehistoric Men*, enlarged 3rd ed. Chicago: Chicago Natural Museum, 1957.

Brailsford, Henry Noel. *Macedonia: Its Races and Their Future*. London: Methuen, 1906.

————. *The War of Steel and Gold: A Study of the Armed Peace*. London: G. Bell and Sons Ltd., 1914.

Branigan, J. J., and Jarrett, H. R. *The Mediterranean Lands*. London: Macdonald and Evans, 1969.

Brass, Paul R. "Ethnic Groups and Nationalities," in Sugar, ed. *Ethnic Diversity*, pp. 1–68.

Bratanič, Branimir. "Some Similarities between Ards of the Balkans, Scandinavia, and Their Methodological Significance," in Anthony F. C. Wallace, ed., *Selected Papers of the Fifth International Congress of Anthropological and Ethnological Sciences, Philadelphia, September 1–9, 1956: Men and Cultures*. Philadelphia: University of Pennsylvania Press, [1960]. Pp. 221–28.

Braudel, Fernand. *Afterthoughts on Material Civilization and Capitalism*, translated by Patricia M. Ranum. Baltimore and London: Johns Hopkins University Press, [1977].

————. "L'Apport de l'histoire des civilisations," in *Encyclopédie Française*, Vol. XX: *Le Monde en devenir (Histoire, Évolution, Prospective)*. Paris, 1959. Pp. 20.10–11 to 20.12–14.

————. *Civilisation matérielle et capitalisme (XVe–XVIIIe siècles)*, Vol. I. Paris: Armand Colin, 1967.

————. *Civilisation matérielle, économie et capitalisme, XVe–XVIIIe siècle*, 3 vols. Paris: Armand Colin, [1979].

————. *Civilization and Capitalism, 15th–18th Century*, 3 vols., translated by Siân Reynolds. London: William Collins Sons; New York: Harper and Row, 1982–84.

————. "La Démographie et les dimensions des sciences de l'homme," *Écrits sur l'histoire*. [Paris]: Flammarion, [1969]. Pp. 193–235. Reprinted from *Annales: Économies, Sociétés, Civilisations*, XV, 3 (May–June 1960), 493–523. Translated by Sarah Matthews as "Demography and the Scope of the Human Sciences," in *On History*. Chicago: University of Chicago Press, [1960]. Pp. 132–61.

————. "Histoire et sciences sociales: La Longue durée," *Annales: Économies, Sociétés, Civilisations*, XIII, 4 (October–December 1958), 725–53.

————. *The Identity of France*, Vol. I: *History and Environment*. New York: Harper and Row, reprinted by arrangement with William Collins Sons and Co., Ltd., 1988. Translated by Siân Reynolds from *L'Identité de la France*, Vol. I: *Espace et histoire*. Paris: Arthaud-Flammarion, 1986.

————. *The Mediterranean and the Mediterranean World in the Age of Philip II*, 2 vols., translated from the French by Siân Reynolds. New York: Harper and Row, 1972.

————. *La Méditerranée et le monde méditerranéen à l'époque de Philippe II*. Paris: Armand Colin, 1949; 2nd ed. revised and enlarged, 2 vols. Paris: Armand Colin, 1966.

————. "Misère et banditisme," *Annales: Économies, Sociétés, Civilisations*, II (April–July 1947), 129–42.

————. "Sur une conception de l'histoire sociale," *Ecrits sur l'histoire*, pp. 175–91. Reprinted from *Annales: Économies, Sociétés, Civilisations*, XIV, 2 (April–June 1959), 308–19.

Braudel, Fernand, and Spooner, Frank. "Prices in Europe from 1450 to 1750," in *The Cambridge Economic History of Europe*, Vol. IV: *The Economy of Expanding Europe in the Sixteenth and Seventeenth Centuries*, edited by E. E. Rich and C. H. Wilson. Cambridge: University Press, 1967. Pp. 374–486.

Brenner, Y. S. *Capitalism, Competition, and Economic Crisis: Structural Changes in Advanced Industrialised Countries*. Washington, D.C.: Kapitan Szabo Publishers, [1984]; first published in Great Britain in 1984 by Wheatsheaf Books, Ltd., a member of the Harvester Press Group.

Brinkmann, Carl. "Mihail Manoïlesco und die klassische Aussenhandelstheorie," *Weltwirtschaftliches Archiv*, XLVIII, 2 (September 1938), 273–86.

Brkić, Jovan. *Moral Concepts in Traditional Serbian Epic Poetry.* 's-Gravenhage: Mouton, 1961.

Broad, William J. "Breakthrough in Nuclear Fusion Offers Hope for Power of Future," *New York Times,* November 11, 1991.

Brooks, C. E. P. *Climate through the Ages: A Study of the Climatic Factors and Their Variations,* 2nd rev. ed. New York: Dover Publications, 1970.

Brown, David. "Ethnic Revival: Perspectives on State and Society," *Third World Quarterly,* XI, 4 (October 1989), 1–17.

Brown[e], Edward (M.D., of the College of London, Fellow of the Royal Society, and physician-in-ordinary to His Majesty). *A Brief Account of Some Travels in Hungaria, Servia, Bulgaria, Macedonia, Thessaly, Austria, Styria, Carinthia, Carniola, and Friuli.* London: B. Tooke, 1673.

Browne, Malcolm W. "Bulgaria Must Fix Run-Down A-Plant," *New York Times,* December 8, 1992.

———. "Scientists at Princeton Produce World's Largest Fusion Reaction," *New York Times,* December 10, 1993.

Browning, Robert. *Byzantium and Bulgaria: A Comparative Study across the Early Medieval Frontier.* Berkeley and Los Angeles: University of California Press, 1975.

Brunner. Otto. *Neue Wege der Sozialgeschichte: Vorträge und Aufsätze.* Göttingen: Vandenhoeck und Ruprecht, 1956.

Bruun, Stanley D. "Future of the Nation-State System," in Taylor and House, eds., *Political Geography,* pp. 149–67.

Bryson, Reid A., and Murray, Thomas J. *Climates of Hunger: Mankind and the World's Changing Weather.* Madison: University of Wisconsin Press, 1977.

Buck, Carl Darling. *Dictionary of Selected Synonyms in the Principal Indo-European Languages: A Contribution to the History of Ideas.* Chicago and London: University of Chicago Press, [1949].

Bulliet, Richard W. *The Camel and the Wheel.* Cambridge, Mass.: Harvard University Press, 1975.

Burg, Steven L. *Conflict and Cohesion in Socialist Yugoslavia: Political Decision Making since 1966.* Princeton, N.J.: Princeton University Press, 1983.

Burgel, Guy. *Athènes: Étude de la croissance d'une capitale méditerranéenne.* Lille: Atelier Reproduction des Thèses, Université de Lille III; Paris: diffusion, Librairie Honoré Champion, 1975.

Burks, Richard V. *The Dynamics of Communism in Eastern Europe.* Princeton, N.J.: Princeton University Press, 1961.

———. "Nationalism and Communism in Yugoslavia: An Attempt at Synthesis," in Birnbaum and Vryonis, Jr., eds., *Aspects of the Balkans,* pp. 396–423.

Burn, Andrew Robert. *The Lyric Age of Greece.* London: Edward Arnold, 1960.

Burns, John F. "Hearts Heavy, Arms Light, They Are Fighting On for Sarajevo," *New York Times,* June 27, 1992.

Burns, Robert K. "The Circum-Alpine Culture Area: A Preliminary View," *Anthropological Quarterly,* XXXVI (1963), 130–55.

Buruma, Ian. "Outsiders," *New York Review of Books,* April 9, 1992, pp. 15–16, 18–19.

Busbecq, Ogier Ghiselin de. *The Life and Letters of Ogier Ghiselin de Busbecq, Seigneur of Busbecque, Knight, Imperial Ambassador,* edited by Charles Thornton Forster and F. H. Blackburne Daniell, 2 vols. London: C. Kegan Paul, 1881.

Busch-Zantner, Richard. *Agrarverfassung, Gesellschaft und Siedlung in Südosteuropa in besonderer Berücksichtigung der Türkenzeit.* Leipzig: Otto Harrassowitz, 1938.

Bušetić, Todor M. *Srpske narodne pesme i igre s melodijama iz Levča,* musical arrangement by Stevan St. Mokranjac, Srpska Kraljevska Akademija, "Srpski Etnografski Zbornik," knj. iii Belgrade, 1902.

Čajkanović, Veselin. *O srpskom vrhovnom bogu*, Srpska Kraljevska Akademija, "Posebna izdanja," knj. cxxxii, "Filosofski i filološki spisi," knj. 34. Belgrade: Štamparija "Mlada Srbija," 1941.

————. *Studije iz religije i folklora*, Srpska Kraljevska Akademija, "Srpski Etnografski Zbornik," knj. xxxi, "Život i običaji narodni," knj. 13. Belgrade, 1924. Especially the articles "Gostoprimstvo i teofanija," pp. 1–24; "Magični smej," pp. 25–42; "Subota—djačka bubuta," pp. 43–55; "Da li su stari Srbi znale za idole?" pp. 99–108; "Sv. Sava i vuci," pp. 157–65.

————. *See also* Mijatović, Stanoje M., and Bušetić, Todor M..

Cameron, Rondo, ed. *Banking and Economic Development: Some Lessons of History.* New York: Oxford University Press.

Campbell, John Kennedy. *Honour, Family, and Patronage: A Study of Institutions and Moral Values in a Greek Mountain Community.* Oxford: Clarendon Press, 1964.

————. "The Kindred in a Greek Mountain Community," in Pitt-Rivers, ed., *Mediterranean Countrymen*, pp. 73–96.

Capodistrias, John, Count (to His Majesty the Emperor). "Aperçu de ma carrière, depuis 1798 jusqu'à 1822," *Sbornik Imperatorskago Russkago Istoricheskago Obshchestva*, III (1868), 163–292.

Carcopino, Jérôme. "Un Retour à l'impérialisme: L'Or des Daces," in *Points de vue sur l'impérialisme romain.* Paris: Le Divan, 1934. Pp. 73–86.

Carpenter, Rhys. *Discontinuity in Greek Civilization.* Cambridge: University Press, 1966.

Carter, Francis W., ed. *An Historical Geography of the Balkans.* London, New York, San Francisco: Academic Press, 1977.

Castellan, Georges. "Éléments d'une sociologie religieuse en Yougoslavie socialiste," *Annales: Économies, Sociétés, Civilisations*, XIV, 4 (October–December 1959), 694–709.

Castellan, Yvonne. *La Culture serbe au seuil de l'Indépendance (1800–1840): Essai d'analyse psychologique d'une culture à distance temporelle.* Paris: Presses Universitaires de France, 1967.

Cazeneuve, Jean. *Sociologie de Marcel Mauss.* Paris: Presses Universitaires de France, 1968.

————. "Technical Methods in the Prehistoric Age," *Diogenes*, No. 27 (1959), pp. 102–24.

Centre de Recherches Néohelléniques, Fondation Nationale de la Recherche Scientifique. *Actes du IIe Colloque international d'histoire, Athènes, 18–25 septembre 1983—Économies méditerranéennes: Équilibres et intercommunications, XIIIe–XIXe siècles*, Vol. I: *Liaisons commerciales et mouvement de navires entre la Méditerranée orientale et occidentale, XVe–XIXe siècles.* Athens, 1985.

Cerfberr de Medelsheim, Samson (*dit* Ibrahim-Manzour-Efendi). *Mémoires sur la Grèce et l'Albanie pendant le gouvernement d'Ali Pacha.* Paris: Paul Ledoux, 1827.

Chaconas, Stephen George. *Adamantios Korais: A Study of Greek Nationalism.* New York: Columbia University Press, 1942.

Chantraine, Pierre. *Dictionnaire étymologique de la langue grecque: Histoire des mots*, 2 vols. Paris: Éditions Klincksieck, [1968].

Charanis, Peter. Comment on the views of Soviet Byzantinists as expressed in "Gorod i derevnia v Vizantii v IV–XII vv," in *Actes du XIIe Congrès International d'Études Byzantines, Ochride (Ohrid), 10–16 septembre 1961.* Belgrade, 1963. Pp. 285–91.

————. "Internal Strife in Byzantium during the Fourteenth Century," *Byzantion* (American Series, I), XV (1940–41), 208–30.

————. "The Transfer of Population as a Policy in the Byzantine Empire," *Comparative Studies in Society and History*, III, 2 (January 1961), 140–54.

Chataigneau, Y. *See* Vidal de la Blache, Paul, and Gallois, L.

Chateaubriand, François René de. *Itinéraire de Paris à Jérusalem, suivi des Voyages en Amérique, en France, en Italie*, 2 vols. Paris: P. H. Krabbe, 1853.

Chaumette des Fossés, Jean-Baptiste-Gabriel-Amédée. *Voyage en Bosnie dans les années 1807 et 1808*. Paris: J. Didot, 1822.

Chernus, Ira. "War and the Enemy in the Thought of Mircea Eliade," *History of European Ideas*, XIII, 4 (1991), 335–44.

Childe, V. Gordon. "Archaeological Documents for the Prehistory of Science," *Cahiers d'histoire mondiale*, I, 4 (April 1954), 739–59.

———. *The Dawn of European Civilization*, 6th ed., rev. New York: Vintage Books, [1957].

———. *The Prehistory of European Society*. Baltimore, Md.: Penguin Books, 1958.

Chirot, Daniel. *Social Change in a Peripheral Society: The Creation of a Balkan Colony*. New York, San Francisco, London: Academic Press, [1976].

Cipolla, Carlo M. *Clocks and Culture, 1300–1700*. New York: Walker and Company, [1967].

———. *Guns, Sails, and Empires: Technological Innovation and the Early Phases of European Expansion, 1400–1700*. New York: Pantheon Books, 1965.

Clarke, Edward Daniel. *Travels in Various Countries of Europe, Asia, and Africa*, 6 vols. London: T. Cadell and W. Davies, 1810–23.

Clissold, Stephen. "Croat Separatism: Nationalism, Dissidence, and Terrorism," *Conflict Studies*, No. 103 (January 1979), pp. 3–21.

Clogg, Richard. "The Byzantine Legacy in the Modern Greek World: The Megali Idea," in Clucas, ed., *The Byzantine Legacy in Eastern Europe*, pp. 253–81.

———. "The Greek Mercantile Bourgeoisie: 'Progressive' or 'Reactionary,'" in Clogg, ed., *Balkan Society in the Age of Greek Independence*. Totowa, N.J.: Barnes and Noble Books, [1981]. Pp. 85–110.

Clucas, Lowell, ed. *The Byzantine Legacy in Eastern Europe*. Boulder, [Colo.]: East European Monographs, distributed by Columbia University Press, New York, 1988.

Codrescu, Andrei. *The Hole in the Flag: A Romanian Exile's Story of Return and Revolution*. New York: William Morrow and Company, [1991].

Coll, Steve. "A Bloody History Reborn: Croatia's President Uses His Country's—and His Own Family's—Violent Past," *Washington Post National Weekly Edition*, March 8–14, 1993, pp. 9–10.

Commission Nationale de la République Populaire d'Albanie. "Note sur les Illyriens," *Cahiers d'histoire mondiale, Journal of World History, Cuadernos de Historia Mundial*, VII, 4 (1963), 955–58.

Commission Nationale Roumaine. *Actes du Colloque International de Civilisations Balkaniques*. International colloquium organized for UNESCO and for the Académie de la République Populaire Roumaine, under the auspices and with the aid of UNESCO, at Sinaïa, July 8–14, 1962.

Condurachi, Emil. *Archéologie roumaine au XXe siècle*, Bibliotheca Historica Romaniae, 3. Bucarest: Académie de la République Populaire Roumaine, 1963.

Condurachi, Emil, and Daicoviciu, Constantin. *Romania*, translated from the French by James Hogarth. Geneva, Paris, Munich: Nagel Publishers, [1971].

Constantelos, Demetrios J. "Philanthropia as an Imperial Virtue in the Byzantine Empire of the Tenth Century," *Anglican Theological Review*, XLIV, 4 (October 1962), 351–65; offprint, pp. 1–15.

Constantine Porphyrogenitus. *De Administrando Imperio*, Greek text edited by Gyula Moravcsik, English translation by R. J. H. Jenkins. Budapest: Pázmány Péter Tudományegyetemi Görög Filológiai Intézet, 1949.

Constas, Dimitri C. "Greek Foreign Policy Objectives, 1974–1986," in Vryonis, Jr., ed., *Greece on the Road to Democracy*, pp. 37–69.

Cook, M. A., ed. *Studies in the Economic History of the Middle East from the Rise of Islam to the Present Day*. London, New York, and Toronto: Oxford University Press, 1970.

Cook, R. M. *The Greeks until Alexander*. New York: Frederick A. Praeger, [1962].

Coon, Carleton S. *The Living Races of Man*. New York: Alfred A. Knopf, 1965.

―――. *The Races of Europe*. Westport, Conn.: Greenwood Press, 1939.

―――. *Racial Adaptations*. Chicago: Nelson-Hall, [1982].

Cornford, Francis Macdonald. *From Religion to Philosophy: A Study in the Origins of Western Speculation*. London: Edward Arnold, 1912.

Coulborn, Rushton. *The Origin of Civilized Societies*. Princeton, N.J.: Princeton University Press, 1959.

Cowell, F. R. *History, Civilization, and Culture: An Introduction to the Historical and Social Philosophy of Pitirim A. Sorokin*. Boston: Beacon Press, 1952.

Crawley, C. W. "John Capodistrias and the Greeks before 1821," *Cambridge Historical Journal*, XIII (1957), 162–82.

Črnja, Zvane. *Kulturna historija Hrvatske: Ideje, ličnosti, djela*. Zagreb: Epoha, 1965.

Crnobrnja, Mihailo. *Le Drame yougoslave*, translated from the English. [Rennes]: Éditions Apogée, [1992].

Čubrilović, Vasa. *Istorija političke misli u Srbiji XIX veka*. Belgrade: Prosveta, 1958.

Cunibert, Barthélemy-Sylvestre (ancien médecin en chef au service du gouvernement serbe, décoré de l'ordre ottoman du mérite). *Essai historique sur les révolutions de l'indépendance de la Serbie depuis 1804 jusqu'à 1850*, 2 vols. Leipzig: F. A. Brockhaus, 1855.

Curticăpeanu, V. *Le Mouvement culturel pour le parachèvement de l'État national roumain (1918)*. Bucarest: Éditions de l'Académie de la République Socialiste de Roumanie, 1973.

Curtius, Ernst Robert. *The Civilization of France*, edited by Olive Wyon. New York: Vintage Books, 1962; printed by arrangement with George Allen and Unwin, Ltd.

Curwen, E. Cecil, and Hatt, Gudmund. *Plough and Pasture: The Early History of Farming*. New York: Collier Books, 1961; copyright 1953 by Henry Schuman, Inc.

Cvetkova, Bistra. "Les *Celep* et leur rôle dans la vie économique des Balkans à l'époque ottomane (XVe-XVIIIe s.)," in Cook, ed., *Studies in the Economic History of the Middle East*, pp. 172–92.

―――. "Changements intervenus dans la condition de la population des terres bulgares (depuis la fin du XVIe jusqu'au milieu du XVIIIe s.)," in *Études historiques*, Vol. V: *À l'occasion du XIIIe Congrès International des Sciences Historiques—Moscou, août 1970*. Sofia: Académie Bulgare des Sciences, 1970. Pp. 291–318.

―――. "Le Service des 'Celep' et le ravitaillement en bétail dans l'Empire Ottoman (XVe-XVIIIe s.)," *Études historiques*, III (1966), 145–72.

Cvijić, Jovan. "Izlazak Srbije na Jadransko More," in *Govori i članci*, 2 vols. Belgrade: Napredak, 1921. II, 9–25.

―――. "Des Migrations dans les pays yougoslaves: L'adaptation au milieu," *Revue des études slaves*, III (Paris, 1923), 5–26.

―――. "O nacionalnom radu," in *Govori i članci*, 2 vols. Belgrade: "Napredak," 1921. I, 51–71.

―――. "O naučnom radu i o našem univerzitetu," in *Govori i članci*, 2 vols., Belgrade, "Napredak," 1921. I, 3–49.

―――. *La Péninsule balkanique: Géographie humaine*. Paris: Armand Colin, 1918.

―――. "The Zones of Civilisation of the Balkan Peninsula," *Geographical Review*, V, 6 (June 1918), 470–82.

Dalton, George. "Primitive, Archaic, and Modern Economies: Karl Polanyi's Contribution to Economic Anthropology and Comparative Economy," in June Helm, Paul

Bohannan, and Marshall D. Sahlins, eds., *Essays in Economic Anthropology Dedicated to the Memory of Karl Polanyi: Proceedings of the 1965 Annual Meeting of the American Ethnological Society*. Seattle: American Ethnological Society, distributed by the University of Washington Press, 1965. Pp. 1–24.

Daly, Herman E. "Introduction to the Steady-State Economy," in Daly, ed., *Economics, Ecology, Ethics*, pp. 1–31.

———, ed., *Economics, Ecology, Ethics: Essays toward a Steady-State Economy*. San Francisco: W. H. Freeman, [1973, 1980]. Pp. 1–31.

Damianov, Simeon. "French Commerce with the Bulgarian Territories from the Eighteenth Century to 1914," in Vacalopoulos, Svolopoulos, and Király, eds., *Southeast European Maritime Commerce*, pp. 13–33.

Danaïlow, Georges T. [Danailov, Georgi Todorov]. *Les Effets de la Guerre en Bulgarie*, Publications de la Dotation Carnegie pour la Paix Internationale. Paris: Presses Universitaires de France; New Haven, Conn: Yale University Press, [1932].

Daničić, Gj. (Djuro). *Korijeni s rječima od njih postalijem u hrvatskom ili srpskom jeziku*. Zagreb: Jugoslavenska Akademija Znanosti i Umjetnosti, 1877.

———. *Rječnik iz književnih starina srpskih*, 3 vols. Belgrade: Državna Štamparija, 1863–64.

Dapontès, Constantin (secretary of Prince Constantino Maurocordato). *Éphémérides daces, ou Chronique de la Guerre de quatre ans (1736–39)*, translated and annotated by Émile Legrand, Vol. II. Paris: Leroux, 1881.

Dascalakis (Daskalakes), Apostolos Vasileiou. *Rhigas Velestinlis: La Révolution française et les préludes de l'indépendance hellénique*. Paris, 1937.

Davies, Oliver. *Roman Mines in Europe*. Oxford: Clarendon Press, 1935.

Deák, István. *Beyond Nationalism: A Social and Political History of the Habsburg Officer Corps, 1848–1918*. New York, Oxford: Oxford University Press, 1992.

Decornoy, Jacques. "La Chevauchée américaine pour la direction du monde," *Le Monde diplomatique*, No. 476, 40e année (November 1993), pp. 8–9.

Dedijer, Jevto. "La Transhumance dans les pays dinariques," *Annales de géographie*, No. 137, XXVe année (September 15, 1916), pp. 347–65.

Dedijer, Vladimir. *Tito*. New York: Simon and Schuster, 1953.

Deffontaines, Pierre. "Notes sur la répartition des types de voiture," reprint without periodical or book title, pp. 169–85.

De Grazia, Sebastian. *Of Time, Work, and Leisure*. New York: Twentieth Century Fund, 1962.

Delaisi, Francis. *Les Deux Europes*, préface de Dannie Heineman. Paris: Payot, 1929.

———. *Political Myths and Economic Realities*. New York: Viking Press, 1927.

Delaunay, Paul. *L'Aventureuse existence de Pierre Belon du Mans*. Paris: Libr. Édouard Champion, 1926.

Demetriades, Vassilis. "Some Thoughts on the Origins of the Devşirme," in Zachariadou, ed., *The Ottoman Emirate*, pp. 23–31.

Demos, Raphael. "The Neo-Hellenic Enlightenment (1750–1821)," *Journal of the History of Ideas*, XIX (1958), 523–41.

Den Hollander, A. N. J. "The Great European Plain: A European Frontier Area," *Comparative Studies in Society and History*, III, 1 (October 1960), 74–88, and III, 2 (January 1961), 155–69.

Dennell, Robin. *European Economic Prehistory: A New Approach*. London, New York: Academic Press, 1983.

Dertilis, Georges B. "Terre, paysans et pouvoir politique, Grèce, XVIIIe–XXe siècle," *Annales: Économies, Sociétés, Civilisations*, XLVIII, 1 (January–February 1993), 85–107.

Despalatović, Elinor Murray. *Ljudevit Gaj and the Illyrian Movement.* Boulder, Colo.: *East European Quarterly,* distributed by Columbia University Press, New York and London, 1975.

d'Eszláry, Charles. "Les Jacobins hongrois et leurs conceptions juridico-politiques," *Revue d'histoire moderne et contemporaine,* VII (October–December 1960), 291–307.

Deutsch, Karl W. *Nationalism and Social Communication: An Inquiry into the Foundations of Nationality,* 2nd ed. Cambridge, Mass.: MIT Press, 1953, 1966.

Devereux, Georges. "Considérations ethnopsychanalytiques sur la notion de parenté," *L'Homme: Revue française d'anthropologie,* V, 3–4 (1965), 224–47.

Dicey, Edward. *The Peasant State: An Account of Bulgaria in 1894.* London: John Murray, 1894.

Dinić, Mihailo. *Srpske zemlje u srednjem veku: Istorijsko-geografske studije,* edited by Sima M. Ćirković. Belgrade: Srpska Književna Zadruga, 1978.

Dion, Michel. "L'Identité ethnique en Roumanie," *Cahiers internationaux de sociologie,* XCIII (July–December 1992), 251–68.

Djilas, Milovan. *The New Class: An Analysis of the Communist System.* New York: Praeger, 1957.

Djordjević, Dimitrije. *Révolutions nationales des peuples balkaniques, 1804–1914,* translated by Margita Ristić. Belgrade: Institut d'histoire, 1965.

Djordjević, Dimitrije, and Fischer-Galati, Stephen. *The Balkan Revolutionary Tradition.* New York: Columbia University Press, 1981.

Djordjević, Tihomir R. *Beleške o našoj poeziji.* Belgrade: n.p., 1939.

———. *Gradja za srpske narodne običaje iz vremena prve vlade Kneza Miloša,* Srpska Kraljevska Akademija, "Srpski Etnografski Zbornik," knj. xiv: "Običaji naroda srpskoga," knj. 2. Belgrade, 1909.

———. *Priroda u verovanju i predanju našega naroda,* 2 vols. Belgrade: Srpska Akademija Nauka, 1958.

———. *Srbija pre sto godina.* Belgrade, 1946.

———. "Uzimanje u rodu u našem narodu," in *Zbornik u čast Bogdana Popovića.* Belgrade: Geca Kon, 1939. Pp. 331–39.

Dockès, Pierre. *Medieval Slavery and Liberation,* translated by Arthur Goldhammer. Chicago: University of Chicago Press, [1982].

Dodds, E. R. *The Greeks and the Irrational.* Berkeley and Los Angeles: University of California Press, 1951, 1963.

Doder, Dusko. "Belgrade Professor [Mihajlo Marković] Who Fought Tito Now Scorned as Serb Leader [by Western Media]," *Chronicle of Higher Education,* April 7, 1993, pp. A37–A38.

Dolukhanov, Paul M. *Ecology and Economy in Neolithic Eastern Europe.* [London]: Gerald Duckworth & Co., [1979].

Domanović, Radoje. *Odabrane pripovetke,* edited by Marijan Jurković. N.p.: Novo Pokoljenje, 1949.

———. "Razmišljanje jednog običnog srpskog vola" (Reflexions of an Ordinary Serbian Ox), in *Odabrane Pripovetke,* edited by Marijan Jurković. N.p.: Novo pokoljenje, 1949. Pp. 110–14.

Douglas, Mary Tew. *Natural Symbols: Explorations in Cosmology.* New York: Pantheon Books, 1970; Vintage Books, 1973.

Dragnich, Alex N. *Serbs and Croats: The Struggle in Yugoslavia.* San Diego, New York, London: Harcourt Brace and Company, a Harvest Book, [1992].

Drakulić, Slavenka. *How We Survived Communism and Even Laughed.* New York: W. W. Norton, 1992; Harper Perennial, a Division of HarperCollins Publishers, 1993.

Driault, Édouard, and Lhéritier, Michel. *Histoire diplomatique de la Grèce de 1821 à nos jours*, Vol. II. *Le Règne d'Othon, la Grande Idée*, by Edouard Driault. Paris: Presses Universitaires de France, 1925. See also L'Héritier.

Dučić, Stevan. *Život i običaji plemena Kuči*, Srpska Kraljevska Akademija, "Srpski Etnografski Zbornik," knj. xlviii, drugo odeljenje. Belgrade, 1931.

Dumézil, Georges. *Le Crime des Lemniennes: Rites et légendes du monde égéen*. Paris: Librairie Orientale Paul Geuthner, 1924.

―――. *L'Idéologie tripartite des Indo-Européens*. Bruxelles: Latomus, 1958.

―――. "Métiers et classes fonctionnelles chez divers peuples," *Annales: Économies, Sociétés, Civilisations*, XIII, 4 (October–December 1958), 716–24.

Dumont, Albert. *Le Balkan et l'Adriatique*, 2nd ed. Paris: Didier et Cie, 1874.

Dumont, René. *Types of Rural Economy: Studies in World Agriculture*, translated from the French by Douglas Magnin. London: Methuen, 1957.

Durham, Mary Edith. *Some Tribal Origins, Laws, and Customs of the Balkans*. London: George Allen and Unwin, 1928; also 1979 reprint.

―――. *Through the Lands of the Serb*. London: Edward Arnold, 1904.

Durkheim, Émile. *Les Règles de la méthode sociologique*, 14th ed. Paris: Presses Universitaires de France, 1960.

Durkheim, Émile, and Mauss, Marcel. "De quelques formes primitives de classification: Contribution à l'étude des représentations collectives," *L'Année sociologique*, VI (1901–02), 1–72.

Duțu, Alexandru. "Assimilations and Continuity in Romanian Culture," Association Internationale d'Études du Sud-Est Européen, *Bulletin* (Bucarest), IX, 1–2 (1971), 41–52.

―――. "Ideas and Attitudes: The Southeast European Revolutions of the Nineteenth Century," *Southeastern Europe/L'Europe du Sud-est*, XI, 1 (1984), 1–11.

Dvornik, Francis. *Byzantine Missions among the Slavs: SS. Constantine-Cyril and Methodius*. New Brunswick, N.J.: Rutgers University Press, [1970].

―――. *The Slavs in European History and Civilization*. New Brunswick, N.J.: Rutgers University Press, 1962.

Dvorniković, Vladimir. *Karakterologija Jugoslovena*. Belgrade: Kosmos, Geca Kon, 1939.

East, Gordon. "The Concept and Political Status of the Shatter Zone," in Pounds, ed., *Geographical Essays*, pp. 1–27.

Ebinger, Julius. *Studien über Bosnien und die Herzegovina*. Demmin: [A. Frantz], 1878.

Edmonds, [E. M.], Mrs. "Introductory and Historical Sketch of the Klephts," in *Kolokotronês the Klepht and the Warrior: Sixty Years of Peril and Daring, an Autobiography*, translated from the Greek with introduction and notes by Mrs. Edmonds. London: T. Fisher Unwin, 1892. Pp. 1–79.

Edwards, Chris. *The Fragmented World: Competing Perspectives on Trade, Money, and Crisis*. London and New York: Methuen, 1985.

Eflaki. *Les Saints des derviches tourneurs*, edited and translated by Cl. Huart, 2 vols. Paris, 1918.

Ehrich, Robert W., ed. *Chronologies in Old World Archaeology*. Chicago and London: University of Chicago Press, 1965.

―――. "Culture Areas and Culture History in the Mediterranean and the Middle East," in Weinberg, ed., *The Aegean and the Near East*, pp. 1–21.

Elezović, Gliša. "Tarapana (Darb-Hane) u Novom Brdu: Turske akče (aspre) kovane u kovnici Novoga Brda," Srpska Akademija Nauka, *Istoriski časopis*, II (1949–50), 115–26.

―――.*Turski spomenici*, knj. I, sveska 1: *1348–1520*, Srpska Kraljevska Akademija, "Zbornik za istočnjačku istorisku i književnu gradju," serija prva, knj. 1. Belgrade: "Zora," 1940.

Eliade, Mircea. *Cosmos and History: The Myth of the Eternal Return*, translated from the French by Willard R. Trask. New York: Harper and Row, copyright 1954 by

Bollingen Foundation. Published in 1954 by Pantheon Books as *The Myth of the Eternal Return*.

―――. *Myths, Dreams, and Mysteries: The Encounter between Contemporary Faiths and Archaic Realities*, translated by Philip Mairet. New York and Evanston: Harper and Row, 1960.

―――. *Zalmoxis, the Vanishing God: Comparative Studies in the Religions and Folklore of Dacia and Eastern Europe*. Chicago and London: University of Chicago Press, [1972].

Eliot, Sir Charles. *Turkey in Europe*. [London]: Frank Cass, 1900, new impression 1965.

Elworthy, Frederick Thomas. *The Evil Eye: The Origins and Practices of Superstition*, introduction by Louis S. Barron. New York: Julian Press, [1958]; originally published by John Murray, London, 1895.

Emerit, Marcel. *Les Paysans roumains depuis le traité d'Andrinople jusqu'à la libération des terres (1829–1864): Étude d'histoire sociale*. Paris: Librairie du Recueil Sirey, 1937.

Emmanuel, Isaac Samuel. *Histoire des Israélites de Salonique*, Vol. I: *(140 a. J. C. à 1640)*. Paris: Librairie Lipschutz, 1936.

Erdeljanović, Jovan. *Etnološka gradja o Šumadincima*, composed on the basis of the author's travel notes by Petar Ž. Petrović, knj. LXIV, četvrto odeljenje, *Rasprave i gradja*, knj. 2. Belgrade, 1951.

Eton, William. *A Survey of the Turkish Empire*. London: printed for T. Cadell, Jun., and W. Davies, 1798.

Evans, Ifor L. *The Agrarian Revolution in Roumania*. Cambridge: University Press, 1924.

Evelpidi, C. (Euelpides, Chrysos). *Les États balkaniques: Étude comparée politique, sociale, économique et financière*. Paris: Arthur Rousseau et Cie, 1930.

Faensen, Johannes. *Die albanische Nationalbewegung*, Osteuropa-Institut an der Freien Institut Berlin, Balkanologische Veröffentlichungen, herausgegeben von Norbert Reiter, Bd. 4. Berlin, 1980, in Kommission bei Otto Harrassowitz, Wiesbaden.

Febvre, Lucien. "La sensibilité et l'histoire: Comment reconstituer la vie affective d'autrefois," in *Combats pour l'histoire*. Paris: Armand Colin, 1953. Pp. 221–38. First published in *Annales d'histoire sociale*, III (1941), 5–20.

Fei, John C. H., and Ranis, Gustav. "Economic Development in Historical Perspective," *American Economic Review*, LIX, 2 (May 1969), 386–400.

Feldman, Arnold S. *See* Moore, Wilbert E.

Félix-Beaujour. *See* Beaujour, Louis-Auguste Félix, baron de.

Fennel, J. L. I. *Ivan the Great of Moscow*. London: Macmillan; New York: St. Martin's Press, 1961.

Ferguson, R. Brian. "Explaining War," in Haas, *The Anthropology of War*, pp. 26–55.

―――. *See also* Whitehead, Neil L.

Ferguson, Yale H., and Mansbach, Richard W. "Between Celebration and Despair: Constructive Suggestions for Future International Theory," *International Studies Quarterly*, XXXV (1991), 363–86.

Ferrières-Sauveboeuf, Louis-François, comte de. *Mémoires historiques, politiques et géographiques des voyages du comte de Ferrières Sauveboeuf, faits en Turquie, en Perse et en Arabie, depuis 1782, jusqu'en 1789*, 2 vols. Paris: Buisson, 1790.

Fewkes, Vladimir J. "Neolithic Sites in the Moravo-Danubian Area (Eastern Yugoslavia)," *American School of Prehistoric Research Bulletin*, No. 12 (May 1936), pp. 5–81.

Filipović, Milenko. "Odlaženje na prehranu" (Les Migrations alimentaires), *Glasnik Grografskog Društva (Bulletin de la Société de Géographic de Belgrade)*, XXVII (1947), 76–93.

Filipović, Nedim. "Pogled na osmanski feudalizam," *Godišnjak Istoriskog Društva Bosne i Hercegovine*, IV (Sarajevo, 1952), 5–146.

Fine, John V.A., Jr. *The Bosnian Church, a New Interpretation: A Study of the Bosnian Church and Its Place in State and Society from the Thirteenth to the Fifteenth Centuries*. Boulder, Colo.: *East European Quarterly*; New York: distributed by Columbia University Press, 1975.

—————. *The Early Medieval Balkans: A Critical Survey from the Sixth to the Late Twelfth Century*. Ann Arbor: University of Michigan Press, [1983].

—————. *The Late Medieval Balkans: A Critical Survey from the Late Twelfth Century to the Ottoman Conquest*. Ann Arbor: University of Michigan Press, [1987].

[Finlay, George]. "The Euthanasia of the Ottoman Empire," *Blackwood's Edinburgh Magazine*, LXXXIX (May 1861), 571–94.

—————. *A History of Greece from Its Conquest by the Romans to the Present Time, B.C. 146 to A.D. 1864*, revised and enlarged ed. 7 vols. Oxford: Clarendon Press, 1877.

Finley, M. I. "Between Slavery and Freedom," *Comparative Studies in Society and History*, VI (1964), 233–49.

Fischer-Galati, Stephen. "The Peasantry as a Revolutionary Force in the Balkans," *Journal of Central European Affairs*, XXIII (1963), 12–22.

—————. *See also* Djordjević, Dimitrije.

Fisher, Jack C. *Yugoslavia—A Multinational State: Regional Difference and Administrative Response*. San Francisco: Chandler Publishing Company, [1966].

Flachat, Jean Claude. *Observations sur le commerce et sur les arts*, 2 vols. Lyon: Jacquenod et Rusand, 1766.

Flam, Harry, and Flanders, M. June. "Introduction," in *Heckscher-Ohlin Trade Theory*, translated, edited, and introduced by Harry Flam and M. June Flanders. Cambridge, Mass.; London: MIT Press, [1991]. Pp. 1–37.

Flatrès, Pierre. "Historical Geography of Western France," in Hugh D. Clout, ed. *Themes in the Historical Geography of France*. London, New York, San Francisco: Academic Press, 1977. Pp. 301–42.

Fortis, Alberto. *Travels into Dalmatia; Containing General Observations on the Natural History of That Country and the Neighbouring Islands; the National Productions, Arts, Manners and Customs of the Inhabitants*, translated from the Italian under the author's inspection. London: printed for J. Robson, 1778.

Foucher, Michel. "Changements et continuité dans la géopolitique du Sud-Est de l'Europe," paper presented at the conference on "The European Community and the Balkans," Corfu, July 2–5, 1993, organized by the Hellenic Centre for European Studies (EKEM) and the Hellenic Foundation for Defence and Foreign Policy (ELIAMEP) with the support of the Commission of the European Community.

Fox, Edward Whiting. *History in Geographic Perspective: The Other France*. New York: W. W. Norton, [1971].

France, Ministère des Affaires Étrangères, Commission de la publication des documents relatifs aux origines de la Guerre de 1914. *Documents diplomatiques français (1871–1914)*, Vol. IV: *(1er octobre 1912–4 décembre 1912)*. Paris: Imprimerie Nationale, 1932; Vol. V: *(5 décembre 1912–14 mars 1913)*. Paris: Imprimerie Nationale, 1933.

Francès, E. "La Féodalité et les villes byzantines au XIIIe et au XIVe siècles," *Byzantinoslavica*, XVI (1955), 76–96.

Frangeš, Otto von. "Die Donaustaaten Südosteuropas und der deutsche Grosswirtschaftsraum," *Weltwirtschaftliches Archiv*, LIII (March 1941), 284–316.

—————. "L'Industrialisation des pays agricoles du Sud-est de l'Europe," *Revue économique internationale*, XXX, 3 (July–September 1938), 27–77.

————. "Die treibenden Kräfte der wirtschaftlichen Strukturwandlungen in Jugoslawien," *Weltwirtschaftliches Archiv*, XLVIII (September 1938), 309–38.

Frazer, Sir James George. *The Golden Bough: A Study in Magic and Religion*, 1-vol. abridged ed. New York: Macmillan, 1951; copyright 1922 by Macmillan Co., copyright 1950 by Barclays Bank.

Fresne-Canaye, Philippe du. *Le Voyage du Levant de Philippe du Fresne-Canaye (1573)*, edited by Henri Hauser, Vol. XVI: *Recueil de voyages et de documents pour servir à l'histoire de la géographie depuis le XIIIe jusqu'à la fin du XVIe siècle*, edited by Charles Schefer and Henri Cordier. Paris: Ernest Leroux, 1897.

Freud, Sigmund. *Civilization and Its Discontents*, newly translated from the German and edited by James Strachey. New York: W. W. Norton, copyright 1961.

Freyre, Gilberto. "On the Iberian Concept of Time," *American Scholar*, XXXII, 3 (Summer 1963), 415–30.

Friedl, Ernestine. *Vasilika: A Village in Modern Greece*. New York: Holt, Rinehart and Winston, 1962.

Frilley, Gabriel, Dr. (officier de la Légion d'Honneur), and Wlahovitj [Vlahović], Jovan (Montenegrin by birth and captain in the Serbian army), *Le Monténégro contemporain*. Paris: E. Plon, 1876.

Frobenius, Léo. *Le Destin des civilisations*, translated from the German by N. Guterman. Paris: Gallimard, 1940.

Frye, Richard N. "Introduction," in Richard N. Frye, ed., *Islam and the West: Proceedings of the Harvard Summer School Conference on the Middle East, July 25–27, 1955*. 's-Gravenhage: Mouton, 1957. Pp. 1–5.

Furtado, Celso. *Accumulation and Development: The Logic of Industrial Civilization*, translated by Suzette Macedo. Oxford: Martin Robertson, 1983.

Gallois, L. *See* Vidal de la Blache, Paul.

Gandev, Christo (Hristo). "L'Apparition des rapports capitalistes dans l'économie rurale de la Bulgarie du Nord-Ouest au cours du XVIIIe s.," in Académie des Sciences de Bulgarie, *Études historiques à l'occasion du XIe Congrès*, pp. 207–17.

Garašanin, Milutin V., and Olga Garašanin. *Arheoološka nalazišta u Srbiji*. Belgrade: Prosveta, 1951.

Garašanin, Milutin V. "Neolithikum und Bronzezeit in Serbien und Makedonien," in Römisch-Germanische Kommission des Deutschen Archäologischen Instituts, *39. Bericht* (1958). Berlin: Walter de Gruyter, 1959.

Gardet, Louis. "Un Problème de mystique comparée," *Revue Thomiste*, LII (1952), 642–79, and LIII (1953), 197–216.

Gasparini, Evel. "La 'Verv' e i 'Sjabry," *Ricerche Slavistiche*, VIII (1960), 3–28.

Gavazzi, Milovan. "Das Kulturerbe der Südslaven im Lichte der Völkerkunde," *Die Welt der Slaven*, I, 1 (1956), 63–81.

Gavrilović, Slavko. "Obnova Slavonskih županija i njihovo razgraničavanje sa Vojnom Granicom (1745–1749)," *Matica Srpska: Zbornik za društvene nauke*, No. 25 (Novi Sad, 1960), pp. 49–92.

Geanakoplos, Deno J. "The Council of Florence (1438–1439) and the Problem of Union between the Byzantine and Latin Churches," in *Byzantine East and Latin West: Two Worlds of Christendom in Middle Ages and Renaissance*. Oxford: Basil Blackwell; New York: Harper and Row, 1966. Pp. 84–111.

Gellner, Ernest. "Ethnicity, Culture, Class, and Power," in Sugar, ed., *Ethnic Diversity*, pp. 237–77.

————. *Nations and Nationalism*. Ithaca, N.Y.: Cornell University Press, [1983].

————. *Plough, Sword and Book: The Structure of Human History*. London: Collins Harvill, 1988; Chicago: University of Chicago Press, 1989.

————. "Scale and Nation," in Barth, ed., *Scale and Social Organization*, pp. 133–49.

Genç, Mehmet. "A Comparative Study of the Life Term Tax Farming Data and the Volume of Commercial and Industrial Activities in the Ottoman Empire during the Second Half of the Eighteenth Century," in Todorov, Valtchev, and Todorova, eds., *La Révolution industrielle dans le Sud-Est européen*, pp. 243–79.

George, Pierre. *L'Europe Centrale*, Vol. II: *Les États*. Paris: Presses Universitaires de France, 1954.

————. "Le Travail au village dans l'ancienne et dans la nouvelle Russie," *Revue des études slaves*, XXVII (1951), 113–23.

————. *See also* Blanc, André.

Georgescu-Roegen, Nicholas. "Economic Theory and Agrarian Economics," *Oxford Economic Papers*, N.S., XII, 1 (February 1960), 1–40.

————. "The Entropy Law and the Economic Problem," in Daly, ed., *Economics, Ecology, Ethics*, pp. 49–60.

Georgiev, Vladimir I. "The Earliest Ethnological Situation of the Balkan Peninsula as Evidenced by Linguistic and Onomastic Data," in Birnbaum and Vryonis, Jr., eds., *Aspects of the Balkans*, pp. 50–65.

————. "The Genesis of the Balkan Peoples," *Slavonic and East European Review*, XLIV (July 1966), 285–97.

Gerlach, Samuel, ed. *Stephan Gerlachs dess Aeltern Tage-Buch*. Franckfurth am Mayn: in Verlegung J. D. Zunners, 1674.

Gerschel, Lucien. "La Conquête du nombre: Des Modalités du compte aux structures de la pensée," *Annales: Économies, Sociétés, Civilisations*, XVII, 4 (July–August 1962), 691–714.

Gerschenkron, Alexander. "Some Aspects of Industrialization in Bulgaria, 1878–1939," in *Economic Backwardness in Historical Perspective*. Cambridge, Mass.: Belknap Press of Harvard University Press, 1962. Pp. 198–234.

Gesemann, Gerhard. *Heroische Lebensform: Zur Literatur und Wesenskunde der Balkanischen Patriarchalität*. Berlin: Wiking Verlag, 1943. With slight modifications, the first sixteen chapters are the author's inaugural address as rector of the German Karls-Universität in Prague, in 1933–34, published under the title *Der montenegrinische Mensch*.

Geštrin, Ferdo. "Économie et société en Slovénie au XVIe siècle," *Annales: Économies, Sociétés, Civilisations*, XVII, 4 (July–August 1962), 663–90.

G. G. "Le développement de la population de Bulgarie," review of D. Balevski and N. Minkov on Bulgarian demography, 1887–1910, in *Population: Revue de l'Institut National d'Études Démographiques*, XIV (1959), 339–44.

Gianaris, Nicholas V. *The Economies of the Balkan Countries: Albania, Bulgaria, Greece, Romania, Turkey, and Yugoslavia*. [New York]: Praeger, 1982.

————. *Greece and Turkey: Economic and Geopolitical Perspectives*. New York, Westport [Conn.], London: Praeger, [1988].

————. *Greece and Yugoslavia: An Economic Comparison*. New York: Praeger, [1984].

Gibb, H. A. R., and Bowen, H. *Islamic Society and the West: A Study of the Impact of Western Civilization on Moslem Culture in the Near East*, Vol. I: *Islamic Society in the Eighteenth Century*, 2 parts. London, New York, Toronto: Oxford University Press, 1950–57.

Gimbutas, Marija. *The Gods and Goddesses of Old Europe, 7000 to 3500 B.C.: Myths, Legends, and Cult Images*. Berkeley and Los Angeles: University of California Press, 1974; new ed. retitled: *The Goddesses and Gods of Old Europe, 6500–3500 BC: Myths and Cult Images*. Berkeley and Los Angeles: University of California Press, 1982.

————. "The Neolithic Cultures of the Balkan Peninsula," in Birnbaum and Vryonis, Jr., eds., *Aspects of the Balkans*, pp. 9–49.

————. *The Slavs*. New York: Praeger, 1971.

Giustiniano, Giovanni Battista. "Itinerario" (1553), in Academia Scientiarum et Artium Slavorum, *Monumenta Spectantia Historiam Slavorum Meridionalium*, VIII, 2: *Annorum 1525–1553*.

Glacken, Clarence J. *Traces on the Rhodian Shore: Nature and Culture in Western Thought from Ancient Times to the End of the Eighteenth Century*. Berkeley, Los Angeles: University of California Press, 1967.

Glenny, Misha. "Bosnia: The Last Chance," *New York Review of Books*, January 28, 1993, pp. 5–6, 8, under the dateline December 30, 1992.

————. "Bosnian Quicksand," *New York Times*, February 18, 1994.

————. *The Fall of Yugoslavia: The Third Balkan War*. New York: Penguin Books, 1993; first published in Great Britain in 1992.

————. "The Massacre of Yugoslavia," *New York Review of Books*, January 30, 1992.

————. "Yugoslavia: The Revenger's Tragedy," *New York Review of Books*, August 13, 1992, pp. 37–43, under the dateline July 16, 1992.

Godechot, Jacques. *La Grande Nation: L'Expansion révolutionnaire de la France dans le monde de 1789 à 1799*, 2 vols. Paris: Aubier, Éditions Montaigne, 1956.

Gogol, N. V. *Sobranie sochinenii*, Vol. V: *Mertvye dushi: Poema*. Moscow: Gosudarstvennoe izdatelstvo khudozhestvennoi literatury, 1953.

Golczewski, Mechthild. *Der Balkan in deutschen und österreichischen Reise- und Erlebnisberichten 1912–1918*. Wiesbaden: Franz Steiner, 1981.

Goldenberg, S. "Peter Hallers Darlehen an Nürnberg," in Schneider et al., eds., *Wirtschaftskräfte und Wirtschaftswege*, I, 549–56.

Gooch, George Peabody, and Temperley, Harold, eds., with the assistance of Lillian M. Penson (Great Britain, Foreign Office). *British Documents on the Origins of the War, 1898–1914*, Vol. IX, Pt. 2. London: printed and published by His Majesty's Stationery Office, 1934.

Good, David. "Modern Economic Growth in the Habsburg Monarchy," in Komlos, ed., *Economic Development in the Habsburg Monarchy*, pp. 201–20.

Gordon, Thomas. *History of the Greek Revolution*, 2 vols., 2nd ed. Edinburgh: William Blackwood; London: T. Cadell, 1844.

Gottwald, Joseph. "Phanariotische Studien," *Leipziger Vierteljahrsschrift für Südosteuropa*, V (1941), 1–58.

Gouldner, Alvin W. "The Norm of Reciprocity: A Preliminary Statement," *American Sociological Review*, XXV, 2 (April 1960), 161–78.

Graham, Stephen. *Alexander of Yugoslavia: The Story of a King Who Was Murdered at Marseille*. New Haven, [Conn.]: Yale University Press, 1939.

Grbić, Savatije M. *Srpski narodni običaji iz sreza Boljevačkog*, Srpska Kraljevska Akademija, "Srpski Etnografski Zbornik," knj. xiv. Belgrade, 1909.

Great Britain (Foreign Office). *See* Gooch, G.P., and Temperley, H.

Great Britain (Parliament). *Sessional Papers*, LXXXII (1883), Sidney Lockock's Report.

————. *Sessional Papers*, LXXXVII (1884), Report by Consul-General J. E. Blunt on the Salonica-Mitrovitza Railway, October 31, 1883, enclosed with his letter to Earl Granville, November 2, 1883, in Commercial No. 16 (1884): "Further Correspondence Relating to Article XXXVIII of the Treaty of Berlin (Balkan Railways)."

Greenwood, Davydd J. "Culture by the Pound: An Anthropological Perspective on Tourism as Cultural Commoditization," in Smith, ed., *Hosts and Guests*, pp. 171–85.

Grégoire, Henri. "Deux étymologies: Vardar, *verēdarius*," *Byzantion*, XXII (1952), 268–69.

————. "L'Origine et le nom des Croates et des Serbes," *Byzantion*, XVII (1944–45), 88–118.

Gregoras, Nicephorus. *Correspondance de Nicéphore Grégoras*, edited by R. Guilland. Paris: Société d'Edition "Les Belles Lettres," 1927.

Greider, William. *Who Will Tell the People? The Betrayal of American Democracy*. New York: Simon and Schuster, [1992].

Grekov, B. D. *Krestiane na Rusi s drevneishikh vremen do XVII veka*. Moscow, Leningrad: Akademiia Nauk SSSR, 1946.

Grenville, Henry. *Observations sur l'état actuel de l'Empire ottoman*, edited by Andrew S. Ehrenkreutz. Ann Arbor, Mich: University of Michigan Press, [1965].

Grmek, Mirko; Gjidara, Marc; and Šimac, Neven. *Le Nettoyage ethnique: Documents historiques sur une idéologie serbe*. [Paris]: Librairie Arthème Fayard, 1993.

Grousset, René. "La Civilisation à travers l'histoire," in *L'Homme et son histoire*. Paris: Plon, 1954.

Grujić, Jevrem. *Zapisi*, 3 vols. Belgrade: Štamparija Budućnost, 1922–23.

Gücer, Lûtfi. "Le Commerce intérieur des céréales dans l'Empire ottoman pendant la seconde moitié du XVIe siècle," *Revue de la Faculté des sciences économiques de l'Université d'Istanbul*, XI (1950), 163–88.

———. "Le Problème d'approvisionnement d'Istanbul en céréales vers le milieu du XVIIIe siècle," *Revue de la Faculté des sciences économiques de l'Universite d'Istanbul*, XI (1950), 153–62.

Guilaine, Jean. *Premiers bergers et paysans de l'Occident méditerranéen*. Paris: Mouton, [1976].

Guilmartin, John Francis, Jr., *Gunpowder and Galleys: Changing Technology and Mediterranean Warfare at Sea in the Sixteenth Century*. London: Cambridge University Press, 1974.

Guldescu, Stanko. *History of Medieval Croatia*. The Hague: Mouton, 1964.

Gumilev, L. N. "Les Fluctuations du niveau de la mer Caspienne," translated by N. Godneff, *Cahiers du monde russe er soviétique*, VI (1965), 331–66.

———. "Heterochronism in the Moisture Supply of Eurasia in the Middle Ages," *Soviet Geography: Review and Translation*, IX, 1 (January 1968), 23–35. Translated from *Vestnik Leningradskogo Universiteta*, No. 18 (1966), pp. 81–90.

Gurvitch, Georges, ed. *Marcel Mauss: Sociologie et anthropologie*, with an "Introduction à l'oeuvre de Marcel Mauss" by Claude Lévi-Strauss. Paris: Presses Universitaires de France, 1960.

Guzina, Ružica. *Knežina i postanak buržoaske države*. Belgrade: Kultura, 1955.

Haas, Jonathan, ed. *The Anthropology of War*. Cambridge: Cambridge University Press, 1990.

Haberlandt, A. "Zur Systematik der Pflugforschung und Entwicklungsgeschichte des Pfluges," *Wiener Zeitschrift für Volkskunde* (vormals *Zeitschrift für österreichische Volkskunde*), XXXVIII (1933), 28–34, 76–79.

Hadjimihali, Angheliki. "Aspects de l'organisation économique des Grecs dans l'Empire ottoman," in *Le Cinq-centième anniversaire de la prise de Constantinople, 1453–1953*, "L'Hellénisme contemporain," 2ème série, VII, fasc. hors série. Athens, May 29, 1953. Pp. 262–78.

Hadrovics, Ladislas. *Le Peuple serbe et son Église sous la domination turque*. Paris: Presses Universitaires de France, 1947.

Hadži Vasiljević, Jovan. *Prosvetne i političke prilike u južnim srpskim oblastima u XIX v. (do srpsko-turskih ratova 1876–78)*. Belgrade: Društvo Sv. Save, Zadužbina Lenke Beljinice, 1928.

Hakluyt, Richard, ed. *Principal Navigations, Voyages, Traffiques and Discoveries of the English Nation*, Vol. II, Pt. 2. London: George Bishop, Alfred Newberie, and Robert Barker, 1599). Published under the same title, by James MacLehose and Son (successor, Jackson Son & Co., Ltd.) of Glasgow, and Everyman's Library edition, published by J. M. Dent & Sons, Ltd., of London and Toronto, and E. P. Dutton and Co. of New York.

Hall, Edith. *Inventing the Barbarian: Greek Self-Definition through Tragedy.* Oxford: Clarendon Press, [1989].

Hall, Edward T. *The Silent Language.* Greenwich, Conn.: Premier Book, Fawcett Publications, 1963. Published originally in 1959 by Doubleday.

Hall, John A. *Powers and Liberties: The Causes and Consequences of the Rise of the West.* Harmondsworth, Middlesex: Penguin Books. First published by Basil Blackwell, 1985.

Hall, Peter. *See* Thünen.

Halpern, Joel M. "The Economies of Lao and Serb Peasants: A Contrast in Cultural Values," *Southwestern Journal of Anthropology,* XVII (1961), 165–77.

———. *A Serbian Village.* New York: Columbia University Press, 1958.

———. "The Zadruga: A Century of Change," *Anthropologica,* N.S., XII, 1 (1970), 83–97.

Hammel, Eugene A. *Alternative Social Structures and Ritual Relations in the Balkans.* Englewood Cliffs, N.J.: Prentice-Hall, [1968].

Hammer-Purgstall, Josef Freiherr von. *Histoire de l'Empire ottoman depuis son origine jusqu'à nos jours,* translated from the German by J.-J. Hellert, 18 vols. and atlas. Paris: Bellizard, Barthes, Dufour et Lowell, 1835–43.

Hammond, N. G. L. *A History of Macedonia,* Vol. I: *Historical Geography and Prehistory.* Oxford: Clarendon Press, 1972.

Haraszti, Endre. *Origin of the Rumanians (Vlach Origin, Migration, and Infiltration to Transylvania).* Astor, Fla.: Danubian Press, [1977].

Harrison, Jane Ellen. *Themis: A Study of the Social Origins of Greek Religion.* Cambridge: University Press, 1912; Cleveland and New York: World Publishing Company, Meridian Books, 1962, by arrangement with Cambridge University Press.

Hartog, François. *The Mirror of Herodotus: The Representation of the Other in the Writing of History,* translated from the French by Janet Lloyd. Berkeley, Los Angeles, London: University of California Press, [1988].

Harva, Uno. *Les Représentations religieuses des peuples altaïques,* translated from the German by Jean-Louis Perret. Paris: Gallimard, [1959].

Hasluck, Frederick William. *Christianity and Islam under the Turks,* 2 vols. Oxford: Clarendon Press, 1929.

Hasluck (née Hardie), Margaret (Mrs. F. W. Hasluck). "The Evil Eye in Some Greek Villages of the Upper Haliakmon Valley in West Macedonia," *Man,* LIII (1923), 160–72.

———. "Historical Sketch of the Fluctuations of Lake Ostrovo in West Macedonia," *Geographical Journal,* LXXXVII (1936), 338–47.

———. *The Unwritten Law in Albania,* edited by J. H. Hutton. Cambridge: University Press, 1954.

Hassan, Fekri A. *Demographic Archaeology.* New York, London, Toronto, etc.: Academic Press, [1981].

Hatt, Gudmund. *See* Curwen, E. Cecil.

Haudricourt, André-G. "Ce que peuvent nous apprendre les mots voyageurs," *Mélanges d'histoire sociale,* I (1942), 25–30.

Haudricourt, André-G., and Jean-Brunhes Delamarre, Mariel. *L'Homme et la charrue à travers le monde.* Paris: Gallimard, [1955].

Haumant, Émile. *La Formation de la Yougoslavie (XVe–XXe siècles).* Paris: Bossard, 1930.

Hauptmann, Ljudmil. "Seobe Hrvata i Srba," *Jugoslovenski Istoriski Časopis,* godina III, sveska 1–4 (1937), pp. 30–61.

Havrylyshyn, Oli. "Yugoslavia," in Demetris Papageorgiou, Michael Michaely, and

Armeane M. Choksi, eds., *Liberalizing Foreign Trade*, Vol. III: *The Experience of Israel and Yugoslavia*. Oxford; Cambridge, Mass.: Basil Blackwell, [1991]. Pp. 157–363.

Hawkes, Jacquetta. *Prehistory*, edited by the International Commission for a History of the Scientific and Cultural History of Mankind as Vol. I, Pt. 1, of its six-volume *History of Mankind*. New York and Toronto: Mentor Book, published by New American Library, copyright 1963 by UNESCO, first Mentor Book printing 1965 by arrangement with George Allen and Unwin.

Heckscher, Eli F. "The Effect of Foreign Trade on the Distribution of Income," in Flam and Flanders, eds. *Heckscher-Ohlin Trade Theory*, pp. 39–69.

Heichelheim, F.M. "Man's Role in Changing the Face of the Earth in Classical Antiquity," *Kyklos*, IX (1956), 318–59.

Heilbroner, Robert. "After Communism," *New Yorker*, September 10, 1990, pp. 91–100.

Helbaek, Hans. "Domestication of Food Plants in the Old World," *Science*, CXXX (August 14, 1959), 365–72.

Helleiner, Gerald K. *International Economic Disorder: Essays in North-South Relations*. Toronto and Buffalo: University of Toronto Press, 1981.

Hencken, Hugh. "Indo-European Languages and Archeology," American Anthropological Association, *American Anthropologist*, LVII, No. 6, Pt. 3, Memoir No. 84 (December 1955).

Hendy, Michael F. *Studies in the Byzantine Monetary Economy c. 300–1450*. Cambridge: Cambridge University Press, 1985.

Herlihy, Patricia. "Russian Grain and Mediterranean Markets, 1744–1861," Ph.D. dissertation, University of Pennsylvania, 1963.

Herodotus, *The Histories*, newly translated and with an introduction by Aubrey de Sélincourt. Baltimore, Md.: Penguin Books, 1954.

Herrenschwand, [Jean (Johann Daniel Caspar)]. *De l'Économie politique moderne: Discours fondamental sur la population*. London: T. Hookham, 1786.

Herskovits, Melville J. "Economic Change and Cultural Dynamics," in Ralph Braibanti and Joseph J. Spengler, eds., *Tradition, Values, and Socio-Economic Development*. Durham, N.C.: Published for the Duke University Commonwealth Studies Center by Duke University Press, 1961. Pp. 127–31.

Hertz, Frederick. *Nationality in History and Politics: A Study of the Psychology and Sociology of National Sentiment and Character*. New York: Oxford University Press, 1944.

Herzfeld, Michael. *Anthropology through the Looking-Glass: Critical Ethnography in the Margins of Europe*. Cambridge: Cambridge University Press, 1987.

———. "Honour and Shame: Problems in the Comparative Analysis of Moral Systems," *Man*, N.S., XV, 2 (June 1980), 339–51.

———. *Ours Once More: Folklore, Ideology, and the Making of Modern Greece*. Austin: University of Texas Press, [1982].

Hess, Andrew C. "The Evolution of the Ottoman Seaborne Empire in the Age of the Discoveries, 1453–1525," *American Historical Review*, LXXV (December 1970), 1892–1919.

———. *The Forgotten Frontier: A History of the Sixteenth Century Ibero-African Frontier*. Chicago: University of Chicago Press, 1978.

Hettich, Ernest L. *A Study in Ancient Nationalism: The Testimony of Euripides*. Williamsport, Pa.: Bayard Press, [1933].

Hettne, Björn. "Europe and the Crisis: The Regional Scenario Revisited," in Marguerite Mendell and Daniel Salée, eds., *The Legacy of Karl Polanyi: Market, State, and Society at the End of the Twentieth Century*. New York: St. Martin's Press, [1991]. Pp. 133–54.

Heusch, Luc de. "Introduction à une ritologie générale," in Centre Royaumont pour une Science de l'Homme, *L'Unité de l'homme*, Vol. III: *Pour une anthropologie fondamentale: Essais et discussions présentées et commentées*. Paris: Éditions du Seuil, 1974. Pp. 213–47.

Heyd, W. *Histoire du commerce du Levant au Moyen-âge*, édition française refondue et considérablement augmentée, Vol. II. Leipzig: Otto Harrassowitz, 1923.

Hicks, Sir John. *A Theory of Economic History*. London: Oxford University Press, 1969.

Hildebrandt, Walter. "Die Stadt in Südosteuropa," *Vierteljahrsschrift für Südosteuropa*, III (1939), 153–77.

Hirschman, Albert O. *The Passions and the Interests: Political Arguments for Capitalism before Its Triumph*. Princeton, N.J.: Princeton University Press, 1977.

Hirschmann, Gerhard. "Kunz Horn (+1517), ein Nürnberger Grosshändler und Frühkapitalist," in Schneider et al., eds. *Wirtschaftskräfte und Wirtschaftswege*, I, 557–80.

Hitchins, Keith. "*Gîndirea* [Thought]: Nationalism in a Spiritual Guise," in Jowitt, ed., *Social Change in Romania*, pp. 140–73.

————. "Historiography of the Countries of Eastern Europe: Romania," *American Historical Review*, IIIC, 4 (October 1992), 1064–83.

————. *Orthodoxy and Nationality: Andreiu Şaguna and the Rumanians of Transylvania, 1846–1873*. Cambridge, Mass.: Harvard University Press, 1977.

————. "Samuel Clain and the Rumanian Enlightenment in Transylvania," *Slavic Review*, XXIII (December 1964), 660–75.

Hobhouse, John Cam [1st Baron Broughton]. *A Journey through Albania, and Other Provinces of Turkey in Europe and Asia, to Constantinople, during the Years 1809 and 1810*, 2nd ed. London: J. Cawthorne, 1813.

Hobsbawm, E. J. *Nations and Nationalism since 1780*. Cambridge, New York, etc.: Cambridge University Press, [1990].

Hočevar, Toussaint. *Slovenski družbeni razvoj: Izbrane rasprave*. New Orleans: Založba Prometej, 1979.

Hofer, Tamas. "Construction of the 'Folk Cultural Heritage' in Hungary and Rival Versions of National Identity," paper presented at the Rutgers Center for Historical Analysis, Department of History, Rutgers University, New Brunswick, N.J., March 6, 1990.

Hoffman, George W. "The Evolution of the Ethnographic Map of Yugoslavia: A Historical Geographic Interpretation," in Carter, ed., *An Historical Geography of the Balkans*, pp. 436–99.

————. *Regional Development Strategy in Southeast Europe. A Comparative Analysis of Albania, Bulgaria, Greece, Romania and Yugoslavia*. New York, Washington, London: Praeger Publishers, [1972].

Hoffmann, Stanley. "Delusions of World Order," *New York Review of Books*, April 9, 1992, pp. 37–43.

Hogarth, William D. "Introduction," in Alexander William Kinglake, *Kinglake's Eothen*, pp. iii–xxi.

Holbach, Maude M. *Bosnia and Herzegovina: Some Wayside Wanderings*, with 48 illustrations from photographs by O. Holbach and a map. London: John Lane, Bodley Head; New York: John Lane Company, 1910.

Holland, Henry. *Travels in the Ionian Isles, Albania, Thessaly, Macedonia, etc., during the Years 1812 and 1813*. London: printed for Longman, Hurst, Orme, and Brown, 1815.

Hollander, A. N. J. Den. *See* Den Hollander, A. N. J.

Hommaire de Hell, Ignace-Xavier-Morand. *Voyage en Turquie et en Perse exécuté par ordre du gouvernement français, pendant les années 1846, 1847 et 1848*, ouvrage accompagné de cartes, d'inscriptions, etc., et d'un album de 100 planches par Jules

Laurens, 4 vols., plus a fifth large in-fol. *Atlas historique et scientifique.* Paris: P. Bertrand, 1854–60.

Hony, H.C. *A Turkish-English Dictionary*, 2nd ed. Oxford: Clarendon Press, 1957.

Horia, Vintilia. "Roumanie," in *Les Grands courants de la pensée mondiale contemporaine*, ouvrage publié sous la direction de Michele Federico Sciacca, Vol. II: *Panoramas nationaux*. Paris: Fischbacher & Marzorati, copyright by "Marzorati" of Milan 1964. Pp. 1067–94.

Hopper, R. J. *Trade and Industry in Classical Greece.* [London]: Thames and Hudson, [1979].

Horecky, Paul L. *Southeastern Europe: A Guide to Publications.* Chicago: University of Chicago Press, 1969.

Hoselitz, Bert F. "Generative and Parasitic Cities," *Economic Development and Cultural Change*, III (April 1955), 278–94.

———. "The Market Matrix," in Moore and Feldman, eds., *Labor Commitment*, pp. 217–37.

House, John. *See* Taylor, Peter.

Houston, J. M. *A Social Geography of Europe.* London: Gerald Duckworth, 1953.

Hubert, Henri. *The Greatness and Decline of the Celts*, translated from the French. London: Routledge and Kegan Paul, 1934.

Hughes, Charles. "Introduction" to Moryson, *Shakespeare's Europe*, pp. i–xlvi.

Hughes, J. Donald. "Ecology in Ancient Greece," *Inquiry*, XVIII, 2 (Summer 1975), 115–25.

Hull, Denison B., trans., with introduction and notes. *Digenis Akritas, the Two-Blood Border Lord*, the Grottaferrata version. Athens, Ohio: Ohio University Press, [1972].

Huntington, Ellsworth. *The Pulse of Asia: A Journey in Central Asia Illustrating the Geographic Basis of History.* Boston and New York: Houghton, Mifflin, and Company, [1907].

Ibrahim-Manzour-Efendi. *See* Cerfberr de Medelsheim, Samson.

Innis, Harold A. *The Bias of Communication*, with an introduction by Marshall McLuhan. Toronto: University of Toronto Press, [1951], reprinted 1964, 1968, in the U.S.A.

Institut National d'Études Démographiques. *See* J. C. C.

Iordanis (Jordanes). "De Origine Actibusque Getarum," in Theodor Mommsen, ed., *Monumenta Germaniae Historica: Auctorum Antiquissimorum*, Vol. V. Berlin: Weidmann, 1882.

———. *De Origine Actibusque Getarum*, edited by Alfred Holder. Freiburg i. Breisgau and Tübingen: J. C. B. Mohr, 1882.

Iorga, Nicolae. *Le Caractère commun des institutions du Sud-est de l'Europe.* Paris: Librairie Universitaire J. Gamber, 1929.

Isnard, Achille-Nicolas. *Catéchisme social, ou Instructions élémentaires sur la morale sociale à l'usage de la jeunesse.* Paris: chez Guillot, 1784.

———. *Observations sur le principe qui a produit les révolutions de France, de Genève & d'Amérique dans le dix-huitième siècle.* Évreux: Imprimerie de la Veuve Malassis, October 1789.

Issawi, Charles, ed. *History of the Middle East, 1800–1914: A Book of Readings.* London: University of Chicago Press, [1966].

Ivić, Pavle. *Die serbokroatischen Dialekte: Ihre Struktur und Entwicklung*, Vol. I: *Allgemeines und die štokavische Dialekt-gruppe*, Slavistic Printings and Reprintings, edited by C. H. van Schooneveld. 's-Gravenhage: Mouton, 1958.

Jackson, Marvin R. *See* Lampe, John R.

Jacob, William. *An Historical Inquiry into the Production and Consumption of the Precious Metals*, 2 vols. London: John Murray, 1831.

Jaeger, Werner. *Paideia: The Ideals of Greek Culture*, translated from second German edition by Gilbert Highet, 3 vols. New York: Oxford University Press, 1943–45.

Jagić, Vatroslav. *Entstehungsgeschichte der kirchenslavischen Sprache*, new rev. and enlarged ed. Berlin: Weidmannsche Buchhandlung, 1913.

Jakobson, Roman. "Medieval Mock Mystery," in A. G. Hatcher and K. L. Selig, eds., *Studia Philologica et Litteraria in Honorem L. Spitzer*. Bern: Francke Verlag, [1958]. Pp. 245–63.

Jakšić, Vladimir. Address to the Srpsko Učeno Društvo in celebration of the fiftieth anniversary of his first publication (1839), in *Glasnik Srpskoga Učenog Društva*, knj. 71 (Belgrade, 1890), pp. 313–25.

Janković, Dragoslav. *O političkim strankama u Srbiji XIX veka*. Belgrade: Prosveta, 1951.

————. "O programima i borbama za lokalne samouprave u Srbiji XIX veka," *Nova Misao*, I, 3 (March 1953), 403–19.

Janković, Nenad Dj. *Astronomija u predanjima, običajima i umotvorinama Srba*, Srpska Akademija Nauka, odeljenje društvenih nauka, "Srpski Etnografski Zbornik," knj. lxiii, drugo odeljenje, "Život i običaji narodni," knj. 28. Belgrade, 1951.

Janković, Velizar. *See* Yankovitch, Velizar.

Janos, Andrew C. "Modernization and Decay in Historical Perspective: The Case of Romania," in Jowitt, ed., *Social Change in Romania*, pp. 72–116.

Jardé, Auguste François Victor. *Les Céréales dans l'Antiquité grecque*, Vol. I: *La Production*. Paris: E. de Boccard, 1925.

————. *The Formation of the Greek People*, translated from the French by M. R. Dobie. New York: Alfred A. Knopf, 1926.

Jarrett, H. R. *See* Branigan, J. J.

J. C. C., "La Population de la Grèce depuis 1860," *Population: Revue de l'Institut National d'Études Démographiques*, XV (1960), 889–93.

Jászi, Oscar. *The Dissolution of the Habsburg Monarchy*. Chicago: University of Chicago Press, 1929; Phoenix Books, 1961.

JAZU. *See* Jugoslavenska Akademija znanosti i umjetnosti.

Jelavich, Barbara. *History of the Balkans*, 2 vols. Cambridge: Cambridge University Press, [1983].

————. "Tsarist Russia and the Balkan Slavic Connection," *Canadian Review of Studies in Nationalism*, XVI, 1–2 (1989), 209–26.

Jelavich, Charles. "Nationalism as Reflected in the Textbooks of the South Slavs in the Nineteenth Century," *Canadian Review of Studies in Nationalism, Revue canadienne des études sur le nationalisme*, XVI, 1–2 (1989), 15–34.

————. "Serbian Nationalism and the Croats: Vuk Karadžić's Influence on Serbian Textbooks," *Canadian Review of Studies in Nationalism, Revue canadienne des études sur le nationalisme*, XVII, 1–2 (1990), 31–42.

————. *Tsarist Russia and Balkan Nationalism: Russian Influence in the Internal Affairs of Bulgaria and Serbia, 1879–86*. Berkeley and Los Angeles: University of California Press, 1958.

Jelavich, Charles, and Jelavich, Barbara, eds. *The Balkans in Transition: Essays on the Development of Balkan Life and Politics since the Eighteenth Century*. Berkeley and Los Angeles: University of California Press, 1963.

Jensen, John H., and Rosegger, Gerhard. "British Railway Building along the Lower Danube, 1856–1869," *Slavonic and East European Review*, XLVI (January 1968), 105–28.

————. "The Danube and Black Sea Railway: An Episode in Balkan Economic Development," typescript, 1961.

————. "Transferring Technology to a Peripheral Economy: The Case of Lower Danube Transport Development, 1856–1928," *Technology and Culture*, XIX, 4 (October 1978).

Jeremić, Risto, Dr. *Zdravstvene prilike u jugoslovenskim zemljama do kraja devetnaestog veka*. Zagreb: Škola Narodnog Zdravlja, 1935.

Jireček, Constantin [Konstantin] Josef. "Albanien in der Vergangenheit," in Ludwig von Thallóczy, ed., *Illyrisch-albansche Forschungen*, 2 vols. München and Leipzig: Verlag von Duncker & Humblot, 1916. I, 63–93.

―――. *La Civilisation serbe au Moyen âge*, translated from the German under the direction of Louis Eisenmann. Paris: Éditions Bossard, 1920.

―――. *Geschichte der Bulgaren*. Prague: F. Tempsky, 1876.

―――. *Die Handelsstrassen und Bergwerke von Serbien und Bosnien während des Mittelalters*. Prag: Verlag der kön. böhmischen Gesellschaft der Wissenschaften, 1879.

―――. *Istorija Srba*, translated and completed by Jovan Radonić, Vol. IV. Belgrade, 1923.

―――. *Istorija Srba*, 2nd rev. and enlarged ed., 2 vols. Belgrade: Izdavačko preduzeće NR Srbije, 1952.

Johnston, R. J. "The Political Geography of Electoral Geography," in Taylor and House, eds., *Political Geography*, pp. 133–48.

Jordan, Sonja. *Die kaiserliche Wirtschaftspolitik im Banat im 18. Jahrhundert*. München: Verlag R. Oldenbourg, 1967.

―――. *Staat und Gesellschaft im mittelalterlichen Serbien*. Vienna: Kais. Akademie der Wissenschaften, 1912–14.

Jovanović, Bogoljub. "Stanje javne nastave u Kraljevini Srbiji za 1877–78 i 1878–79 školsku godinu," *Glasnik Srpskoga Učenog Društva*, LXXI (1890), 72–157.

Jovanović, Branislav. "O šumama Srbije početkom XIX veka," in Srpsko Geografsko Društvo, *Geografski lik Srbije u doba Prvog ustanka*, fasc. 32. Belgrade, 1954. Pp. 17–35.

Jovanović, Dragoljub. "Les Classes moyennes chez les Slaves du Sud," in *Inventaire III: Classes moyennes*, Centre de Documentation sociale de l'École Normale Supérieure. Paris: Félix Alcan, 1939.

―――. *Les Effets économiques et sociaux de la Guerre en Serbie*, Histoire Économique et Sociale de la Guerre Mondiale, Série Serbe. Paris: Presses Universitaires de France; New Haven: Yale University Press, 1930.

―――. *Kult rada*. Belgrade: Rad, 1927.

Jovanović, Slobodan. *O državi: Osnovi jedne pravne teorije*, 3rd rev. and enlarged ed. Belgrade: Geca Kon, 1922.

―――. *Iz naše istorije i književnosti*. Belgrade: Srpska Književna Zadruga, 1931.

―――. *Svetozar Marković*, 2nd rev. ed. Belgrade: Geca Kon, 1920.

―――. *Ustavobranitelji i njihova vlada (1838–1858)*. Belgrade: Državna Štamparija, 1912.

Jowitt, Kenneth, ed. *Social Change in Romania, 1860–1940: A Debate on Development in a European Nation*. Berkeley: University of California, Institute of International Studies, [1978].

Judt, Tony. "The Rediscovery of Central Europe," *Daedalus*, CXIX (Winter 1990), 23–54.

Jugoslavenska Akademija znanosti i umjetnosti. *Rječnik hrvatskoga ili srpskoga jezika*. Zagreb, 1880–.

Jutikkala, Eino. "The Great Finnish Famine in 1696–97," *Scandinavian Economic History Review*, III (1955), 48–63.

Kadić, Ante. *The Tradition of Freedom in Croatian Literature: Essays*. Bloomington, Ind.: The Croatian Alliance, 1983.

Kaldor, Mary. "Yugoslavia and the New Nationalism," *New Left Review*, No. 197 (January–February 1993), pp. 96–112.

Kamenka, Eugene, ed. *Nationalism: The Nature and Evolution of an Idea*. Canberra: Australian National University Press, 1973.

Kant, Immanuel. "Idea for a Universal History from a Cosmopolitan Point of View," translated by Lewis White Beck, in *On History*, edited, with an introduction by Beck, translated by L. W. Beck, Robert E. Anchor, and Emil L. Fackenheim. Indianapolis, New York: The Library of Liberal Arts, published by Bobbs-Merrill, copyright 1963. Pp. 11–26.

Karadžić, Vuk Stefanović. *Danica: Zabavnik za godinu 1827*, Vol. II. Vienna: Printing Press of the Armenian Monastery, 1827.

————. *Pisma*. Belgrade: Prosveta, 1947.

————. *Srpske narodne poslovice i druge različne kao one u običaj uzete riječi i zagonetke*, 2nd state ed. Belgrade: Državna Štamparija Kraljevine Jugoslavije, 1933.

Karal, E. Ziya. "La Transformation de la Turquie d'un Empire oriental en un État moderne et national," *Cahiers d'histoire mondiale, Journal of World History, Cuadernos de Historia Mundial*, IV (1958), 426–45.

Karavelov, Liuben. *Bolgary starogo vremeni*. Moscow: Gos. izd. khudozhestvennoi literatury, 1950.

Kardelj, Edvard. *Razvoi slovenskega narodnega vprašanja*, 2nd rev. and enlarged ed. Ljubljana: Državna založba Slovenije, 1957. Translated into Serbo-Croatian by Zvonko Tkalec as *Razvoj slovenačkog nacionalnog pitanja* (Belgrade: Kultura, 1958). A revision of the author's work (under the pseudonym Sperans) bearing the same Slovenian title, Ljubljana: Naša založba, 1939.

Karger, Adolf. *Die Entwicklung der Siedlungen im westlichen Slawonien: Ein Beitrag zur Kulturgeographie des Save-Drau-Zwischenstromlandes*, Kölner Geographische Arbeiten, Heft 15. Wiesbaden: Franz Steiner Verlag, 1963.

Karić, V. *Srbija: opis zemlje, naroda i države*. Belgrade: Kraljevskosrpska Državna Štamparija, 1887.

Kaser, Karl. "Karl Kaser on Austria and the Crisis in Yugoslavia," interview by the Center for Austrian Studies at the University of Minnesota, *Austrian Studies Newsletter*, IV, 1 (Winter 1992), 7.

Katić, Relja. *Medicina kod Srba u srednjem veku*. Belgrade: Srpska Akademija Nauka, 1958.

Kautsky, John H. "The Politics of Traditional Aristocratic Empires and Their Legacy," *International Journal of Comparative Sociology*, XXIV, 1–2 (1983), 47–60.

Kavadias, Georges B. *Pasteursnomades méditerranéens: Les Saracatsans de Grèce*. Paris: Gauthier-Villars, 1965.

Kayser, Bernard. "La Carte de la distribution géographique de la population grecque en 1961," *Annales: Économies, Sociétés, Civilisations*, XX, 2 (March–April 1965), 301–8.

Kedourie, Elie. *Nationalism*, 3rd ed. London: Hutchinson University Library, 1966.

Keller, A. G. "A Byzantine Admirer of 'Western' Progress: Cardinal Bessarion," *Cambridge Historical Journal*, XI (1955), 343–48.

Kemp, Phyllis. *Healing Ritual: Studies in the Technique and Tradition of the Southern Slavs*. London: Faber and Faber, published in conjunction with the School of Slavonic and East European Studies, University of London, 1935.

Kennan, George F. "The Balkan Crisis: 1913 and 1993," *New York Review of Books*, July 15, 1993, pp. 3–7, the introduction to the Carnegie Endowment for International Peace, *The Other Balkan War: A Carnegie Endowment Inquiry in Retrospect, with a New Introduction and Reflections on the Present Conflict by George F. Kennan*, distributed by the Brookings Institution, 1993.

Keppel, George Thomas, Earl of Albemarle. *Narrative of a Journey across the Balcan, by the Two Passes of Selimno and Pravadi; Also of a Visit to Azani, and Other Newly Discovered Ruins in Asia Minor, in the Years 1829–30*, 2 vols. London: Henry Colburn and Richard Bentley, 1831.

Kevles, Daniel J. "Some Like It Hot," *New York Review of Books*, March 26, 1992, pp. 31–34, 36–39.

Kinglake, Alexander William. *Kinglake's Eothen*, introduction by William D. Hogarth. London: Henry Frowde, 1906.

Király, Béla K., ed. *East Central European Society in the Era of Revolutions, 1775–1856*. New York: Social Science Monographs, Brooklyn College Press, distributed by Columbia University Press, © 1984 by Atlantic Research and Publications.

Kirschbaum, Stanislav J., ed. *East European History: Selected Papers of the Third World Congress for Soviet and East European Studies*. [Columbus, Ohio]: Slavica Publishers, [1988].

Kissling, Hans Joachim. "The Sociological and Educational Role of the Dervish Orders in the Ottoman Empire," in G. E. Von Grunebaum, ed., *Studies in Islamic Cultural History*, published as Vol. LVI, No. 2, Pt. 2, Memoir No. 76, of *American Anthropologist* (No. 2 of "Comparative Studies of Cultures and Civilizations") (1954). Pp. 23–35.

Kitroeff, Alexander. "Approaches to the Study of the Holocaust in the Balkans," in Saul S. Friedman, ed., *Holocaust Literature: A Handbook of Critical, Historical, and Literary Writings*, foreword by Dennis Klein. Westport, Conn.: Greenwood Press, 1993. Pp. 301–20.

―――. "Émigration transatlantique et stratégie familiale en Grèce," in Stuart Woolf, ed., *Espaces et familles dans l'Europe du Sud à l'âge moderne*. Paris: Éditions de la Maison des Sciences de l'Homme, 1993. Pp. 241–70.

Kitromilides, Paschalis M. "The Enlightenment East and West: A Comparative Perspective on the Ideological Origins of the Balkan Political Traditions," *Canadian Review of Studies in Nationalism, Revue canadienne des études sur le nationalisme*, X, 1 (Spring/printemps 1983), 51–70.

―――. " 'Imagined Communities' and the Origins of the National Question in the Balkans," *European History Quarterly*, XIX, 2 (April 1989), 149–92.

Kitto, H. D. F. *The Greeks*, rev. ed. Baltimore, Md.: Penguin Books, 1957.

Kluckhohn, Clyde. *Anthropology and the Classics*. Providence, R.I.: Brown University Press, 1961.

―――. *See also* Kroeber, Alfred Louis.

Knežević, Božidar. *History, the Anatomy of Time: The Final Phase of Sunlight*, translated by George Vid Tomashevich, in collaboration with Sherwood A. Wakeman, and with a preface by W. Warren Wagar. New York: Philosophical Library, [1980]. A translation of Knežević's own abridgment (1904) of his two-volume work.

―――. *Misli*, edited by Paulina Lebl-Albala, introduction by Ksenija Atanasijević, 4th ed. Belgrade: Srpska Književna Zadruga, 1931.

Kolarić, Miodrag. "Modernazacija srpskog slikarstva u razdoblju zografa i molera," *Zbornik Matice Srpske*, social science series, No. 8 (Novi Sad, 1954), pp. 87–98.

Koledarov, Petŭr. "Place-Name Classification in the Central Part of the Balkan Peninsula in the Middle Ages," in Association Internationale d'Études du Sud-est Européen, *Actes du Premier Congrès International des études balkaniques*, III, 277–85, and comment by Traian Stoianovich, p. 288.

Koliopoulos, John S. "Brigandage and Irredentism in Nineteenth-Century Greece," *European History Quarterly*, XIX, 2 (April 1989), 193–228.

―――. *Brigands with a Cause: Brigandage and Irredentism in Modern Greece, 1821–1912*. Oxford: Clarendon Press, 1987.

Koljević, Svetozar. *See* Pennington, Anne.

Kolokotrones, Theodoros. *See* Edmonds.

Komlos, John, ed. *Economic Development in the Habsburg Monarchy and in the Successor States: Essays*. Boulder, Colo.: East European Monographs, distributed by Columbia University Press, New York, 1990.

Kortepeter, Carl Max. *Ottoman Imperialism during the Reformation: Europe and the Caucasus*. New York: New York University Press, 1972.

Kosminskii, Evgenii Alekseevich, and Levandovskii, A. P., eds., *Atlas istorii srednikh vekov*. Moscow: Glavnoe upravlenie gedezii i kartografii pri Sovete Ministrov SSSR, 1951.

Kostanick, Huey Louis. "The Geopolitics of the Balkans," in Jelavich and Jelavich, eds., *The Balkans in Transition*, pp. 1–51.

Kostić, Cvetko. "Postanak i razvitak 'čaršije' (primer 'čaršije' Bajine Bašte)," *Glasnik Etnografskog Instituta Srpske Akademije Nauka (Bulletin de l'Institut Ethnographique de l'Académie Serbe des Sciences)*, knj. IV–VI (1955–57), pp. 123–49, with a résumé in French.

Kostić, K. N. "Domaće životinje kao transportna sredstva u srpskim zemljama za turskog vremena," *Glasnik Srpskog Geografskog Društva (Bulletin de la Société Serbe de Géographie)*, god. III, sv. 3 and 4 (April 1914), pp. 57–81.

Kostić, Mita. *Dositej Obradović u istoriskoj perspektivi XVIII i XIX veka*, Srpska Akademija Nauka, "Posebna izdanja," knj. CXC, Istoriski Institut, knj. 2. Belgrade: Naučna Knjiga, 1952.

————. "Nekoliko idejnih odraza Francuske Revolucije u našem društvu krajem 18 i početkom 19 veka," *Zbornik Matice Srpske*, serija društvenih nauka, No. 3 (November 1952), pp. 5–20.

Koty, John. "Greece," in Arnold M. Rose, ed., *The Institutions of Advanced Societies*. Minneapolis: University of Minnesota Press, [1958]. Pp. 330–83.

Kourvetaris, George A. "Greek Armed Forces and Society in the Nineteenth Century, with Special Emphasis on the Greek Revolution of 1821," in Király, ed., *East Central European Society*, pp. 271–302.

Kovačević, Desanka. "Dans la Serbie et la Bosnie médiévales: Les Mines d'or et d'argent," *Annales: Économies, Sociétés, Civilisations*, XV, 2 (March–April 1960), 248–58.

————. "O Janjevu u doba srednjovekovne srpske države," *Istoriski Glasnik*, Nos. 3–4 (1951), pp. 121–26.

Kozyrev, Andrei. "Don't Threaten Us," *New York Times*, March 16, 1994.

Krallert, Wilfried. "Die Verstädterung in Südosteuropa und ihre sozialen und wirtschaftlichen Auswirkungen," in *Wirtschaft und Gesellschaft Südosteuropas: Gedenkschrift für Wilhelm Gülich*, "Südosteuropa: Schriften der Südosteuropa-Gesellschaft," edited by Rudolf Vogel, Band II. München: Südosteuropa Verlagsgesellschaft, 1961. Pp. 278–95.

Krappe, Alexander Haggerty. *The Science of Folk-Lore*. London: Methuen, 1930.

Krauss, Friedrich S. "Aux temps anciens *(Župa, pleme, občina [sic])*," in Paul Henri Stahl, ed., *Ethnologie de l'Europe du Sud-est*, pp. 177–92. Translated by Eugénie Boeuve from Krauss, *Sitte und Brauch der Südslaven: Nach heimischen, gedruckten und ungedruckten Quellen*. Wien, 1885.

Krejci, Jaroslav. "Ethnic Problems in Europe," in Salvador Giner and Margaret Scotford Archer, eds., *Contemporary Europe: Social Structures and Cultural Patterns*. London, Henley-on-Thames, Boston: Routledge and Kegan Paul, [1978]. Pp. 124–71.

Krekić, Bariša. "Venetian Merchants in the Balkan Hinterland in the Fourteenth Century," in Schneider et al., eds., *Wirtschaftskräfte und Wirtschaftswege*, I, 413–29.

Kremenliev, Boris A. *Bulgarian-Macedonian Folk Music*. Berkeley and Los Angeles: University of California Press, 1952.

Kreševljaković, Hamdija. "Gradska privreda i esnafi u Bosni i Hercegovini (od 1463 do 1851)," *Godišnjak Istoriskog Društva Bosne i Hercegovine*, I (Sarajevo, 1949), 168–209.

————. "Kapetanije i kapetani u Bosni i Hercegovini," *Godišnjak Istoriskog Društva Bosne i Hercegovine*, II (Sarajevo 1950), 89–141.

————. *Kapetanije u Bosni i Hercegovini*, Naučno društvo NR Bosne i Hercegovine, "Djela," knj. V, odjeljenje Istorisko-filoloških nauka, knj. 4. Sarajevo, 1954.

Kritovoulos. *History of Mehmed the Conqueror*, translated from the Greek by Charles T.

Riggs. Princeton, N.J.: Princeton University Press, 1954.

Kroeber, Alfred Louis, and Kluckhohn, Clyde, with the assistance of Wayne Untereiner. *Culture: A Critical Review of Concepts and Definitions*, appendices by Alfred G. Meyer. Cambridge, Mass.: Peabody Museum, 1952.

Krulic, Joseph. "Deux sociétés civiles, plusieurs nations: Les luttes nationales dans la Yougoslavie post-titiste," *Le Débat*, No. 59 (March–April 1990), pp. 31–49.

Kukiel, Marian. *Czartoryski and European Unity, 1771–1861*. Princeton, N.J.: Princeton University Press, 1953.

Kulischer, Eugene M. *Europe on the Move: War and Population Changes, 1917–47*. New York: Columbia University Press, 1948.

Kunst, Jaap. *Cultural Relations between the Balkans and Indonesia*. Amsterdam: Royal Tropical Institute, 1954.

Kurath, Gertrude Prokosch. "Dance Relatives of Mid-Europe and Middle America: A Venture in Comparative Choreology," in Lord, ed., *Slavic Folklore*, pp. 88–100.

Kuripešić, Benedikt. *Putopis kroz Bosnu, Srbiju, Bugarsku i Rumeliju 1530*, translated from the Latin of the first German ed. by Djordje Pejanović. Sarajevo: Svjetlost, 1950.

Kuželj, Sreten. *Zur Entwicklung der Handwerkerfrage im gegenwärtigen Serbien*. Erlangen, 1909.

La Gorce, Paul-Marie de. "Les Divergences franco-allemandes mises à nu," *Le Monde diplomatique*, No. 474, 40e année (September 1993), pp. 10–11.

Laiou, Angeliki E. "Population Movements in the Greek Countryside during the Civil War," in Bærentzen, Iatrides, and Smith, eds., *Studies in the History of the Greek Civil War*, pp. 55–103.

Lamansky, Vladimir. *Secrets d'État de Venise: Documents, extraits, notices et études servant à éclaircir les rapports de la Seigneurie avec les Grecs, les Slaves et la Porte ottomane à la fin du XVe et au XVIe siècle*, 2 vols. New York: Burt Franklin, 1968; originally published in 1884 by the Imperial Academy of Sciences in St. Petersburg.

Lamartine, Alphonse-Marie-Louis de. *Voyage en Orient: Souvenirs, impressions, pensées et paysages pendant un voyage en Orient, 1832–1833*, Vol. II. Paris: Hachette, 1911.

Lampe, John R. *The Bulgarian Economy in the Twentieth Century*. London and Sydney: Croom Helm, [1986].

———. "Serbia, 1878–1912," in Cameron, ed., *Banking and Economic Development*, pp. 122–67.

Lampe, John R., and Jackson, Marvin R. *Balkan Economic History, 1550–1950: From Imperial Borderlands to Developing Nations*. Bloomington: Indiana University Press, [1982].

Lamprecht, Karl. *Zur jüngsten deutschen Vergangenheit*, 4th unrevised ed., Vol. II. Berlin: Weidmannsche Buchhandlung, 1922.

———. *What Is History? Five Lectures on the Modern Science of History*, translated by E. A. Andrews. New York: Macmillan, 1905; first published in Freiburg, Germany, as *Moderne Geschichtswissenschaft*.

Landes, David S. *The Unbound Prometheus: Technological Change and Industrial Development in Western Europe from 1750 to the Present*. Cambridge: University Press, 1969.

Lane, Frederic C. "Economic Consequences of Organized Violence," *Journal of Economic History*, XVIII (June 1958), 401–10.

———. "The Role of Governments in Economic Growth in Early Modern Times," *Journal of Economic History*, XXXV, 1 (March 1975), 8–17.

———. "The Venetian Galleys to Alexandria, 1344," in Schneider et al., eds., *Wirtschaftskräfte und Wirtschaftswege*, I, 431–40.

Lang, Rikard; Macesich, George; and Vojnić, Dragomir., eds., *Essays on the Political Economy of Yugoslavia*. Zagreb: Center for Yugoslav-American Studies, Research, and Exchanges at the Florida State University, Ekonomski Institut Zagreb, and Informator Zagreb, 1982.

Lanternari, Vittorio. *The Religions of the Oppressed: A Study of Modern Messianic Cults*, translated by Lisa Sergio. New York: Alfred A. Knopf, 1963.

Lapčević, Dragiša. *Istorija socijalizma u Srbiji*. Belgrade: Geca Kon, 1922.

Latouche, Robert. "Aspect démographique de la crise des grandes invasions," *Population: Revue de l'Institut National d'Études Démographiques*, II (1947), 680–90.

Lattimore, Owen. "La Civilisation, mère de barbarie?" *Annales: Économies, Sociétés, Civilisations*, XVII, 1 (January–February 1962), 95–108.

Lauterer, Georg, and Mihanovich, Franz. "Relation uiber die Reise des Hauptmann Georg Lauterer und Unterlieutenant Franz Mihanovich, beide von Pontoniers-bataillon, von Constantinopel bis Durrazzo, nebst der Fortsetzung des letztern von Durrazzo nach Semlin, im Jahr 1783," in Pantelić, "Vojno-geografski opisi Srbije," pp. 1–153.

Lawless, Richard A. "The Economy and Landscapes of Thessaly during Ottoman Rule," in Carter, ed., *An Historical Geography of the Balkans*, pp. 501–33.

Lawson, Cuthbert John. *Modern Greek Folklore and Ancient Greek Religion: A Study in Survivals*. Cambridge: University Press, 1910.

Lebel, Germaine. *La France et les Principautés danubiennes (du XVIe siècle à la chute de Napoléon Ier)*. Paris: Presses Universitaires de France, 1955.

Lechevalier, I. B. *Voyage de la Propontide et du Pont-Euxin*, 2 vols. Paris: Dentu, an VIII.

Lederer, Ivo J. *Yugoslavia at the Paris Peace Conference: A Study in Frontiermaking*. New Haven, Conn.: Yale University Press, 1963.

Lee, Dorothy Demetracopoulou. "Studies of Whole Cultures: Greece," in Mead, ed., *Cultural Patterns*, pp. 77–114.

———. "View of the Self in Greek Culture," in *Freedom and Culture*. Englewood Cliffs, N.J.: Prentice-Hall, [1959]. Pp. 141–53. Adapted from the foregoing.

Lefebvre des Noëttes, Richard. *L'Attelage: Le Cheval de selle à travers les âges, contribution à l'histoire de l'esclavage*, 2 vols. Paris: A. Picard, 1931.

Lencek, Rado L. "The Enlightenment's Interest in Languages and the National Revival of the South Slavs," *Canadian Review of Studies in Nationalism, Revue canadienne des études sur le nationalisme*, X, 1 (Spring/printemps 1983), 111–34.

Leon, George B. "The Greek Merchant Marine (1453–1850)," in Papadopoulos, ed., *The Greek Merchant Marine*, pp. 13–52.

Leontief, Wassily. "Environmental Repercussions and the Economic Structure: An Input-Output Approach," *Review of Economics and Statistics*, LII, 3 (August 1970), 262–71.

Lerner, Daniel, with the collaboration of Lucille W. Pevsner and an introduction by David Riesman. *The Passing of Traditional Society: Modernizing the Middle East*. Glencoe, Ill.: Free Press, 1958.

Leroi-Gourhan, André. *Le Geste et la parole*, Vol. II: *La Mémoire et les rythmes*. Paris: Albin Michel, 1965.

———. *Milieu et techniques*. Paris: Albin Michel, [1945].

Le Roy Ladurie, Emmanuel. *Histoire du climat depuis l'an mil*. Paris: Flammarion, 1967, with a revised and updated English translation by Barbara Bray entitled *Times of Feast, Times of Famine: A History of Climate since the Year 1000*. Garden City, N.Y.: Doubleday, 1971.

———. "Histoire et climat," *Annales: Économies, Sociétés, Civilisations*, XIV, 1 (January–March 1959), 3–34.

———. "Pour l'histoire de l'environnement: La Part du climat," *Annales: Économies, Sociétés, Civilisations*, XXV, 5 (September–October 1970), 1459–70.

Leskien, August. *Handbuch der altbulgarischen (altkirchenslawischen) Sprache*. Weimar: H. Böhlau, 1871.

Lettenbauer, Wilhelm. "Bemerkungen in Volksglauben und Brauchtum der Südslawen," *Südost-Forschungen,* XVIII (1958), 68–82.

Lévi-Strauss, Claude. *Mythologiques,* Vol. I: *Le Cru et le cuit.* Paris: Plon, [1964].

———. "Le Temps retrouvé," *Les Temps modernes,* XVII (April 1962), 1402–31.

———. *The View from Afar,* translated from the French by Joachim Neugroschel and Phoebe Hoss. New York: Basic Books, [1985].

———. *See also* Gurvitch, Georges.

Lewis, Bernard. "The Impact of the French Revolution on Turkey: Some Notes on the Transmission of Ideas," *Cahiers d'histoire mondiale, Journal of World History, Cuadernos de Historia Mundial,* I, 2 (October 1953), 105–25.

Lewis, Paul. "U.N. Yields to Plans by Germany to Recognize Yugoslav Republics," *New York Times,* December 16, 1991.

L'Héritier, Michel. *La Grèce.* Paris: F. Rieder, 1921.

———. *See also* Driault, Édouard.

Liddell, Henry George, and Scott, Robert, comps. *A Greek-English Lexicon,* new ed., revised and augmented by Henry Stuart Jones and Roderick McKenzie, 2 vols. Oxford: Clarendon Press, [1925–40].

Liebel, Helen P. "History and the Limitations of Scientific Method," *University of Toronto Quarterly,* XXXIV, 1 (October 1964), 15–29.

Lindsay, Jack. *Byzantium into Europe.* London: Bodley Head, 1952.

Lockwood, William G. "Bride Theft and Social Maneuverability in Western Bosnia," *Anthropological Quarterly,* XLVII, 3 (July 1974), 253–69.

Löfgren, Orvar. "The Nationalization of Culture," *Ethnologia Europaea: Journal of European Ethnology,* XIX, 1 (1989), 5–24.

Logio, George Clinton. *Bulgaria Past and Present.* Manchester: Sherratt and Hughes, 1936.

Lombard, Maurice. "Les Bases monétaires d'une suprématie économique: L'Or musulman du VIIe siècle au XIe siècle," *Annales: Économies, Sociétés, Civilisations,* II, 2 (April–June 1947), 143–60.

———. "Caffa et la fin de la route mongole," *Annales: Économies, Sociétés, Civilisations,* V, I (January–March 1950), 100–103.

———. *Les Métaux dans l'ancien monde du Ve au XIe siècle.* Paris, La Haye: Mouton, 1974.

———. "Un Problème cartographié: Le Bois dans la Méditerranée musulmane (VIIe–XIe siècles)," *Annales: Économies, Sociétés, Civilisations,* XIV, 2 (April–June 1959), 234–54 and map at end of periodical.

Lopez, Robert Sabatino. "Market Expansion: The Case of Genoa," *Journal of Economic History,* XXIV (1964), 445–64.

———. "The Trade of Medieval Europe: The South," *The Cambridge Economic History of Europe from the Decline of the Roman Empire,* Vol. II: *Trade and Industry in the Middle Ages,* edited by M. Postan and E. E. Rich. Cambridge: University Press, 1952. Pp. 257–338.

Lord, Albert Bates, ed., "Nationalism and the Muses in Balkan Slavic Literature in the Modern Period," in Jelavich and Jelavich, eds., *The Balkans in Transition,* pp. 258–96.

———, ed. *Slavic Folklore: A Symposium.* Philadelphia: American Folklore Society, 1956.

Lorimer, H. L. "The Country Cart of Ancient Greece," *Journal of Hellenic Studies,* XXIII (1903), 132–51.

Lot, Ferdinand. *L'Art militaire et les armes au Moyen âge en Europe et dans le Proche Orient,* 2 vols. Paris: Payot, 1946.

Lotić, Ljubomir. *Prilozi o ekonomskom stanju u Ugarskoj i u našem narodu.* Novi Sad: Matica Srpska, 1908.

Lowie, Robert H. *An Introduction to Cultural Anthropology,* 2nd ed., new and enlarged. New York: Rinehart, 1940.

Ludat, Herbert. "Farbenzeichnungen in Völkernamen," *Saeculum*, IV (1953), 138–55.

Lydall, Harold. *Yugoslavia in Crisis*. Oxford: Clarendon Press, 1989.

Macartney, C. A. *The Magyars in the Ninth Century*. Cambridge: University Press, 1930.

Macaulay, Thomas Babington, Lord. "Machiavelli," in *The Miscellaneous Works of Lord Macaulay*, 10 vols., edited by his sister, Lady Trevelyan, Whitehall ed. New York and London: G. P. Putnam's Sons, n.d. I, Pp. 68–122.

McClellan, Woodford D. *Svetozar Marković and the Origins of Balkan Socialism*. Princeton, N.J.: Princeton University Press, 1964.

Macesich, George. *Economic Nationalism and Stability*. New York: Praeger, 1985.

———. "The Yugoslav Model in Perspective," in George Macesich, ed., with the assistance of Rikard Lang and Dragomir Vojnic [*sic*], *Essays on the Yugoslav Economic Model*. New York: Praeger, [1989]. Pp. 1–7.

MacIver, R. M. "Group Images and Group Realities," in R. M. MacIver, ed., *Group Relations and Group Antagonisms: A Series of Addresses and Discussions, Institute for Religious [and Social] Studies*, Jewish Theological Seminary of America. New York: Peter Smith, reprinted, 1951, by permission of Harper and Brothers; copyright, 1944, by Institute for Religious Studies. Pp. 3–9.

[MacKenzie, G. Muir]. *Notes on the South Slavonic Countries in Austria and Turkey in Europe, Containing Historical and Political Information Added to the Substance of a Paper Read at the meeting of the British Association at Bath, 1864*, edited, with a preface, by Humphrey Sandwith. Edinburgh and London: William Blackwood and Sons, 1865.

MacLean, Fitzroy. *The Heretic: The Life and Times of Josip Broz-Tito*. New York: Harper, 1957.

McNeill, William H. "The Care and Repair of Public Myth," in *Mythistory and Other Essays*. Chicago and London: University of Chicago Press, [1986]), pp. 23–42, reprinted from *Foreign Affairs*, LXI (Fall 1982), 1–13, copyright 1982 by the Council on Foreign Relations.

———. "Control and Catastrophe in Human Affairs," *Daedalus*, CXVIII (Winter 1989), 1–12.

———. "Dilemmas of Modernization," *Massachusetts Review*, IX (Winter 1968), 133–46.

———. "The Eccentricity of Wheels, or European Transportation in Historical Perspective," *American Historical Review*, XCII, 5 (December 1987), 1111–26.

———. *Europe's Steppe Frontier, 1500–1800*. Chicago and London: University of Chicago Press, [1964].

———. *The Great Frontier: Freedom and Hierarchy in Modern Times*. Princeton, N.J.: Princeton University Press, [1983].

———. *Greece: American Aid in Action, 1947–1956*. New York: The Twentieth Century Fund, 1957.

———. *The Metamorphosis of Greece since World War II*. Chicago: University of Chicago Press, 1978.

———. "The Ottoman Empire in World History," in *Meletēmata stē mnēmē Basileiou [Vasileiou] Laourda: Essays in Memory of Basil Laourdas*. Thessaloniki, 1975. Pp. 374–85.

———. *Population and Politics since 1750*. Charlottesville and London: University Press of Virginia, [1990].

———. *The Pursuit of Power: Technology, Armed Force, and Society since A.D. 1000*. Chicago: University of Chicago Press, 1978.

———. *See also* Smothers, Frank.

McNeill, Elizabeth Darbishire. *See* Smothers, Frank.

McVicker, Charles P. *Titoism, Pattern for International Communism*. New York: St. Martin's Press, 1957.

Mączak, Antoni. "Progress and Underdevelopment in the Ages of Renaissance and Baroque Man," translated by S. Makowiecki, in *Studia Historiae Oeconomicae*, IX (1974), 77–94.

———. "Travel Expenses and Living Costs in Sixteenth Century Europe," typescript working paper, n.d.

———. "Un Voyageur témoin des prix européens à la fin du XVIe siècle," in *Mélanges en l'honneur de Fernand Braudel*, Vol. I: *Histoire économique du monde méditerranéen 1450–1650*, with an introduction by Ernest Labrousse. [Toulouse]: Édouard Privat, [1973]. Pp. 327–36.

Maddison, Angus. *Dynamic Forces in Capitalist Development: A Long-Run Comparative View*. Oxford, New York: Oxford University Press, 1991.

———. *Economic Growth in the West: Comparative Experience in Europe and North America*. New York: W. W. Norton, [1964].

Malet, Albert (ancien professeur du Roi Alexandre Ier et professeur agrégé au Lycée Voltaire). *En Serbie (Serbie, Bosnie, Herzégovine)*, conférence faite pour l'École Internationale des Expositions le 27 juin 1900. Paris: Arthur Rousseau, 1901.

[Maletić, Djordje]. *Gradja za istoriju srpskog narodnog pozorišta u Beogradu*, Čupićeva Zadužbina, knj. xxii. Belgrade: Kraljevsko-Srpska Državna Štamparija, 1884.

Małowist, Marian. "Saraï la Nouvelle, capitale de la Horde d'Or," in Schneider et al., eds., *Wirtschaftskräfte und Wirtschaftswege*, I, 15–29.

Manoilescu (Manoïlesco), Mihail. "Arbeitsproduktivität und Aussenhandel," *Weltwirtschaftliches Archiv*, XLII, 1 (July 1935), 13–43.

Mantran, Robert. *Istanbul dans la seconde moitié du XVIIe siècle: Essai d'histoire institutionnelle, économique et sociale*. Paris: Librairie d'Adrien Maisonneuve, 1962.

Marcovitch, Lazare. "Two Anniversaries of Serbian Law: The Civil Code of 1844 and the Zakonik of Dushan," *Journal of Central European Affairs*, XIV, 3 (October 1954), 270–73.

Marcovitch, Micha, ed. *Livre jubilaire des chemins de fer d'État du Royaume de Yougoslavie*. Belgrade: Imprimerie "Vreme," 1929. Article by Marcovitch, "Création et developpement des chemins de fer dans le Royaume de Serbie, 1867–1918," pp. 151–64.

Marcuse, Hugo. *Serbien und die Revolutionsbewegung in Makedonien*. Berlin: Verlag Willy Kraus, 1908.

Mardin, Şerif (Sherif). *The Genesis of Young Ottoman Thought: A Study in the Modernization of Political Ideas*. Princeton, N.J.: Princeton University Press, 1962.

———. "The Mind of the Turkish Reformer, 1700–1900," *Western Humanities Review*, XIV, 4 (Autumn 1960), 413–36.

———. "Power, Civil Society and Culture in the Ottoman Empire," *Comparative Studies in Society and History*, XI, 3 (June 1969), 258–81.

Mardin, Şerif, and Zartman, I. William. "Ottoman Turkey and the Maghreb in the 19th and 20th Centuries," Social Science Research Council, *Items*, XXX, 4 (December 1976), 61–66.

Margat, J. "L'Eau dans les pays balkaniques (Albanie, Bulgarie, Grèce, Turquie d'Europe, ex-Yougoslavie)," paper presented at a conference on The European Community and the Balkans, Corfu, July 2–5, 1993, organized by the Hellenic Centre for European Studies (EKEM) and the Hellenic Foundation for Defence and Foreign Policy (ELIAMEP) with the support of the Commission of the European Community.

Maricq, André. "Notes sur les Slaves dans le Péloponnèse et en Bithynie et sur l'emploi de 'slave' comme appellatif," *Byzantion*, XXII (1952), 337–56.

Maringer, Johannes. *The Gods of Prehistoric Man*, edited and translated from the German, originally published in Dutch in 1952 and enlarged and revised in German in 1956. New York: Alfred A. Knopf, 1960.

Marinović, Ante. "Prilog poznavanju dubrovačkih bratovština," *Anali Historijskog Instituta u Dubrovniku*, I (1952), 233–45.

Markert, Werner, ed. *Osteuropa-Handbuch: Jugoslawien.* Köln/Graz: Böhlau-Verlag, 1954.

Marković, Miša. *See* Marcovitch, Micha.

Marković, Svetozar. *Celokupna dela,* 8 vols. Vols. I–II, edited by Lj. Joksimović. Belgrade: Moderna Štamparija Milivoja Bodjanskog, 1911–12. Vol. III, edited by the Committee for the Publication of the Complete Works of Svetozar Marković. Belgrade: Izdavačka Knjižarnica Rajkovića i Cukovića, n.d. Vols. IV–VIII, edited by Lj. Joksimović, text prepared by the Committee for the Publication of the Complete Works of Svetozar Marković. Belgrade: Parna Štamparija Narodne Radikalne Stranke, 1893.

———. *See also* Masleša, Veselin.

Marsenic [*sic*], Dragutin. "Accumulation and Investment in the Yugoslav Economy: The Developmental and Systemic Aspects," in Macesich, ed., *Essays on the Yugoslav Economic Model,* pp. 82–100.

Martinet, André. *Des Steppes aux océans: L'Indo-européen et les "Indo-Européens."* Paris: Payot, 1987.

Martonne, Emmanuel de. *La Valachie: Essai de monographie géographique.* Paris: Armand Colin, 1902.

März, Josef. *Jugoslawien: Probleme aus Raum, Volk und Wirtschaft,* introduction by Karl Haushofer. Berlin: Deutscher Verlag für Politik und Wirtschaft, 1938.

Masleša, Veselin, ed. *Odabrani spisi [Svetozara Markovića].* Zagreb: Prosvjeta, 1950.

Mathias, Peter. *The First Industrial Nation: An Economic History of Britain, 1700–1914.* New York: Charles Scribner's Sons, [1969].

Mathiex, Jean. "Trafic et prix de l'homme en Méditerranée aux XVIIe et XVIIIe siècles," *Annales: Économies, Sociétés, Civilisations,* IX, 2 (April–June 1954), 157–64.

Matković, Petar. "Putovanje na Balkanskom poluotoku XVI. vieka," xiii, "Putopisi Stj. Gerlacha i Sal. Schweigera, ili opisi carskih poslanstva u Carigrad, naime Davida Ungnada od g. 1573–78 i Joach. Sinzendorfa od g. 1577," *Rad Jugoslavenske Akademije znanosti i umjetn'osti,* knj. CXVI, filologičko-historički i filosofičko-juridički razredi, XXXIX (Zagreb, 1893).

Matossian, Mary Kilbourne. "In the Beginning God Was a Woman," *Journal of Social History,* VI, 3 (Spring 1973), 325–43.

Matvejević, Predrag. "Central Europe Seen from the East of Europe," in George Schöpflin and Nancy Wood, eds., *In Search of Central Europe.* [Cambridge]: Polity Press, [1989]. Pp. 183–90.

Maurizio, Adam (professor of botany at the Higher Technical School of Lemberg or Lwów). *Die Geschichte unserer Pflanzennahrung von den Urzeiten bis zur Gegenwart.* Berlin: Verlagsbuchhandlung Paul Parey, 1927.

———. *Histoire de l'alimentation végétale depuis la préhistoire jusqu'à nos jours,* trans. Dr. F. Gidon. Paris: Payot, 1932.

Mauss, Marcel. "Une Catégorie de l'esprit humain: La Notion de personne, celle de 'moi,'" in Gurvitch, ed., *Marcel Mauss,* pp. 331–62.

———. *Manuel d'ethnographie.* Paris: Payot, 1947.

———. *Oeuvres,* présentation de Victor Karady, 3 vols. Paris: Les Éditions de Minuit, [1968–69].

———. "Les Techniques du corps," in Gurvitch, ed., *Marcel Mauss,* pp. 363–86, first published in *Journal de psychologie,* XXXII, 3–4 (March 15–April 15, 1936).

———. *See also* Durkheim, Émile.

May, Jacques Meyer. *The Ecology of Malnutrition in Five Countries of Eastern and Central Europe (East Germany, Poland, Yugoslavia, Albania, Greece),* Studies in Medical Geography, No. 4. New York: Hafner, 1963.

Mead, Margaret, ed., *Cultural Patterns and Technological Change,* manual prepared by World Federation of Mental Health. Paris: UNESCO, 1953.

Mehlan, Arno. "Über die Bedeutung der mittelalterlichen Bergbaukolonien für die slavischen Balkanvölker," *Revue internationale des études balkaniques*, IIIe année, t. II (6) (Belgrade, 1938), pp. 383–404.

Meillet, Antoine. *Etudes sur l'étymologie et le vocabulaire du vieux slave*, 2 vols. in one. Paris: É. Bouillon, 1902–05.

Ménage, V. L. "Devshirme," *Encyclopaedia of Islam*, new ed., edited by B. Lewis, Ch. Pellat, and J. Schacht. Leiden: E. J. Brill; London: Luzac, 1965, II, 210–13.

Meyendorff, Jean. *St. Grégoire Palamas et la mystique orthodoxe*. Paris: aux Éditions du Seuil, [1959].

———. *See also* Palamas, Gregory.

Michoff, Nicholas V. *See* Mikhov, Nikola V.

Mićić, Ljubomir Ž. "Zlatibor: Antropogeografska ispitivanja," Srpska Kraljevska Akademija, *Srpski Etnografski Zbornik*, xxxiv, Section 1: "Naselja i poreklo stanovništva," 19, edited by Jovan Cvijić. Belgrade, 1925. Pp. 397–501.

Mihanovich, Franz. *See* Lauterer, Georg.

Mijatović, Čedo or Čedomilj (Chedo or Chedomille Mijatovich), Count. *Izvod iz politične ekonomike*. Belgrade: Državna Štamparija, 1867.

———. *The Memoirs of a Balkan Diplomatist*. London, New York, Toronto, and Melbourne: Cassell and Company, 1917.

———. *Nauka o državnom gazdinstvu ili nauka o financiji, po Lorencu Štajnu i drugima*. Belgrade: Državna Štamparija, 1869.

———. *Servia and the Servians*. Boston: L. C. Page, 1908; new ed. London: Sir Isaac Pitman and Sons, 1911.

Mijatović, Stanoje M. *Zanati i esnafi u Rasini*, edited by Tihomir R. Djordjević, Srpska Kraljevska Akademija, "Srpski Etnografski Zbornik," knj. XLII, drugo odeljenje, "Život i običaji narodni," knj. 17. Belgrade, 1928.

Mijatović, Stanoje M., and Bušetić, Todor M. "Tehnički radovi Srba seljaka u Levču i Temniću," in Tihomir R. Djordjević and Veselin Čajkanović, eds., *Različita gradja za narodni život i običaje*, Srpska Kraljevska Akademija, "Srpski Etnografski Zbornik," xxxii, drugo odeljenje, knj. 14. Belgrade, 1925. Pp. 1–168.

Mikhov, Nikola V. *Beiträge zur Handelsgeschichte Bulgariens (Offizielle Dokumente und Konsularberichte)*, Vol. I. Sofia, 1943.

———. *Contribution à l'histoire du commerce bulgare*, Vol. I: *Rapports consulaires belges*. Sofia, 1941.

———. *Contribution à l'histoire du commerce de la Turquie et de la Bulgarie*, Vol. VI: *Auteurs français, allemands et anglais*. Sofia: Bŭlgarska Akademiia na Naukite, 1970.

Miklosich, Franz. *Lexicon Palaeoslovenico-graeco-latinum*. Wien: Wilhelm Braumueller, 1862–65.

Milenković, Petar. *Istorija gradjenja železnica i železnička politika kod nas (1850–1935)*. Belgrade: n.p., 1936.

Milenković, Vladislav. *Ekonomska istorija Beograda do Svetskog rata*. Belgrade: Za Narodnu Štampariju Mirko Drobac, 1932.

Milev, Aleksandŭr. "Grŭtskite i latinskite dumi v Istoriiata na Paisii Khilendarski," in Academia Litterarum Bulgarica, Institutum Historicum, ed., *Paisii Khilendarski i negovata epokha (1762–1962): Sbornik ot izsledovaniia po sluchai 200-godishninata ot Istoriia Slavianobŭlgarska*. Sofia: Izdatelstvo na Bŭlgarskata Akademiia na Naukite, 1962. Pp. 401–11.

Milićević, Milan Djuro. *Dodatak pomeniku od 1888: Znameniti ljudi u srpskoga naroda koji su preminuli do kraja 1900 g.* Belgrade: Čupićeva Zadužbina, 1901).

———. *Kneževina Srbija*, 2 vols. Belgrade: Državna Štamparija, 1876.

———. *Kraljevina Srbija: Novi krajevi*. Belgrade: Državna Štamparija, 1884.

————. "Pregled zadružnog stanja Srba seljaka," in *Glasnik Društva Srbske Slovesnosti*, otdel 1, IX (1856), 145–61.

————. *Život Srba seljaka*, 2nd ed., rev. and enlarged. Belgrade: Srpska Kraljevska Akademija, 1894.

Miller, Dean A. *Imperial Constantinople*. New York, London, Sydney, Toronto: John Wiley and Sons, 1969.

Miller, Judith. "Strangers at the Gate," *New York Times Magazine*, September 15, 1991, pp. 33–37, 49, 80–81, 86.

Miller, Nicholas J. "R. W. Seton-Watson and Serbia during the Reemergence of Yugoslavism, 1903–1914," *Canadian Review of Studies in Nationalism, Revue canadienne des études sur le nationalisme*, XV, 1–2 (1988), 59–69.

Miller, William. "Greece under the Turks, 1571–1684," *English Historical Review*, XIX (1904), 646–68.

Minc, Alain. *Le Nouveau Moyen âge*. Paris: Gallimard, 1993.

Minkov, N. *See* G. G.

Mirković, Mijo. *Ekonomska historija Jugoslavije*. Zagreb: Ekonomski Pregled, 1958.

Mireaux, Émile. *Daily Life in the Time of Homer*, translated from the French by Iris Sells. London: George Allen and Unwin, 1959.

Mišić, Dimitrije. "Industrija Jugoslavije do Drugog svetskog rata," in *Iz istorije Jugoslavije 1918–1945*. Belgrade: Nolit, 1958.

Mitrany, David. *The Effect of the War in Southeastern Europe*, Economic and Social History of the World War, General Series. New Haven: Yale University Press; London: Oxford University Press, published for the Carnegie Endowment for International Peace, Division of Economics and History, 1936.

————. *The Land and the Peasant in Rumania: The War and Agrarian Reform (1917–1921)*. London: H. Milford, 1930.

Mitteis, Heinrich. "Land und Herrschaft: Bemerkungen zu dem gleichnamigen Buch Otto Brunners," in Hellmut Kämpf, ed., *Herrschaft und Staat im Mittelalter*. Darmstadt: Wissenschaftliche Buchgesellschaft, 1974. Pp. 20–65. Review article first published in *Historische Zeitschrift*, CLXIII (1941), 255–81, 471–89.

Mittesser, Josef Paul. "Militairische Beschreibung," in Pantelić, "Vojno-geografski opisi Srbije," pp. 57–102.

Modelski, George. "The Long Cycle of Global Politics and the Nation-State," *Comparative Studies in Society and History*, XX, 2 (April 1978), 214–38.

Mollat du Jourdan, Guy. *L'Âme des cités*, preface by Albert Mousset, color illustrations by Étienne Morin. Paris: Les Éditions Internationales, 1946.

Montagu, Mary (Pierrepont) Wortley, Lady. *The Complete Letters of Lady Mary Wortley Montagu*, edited by Robert Halsband, 3 vols. Oxford: Clarendon Press, 1965–1967.

Montias, John Michael. "Notes on the Romanian Debate on Sheltered Industrialization: 1860–1906," in Jowitt, ed., *Social Change in Romania*, 53–71.

Moore, John A. *Sophocles and Aretē*. Cambridge, Mass.: Harvard University Press, 1938.

Moore, Wilbert E., and Feldman, Arnold S., eds. *Labor Commitment and Social Change in Developing Areas*. New York: Social Science Research Council, 1960.

Moreau, Joseph. "Les Théories démographiques dans l'Antiquité grecque," *Population: Revue de l'Institut National d'Études Démographiques*, IV (1949), 597–614.

Morin, Edgar. "De la culturanalyse à la politique culturelle," *Communications*, No. 14 (1969), pp. 5–38.

Morison, Walter Angus. *The Revolt of the Serbs against the Turks (1804–13): Translations from the Serbian National Ballads of the Period*. Cambridge: University Press, 1942.

Moryson, Fynes. *An Itinerary Containing His Ten Yeeres Travell through the Twelve Dominions of Germany, Bohmerland, Switzerland, Netherland, Denmarke, Poland,*

Italy, Turkey, France, England, Scotland & Ireland, 4 vols. Glasgow: James MacLehose and Sons, 1907–08; reprint of the original 1617 edition.

————. *Shakespeare's Europe: [Some] Unpublished Chapters of Moryson's Itinerary, Being a Survey of the Condition of Europe at the End of the 16th Century,* with an introduction and an account of Moryson's career by Charles Hughes. London: Sherratt and Hughes, 1903.

Mougenot, Pierre, dir. *Grand atlas historique,* édition française. Paris: Librairie Stock, [1968].

Mouradgea d'Ohsson, Ignace [Ignatius]. *Tableau général de l'Empire othoman,* 7 vols. Paris: Firmin Didot, 1788–1824.

Mousset, Jean. *La Serbie et son Église (1830–1904).* Paris: Institut d'Études Slaves de l'Université de Paris, 1938.

Mouzelis, Nicos P. *Modern Greece: Facets of Underdevelopment.* New York: Holmes and Meier Publishers, [1978].

Müller, Elli. "Die Herdenwanderungen in Mittelmeergebiet (Transhumance)," *Petermanns Geographische Mitteilungen,* LXXXIV, 12 (December 1938), 364–70 and accompanying map.

Murphy, Alexander B. "Urbanism and the Diffusion of Substate Nationalist Ideas in Western Europe," *History of European Ideas,* XV, 4–6 (August 1992), 639–45.

Murray, Thomas J. *See* Bryson, Reid A.

Musson, A. E., and Robinson, E. "The Origins of Engineering in Lancashire," *Journal of Economic History,* XX, 2 (June 1960), 209–30.

Musto, Stefan A. "The European Community in Search of a New Mediterranean Policy: A Chance for a More Symmetrical Interdependence," in Pinkele and Pollis, eds., *The Contemporary Mediterranean World,* pp. 151–74.

Mutafchieva, Vera P. "Feodalnite razmiritsi v severna Trakiia prez kraia na XVIII i nachaloto na XIX v.," in Academia Litterarum Bulgarica, Institutum Historicum. *Paisii Khilendarski i negovata epokha (1762–1962): Sbornik ot izsledovaniia po sluchai 200-godishninata ot Istoriia Slavianobŭlgarska.* Sofia: Izdatelstvo na Bŭlgarskata Akademiia na Naukite, 1962.. Pp. 167–210.

Myres, John L. "An Attempt to Reconstruct the Maps Used by Herodotus," *Geographical Journal,* VIII (1896), 606–31.

————. *Geographical History in Greek Lands.* Oxford: Clarendon Press, 1953.

Narodna Odbrana (Serbia). "Nationalism in Action: Program of the Society of National Defense 1911," in Anderson, Pincetl, and Ziegler, eds., *Europe in the Nineteenth Century,* II, 304–35.

Narodni Muzej (Belgrade, Serbia). *Neolit Centralnog Balkana,* 2 vols. Belgrade: Musée National, 1968.

Nash, June, "Ethnographic Aspects of the World Capitalist System," *Annual Review of Anthropology,* X (1981), 393–423.

Nef, John U. *Western Civilization since the Renaissance: Peace, War, Industry, and the Arts.* New York and Evanston: Harper and Row, [1963], published originally in 1950 by the Harvard University Press under the title *War and Human Progress.*

Nenadović, Matija. *Memoari.* Belgrade: Prosveta, 1947.

Newbigin, Marion I. *Geographical Aspects of Balkan Problems.* New York: Putnam, 1915.

————. *Southern Europe: A Regional and Economic Geography of the Mediterranean Lands,* 3rd ed., revised under the editorship of R. J. Morrison Church. London: Methuen; New York: E. P. Dutton, 1949.

"New Problem Cripples Bulgarian Atom Plant," *New York Times,* February 24, 1992.

Nicolay, Nicolas de, seigneur d'Arfeuille. *Les Navigations, peregrinations et voyages faicts en la Tvrqvie,* par Nicolas de Nicolay, Daulphinois, Seigneur d'Arfeville, valet de chambre & geographe ordinaire du Roy de France, contenants plusieurs singularitez que l'Autheur y a veu & obserué, le tout distingué en quatre Liures. Anvers: Guillaume Silvius, 1576.

Niederle, Lubor. *Manuel de l'Antiquité slave*, 2 vols. Paris: Librairie Ancienne Honoré Champion, 1923–26.

Nikitin, S. A., et al., eds. *Istoriia Iuzhnykh i Zapadnykh Slavian* Moscow: Moskovskii Universitet, 1957.

Nopcsa, Franz, Baron. "Zur Genese der primitiven Pflugtypen," *Zeitschrift für Ethnologie*, Organ der Berliner Gesellschaft, LI (1919), 234–42.

Novak, Viktor. *Antologija jugoslovenske misli i narodnog jedinstva (1390–1930)*. Belgrade: Author, 1930.

Novak, Vilko. "Structure de la culture populaire slovène," in International Commission on Folk Arts and Folklore and the Swedish Organizing Committee, *Papers on the International Congress of European and Western Technology, Stockholm 1951*. Stockholm, 1955. Pp. 85–94.

Novaković, Miodrag. *Racionalizacija (Naučna organizacija rada)*. Belgrade: Štamparija "Privrednik," 1931.

Novaković, Stojan. "Djuvendija," *Archiv für slavische Philologie*, XXVII (1905), 175–81.

———. *Istorija srpske književnosti: Pregled ugadjan za školsku potrebu*. Belgrade, 1867.

———. "Selo," Srpska Kraljevska Akademija, *Glas*, XXIV (Belgrade, 1891), viii–261.

———. "Srbija u godini 1834; pisma grofa Boa-le-Konta de Rinji ministru inostranih dela u Parizu o tadašnjem stanju u Srbiji," Srpska Kraljevska Akademija, *Spomenik*, XXIV (Belgrade, 1894), 1–64.

———. *Zakonik Stefana Dušana cara srpskog 1349 i 1354*, izdanje Zadužbine Ilije M. Kolarca, 91. Belgrade: Državna Štamparija, 1898.

Nove, Alec; Höhmann, Hans-Hermann; and Seidenstecher, Gertrud, eds. *The East European Economies in the 1970s*. London, Boston, Durban: Butterworths, 1982. Pp. 280–314.

Noyes, George Rapall. *See* Obradović, Dositej.

Nušić, Branislav. Foreword to his play *Gospodja Ministarka*, in Vol. I, pp. 7–11, and his plays *Svet* in Vol. VI, and *Narodni Poslanik*, in Vol. XII, of his *Sabrana dela*. Belgrade: Geca Kon, 1931–32.

Obolensky, Dmitri. "Bogomilism in the Byzantine Empire," in *Actes du VIe Congrès International d'études byzantines, Paris, 27 juillet–2 août 1948*, Vol. I. Paris, 1950.

———. *The Bogomils: A Study in Balkan Neo-Manichaeism*. Cambridge: University Press, 1948.

Obradović, Dositej. *Dela Dositeja Obradovića*, edited by Jovan Skerlić, Milutin K. Dragutinović, and Miloš Ivković., 5th state, ed. Belgrade: Državna Štamparija Kr. Srbije, 1911.

———. *The Life and Adventures of Dimitrije Obradović, Who as a Monk Was Given the Name Dositej, Written and Published by Himself*, ed. George Rapall Noyes. Berkeley and Los Angeles: University of California Press, 1953.

———. "Sovjeti zdravago razuma" (Counsels of Sound Reason), in *Dela*, pp. 95–131, published originally by Breitkopf in Leipzig in 1784.

Ogilvie, Alan G. *Europe and Its Borderlands*. Edinburgh and London: Thomas Nelson and Sons, 1957.

Ohlin, Bertil. "The Theory of Trade," in Flam and Flanders, eds., *Heckscher-Ohlin Trade Theory*, pp. 71–214.

Oliva, Pavel. *Pannonia and the Onset of Crisis in the Roman Empire*, translated from the Czech by Iris Irwin. Praha: Czechoslovak Academy of Sciences, 1962.

Olivier, Guillaume Antoine. *Voyage dans l'Empire othoman, l'Égypte et la Perse, fait par ordre du Gouvernement, pendant les six premières années de la République*, Vol. I. Paris: chez H. Agasse, an 9.

Olson, Mancur. *The Rise and Decline of Nations: Economic Growth, Stagflation, and Social Rigidities*. New Haven and London: Yale University Press, [1982].

Onians, Richard Broxton. *The Origins of European Thought: About the Body, the Mind, the Soul, the World, Time, and Fate—New Interpretations of Greek, Roman, and Kindred Evidence; Also Some Basic Jewish and Christian Beliefs*. Cambridge: University Press, 1951; New York: Arno Press, 1973, reprint of the 1951 edition.

Origo, Iris. "The Domestic Enemy: The Eastern Slaves in Tuscany in the XIV and XV Centuries," *Speculum*, XXX (1955), 321–66.

Ostrogorsky, George. *History of the Byzantine State*, translated from the German by John Hussey, with a foreword by Peter Charanis. New Brunswick, N.J.: Rutgers University Press, 1957; rev. ed. 1969.

Pach, Z. P. "Zur Geschichte des levantinischen Pfefferhandels um 1500," in Schneider et al., eds., *Wirtschaftskräfte und Wirtschaftswege*, I, 521–29.

Paikert, G. C. *The Danube Swabians: German Populations in Hungary, Rumania and Yugoslavia and Hitler's Impact on Their Patterns*. The Hague: Martinus Nijhoff, 1967.

Palairet, Michael. "Farm Productivity under Ottoman Rule and Self-Government in Bulgaria, c. 1860–90," in Kirschbaum, ed., *East European History*, pp. 89–124.

Palamas, Gregory. *Grégoire Palamas: Défense des saints hésychastes*, introduction, texte critique, traduction et notes de Jean Meyendorff. Louvain: Spilegium Sacrum Lovaniense, 1959.

Palmer, Robert R. *The Age of the Democratic Revolution: A Political History of Europe and America, 1760–1800*, Vol. I: *The Challenge*. Princeton, N.J.: Princeton University Press, 1959.

Pantazopoulos, Nikolaos. "Human Liberties in the Pre-Revolutionary Greek Community System," *Balkan Studies*, XXX, 1 (Thessaloniki, 1989), 5–32.

Pantelić, Dušan. "Vojno-geografski opisi Srbije pred Kočinu Krajinu 1783 i 1784 god.," in Srpska Kraljevska Akademija, *Spomenik*, LXXXII, drugi razred, knj. 64 (Belgrade, 1936), pp. 1–153.

Papadopoullos, Theodore. *Studies and Documents Relating to the History of the Greek Church and People under Turkish Domination*. Brussels: Wetteren, 1952.

Papadopoulos, Stelios A., ed. *The Greek Merchant Marine (1453–1850)*. Athens: National Bank of Greece, [1972].

Papaioannou, Kostas. "Nature and History in the Greek Conception of the Cosmos," *Diogenes*, No. 25 (1949), pp. 1–27.

Papathanassopoulos, Constantinos. "The State and the Greek Commercial Fleet during the Nineteenth Century," in Vacalopoulos, Svolopoulos, and Király, eds., *Southeast European Maritime Commerce*, pp. 177–87.

Parry, M. L. *Climatic Change, Agriculture, and Settlement*. [Folkestone, Kent, Eng.: William Dawson and Sons; Hamden, Conn.: Archon Books, Shoe String Press, 1978].

Paskaleva, Virginia. "Les Relations commerciales des contrées bulgares avec les pays occidentaux et la Russie au cours de la première moitié du XIXe s.," in Académie des Sciences de Bulgarie, *Études historiques*, pp. 253–83.

Passarge, Siegfried. "Probleme einer Geschichtsgeographie auf landschaftskundlicher Basis," *Forschungen und Fortschritte*, XXVI, Heft 21/22 (November 1950), pp. 271–73.

Patlagean, Evelyne. "Ancienne hagiographie byzantine et histoire sociale," *Annales: Économies, Sociétés, Civilisations*, XXIII, 1 (January–February 1968), 106–26.

———. "Une Représentation byzantine de la parenté et ses origines occidentales," *L'Homme: Revue française d'anthropologie*, VI, 4 (December 1966), 59–81.

Paton, Andrew Archibald. *Researches on the Danube and the Adriatic; or, Contributions to the Modern History of Hungary and Transylvania, Dalmatia and Croatia, Servia and Bulgaria*, 2 vols. London: Trübner and Co., 1862.

————. *Servia, the Youngest Member of the European Family, or, A Residence in Belgrade, and Travels in the Highlands and Woodlands of the Interior, during the Years 1843 and 1844.* London: Longman, Brown, Green, and Longmans, 1845.

Pavlowitch, Stevan K. *Anglo-Russian Rivalry in Serbia, 1837–39: The Mission of Colonel Hodges.* Paris, The Hague: Mouton, 1961.

————. *The Improbable Survivor: Yugoslavia and Its Problems, 1918–1988.* Columbus: Ohio State University Press, [1988].

Paxton, Roger Viers. "Nationalism and Revolution: A Re-examination of the Origins of the First Serbian Insurrection, 1804–1807," *East European Quarterly,* VI (September 1972), 337–62.

Pennington, Anne, and Levi, Peter, trans. *Marko the Prince: Serbo-Croat Songs,* with introduction and notes by Svetozar Koljević. New York: St. Martin's Press, [1984].

Petrakis, P. E., with the collaboration of H. Panorios. "Economic Fluctuations in Greece: 1844–1913," *Journal of European Economic History,* XXI, 1 (Spring 1992), 31–46.

Petrović, Petar Ž. *Život i običaji narodni u Gruži,* Srpska Akademija Nauka, "Srpski Etnografski Zbornik," knj. lviii. Belgrade, 1948.

Petrović, Vukašin J., and Petrović, Nik. J. *Gradja za istoriju Kraljevine Srbije: Vreme prve vlade Kneza Miloša Obrenovića,* 2 vols. Belgrade, 1882–1884.

Petrovich, Miodrag B. "*Srpski Književni Glasnik* and the Yugoslav Idea, 1901–1914," in Kirschbaum, ed., *East European History,* pp. 141–56.

Philip, André. *L'Europe unie et sa place dans l'économie internationale,* Publications de l'Université de la Sarre. Paris: Presses Universitaires de France, 1953.

Philippson, Alfred. *Das Mittelmeergebiet: Seine geographische und kulturelle Eigenart,* 3rd ed. Leipzig and Berlin: B. G. Teubner, 1914.

Piaget, Jean. *Le Structuralisme,* 2nd ed. Paris: Presses Universitaires de France, 1968.

Picard, Charles. "Nouvelles observations sur diverses représentations du héros cavalier des Balkans," *Revue d'histoire des religions,* LXXVe année, CL (1956), 1–26.

Piccone, Paul, and Ulmen, G. L. "Schmitt's 'Testament' and the Future of Europe," *Telos,* No. 83 (Spring 1990), pp. 3–34.

Pieper, Josef. *Leisure the Basis of Culture,* translated by Alexander Dru, with an introduction by T. S. Eliot. New York: Pantheon Books, [1952].

Piggott, Stuart. *The Earliest Wheeled Transport from the Atlantic Coast to the Caspian Sea.* Ithaca, N.Y.: Cornell University Press, [1983].

Pinkele, Carl F., and Pollis, Adamantia, eds. *The Contemporary Mediterranean World.* [New York]: Praeger, 1983.

Pinto, V. de S. "Bulgaria," in *Contrasts in Emerging Societies: Readings in the Social and Economic History of South-Eastern Europe in the Nineteenth Century,* selected and translated by G. F. Cushing, E. D. Tappe, V. de S. Pinto, and Phyllis Auty, and edited by Doreen Warriner. Bloomington: Indiana University Press, 1965. Pp. 205–80.

Pipes, Richard. *Russia under the Old Regime.* New York: Charles Scribner's Sons, [1974].

Pitcher, Donald Edgar. *An Historical Geography of the Ottoman Empire from Earliest Times to the End of the Sixteenth Century,* with detailed maps to illustrate the expansion of the Sultanate. Leiden: E. J. Brill, 1972.

Pittard, Eugène. *Les Peuples des Balkans: Recherches anthropologiques dans la péninsule des Balkans, spécialement dans la Dobroudja.* Genève et Lyon: Éditions Georg et Cie; Paris: Éditions Leroux, 1920.

————. *Race and Culture: An Ethnological Introduction to History,* translated by V. C. C. Collum. London: Kegan Paul, Trench, Trubner and Co.; New York: Alfred A. Knopf, 1926.

————. *Les Races et l'histoire: Introduction ethnologique à l'histoire.* Paris: La Renaissance du Livre, 1924.

Pittioni, Richard. "Southern Middle Europe and Southeastern Europe," in Braidwood and Willey, eds., *Courses toward Urban Life*, pp. 211–26.

Pitt-Rivers, Julian A., ed. *Mediterranean Countrymen: Essays in the Social Anthropology of the Mediterranean*. Paris, La Haye: Mouton, 1963.

———. *The People of the Sierra*. Chicago and London: University of Chicago Press— Phoenix Books, 1961.

Plamenatz, John. "Two Types of Nationalism," in Kamenka, ed., *Nationalism*, pp. 22–36.

Planhol, Xavier de. *The World of Islam*. Ithaca, N.Y.: Cornell University Press, 1959. A translation, with corrections, additions, and revisions, of Planhol's *Le Monde islamique: Essai de géographie religieuse*. Paris: Presses Universitaires de France, 1957.

Plato. *The Republic*, translated by Benjamin Jowett, with the Jowett notes and marginalia, illustrated by Laszlo Matulay, with an introduction by Scott Buchanan. Cleveland: Fine Arts Editions Press, [1946].

Plinius Secundus, C. *Naturalis Historiae*, libri XXXVII, ed. Carolus Mayhoff, 6 vols. Stuttgart: B. G. Teubner, 1967–70.

Polanyi, Karl. "The Economy as Instituted Process," in Karl Polanyi, Conrad M. Arensberg, and Harry W. Pearson, eds., *Trade and Market in the Early Empires: Economies in History and Theory*. New York: Free Press, 1957. Pp. 188–217.

———. *The Great Transformation*, foreword by Robert W. MacIver. Boston: Beacon Press, paperback, published by arrangement with Rinehart and Company, copyright 1944 by Karl Polanyi.

———. "Ports of Trade in Early Societies," *Journal of Economic History*, XXIII (March 1963), 30–45.

Pollis, Adamantia. "Social Change and Nationhood," *Massachusetts Review*, IX (Winter 1968), 123–32.

———. "The Southern European Semiperiphery and the European Community," in Pinkele and Pollis, eds., *The Contemporary Mediterranean World*, pp. 202–20.

Polyzos, N. J. *Essai sur l'émigration grecque*. Paris: Librairie Recueil Sirey, 1946.

Popov, Nil. *Srbija i Rusija od Kočine Krajine do Andrejevske Skupštine*, 2 vols. Belgrade: Državna Štamparija, 1870.

Popović, Bogdan. *Ogledi iz književnosti i umetnosti*. Belgrade: S. B. Cvijanović, 1914.

Popović, Dušan J. *O Cincarima: Prilozi pitanju postanka našeg gradjanskog društva*, 2nd rev. and enlarged ed. Belgrade: Drag. Gregorić, 1937.

———. *O Hajducima*, 2 vols. Belgrade: Narodna Štamparija, 1930–1931.

———. *Srbija i Beograd od Požarevačkog do Beogradskog mira (1718–1739)*. Belgrade: Srpska Književna Zadruga, 1950.

Popović, Sreten L. *Putovanje po novoj Srbiji (1878 i 1880)*. Belgrade: Srpska Književna Zadruga, 1950.

Popović, Vasilj. "Trgovina i promet u Napoleonovo doba," in Srpska Kraljevska Akademija, *Spomenik*, LXIX, drugi razred, knj. 54. Belgrade, 1929. Pp. 83–91.

Popovitch (Popović), Vladislav. "Sur la chronologie de la civilisation proto-historique dans la péninsule des Balkans," *Revue archéologique*, XLIX (1957), 129–46, and L (1957), 1–24.

Porphyrogenitus, Constantine. *See* Constantine Porphyrogenitus.

Portal, Roger. *Les Slaves: Peuples et nations*. Paris: Armand Colin, 1965.

Post, John Dexter. *Food Shortage, Climatic Variability, and Epidemic Disease in Preindustrial Europe: The Mortality Peak in 1743*. Ithaca, N.Y.: Cornell University Press, [1985].

———. *The Last Great Subsistence Crisis in the Western World*. Baltimore and London: Johns Hopkins University Press, [1977].

———. "Meteorological Historiography," review article, *Journal of Interdisciplinary History*, III (Spring 1973), 721–32.

————. "A Study in Meteorological and Trade Cycle History: The Economic Crisis Following the Napoleonic Wars," *Journal of Economic History*, XXXIV, 2 (June 1974), 315–49.

Pounds, Norman J. G., ed., *Geographical Essays on Eastern Europe*, Indiana University Publications, Russian and East European Series, Vol. XXIV. Bloomington, published by Indiana University through Mouton and Co., The Hague, 1961.

————. *Hearth and Home: A History of Material Culture*. Bloomington and Indianapolis: Indiana University Press, [1989].

Pouqueville, François-Charles-Hugues-Laurent. *Voyage dans la Grèce*, 5 vols. Paris: Firmin Didot, 1820–21; *Voyage de la Grèce*, 2nd ed., 6 vols. Paris: Firmin Didot père et fils, 1826.

————. *Voyage en Morée, à Constantinople, en Albanie, et dans plusieurs autres parties de l'Empire othoman, pendant les années 1798, 1799, 1800 et 1801*, 3 vols. Paris: Cabon et Cie, 1805.

Preziosi, Donald. "Introduction: The Mechanisms of Urban Meaning," in Bierman, Abou-el-Haj, and Preziosi,*The Ottoman City*, pp. 3–11.

Pribić, Nikola R. "Dositej Obradović (1742–1811): Enlightenment, Rationalism, and the Serbian National Tongue," *Canadian Review of Studies in Nationalism, Revue canadienne des études sur le nationalisme*, X, 1 (Spring/printemps 1983), 41–49.

Protić, Ljubiša. "Neki običaji oko kupovine, prodaje i trampe," *Glasnik Etnografskog Muzeja u Beogradu (Bulletin du Musée Ethnographique de Beograd)*, XI (Belgrade, 1936), 17–30, and XII (1937), 40–60.

————. *Razvitak industrije i promet dobara u Srbiji za vreme prve vlade Kneza Miloša*. Belgrade: Rad, 1953.

Pye, Lucian W. "Political Culture and Political Development," in Pye and Verba, eds. *Political Culture*, pp. 3–26.

Pye, Lucian W., and Verba, Sidney, eds. *Political Culture and Political Development*. Princeton, N.J.: Princeton University Press, 1965.

"Quiet Voices from the Balkans," *New Yorker*, March 15, 1993, pp. 4, 6.

Rabbe, Alphonse. "Introduction: Esquisse des révolutions de la Grèce depuis l'établissement de la domination romaine jusqu'à la chute du Bas-Empire; et Tableau de l'état de la nation grecque sous les Turcs," in Raybaud, *Mémoires sur la Grèce*, I, 1–184.

Rabelais, François. *The Histories of Gargantua and Pantagruel*, translated and with an introduction by J. M. Cohen. Baltimore, Md.: Penguin Books, this translation first published in 1955.

Rački, Franjo. "Nutarnje stanje Hrvatske prije XII stoljeća," Jugoslavenska Akademija znanosti i umjetnosti, *Rad*, LXX (1884), 153–90; LXXIX (1886), 135–84; IXC (1888), 125–80; IC (1890), 73–128; CV (1891), 202–38; CXV (1893), 37–67; CXVI (1893), 175–229.

Radić, Stjepan. *Moderna kolonizacija i Slaveni*, Poučna Knjižnica "Matice Hrvatske," Vol. XXX. Zagreb: Matica Hrvatska, 1904.

Raditsa, Bogdan. Review of O. Dominik Mandić, *Bogomilska crkva bosanskih Krstjana* (Chicago: Croatian Historical Institute, 1962), in *Journal of Central European Affairs*, XXIII (1963), 86–88.

Radojčić, Nikola. "Dositejevo pismo o uredjenju i prosvećenju Srbije," *Letopis Matice Srpske*, CCC (1921), 8–33.

Radojković, Borislav M. *O Sokalnicima: Rasprava iz socijalnih odnosa u staroj srpskoj državi srednjeg veka*. Belgrade: Srpska Kraljevska Akademija, 1937.

Radonić, Jovan. *Fontes rerum Slavorum meridionalium*, first series, *Acta et diplomata ragusina*, Vol. II, fasc. 1. Belgrade, 1935.

Radovanović, V. "Novo Brdo," in *Narodna Enciklopedija srpsko-hrvatsko-slovenačka*, edited by St. Stanojević. Zagreb, 1928, III, 170–73.

Raeff, Marc. *Understanding Imperial Russia: State and Society in the Old Regime*, translated from the French by Arthur Goldhammer, foreword by John Keep. New York: Columbia University Press, 1984.

Rafo, Ferri. "Prilog poznavanju ilirske mitologije," *Anali Historijskog Instituta u Dubrovniku*, II (1953), 419–29.

Raicevich, J. [Étienne-Ignace, Stephen Ignatius]. *Osservazioni storiche naturali, e politiche intorno: La Valachie, e Moldavia.* Napoli: G. Raimondi, 1788.

Ramet, Pedro. "Kosovo and the Limits of Yugoslav Socialist Patriotism," *Canadian Review of Studies in Nationalism, Revue canadienne des études sur le nationalisme*, XVI, 1–2 (1989), 227–50.

————. "From Strossmayer to Stepinac: Croatian National Ideology and Catholicism," *Canadian Review of Studies in Nationalism, Revue canadienne des études sur le nationalisme*, XII (1985), 123–39.

Ramet, Sabrina P. (earlier known as Pedro). "The Breakup of Yugoslavia," *Global Affairs*, VI, 2 (Spring 1991), 93–110.

————. *Nationalism and Federalism in Yugoslavia, 1962–1991*, 2nd ed. Bloomington and Indianapolis: Indiana University Press, [1992].

Ranis, Gustav. *See* Fei, John C. H.

Ranke, Leopold. *The History of Servia, and the Servian Revolution, with a Sketch of the Insurrection in Bosnia*, translated from the German by Mrs. Alexander Kerr. London: Henry G. Bohn, 1853.

Raybaud, Maxime. *Mémoires sur la Grèce pour servir à l'histoire de la guerre de l'Indépendance*, 2 vols. Paris: Tournachon-Molin, 1824–25.

Redfield, Robert. "The Little Community," in *The Little Community and Peasant Society and Culture*. Chicago and London: Phoenix Books—University of Chicago Press, [1960]. Pp. 1–182.

Reinert, Stephen W. "From Niš to Kosovo Polje: Reflections on Murād I's Final Years," in Zachariadou, ed., *The Ottoman Emirate*, pp. 169–211.

Reljković, Matija Antun. *Satir iliti divji čovik*, edited by David Bogdanović. Zagreb: Tisak Kralj. Zemaljske Tiskare, 1909.

Renfrew, Colin. *Archaeology and Language: The Puzzle of Indo-European Origins.* New York: Cambridge University Press, 1988; first published by Jonathan Cape, 1987.

Renouard, Yves. "Information et transmission des nouvelles," in Charles Samaran, ed., *L'Histoire et ses méthodes*, "Encyclopédie de la Pléiade," XI. Paris: Gallimard, 1961. Pp. 95–142.

Rey, Abel. *La Jeunesse de la science grecque.* Paris: La Renaissance du Livre, 1933.

Rey, Violette. *La Roumanie: Essai d'analyse régionale.* Paris: Société d'Enseignement Supérieur, [1975].

Ricardo, David. *The Principles of Political Economy and Taxation.* London: J. M. Dent and Sons; New York: E. P. Dutton and Co., 1911.

Richta, Radovan, and a Research Team. *Civilization at the Crossroads: Social and Human Implications of the Scientific and Technological Revolution*, 3rd expanded edition, translated by Marian Šlingová. White Plains, N.Y.: International Arts and Sciences Press, 1969.

Riquet, Michel. "Christianisme et population," *Population: Revue de l'Institut National d'Études Démographiques*, IV (1949), 615–30.

Roberts, Henry L. *Rumania: Political Problems of an Agrarian State.* New Haven: Yale University Press; London: Oxford University Press, 1951; reprinted 1969 by Archon Books.

Rodden, Robert J. "An Early Neolithic Village in Greece," *Scientific American*, CCXII (April 1965), 83–92.

Rodocanachi, E. *Bonaparte et les îles Ioniennes: Un Épisode des conquêtes de la République et du Premier Empire (1797–1816).* Paris, 1899.

————. "Les Îles Ioniennes pendant l'occupation française (1797–1799)," *La Nouvelle revue*, CXII (May–June 1898), 438–53, 595–610, and CXIII (1899), 76–89, 315–29.

Rogel, Carole. "Edward Kardelj's Nationality Theory and Yugoslav Socialism," *Canadian Review of Studies in Nationalism, Revue canadienne des études sur le nationalisme*, XII, 2 (1985), 343–57.

Roglić, Josip. "The Geographical Setting of Medieval Dubrovnik," in Pounds, ed., *Geographical Essays on Eastern Europe*, pp. 141–59.

Romaios, C. A. *Cultes populaires de la Thrace: Les Anasténaria, La Cérémonie du Lundi Pur*, translated from the Greek by I. Tissaméno. Athens: Institut Français d'Athènes, 1949.

Rosecrance, Richard. *The Rise of the Trading State: Commerce and Conquest in the Modern World*. New York: Basic Books, [1986].

Rothenberg, Gunther Erich. *The Austrian Military Border in Croatia, 1522–1747*. Urbana: University of Illinois Press, 1960.

————. "Christian Insurrections in Turkish Dalmatia, 1580–96," *Slavonic and East European Review*, XL, No. 94 (December 1961), pp. 136–47.

Rothschild, Joseph. *The Communist Party of Bulgaria: Origins and Development, 1883–1936*. New York: Columbia University Press, 1959.

Rotstein, Abraham. "Karl Polanyi's Concept of Non-Market Trade," *Journal of Economic History*, XXX (1970), 117–26.

Roucek, Joseph S. *The Politics of the Balkans*. New York and London: McGraw-Hill, 1939.

Royal Institute of International Affairs (specially prepared for, and with the assistance of, the Information Department). *The Balkan States*, Vol. I: *Economic: A Review of the Economic and Financial Development of Albania, Bulgaria, Greece, Roumania, and Yugoslavia since 1919*. Oxford: University Press; London: Humphrey Milford, 1936.

Rusinow, Dennison. *The Yugoslav Experiment, 1948–1974*. Berkeley and Los Angeles: University of California Press, published for the Royal Institute of International Affairs, London, 1977.

Russell, J. C. "Late Ancient and Medieval Population," *Transactions of the American Philosophical Society*, New Series, Vol. XLVIII, Pt. 3 (June 1958).

————. "The Medieval Balkan and Asia Minor Population," *Journal of the Economic and Social History of the Orient*, III (October 1960), 265–74.

Rustow, Dunkwart A. "Turkey: The Modernity of Tradition," in Pye and Verba, eds., *Political Culture*, pp. 171–98.

Rutkowski, Jan. "Medieval Agrarian Society in Its Prime," in *The Cambridge Economic History of Europe from the Decline of the Roman Empire*, Vol. I: *The Agrarian Life of the Middle Ages*, edited by J. H. Clapham and Eileen Power. Cambridge: University Press, 1941. Pp. 398–417.

Rycaut, Sir Paul. *The History of the Turkish Empire from the Year 1623 to the Year 1677*. London: John Starkey, 1680.

————. *The History of the Turkish Empire, from the Year 1623 to the Year 1677, Containing the Reigns of the Three Last Emperors, viz. Sultan Morat or Amurat IV., Sultan Ibrahim, and Sultan Mahomet IV, His Son, the Thirteenth Emperor, Now Reigning*. London: printed by J. D. for Tho. Basset, R. Clavell, J. Robinson, and A. Churchill, 1687.

Sadat, Deena R. "Rumeli Ayanlari: The Eighteenth Cenury," *Journal of Modern History*, XLIV, 3 (September 1972), 346–63.

Sadnik, L., and Aitzenmüller, R. *Handwörterbuch zu den altkirchenslavischen Texten*. 's-Gravenhage: Mouton, 1955.

Sahlins, Marshall D. *Tribesmen*. Englewood Cliffs, N.J.: Prentice-Hall, 1968.

Sahlins, Peter. *Boundaries: The Making of France and Spain in the Pyrenees*. Berkeley, Los Angeles, Oxford: University of California Press, [1989].

Ste.-Croix, C. E. M. de. "Greek and Roman Accounting," in A. C. Littleton, ed., *Studies in the History of Accounting*. Homewood, Ill.: Richard D. Irwin, 1956. Pp. 14–74.

Sakazov, Ivan. *Bulgarische Wirtschaftsgeschichte*. Berlin and Leipzig: Walter de Gruyter, 1929.

Šamić, Midhat. "Un Consul français en Bosnie et la 'Chronique de Travnik' de M. Ivo Andrić," *Annales de l'Institut Français de Zagreb*, 2e série, No. 1 (1952), pp. 69–80.

———. *Les Voyageurs français en Bosnie à la fin du XVIIIe siècle et au début du XIXe et le pays tel qu'ils l'ont vu*, "Études de littérature étrangère et comparée," 32. Paris: Didier, [1960].

Sanders, Irwin T. *Balkan Village* (Dragalevtsy, near Sofia). Lexington, Ky.: University of Kentucky Press, 1949.

———. *Rainbow in the Rock: The People of Rural Greece*. Cambridge, Mass.: Harvard University Press, 1962.

Sapir, Edward. "Culture, Genuine and Spurious," in David B. Mandelbaum, ed., *Culture, Language, and Personality: Selected Essays*. Berkeley and Los Angeles: University of California Press, 1957. Pp. 78–119.

Sarç, Ömer Celal. "Ottoman Industrial Policy, 1840–1914," in Issawi, ed., *History of the Middle East*, pp. 46–59.

Sarkisyanz, Emanuel. *Geschichte der orientalischen Völker Russlands bis 1917*. München: R. Oldenbourg, 1961.

Schieder, Theodor. "Typologie und Erscheinungsformen des Nationalstaats in Europa," *Historische Zeitschrift*, CCII (1966), 58–81.

Schischmanoff, Lydia, trans. *Légendes religieuses bulgares*. Paris: Ernest Leroux, 1896.

Schlemmer, Oskar. "Warum triadisch?" in Kunstgewerbemuseum, Zürich, *Oskar Schlemmer und die abstrakte Bühne*, catalogue of an exhibit, June 8 to August 23, 1961.

Schlote, Werner. *British Overseas Trade from 1700 to the 1930s*. Oxford: Basil Blackwell, 1952.

Schmidt, Charles. "Napoléon et les routes balkaniques," *La Revue de Paris*, XIX (November 1952), 335–52.

Schmieder, Oskar. *Die alte Welt: Anatolien und die Mittelmeerländer Europas*, 2 vols. Kiel: Verlag Schmidt & Klaunig, 1969.

Schmitt, Carl. *The Concept of the Political*, translation, introduction, and notes by George Schwab, with comments on Schmitt's essay by Leo Strauss. New Brunswick, N.J.: Rutgers University Press, [1976]. Published originally as "Der Begriff des Politischen," in *Archiv für Sozialwissenschaft und Sozialpolitik*, LVIII, 1 (1927), 1–33, revised under the same title and published in 1932 by Duncker & Humblot in Munich. The English translation is based on the 1932 editiion.

———. "The Plight of European Jurisprudence," translated by G. L. Ulmen, *Telos*, No. 83 (Spring 1990), pp. 35–70.

Schmitt, Jean-Claude. "L'Histoire des marginaux," in Jacques Le Goff, Roger Chartier, and Jacques Revel, eds., *La Nouvelle Histoire*. Paris: CEPL, Les Encyclopédies du savoir moderne, 1978. Pp. 344–69.

Schmitter, Philippe C. "Reflections on Mihail Manoilescu and the Political Consequences of Delayed-Dependent Development on the Periphery of Western Europe," in Jowitt, ed., *Social Change in Romania*, pp. 117–39.

Schneeweis, Edmund. *Serbokroatische Volkskunde*, Vol. I: *Volksglaube und Volksbrauch*. Berlin: Walter de Gruyter, 1961.

Schneider, Jane. "Of Vigilance and Virgins: Honor, Shame, and Access to Resources in Mediterranean Societies," *Ethnology*, X, 1 (January 1971), 1–24.

Schneider, Jürgen, et al., eds., *Wirtschaftskräfte und Wirtschaftswege: Festschrift für Hermann Kellenbenz*, 5 vols. Stuttgart: Klett-Cotta, 1978–1979. Vols. I and II. *See also* the review by Stoianovich, Traian.

Schöpflin, George. "The Ideology of Croatian Nationalism," *Survey: A Journal of East and West Studies*, XIX, 1/86 (Winter 1973), 123–46.

———. "The Political Traditions of Eastern Europe," *Daedalus*, CXIX, 1 (Winter 1990), 55–90.

Schultze Jena, Leonhard. *Makedonien: Landschafts- und Kulturbilder*. Jena: Verlag Gustav Fischer, 1927.

Schumpeter, Joseph Alois. "The Crisis of the Tax State," *International Economic Papers*, No. 4. London, New York: Macmillan, 1954. Pp. 5–38. Translated by W. F. Stolper and R. A. Musgrave from Joseph A. Schumpeter, *Die Krise des Steuerstaats*. Graz and Leipzig: Leuschner & Lubensky, 1918.

Schwab, George. "Enemy or Foe: A Conflict of Modern Politics," *Telos*, No. 72 (Summer 1987), pp. 194–201.

Schwartz, Theodore. "The Size and Shape of a Culture," in Barth, ed., *Scale and Social Organization*, pp. 215–52.

Sciolino, Elaine. "As U.S. Sought a Bosnian Policy, the French Offered a Good Idea," *New York Times*, February 14, 1994.

———. "Who Can Make Peace in Bosnia? The U.S. Says France. No, Only the Bosnians, Says the U.S.," *New York Times*, January 28, 1994.

Seers, Dudley; Schaffer, Bernard; and Kiljunen, Marja Liisa, eds. *Underdeveloped Europe: Studies in Core-Periphery Relations*. Atlantic Highlands, N.J.: Humanities Press, copyright 1979 by the Institute of Development Studies at the University of Sussex.

Segalen, Martine. "Breton Identity: Local Types and Regional Stereotypes," papers presented at the Rutgers Center for Historical Analysis, 1989–1991 Project: The Historical Construction of Identities, New Brunswick, N.J., February 13, 1990.

Seligman, Miles. "Those Who Own the Papers Also Own this Land," *Conjecture* (New Brunswick, N.J.) (April–May 1992), pp. 17–21.

Semple, Ellen Churchill. *The Geography of the Mediterranean Region: Its Relation to Ancient History*. New York: Henry Holt, [1931].

Serbia, Ministarstvo Finansije (Narodne Privrede). *Državopis Srbije (Statistique de la Serbie)*, Vols. IX–XVI. Belgrade, 1879–89.

———. Ministarstvo Narodne Privrede (Statističko odeljenje). *Prethodni resultati popisa stanovništva u Kraljevini Srbiji 31. decembra 1890 godine*, preliminary results of the Serbian census of December 31, 1890. Belgrade, 1891.

———. *Prethodni resultati Stanovništva u Kaljevini Srbiji 31. decembra 1895 godine*, preliminary results of the 1895 census. Belgrade, 1896.

———. Narodna Skupština (National Assembly). *Stenografske beleške o sednicama Narodne Skupštine držane u Beogradu 1874/5 godine*, 2 vols. Belgrade: Državna Štamparija, 1875.

Sevin, François (abbé). *Lettres sur Constantinople*. Paris: chez Obré, an X [1802].

Shonfield, Andrew. *Modern Capitalism: The Changing Balance of Public and Private Power*. New York and London: Oxford University Press, issued under the auspices of the Royal Institute of International Affairs, 1965.

Simons, Marlise. "For Black Sea, Slow Choking by Pollutants," *New York Times*, November 24, 1991.

———. "West Urges Bulgarians to Shut Reactors," *New York Times*, July 10, 1991.

Singleton, Fred. "Objectives and Methods of Economic Policies in Yugoslavia, 1970–1980," in Nove, Höhmann, and Seidenstecher, eds., *The East European Economies*, pp. 280–314.

Sion, Jules. "Quelques problèmes de transports dans l'Antiquité: Le Point de vue d'un géographe méditerranéen," *Annales d'histoire économique et sociale*, VII (1935), 628–33.

————. *See also* Vidal de la Blache, Paul.

Sivignon, M. "The Demographic and Economic Evolution of Thessaly (1881–1940)," in Carter, ed., *An Historical Geography of the Balkans*, pp. 379–407.

Sjöberg, Örjan, and Wyzan, Michael L. "The Balkan States: Struggling along the Road to the Market from Europe's Periphery," in Sjöberg and Wyzan, eds., *Economic Change in the Balkan States*, pp. 1–15.

————, eds. *Economic Change in the Balkan States: Albania, Bulgaria, Romania and Yugoslavia.* New York: St. Martin's Press, [1991].

Sjoestedt, Marie-Louise. *Dieux et héros des Celtes.* Paris: Leroux, 1940.

Skendi, Stavro, with the assistance of Mehmet Beqiraj, George Bossy, Fred Pisky, and Qemal Vokopola. *Albania.* New York: published for the Mid-European Studies Center of the Free Europe Committee by Frederick A Praeger, [1956].

————. *The Albanian National Awakening, 1878–1912.* Princeton, N.J.: Princeton University Press, 1967.

————. *Albanian and South Slavic Oral Epic Poetry.* Philadelphia: American Folklore Society, 1954.

————. "Religion in Albania during the Ottoman Rule," *Südost-Forschungen*, XV (1956), 311–27.

Skerlić, Jovan. *Istorija nove srpske književnosti*, 3rd ed. Belgrade: Rad, 1953.

Skerlić, Jovan; Dragutinović, Milutin K.; and Ivković, Miloš, eds., *Dela Dositeja Obradovića*, 5th ed. Belgrade: Državna Štamparija Kr. Srbije, 1911.

Sklair, Leslie. *Sociology of the Global System.* Baltimore: Johns Hopkins University Press, 1991.

Škrivanić, Gavro A. "Mreža puteva prema Svetostefanskoj (1313–1318), Gračaničkoj (1321), Dečanskoj (1330) i Svetoarhandjelovskoj (1348–1352) povelji," *Istoriski Časpopis*, V (1956), 387–97, with a summary in English.

————. *Oružje u srednjovekovnoj Srbiji, Bosni i Dubrovniku.* Belgrade: Srpska Akademija Nauka, 1957, with a summary in English: "Armour and Weapons in Medieval Serbia, Bosnia, and Dubrovnik," pp. 201–5.

Slijepčević, Pero. "Jovan Dučić," in *Zbornik u čast Bogdana Popovića.* Belgrade: Geca Kon, 1929. Pp. 148–57.

Smith, Alan. "Is There a Romanian Economic Crisis? The Problems of Energy and Indebtedness," in Jan Drewnowski, ed., *Crisis in the East European Economy: The Spread of the Polish Disease.* London and Canberra: Croom Helm; New York: St. Martin's Press, [1982]. Pp. 103–30.

Smith, Anthony D. *The Ethnic Origins of Nations.* Oxford, New York: Basil Blackwell, [1986].

————. "Nationalism and the Historians," *International Journal of Comparative Sociology*, XXXIII, 1–2 (1992), 58–80.

————. *Theories of Nationalism*, 2nd ed. [London]: Gerald Duckworth, [1983].

Smith, Valene L., ed. *Hosts and Guests: The Anthropology of Tourism*, 2nd ed. Philadelphia: University of Pennsylvania Press, [1989].

Smothers, Frank; McNeill, William; and McNeill, Elizabeth Darbishire. *Report on the Greeks: Findings of a Twentieth Century Fund Team Which Surveyed Conditions in Greece in 1947.* New York: Twentieth Century Fund, 1948.

Šobajić, Petar. "Povodom dvaju najnovijih priloga proučavanju plemena u staroj Hercegovini," *Glasnik Etnografskog Društva*, I, 1–2 (Belgrade, 1952), 257–78.

Soetbeer, Adolf. "Edelmetall-Produktion und Werthverhältniss zwischen Gold und Silber seit der Entdeckung Amerika's bis zur Gegenwart, *Perermann's Mittheilungen*, Ergänzungsheft 57 (Gotha: Justus Perthes, 1879).

Solmsen, Friedrich. *Hesiod and Aeschylus.* Ithaca, N.Y.: Cornell University Press, 1949.

Soloviev, Alexander (Aleksandar Solovjev). "Bogomilentum und Bogomilengräber in den südslawischen Ländern," in Wilhelm Gülich, *Völker und Kulturen Südosteuropas*. München: Südosteuropa—Gesellschaft, 1959. Pp. 173–98.

————. "Nestanak bogomilstva i islamizacija Bosne," *Godišnjak Istoriskog Društva Bosne i Hercegovine*, I (Sarajevo, 1949), 42–79.

————. "Le Témoignage de Paul Ricaut sur les restes du bogomilisme en Bosnie," *Byzantion*, XXIII (1953), 73–86.

Sombart, Werner. *Le Bourgeois: Contribution à l'histoire morale et intellectuelle de l'homme économique moderne*, translated from the German by S. Jankélévitch. Paris: Payot, 1926.

Soper, Edmund Davison. *The Religions of Mankind*, 3rd ed. rev. New York: Abingdon Press, 1921, 1938, 1951.

Soutsos, Prince Nikolaos. *Mémoires du Prince Nicolas Soutzo (Grand-Logothète de Moldavie), 1798–1871*, publiés par Panaïoti Rizos. Vienne: Gerold & Cie, 1899.

Sozan, Michael. *The History of Hungarian Ethnography*. [Washington, D.C.]: University Press of America, [1979].

Spandonidis (Spandonides), Petros S. "Le Clefte," *L'Hellénisme contemporain*, 2nd ser., VIII (1954), 3–17.

Spasić, Milovan. "Neki podaci o osnovnim školama u Srbiji od 1845 do 1861 godine," *Glasnik Srpskog Učenog Društva*, LXXIII (1892), 187–217.

Spector, Sherman David. *Rumania at the Paris Peace Conference: A Study of the Diplomacy of Ioan I. C. Brătianu*. New York: Bookman Associates, 1962.

Spencer, Edmund. *Travels in European Turkey in 1850, through Bosnia, Servia, Bulgaria, Macedonia, Thrace, Albania, and Epirus; with Visit to Greece and The Ionian Isles*, 2 vols. London: Colburn and Co., 1851.

Spiridonakis, B. G. *Essays on the Historical Geography of the Greek World in the Balkans during the Tourkokratia*. Thessaloniki: Institute for Balkan Studies, 1977.

Spitzer, Alan B. *The French Generation of 1820*. Princeton, N.J.: Princeton University Press, [1987].

Spulber, Nicolas. "Changes in the Economic Structures of the Balkans, 1860–1960," in Jelavich and Jelavich, *The Balkans in Transition*, pp. 346–75.

————. "The Role of the State in Economic Growth in Eastern Europe since 1860," in Hugh G. J. Aitken, ed., *The State and Economic Growth: Papers of a Conference Held on October 11–13, 1956, under the Auspices of the Committee on Economic Growth*. New York: Social Science Research Council, 1959. Pp. 255–86.

Stadtmüller, Georg. *Geschichte Südosteuropas*. Munich: R. Oldenbourg, 1950.

Stahl, Henri H., ed. *Nerej, un village d'une région archaïque*, 3 vols. Bucarest: Institut de Sciences Sociales de Roumanie, [1939].

————. *Traditional Romanian Village Communities: The Transition from the Communal to the Capitalist Mode of Production in the Danube Region*, translated by Daniel Chirot and Holley Coulter Chirot. Cambridge: Cambridge University Press; Paris: Éditions de la Maison des Sciences de l'Homme, [1980]. Originally published in French in 1969 by Éditions de l'Académie de la République Socialiste de Roumanie and Éditions du Centre National de la Recherche Scientifique.

Stahl, Paul Henri, ed. *Ethnologie de l'Europe du Sud-est: Une anthologie*. Paris, La Haye: Mouton, [1974].

————. *Household, Village, and Village Confederation in Southeastern Europe*, translated by Linda Scales Alcott. New York: East European Monographs, distributed by Columbia University Press, 1986.

Štampar, Slobodan. "Borba jedrenjača s parobrodima u hrvatskom Primorju," *Historijski Zbornik*, II (1949), 47–76.

Stanojević, Milenko. "Iz narodnog života na Timoku: Verovanja i praznoverice," *Glasnik*

Etnografskog Muzeja u Beogradu (Bulletin du Musée Ethnographique de Beograd), VIII (Belgrade, 1933), pp. 59–71, with a résumé in French, "Croyances et superstitions dans le Timok."

Starr, Chester G. *The Origins of Greek Civilization, 1100–650 B.C.* New York: Alfred A. Knopf, 1961.

Stavrianos, Leften S. "Antecedents to the Balkan Revolutions of the Nineteenth Century," *Journal of Modern History*, XXIX, 4 (December 1957), 335–48.

————. *Balkan Federation: A History of the Movement toward Balkan Unity in Modern Times*, Smith College Studies in History, XXVII, Nos. 1–4, October 1941–July 1942. Menasha, Wis.: printed by George Banta Publishing Co., 1944.

————. *The Balkans since 1453*. New York: Holt, Rinehart, and Winston, 1958.

————, ed. *The Epic of Modern Man: A Collection of Readings*. Englewood Cliffs, N.J.: Prentice-Hall, 1966.

————. "The Influence of the West on the Balkans," in Jelavich and Jelavich, eds., *The Balkans in Transition*, pp. 184–226.

————. *Lifelines from Our Past: A New World History*. Armonk, N.Y.: M. E. Sharpe, [1992], paperback edition published by arrangement with Pantheon Books.

Stead, Alfred, ed. *Servia by the Servians*. London: William Heinemann, 1909.

Stearns, Peter N., ed. *Encyclopedia of Social History*. New York: Garland Publishing Company, 1994.

Steed, Henry Wickham. *The Hapsburg Monarchy*, 4th ed. London: Constable and Company, 1919.

Ştefănescu, Şt.; Mioc, D.; and Chircă, H. "L'Évolution de la rente féodale en travail en Valachie et en Moldavie aux XIVe-XVIIIe siècles," *Revue roumaine d'histoire*, I, 1 (1962), 39–60.

Stevović, I. "U straha su velike oči," Srpska Akademija Nauka, *Naš jezik*, N.S., knj. ii, sv. 1–2 (Belgrade, 1950), pp. 50–52.

Stipetić, Vladimir. "Agriculture in Yugoslavia: Problems and Prospects," in Lang, Macesich, and Vojnić, eds., *Essays on the Political Economy of Yugoslavia*, pp. 327–48.

Stoianovich, Traian. "Arithmetic and Ethnography of Balkan Foods," in John S. Langdon, Stephen W. Reinert, Jelisaveta Stanojevich Allan, and Christos P. Ioannides, eds., *Studies in Honor of Speros Vryonis, Jr.*, 2 vols. New Rochelle, N.Y.: Aristide D. Caratzas, 1993–. Vol. II, edited by Stanojevich Allan, Ioannides, Langdon, and Reinert, forthcoming.

————. "Before and After 1789: A Cantonal Markets Economy," *History of European Ideas*, XV, No. 1–3 (1992), pp. 171–76.

————. *Between East and West: The Balkan and Mediterranean Worlds*, 4 vols. New Rochelle, N.Y.: Aristide D. Caratzas, 1992–1994. Vols. III and IV, forthcoming.

————. "Cities, Capital Accumulation, and the Ottoman Command Economy, 1500–1800," in Charles Tilly and Wim P. Blockmans, eds., *Cities and the Rise of States in Europe, A.D. 1000–1800*. Boulder, Colo.: Westview Press, forthcoming.

————. "The Conquering Balkan Orthodox Merchant," *Journal of Economic History*, XX (June 1960), 234–313.

————. "L'Espace maritime segmentaire de l'Empire ottoman," in Centre de Recherches Néohelléniques, Fondation Nationale de la Recherche Scientifique, *Actes du IIe Colloque international d'histoire, Athènes, 18–25 septembre 1983*, pp. 203–18.

————. "Europe and the Balkans: An Asymmetry of Economies, 1500–1900," paper presented at a conference on "The European Community and the Balkans," Corfu, July 2–5, 1993, organized by the Hellenic Centre for European Studies (EKEM) and the Hellenic Foundation for Defence and Foreign Policy (ELIAMEP) with the support of the Commission of the European Community.

_____. "Factors in the Decline of Ottoman Society in the Balkans," *Slavic Review*, XXI (December 1962), 623–25.

_____. *French Historical Method: The "Annales" Paradigm*. Ithaca, N.Y.: Cornell University Press, 1976.

_____. "Land Tenure and Related Sectors of the Balkan Economy, 1600–1800," *Journal of Economic History*, XIII, 4 (Fall 1953), 398–411.

_____. "Longue durée," in Stearns, ed., *Encyclopedia of Social History*, pp. 426–28.

_____. "Le Maïs dans les Balkans," *Annales: Économies, Sociétés, Civilisations*, XXI (1966), 1026–40.

_____. "Material Foundations of Preindustrial Civilization in the Balkans," *Journal of Social History*, IV, 3 (Spring 1971), 205–62.

_____. "The Pattern of Serbian Intellectual Evolution, 1830–1880," *Comparative Studies in Society and History*, I, 3 (March 1959), 242–72.

_____. "Raguse—société sans imprimerie," in Association Internationale d'Études du Sud-est Européen, ed., *Structure sociale et développement culturel des villes sud-est européennes et adriatiques aux XVIIe et XVIIIe siècles*. Bucarest: AIESEE, 1975. Pp. 43–73.

_____. "Routes as Sources of Information: The Via Egnatia under Ottoman Rule as a Route Type," Institute for Mediterranean Studies, Foundation for Research and Technology—Hellas, Rethymnon (Crete), Greece. Symposium on "The Via Egnatia under Ottoman Rule," January 9–11, 1994.

_____. "Russian Domination in the Balkans," in Taras Hunczak, ed., *Russian Imperialism from Ivan the Great to the Revolution*. New Brunswick, N.J.: Rutgers University Press, [1974]. Pp. 198–238, 352–62.

_____. "The Segmentary State and *La Grande Nation*," in Eugene D. Genovese and Leonard Hochberg, eds., *Geographic Perspectives in History*. Oxford, Eng.: Basil Blackwell, 1989. Pp. 256–80.

_____. "The Social Foundations of Balkan Politics, 1750–1941," in Jelavich and Jelavich, *The Balkans in Transition*, pp. 297–345.

_____. "Social History: Perspective of the *Annales* Paradigm," *Review: A Journal of the Fernand Braudel Center for the Study of Economies, Historical Systems, and Civilizations*, I, 3–4 (Spring 1978), 19–48.

_____. *A Study in Balkan Civilization*. New York: Alfred A. Knopf, 1967.

_____. *See also* Koledarov, P.; Schneider, Jürgen; Vucinich, Wayne S.

Stojanović, Ljubomir. *Stare srpske povelje i pisma*, Vol. I: *Dubrovnik i susedi njegovi*, Pt. 2. Belgrade, 1934.

_____. *Stari srpski zapisi i natpisi*, 3 vols. Belgrade: Srpska Kraljevska Akademija, 1902–05.

Stojančević, Vladimir. A critical review of Serbia's office of statistics (Zavod za statistiku) on the demography of Serbia, 1718–1813 (*Prilozi statističkom proučavanju Prvog srpskog ustanka NR Srbije*), in *Istoriski Glasnik*, No. 2 (1956), pp. 98–100.

Strabo. *The Geography of Strabo*, literally translated, with notes, the first six books by H. C. Hamilton and the remainder by W. Falconer, 3 vols. London: G. Bell and Sons, 1912 for Vol. I, 1903 for Vol. II, and 1906 for Vol. III.

Stranjaković, Dragoslav. "Kako je postalo Garašaninovo 'Načertanije,'" Srpska Akademija Nauka, *Spomenik*, XCI, drugi razred, knj. 70 (Belgrade, 1939), pp. 3–12 (alternately numbered, 65–74).

Strauss, William, and Howe, Neil. *Generations: The History of America's Future, 1584 to 2069*. New York: William Morrow and Company, 1991.

Stripling, George William Frederick. *The Ottoman Turks and the Arabs, 1511–1574*, Illinois Studies in the Social Sciences, XXVI, 4. Urbana: University of Illinois Press, 1942.

Stulli, Joakim. *Rjecsoslòxje slovinsko-italiansko-latinsko*, 2 vols. Dubrovnik: A. Martekini, 1805.

Subotić, Dragutin. "The Serbia of Prince Miloš," *Slavonic Review*, III (June 1924), 156–65.

Sučević, Branko P. "Razvitak 'vlaških prava' u Varaždinskom Generalatu," *Historijski Zbornik*, VI (Zagreb, 1953), 33–70.

Šufflay, Milan. *Srbi i Arbanasi (njihova simbioza u srednjem vijeku)*. Belgrade, 1925.

Sugar, Peter F., ed. *Ethnic Diversity and Conflict in Eastern Europe*. Santa Barbara, Calif.: ABC-Clio; Oxford: Clio Press, [1980].

———. *Industrialization of Bosnia-Hercegovina, 1878–1918*. Seattle: University of Washington Press, 1963.

———. "The Roots of Eastern European Nationalism," in *Premier Congrès International des Études Balkaniques et Sud-est Européennes, Sofia, 26 août–1-er septembre 1966: Résumés des communications, Histoire moderne et contemporaine*, edited by Association Internationale d'Études du Sud-est Européen. Sofia, 1966. Pp. 162–94.

———. *Southeastern Europe under Ottoman Rule, 1354–1804*. Seattle and London: University of Washington Press, [1977].

Sumner, Benedict Humphrey. *Russia and the Balkans, 1870–1880*. Oxford: Clarendon Press, 1937.

Šurmin, Dj. "Dokumenti o Srbiji od 1842–1848," in Srpska Kraljevska Akademija, *Spomenik*, LXIX, drugi razred, 54 (1929), 19–82.

Susman, Warren I. "Culture and Communications," in *Culture as History: The Transformation of American Society in the Twentieth Century*. New York: Pantheon Books, copyright 1973, 1984, by Warren I. Susman. Pp. 252–70.

Sutton, Francis K. "Development Ideology: Its Emergence and Decline," *Daedalus*, CXVIII (Winter 1989), 35–58.

Svoronos, Nicolas G. *Le Commerce de Salonique au XVIIIe siècle*. Paris: Presses Universitaires de France, 1956.

———. *Histoire de la Grèce moderne*, "Que sais-je?" 578. Paris: Presses Universitaires de France, 1953.

Sweet-Escott, Bickham. *Greece: A Political and Economic Survey, 1939–1953*. London and New York: Royal Institute of International Affairs, 1954.

Tacitus. *Tacitus on Britain and Germany*, a translation of the "Agricola" and the "Germania" by H. Mattingly. Baltimore, Md.: Penguin Books, 1948.

Tadić, Jorjo. *Dubrovački portreti*. Belgrade, 1948.

———. *Španija i Dubrovnik u XVI v*. Belgrade, 1932.

Tafel, Théophile Lucas Frédéric. *De Via Militari Romanorum Egnatia Qua Illyricum, Macedonia et Thracia lungebantur: Dissertatio Geographica*. Tubingae: apud H. Leupp, 1842.

Tanović, Stevan. "Domaće vaspitanje u Južnoj Makedoniji," in *Zbornik Etnografskog Muzeja u Beogradu 1901–1951*. Belgrade: Naučna Knjiga, 1953. Pp. 348–51, with résumé in English, "Domestic Education in South Macedonia."

Tăpkova-Zaimova, Vasilka. "L'Idée byzantine de l'unité du monde et l'État bulgare," in Association Internationale d'Études du Sud-est Européen, ed. *Actes du Premier Congrès International des études balkaniques*, III, 291–98.

Tavernier, Jean. *Les Six voyages de Jean Tavernier, écuyer baron d'Aubonne, en Turquie, en Perse, et aux Indes, faits pendant l'espace de quarante ans*, 3 vols. La Haye: chez Henri Scheurleer, 1718.

Taylor, Peter, and House, John, eds. *Political Geography: Recent Advances and Future Directions*. London and Sydney: Croom Helm; Totowa, N.J.: Barnes and Noble Books, 1984.

Teichova, Alice. "Structural Change and Industrialisation in Inter-War Central-East Europe," in Bairoch and Lévy-Leboyer, eds., *Disparities in Economic Development*, pp. 175–86.

Tekeli, Ilhan. "On Institutionalized External Relations of Cities in the Ottoman Empire: A Settlement Models Approach," *Études balkaniques*, VIII, 2 (1972), 49–72.

Tenenbaum, Edward. *National Socialism vs. International Capitalism*. New Haven, Conn.: Yale University Press; London: Humphrey Milford, Oxford University Press, 1942.

Tenney, Frank, et al., eds. *An Economic Survey of Ancient Rome*, 5 vols. Baltimore, Md.: Johns Hopkins Press, 1933–1940. Vol. V by Frank Tenney, *Rome and Italy of the Empire*.

Teodorescu, Alin. "The Future of a Failure: The Romanian Economy," in Sjöberg and Wyzan, eds., *Economic Change in the Balkan States*, pp. 69–88.

Théodoridès, J. "La Science byzantine," in René Taton, ed., *Histoire générale des sciences*, Vol. I: *La Science antique et médiévale (des origines à 1450)*. Paris: Presses Universitaires de France, 1957. Pp. 490–502.

Thompson, Jon. "East Europe's Dark Dawn: The Iron Curtain Rises to Reveal a Land Tarnished by Pollution," *National Geographic*, CLXXIX, 6 (June 1991), 36–68.

Thompson, Robert A., and Thompson, Louise S. *Ecoshell: Planetary Individualism Balanced within Planetary Interdependence*. Buffalo, N.Y.: Prometheus Books, [1987].

Thomson, George. *Studies in Ancient Greek Society: The Prehistoric Aegean*. London: Lawrence & Wishart, 1949; also *Studies in Ancient Greek Society*, Vol. I: *The Prehistoric Aegean*. New York: Citadel Press, 1965.

Thünen, Johann Heinrich von. *Von Thünen's Isolated State*, an English edition of *Der Isolierte Staat* translated by Carla M. Wartenberg, edited with an introduction by Peter Hall. Oxford, Edinburgh, New York: Pergamon Press, [1966].

Tildesley, Miriam L. "The Albanians of the North and South," *Biometrika*, XXV (1933), 21–29.

Tilly, Charles, and Blockmans, Wim P., eds., *Cities and the Rise of States in Europe A.D. 1000–1800*. Boulder, Colo.: Westview Press, forthcoming.

Tocqueville, Alexis de. *Souvenirs*, préface de Fernand Braudel, postface de J. P. Mayer, texte établi par Luc Monnier et annoté par J. P. Mayer et B. M. Wicks-Boisson. Paris: Gallimard, [1978]).

Todorov, Nikolai. *Balkanskiiat grad, XV–XIX vek, sotsialno-ikonomichesko i demografsko razvitie*. Sofia: Nauka i izkustvo, 1972.

———. "La Révolution industrielle en Europe occidentale et les provinces balkaniques de l'Empire ottoman: Le Cas bulgare," in Todorov, Valtcher, and Todorova, eds., *La Révolution industvielle*, Pp. 140–62.

Todorov, Nikolay [Nikolai]; Valtchev, Alexander; and Todorova, Maria, eds. *La Révolution industrielle dans le Sud-est européen, XIXe siècle*, rapports présentés au Colloque International de la Commission de l'AIESEE sur l'histoire sociale et économique, Hambourg, 23–26 mars 1976. Sofia: Institut d'Études Balkaniques, Musée Polytechnique, 1977.

Todorova, Maria. "Historiography of the Countries of Eastern Europe: Bulgaria," *American Historical Review*, IIIC, 4 (October 1992), 1105–17.

Toledano, Ehud R. *The Ottoman Slave Trade and Its Suppression: 1840–1890*. Princeton, N.J.: Princeton University Press, [1982].

Tomasevich, Jozo. *Peasants, Politics, and Economic Change in Yugoslavia*. Stanford: Stanford University Press; London: Geoffrey Cumberlege, Oxford University Press, 1955.

Tomashevich, George Vid. "Božidar Knežević: A Yugoslav Philosopher of History," *Slavonic and East European Review*, XXXV (June 1957), 443–61.

———. *See also* Knežević, Božidar.

Tomasic, Dinko. "Ideologies and the Structure of Eastern European Society," *American Journal of Sociology*, LIII (1947–48), 367–75.
———. *Personality and Culture in Eastern European Politics*. New York: George W. Stewart, 1948.
Topping, Peter. "Greek Historical Writing on the Period 1453–1914," *Journal of Modern History*, XXXII, 2 (June 1961), 157–73.
Toynbee, Arnold J. *Constantine Porphyrogenitus and His World*. London: Oxford University Press, 1973.
———. *A Study of History*, Vols. II and III. London: Oxford University Press; London: Humphrey Milford, 1934.
Tozer, H. F. "Byzantine Satire," *Journal of Hellenic Studies*, II (1881), 233–70.
Trojanović (Troyanovitch), Sima. "Manners and Customs," in Stead, ed., *Servia by the Servians*, pp. 169–98.
———. "Naše kiridžije," in Srpska Kraljevska Akademija, *Srpski Etnografski Zbornik*, knj. xiii, "Etnološka i etnografska gradja." Belgrade, 1909. Pp. 1–154.
———. *Psihofizičko izražavanje srpskog naroda poglavito bez reči*. Belgrade: Srpska Kraljevska Akademija, 1935.
———. *Vatra u običajima i života srpskog naroda*. Belgrade: Srpska Kraljevska Akademija, 1930.
Tsvetkova, Bistra. *See* Cvetkova, Bistra.
Tuan, Yi-Fu. *Topophilia: A Study of Environmental Perception, Attitudes, and Values*, with a new preface by the author. New York: Columbia University Press, [1990]; originally published by Prentice-Hall, Englewood Cliffs, N.J., 1974.
Turgot, Anne-Robert-Jacques. "Plan de deux discours sur l'histoire universelle: Plan du premier discours, sur la formation des gouvernements et le mélange des nations" (1750), in *Oeuvres de Turgot*, nouvelle édition classée par ordre de matières, avec les notes de Dupont de Nemours, augmentées de lettres inédites, des questions sur le commerce, et d'observations et de notes nouvelles par MM. Eugène Daire et Hippolyte Dussard et précédée d'une notice par M. Eugène Daire, 2 vols. Paris: Guillaumin, 1844. II, 628–42. In *Oeuvres de Turgot et documents le concernant avec biographie et notes*, par Gustave Schelle (Paris: Félix Alcan, 1913), I, 277–98, the date of Turgot's essay is given as "*vers* 1751."
Turner, William. *Journal of a Tour in the Levant*, 3 vols. London: John Murray, 1820.
Turnock, David. *The Human Geography of Eastern Europe*. London and New York: Routledge, 1989.
———. "The Industrial Development of Romania from the Unification of the Principalities to the Second World War," in Carter, ed., *An Historical Geography of the Balkans*, pp. 319–78.
Turrill, William Bertram. *The Plant Life of the Balkan Peninsula: A Phytogeographical Study*. Oxford: Clarendon Press, 1929.
Ubicini, Jean-Henri-Abdolonyme. *Les Serbes de Turquie: Études historiques, statistiques et politiques sur la principauté de Serbie, le Montenegro et les pays serbes adjacents*. Paris: E. Dentu, 1865.
Ulmen, G. L. "American Imperialism and International Law: Carl Schmitt on the US in World Affairs," *Telos*, No. 72 (Summer 1987), pp. 43–71.
———. "Return of the Foe," *Telos*, No. 72 (Summer 1987), pp. 187–93.
———. *See also* Piccone, Paul.
Unbegaun, Boris. *Les Débuts de la langue littéraire chez les Serbes*. Paris: Librairie Honoré Champion, 1935.
Urquhart, David. *Progress of Russia in the West, North, and South, by Opening the Sources of Opinion and Appropriating the Channels of Wealth and Power*, 4th ed. London: Trübner, 1853.

Uspenskii, Fedor Ivanovich. *Obrazovanie Vtorago Bolgarskago Tsarstva,* "Zapiski Imperatorskago Novorossiiskago Universiteta," XXVII. Odessa: G. Ulrich, 1879.

Utterström, Gustaf. "Climatic Fluctuations and Population Problems in Early Modern History," *Scandinavian Economic History Review,* III, 1 (1955), 3–47.

Vacalopoulos, Apostolos E. *The Greek Nation, 1453–1669: The Cultural and Economic Background of Modern Greek Society,* translated from the Greek by Ian Moles and Phania Moles. New Brunswick, N.J.: Rutgers University Press, [1976].

―――. "La Retraite des populations grecques vers les régions éloignées et montagneuses pendant la domination turque," *Balkan Studies,* IV, 2 (1963), 265–76.

Vacalopoulos, Apostolos E.; Svolopoulos, Constantinos D.; and Király, Béla K., eds., *Southeast European Maritime Commerce and Naval Policies from the Mid-Eighteenth Century to 1914: Proceedings of the XVIIth Conference on War and Society in East Central Europe, Thessaloniki, 6–8 June 1985,* "War and Society in East Central Europe," Vol. XXIII. Boulder, Colo.: Social Sciences Monographs; Highland Lakes, N.J.: Atlantic Research and Publications, distributed by Columbia University Press; co-publisher: Institute for Balkan Studies, Thessaloniki, 1988.

Vacalopoulos, Constantin A. "Commercial Development and Economic Importance of the Port of Thessaloniki from the Late Eighteenth Century to 1856," in Vacalopoulos, Svolopoulos, and Király, eds., *Southeast European Maritime Commerce,* pp. 301–7.

Vakarelski, Hr. (Khr.). "Iz veshtestvenata kultura na Bŭlgarite," in Narodniia Etnografski Muzei (Sofia), *Izvestiia,* XII (1936), 55–109 (on the ard) and 130–65 (on the harrow).

Valaoras, Vasilios G. "A Reconstruction of the Demographic History of Modern Greece," *Milbank Memorial Fund Quarterly,* XXXVIII, 2 (April 1960), 115–39.

Valério, Nuno. "Some Remarks about Growth and Stagnation in the Mediterranean World in the XIXth and XXth Centuries," *Journal of European Economic History,* XXI, 1 (Spring 1992), 121–33.

Valéry, Paul. *Tel quel,* Vol. II. [Paris]: Gallimard, [1943].

Vambéry, Arminius. *Western Culture in Eastern Lands.* London: J. Murray, 1906.

Varagnac, André. *Civilisation traditionnelle et genres de vie.* Paris: Albin Michel, [1948].

Vasić, Miloje M. "Htonski kult, Vinča i naš folklor," *Zbornik Etnografskog Muzeja u Beogradu 1901–1951.* Belgrade: Naučna Knjiga, 1953. Pp. 267–69, with résumé in French: "Culte chthonien, Vinča et notre folklore."

Vasiljević, Jovan Hadži. *See* Hadži Vasiljević, Jovan.

Verdery, Katherine. *National Ideology under Socialism: Identity and Cultural Politics in Ceauşescu's Romania.* Berkeley, Los Angeles, Oxford: University of California Press, [1991].

―――. *Transylvanian Villagers: Three Centuries of Political, Economic, and Ethnic Change.* Berkeley, Los Angeles, London: University of California Press, [1983].

Veremis, Thanos. "From the National State to the Stateless Nation, 1821–1910," *European History Quarterly,* XIX, 2 (April 1989), 135–48.

Vergopoulos, Kostas. *Le Capitalisme difforme et la nouvelle question agraire: L'Exemple de la Grèce moderne,* présentation de Samir Amin. Paris: François Maspero, 1977.

Verlinden, Charles. "La Colonie vénitienne de Tana, centre de la traite des esclaves au XIVe et au début du XVe siècle," in *Studi in Onore di Gino Luzzatto,* Milano: Dott. A. Giuffrè, 1950. II, 1–25.

―――. "La Crète, débouché et plaque tournante de la traite des esclaves aux XIVe et XVe siècles," in *Studi in Onore di Amintore Fanfani,* Vol. III. Milano: Giuffrè, 1962.

―――. "Le Franc Samo," *Revue belge de philologie et d'histoire,* XI (1933), 1090–95.

Vermaseren, Maarten J. *Mithras, the Secret God,* translated from the Dutch by Therese and Vincent Megdaw. London: Chatto and Windus, 1963.

Vernant, Jean-Pierre. "Du Mythe à la raison: La Formation de la pensée positive dans la Grèce archaïque," *Annales: Économies, Sociétés, Civilisations*, XII, 2 (April–June 1957), 183–206.

Vidal de la Blache, Paul, and Gallois, L., eds. *Géographie universelle*, VII. *Méditerranée*, Pt. 2. Paris: Armand Colin, 1934. Section on "Pays balkaniques" by Y. Chataigneau and Jules Sion.

Villari, Luigi. *The Republic of Ragusa*. London: J. M. Dent, 1904.

Vinaver, Vuk. "Trgovina bosanskim robljem tokom XIV veka u Dubrovniku," *Anali Historijskog Instituta u Dubrovniku*, II (1953), 125–47.

Vining, Rutledge. "A Description of Certain Spatial Aspects of an Economic System," *Economic Development and Cultural Change*, III, 2 (January 1955), 147–95.

Violich, Francis. *The Search for Cultural Identity through Urban Design: Dalmatian Towns to Berkeley Planning*. Berkeley Center for Environmental Design Research, College of Environmental Design, University of California, n.d.

Viorst, Milton. "The Yugoslav Idea," *New Yorker*, March 18, 1991, pp. 58–79.

Vivian, Herbert. *Servia, the Poor Man's Paradise*. London, New York, and Bombay: Longmans, Green, and Co., 1897.

Vlachos, Evan. "Transboundary Water Challenges in the Balkans: Some Preliminary Remarks," paper presented at a conference on "The European Community and the Balkans," Corfu, July 2–5, 1993, organized by the Hellenic Centre for European Studies (EKEM) and the Hellenic Foundation for Defence and Foreign Policy (ELIAMEP) with the support of the Commission of the European Community.

Vlahović, Jovan. *See* Frilley, Gabriel, Dr.

Vlajinac (Wlaïnatz), Milan Z. *Die agrar-rechtlichen Verhältnisse des mittelalterlichen Serbiens*. Jena: Gustav Fischer, 1903.

———. *Moba i pozajmica: Narodni običaji udruženoga rada—opis, ocena i njihovo sadašnje stanje*, Srpska Kraljevska Akademija, "Srpski Etnografski Zbornik," knj. xliv, drugo odeljenje, "Život i običaji narodni," knj. 18. Belgrade, 1929.

———. *Rečnik naših starih mera u toku vekova*, 4 vols. Belgrade: Srpska Akademija znanosti i umetnosti, 1961–74.

Volney, Constantin-François Chasseboeuf de. *The Ruins, or a Survey of the Revolutions of Empires*, 5th ed. London: printed for Thomas Tegg, 1811.

Von Grunebaum, G. E. "Islamic Studies and Cultural Research," in G. E. Von Grunebaum, ed., *Studies in Islamic Cultural History*, published as Vol. LVI, No. 2, Pt. 2, Memoir No. 76, of *American Anthropologist* (No. 2 of "Comparative Studies of Cultures and Civilizations") (1954). Pp. 1–22.

Vryonis, Speros, Jr. "The Byzantine Legacy in Folk Life and Tradition in the Balkans," in Clucas, ed., *The Byzantine Legacy*, pp. 107–45.

———, ed. *Greece on the Road to Democracy: From the Junta to PASOK, 1974–1986*. New Rochelle, N.Y.: Aristide D. Caratzas, published under the auspices of the Speros Basil Vryonis Center for the Study of Hellenism, [1991].

———. "Introductory Remarks on Byzantine Intellectuals and Humanism," *Skepsis*, II (Athens: Olympia, 1991), 104–40.

———. "Nomadization and Islamization in Asia Minor," *Dumbarton Oaks Papers*, XXIX (1975), 41–71.

———. "The Question of the Byzantine Mines," *Speculum*, XXXVII, 1 (January 1962), 1–17.

———. "Religious Changes and Patterns in the Balkans, 14th–16th Centuries," in Birnbaum and Vryonis, Jr., eds., *Aspects of the Balkans*, pp. 151–76.

Vucinich, Wayne S., ed., *The First Serbian Uprising, 1804–1813*, Social Science Monographs, Boulder, Colo.: Brooklyn College Press, distributed by Columbia University Press, 1982.

————. "Marxian Interpretations of the First Serbian Revolution," *Journal of Central European Affairs*, XXI, 1 (April 1961), 3–14.

————. "The Nature of Balkan Society under Ottoman Rule," *Slavic Review*, XXI (December 1962), 597–638, with comments by Stanford J. Shaw and Traian Stoianovich.

————. *Serbia between East and West: The Events of 1903–1908.* Stanford, Calif.: Stanford University Press, 1954.

————. *A Study in Social Survival: Katun in the Bileća Rudine*, Monograph Series in World Affairs, 13. Denver: University of Denver, 1975.

Vučo, Nikola. *Privredna istorija naroda FNRJ do Prvog svetskog rata.* Belgrade: Izdavačko preduzeće NR Srbije, 1948.

————. *Privredna istorija Srbije do Prvog svetskog rata.* Belgrade: Univerzitet u Beogradu—Naučna Knjiga, 1955.

Vujić, Joakim. *Putešestvije po Serbiji*, 2 vols. Belgrade, 1901–02.

Wace, Alan John Bayard, and Thompson, Maurice Scott. *The Nomads of the Balkans: An Account of Life and Customs among the Vlachs of the Northern Pindus.* New York: E. P. Dutton, [1913–14]; London: Methuen; New York: Biblo and Tannen, 1972.

Wagemann, Ernst Friedrich. *Der neue Balkan: Altes Land, junge Wirtschaft.* Hamburg: Hanseatische Verlagsanstalt, [1939].

————. *Die Zahl als Detektiv*, 2nd ed. Bern: A. Francke, 1952.

Wagstaff, J. M. "A Possible Interpretation of Settlement Pattern Evolution in Terms of 'Catastrophe Theory,'" Institute of British Geographers, *Transactions*, N.S., III, 2 (1978), 165–78.

————. "War and Settlement Desertion in the Morea, 1685–1830," Institute of British Geographers, *Transactions*, N.S., III, 2 (1978), 295–308.

Wallace, Anthony F. C. *Culture and Personality.* New York: Random House, 1961.

————. *See also* Bratanič, Branimir.

Wallerstein, Immanuel. *The Modern World-System: Capitalist Agriculture and the Origins of the European World-Economy in the Sixteenth Century.* New York and London: Academic Press, [1974].

Wallerstein, Immanuel; Decadeli, Hale; and Kasaba, Reşat. "The Incorporation of the Ottoman Empire into the World-Economy," paper presented at the International Conference on Turkish Studies, University of Wisconsin, Madison, May 25–27, 1979.

Walsh, Robert, Rev. *Narrative of a Journey from Constantinople to England.* Philadelphia: Carey, Lea, and Carey, 1828.

Walters, A. Harry. *Ecology, Food and Civilisation.* London: Charles Knight and Co., Ltd., 1973.

Warriner, Doreen, ed. *See* Pinto, V. de S.

Wassermann, Felix M. "Thucydides and the Disintegration of the Polis," in *Transactions and Proceedings of the American Philological Association*, LXXXV (1954), 46–54.

Waterbolk, H. T. "The Lower Rhine Basin," in Braidwood and Willey, eds., *Courses toward Urban Life*, pp. 227–53.

Weber, Eugen. *Peasants into Frenchmen: The Modernization of Rural France, 1870–1914.* Stanford, Calif.: Stanford University Press, 1976.

Wegner, Max. *Land der Griechen: Reiseschilderungen aus sieben Jahrhunderten.* Berline: Walter de Gruyter, 1943.

Weinberg, Saul S., ed., *The Aegean and the Near East: Studies Presented to Hetty Goldman on the Occasion of Her Seventy-Fifth Birthday.* Locust Valley, N.Y.: J. J. Augustin Publisher, 1956, publication supported by Institute for Advanced Study, Princeton.

————. "The Relative Chronology of the Aegean and Early Bronze Ages," in Ehrich, ed., *Chronologies in Old World Archaeology*, pp. 285–320.

Wenzel, Marian. "Bosnian and Herzegovinian Tombstones—Who Made Them and Why," *Südost-Forschungen*, XXI (1962), 102–43.

———. "The Dioscuri in the Balkans," *Slavic Review*, XXVI, 3 (September 1967), 363–81.

Werner, Ernst. "Yürüken und Wlachen," in Association Internationale d'Études du Sud-est Européen, *Actes du Premier Congrès International des études balkaniques*, III, 605–7.

Westermann, Ekkehard. "Zur künftigen Erforschung der Frankfurter Messen des 16. und frühen 17. Jahrhunderts: Ein Wegweiser zu ungenutzter Quellen," in Schneider et al., eds., *Wirtschaftskräfte und Wirtschaftswege*, II, 245–70.

Wheelwright, Philip. *Heraclitus*. Princeton, N.J.: Princeton University Press, 1959.

White, Hayden. *Tropics of Discourse: Essays in Cultural Criticism*. Baltimore and London: Johns Hopkins University Press, [1978].

White, Lynn, Jr. "The Historical Roots of Our Ecologic Crisis," *Science*, CLV (March 10, 1967), 1203–07.

———. *Medieval Technology and Social Change*. New York: Oxford University Press, 1962; Galaxy Book, 1966.

Whitehead, Neil L., and Ferguson, R. Brian. "Deceptive Stereotypes about 'Tribal Warfare,'" *Chronicle of Higher Education*, November 10, 1993, p. A48.

Wilford, John Noble. "Site in Turkey Yields Oldest Cloth Ever Found," *New York Times*, July 13, 1993, pp. C1, C8.

Wilhelmy, Herbert. *Hochbulgarien*, Vol. I. *Die ländlichen Siedlungen und die bauerliche Wirtschaft*; Vol II. *Sofia: Wandlungen einer Grossstadt zwischen Orient und Okzident*, Schriften des Geographischen Instituts der Universität Kiel. Kiel, 1935–36.

Willey, Gordon R. *See* Braidwood, Robert J.

Winnifrith, T. J. *The Vlachs: The History of a Balkan People*. New York: St. Martin's Press, [1987].

Wittek, Paul. "Devshirme and Shari'a," University of London, *Bulletin of the School of Oriental and African Studies*, XVII, pt. 2 (1955), 271–78.

Wolff, Robert Lee. "The Second Bulgarian Empire: Its Origin and History to 1204," *Speculum*, XXIV (1949), 167–206.

Wood, A. C., ed., *Mr. Harrie Cavendish: His Journey to and from Constantinople by Fox, His Servant*, Camden Miscellany, XVII, Camden Third Series, LXIV. London: Offices of the Royal Historical Society, 1940.

Woodhouse, Christopher Montague. *The Greek War of Independence*. London, New York, Melbourne, Sydney, and Capetown: Hutchinson's University Library, 1952.

Woodward, Susan L. "Political Changes in the European Mediterranean Arena: An Overview of Considerations for Policy Makers," in Pinkele and Pollis, eds., *The Contemporary Mediterranean World*, pp. 175–201.

Wright, John K. "Terrae Incognitae: The Place of Imagination in Geography," *Annals of the Association of American Geographers*, XXXVII, 1 (March 1947), 1–15.

Wuthnow, Robert. "The Voluntary Sector: Legacy of the Past, Hope for the Future?" in Robert Wuthnow, ed., *Between States and Markets: The Voluntary Sector in Comparative Perspective*. Princeton, N.J.: Princeton University Press, [1991]. Pp. 3–29.

Wyzan, Michael L. *See* Sjöberg, Örjan.

Xenopol (Xénopol), Alexandru Dimitrie. *Une énigme historique: Les Roumains au Moyen-âge*. Paris: Ernest Leroux, 1885.

———. *La Théorie de l'histoire: Deuxième édition des Principes fondamentaux de l'histoire*. Paris: Ernest Leroux, 1908.

Yankovitch, Velizar. "Le Problème de notre navigation fluviale," in Marcovitch, ed., *Livre jubilaire des chemins de fer*, pp. 268–77.

Young, George. *Corps de droit ottoman*, 7 vols. Oxford: Clarendon Press, 1905–06.

Yovanovitch, Dragolioub. *See* Jovanović, Dragoljub.

Yriarte, Charles. *Bosnie et Herzégovine: Souvenirs d'un voyage pendant l'insurrection.* Paris: Plon, 1876.

Yugoslavia. "Memorandum of the Government of Yugoslavia on the Yugoslav Crisis," addressed to the Secretary General of the United Nations, January 28, 1992, in *Yugoslav Survey*, XXXIII, 1 (1992), 77–106.

Zachariadou, Elizabeth, ed. *The Ottoman Emirate (1300–1389)*, Institute for Mediterranean Studies: "Halcyon Days in Crete I," a symposium held in Rethymnon, 11–13 January 1991. Rethymnon: Crete University Press, 1993.

Zagoroff, Slavtcho D.; Végh, Jenö; and Bilimovich, Alexander D. *The Agricultural Economy of the Danubian Countries, 1935–45.* Stanford, Calif.: Stanford University Press, 1955.

Zartman, I. William. *See* Mardin, Şerif.

Zavod za statistiku NR Srbije. *Prilozi statističkom proučavanju Prvog srpskog ustanka NR Srbije*, Prilozi 14. Belgrade, 1955.

Zedlitz-Neukirch, Leopold Freiherr von. *Europa im Jahre 1829: Ein genealogisch-statistisch-historisches Handbuch.* Berlin: im Verlage der Vossischen Buchhandlung, n.d.

Zeune, [Johann] August. *Gea: Versuch einer wissenschaftlichen Erdbeschreibung.* Berlin: bei L. W. Wittich, 1808.

Zinkeisen, Johann Wilhelm. *Geschichte des osmanischen Reiches in Europa*, Vol. II. *Das Reich auf der Höhe seiner Entwicklung 1453–1574.* Gotha: bei Friedrich Andreas Perthes, 1854.

Zipf, George Kingsley. *National Disunity: The Nation as a Bio-Social Organism.* Bloomington, Ind.: Principia Press, 1941.

Zlatarski, V. N. *Istoriia na bŭlgarskata dŭrzhava prez srednite vekove*, Vol. II: *Bŭlgariia pod vizantiisko vladichestvo (1018–1187)*, pt. 1. Sofia: Bŭlgarska Akademiia na naukite, 1934.

Zur, Ofer. "The Love of Hating: The Psychology of Enmity," *History of European Ideas*, XIII, 4 (1991), 345–69.

INDEX

About the Author

Traian Stoianovich was born in a small village in Yugoslav Macedonia. Educated in the United States and in France, he was for four decades a teacher of European and world history at Rutgers University. He has also taught at New York University, the University of California (Berkeley), Stanford University, and Sir George Williams University (Montreal). In addition to the present work, his publications include *French Historical Method: The 'Annales' Paradigm* and *Between East and West: The Balkan and Mediterranean Worlds.*